TRANSLOCALITIES/
TRANSLOCALIDADES

TRANSLOCALITIES/
TRANSLOCALIDADES

FEMINIST POLITICS OF TRANSLATION IN THE LATIN/A AMÉRICAS

SONIA E. ALVAREZ
CLAUDIA DE LIMA COSTA
VERÓNICA FELIU
REBECCA J. HESTER
NORMA KLAHN
AND MILLIE THAYER, EDITORS

with Cruz Caridad Bueno

Duke University Press / Durham and London / 2014

Library of Congress Cataloging-in-Publication Data
Translocalities/translocalidades : feminist politics of translation
in the Latin/a Américas / Sonia E. Alvarez, Claudia de Lima Costa,
Verónica Feliu, Rebecca J. Hester, Norma Klahn, and Millie Thayer,
editors ; with Cruz Caridad Bueno.
pages cm
Includes bibliographical references and index.
ISBN 978-0-8223-5615-8 (cloth : alk. paper)
ISBN 978-0-8223-5632-5 (pbk. : alk. paper)
1. Women—Political activity—Latin America. 2. Feminism—
Latin America. 3. Latin America—Politics and government.
4. Democracy—Latin America. 5. Democratization—Latin
America. I. Alvarez, Sonia E., 1956– II. Costa, Claudia de Lima.
III. Feliu, Verónica. IV. Hester, Rebecca J. V. Klahn, Norma.
VI. Thayer, Millie. VII. Caridad Bueno, Cruz.
HQ1236.5.L29T73 2014
305.42098—dc23
2013041396

CONTENTS

This collaborative project emerged out of an interdisciplinary feminist working group first brought together by Hemispheric Dialogues, a program supported by the Ford Foundation's Rethinking Area Studies initiative, based at the Chicano/Latino Research Center at the University of California, Santa Cruz (UCSC), which was aimed at bridging Latin American and Latina/o studies through curricular innovation and action–research partnerships. That program gave rise to a Greater Bay Area research group of Chicana/Latina and Latin American(ist) feminist scholars — cofounded by Sonia E. Alvarez, together with Claudia de Lima Costa, Norma Klahn, Lionel Cantú, Verónica Feliu, Patricia Zavella, Lourdes Martínez-Echazabal, Teresa Carrillo, and several other Latin/a American and feminist faculty and graduate students of color—which ultimately inspired this anthology. The editors and many of the contributors formed part of that group, which met in Santa Cruz over a number of years. Most other contributors also participated at one point or another in one of the several sessions on the travels and translations of feminist theories in the Americas that we organized for Congresses of the Latin American Studies Association in 2000, 2001, 2003, 2004, 2006, and 2007 and in various conferences and seminars we have held on the topic in a variety of locations, including UCSC and the Federal University of Santa Catarina in Brazil. In 2006, the project traveled to the East Coast, and this book began to be collectively imagined during a transcoastal, translocal conference, held at the University of Massachusetts, Amherst, that spring. The always productive and provocative conversations among our authors have been sustained virtually in more recent years. We thank all the contributors for their hard work and dedication to the project as the book underwent revisions.

Sonia E. Alvarez wishes to thank the University of Massachusetts graduate research assistants who have worked tirelessly over the years to help make this project successful and this book a reality: Cruz Caridad Bueno, Casey Stephen, Alper Yagci, Irem Kok, Amy Fleig, Martha Balaguera, and Alyssa Maraj Graham. The Center for Latin American, Caribbean and Latino Studies at UMass-Amherst provided crucial support. Alvarez also is especially indebted to Claudia de Lima Costa for the invitation to travel/*viajar* with her on questions of feminist translation. Without our own frequent and intense trans/dislocations and without her wide-ranging command of cultural translation, this collective project would not have been possible.

Claudia de Lima Costa would like to thank CNPq for the continuing support for her research on the travels and translations of feminist theories. She is also grateful to the Chicano/Latino Research Center at UCSC and the Center for Latin American, Caribbean and Latino Studies at UMass-Amherst for the warm welcome and institutional backing she received at different stages of this book project. Finally, without the unabating encouragement, relentless commitment, and personal involvement of Sonia E. Alvarez, this book project would not have been sustained and come to completion.

Verónica Feliu extends many thanks to Sonia and the other *translocas* in Chile: Perla Wilson from Radio Tierra; Carolina Stefoni from Universidad Alberto Hurtado; Rosalba Todaro from Centro de Estudios de la Mujer (CEM); Praxedes Peña from Fundación para la Promoción y Desarrollo de la Mujer (PRODEMU); Ruth Díaz from Asociación de Empleadas de Casa Particular (ANECAP); and Andrea Manqui from Corporación Nacional de Desarrollo Indígena (CONADI).

Rebecca Hester thanks all of the translocas, especially Pascha Bueno Hansen for her support early on and Sonia for including her in this project. She would not have begun to study health and migration if it were not for Pat Zavella. She has greatly benefited from Zavella's help and support along the way. Jonathan Fox was instrumental in her choice to work with indigenous migrants from Oaxaca. Hester can't thank him enough for opening that door. Finally, she thanks the Chicano/Latino Research Center (CLRC) at UCSC for supporting this work and the Department of Latino Studies at the University of Illinois, Urbana-Champaign, for providing a space to complete her editorial duties.

Norma Klahn thanks her coeditors, most especially Sonia, her graduate research assistants, and the Center for Latin American, Caribbean and Latino Studies at UMass-Amherst, without whom this book would not have come to light. Due recognition should be given to the Ford Foundation and the CLRC at UCSC for their crucial support in the early stages of this project. Klahn's chapter owes much to the exchange of ideas with all the participant translocas, to the members of the IAFR (Institute of Advanced Feminist Research at UCSC, 2004–2010), and not least to the activist feminists around the project of *Mujeres*

Creando in Bolivia, among them Ana Rebeca Prada and Elizabeth Monasterios, as well as the relentless team of *Debate Feminista* under the guidance of Marta Lamas.

Millie Thayer gives profound thanks to the members of sos Corpo and the Rural Women Workers' Movement—in particular, Vanete Almeida—for their willingness to share their time and their struggles. She is also indebted to the *Feminist Studies* editors and reviewers for their insightful comments, and to her fellow translocas for many years of generative feminist conversations.

We all thank each other for mutual support as well our editors at Duke University Press, Valerie Millholland and Gisela Fosado, for their unwavering and enthusiastic support for this project. The Diebel Monograph Fund of the Institute for the Medical Humanities at the University of Texas Medical Branch underwrote the preparation of the index. The Leonard J. Horwitz Endowment of the University of Massachusetts at Amerst provided generous support for all stages of the production of this book.

INTRODUCTION TO THE PROJECT AND THE VOLUME/
ENACTING A TRANSLOCAL FEMINIST POLITICS OF TRANSLATION

SONIA E. ALVAREZ

This book explores how feminist discourses and practices travel across a variety of sites and directionalities to become interpretive paradigms to read and write issues of class, gender, race, sexuality, migration, health, social movements, development, citizenship, politics, and the circulation of identities and texts. The notion of translation is deployed figuratively to emphasize the ways these travels are politically embedded within larger questions of globalization and involve exchanges across diverse localities, especially between and among women in Latin America and Latinas in the United States. The contributors—including authors from Argentina, Brazil, Bolivia, Chile, and Mexico, as well as East and West Coast–based Latinas of Cuban, Puerto Rican, Mexican, Chilean, Peruvian, and Dominican descent and other U.S. women of color and allies—enact a politics of translation by unabashedly trafficking in feminist theories and practices across geopolitical, disciplinary, and other borders, bringing insights from Latina/women of color/postcolonial feminisms in the North of the Américas to bear on our analyses of theories, practices, cultures, and politics in the South and vice versa.

Translation is politically and theoretically indispensable to forging feminist, prosocial justice, antiracist, postcolonial/decolonial, and anti-imperial political alliances and epistemologies because the Latin/a Américas—as a transborder cultural formation rather than a territorially delimited one—must be understood as translocal in a dual sense. The first sense we deploy—that of translocation—builds on but moves beyond U.S. Third World feminist conceptions of the "politics of location." Because a feminist politics of location involves "a temporality of struggle, not a fixed position," as Claudia de Lima Costa argues in the Introduction to Debates about Translation, we must be attentive to the social and power relations that "produce location and situated knowledges."[1] Yet as Agustín Lao-Montes suggests, Latina/os, and Afro-Latina/

os in particular, are best conceptualized as "translocal subjects." In his reading, the politics of location, as developed by U.S. women of color feminisms, "relates the 'multiple mediations' (gender, class, race, etc.) that constitute the self to diverse modes of domination (capitalism, patriarchy, racism, imperialism) and to distinct yet intertwined social struggles and movements" (2007, 122). The notion of translocation takes us a step further, linking "geographies of power at various scales (local, national, regional, global) with subject positions (gender/sexual, ethnoracial, class, etc.) that constitute the self" (see chapter 19 of this volume). Here we wish to extend this conception of translocation to encompass not just U.S. Latina/os but all of the Latin/a Américas.

A hemispheric politics of translocation would be attentive to the heterogeneity of Latinidades within the United States *and* within and among Latin American and Caribbean peoples, as well as to the diverse positionalities that shape Latina/o American lives across multiple borders. In the twenty-first century, "political borders cannot contain cultural ones, just as within political borders, different nations, cultures and languages cannot be suppressed in the name of national (understood) as monolithic unity," as Norma Klahn argues pointedly in chapter 1. Many sorts of Latin/o-americanidades—Afro, queer, indigenous, feminist, and so on—are today constructed through processes of translocation. *Latinidad* in the South, North, and Caribbean "middle" of the Américas, then, is always already constituted out of the intersections of the intensified cross-border, transcultural, and translocal flows that characterize contemporary transmigration throughout the hemisphere—from La Paz to Buenos Aires to Chicago and back again. Many such crossings are emotionally, materially, and physically costly, often dangerous, and increasingly perilous. Yet cross-border passages also always reposition and transform subjectivities and worldviews.

Rather than immigrating and "assimilating," moreover, many people in the Latin/a Américas increasingly move back and forth between localities, between historically situated and culturally specific (though increasingly porous) places, across multiple borders, and not just between nations (as implied in the phrase "transnational migration," for instance). We therefore deploy the notion of translocal in a second sense, which we call translocalities/*translocalidades*, precisely to capture these multidirectional crossings and movements.

Many, if not all, of the contributors to this anthology regularly transit across an array of intimate, familial, personal, libidinal, consumer, financial, cultural, political, and labor circuits in and through different locales of the Latin/a Américas and beyond. Our feminism, as Márgara Millán suggests in chapter 7, is a "multilocated practice." Like "travelling theories" (Said 1983, cited in de Lima Costa, Introduction to Debates, this volume) and today's transmigrants, our own crossings—theoretical, political, personal, and intimate—are heavily patrolled and often constrained or obstructed by various kinds of (patriarchal, disciplinary, institutional, capitalist/neoliberal, geopolitical, sexual, and so on) gatekeepers.

Crucially for the politics of translation, our multiple locations or subject positions shift, often quite dramatically, as we move or travel across spatio-temporal localities. Our subjectivities are at once place-based and mis- or displaced.[2] Whereas I am an ethnicized Cuban American in south Florida and a racialized Latina in New England, for instance, whenever I deplane in São Paulo I instantly "become white." But I necessarily embody my provisional whiteness uncomfortably, as I am all too painfully aware of the injuries inflicted by racism in both the North and South of the Américas. Though less flexible for the darkest bodies because of "the fact of blackness," as Frantz Fanon rightly insisted, race can be a mobile signifier across borders. "Race is not a fixed marker of identity, but one that varies as people inhabit particular spaces," as Brazilian anthropologist Suzana Maia makes clear in chapter 13. Indeed, as Chilean émigré Verónica Feliu reminds us (chapter 12), our translocalized understandings of race often force us to "deal with our own ghosts, our own repressed memories, and, finally, as Cherríe Moraga so poignantly said, with that racism we have internalized, the one we aimed at ourselves." Challenging racisms within Latino/America means interrogating the "possessive investment in whiteness" (Lipsitz in Gómez-Barris, chapter 10 in this volume) that translates as emblanquecimiento and the related "possessive investment in colonialism," which, as another Chilean contributor, Macarena Gómez-Barris, aptly puts it, has historically looked toward Europe "as a site of insatiable material consumption, as a way to devour a whiteness of being."

Because our transit across multiple boundaries disrupts the prevailing common sense in many of the localities through which we move in ways that sometimes make us seem outright mad (in a double sense), we early on adopted the nickname Translocas for the cross-disciplinary, cross-border research group of Latina and Latin American(ist) feminists who brought this edited collection into being. Like the Afro-Chilean vocalist and composer Moyenei Valdés, whose work is analyzed here by Gómez-Barris, our politics and theorizing seek to interrupt "the hegemonic drone of economic neoliberalism," heteronormative patriarchal racisms, and racist sexisms across the Latin/a Américas. We deploy the metaphor Translocas to capture both the movements of bodies, texts, capital, and theories in between North/South and to reflect the mobile epistemologies they inspire in growing numbers of subjects in contemporary times. The metaphor is deployed with a double meaning—both women trans/dislocated in a physical sense, and the (resulting) conceptual madness linked to attempts to understand unfamiliar scenarios with familiar categories: women and categories out of place. We embrace the transgressive, queer, transgendered sense of the term as well.[3] With this book, we wish to propose Translocas as both a political project and an episteme for apprehending and negotiating the globalized Américas, one that can potentially be embraced widely across the hemisphere and beyond.

"The increased mobility and displacement of peoples, their cultures and languages and the global interconnectedness made possible by technology," as Norma Klahn insists, "are deconstructing conceptual mappings of North to South/South to North routes, let alone their translations and reception." Indeed, with the intensification of transmigration, growing numbers of Latin@s and Latin Americans today *embody* similarly shifting registers, positionalities, and epistemes due to our intermittent movement in and across diverse localities in the North and South of the Américas. Growing numbers of folks are, in effect, "becoming Transloc@s."[4] We are expanding exponentially.

Translocas in the Américas and other globalized places defy "the 'us' and 'them' paradigm that stems from modernist/[colonial] modes of description and representation" because we are simultaneously and intermittently self and other, if you will (Grewal and Kaplan 1994a, 7). As Karina Céspedes suggests, many in the Latin/a Américas are "world travelers" as "a matter of necessity and survival" (Céspedes 2007, 107; Lugones 1990). Translocas' travels and translation efforts are also driven by affect, passion, solidarity, and interpersonal and political connectedness. What's more, we travel across multiple worlds *within* ourselves. Rather than W. E. B. Du Bois's "double consciousness," our translocalities enable a multiple, intersectional, multisited consciousness—a translocated version of Chela Sandoval's "differential" or "oppositional" consciousness (1991, 2000b). Many of us become "double insiders," as Kiran Asher refers to her own "translocation" as a South Asian feminist researching and working with Afro-Colombian women (chapter 9).

As Simone Schmidt maintains, displacement is altogether too familiar to many subjects in late modern times, and the feeling of "dislocation," or in this case translocality, often leaves Translocas and other diasporic subjects with the sensation that our communities of origin have become "unrecognizable" because "history, somehow intervened irrevocably" and we are not at home any place (Hall 2003, 27, cited in Schmidt, chapter 3 in this volume). She proposes that it may be more appropriate to "think of coming home as impossible, because home no longer exists. The road leaving home is one of no return." Perhaps like Gloria Anzaldúa, who claimed she carried her home on her back like a turtle, Translocas bear our multiple localities on ours as well.

Our dislocations across a variety of "heres" and "theres," our "travels to and from different contexts of knowledge production and reception," as de Lima Costa suggests, afford Translocas "certain types of analytical baggage that can alter one's perceptions of subalternity, privilege, intellectual work and feminism" (Costa 2000, 728). Our translocalities fuel endless epistemic traveling as well. Together with contributor Ester Shapiro (chapter 17), many of us "strive to learn from our shifting re-locations . . . as cultural outsiders in ethnocentric U.S. feminist organizations; as women in sexist Latino community-based organizations; as women of the 'Third World' whose Spanish is too Caribbean and primitive for European sensibilities; and as 'Latina gringas' whose Spanglish marks us as undereducated in our nation of origin language, culture and politics."

Because of our manifold circuits, travels, and dis/mis-placements, Translocas are more than diasporic subjects; we are necessarily translators. For starters, we have to translate *ourselves* across our differing locales of attachment and commitment. Indeed, for those of us who are based in the United States, translation is "an untiring game," a "way of life, a strategy for survival in the North" (Zavalia 2000, 199, in Espinal, chapter 4 in this volume). For many of us who were born in the United States or immigrated as children with parents who spoke no English, "translation starts practically in infancy," as Isabel Espinal reminds us in her chapter. Translocas straddle and transform languages and cultures, as neither our "mother tongue" nor our "other" language(s) is either "really foreign" or our own, as Espinal further notes. Like Donna Kaye Ruskin, whose "The Bridge Poem" opens *This Bridge Called My Back: Writings by Radical Women of Color*, we all do "more translating / Than the Gawdamn U.N." Ruskin complained of being tired of translating:

I've had enough
I'm sick of seeing and touching
Both sides of things
Sick of being the damn bridge for everybody

Nobody
Can talk to anybody
Without me

Right?

I explain my mother to my father my father to my little sister
My little sister to my brother my brother to the white feminists
The white feminists to the Black church folks the Black church folks

To the ex-hippies the ex-hippies to the Black separatists the
Black separatists to the artists the artists to my friends' parents . . .

Then I have to explain myself
To everybody.

I was drawn to revisit Ruskin's poem in the process of writing this introduction and readily came up with a "personalized Translocas adaptation":

I sometimes grow weary of seeing and touching
Multiple sides of things

I explain the *Americanos* to the Cubans the Cubans to the Brazilians the Brazilians (and Cubans and other Latin Americans) to the U.S. Women of Color feminists the U.S. Women of Color feminists to Latino men the Latino men to the U.S. white feminists the U.S. white feminists to the Latin American Black feminists and to the Latin American white feminists who don't identify as white the Latin American white feminists to queer U.S. Latinas . . .

Then I try to explain myself
To everybody.

As Espinal laments, this kind of multidirectional translating "can simply become tedious and we become *hartos* of this role." Translocas like Espinal and me cannot afford to tire of translation, however. In the face of the increasing entrapment of local cultures and knowledges in the global flows of capital and commodities, as many of our contributors insist, there is a growing need for feminists to engage in productive dialogue and negotiations across multiple geopolitical and theoretical borders. As Millie Thayer suggests in her contribution (chapter 20), the stakes in feminist translations are high; translations themselves, she maintains, are objects of struggle and "translation, or its refusal, is a strategic political act in the hands of social movements, whether it involves sharing knowledge to foster an alliance or interrupting a dominant discourse to defend autonomy."

If women's movements in the Latin/a Américas and elsewhere in the global South share a "common context of struggle" (Mohanty 1991a), as Thayer contends, then "their encounters with the 'scattered hegemonies' represented by states, development industries, global markets, and religious fundamentalisms create powerful (if only partially overlapping) interests and identities" that make the project of translation among them both possible and all the more pressing. Pascha Bueno-Hansen (chapter 16) argues that cultural translation can facilitate dialogue between ostensibly incompatible political positions in different locations through a "dynamic and necessarily incomplete process of mediation across discursive, political, linguistic, and geographic borders and power asymmetries." Theorizing the practice of what she dubs "translenguas," Maylei Blackwell (chapter 15) further proposes that translocal translation is a "key step in coalition building," especially critical for actors who are "multiply marginalized in their national contexts, creating linkages with social actors across locales to build new affiliations, solidarities, and movements."

We all need to devise better "bridging epistemologies" (Lao-Montes 2007, 132) so as to confront the mistranslations or bad translations that have fueled misunderstandings and obstructed feminist alliances, even among women who share the same languages and cultures — like U.S.-based Latinas and Latin Americans. As Costa argues pointedly, "in the interactions between Latina and Latin American feminisms, the travels of discourses and practices encounter formidable roadblocks and migratory checkpoints." She recounts our Translocas group's incessant wrestling (and frustration) with, on the one hand, the untranslatability of the U.S. concept of "women of color"—whether as a political project or an identity category—when carried to other topographies and, on the other hand, with the obliteration of questions of sexuality, race, and class in the production of "a universal subject of [early] Latin American feminism," "self-referential," and exclusive of "perspectives that question the very notion of 'women' as a collective identity" (Feliu, chapter 12), until recent years — itself a product of the operations of what Millán, following Hernández Castillo (2001; cited in Millán, chapter 7 in this volume) calls "hegemonic feminism" in the North-within-the-South of the Américas.

As chapters that deal extensively with Afro-Latin American women's movements and feminisms (Asher, Gómez-Barris, and Lao-Montes and Buggs), indigenous women (Belausteguigoitia, Millán, Bañales, Prada, Feliu, Hester, Blackwell), and Latina/U.S. women of color coalitional politics (Lao-Montes and Buggs, Blackwell, Bueno-Hansen, and Shapiro) make patently evident, Latin/a América is made up of multiple and multidirectional, and often overlapping, "intertwined diasporas" (Lao-Montes and Buggs, chapter 19 in this volume). Latin@ people of color theorists and activists, especially antiracist, feminist, indigenous, and Afro-Latino rights advocates, therefore are particularly well "translocated" to help foster the spread of bridging identities and epistemologies throughout the Américas. Lao-Montes and Mirangela Buggs maintain, for instance, that Afro-Latina difference can be a crucial component of a coalitional political community and a significant element within fields of intellectual production and critique. As Shapiro suggests, U.S. Latina immigrants also can make "distinctive contributions in translating feminist activisms across U.S. divides of race, ethnicity, class, and educational status, while remaining associated with global Third World feminisms through nation of origin connections."

Translocas also are more than world-traveling translators; we are cultural, political, theoretical mediators. We are agents of transculturation. As a counterpoint to assimilationist theories of "acculturation," Fernando Ortiz's notion of transculturation "necessarily involves the loss or uprooting of a previous culture, which could be defined as deculturation . . . [and] carries the idea of a consequent creation of a new cultural phenomena" (quoted in Renta 2007). As Costa suggests is the case with traveling theories and other cross-border flows, translocal feminism at least potentially "disfigures, deforms and transforms the culture and/or discipline that receives it" (see Introduction to Debates).

Translocas interrogate and thereby destabilize received meanings of race, class, sexualities, genders, and other "locational politics" on all sides of compound borders, as these meanings shift as we move across diverse localities. Bodies and desires are (re)produced and transformed through processes of translocal translation, as contributions by Hester, Maia, Bueno-Hansen, Schmidt, and Shapiro make clear. Like the Brazilian erotic dancers analyzed by Maia and the women of Fortaleza, Brazil, who engage with sex tourism, discussed in Adriana Piscitelli's contribution (chapter 14), Translocas refashion new racial and sexual *selves* as we cross multiple borders.[5] Our "remittances" —of which women are the most faithful senders, as Teresa Carrillo notes in her chapter (chapter 11)—are sociocultural and political, as well as material (Duany 2008).

A Translocas conception of transculturation—understood as promoting *intracultural* as well as cross-cultural processes of multidirectional transformation and multilevel processes of "deculturation" and cultural refoundation— also aims to engage productively with contemporary theorizing on the coloniality of power and *interculturalidad*, or "interculturality" (Quijano 2000; Mignolo 2006; Lugones 2007; Moraña, Dussel, and Jáuregui 2008; Costa 2009).[6] As Norma Klahn proposes in chapter 1, to better understand the "coloniality of power" one must "comprehend the unequal traveling and translation of feminist practices, theories, and texts and their reception." Citing Boaventura de Sousa Santos (2002), Schmidt similarly insists that postcolonial/decolonial theory requires "a dense articulation with the question of sexual discrimination and feminism" to reveal the sexist norms of sexuality that "'tend to lay a white man down on the bed with a black woman, rather than a white woman and a Black man.'" Though a translocal translational politics arguably is crucial to the "decolonial turn," the failure to engage feminist theory can result in homogenizing views of subaltern cultures that ignore or underplay sexual, gendered, racialized, class, age, and other differences and power relations that sustain hierarchies even among decolonial subjects like indigenous and Afro-descendant peoples.

Lao-Montes and Buggs nonetheless insist that a "decolonial politics of translocation" is essential to dismantling "hierarchies of rule" and the "colonial legacies of race, gender, class, sexuality, and nation that have shaped the lives, structural predicaments, and identities of women of color" and of "Afro-America." Blackwell shows, moreover, that an anti-imperial, decolonial Third World imaginary was at the core of early women of color organizing in the United States, as it is today among many indigenous and antiracist activists in the Latin American region. In her postcolonial reading of black women's struggles in Colombia, Asher further notes that postcolonial/decolonial politics and epistemes are crucial to challenging the "binaries (theory versus practice, power versus resistance, discourse versus materiality, victims versus guardians, etc.) that plague and limit so much thinking in the field of Third World women, gender, and development," arguing cogently that, like colonial discourses, such binaries "occlude the complex, contradictory, incomplete, and power-laden processes and practices against and within which women emerge and act."

THE CHAPTERS ARE GROUPED into four parts. The Introduction to Debates about Translation is Costa's essay, "Lost (and Found?) in Translation: Feminisms in Hemispheric Dialogue," which served as the concept paper that provided the theoretical backdrop for our collective project, and provides an incisive overview of feminist and other translation theorists' reflections on the travels and translations of feminist theories in the Américas. Drawing on our Translocas group's collective theoretical and political ruminations, it explores issues concerning feminism, translation, and transnationalism/translocalities with the aim of building feminist alliances among different constituencies not only across the North–South axis but in other latitudinal and longitudinal directions as well.

Part I, "Mobilizations: Mobilizing Theories/Texts/Images," presents essays centered on how actual texts, theories, authors, and theorists have traveled and been translated, and how the mobilization of such translations affects the translocal making of feminist meanings in the Américas. Chapters in this part further reveal the transgressive potential of translocated readings and pedagogies, proposing provocative strategies for reading across multiple borders.

In chapter 1, Chicana critic Norma Klahn offers an exacting analysis of women's writing in Latin/a América since the 1970s, illustrating how it has been a "site actively marked by gender, but where questions of class, ethnicity, sexuality, nation, and generation have been inexorably present." She insists that these writings — *testimonios*, autobiographical fictions, essays, and novels — constitute "poetic/political interventions," that are at once "aesthetic/ ethical ones linked to contestatory practices."

Similarly concerned with mapping the travels of feminist writings in the Latin/a Américas, Bolivian literary theorist Ana Rebeca Prada explores the question of whether Anzaldúa is "translatable in Bolivia." Effecting what we could call a transgressively "faithless appropriation" (Tsing 1997), Prada, like Klahn, seeks to open new "scenarios of conversation" and propose "new horizons for dialogue" across the Latin/a Américas by facilitating an unprecedented conversation between radical feminist queer mestizas and indigenous feminists across Texas and La Paz, Bolivia. Such translocal reappropriations of traveling theories, she argues, enable us to reimagine how feminist discourses and practices, as well as texts, might be able to travel North–South and South–North. Like the radical Bolivian feminist collective she discusses, Mujeres Creando, many translocal subjects "insist on staying on the border, living the body created by the colonial, racist divide, transgressing it, re-creating it, decolonizing it while staying *atravesado*, queer — therefore, *un-institutionable*." Noting that the history of feminism in Brazil "often runs against the grain of postmodernity" and "was written in painful struggles" in which class and race were necessarily articulated with gender, "each putting its entire set of urgencies on the order of the day even before such elaborations come to figure on the agenda of metropolitan feminisms," Brazilian literary critic Simone Schmidt's contribution explores "the tense and poorly resolved legacy of slavocratic patriarchy" and its consequences in terms of racial, class, sexual, and gendered inequalities and violence. The fruit of that violence, she pointedly notes, is the *corpo mestiço*, the racially mixed body, which constitutes a veritable battleground on which the multiple, inherent contradictions of race and racism in the Lusophone postcolonial world unfold. Working to translate the postcolonial agenda into Portuguese, Schmidt's chapter probes how the mestiça body is represented in several fictional texts by Brazilian women writers. Similarly seeking to interpret "Euro-centric translation theories" so as to better apprehend the position of an immigrant Dominican woman from New York translating the Spanish-language poems of Yrene Santos, another Dominican York woman, Espinal offers a poignant and insightful discussion of how and why translation for both her and Santos is "a matter of politics and an act of faith."

Closing this part of the book, Mexican cultural critic Maritza Belausteguigoitia argues for approaching feminist translation as a pedagogy, as "a way of reading," and reading as a recasting of distances and scales. Advocating a "pedagogy of the double" as a productive approach to reading transnationally, she pursues a paired reading of border-thinkers Gloria Anzaldúa and Subcomandante Marcos, placing "Chicanas and Zapatistas, face to face, mask to mask, ink to ink with one another," Indians and migrants, "two subjects that the nation refuses to fully integrate," as they represent "the unstranslatable, due to an excessive difference in color, tongue, and culture." Belausteguigoitia's essay, like the other chapters in this section, illustrates the powerful political and epistemological possibilities opened up when translocal readings disrupt the "process of transfer of the negative veil to the 'other,'" inducing a "two-way" circulation of significance: Chicana and Mexican, United States and Mexico, Marcos and Anzaldúa, "recasting signification from one to another."

The chapters in part II, "Mediations: National/Transnational Identities/ Circuits," turn to considerations of the venues, circuits, institutions, agents, and "theory brokers" that facilitate or obstruct the movements and mobilizations of specific feminist discourses and practices, privileging some, silencing others. Brazilian feminist theorist Costa's contribution to this section explores how Brazil's premier feminist studies journal, Revista Estudos Feministas (REF), has been a key component of the "material apparatus" that organizes the translation, publication, and circulation of feminist theories. She maintains that REF in fact had a constitutive role in the field it claims only to represent and that its editors and editorial committees, as well as the agendas of the journal's funders, exert "the function of gatekeepers of the feminist academic community, policing the many local appropriations/translations" of metropolitan theories. The journal has produced a "gender studies canon" that affords easier transit and greater visibility to authors and theories "closest to the international circuits of academic prestige and situated at privileged racial, geographical (Rio de Janeiro and São Paulo), and class sites." To promote more symmetry in the global flows of feminist theories, she contends, academic feminist journals must work to establish "epistemological countercanons" and "engage in practices of translation that 'translate with a vengeance.'" Mexican anthropologist Márgara Millán also focuses on three feminist magazines — Fem, Debate Feminista, and La Correa Feminista — as venues that control the flux of feminist discourses and practices, particularly those concerning race, ethnicity, and indigeneity. Closely examining the translational politics of those publications, the theories and authors they translate, and the ways they align with local political contexts, she argues that feminist journals are particularly relevant in shaping communication between different kinds of practices and are privileged places from which to understand the relationship between feminist theory, activism, and national politics.

The two chapters that follow, by political scientists Rebecca Hester and Kiran Asher, explore how the lives of indigenous Mexican immigrant women in the United States and Afro-Colombian women in the Chocó Valley are represented by "health promotion" and development discourses, respectively. Examining how Mixtec and Triqui women translate dominant medical and health care models and local patriarchies in caring for themselves and their families, Hester analyzes how indigenous migrant women's bodies are "*written* by and through the forces they engage within their daily lives" (Price and Shildrick 1999, quoted in Hester, chapter 8 this volume), while showing how they also "become agents in that writing." Although "health promotion" as a global discourse and practice is touted as particularly well suited to reaching and serving marginalized, "at-risk" populations, Hester cautions against its untranslated adoption as a strategy for promoting indigenous migrant women's "empowerment." Asher similarly warns that dominant discourses of "women and development" fail to appreciate the contradictions and complexities of Afro-Colombian women's experiences. Analyzing the texts—interviews, statements, poetry, songs, stories—of Matamba y Gausa, a network of black women in the Cauca region of Colombia, she argues that "gender experts" mistranslate local women's engagements with development and the environment. Asher suggests that postcolonial feminist approaches complicate our understanding of black women's activism, highlighting how they are shaped differentially, unequally, and discursively and can thereby contribute to developing more nuanced readings of Afro-descendant women's "texts in context."

Sociologist Macarena Gómez-Barris, a second-generation Chilean American, examines how feminist and antiracist discourses and practices flow through music and performance. Exploring music as translation through the work of Afro-Chilean performer Moyeneí Valdés, she analyzes how this performer's powerful enactments of cultural politics showcase African-descendant sensibilities and aesthetics. Analyzing how sound-break politics "are cultural efforts that rupture the hegemonic drone of economic neoliberalism that produce a visual and sound economy of commercialization, white noise, and an endless barrage of products," Gómez-Barris offers a unique window onto how transnational political and musical histories, especially feminist and antiracist formations, can influence the terrain of cultural politics even in situations of neoliberal hegemony.

Part III, "Migrations: Disrupting (B)Orders," draws attention to the translocalities and translations enacted in the movement of/across gendered, sexualized, class-based, and racialized bodies and borders. Teresa Carrillo provides a richly detailed account of the growing "feminization of migration" and the increased reliance on migrant domestic service workers to meet the "care deficit" of the global North (and as Verónica Feliu's chapter shows, of the North within the South). Arguing that a globalized "regime of social reproduction" systematically devalues the care work largely supplied by immigrant and diasporic women, she mounts a trenchant critique of the patriarchal, racist, and nativist discourses that pervade immigration policy debates in the United States and documents how the policies of both sending and receiving countries systematically disadvantage and diminish migrant women. Translations occur daily "from within the employee–employer relationship of domestic service," yet she, like Feliu, insists that that the "disempowering trends . . . rooted in a fundamental devaluation of domestic work (aka women's work) have not translated into feminist discourse in the North or South."

Feliu's contribution (chapter 12) demonstrates that the racialized, patriarchal devaluation of domestic service workers respects no geopolitical boundaries and is amply evident in southern latitudes of the Américas as well. Struggling to translate Chilean feminist "silences" surrounding the "labor women perform for other women," she undertakes a detailed (and largely unprecedented) analysis of Chilean domestic service work—principally performed by indigenous Chileans and Peruvian migrants. She maintains that despite (or perhaps because of) the feminist silences she documents, *empleadas* have played an "essential role" in the development of feminism by performing the care work from which middle-class feminists have been "liberated."

Two chapters in this part of the book explore how women in the Latin/a Américas redefine and rearticulate their racial, class, and sexual subjectivities as they translate themselves in sexual/erotic encounters in/from new latitudes. Brazilian anthropologist Suzana Maia examines how women who work as erotic dancers in New York City "deploy racial categories such as morena to articulate the tensions in their shifting identity as they move across nation-states." She argues that using a language of racial mixture and "mimetically incorporating icons of Brazilian sexuality and race" are central to the dancers' "sense of self" and "ways of experiencing the body," revealing "how racial configurations are defined transnationally." In an equally rich ethnographic account of "sex travels" in Fortaleza, Brazil-based Argentine anthropologist Adriana Piscitelli shows that local residents who work in sex tourism "translate themselves to suit the sex travelers' expectations." In such translocal circuits, race and gender are crucial to the performance of national identity. Accommodating sex tourists' desires for a "racialized, intense *tropical sexuality*," local women seeking relationships with sex travelers embody and reconfigure sexualized notions about Brazil, "performing the racialized identity allocated to them by foreigners."

"Movements: Feminist/Social/Political/Postcolonial, the fourth and final part of the book, offers a set of essays analyzing how and why particular theories and discourses do or do not translate in the political and cultural practices of Latina and Latin American feminisms. This part opens with an analysis of transborder, multiscalar flows across three movement formations: the indigenous women's movement, the lesbian feminist movement in Mexico, and Chicana and U.S. women of color feminisms in the United States, by Native American/Thai cultural theorist Maylei Blackwell. She introduces "unaligned geographies of difference" as a theoretical framework for analyzing the possibilities and challenges implicated in forging feminist coalitions and movement-building across borders and theorizes a practice she dubs *translenguajes* (translanguages/tongues) "to identify the ways activists are translating, reworking, and contesting meaning in the transnational flow of discourses between social movement actors in three different cross-border formations." Analyzing how marginalized political actors have to navigate local entrapments of power to reach the transnational level, Blackwell demonstrates that local negotiations and configurations of power, especially those shaped by gender, race, and sexuality, necessarily mediate transborder exchanges among movements. Exploring the high stakes always implicated in the transnational politics of translation and mistranslation, she shows that translocal social movements often entail translating notions of identity that involve struggles over meaning, regional identities, and local autonomy. Like the other chapters in this section of the book, Blackwell's concludes that transnational organizing that recognizes "how power is structured in each [local] context, and negotiates rather than glosses over power differences, requires a critical practice of translation of everyday political meanings, practices, and organizing logics."

Peruvian American political scientist Pascha Bueno-Hansen at once explores and facilitates a "virtual dialogue" between *movimientos de lesbianas feministas* and queer women of color feminist movements in the Américas. Her analysis highlights how the meanings of terms like *lesbiana* and *queer* shift as they travel across borders and through distinct political-cultural contexts and different movement spaces, marked by power asymmetries that include accelerated transcultural flows, usage of international and regional forums and networks, and increased migration. Deploying a "friendship model for feminist solidarity," the virtual dialogue she develops explores how two distinct feminist activist formations "might negotiate the tension between essentialist and deconstructivist approaches to making identity claims, naming themselves, and struggling for visibility on their own terms."

Ester Shapiro's chapter turns to a consideration of how traveling texts can both facilitate and obstruct cross-border coalitional politics, analyzing her own and other U.S. Latinas' accomplishments and disillusionments in "translocating" *Our Bodies, Ourselves* into *Nuestros Cuerpos, Nuestras Vidas* as a text "deliberately designed to be read, interpreted, and used differently as it traveled, engaging Spanish-speaking readers in multiple spaces and building empathy, recognition, and political connections across borders." Applying concepts from U.S. border-crossing and Third World feminism, the chapter demonstrates how the inclusion of U.S. Latina perspectives "helped re-vision the text's relationship to both local and transnational feminist movements, creating an empowering world-traveling text, 'translocating' knowledge while identifying opportunities for transformative political action."

Through a translocal feminist reading of another widely circulated text, *I, Rigoberta Menchú*, Chicana literary critic Victoria Bañales examines how indigenous women's revolutionary struggles "openly defy and challenge dominant racialized gender and sexuality discourses that represent indigenous women as essentially passive, penetrable, and apolitical." Noting that most critical work on the text treats gender as secondary to other ethnic, cultural, or class dimensions of Menchú's testimonio, Bañales's examination of the representational possibility of indigenous "women with guns" in that testimonio "illuminates the ways power relations are never fixed and immutable but rather the historical, man-made (literally and figuratively) products of complex social institutions that can be ultimately challenged, resisted, and reconfigured." Through a richly detailed analysis of the complex representations of gender in the text, Bañales helps "unearth and recuperate some of the text's buried gender 'truth effects,' which have remained, for one reason or another, heavily lost in translation."

Further advancing keen theorizations of "translocation" and "intertwined diasporas," Afro-Puerto Rican sociologist Agustín Lao-Montes and U.S. African American feminist educator Mirangela Buggs explore similar questions through a discussion of U.S. women of color feminisms and Afro-Latin@ movements. They undertake a "gendering [and Latin/a Americanization] of African diaspora discourse," analyzing the African diaspora as a black borderland, as a geohistorical field with multiple borders and complex layers. Lao-Montes and Buggs also engage black feminist and queer perspectives on the African diaspora that reveal the particularly profound forms of subalternization experienced by women of color and black queers.

Examining the complex politics of translation in what she dubs "transnational feminist publics," Anglo-American feminist sociologist Millie Thayer caps off this final part of the book with a richly textured ethnographic analysis of the tortuous travels of feminist discourses and practices among women's movements in Recife and their allies and donors beyond Brazil. Examining the discursive circuits and flows between differentially (trans)located women in feminist counterpublics, Thayer argues that "local" movement politics always entails manifold and multidirectional translations among diverse women "linked to . . . publics organized around other markers, such as race, class, and local region, [who] speak distinctive 'dialects' or, sometimes, even 'languages.'"

THIS COLLECTION ASPIRES to take its place in a tradition of collaborative writing and anthologizing practices among Latina and women of color feminists in the United States, documented in chapters by Bueno-Hansen, Shapiro, and Blackwell.[7] It also represents an exercise in translocal knowledge production and collective, collaborative framework building which, as Arturo Escobar rightly insists, always "pays off in terms of theoretical grounding, interpretive power, social relevance, and sense of politics" (2008, xii). We've learned a great deal from one another's *translocuras*.

Our anthology transgresses disciplinary borders as shamelessly and energetically as it does geopolitical ones. The authors are based in a variety of disciplines, from media studies to literature to Chican@ studies to political science; most span a range of disciplinary knowledges and theoretical perspectives in a single chapter. Moreover, because our contributors have been engaged in sustained dialogue, readers should find that the essays collected here are in implicit or explicit conversation with one another. That conversation is intergenerational as well as interethnic, international, and interdisciplinary, requiring all of us to interrogate some of our most dearly and steadfastly held assumptions and inspiring many to learn to read and translate in new ways.

Whereas (too) many edited collections published nowadays are hastily cobbled together after a one- or two-day conference, this anthology is the carefully cultivated and matured fruit of a multiyear collaborative process stretching across a number of countries, institutions, disciplines, and generations and involving Latin American(ist) and Latina feminist scholars from the North and South of the Américas. The editors and many of the contributors formed part of a Greater San Francisco Bay Area research group that met at the University of California at Santa Cruz (UCSC) over a number of years, under the auspices of the Chicano/Latino Research Center. Most others also participated at some point in one of the several sessions on the travels and translations of feminist theories in the Américas we organized for the 2000, 2001, 2003, 2004, 2006, and 2007 Congresses of the Latin American Studies Association or in one of several conferences and seminars we've held on the topic at UCSC, the Federal University of Santa Catarina in Brazil, and at the University of Massachusetts–Amherst (May 5–6, 2006).

We originally emerged as a network of scholar-activists articulated across the particular locations of southern Brazil, northern California, and, later, New England. What brought us together initially and subsequently brought others (Prada, Maia, Millán, Piscitelli, and Belausteguigoitia among them) into our translocal circuit of theorizing feminisms was the urgency of seeking new epistemes for reading culture, politics, gender, race, and so on that were not based on binary markers such as North and South. Indeed, a major goal of the anthology was to destabilize the North–South dichotomy and highlight how translocal subjects and theories are constituted in the spaces in between. Some of the contributors are from the South speaking in the North about the South, in the South speaking about the North, in the South speaking about the South, or in the North speaking from a translocal position that is neither North nor South.

This book thereby provides unprecedented insights into the travels and translations of feminist theories, practices, and discourses in and across the Américas, offering fresh perspectives on questions typically framed in terms of transnationalism and new ways of thinking about translocal connections among feminisms in the global North and (within and across the) global South. Our project aims to foster a renewed feminist and antiracist episteme for reimagining and retheorizing a revitalized Latina/o Américan feminist studies *travestida* (cross-dressed) for the globalized, transmigrant Américas of the twenty-first century. It also signals the possibilities of a transformed "U.S. American studies" and a Latin American studies that would understand the Américas as a dynamic transborder, translocal cultural formation rather than a clearly delineated geopolitical space. We entreat activists, cultural workers, and knowledge producers inside and outside the academy to join us in translating and translocating hegemonic and subaltern discourses, policies, and practices and in building alliances to forge a genuinely inclusive, socially, sexually, racially, economically, environmentally just, and *feminist* Latin/a Américas.

Notes

A partial, earlier version of this essay appeared in Portuguese as "Constituindo uma Política Feminista Translocal de Tradução" (Enacting a Translocal Feminist Politics of Translation), *Revista Estudos Feministas* (Brazil), 17, no. 3 (2009). I am especially indebted in this essay and this project as a whole to Claudia de Lima Costa. I am also grateful to my research assistants and faithful interlocutors, Cruz Caridad Bueno, Casey Stevens, Amy Fleig, Stephanie Gutierrez, Irem Kok, Alyssa Maraj-Grahame, Martha Balaguera, and especially Alper Yagci, for their indefatigable efforts to help us see this project through to publication.

1. For a succinct overview of feminist debates about the politics of location, see Davis (2007, 7–11).

2. On the feminist politics of place, see especially Harcourt and Escobar (2005).

3. Lionel Cantú was the first to call our group Translocas and was among the most enthusiastic and insightful founding members of our Transnational Feminist Politics of Translation research group, the "most *loca* of all," as he liked to say. This book is dedicated to his memory. His untimely death in the early stages of this project was an inestimable emotional and intellectual loss for Translocas and all those who knew and loved him.

4. Other scholars have similarly emphasized the transnational/translocal constitution of subjectivities that is central to our own conception of Translocas. Lynn Stephen (2007) proposes the concept of "transborder lives," for instance, to refer to subjects who migrate among multiple sites in the United States and Mexico, and Patricia Zavella (2011) advances the notion of "peripheral vision" to refer to subjectivities and imaginaries fashioned by migrants and Latina/os who do not migrate but reside in locales with migrants and links to "sending regions" in the Americas. Lawrence La Fountain-Stokes has used the term "translocas" to discuss Puerto Rican drag (2008, 2011).

5. As Ginetta Candelario (2007) finds in her compelling account of racialization processes among Dominicans in New York City, Washington, and Santo Domingo, nationally rooted racial self-perceptions and identities can also be quite resilient even as subjects move across localities.

6. For recent works by the various authors associated with the decolonial studies group, see the special issue of *Cultural Studies* on "The Coloniality of Power and De-colonial Thinking" (2007) and Moraña, Dussel, and Jáuregui (2008).

7. Among those most frequently cited in our contributors' chapters are *This Bridge Called My Back: Writings by Radical Women of Color* (Moraga and Anzaldúa 1983 [1981]); *All the Women Are White, All the Blacks Are Men, But Some of Us Are Brave; Home Girls: A Black Feminist Anthology* (Hull, Bell-Scott, and Smith 1982); and *Telling to Live: Latina Feminist Testimonios* (Latina Feminist Group 2001b). Our book also follows in the anthologizing tradition of Latina and Latin Americanist feminist scholars who produced collaborative texts about feminist thought and activism, such as *Women, Culture and Politics in Latin America* (Seminar on Feminism and Culture in Latin America 1990) and *Chicana Feminisms: A Critical Reader* (Arredondo et al. 2003).

INTRODUCTION TO DEBATES ABOUT TRANSLATION/
LOST (AND FOUND?) IN TRANSLATION/FEMINISMS IN HEMISPHERIC DIALOGUE

CLAUDIA DE LIMA COSTA

This chapter is a reprint of an article originally published in *Latino Studies* 4, no. 1 (2006). It was initially written as a concept paper on feminism and translation to capture and systematize the conversations and inquiries that had for several years informed the agenda of our Latina and Latin American(ist) feminist research group on questions of translation and translocation. In meetings marked by lively and provocative conversation, the group explored how the notion of translation could be deployed to track the movements of feminist concepts and political strategies across localities, especially between and among U.S. Latina and Latin American feminisms. We decided to include this concept paper in its original form to mark the theoretical ground from which many of the discussions in the ensuing chapters of this anthology departed, exploring the ways the idea of cultural translation plays out in a multiplicity of transnational, national, regional, and local arenas of feminist struggles and interventions.

Since the original publication of this concept paper, and with the increasing importance and visibility that the notion of cultural translation (and translation in general) acquired vis-à-vis the global shuttling of peoples, ideas, and commodities, a plethora of journal articles, book chapters, and books have appeared on the subject. My other contribution to this anthology (chapter 6) incorporates more recent debates on translation, as do many of the chapters that follow. While reading those, it is important not to forget what Spivak (2012, 242) teaches us—that the very notion of translation, that is, of one word or idea standing in for another, dislodges any possibility of literal translation. In the sense that the concept is deployed throughout this volume, translation can only be understood as a catachresis, as an always already misuse of words, an impropriety and inadequacy that underpins all systems of representation.

In contemporary globalized postcolonial formations, in light of the reconfiguration of knowledges and the contemporary remapping of all kinds of borders (geographic, economic, political, cultural, libidinal, among others), the problematic of translation has become an important, as well as recent, domain of feminist contention.[1] In the context of "diverse, interconnected histories of travel and displacement" (Clifford 1997, 18) and the transnational traffic in theories and concepts, the question of translation becomes quite pertinent and constitutes a unique space from which, on the one hand, to take on critical analyses of representation and power and the asymmetries between languages and, on the other, to examine the knowledge formations and institutionalities in/through which these theories and concepts travel. In summary, at this moment when "mobility, proximity, approximation" (Chow 1995), promoted by the movements of capital and the transnationalization of culture, have signaled the entrance of increasingly disparate regions into a forced and homogeneous modernity, to theorize the process of translation (to translate translation) requires an analysis of the various economies within which the sign of translation circulates.

I should begin clarifying that the use of the term translation is borrowed from Tejaswini Niranjana's (1992) deployment of the concept, that is, it does not refer exclusively to discussions about the strategies for semiotic processes in the area of translation studies but to debates on cultural translation. The notion of cultural translation (drawing on debates on ethnographic theory and practice) is premised on the view that any process of description, interpretation, and dissemination of ideas and worldviews is always already caught up in relations of power and asymmetries between languages, regions, and peoples.[2] Much ink has been spilled about the travels of theories across different topographies and through itineraries that are ever more complex. The metaphor of "traveling theory" was first introduced by Edward Said (1983), who looked at the movement of theories as embedded in other cultural practices, larger historical contexts, and power struggles. Since then, it became a traveling metaphor taken up by many other theorists who wanted to examine the conditions shaping the constitution of knowledge formations through the traffic of ideas and concepts, including the changing conditions of traveling in increasingly transnationalized, yet unequal, world economy and academic markets.[3] In the traffic of theories, Mary E. John (1996) argues, those that travel more easily articulate such a high level of abstraction that any question of context is rendered irrelevant (e.g., deconstruction, poststructuralism, psychoanalysis). While crossing territories, theories are continuously appropriated and transformed by their local readings, acquiring a more composite structure. Feminist theories fall under this category, for in making simultaneous use of several registers (material, political, cultural frameworks), they are forged at different levels of abstraction.[4]

In the context of the Americas, in the interactions between Latina and Latin American feminisms, the travels of discourses and practices encounter formidable roadblocks and migratory checkpoints when they attempt to cross borders. This is in part due not only to the existence of certain dominant and exclusionary institutional configurations but also to the fact that different historiographies have excluded subjects and subjectivities from both sides of the North–South divide (and within each side), making the possibility of productive dialogue a daunting political and epistemological challenge. Given these difficulties, the questions posed early on in our conversation were as follows. How is academic knowledge conveyed from one hemisphere to another? What is lost in translation, and why, in conversations between Latinas and Latin American feminists?

The point of departure of this chapter—and of our research cluster interrogations—was the insight that the relationalities and attachments that different analytical categories have as they travel will greatly influence their ability to translate. For instance, although the project of subaltern studies was in a first moment anchored to theory and detached from projects of race and gender, the project of women of color from the start has been anchored to race. However, race is a category that is "read" in specific ways in different racial formations, hence the (un)translatability of the U.S. concept "woman of color" when carried to other topographies.[5] Likewise, resistance to Latinas' and Chicanas' concerns in some Latin American feminist quarters, which were often racialized and quickly dismissed as not serious or relevant to Latin American matters, indicate how questions of sexuality, race, and class are obliterated at the same time that a universal subject of Latin American feminism is produced. An important issue facing feminists engaged in the process of translation while crossing borders, then, is to mediate linguistic, cultural, racial, and other barriers so as "to create sites for alliances and cross-border talk that does not lead to cross-talk" (Carrillo 1998).

The recent polemic spurred by an article by Pierre Bourdieu and Loïc Wacquant (1999), in which these two sociologists criticize the transnational circulation and importation of U.S.-based ideas and models, serves as an illustration of the problematic of translation when some categories are transported from one context to another. As John D. French (2003, 376) has incisively put it, Bourdieu and Wacquant describe the global export of concepts (including the imposition, for instance, of a U.S. black-and-white model of race relations in Brazil) as the proliferating McDonaldization of out-of-place ideas, hence "neglecting the dynamics of 'reading' and 'translation' through which 'foreign' ideas come to be incorporated into national intellectual fields, each with its own historical trajectory, cultural formation, and social mythologies." According to French, "Their simplistic model of US domination/imposition and subaltern submission/complicity is empirically and theoretically wrongheaded. It erases the process of local appropriation while vastly exaggerating the power and influence that US-based notions have had or can have in Brazil. In summary, they make a fetish of the 'foreign' origin of ideas (itself questionable) while depicting the process of transnational exchange as inherently one-sided. Worst of all, their call for resistance is vitiated by their own preference for taking refuge behind flimsy nationalist barricades rather than conducting serious transnational intellectual and political debate" (French 2003, 376).

To engage in debates about the appropriation/translation of ideas necessitates an exploration of how theories travel through the North–South axis. An example is given by Francine Masiello's (2000, 55) reading of the pages of Las/12, the feminist supplement of the Argentinean daily Pagina/12, to examine "how materials of cultural theory move from one language to another, and how the screen aura of celebrities can be reread from the Southern margin, how sexuality is resemanticized when it crosses the borders of home and state." Masiello's keen analysis of Las/12 reveals that through the mechanisms of sensationalism and satire, which stress the artifice of representation, and in a playful language aimed at a mass reading public, its editors and collaborators interrogate, through the perspective of a (Latin American) lesbian gaze, the relationship between gender, sexuality, and translation so as to sabotage the normative North–South flow of meanings established by the neoliberal market economy. The cultural translations and (mis)appropriations of market constructions of gender in the pages of Las/12 (such as, for instance, representations of Latinas in Hollywood cinema, the culture of Hollywood celebrities, the imposition of fashion on the female body) not only offer readers alternative reflections about female identity but also upset the North–South traffic of commodity culture by "dismantl[ing] a sense of 'woman' as projected by mass media venues and academic theory" (Masiello 2000, 54): "La mujer no es un suplemento" (woman is not a supplement) (2000, 52).

Turning from daily supplement to literary texts, Nora Domínguez (2000) reads some Latin American fictional narratives[6] to explore how these texts, by interpellating a nomad subject, construct a space in between different languages — national and foreign, private and political, written and oral, the language of exile and the language of the return — as well as in-between systems of meanings and contact zones (North America, Latin America, Europe). For the novels' narrators in question, it is from these interstitial spaces and through the metaphor of translation that an appropriate understanding of the mechanisms forging gendered social identities through continuous processes of translation can be built, revealing how "foreign" theories and concepts are brought into friction and dialogue with local experiences so as to enable identifications and deidentifications, as well as configurations of alternative theoretical cartographies.

Another example of the processes of identification and deidentification entailed by strategies of translation is discussed by Kathy Davis (2002). In her scrutiny of the worldwide dissemination of the book *Our Bodies, Ourselves* (Boston Women's Health Book Collective 1971)—considered a North American artifact and at the time one of the most important and progressive references for women's health both in the United States and abroad—the author probes the extent to which Western (U.S.-based) feminism (under the garb of global feminism) is imposed on the bodies and minds of women situated in other contexts, Western and non-Western. Addressing the "feminism-as-cultural-imperialism" critique, articulated by several U.S. feminists engaged in the deconstruction of the notion of a global sisterhood, the author assesses the pitfalls of global feminism and "the possibilities of transnational alliances for the circulations of feminist knowledges and body/politics" (Davis 2002, 229). Davis (2007) examines the border crossings of *Our Bodies, Ourselves* in the West–East, North–South directions to argue that different local material conditions—ranging from availability of funding resources for translators, computer equipment, to publishing houses—coupled by ideological configurations, the presence of philanthropic foundations, international donors, women's groups, and/or feminist nongovernmental organizations (NGOs) greatly influenced translation strategies of the book to better adapt it to the needs and experiences of different women's constituencies. Looking at these travels and translations of *Our Bodies, Ourselves* (OBOS), Davis concludes that

the translations which emerged in the three decades following the first edition of OBOS indicate that it was not the notion of "global sisterhood" which traveled (y). On the contrary, what traveled was how the original collective wrote the book. The image of a group of (lay)women collectively sharing knowledge about their embodied experiences seems to be what fired the imagination of women in different parts of the world and served as an invitation to do the same. While the notion of "global sisterhood" creates a spurious universality, which denies differences among women, the process by which the original collective wrote their book could be taken up fairly easily by a diversity of women and adapted to their specific circumstances. It was the method of knowledge sharing and not a shared identity as women which appeared to have a global appeal, making OBOS a case in point for a transnational feminist body/politics based on oppositional practices rather than identity politics. (Davis 2007, 240, 241)

Looking at the travels of *Our Bodies, Ourselves*, as well as the gender concept in the Latin American context (more specifically, in Brazil), Millie Thayer (2000) focuses on the complex articulations of political, economic, racial, and ideological factors constitutive of these localities and their relation to larger, more globalized forces. Taking as its point of departure the NGO SOS Corpo in Recife, northeast Brazil, Thayer analyzes the initial appropriation of the book by its feminist constituency and the ways in which, in the span of two decades (1980–1990s) and against the background of military dictatorship, followed by transition to democracy and democratic consolidation, its resemantization responded to varying local social movement practices and discourses around political demands for citizenship rights. The author examines how the concept of the individual body in the pages of *Our Bodies, Ourselves* is articulated by the SOS Corpo feminists to the idea of the political body as a platform for demands for basic (citizenship) rights, therefore showing how translations are the result of ongoing processes of negotiation and not one-way impositions. However, as Thayer acutely observes, despite having originated in the context of the SOS Corpo practices and discussions, the local meanings of the concept of citizenship were also influenced by international donors and transnational feminisms. Thayer concludes by arguing that economic and discursive barriers prevent feminist theories and concepts from treading in the South–North direction. It is incumbent on the transnational feminist movement and the diasporic intellectual to open up spaces that would allow for more horizontality and symmetry in the global flux of theories, concepts, discourses, and identities.

In the contemporary scenario of fragmented identities, contact zones, and border epistemologies, it is incumbent on feminist critics to scrutinize the processes of cultural translation of feminist theories/concepts so as to develop what has been dubbed "a geopolitical or transnational ability to read and write" (Friedman 1998; Spivak 1992) toward the articulation of "transnational feminisms" (Grewal and Kaplan 1994a). This task demands mapping the dislocations and continual translations of feminist theories/concepts, as well as the constraints mechanisms of mediation and technologies of control imposed in the transit of theories across geopolitical borders. For example, Rosi Braidotti

(2000, 720), scrutinizing the problematic export of French poststructuralism to the highly commodified U.S. academic market (where it is profoundly de-politicized in its reception), argues that a full-scale analysis of the travels/translations of theories needs to take account of "the nature of the institutions of learning, the centralized status of theory, [and] the norms and taboos of representation" at the point of arrival.[7] However, as has been previously argued by Robert Stam (2001) and Ella Shohat (2002), to locate the emergence of poststructuralism in the West is itself an effect of translation. For these authors, to ignore the contribution of anticolonial and subaltern theorizing in the decentering of Euro-centric master narratives, thereby occluding how Third Worldist thinking was codified by those associated with structuralism and poststructuralism, is to give this theoretical corpus a white coating and a French accent.[8] Therefore, a close scrutiny of the traffic in theories or the transportation of texts might also reveal the operations of "intellectual, conceptual imperialism . . . most notably in the forms of racism and colonialism" (Jardine 1988, 14).

One of the pertinent questions to ask of the travels and translations of feminist theories and practices would be the following. By what means and through which institutionalities do feminist concepts/discourses/practices gain temporary (or even permanent) residence in different representational economies? It is well known that texts do not travel across linguistic contexts without a "visa" (translations always entail some sort of cost). Their dislocation can only take place if there is also a material apparatus organizing their translation, publication, circulation, and reception. This materiality—which is at the same time constituted by and constitutive of the contexts of reception—influences in significant ways which theories/texts get translated and are resignified for a better fit with local intellectual agendas. Acts of reading (modes of reception) are acts of appropriation carried out in contexts of power (institutional, economic, political, and cultural).

In the travels of feminist theories in the Americas, there are several "theory brokers" ranging from academics, international, and national donors situated in state and philanthropic organizations, feminist NGOs, and grassroots women's organizations and movements. These different and diverse mediators—as Thayer (2001) and Sonia E. Alvarez (2000) have convincingly shown (and whose arguments will be explored later)—have a certain agency in the cross-border movement of feminist theories/discourses. In both the United States and Latin America, the academy and feminist NGOs are the two most important locales for the production, circulation, and reception of feminisms. However, ongoing economic crises in Latin America have put serious constraints in the circulation of feminist theories, and within the United States, Chicana/ Latina productions have not always counted on effective apparatuses of dissemination, given the still pervasive dismissal of subaltern knowledges within the U.S. academy.

Translation Practices and the Traffic in Gender

One way of assessing the political gains and/or losses in the traffic in theories within feminism is to look at the uneven migrations of one of its foundational categories, gender.[9] Some versions of U.S. feminist theories' emphasis on difference (a response, in the social terrain, to political pressures from women of color and lesbian feminists in the United States), together with the deconstruction of identity categories (an outcome, in the epistemological terrain, of the advent of poststructuralism), led many U.S. academic feminists to proclaim the disintegration of gender in light of the fractures of class, race, sexuality, age, historical particularity, and other individual differences constitutive of the postmodern heteroglossia.

Other feminists, contesting the dispersal of both woman and gender, amply criticized what they viewed as a dangerous trend in the 1990s: the emergence of "feminism without women" (Modleski 1991). There are still others, including many Latina feminists, who, when confronting a devastating scenario of volatile bodies and evasive analytical categories — in which everything is reduced to parodic performances — reaffirm the need to fight against the atomization of differences by asserting a positive identity for women through the articulation of differences among women with the structures of domination that helped produce those differences in the first place (Benhabib 1995).[10]

While these theoretical debates on gender took hold in the U.S. academy, states and intergovernmental agencies in the Americas amply adopted the gender category in their public policies and social programs directed toward promoting "gender equity." Alvarez (1998a), analyzing feminist incursions in the state during the political opening toward gender, for instance, argues that feminist critiques of women's oppression and subordination become diluted and neutralized in the discourses and practices of these institutions. In her words, "despite the local and global feminist lobbies' central role in advocating for the changed international gender norms that helped foster such apparently gender-friendly State policies and discourses, however, the terms of women's, especially poor women's, incorporation into neoliberal State policies are not necessarily feminist-inspired. One Colombian local government official neatly summed up how feminists' political indictment of women's subordination is too often translated or tergiversated by State bureaucrats when she told me:

'now things have changed, it's no longer that radical feminism of the 1970s, now it's public policies with a gender perspective'" (*políticas públicas con perspectiva de género*) (Alvarez 1998a, 271). However, as Alvarez (2000) points out, in the arena of policy advocacy at a supranational level feminism has proven to be most successful in the task of translation and fashioning local feminist political grammars and symbolic maps. Analyzing Latin American feminist movement's *encuentros* and international policy advocacy networks, Alvarez identifies two logics intersecting these different, yet interconnected terrains: identity-solidarity logic (oriented toward creating an imagined feminist community, politicized identities, and ideological affinities) and transnational intragovernmental advocacy logic (oriented toward influencing gender policies through venues such as the UN conferences).

These logics feed into one another in complex ways. According to the author, feminist encuentros help local activists build international ties of solidarity, political affinities, and shared identities with positive repercussions for their local movement practices and struggles. Participating in arenas such as the UN conferences requires specialized skills at policy advocacy that many feminist activists did not (and do not) necessarily have. However, given that the encuentros have "facilitated the formation of transnational social networks and nurtured intense personal and political bonds among feminists in far-flung reaches of Latin America, [thus contributing to] the creation of policy-focused networks and regional advocacy coalition" (Alvarez 2000, 43), involvement in the transnationalized gender policy advocacy has, in turn, reverberated back on the home front in the local translations and deployments of internationally sanctioned political scripts.[11] Despite the two-way flows of these logics, these translations, Alvarez alerts, have not always been unproblematic. Often the local appropriations/resignifications of the transnational advocacy logic "exacerbat[ed] existing power imbalances among activists and organization" (2000, 56). Asymmetries result when greater local political capital and resources are accrued to activists and organizations with easier access (due to various reasons) to the transnational public spaces of policy advocacy. Notwithstanding these imbalances, more frequently than not we can witness Southern-inspired appropriations of Northern-based women's lobby. In the words of one of Alvarez's interviewees, "though she initially found the [advocacy] concept abstract and foreign, It has been mixing with my Latin American *mestizaje* (mestiza identity), and I have appropriated it and ascribed it new meaning from Latin America and from my own experience" (2000, 56).

While states and intergovernmental agencies unabashedly embraced gender, the Vatican, during its preparation for the 1995 Conference on Women in Beijing, and fearful of the consequences that the use of the word *gender* might entail—such as the acceptance of homosexuality, the destruction of the (patriarchal) family, and the dissemination of feminism—was orchestrating an intractable attack to the concept of gender, associating it to a "sinister foreign influence" (Franco 1998). As Jean Franco tells us, in the warning of the auxiliary bishop of Buenos Aires, the use of the word *gender* as "a purely cultural construct detached from the biological . . . would make us into fellow travelers of radical feminism" (1998, 281).

Although it would be a clear exaggeration to say that gender was a "sinister influence" (much to the contrary), as an analytical category it did leave room for depoliticizing moves. Since, in the Brazilian academy, the words *feminism* and *feminist theories* conveyed a radical attitude, many Brazilian feminist academics adopted the gender studies rubric to describe their scholarly activities so as to retain credibility vis-à-vis the scientific community. A focus on gender studies, as opposed to feminist studies, allowed them some modicum of "rigor" and "excellence" (according to positivist definitions) and secured them a (somewhat) safe place in the canon, which in turn was not challenged. In the scenario of gender studies in Brazil, one could study women's oppression and the unequal power relations between women and men without necessarily being engaged in a feminist political project. In the supposedly neutral terrain of gender, there was no need to politicize theory and theorize politics.

To understand this contextual take on gender, it is important to realize that Brazilian academic feminism remains poised at the crossroads of two very distinct theoretical currents. One road takes us to French structuralism, with its emphasis on complementarity (along with the ideal of equality and denial of difference), whereas the other summons us toward North American poststructuralism, with its emphasis on otherness and the politicization of difference (Machado 1997).

One of the outcomes of this particular mix of theoretical tendencies in Brazilian feminism is that a large number of its practitioners in the social sciences (in contrast to many, if not most, feminist scholars in the humanities) embraced the term *gender studies* more willingly than their literary counterparts, who still held on to the signifier *woman*.[12] For the former group, gender was perceived as being a more scientifically rigorous term than either women's or feminist studies. Women's studies seemed too essentialist, and feminist studies sounded too militant, therefore not objective or systematic.[13] This controversy nicely captures the fact that, to gauge how well gender travels, one needs to thoroughly examine the analytic and historical constraints inhabiting the articulation of difference (John 1996).[14] As Joan Scott herself put it, worried about the ease with which gender had entered the academy, "gender seems to fit within the scientific terminology of social science and thus dissociates itself from the (supposedly strident) politics of feminism. It does not carry with it a necessary statement about inequality or power nor does it name the aggrieved (and hitherto) invisible party" (1988, 31).

At present this proclivity in gender studies in the Brazilian academy is fully consolidated through the fashionable and rapidly spreading field of masculinities studies (which are not necessarily articulated with a feminist critical perspective), largely due to generous grants from government agencies and national and international philanthropic institutions. However, I should note that there have been other, more politically progressive appropriations of gender in the Brazilian context. One example comes from Thayer's (2000) incisive study of the North–South travels of the concept. Thayer shows how the discursive migration of gender and its eclectic and contextually specific translations were more radical than allowed by most models of unilateral transmission between North and South of the Americas, hence illuminating the diversity of forces (e.g., financing from international institutions) and discourses (e.g., discourses about citizenship and rights) implicated in such geographical dislocations. She makes evident how these factors complicate endlessly any movement of concepts and categories across geographic, political, and epistemological boundaries.

Translation as Discursive Migration

Owing to the intense migration of concepts and values that accompany the travels of texts and theories, it is often the case that a concept with a potential for political and epistemological rupture in a particular context, when carried over to another context, may become depoliticized. For J. Hillis Miller (1996), this happens because any concept carries within itself a long genealogy and a silent history that, transposed to other topographies, may produce unanticipated readings. However, a theory's openness to translation is a result of the performative, not cognitive, nature of language (every reading is, after all, a misreading). According to Miller, theories are ways of doing things with language, one of them being the possibility of activating different readings of the social text. When introduced to a new context, the kinds of readings a theory will enact may radically transform this context. Therefore, translations, besides being intrinsically mistranslations, as Walter Benjamin (1969) had also pointed out, will always entail defacement; when a theory travels, it disfigures, deforms, and transforms the culture and/or discipline that receives it.

> A theoretical formulation never quite adequately expresses the insight that comes from reading. That insight is always particular, local good for this time, place, text, and act of reading only. The theoretical insight

is a glimpse out of the corner of the eye of the way language works, a glimpse that is not wholly amenable to conceptualization. Another way to put this is to say that the theoretical formulation in its original language is already a translation or mistranslation of a lost original. This original can never be recovered because it never existed as anything articulated or able to be articulated in any language. Translations of theory are therefore mistranslations of mistranslations, not mistranslations of some authoritative and perspicuous original. (Miller 1996, 223)

In the travels of theories in the Americas, one of the recurring challenges for hemispheric dialogue lies in the attempt to translate concepts that resist appropriation. How do we translate ideas and concepts that have not traveled? In the politics of translation, the concern must be not only with the travels and appropriations of terms/discourses but with the extent to which one wants to open the translated sign and to whom should it be open. The "sheer convenience of incomprehension," as Timothy Brennan notes, punctuates the silence on the other side of the translation process, emphasizing the fact that "acts of translation do not always seek ways to communicate more accurately, but instead to mistranslate meaning subversively in order to ensure an incommunicability" (2001, 53) that, in the last instance, signals the possibility of cultural survival. For Emily Apter, the silence of incommunicability represents an active resistance "against simplistic models of translation transnationalism that idealize the minority language as an object of ecological preservationism" (2001b, 7).

Many feminists, in trying to find productive ways of establishing dialogues across diverse and dispersed feminist communities in the articulation of transnational alliances, have resorted to the practice of translation as a privileged site for the negotiation of difference in a world of increasing cross-border movements and cross-cultural contacts. However, their strategies in negotiating these multiple and discrepant feminist audiences, situated in different "temporalit[ies] of struggles" (Mohanty 1987, 40), have greatly varied.

Inderpal Grewal and Caren Kaplan (1994b), for instance, rely on the notion of a politics of location (conceived as a temporality of struggle, not a fixed position) to develop some key practices of feminist deconstructive projects, including scrutiny of the specific social relations that produce location and situated knowledges.[15] Tropes of travel/displacement (such as nomadism, tourism, exile, and homelessness) deployed in modernist critical discourses often romanticize the terms of travel and elide the material conditions that produce displacement in the contemporary world. In assessing how location and positionality need to be explored in relation to the production and reception of knowledge, Lata Mani (2003) calls for a strategy of multiple mediations when feminists confront the dilemmas of speaking to discrepant audiences within different historical moments. In presenting her work to groups in the United States, Britain, and India, Mani realized how audiences in each location perceived as politically significant entirely different aspects of her work, as well as how diverse agendas in these locations guided its reception. As she puts it, "these responses in turn have caused me to reflect on how moving between different 'configurations of meaning and power' can prompt different 'modes of knowing'" (2003, 367).

Anna Lowenhaupt Tsing (1997), in a similar vein, has asked how feminists should build alliances "that do not squash diversity." Drawing on the Benjaminian (and Derridean) notion of "faithless translation" (whereby texts are appropriated and rewritten so that new meanings are forged by the interaction of languages), she details how translation technologies have produced intellectual histories of feminism and environmentalism as intrinsically Western, following a West-to-the-rest pattern of development and, in this process, creating Western histories and non-Western cultures. Her strategy to avoid such history involves embracing three methodological caveats to emphasize how both feminism and environmentalism are continuously forged out of heterogeneous encounters and interactions: "First, instead of tracing a Western history of social thought, we can trace the moves in which lists of Western thinkers appear to be History; second, instead of following Western originals across non-Western cultural transformations, we can follow the narrative contexts through which foci of cultural difference are identified. Third, instead of debating the truth of Western-defined universals, we can debate the politics of their strategic and rhetorical use across the globe" (Tsing 1997, 254). To avoid a framework that relies on West-to-the-rest narratives, feminists should build diverse alliances that, in developing more South-South–oriented dialogues, would rely on processes of continuous (and faithless) translation that "would work with, rather than exclude, each other" (Tsing 1997, 269).[16]

A concern for the inclusion, not exclusion, of the other in cross-border dialogues and in the building of communities-in-relation also guides the theoretical project of Ofelia Schutte (2000) and Ella Shohat (2002). Drawing on the philosophical notion of incommensurability and the phenomenological-existentialist concept of alterity, Schutte claims that communicating with the other feminists would require recognizing the multiple and disjunctive temporalities in which all the interlocutors are situated. Awareness of these multiple layers both within the self and between the self and the other, Schutte argues, may facilitate the positive reception "of the richness and incommensurability of cultural difference where the other's differences, even if not fully translatable into the terms of our own cultural horizons, can be acknowledged as sites of appreciation, desire, recognition, caring, and respect" (2000, 52).[17] In doing so, the history of identity construction, which will vary geographically and culturally, needs to be highlighted in every process of translation.

For example, as previously pointed out, political labels such as "women of color" are not always translatable in Latin America, especially in certain contexts (e.g., Brazil) and in relation to more "fluid" markers of race and, precisely, "color." Similarly, our readings of foundational Latin American feminist texts, such as the writings of Chilean feminist theorist Julieta Kirkwood, revealed an engagement with class and "revolutionary transformation" that was incommensurable in a U.S. context. Kirkwood's writings nonetheless tellingly reproduced the Occidentalist, universalizing deployments of "women" found in some early "white" feminist theoretical texts in the United States. This same universalizing textual move is also present in many earlier Brazilian feminist texts, as Sandra Azeredo (1994) and Kia L. Caldwell (2000) have pointed out. According to the latter, "it is also important to note the extent to which critiques of feminist essentialism by black Brazilian women have gone unheeded by the majority of Women's Studies scholars in Brazil. Although Afro-Brazilian feminists have attempted to address the specificities of black women's lives since at least the early-1980s, their critical insights regarding the intersection of race and gender have not been made central to the research objectives and priorities of Women's Studies. Instead, if and when the issue of racial difference has been addressed, it has largely been done by black feminist scholars and activists" (Caldwell 2000, 95). Shohat pushes further Schutte's argument on incommensurability (untranslatability) by asking that feminists analyze how theories and actions are translated from one context to another in building relational maps of knowledge. Instead of subscribing to a cultural relativist framework that positions the other (women) within "tradition" and in need of being rescued, Shohat advances a multicultural feminism as a situated practice of translation in which "histories and communities are [viewed as] mutually co-implicated and constitutively related" (2002, 75), hence countering segregated notions of temporality and spatiality.

The need for translation, troped as cannibalism, is also stressed by Sneja Gunew (2002) in her assessment of the intellectual project undergirding U.S. women's studies interdisciplinary programs. Asking whether the cultural differences permeating global feminism can be translated so that a common cultural literacy can be found, Gunew contends that to understand the varieties of feminisms and women's studies projects, we need to explore the slippages between languages and texts through a process of "faithless translation" (pace Tsing 1997). For her, the trope of cannibalism (problematically borrowed from the symbolic framework of Brazilian anthropophagi)[18] should be deployed as a translating tactic to move us beyond the "paralyzing battles" about identity, difference, and critique. It remains an apt (albeit violent, I would add) metaphor of the power differentials inherent in all translation events, including the translations/cannibalisms that happen in inter/transdisciplinary reconfigurations of our ways of knowing. According to Gunew, "The image of the cannibal, that most abject of humans (indeed, to designate someone as cannibal is to mark her or him as abject, beyond the pale) looking and speaking back to the taxonomists, the legislators or those in the know, could well function as a galvanizing icon or mascot for our future projects and our potential attainment of common cultural literacies" (Gunew 2002, 65).

Finally, as Katie King (2001) reminds us, feminist theories, discourses, and practices travel across different communities of practices. What is considered "theory" in one community of practice may not be seen as "theory" in another, so there are different meanings attached to this word. Therefore, it is important to rethink categories in transnational frames, emphasizing their movement across communities of practice, as well as new ways of creating alliances with, through, about, and over the meanings of "feminist theory."[19]

As this chapter has argued, in the present times, characterized by the deepening of the linguistic turn into the translation turn, feminists in the North and South can disturb hegemonic narratives of the other, gender, and feminism itself through practices of translation that make visible the asymmetrical geometries of power along the local-regional-national-global nexus. It is through translation as "world-traveling,"[20] as constant mediation between worlds, that feminists on both sides of the hemisphere are able to develop, heeding Shohat's call, critical multiaxis cartographies of knowledge in webs of relationality—and not in cauldrons of cannibalism (where the difference of the other is ultimately assimilated into the sameness of the self)—as a first and necessary step toward social transformation. Yet challenges remain. How can we think through the gap of translation and account for the multiple forces that overdetermine translation practices along with its strategies of containment? How can translation produce continuity across heterogeneity? These were just a few of the conundrums that have fueled our efforts to think through the vexing linkages between feminisms and transnationalisms in the translation zone.

Notes

This study was carried out in collaboration with Verónica Feliu.

1. The project behind this conceptual effort began as the result of a Latin American Studies Association (LASA) congress panel in 2000, put together by Sonia E. Alvarez and Claudia

de Lima Costa, and with the participation of scholars from the University of California, Santa Cruz (UCSC), as well as other universities in the Greater Bay Area. Papers from this panel were later revised and published in a special section of the *Revista Estudos Feministas* 8, no. 2 (2000), accessible at www.portalfeminista.org.br. Shortly after the congress panel, a one-day mini-conference was held at UCSC in February 2001, and a UCSC Chicano and Latino Research Center (CLRC) research cluster was constituted to explore issues concerning feminism, translation, and transnationalism. Since then, our research cluster has been meeting regularly in workshops at UCSC under the auspices of CLRC and has organized subsequent LASA panels (Washington, 2001; Dallas, 2003; Las Vegas, 2004; Puerto Rico, 2006). We are currently working on an edited collection on feminist transnational translations. The present chapter is the result of several conversations that took place during these workshops, and I acknowledge the invaluable contributions by the research cluster participants. I am also grateful to Sonia E. Alvarez, Patricia Zavella, and two anonymous reviewers for their incisive readings and suggestions for revisions of earlier versions of this manuscript. I thank the Brazilian government research council, CNPq, for financial support for this ongoing research.

2. The importance and relevance that languages as tools and apparatuses of power have in all processes of translation should not be neglected, of course.

3. Gudrun-Axeli Knapp (2005) observes that these days and in certain regions of the globe, *smuggling* may be a more appropriate term to describe the movement of theories.

4. Discussions of feminist ethnographies have shown that because feminism derives its theory from a practice grounded in the materiality of women's oppression (regardless of the complexity of this category), the political dimensions of the ethnographic text are always already articulated to its emplotment in contingent, conjunctural translations of the other. Ethical, political, and epistemological dilemmas apart—feminist or otherwise—I concur with Judith Stacey (1988) in that the exchange and reciprocity encountered in the fieldwork process will always be asymmetrical, especially if the other being studied finds herself in a situation of utter fragility and powerlessness. However, as Millie Thayer (2001) has pointed out, in other settings—such as conducting interviews with social movement leaders and activists—the geometries of power may be entirely different, and the so-called subaltern may be, after all, quite empowered by her or his engagement in a collective struggle for social rights and justice, self-representation and self-determination.

5. For an interesting discussion of the travels of the concept of race from the North American context to Germany, see Knapp (2005).

6. The Latin American writers examined by Domínguez are Diamela Eltit, Tunuma Mercado, Matilde Sánchez, and Clarice Lispector.

7. In Latin America, however, we have witnessed an opposite trend within feminist circles and in the context of dictatorship and postdictatorship: there have been highly politicized appropriations of so-called Western-based theories such as, for instance, those of Michel Foucault and Pierre Bourdieu.

8. Stuart Hall (1996) makes a similar argument concerning the contested space in which the postcolonial operates. To prevent the concept from becoming another way the West appropriates the non-West to think about itself, Hall, instead of jettisoning the concept altogether, suggests that it should be deployed in a way that forces us to reread binarisms (e.g., before/after, here/there, colonize/colonized, center/periphery) as forms of cultural

translation responding to the new relations of power in the aftermath of independency and decolonization. The postcolonial, hence, is a way of rereading colonization as part of a transnational and transcultural global process with the result of producing a decentered account of the imperial narratives of the past anchored in the nation. See also Pal Ahluwalia (2005) for a fascinating discussion of the African roots of poststructuralism through the reading of Jacques Derrida's and Hélène Cixous's autobiographies.

9. In earlier work (Costa 1998b), I reflected on the travels of the category of experience from the context of U.S. poststructuralist feminist theory into the context of Brazilian *sem teto* (homeless) women.

10. For a sampling of pointed theoretical interventions by Latina feminists that revert the trend of some versions of "postmortem" feminisms, see the debates on experience from the perspective of a postpositivist realism as articulated by Moya and Hames-García (2000), Stone-Mediatore (2000), Sandoval (2000b), and Moya (2002).

11. To be true to Alvarez's arguments, there are more dimensions and complexities to these intersecting logics than is reflected in this brief summary.

12. According to Lia Zanotta Machado (1997), French feminism and its foregrounding of difference through deconstruction did not fully enter the fields of anthropology, sociology, and history in France. As in Brazil, its institutional place remained in literary and psychoanalytic studies.

13. For an illustration of these debates, see the "state of the art" article by anthropologist Maria Luisa Heilborn and sociologist Bila Sorj (1999). However, insofar as the problematic of translation is foregrounded here, it is somewhat remarkable that, when writing about the travels of gender studies into the Brazilian academic context, Heilborn and Sorj refer almost exclusively to North American debates on gender and do not offer any reflections on how such debates were interpreted locally.

14. Another crucial constraint, which I explored in an earlier article (Costa 2000), is the fact that Brazilian universities are, to this day, among the most elitist (therefore whitest) of institutions.

15. Lawrence Venuti (1998) uses the expression "ethics of location" in translation as a way of protecting linguistic minorities and counterweighing cosmopolitan literariness.

16. More often than not in debates about the travels and translations of feminist theories in the Americas, a tacit assumption is that there is an original moment in the journey and it is located in the United States, thus occluding the fact that U.S. feminist theories have been deeply informed by other currents as well, making its genealogy far more complex than initially recognized.

17. A similar argument about transnational encounters is advanced by Shu-Mei Shih (2002). Reflecting on such encounters and the subject position of the diasporic intellectual as translator of cultural difference, Shih contends that a way to avoid incommensurability (understood by her as the result of ignorance) is to "practice an ethics of transvaluational relationality" (2002, 119). This entails "to situate oneself in both one's own position and the Other's position, whether on the plane of gender, historical contexts, and discursive paradigms. In practice, this could mean that the Western feminist is asked to speak about China's problems by shifting her position from Western universalism, returning Chinese women to their original contexts and using the multiple and contradictory discursive paradigms used there" (2002, 118).

18. Anthropophagi, especially as conceived by the Brazilian modernist poet and critic Oswald de Andrade, refers to a radical strategy of resistance to cultural colonialism, articulated by the Brazilian modernist movement in 1922, in which artists should digest foreign cultural products and influences, and recycle them in the construction of a synthesis that would represent Brazilian national identity. In short, the colonized artist critically devours the culture of the colonizer (difference) to create a culture that uses and resists what is other to itself. One of the problems with this metaphor, as Heloísa Buarque de Hollanda (1998) points out, is that *anthropophagi* "stretched to the limit the notion that one must not identify with the 'Other,' but assimilate only what is worthy from the Other and eliminate what is not. And it specified the way this partial assimilation should occur: it should be done by chewing, processing, and digesting the desired parts of the 'Other.' That is, by destroying the Other's uniqueness. Here we can clearly see the Brazilian's preference for swallowing difference rather than confronting it." Another problem is that this "elaborate discursive technology for processing otherness, erasing conflicts and avoiding confrontation," in a country of glaring racial inequalities and pervasive "cordial racism," makes the anthropophagic discourse into a ruse for silencing the (racialized and gendered) other. It not only hides "a situation of racial and sexual domination but mak[es] the task of denouncing it even more difficult—if not impossible."

19. As several participants in my workshops suggested, the problem of translating sexuality across diverse geopolitical contexts serves as a case in point, for depending on the community of practice, sexual categories, identities, and experiences do not translate easily or smoothly (the term *queer* and the challenges its translation into other languages pose come to mind here).

20. See Maria Lugones (1997) for the notion of "world" traveling.

PART I

MOBILIZATIONS/MOBILIZING THEORIES/TEXTS/IMAGES

CHAPTER ONE/LOCATING WOMEN'S WRITING AND TRANSLATION IN THE AMERICAS IN THE AGE OF LATINAMERICANISMO AND GLOBALIZATION

NORMA KLAHN

> A bridge (made of stories, ideas, theories) is knowledge.
> It is public; it is communal: it is where our paths converge.
> —GLORIA ANZALDÚA, *This Bridge Called My Back*

Women's writing in Latin/Latina America—that of major figures who emerged after the 1970s, many of whom consolidated their work in the 1980s and 1990s, and who were joined by a younger generation at the turn of the century—has been a site actively marked by gender, but where questions of class, ethnicity, sexuality, nation, and generation have been inexorably present. Latin/Latina American women's writings, I suggest, represented a major shift that defined them as both products and producers of what has been called the cultural turn, a defining critical moment that deconstructed the centrality of modernist epistemologies and the binary and hierarchical categories that sustained them. Center–periphery, elite–popular, male–female opposites were critiqued in the postmodernist turn as constructed antinomies that upheld hegemonic power relations privileging Anglo-Euro-centrism, patriarchal structures, and an aestheticist view of the literary (read: nonpolitical). These writings (*testimonios*, autobiographical fictions, poetry, essays, novels) linked to political mobilizations and social movements have been fundamental in the theorizing and construction of a sui generis practice. Latin American and Latina feminists readapted feminist liberation discourses from the West, resignifying them in relation to self-generated practices and theorizations of gender empowerment that have emerged from their lived experiences, particular histories and contestatory politics. Their interventions range from denouncing sexist practices, exclusionary nation-state structures, and xenophobic ideologies to state-sponsored violence and authoritarian regimes. From these loci, women writers can be seen as actively participating in the larger global project of an inclusive democratization process demanding full equality and dignity for women and other excluded minorities.

Whether as storytelling (fiction) or life writing, in its multiple forms, Latin American and Latina feminist work constitute poetic and politicized interventions that have opened a discursive space for self-awareness, for self-inclusion in nation-state projects, and for their role in an increasingly globalized world. In their desire to redefine and reinvent the nation-state, their writing opened a symbolic space in the 1970s, forging new political identities and subjectivities. As interventions/inventions, the prolific writings of Latin American/ Latina women of the latter part of the twentieth century and first decade of the twenty-first century represent a feminist practice that persistently addresses, especially since the 1990s, the endured disparities and unequal power relations sustained by hegemonic discourses and neoliberal policies that have shown to be—since the Great Recession of 2008—bankrupt. Their writings continue to situate them as central players in processes that point to the need to enact and strengthen renewed democracies.

Given these recent developments, this chapter is a critical attempt at locating and understanding the journeys of feminist literary (broadly conceived) texts, their travels and translations, their readings and misreadings. This is not an exhaustive list nor a detailed analysis, but a mapping of several authors and texts that might illustrate the particular ways women's writings, grounded in distinct temporalities and cultural and historical legacies, circulate beyond (outside) and within (inside) their localities. My reading identifies the writings (testimonios, autobiographical fictions, essays, novels) as poetic/political interventions or, if you wish, aesthetic/ethical ones linked to contestatory practices.

Redefining the Nation: Testimonio as Mobilizing Texts

The shift that occurred internationally in the 1960s and 1970s as civil rights and social movements based on group identifications fought for recognition and built transnational alliances in solidarity with others based on shared experiences of disenfranchisement can be seen, I suggest, as a postnationalist moment. I understand it as constituting a critique of the politics of the modern nation-state whose nationalist discourses of an imagined monocultural community were, in effect, based on exclusionary practices and universalist assumptions of being. This paradigm shift that brought about gender and ethnic awareness produced texts in the post-1968 period in Latin America of a different kind than those of the modern period that were generated by the internationally acclaimed, and mainly male, writers of the Latin American avant-garde and "boom." Their critical texts, foregrounding questions of national identity, no doubt opened the space for translating and marketing Latin American literature worldwide. Their translators understand the complexity of their project and note what they consider most important as they transfer meaning from the source text into the target language to render as close as possible a parallel relationship of their acknowledged "rewriting" of the source. I mention some who have been duly recognized. For Gregory Rabassa, central to his translation is transferring the culture (1991, 44); for Edith Grossman, conveying the original meaning (Salisbury 1993, 11); for Susanne Jill Levine, capturing the voice (Estrada 2010, 7). Value was placed in the ability of the translated text to reproduce the original for a domestic audience. As their translations reinterpreted the source text for English-English speaking audiences, they familiarized and transmitted to readers the author's rendition of essentialized national cultures. The poststructuralist turn that deconstructed absolutes saw individuals or collectivities as fluid, thus privileging the instability of meaning, informing new modes of engaging translation that shifted the focus of attention to broader issues of context, history, and convention and not just to debating the meaning of faithfulness in translation (Bassnett 2007, 13).

Translation studies began, Susan Bassnett states, to "pay attention to the ideological implications of translation and the power relationships that are involved as a text is transferred from one context to another . . . and where the function that translation is meant to fulfill in the target culture enables that translator to make certain choices" (2007, 14). This, says Lawrence Venuti, moved theorists toward an ethical reflection: "When motivated by this ethical politics of difference, the translator seeks to build a community with foreign cultures, to share an understanding with and of them and to collaborate on a project founded on that understanding to allow it to revise and develop domestic values and institutions. The very impulse to seek a community abroad suggests that the translator wishes to extend or complete a particular domestic situation, to compensate for a defect in the translating language and literature, in the translating cultures" (2000, 469).

For Latin America, one can say that post-1968 and post-1989 realities and politics and international feminist movements, both in dialogue and disruption, brought about shifts crucial to the collaboration of women across borders that assured the traveling of women, their writings, and translations. If early paradigms adhered to stable notions of womanhood, the genre of testimonio, bringing in ethnicity and class, was a destabilizing force that sharply pointed to the need of different translating/translocating theories and practices. The shift from a surrealist to a realist aesthetic that prompted a return to the referent, whether by engaging in testimonio or novelas testimonio (nonfiction novels), was brought about by transformed realities (civil rights movements) that generated transformed expressive venues, which could not but point to the importance of contexts. The particular social/political realities from which the new texts emerged made clear that earlier translating practices that were source text–oriented, and focused only on felicitous linguistic translation and transference, were no longer tenable. In the case of post-1968 testimonio or literary texts from Latin America that privileged the recording of witnessed realities as political critique, translators had to rethink strategies that would responsibly transfer not only the cultural content but the intended goals of the source text to the target culture.

Translation, say Piotr Kuhiwczak and Karin Littau, "maintains an apriori dialogue between outside–inside of cultures, languages, histories," and that we practice translation each time we theorize connection (2007, 6). In that case, we suggest, that Domitila Barrios de Chungara anticipated and participated in the shifts that occurred in rethinking translating practices when in 1975 in the first UN international meeting on the rights of women, held in Mexico City, she confronted and corrected Betty Friedan's call for an international sisterhood by insisting on the specificity of class historical experiences in particular sites. A watershed encounter, it made clear, says Karin Monasterios, that the condition of possibilities for feminism in Bolivia, a nation with a large indigenous population, "produce identidades específicas de género y formas sui generis de patriarcado . . . a partir de la condición colonial y periférica del pais" (produces sui generis identities of gender and patriarchy given colonial and peripheral condition of the country) (2007, 129).

This ethnic/gender paradigm critiquing colonial patriarchal structures found, in the emergence and practice of testimonio, a vehicle for expressing dissension and human rights abuses and establishing community. The genre, mediated by Western intellectuals in solidarity with the individual whose voice represented a collectivity, was meant to provoke immediate political responses. In the crisis of traditional/modern ethnography that was critiqued for objectifying the "other" in the 1970s, the politically urgent interventions of the testimonios of Domitila Barrios de Chungara in 1977 and that of Rigoberta Menchú in 1983 were successful in their travels and translations. In the case of Domitila Barrios, a miner's housewife turned activist, her testimony served as a catalyst for the hunger strikes that followed and brought down the military dictatorship of Hugo Banzer in Bolivia. The result of Menchú's testimony led to the recognition of the indigenous subject without rights that became a UN concern, so much so that in 1993, the decade of indigenous peoples was proclaimed for 1995 to 2004.

These testimonios were working toward the systematic transformation of structures rooted deeply and connected to what Anibal Quijano calls the "coloniality of power," defined as the space where a conflict of knowledges and structures of power occur (1997). I understand this as the ways state, church, and political social elites transposed/imposed and finally negotiated a hierarchical structure that worked in complicated ways to ensure the hegemony of patriarchal colonial powers, still very much in sight and in situ. To understand this "coloniality of power" means also to comprehend the unequal traveling and translation of feminist practices, theories and texts, and their reception. The testimonios by Rigoberta and Domitila made clear the untranslatability of Western feminism (not necessarily understood as a place on a map), pointing to the differentiated projects at work that positioned women differently in Latin America in accordance with their ethnic, class, sexual, religious, historical and political situatedness, and even generational affiliation and that deconstructed any essentializing that posited "woman" as a universal category.

These represented interesting cases in which the protagonists' oral histories are already translations/transferences from their indigenous languages and transculturated communities into variants of Spanish. The language of empire, that the ethnographers, as mediating facilitators, then rewrote and reproduced, and that in turn found English translators, ended as critique and in solidarity with their political projects. For Francesca Miller, what distinguished the work on and by Latin American women, especially that of feminist scholars, was a commitment to Freyrian *concientización*, and the need to collect and distribute more accurate information on women's lives, a basic premise of the United Nations Decade for Women, 1976–85 (Miller 1991, 231). Once the testimonies of Domitila and Rigoberta were translated—by Victoria Ortiz (Chungara and Viezzer 1978) and by Ann Wright (Menchú and Burgos-Debray 1984), respectively—informed women reviewers ensured their circulation by contextualizing the texts and rendering them intelligible to wider audiences. A case in point was the review by Nirmala Banerji (1981), who brought in comparable contexts such as those of English coal miners in the nineteenth century, the story/film *Norma Rae* in the United States, and most interestingly drew parallels between poor women in Bolivia and India, positing a global South connection. In the case of reviews for Rigoberta's story, in later editions, Linda Larson states its importance for feminist and indigenous politics and women's cultural roles (1994, 106), whereas Ximena Bunster signals its contribution to women's and human rights studies (1985, 12). In most cases, the reviews do not address the processes of translation. Banerji offers a one-line comment that the translation "misses out on the earthiness and the originality of Domitila's dialect" (Banerji 1981, 1653). It seems most reviewers were engaged in constructing interest around the texts and building community, rather than attending to the technicalities of transference.

The translocated testimonio of Rigoberta found felicitous readings, and also misreadings, disregarding the long line of *literatura de denuncia*, a genre of denouncement that from Bartolomé de Las Casas's *Brief History of the Destruction of the Indies* (1552) to testimonio calls for urgent action, privileging rhetorical strategies rather than "facts" to capture the racism and atrocities being experienced. Anthropologist David Stoll's insistence on an empiricist reading from the generic conventions of journalist documentation was in fact seeking equivalences between the origin (reality) and the text (constructed reality) in "modern" terms, searching for a faithful reproduction rather than what the text was trying to achieve—the continued existence for the community being destroyed and the transmission of the story to guarantee the first. In an important book that spoke directly to the subject of "translating" Latin America culturally and linguistically, Javier Sanjinés alerted us to the generic difference that Stoll's cultural misreading represented as other issues came into play, that is the poetic/political perspective that privileged a collective identity not as "an ancestral reconciliation, but a cultural and political practice necessary for future survival (1991, 186). Stoll had reduced otherness to sameness and used similar judgment tools in his (mis)reading rather than understanding the appeal of the narrative to human rights abuses that were foregrounding questions of ethics rather than accuracy. An understanding of colonialism's legacies could have rendered an ethical response to alterity.

Reading in translation or in translating cultures, we are reminded, requires not only contextual social and political awareness but knowledge of differentiated literary/cultural histories and systems and acknowledgment of divergent generic expectations to make possible a more productive reading at the receiving end. Not much attention had been paid to shifting translation practices. In fact, in reviews of the English translation of testimonios by Rigoberta and Domitila, there is a scarcity of commentaries on the subject of the translations themselves. Kathleen Logan, in her review of the English translations of the aforementioned testimonios, did raise the issue of authorship: whereas in the Spanish texts, the anthropologists appear as the authors, in the English version, the authorship is properly, she says, attributed to the women telling the testimony. "Burgos," she assertively adds, "is appropriately listed as editor," and goes as far as suggesting that a correction be made in the Spanish publications (Logan 1997, 205).

Texts, if felicitous, survive in translation and transit, in what Walter Benjamin and translation theorists following him have called an "after-life." They believe not so much in the property of the original but in its potentiality, a prolongation that continues to extract shifting and redefined meaningful reading experiences. For them, the historical significance of the original is ensured by its translatability, which "constitutes a *way—way of signifying*—rather than a *what*" (Weber 2005, 74, 75). Translations, then, set texts on routes "away from" rather than "back to," with the idea of recovering a "lost" meaning, joining a complex circulation of texts that generate a continued discussion of the goals set out as ways of signifying and expanding its possibilities.

Domitila's testimonio is a case in point that shows the intricate path her text set in motion as transnational alliances of progressive women produced a complex network of signification away from the original, producing uncharted effects and detectable effectiveness. In homage to Betty Friedan after her death, Marta Lamas, feminist activist and editor of *Debate Feminista*, in an article of 2006, revisits the publication of *The Feminine Mystique* (1963) and reflects on its impact on women in the United States and the foundation of the National Organization for Women. Lamas focused on radical feminist criticism of Friedan for her reformist liberal positions. That view, Lamas continues, was shattered by Daniel Horowitz (1998) in a book that "uncovers" Friedan's activities from 1938 to 1953, in which she is depicted as a radical activist, connected to the U.S. Communist Party, and engaged in labor and Afro-American struggles. As a journalist for the leftist Federated Press, she early on denounced racism, sexism, and exploitable labor policies. Lamas, translating Horowitz, interprets Friedan's later silence as a strategy to prevent the contamination of the feminist movement with the stigma that communism signified in the United States during the McCarthy era. As Lamas pays homage to Friedan's radical feminism, one feels the necessity to rethink the now clear mis/communication with Domitila Barrios de Chungara, the miner's wife familiarized, as Friedan was, with radical union organizing. Lamas's rescuing of Friedan is telling of the ways history or the past is never completed nor settled but always in flux in relation to the present and therefore the future. The continued relevance of Rigoberta's and Domitila's testimonios points to the ways their texts, in conjunction with their activist traveling, constituted a major shift as part of the cultural/ethical turn that also brought about an awareness of "the other" to a U.S. audience, and consequently a shift challenging textual and reading practices. However, one has to heed any idealist acquiescence, as Nelly Richard reminds us, in this ethical response to alterity, because in the poststructuralist vindication of metropolitan discourses "the other" becomes, rather than a subject in his or her own right, the object of the discourse of the other, who speaking from the position of privilege manages the rhetoric and appropriates the representation (1993, 80).

Indeed, Elizabeth Burgos and Moema Viezzer inspired other social scientists, and later cultural critics—in fact, even fiction writers who assumed the role of journalists, mediators, and ethnographers in their novels—to continue documenting the lives of marginalized women. A cultural text that represented an important contribution in this area was *La flor más bella de la maquiladora* (Iglesias 1985). The representations of working-class women portrayed in this seminal book emerged from the oral histories *qua testimonios* collected by Norma Iglesias. It brought into public view a line-up of emergent protagonists, the *maquiladora* (sweatshop) workers as the flexibility and feminization of labor became the new reality of early neoliberalism, industrial reconversion, and free trade. Speaking from a degree of empowerment, their narratives presented confident plots, as hopeful voices register some faith in a different future. Many of these women believed that through their full integration into the labor force, the paradigms that maintained them in oppressive conditions would change. Says Iglesias:

> Para muchas obreras de las maquiladoras que son migrantes y/o madres solteras, este trabajo significa "la independencia" económica. . . . La mayoría de las migrantes han expresado y consideran que llegar a Tijuana y trabajar en las maquiladoras ha sido un avance, dado que están libres del padre, la madre, esposo o hermanos. . . . En otras palabras a partir de que la mujer participa en la vida productiva, se modifican los patrones de comportamiento; se modifica, de alguna manera, la estructura familiar, sin estar por ello menos explotada u oprimida. (Iglesias 1985, 70–71)

> For many of the maquiladora workers who are migrants or single mothers or both, their employment signifies economic "independence." . . . The majority of migrant female workers asserts and believes that to make it to Tijuana and work in the maquiladoras has been an improvement as they have freed themselves of the influence of their father, mother, brother, or husband. . . . So as a woman begins to participate in economically productive activity, behavioral patterns change, modifying the family structure in some ways, without, however, diminishing women's own exploitation or oppression. (Iglesias 1997, 35)

This well-received and influential book in Mexico was finally translated in 1997 with the subtitle *Life Histories of Women Workers in Tijuana*. Even as it broke what Tillie Olsen (1979) has called "the unnatural silences" in literature, most especially of women, and among them those of working class origins," the translation twelve years later, temporally bounded, can only be read as a historical accounting of a rapid industrial modernization and violent time period that seems to have concluded when in fact it represented the beginning of an ongoing process that has found its worsening reality in Ciudad Juárez as I write today. In turn, however, with the shift in translation practices, the translators of the book, Michael Stone and Gabrielle Winkler, contextualize the importance of Iglesias's testimonio as signaling what "David Harvey sees as a corporate shift from Fordism to a global regime of flexible accumulation" (Iglesias 1997, xiii). The foreword by the anthropologist Henry Selby identifies the downturn of the Mexican economy, the masculinization of the industry, and the loss of union power. More focused on labor itself, however, there is no echo to either the feminist project presented by Iglesias originally or the women's voices, whose entrance into the workforce, even in its exploitive conditions, was seen as a step forward at the time. The introduction does refunction the text for its audience by illustrating the ways it exemplifies the workings of late capitalism and globalization in situ. There is at least a reference to the translation itself. Selby speaks to its excellence, which I share, commenting that "the young women come across very much as they are. . . . They retain the workers' dignity and their point of view, as well as the freshness of their voices" (Iglesias 1997, xii).

Literary fiction joined testimonio in documenting the increased violence at the U.S.–Mexico border. The majority of workers that offered their testimony in *La flor más bella* in the early 1980s were mothers, and their reproductive roles in the private sphere, according to several of them, were going to enrich their productive role in the public arena. Later, the short stories on working women by Rosina Conde narrated a different reality from the testimonios collected by Iglesias as women workers cautiously denied their reproductive powers, considered an obstacle. The protagonist in "Gaviota" pleads with a co-worker to keep her motherhood a secret, because women with children are not allowed to work in the maquiladoras (Conde 1994, 20). The story highlights the ways the discourses of production/reproduction in the case of women workers were being manipulated by the system: the empowering language of *La flor más bella de la maquiladora* is absent. This is also the case in the stories of Dora Elia Rodríguez (1998) from Matamoros, Mexico, who narrates the impact of drug trafficking, the effects of crude labor exploitation, continued sexual harassment, and systemic corruption. In the age of globalization, a different story that plots the disillusioned fate of *maquila* workers is told. In Rodríguez's narratives there is sharp criticism of existing social cultural paradigms, where lack of security for the average citizen and a persistent impunity have drastically upset the normativity of daily life as previously experienced. While these stories await translation, cross-border solidarity has Latinas picking up the slack by publishing in English. Violence at the border deepens as it is examined in the critical mystery novel *Desert Blood: The Juárez Murders*, by Alicia Gaspar de Alba (2005), who explores the horror of the events taking place in that city through the lens of a hybrid genre (detective and autobiographical fiction).

In 1985, the same year *La flor más bella de la maquiladora* was published, Mexico City suffered a devastating earthquake. In its aftermath, thousands of seamstresses working in hidden urban maquilas were buried and literally unearthed and made visible. Getting paid much less than the minimum wage, a number of them had been working for as long as twenty years with a daily schedule of ten hours or more. Four hundred maquiladoras were destroyed or damaged, and eight hundred seamstresses were found dead. The committed writer and feminist intellectual Elena Poniatowska published *Nada/Nadie* (1988), chronicling the organizational power of the seamstresses, denouncing the inept bureaucracy, and capturing the beginnings of their protagonism in union building. The book, translated in 1995 as *Nothing/Nobody* by Aurora Camacho de Schmidt and Arthur Schmidt, marked the first of the series Voices of Latin American Life by Temple University Press, opening with an excellent introduction contextualizing the book and establishing its relevance to the ways civil society organized itself. It includes a helpful glossary.

These pathbreaking prior texts, among others, no doubt had created enough awareness about the importance of documenting women's lives and struggles. When the Zapatista insurgency of January 1, 1994, exploded, the participation of Indigenous women (Tojolobal, Chol, Tzotzil, and Tzeltal) demanding land and ethnic rights, alongside the democratization of gender relations within the family, the community, and the organization through the so-called Women's Revolutionary Law, found feminist international support. *Mujeres de maíz* (1997) by Guiomar Rovira was translated three years later by Anne Keene. However, *Las alzadas* (The rebellious ones; Lovera and Paloma 1997), which also spoke to women's participation in the Zapatista uprising, is still awaiting translation. Both texts remain strong indictments of continued gender/ethnic struggles.

It is important to note an earlier literary critique of colonialism in Chiapas, as is the case of Rosario Castellanos, whose autobiographical fiction *Balún Canán* (1989 [1959]) rendered visible the invisibility of ethnic and gendered subjectivities. The first translation into English by Irene Nicholson went unrecognized—perhaps a pre-1968 audience was not yet attuned to a feminist/postcolonial text. Feminist literary critics rescued her work in the 1970s, demonstrating how a literary period can be rewritten if studied from a different temporal and theoretical perspective and confirming Benjamin's idea of an afterlife in the travels of texts. Coinciding with the five hundred years of conquest and appearing in 1992 with its translated title from the Mayan, *Nine Guardians* has enjoyed increased circulation, especially since the Zapatista rebellion of 1994. Nowadays it is read as a text whose unresolved ending predicted an unfinished history that would eventually and inevitably have to unfold as it has.

Anthropologist/activist Aída Hernández Castillo, who has also collected indigenous women's oral testimonies, offers encouraging words today: "To speak of indigenous feminisms would have been unthinkable fifteen years ago. Nevertheless, whether they identify as feminists or not, beginning with the 1990s we have seen the emergence of indigenous women's movements in different Latin American countries that are struggling on different fronts" (2006, 231).

Remembering that even as everyone has a life, a life is not a story, these testimonios do tell a story, the story of a collectivity rendered invisible, whose histories — or better, "herstories"—and knowledge systems had gone unrecognized. In the United States, these life-stories could be read not as removed and distanced Third World narratives but as practices and re/presentations that point to the discrepancies between the monocultural and hegemonic discourses of nation-states, be they Mexico or the United States, and the actual pluricultural, plurilingual existing social realities.

Memorializing Texts: Fictional Feminist Writings

As academics in the United States fought the culture and literary canon wars and feminist scholars recovered women's writing from previous periods, women's fiction writing showed a prolific number of publications in the 1980s, which continued into the 1990s and has not stopped, establishing a feminist canon in Latin America and a new wave of translations in English. As feminists, whether self-identified or not, their texts rethink modern paradigms, contesting hegemonic exclusionary practices linked to gender roles and nationalist discourses. The differently located women writers showed the complexity of Latin American women's writing, which from multiple representational strategies and aesthetic practices critically responded to patriarchal power structures, ranging from middle-class autobiographical fictions — where women gained agency through self-awareness, constructing new subjectivities, and altering the male canon — to women's representations of survival strategies under dictatorial regimes. A compelling form of identity/identification, feminism sought alliances through many venues, literary translation being one of them.

Post-1968 women's texts from Latin America, however, had to open a space for their work at a time when an Anglo public was enthusiastically and belatedly reading the works of mainly male authors in translation, whose experimental avant-garde and surrealist aesthetic had emerged early in the twentieth century. Characterized as "magical realism"—a mode that had already exhausted itself, finding its excellent, ultimate, and final expression in 1967 with *Cien años de soledad* (*One Hundred Years of Solitude*)—and read ahistorically, the texts were depoliticized, rendering Latin America as an exotic, eccentric periphery. Magic realism, argued Sylvia Molloy, became for the outside "a mode of Latin American representation, not [what it was] a self-conscious mode of Latin American production" (2005, 375). This expectation for fiction was crucial in selecting texts from Latin America for translation that would be representative of that particular aesthetic, both reasserting "the other" as stereotypically imagined by the receiving culture while ensuring commercial profitability. For example, Molloy sees Isabel Allende's success outside of Latin America as fulfilling these readerly expectations (Molloy 2005, 375).

Although this may be true, it is also important to note that Allende, no doubt one of the most successful writers in translation, began her first book, *La casa de los espíritus* (1982), in the mode of "realismo mágico" as the story—a pastiche of *One Hundred Years of Solitude*—of four generations of women is told, but shifts in medias res to a realist mode, as it narrates the story of the 1973 military coup that ousted Salvador Allende and brought in the dictatorship of Augusto Pinochet. Translated by Magda Bogin, it appeared in 1985 by a major publishing house. During that same year, its selection as a Book of the Month guaranteed a wide audience. A success story, Margaret Sayers Peden, who concurs with Jorge Luis Borges in the belief that all translation is "approximation" (Peden 1987, 163), has become Allende's official translator and HarperCollins her publisher. Allende's books appear now almost simultaneously in both languages as U.S. publishing houses have also become aware of a growing Spanish-speaking and Spanish-reading audience. Her books continue to have felicitous translations as she strategized to fulfill audience expectations since her first success. In recent years, whether writing about the gold rush–that provoked Chilean migration to California in *Hija de la fortuna* (1999), or *Retrato en sepia* (2000), or about hero/bandits such as in *Zorro* (2005), her novels have entered neoregionalist canons, literatures studied outside nationalist paradigms, illustrating the world system history of diverse cultures that California studies supports. Although this can be seen as deconstructing U.S. monoculturalist agendas, her deployment of historical romance and out-of-the-ordinary characters, if now not distant in space but in time, might raise with its exotic connotations certainly a larger public and also the potential for stereotypical casting (Molloy 2005, 375). Even as edited books, critical companions, and approaches to teaching her work appear, Harold Bloom, in his edited series on authors, understands this as he posits questions other readers may consider: "Is Isabel Allende truly comparable to Gabriel García Márquez, or are we to seek her peers at a very different level, in the cosmos of supermarket fiction?" (Bloom 2002, 3).

Interest in successful women's fiction from Latin America, whether for market or more ideological motives, grew, and it continued to be translated through the 1990s. Laura Esquivel's *Como agua para chocolate* (1989) reached a wide Spanish-speaking and Spanish-reading public in Mexico and was published in the early 1990s in both Spanish and its translation in English in the United States by Doubleday. If it touched grassroots neonationalist sentiment inside the Mexican nation—as, I suggest, contestatory discourse to the neoliberal agenda of pro-NAFTA president Carlos Salinas de Gortari—its conscious and strategic use of romance and parodic magical realism, in addition to movie rights, guaranteed its success outside the nation and the national.

An innovative writing that had appeared earlier, to locate a different way of belonging to the Mexican nation, had also traveled successfully for different reasons: this is the case for the pioneering autobiographical fictions of Margo Glantz, *Las genealogías* (1981), translated as *The Family Tree* (1991) by Susan Bassnett; and Barbara Jacobs's *Las hojas muertas* (1987), translated as *The Dead Leaves* (1993) by David Unger. Both found productive routes as Glantz joined the canon of Jewish writers and Jacobs the emergent canon of migrancy and displacement world narratives. Their texts represented poetic/political interventions that made evident the pluricultural and plurilingual nature of the nation-state. Likewise, Rosario Ferré's *Papeles de pandora* (1976), translated as *The Youngest Doll* (1991), and Luisa Valenzuela's *Cola de lagartija* (1983), published in the United States as *The Lizard's Tail* (1999), also expanded the growing reading public of women's writing, given that they were translated by Gregory Rabassa, who had introduced the major writers of the Latin American avant-garde to a U.S. audience.

While a translation industry was growing—agents, editors, and translators —ensuring the success of the boom authors (Lowe and Fitz 2007, xiii), other emergent women writers, who continued to narrativize "witnessing as critique," were fortunate to have found venues and translators interested in their work. Of major importance early on was Elena Poniatowska's classic *Noche de Tlatelolco* (1971), which registered the tragic events in Mexico where a student demonstration was violently suppressed on October 2, 1968. As critique of state-sponsored violence, the topic became the subject of much post/dictatorial literature writing during the years of military dictatorships or its memorializing, as evidenced by Marta Traba (*Conversación al sur*, 1981), Cristina Peri-Rossi (*La nave de los locos*, 1984), Luisa Valenzuela (*Cambio de Armas*, 1982), and from a younger generation Diamela Eltit, with most of her books translated into English and whose neo–avant-garde, antimimetic, fragmented, and densely rich poetic prose has not discouraged an ever-increasing specialized audience. Extremely successful in Spanish, as evidenced by the critical reception their work has produced, their reconstructions of the traumatic experiences of dictatorship, their daring critiques of authoritarian regimes and the extreme patriarchal military structures that forcefully implemented rigid sexual roles, however, have had a limited readership in English outside Latin Americanists.

For the uninformed, the difficult and painful-to-read subject matter was not, it seems, in sync with the majority of the receiving public, whether because of the unwillingness of the "North" to question/acknowledge its role in interventionist politics or because, as Deborah Treisman points out, "so much of American literature is tailored to be meaningful for American people—very little gets written from a truly international perspective—partly because the publishing industry has an ingrained fear of translations and doesn't always do enough to promote them" (quoted in Kinzer 2003, 19). I suggest that their translated readings would require an informed public that could pay attention to difference, to the lack of existing economic and political coevalness, to questions of human rights disparities, in fact, to otherness, outside the concept of fixity, as in testimonio, foregrounding the necessity of critical presentations that historicize the story being translocated.

It is important to note that in both the cases of Traba's English translation, *Mother and Shadows* (1986) and Peri-Rossi's *Ship of Fools* (1989), there was a lack of any foreword or notes by the author, editor, or translator to contextualize the reading and address questions of translatability. This seems to be the case, I found, in most translations, which in fact almost never include the translator's name on the cover. Ignoring the task of translating, it indicates a lack of awareness of who the receiving audience is and/or might become if enlightened. I am referring to a general public, not a specialized one, because as women's literature proliferated and gained increased attention in Spanish and English in the 1990s, it generated numerous critical books and reviews. This period also saw an increase in male translators joining female translators, who in some cases considered the act of translation as a feminist project of alliances. Sherry Simon points out that "While some feminist translators have suggested that they might best deal with the discomforts of a negative legacy by ensuring that women's texts are translated only by women translators, men's by men, this solution could not be a long-term one" (Simon 1996, 3). She then quoted Lori Chamberlain, who insisted that what needed subversion was the process by which translation complies with gender constructs (Simon 1996, 4). Two cases in point are the novels by celebrated Mexican authors Carmen Boullosa (*Son vacas, somos puercos*, 1991) and Cristina Rivera Garza (*Nadie me verá llorar*, 1999), both translated by males.

This concerted effort by literary scholars and translators to make available other women writers' works became, especially in response to neoliberal policies, a project whose goals, by the turn of the century, were directed at critiquing not only the gendered categories of marginality but the political, ethnic, sexual, social, and political ones as well. It constituted an effort to notably alter consciousness in the exporting writing culture and the importing reading culture. The more disseminated findings of translation studies, now linked to postcolonial studies, were also making translators more aware of the importance of making the public aware of their role as mediators between the "foreign" culture and the "home" one. Relevant examples are the novels of Diamela Eltit, in particular, *Lumpérica* (1983), translated as *E. Luminata* (1997), which won the Kayden National Translation Award First Prize. The foreword by Eltit speaks from a corporeal gendered subjectivity situating hers with others on the margins of the military dictatorship she survived and wrote under. Conceptualizing literature as revolutionary activism, she renders an intense analysis of her novel and the writing process. An afterword by the head translator, Ronald Christ, delves into the language of the work and the translational process required to render the English version. I suggest that this historically and literarily contextualized text could serve as a model for publishing translated texts, not in its appeal in this case to a more specialized reading public but in the framing used to guide the unfamiliarized reader.

Complementing the aforementioned writings, I would add other sites that have been especially important in furthering national and global feminist agendas and alliances, responding, in the period studied, consistently and critically (at times radically) to structures of unequal power. A case in point is the circulation and translation of articles from worldwide feminists in *Debate Feminista*, an academic journal published in Mexico City (founded and directed by Marta Lamas since 1989), that has opened an important space for feminist critical thinking and creative writing. Such writings made visible the virtual linkages that connect places and people, positing what Chandra Talpade Mohanty (2003a, 55) calls "oppositional agency," and working against what Caren Kaplan (1996) names "scattered hegemonies."

Oppositional feminist practices that privilege performance have also accompanied women's writings. Relevant is the artistic performance of Jesusa Rodríguez in Mexico City's El Hábito, a political cabaret that from 1991 through 2004 deconstructed national myths and critiqued normative sex/gender paradigms (Franco 1994) and has translated well among Latinos and performance artists in the United States. The poetry, street graffiti, and performances of

Mujeres Creando in Bolivia, a group of radical feminist activists and street per-formers, were crucial in raising issues of women's subordinate position and linking these to issues of race, class, and sexuality (Monasterios 2006). The presence of some of their members at the International Congress of LASA, the Latin American Studies Association, in Dallas (2003), as well as their invita-tions to U.S. universities, has been crucial in raising awareness in the North of continued gender/ethnic struggles in the South, now complicated by pervasive globalization. It is evident that whether through writing or performances or both, these women are insistent on a radical redemocratization where gender, ethnicity, race, and sexual preference become essential to the redefinition of a body politic.

Migrating Texts: Bordering Stories

The deconstruction of a "modernist" conception of center–periphery in dis-course analysis by both globalization and postcolonial theory, as I have argued in this chapter, offered a new epistemological agenda that brings Latin Amer-ican texts to the center of the literary world systems. This has opened a space to place texts from the "global South" in circulation with Latina and women's production in the "peripheries of the global North," whose projects cannot be separated from gender, ethnic, and class constructs as they critique unequal power relations and the persistent exclusionary practices of nation-state ide-ologies. The feminist writings of Third World women, whether in the global South or within the United States, have at times encountered the same resis-tance in their travels and cultural or linguistic translations. The increased mobility and displacement of peoples, their cultures, and languages and the global interconnectedness made possible by technology are deconstructing conceptual mappings of North to South/South to North routes, let alone their translations and reception. Texts written in English by Latina writers such as Sandra Cisneros, Norma Cantú, Cristina García, Julia Alvarez, and Esmeralda Santiago, among many others, are complicating prior mappings that separate the here and there, positing the circulation of a feminist cultural imaginary that finds resonance in the heritage nation.

At the beginning of the twenty-first century, political borders cannot con-tain cultural ones, just as within political borders, different nations, cultures, and languages cannot be suppressed in the name of national (understood) as monolithic unity. In a world of massive displacements and the multiplication of free "exchange zones," places where distinct cultures *survive* through daily strategies of negotiation, the distinction between foreign and native, migrant and settled, indeterminate and legitimate belonging become questions rooted in rights: human and citizen's rights. This complexity also raises the issues of translating languages and cultures when distances have collapsed, most especially in the case of Spanish, where its status as the unofficial second language in the United States is fast becoming a reality. Texts translated into English from well-known publishing houses, independent editors, and university presses that offer translation series circulate simultaneously with those published in Spanish by Penguin, HarperCollins, and Random House (among others), which recognize the ever-increasing presence of a Spanish-reading public, Latino or Anglo, who read in the original. To this, I add the question of bilingual texts that are, in the words of Molloy, "aesthetic choices demanding competent readings" (Molloy 2005, 376). Living proof of the aforementioned are *Borderlands / La Frontera: La New Mestiza* (Anzaldúa 1987), *Yo-Yo Boing!* (Braschi 1998), *Killer Crónicas: Bi-Lingual Memories* (Chávez-Silverman 2004), and *Scenes from la Cuenca de Los Angeles and Otros Natural Disasters* (Chávez-Silverman 2010). Their bilingual speech is literally untranslatable. Theirs and the writings of Latinas and Latin Americans in the United States can be seen as challenging the homogenizing forces of the nation-state from within and materializing "Nuestra América"—José Martí's reference to "Hispano" America—now inside the belly of the globalizing "beast."

Translocational Politics / Translational Poetics

The turn to translation studies as an area of academic specialization, linked to both inter-American and world literature programs, seems to guarantee the continued interest in the translation of women's writing from Latin America. The question is whether this represents a curriculum of studies that reads the literature contextually, outside homogenizing paradigms, that is, paying attention to its site of production and imagining the "other" not solely as an object of consumption but as a subject speaking and being heard from a specific differentiated sense of place and history; or does it re-present an imperial turn substituting reading in the original, crucial, as Robert Scholes says, "to know how their languages represent the world" (Lowe and Fitz 2007, 173). The appropriation of "other" literatures through translation in the reorganization of U.S. literary systems, outside of a tangible trans/inter/national dialogue, would give short shrift to the long line of women's expressive interventions from Latin America. They have spoken, written, or performed to undo vertical power structures, including that of the imperial North (core) as it positions itself vis-à-vis the South (periphery).

For the record, in this moment of intensified xenophobia, we would do well to remember the words of André Lefevere in his definition of the projects of translation as "not just a window opened on another world [but] a channel opened, often not without a certain reluctance, through which foreign influences can penetrate the native culture, challenge it, and even contribute to subverting it" (1992, 2). If this is so, then the cultural/translation turn could constitute a truly ethical one.

CHAPTER TWO/IS ANZALDÚA TRANSLATABLE IN BOLIVIA?

ANA REBECA PRADA

This essay is a reflection on the possibilities and consequences of theory's travel and translation in the context of radical feminist politics and writing in the North and the South of the Americas. I first give a description of the institutional and political context in Bolivia to discuss the translation, teaching, and reading of Gloria Anzaldúa's work in the public university of La Paz and the (possible) incorporation of her work into radical feminist discourse and action. I argue that the essential connection of Anzaldúa with Bolivia is Mujeres Creando, the radical feminist movement group active since the beginning of the 1990s—and now working separately, as María Galindo and Julieta Paredes (founders of the group) have formed independent projects. In the process of creating this connection, I describe in detail the significance of Mujeres Creando's discourse and action in Bolivia and beyond, especially in relation to complex political issues linked to the profound state and social crisis triggered by President Gonzalo Sánchez de Losada's flight from Bolivia in October 2003 to the election of Evo Morales as president in December 2005 and, more specifically, to his government's insistence on the establishment of the Asamblea Constituyente (for the re-founding of the nation) in August 2006—and the consequent promulgation of the Nueva Constitución Política del Estado in February 2009. It is important to examine the implications of Mujeres Creando's radical feminist interventions in socialist state politics—after analyzing their emergence and role during the previous neoliberal period—and in the context of an ill-born but finally concluded Asamblea Constituyente, always with the aim of finding the links between Chicana queer thinking and this particular form of Bolivian feminist politics.

Late in 2001, more than a year after translating the "unreadable" parts of Anzaldúa's "Crossing Borders" of *Borderlands / La Frontera* (I wouldn't dare get into her poetry!) for my students in the Universidad Mayor de San Andrés (UMSA), La Paz, I realized what that strictly practical operation really meant. I was not only betraying Anzaldúa's essential intention—to create a radical minor language—I was unintentionally participating in a dilemma of Chicana theory that had to do with creating a language of its own, unique and absolutely new, "untranslatable," if you will. This politics of theoretical language was not totally erased in my naive translation, because the discussion of concepts included necessarily the mixed code issue, the mixture of different Spanishes, and therefore the issue of "the configuration of a new language" (Anzaldúa 1987, preface). Nevertheless, my students could not experience Anzaldúa's language in all its force, because it is still partly mediated by the language of the North, a language very few students in the public university read, especially those who come from the poorer Aymara homes of El Alto and the *laderas* of La Paz. Paradoxically, in the context of these students' possibilities of accessing *Borderlands / La Frontera* in all its dimensions, Anzaldúa's book becomes part of the theory that originates in the North and needs the mediation of elite intellectuals to reach students in public schools.[1] It becomes part of the sophisticated theoretical corpus about which many of us are so wary. There is no place, however, for naiveté for the mediator, because a naive mediation/translation in this instance would constitute a double betrayal. In any case, the problem remains: beyond the need for this essentially political operation of the elite mediator, Anzaldúa's *Borderlands* risks being subsumed in a very sophisticated corpus of theory arriving in the South and being critically challenged by cultural and social analysts. This happened with Silvia Rivera Cusicanqui, the Bolivian cultural critic who challenged the ways Walter Mignolo incorporates Bolivian theoretical and cultural material into his work, thus perpetuating Latin America as an object and not a subject constructing knowledge in dialogue. It happened with Nelly Richard challenging U.S. academics—such as John Beverley—who were theorizing *testimonio* after inventing it as an object for the sake of and within Northern academic agendas, without either having the Latin American production of testimonios as active interlocutors or considering the diverse forms of testimonio produced in Latin America. It is all about postcolonial theory's major objective: contesting the way the South is consumed and conformed by the North to enrich its theory, to counteract its own "depletion."

Many may wonder what challenging Northern theory has to do with Anzaldúa, because the "South" and the "Third World" from which she theorizes are located within the North itself. However, she has opened a passage, a bridge for the Southern and Northern Third World's' wounded bodies and histories of resistance to dialogue and connect. It should also be added that the extremely problematic presence of the North (Northern politics and economics) in a very poor country like Bolivia strongly influences the predisposition of Bolivians to consume Northern products neutrally or sympathetically. When cultural studies arrived at the public university in Bolivia during the 1990s, it was challenged by many as another Northern import artificially integrated into university curricula, not as a possibility for enriching cultural-social analysis or for countering traditional, conservative views, which could also be read as a conservative nationalistic move. Moreover, initiatives like the Bolivian Studies Association—created by Bolivian and Bolivianist professors in the North to establish a direct dialogue with intellectuals working in Bolivia—have also had their problems. A friend participating in a panel in the second congress of the association organized in La Paz in 2004, once said to me jokingly, "I am not a Bolivianist, I am a Bolivian." This apparently inoffensive joke deals with something very serious: the South is tired of being involved in knowledge production in which it is always the object, its raw material. A Bolivianist would be somebody who does precisely that.

Postcolonial theory was integrated more in a South-to-South operation, mitigating its Northern universities transit and circulation—as, for example, in the anthology *Debates Post Coloniales* (Cusicanqui and Barragán 1997),[2] or the seminar "'Alternative' Histories and Non-Written Sources: New Perspectives from the South," organized by Silvia Rivera Cusicanqui with SEPHIS funds in 1999.[3]

This apparently unconnected problem in a discussion on Anzaldúa becomes central—in terms of the asymmetrical flow of theories—especially when the possibilities of a North–South enriching and critical consumption of theory is interfered with by a long history of coloniality and exploitation. The opposition to Northern political and economic colonialism—reconfigured and reconfirmed by its latest version, globalized neoliberalism (that is, a neoliberalism the South understands as heavily North American)—affects the way universities and intellectuals consume theory and construct their agendas. It explains why major autonomous thinkers and radical intellectuals in Bolivia largely resort to intellectual traditions other than North American (mostly European and Latin American, of course), because—and this has to be emphasized—there are definitively two Norths in the eyes of Southern intellectuals. It also accounts for why what comes from North America—especially in terms of the new trends, such as cultural analysis and identity politics—is seen by many such intellectuals as part of an "academic fashion" that is mobile, changing, capricious, and linked to an academic life ultimately divorced from larger social and economic issues.

All this obviously connects to the discussion of self-determined knowledge (*conocimiento autodeterminado*) and autonomous knowledge (*conocimiento autónomo*), the decolonization of knowledge, dealing with the recovery of radical local knowledges and thought not only from the tradition of middle-class radicals but also from indigenous local knowledges. This project underlies Anzaldúa's writings, as well as the work, for decades, of many radical intellectuals in Bolivia. As a matter of fact, autonomy cannot be discussed in the Bolivian case without taking into consideration the autonomy of cultural forms such as, for example, the *ayllus* (the ancient and still existing forms of community organization in the Andes) and the Amazonian indigenous community organizations as well as Aymara and Guaraní forms of self-government and legal systems. That is to say, we live very real and vital forms of actual autonomy in our cultures. Living in La Paz — if we do not want to resort to the case of Indian or peasant communities as extreme examples — is an experience of day-to-day autonomy. You can live in "Western" La Paz if you choose, but you can also live in a La Paz of extreme informal economic practices and in an Aymara urban organization of social life. The latter constitutes an autonomous practice in the sense that the state has not been able, for example, to incorporate either Aymara merchants and solidarity economic nets into the formal economy or Aymara society and social behavior to the norms of citizenship stipulated by a Western model of city life and social organizations. La Paz is a city occupied by Aymara immigrants and their descendants, even if many choose not to perceive it as such.[4] Having an Aymara president, elected and reelected by impressive percentages since 2005, in any case, has had an enormous impact on the way perceptions are constructed.

The natural way of saving *Borderlands / La Frontera* from this very messy arena of the politics of traveling theory and theory consumption would be to link it to the work and research practices of feminists. As a matter of fact, it was a feminist who lent me her photocopy of *Esta Puente, Mi Espalda* (Moraga and Castillo 1988) when I was planning to translate Anzaldúa's chapter, "Crossing Borders." To a certain extent, feminism tends to find alternate circuits of discussion and translation of theories. It did not surprise me, then, that this woman had access to a copy of that groundbreaking anthology edited by Cherríe Moraga and Ana Castillo. As a matter of fact, this is the only theoretical book which includes Anzaldúa's writing that has been translated into Spanish—the other translations being Anzaldúa's books written for children. When Karin Monasterios and I were organizing the panels on Mujeres Creando for the Latin American Studies Association (LASA) International Congress in 2003, I told Julieta

Paredes and María Galindo, the founders and main activists of Mujeres Creando, that LASA would be a great opportunity to contact Chicana theorists—I had already sensed the profound potential dialogues between their work and the work of Anzaldúa and other Chicanas. They told us they had not read the work of Chicanas.[5] Recent Chicana theory is not being translated into Spanish. This generation of Chicanas, to a great extent, speaks English; it is difficult to think of a natural, immediate contact with them from the Spanish-speaking side of the South.[6]

In a comparative literature seminar I taught in 2001, for which I "translated" Anzaldúa,[7] I explored and articulated possible connections between heterosexual women and lesbian "extreme" writings from the United States and women and gay writers from the Southern Cone (Chile and Argentina). By *extreme writing* I meant texts emerging from pain, fury, erasure, wounded memory, and political and cultural violence. From the North, we read Julia Álvarez, Cristina García, Sandra Cisneros, Gloria Anzaldúa, the Latinas from *Esta Puente, Mi Espalda*, along with critical texts by Norma Klahn, bell hooks, and Yvonne Yarbro-Bejarano. From the South, we read Diamela Eltit and Tununa Mercado, Néstor Perlongher and Pedro Lemebel, along with critical texts by Nelly Richard and Beatriz Sarlo—these readings in general being strictly defined by the existence of Spanish translations in the case of English and by my own translations. I did not cover Bolivian writers in the seminar. However, in late 2002, working on the Mujeres Creando panels for the 2003 LASA congress, it dawned on me that the seminar should have connected the Chicana writings with Mujeres Creando activism and writing.

The translation of Anzaldúa's "Crossing Borders" began to resonate, not for the Argentinean and Chilean cases but for a very specific instance of radical feminism in Bolivia. The irony was that I had led my students—many of them of Aymara descent and fascinated by *Borderlands*, probably because of obvious connections with their daily lives—to read destitution, violence, and alternative, radical strategies of representation by the aforementioned writers at both extremes of the continent without having dealt with the Bolivian experience. I had not appropriated these texts to look at ourselves. It was probably because the course emphasized literature, and in that context I was not finding any Bolivian women's literature that could dialogue with Anzaldúa as richly and intensely as Eltit's, Lemebel's, and Mercado's postdictatorship narratives did.

Later it became clear to me that it was not in literature but mainly in feminist militancy and political-poetic actions that a true connection between Bolivian women's experience and Anzaldúa's writing could be found. In terms of poetry, Anzaldúa's poetry can be read through the poetry of Julieta Paredes. Also, Domitila Chungara's testimony, "Si me permiten hablar" (Chungara and

Viezzer 1978), resonates with Anzaldúa's critique of white, middle-class feminism. Domitila, a poor mestizo woman from the Bolivian mines, realized at a feminist convention in Mexico that feminism is middle class, and she decided it was time to tell the story of working-class women such as herself, therefore decisively intervening in hegemonic feminist discourses. The reading of her testimonio had privileged more a political and literary (discursive) point of view rather than a feminist one, since at the time she was not necessarily viewed as countering the class determinant of feminist thought and practice. This might have been largely due to the fact that, being a working-class woman, she did not separate women's struggle from their communities' fight for justice.

Even today, many of the grassroots women with which nongovernmental organizations (NGOs) worked during the deceitful bonanza years of the 1990s—as one feminist told me in La Paz—have been "regressing" to a nongendered type of vision of the struggle given the extreme economic crisis of today. This seems to raise the issue of poor women, who may be seeing their separate, gendered processes of consciousness formation as a luxury rather than, in practical and real terms, as the need to focus on the more basic needs of all. In this sense it would be more than a "regression," a basic conception that their own well-being cannot disconnect itself from the well-being of the community—a "cultural abnegation" that I think underlies gender structures in Bolivia.

I could have also turned to the work of Rivera Cusicanqui, who for some time now has incorporated gender as an analytical and creative category in her groundbreaking work on internal colonialism and Indian rebellion in the Bolivian Andes and in her visual undertakings. Finally, and not to tire readers with this extensive list of what I could have done, I could have explored María Eugenia Choque's work on Aymara women, as it is analyzed by Marcia Stephenson's (2003) piece connecting it, as a matter of fact, to Anzaldúa's work as viewed by Norma Alarcón. This consideration would have given me the opportunity to address the work of one—if not the only—of very few Aymara women intellectuals writing on gender issues. Choque, a member at the time of Taller de Historia Oral Andina (THOA), an international spokesperson for the Aymara people, a member of international indigenous organizations, an activist in the realm of Aymara women empowerment, and for a time vice secretary of Rights and Policy for Indian and Originary Peoples, has written on "colonial domination and the subordination of the indigenous woman in Bolivia" (as an article of hers is titled), that is, on the double domination suffered by Aymara women: the colonial society's domination of the Aymara people and the Aymara patriarchal domination of Aymara women. She deconstructs widely cited and studied notions of "duality" and the "complementary nature of the relationship between men and women" in terms of women's actual subordination (Choque 1998).

The hopeful tone in the last section of Choque's article, where immigrant Aymara women's conditions in the cities are seen as the possible transition to autonomy and liberation, allows me to concentrate on the work of Mujeres Creando, who describe themselves precisely as *imillas, cholas, chotas,* and *birlochas,* which are the racist names given to immigrant Indian women living in the cities and marked by skin color, racial features, and different levels of adherence to Indian ways and clothing. Mujeres Creando dislocate these racist categories, conferring on them self-validating meaning. Not only have Galindo and Paredes rooted their political-poetic action, militancy, and discourse against the neocolonial racism, intolerance, and authoritarianism of Bolivia's societies and cultures in the body of this new mestiza, they were pressed to create an alternative space to act and speak from the queer body and voice and to include and embrace other destitute subjectivities, such as the *puta,* the *alzada,* the *rechazada,* the *desclasada,* the *extranjera*[8] —a space opened over the colonial wound, which separates the "white," Westernized, modernized society and the Indian and *cholo,* the mixed society.

I could refer here to Homi Bhabha's third space very productively, especially in terms of those other positions emerging within it, of an articulation of "productive . . . space that engenders new possibility" as "interruptive, interrogative, and enunciative," where cultural meaning and representation have no "primordial unity or fixity"; where there is the enunciation, transgression, and subversion of dualistic categories going beyond the realm of colonial binary thinking and oppositional positioning (Rutherford, Bhabha, and Law, quoted by Meredith 1998). There is the need, however, to stick to Anzaldúa's argument regarding the new mestiza, her particular way of living borderlands and "continually walk(ing) out of one culture and into another," in a way that once recognized and politicized turns into a possibility of achieving an antiracist consciousness. By not staying in the place, in the definition, in the fragment of the binary colonial script she was always told to occupy, by not living it painfully but as possibility, the mestiza becomes the body of this consciousness.[9] I gather this is what Anzaldúa meant by Nepantla, a space which the mestiza could inhabit as a torn subject (Anzaldúa 1987, 78), but also an "overlapping space between different perceptions and belief systems . . . aware of the changeability of racial, gender, sexual, and other categories rendering the labelings obsolete" (Anzaldúa and Keating 2002, 541).

This is why I think Choque's view is important, but not as in dialogue with

Anzaldúa as Mujeres Creando. The latter always emphasize their interest in the *queer* in Anzaldúa's sense, *los atravesados*. Whereas Choque's emphasis is "the urban Aymara woman, in the process of 'empowerment,' as an active subject in contrast to her traditional role as mother, virgin, seductress, and victim," developing "new work spaces, self-realization, levels of decision making, power, and political participation, all in the time of change" (Choque 1998), Mujeres Creando explore the histories and potentialities of putas, desclasadas, *lesbianas*, and *maricones* as well. This is not in terms of an empowerment that would aspire to enter the power structure of the state, as Choque herself has done—very legitimately—but to work for dignity, freedom, and creativity within queerness, within the experience of destitution *as* prostitute, *as* lesbian, *as* a fugitive from a social class, *as* a gay person. In a way Choque would be working to cross the border into the patriarchal power structure to destructure it from within, institutionally. Mujeres Creando insist on staying on the border, living the body created by the colonial, racist divide, transgressing it, re-creating it, decolonizing it while staying atravesado, queer—therefore, *uninstitutionable*. They insist that imillas, cholas, and birlochas became *deslenguadas* (one of the last articles I received from María on the Internet, ended in the following graffiti: "Me gustan las imillas alzadas, las cholas boconas y las birlochas contestonas").

This border discourse is a locus of creation and politics, of perception and noninstitutional, nonacademic knowledge (*saber*, not *conocimiento*), the nightmare of those living on one side *or* the other—I refer here to their graffiti, "Our dreams are your nightmares"—NGO officials and NGO-affiliated intellectuals, especially "institutional feminists" or "gender technocrats," who depoliticize the categories (and struggle) of women and race, transforming them into "gender" and "ethnicity," terms used by NGOs and the local and foreign intelligentsia working for them. Since the beginning of the 1990s and especially during the process of the Asamblea Constituyente, to this day, in the context of a leftist government, Mujeres Creando construct themselves as the nightmare of the patriarchal left and social movements—even the most radical—incapable of structurally incorporating women, sexuality, and sexual orientation into their agendas. They represent the nightmare of homophobes, traditional and intolerant men and women on both sides of the border, of fascists, racists, and *machistas* of all sorts of colors and flavors. The great effect of their actions and writings responds, among other things, to the enthusiastic receptiveness of intellectuals, writers, artists, and a young public willing to go beyond these discriminations and exclusions.

The Emergence of Mujeres Creando in the
Heyday of Neoliberalism in Bolivia

Neoliberalism, formally installed in the state by Víctor Paz Estenssoro in 1985, had a profound impact on the production of knowledge in Bolivia. Many intellectuals were incorporated into the social area of state and government transformation: Reforma Educativa, Participación Popular, Viceministerio de Asuntos Indígenas, de Género y Generacionales, and so on. Nongovernmental organizations and the new social areas in government were two forms of intellectual "cooptation," as some like to call it, which mitigated the truly radical edge of progressive thinking, generating a sort of state- and NGO-sponsored intelligentsia. It justified and in some cases gave the conceptual basis for the general project of reform which, on its economic level, meant selling to transnational corporations all former state-owned and -run industries and services: mining, airlines, communications, water, electricity, and, worst of all, oil. A few intellectuals remained aware of the danger of incorporating themselves into these new dynamics of production of thought and action, notably, Mujeres Creando—as I just elaborated—but also the already mentioned Cusicanqui, the THOA collective, Choque, one of its former directors, and the Comuna collective, which included, among others, Raúl Prada Alcoreza, Álvaro García Linera,[10] and Luis Tapia.[11]

It is important to emphasize that fact, as Evo Morales's vice president, García Linera, created the seminar "Pensando el mundo desde Bolivia" in 2007, which was a series of yearly public events for the discussion of world and regional history, politics, economics, and culture. Key world thinkers and intellectuals have participated, such as Toni Negri, Judith Revel, Michael Hardt, Giuseppe Cocco, Gayatri Spivak, Immanuel Wallerstein, Hugo Zemelman, Enrique Dussel, Ernesto Laclau, Slavoj Žižek, Boaventura de Sousa Santos, and Samir Amin, among others. These are some of the writers that the very influential Comuna collective read when thinking about Bolivia's politics and about the potential for radical change. García Linera has made it an official activity to invite these intellectuals to think in Bolivia (in a Bolivia undergoing radical change, according to him—but not anymore according to the other members of Comuna) about the world. In terms of the discussion on theory travel, consumption, and translation, García Linera's gesture reverses the traditional process: it is key theorists coming to think the world from and in Bolivia, not Bolivia going everywhere, after key thinkers, to think itself.

During the heyday years of neoliberalism in Bolivia, the 1990s, the anarchist feminists Mujeres Creando stormed La Paz and other national and international scenarios with their street actions (the street being the noninstitutional site par excellence), political/poetic performance, participation in national and international women's fora and discussions, graffiti, heterodox publications and videos, street protests, and so on. They focused on disturbing the whole spectrum of political thinking and action from the position of the uncompromisingly subversive queer body. They exercised a radical feminism that disrupted gender and ethnicity research and action by aggressively inserting the crucial elements of racist, colonialist social relations, violent machismo, and rampant sexual intolerance—much like some radical Chicana feminists have done—into an antiacademicist approach privileging the street and its anonymous people as their natural environment and audience. The group's name has sometimes been erroneously translated into English as "Women's Initiative." Erroneously because the word *creando* (creating) is crucial to understand them and their politics of creation, their politics as creation, and their creation of a new politics (which I also see as essential in Anzaldúa) but also due to the gerund: creating is a *process*, something always in movement, lucid and attentive to the extremely complex daily life of people in an Andean politics and society in neoliberal times.

The Mujeres Creando movement—some people prefer to call them *women in movement* rather than a women's movement—has had an enormous impact on the everyday life of La Paz (where they mainly operate) for the past two decades.[12] It has shown the possibilities of autonomous, creative, ethical action in a context where the legitimacy of political representation and legal institutions, and the overall credibility of the democratic system, reached its absolute crisis and collapsed in the overthrow of President Sánchez de Losada in October 2003. Many social movements gained and regained momentum in this context. The difference lies in the fact that Mujeres Creando question the epistemological foundations of such movements—even the most radical, as I said—as patriarchal, homophobic, and misogynistic. This is definitely the strength of their critique and action then and today (in the very different direction of radical feminist action Galindo and Paredes have taken after their separation), even if the political context has changed considerably. For them patriarchy, homophobia, and misogyny have simply changed color and have gained strength in a way: women in powerful positions in government today do not necessarily mean real change. In their view, socialist machismo is not too different from neoliberal machismo, the former being worse in the sense that socialist discourse emphasizes equality, justice, and change.

In this very tense relationship with other radical political initiatives, Mujeres Creando constructed their coherence around a decisive intervention on issues of social and political urgency, essentially involving destitute, extremely vulnerable women. The range of their interventions spans years and represents different and complex struggles. These go from involvement in 2002 in a revolt by small debtors, the occupation of the Superintendencia de Bancos to pressure private bankers to renegotiate debts suffocating poor women's economies, to the 2004 DVD production of *Las exiliadas del neoliberalismo*, which deals with illegal poor Bolivian female immigrants in Spain. It also includes the 2009 documentary *Amazonas: Mujeres indomables*, on female migrants and poor women in Argentina. They have also been aggressively active in the streets, demanding justice for the rape and murder of poor girls in La Paz. They created the TV series *Mamá no me lo dijo* (2003), which deals with issues of colonial scripts of beauty, behavior, and identity engraved on the bodies of imillas, chotas, birlochas, and cholas, and, among many other things, the recuperation of joy, pleasure, and humor in the process of liberation. This does not exclude an important bibliographic production that goes from weekly newspapers (*Mujer pública* and *Cara a cara*) and books on sexual reeducation for male and female adolescents and mothers to books recuperating more than a decade of political and performative interventions.

Galindo's Mujeres Creando have been working with the same energy and intransigence in the street, or on the sidewalks outside the main institutions in La Paz, as they do in the Reina Sofía Museum of Madrid (1999) or the Camden Arts Centre in London (2005), institutions to which they enter as "impostors," because the "outside" is their arena, the source of their energy and creativity. Since the 1990s, this "outside" was constructed as mainly the outside place where thousands of Aymara and mestizo women in La Paz work all day from dawn to night, selling, manufacturing, cooking all sorts of things. It is the "outside" where the main struggles have been carried out against abuse, injustice, racism, and exclusion. Because even if one can identify their discourse and modalities of intervention with certain strands of radical feminism at a more international level, they insist that their genealogy intersects with the history of resistance of these women in the streets of La Paz.

There is a long history of women's radicalism in Bolivia—only recently recuperated from erasure by a very vigorous generation of women social scientists and historians—mainly led by the libertarian organizations of flower and food merchants at the beginning of the twentieth century, by the miners' wives' decisive participation in overthrowing the dictatorship in the 1970s (Domitila Chungara being one of them), and the women's day-to-day resistance in their informal work in the streets, contradicting every basic principle of a formal, liberal economy. Not only are the struggle and survival tactics of women in the streets of La Paz part of their genealogy, but Mujeres Creando find in these women (these *indias* and mestizas), the basic inspiration for their work—referring to themselves as their "apprentices."

> Our discovered treasures are those unique and yet prohibited alliances that we have made.
> By destroying all possible preconceived scripts, we offer these unique alliances with an unprecedented originality in order to be able to embrace each other and to make commitments to one another.
> We offer these unique alliances as a revolutionary proposal and against those preconceived scripts attributed to us as fossilized and objectified identities. These identities, which have been turned into walls which separate and divide love, loved ones and skins.

> *Strategies without license*
> Our strategies are alien to the art world,
> Our strategies are illiterate and anonymous,
> Our strategies are unambiguous and outside of legality,
> These strategies are like children that learned their skills from others,
> In this sense we recreate strategies,
> Strategies multiply.
> Our strategies come incessantly from the streets, the city, from the world outside. They come from the survival skills of women working at market stalls, of women working in the center of the city, their shelters forming a barricade raised against the sun and the heat, and against the encroachment of globalization.
> (Galindo and Adrián 2005, 19–20)

I imagine Anzaldúa would have enjoyed watching the actions and performances of María and Julieta and the other Mujeres Creando women, the mestizas who work with them. They would have shared a strong conversation on how "difficult and painful" it is to navigate "the cracks between the worlds" in search of reconstructing a new life (Anzaldúa 2000, 255). They would have recognized the particularities of the wounds from which both projects emerge, the creative, courageous, intransigent, persistent activity, and the "tremendous amount of energy" it takes to "make changes or additions to the model"—to use Anzaldúa's words (Anzaldúa 2000, 253). These women would have recognized the groundbreaking, foundational character of their endeavors and would have joked around Anzaldúa's idea that "it's like this little fish going against the Pacific Ocean." I can almost hear María or Julieta responding, "No, Gloria, not little fish: like sharks, mad female sharks."

Bolivia, as stated before, has gone through amazing political and social change if one looks at recent history from Sánchez de Losada's terms in office (1993–97, 2002–3) to Evo Morales's terms in office (2005–9, 2010–15).

What does it mean to analyze feminist resistance politics and discourses in a context in which social movements, usually in antagonism with the state and government, have seized the state through constitutional vote? What happens to resistance politics when what you resisted has been ousted and social movements, of which you consider yourself a part, are now in government? What happens when a new constitution has been promulgated after a very conflictive process of the Asamblea Constituyente (2006–8), where the majority of its members came from socialist politics and social movements and are members of Evo Morales's political party, and where a woman, Silvia Lazarte, a Quechua union leader and Movimiento al Socialismo (MAS) militant, was designated president of the Asamblea? What happens when a new constitution, which locates the rights of Indigenous, workers, and subaltern populations in the center of the document, declaring Bolivia a pluricultural state, is promulgated? What happens—finally—when indigenous and women workers have come to occupy the highest offices in government, becoming *ministras* of the president?

Both Galindo and Choque ran for seats at the Asamblea, but did not get elected. One could say that they saw this participation as a possibility of real change; they connected their particular and very different ways of activism, as I have discussed, to the institutional changes promoted by the Morales government. Galindo, however, was extremely critical of the election logic of the members of the Asamblea. She wrote that the logic of election of *asambleístas* has given old politics (excluded from the political arena with the defeat of Sánchez de Losada) the opportunity to make a comeback—which was finally not the case—betraying the popular demand for radical change through a new constitution. Evo Morales and his team, she said, also betrayed the clamor for direct political representation, given the defeat of traditional political representation in the events of 2002–6.

The major betrayal has to do with women, Galindo added: they were forced to run through a "biological quota" logic (typical of "neoliberal, technocratic criteria"), which converts them into a necessary percentage, being forced, furthermore, to alternate with a male colleague and not with another woman. Within a complex argument against Evo Morales's Asamblea Constituyente, Galindo thought that it would become a space for mere reform, not of transformation, given the fact that Evo Morales made sure MAS had the majority of seats at the Asamblea, blocking all possibility for dissidence, autonomy, and real debate. She saw a logic of exclusion and silencing in the Constituy-ente, and the emergence of a monological scenario in Bolivian democracy (the MAS monologue). "Today in Bolivia, both indigenist and Leftist politics repeat themselves and coincide with neoliberal politics in the same phallic and patriarchal posture, which ratifies the confusion between social project and "power" project, society control, the subjection of the masculine Other and the feminine Other, as the only interest around which history and politics should turn" (Galindo 2006).[13] It took Galindo less time than the other intellectuals mentioned before to recognize the obvious and early signs of failure of the new government in terms of its promises of real socialist change.

Paredes did not run for a seat at the Constituyente. Since 2004, she worked on the Asamblea Feminista, which she described as emerging directly from the tragic/heroic events of October 2003 in Bolivia that resulted in Sánchez de Losada fleeing the country. Always differentiating her tactics from Galindo's and her Mujeres Creando, Paredes defines the Asamblea Feminista as follows:

> What's fundamental is to transform society. . . . The Asamblea Fem-inista emerges as the need of a larger space [than Mujeres Creando's space]. . . . October occurs and the people show us how something like that could occur. It shows us how *asambleas zonales* worked. Everybody discussed in those asambleas and in the vigils. And in the street political action, because the vigils occurred in the streets, at night, the asambleas zonales in the morning, the demonstrations at 11 in the morning. We then began to work around the idea of the asamblea, as a space of con-junction, of unity of diverse men and diverse women, but also as a place for proposals. . . . A space of convergence of so many ideas. In our idea of the asamblea, people from the street had to attend, because that was the way things worked in October. (Paredes 2005b, my translation)

Julieta is talking about the tradition of street political action of the Aymara residents of El Alto,[14] of the asamblea—an open meeting where everybody can express his or her opinion and propose action and which is related to worker unions' political practices—and how that practice can be adopted to promote a "non-Western feminism, another feminism, a feminism we are constructing." She is not talking, then, of the Asamblea Constituyente but of a radically dif-ferent sort of asamblea.

Paredes goes on to explain that women from all walks of life participate: those who come from political activity, from the *sin tierra* movements, from the street vendors' unions, neighborhood organizations, young women who work at the university and in their neighborhoods. She differentiates the con-tributions women can make to change from the contributions men make. "We have a different conception of politics," she affirms, and this difference and its practices have been historically silenced, have not been documented, "but Humanity has benefited from them" (Paredes 2005b). The specific contribution made by women from the South, in this case Mujeres Creando, is different from anything in the North because of the South's colonial condition, because it is a region of looted countries that have been made invisible, where language and thought have not been respected but usurped. She insists that a woman in the North might suffer from patriarchy and machismo, but she will never undergo the same social and political conditions as women in the South. This takes us back to Anzaldúa and a strand of what Moraga and Castillo conceive of as Third World North American feminism in *This Bridge Called My Back*, which definitely converses with Mujeres Creando's feminism. Paredes's statement has obviously a strategically political purpose: to connect her project to the specificity of Bolivia's colonial, subaltern history, which is basic to her discourse. It also expresses and connects with the very strong anti-American strand of resistance politics (and now turned into an official politics) in Bolivia. Paredes has expressed that she had read (obviously in translation) the feminist poet Audre Lorde, an African American lesbian to whom she felt very connected. Lorde is conceived by Paredes most probably as an extranjera, a pariah in her own land, and therefore not part of the North she is speaking about.

What position did Paredes take toward the Asamblea Constituyente? She accepted invitations to several fora where the Asamblea was discussed and prepared, expressing there the position of the *Asamblea Feminista*. Later, in March 2006, during the celebration of International Women's Day, Paredes and other members of the Asamblea Feminista were arrested in the Plaza Murillo (in front of the National Congress Building and the Presidential Palace) for peacefully protesting against the way Evo Morales was handling the Asamblea Constituyente elections: they were publicly protesting against what they called la *traición del MAS* (the MAS party betrayal). They held a banner saying: "Se ha promulgado la ley de convocatoria a la TRAICIÓN" (The law calling for treason has been promulgated). This critique was directed against Evo Morales for ignoring the proposals sent to him by the Asamblea Feminista and for forcing social organizations to participate in the elections through political parties.[15] Moreover, they were most critical of his not guaranteeing gender parity in the election of the Asambleístas. Morales answered that he would guarantee 33 percent of women in the Asamblea[16]—although, he recognized, women make up far more than 50 percent of Bolivia's population—and that he appointed several women to very important government positions during his short time in office, "because I am convinced they are not as corruptible as men" (*La Jornada* 2006). Paredes and her Asamblea Feminista did not participate in the elections,

as Galindo did, obviously manifesting the belief that participating in the Constituyente meant participating in the betrayal.[17] It is clear, though, that Paredes
made sure to take her protest against this exclusionary move to the streets,
rallying against the return to old political paradigms in a context where everybody was expecting radically democratic, direct, open, and inclusive elections
for the Asamblea.

Some Conclusions on Radical Feminism and Translation

Given the stand taken by both groups of Mujeres Creando, where would the
connection with Anzaldúa's writing stand? Her writing discovered and uncov-
ered for the world a historical, social, political wound suffered by women of
color in such a way that it can be compared without difficulty to the wounds
Mujeres Creando have worked so hard to reveal. Like Anzaldúa, Galindo and
Paredes have created the possibility of a new feminist politics localized and
centered in the specific body of the mestiza, of the queer, politicizing this
body to explode powerful scripts that insist on trying to make it invisible or, if
visible, ugly and shameful; to victimize it, to subjugate it. Given very different
contexts of action and discourse, I think this dialogue between the queer mestiza from Texas and the queer mestiza from La Paz has to be explored further.
As a matter of fact, Galindo has begun to do it directly, with no need of academic intermediaries (such as myself).

After Anzaldúa's death in 2004, Galindo published an homage to her.[18] She
includes the translation of pages 38 to 40 of *Borderlands / La Frontera* (1999, 2nd
edition), introducing it as follows: "By Gloria Anzaldúa (1942–2004). (Homage)." Allowing Anzaldúa to speak for herself, she translates the fragment into
Spanish (or reproduces somebody else's translation) without adding any specific comment. Galindo lets her talk to a Spanish-speaking audience, a larger
audience than the one I translated *Atravesando fronteras/Crossing Borders* for: the
not necessarily (but probably also) academic audience of her homage. Galindo
finds no reason to write anything about the fragment, and I ask myself to what
extent this other translation (identical in linguistic terms but different in context, purpose, and readership) overcomes my "betrayal" of Anzaldúa's intentions and of her language's search for untranslatability and uniqueness. Does
Galindo's translation lack my naiveté because it is done in a context of political
discussion, of feminist politics, and not in an academic context? Is Galindo
an intellectual mediator in her own context as I am (or in the way I am) at the
university? To what extent does her inclusion of Anzaldúa in a strategic politics
of affinity in the Mujeres Creando project go beyond the possible *erasures* I perceive in my own translation at the beginning of this essay? To what extent does

Anzaldúa's "language of the North," included in the gamut of appropriations in Galindo's discourse, and incorporated de facto in a transnational feminism which (as Mujeres Creando stipulated since its beginnings) have no frontiers but the ones that patriarchy, racism, and homophobia insist on—anarchy being the belief in a humanity without frontiers, without state, without authoritarian divisions of social life?[19] In what way does Anzaldúa's dedication in *Borderlands* become true much further to the South ("This book is dedicated a todos mexicanos on both sides of the border"), not in the sense of an elitist university consumption but of a radical politics of affinity?

My 2001 translation of *Atravesando fronteras/Crossing Borders* had the strangest way of "traveling." I realized that some colleagues had gotten hold of it and had used it for their own work, but also that it had broken out of the university, reaching other people and their own work—most notably, a feminist friend who was excited by the fact that a male colleague of mine had given her a translation of *Borderlands* (not knowing it was mine). Interestingly or coincidentally, this was the same friend who had lent me the photocopy of the translation of *This Bridge Called My Back* some time before, introducing me to Anzaldúa and other Third World writers of the North. This circulation of my translation might have, by those channels, reached other feminists as well. This process challenges the idea that my translation (or any such academic project) necessarily circulated exclusively at the university or that knowledge from the North necessarily stays confined to academics in its dissemination.

Furthermore, Elizabeth Monasterios's initiative of taking Galindo and Paredes to LASA 2003 in Dallas had to have an effect on both of them, because many panels included discussion of Anzaldúa's work. As I mentioned before, in the preparatory meetings of the LASA panels in La Paz before we traveled North, I told them that LASA would be an excellent occasion for getting to know Chicana feminists and scholars. They expressed their familiarity with Audre Lorde's work and with *The Gay and Lesbian Studies Reader*. They did not express an interest in going beyond that. It becomes obvious that what you read and what you accept (or don't accept) you've read are political options, especially in a context, the Mujeres Creando context, where affiliations and affinities have great ideological weight and consequence.

Translating, then, becomes much more complex. It has to do with linguistic translation, yes, but also with making a work available (with all the consequences this might have, all the "betrayals" and "erasures" it might include) to other audiences and letting it travel. It also has to do with opening scenarios of conversation and proposing new horizons for dialogue. It means opening your choices, your tastes, your affinities to others—which in politics (as in Mujeres Creando's) can compromise (or strengthen) your principles. Translation in those terms becomes rigorously "strategic and selective" (Prada 2002, 286). Teaching literature, on the other hand, leaves much more room for exploration, for erratic wanderings, for distance from political discourses and practices that sometimes become too strategic and selective.

What is most important now is to maintain the flow of translations, readings, and conversations open and ongoing and to understand the politics of reading, writing, and translating across borders, and the differences (and connections) of theories traveling within oppositional political discourses and within academic discourses.

The arrival of Gayatri Spivak to La Paz in 2008 revealed that Bolivians—who packed the large auditoriums where the two events organized for her took place—are reading postcolonial thinkers and making, I am sure, complex connections with Bolivia's reality. Paredes was present, in the public. One of Spivak's talks was translated simultaneously by Silvia Rivera Cusicanqui, a postcolonial thinker herself. When trying (with difficulty) to translate certain terms used by Spivak, Rivera resorted to Aymara concepts in an attempt to make them clearer to the Bolivian audience. The complexities and possibilities of the translation—and the traveling of theories—I am talking about were actually performed that night.[20]

In this chapter I tried to show that Anzaldúa's (and Spivak's and Lorde's) writings are finding their way into Bolivian feminist, academic, and political thinking today. Mujeres Creando's feminism has been essential for it to happen, for they have introduced in Bolivia the epistemological ground and tactics for radical thought specifically created by lesbian feminists of color, widening the way we conceive oppositional politics of knowledge in terms of the gendered bodies who suffer racism, discrimination, rejection, and violence. The inclusion of Anzaldúa's writings in classes at the public university and in the publications of Mujeres Creando has been as important as the vice president's project of rethinking the world from within the context of social and political change in Bolivia. In these very different contexts of activism, reading, teaching, and thinking, Anzaldúa and oppositional women writers like her are being incorporated into the work of Bolivian feminists, university professors, and leftist intellectuals outside and inside the government in what I hope to be an important enrichment of our understanding of subaltern women's struggles in Bolivia and around the world. Their presence in Bolivia points to an increasingly healthy and very diverse promotion of the travel of theories.

Notes

1. Anzaldúa herself reflected on the monolingual students in the United States, monolingual not only—to her sorrow—linguistically but mentally (2000, 261).

2. The translation of subaltern studies theorists from India—Rajanit Guha, Gyanendra Pandey, Shahid Amin, Dipesh Chakrabarty, Partha Chatterjee, and Gayatri Spivak—most certainly had an effect in the work of humanities and social sciences researchers in Bolivia. Indian postcolonial theorists translated in Bolivia is an example of specific theory importation and specific intervention in academic and political agendas in the South.

3. SEPHIS, an organization from the Netherlands, stands for the South-South Exchange Programme for Research of the History of Development.

4. A person can live in the wealthier southern neighborhoods of the city without having to visit or acknowledge the mainly Aymara and mestizo neighborhoods located in the mountain slopes and northern areas of the city, living in denial of the heavy mark of the Aymara culture and presence in all aspects of city life, even in the new political scenario.

5. Not reading Chicanas because of the language barrier would have to do with Paredes more specifically, because she comes from an Aymara and poorer background. Galindo comes from a higher middle-class and white background and reads English. The image of them as an anarchist feminist lesbian couple was very powerful during the 1990s for this difference of social and ethnic backgrounds. The term *desclasada* has very direct reference to Galindo's attitude of rejection vis-à-vis her own class.

6. When writing in the North, probably scholars think that their English written production could travel around the world with great ease. This is not true—at least not so in Bolivia, and not in the public university. People do not necessarily speak English—very few students in my classes do. The wealthier classes in La Paz have access to the language in private schools and in their study trips to the North; people who do not attend private schools or travel to the North reveal that the language barrier is more consistent and important than usually thought of. It is not only a matter of not being able to study the language because of economic reasons. One of the prerequisites to graduate in the Licenciatura program in the Literature Department where I worked is a proficiency test in a foreign language. Few students choose English—other Romance languages are preferred.

7. It was a seminar called "Escrituras extremas del extremo norte y del extremo sur" (Extreme writings of the extreme North and the extreme South).

8. The puta would be the whore; the alzada, the rebellious, the indomitable; the rechazada, the rejected; the desclasada, the one that denies her social class; the extranjera, the foreigner.

9. I cannot but think of the public university Aymara students who actively live crossing from the Aymara urban world, their homes, their activities, into the Westernized institutions, let's say, the university, its Spanish, its writing, its theoretical formal thinking, and back on a daily basis.

10. When I began writing this piece in spring 2005, to be delivered at the Chicano-Latino Research Center of the University of California at Santa Cruz on April 1, I did not even dream that Carlos Mesa, the vice president who inherited the presidency when Gonzalo Sánchez de Losada escaped from Bolivia in October 2003, would resign in June 2005 and leave the presidency to Rodríguez Veltzé, a Supreme Court judge, and even less that in the

presidential elections held in December 2005, Evo Morales would win with more than 50 percent of the vote, that Álvaro García Linera would run as vice president, and that they would be reelected in 2009 with an overwhelming 64 percent of the national vote.

11. These three important leftist intellectuals, all of them professors at the public university, were crucial in providing a theoretical foundation to Evo Morales's rise to power, to the point that Evo Morales asked García Linera to run as his vice president. Prada Alcoreza's involvement with the government's MAS party was extensive: he was representative for the party at the Asamblea Constituyente and he then became Viceministro de Planificación. Currently, after a series of very serious disappointments, he has become one of the most radical critics of Evo Morales's government. Luis Tapia, never leaving his post at the postgraduate program in Social Sciences (CIDES) at UMSA, and after a process of similar serious disappointments, has recently published El estado de derecho como tiranía (The Rule of Law as Tyranny, 2011), expressing the tyrannical bent gradually taken by the government since 2005. Silvia Rivera Cusicanqui, who for some time was an adviser to the government, has also become one of its toughest critics.

12. As I already mentioned, Paredes and Galindo have not been working together for many years now. They continue to work as Mujeres Creando (neither of them has renounced the name), but there is the Paredes Mujeres Creando and the Galindo Mujeres Creando. They do not have any contact with each other and are very critical of each other. In an interview published in Feminismos en Latinoamerica (www.americalatinagenera.org), when Paredes attended the XI Encuentro Feminista Latinoamericano in Mexico in March 2009, she called her group Comunidad Mujeres Creando, emphasizing the communal root of political organization and daily life of many mestizo and indigenous women in the Andes and also the communal practice as a way of life in contrast to patriarchal individualism. Paredes defines herself as feminista comunitaria of Aymara descent. This interview narrates the creation of Mujeres Creando, their work during the 1990s, and their split in 2002.

13. A necrological sign was hung in 2007 in front of La Virgen de los Deseos, the house of Galindo's Mujeres Creando: it announced the death of the Asamblea Constituyente. According to her, the logic that defined elections and the party-oriented actions conducting the Asamblea have determined its death.

14. El Alto has been an emblematic scenario of resistance to neoliberal politics. The last order of Sanchez de Losada before fleeing the country in October 2003 was to shoot at protesters in the streets. Several dozen El Alto residents were killed in what is now remembered as Black October.

15. A note written by the Asamblea Feminista explains their accusation of treason and sums up the proposal ignored by Evo Morales: "TREASON to 50 percent participation of women, TREASON to the direct participation of men and women from the social movements, TREASON to the direct participation of women and men from our Indian peoples. Our people have shaken and weakened the five hundred year long political hegemony of the white bourgeois oligarchies in our country, but we do not have a political project agreed upon by all, men and women, an inclusive project which would recognize differences and which would draft, from our bodies, the type of country we want now. In order to achieve this we choose to organize a re-founding Asamblea Constituyente and this time with direct participation of always excluded women and men like us: us, who cornered the oligarchs

in the streets. The present law calling for elections of asambleístas is a copy of Parliament elections, giving political parties the function of representing us again, when we—men and women—want to speak with our own and direct voices" (indymedia romania, "Denuncia de la represión policial contra feministas en el 8 de marzo").

16. Thirty-three was the percentage fought for (and won) by women in Parliament during the Sánchez de Losada government years. Mujeres Creando answered to this victory in a graffiti: "Queremos todo el paraíso, no el 30 percent del infierno neoliberal" (We want the whole paradise, not 30 percent of the neoliberal hell).

17. In this case, Paredes acted more on the logic of the Mujeres Creando of the 1990s during important events involving women's issues: creating a parallel event that collided ideologically, politically, methodologically with the main event, acting many times with disruptive intention (as in the UN World Summit in Beijing in 1995, where a parallel women's summit was organized by radical feminists, or the VII Encuentro Feminista Latinoamericano y del Caribe en Cartagena, Chile, in 1996, which was literally taken by radical feminists). In this case, the Asamblea Feminista would be a parallel forum for direct political discussion and practice, a forum impossible to include in the logic of the Asamblea Constituyente. Galindo also still opts for these disruptive, radically oppositional practices: her group's disruptive actions in the Primer Encuentro de Movimientos Sociales e Intelectuales Latinoamericanos in Cochabamba (November 2005) were considered by some as illogical and contradictory in a context where social movements were trying to discuss and propose the creation of a Coordinadora for participating Latin American indigenous and workers social movements (see http://bolivia.indymedia.org/es/2005/11/23731.shtml). Oppositional intellectuals who usually have been supportive of Galindo's work became perplexed at the paradox of acting oppositionally in a place where radically oppositional organizations were trying to find common ground for discussion and action.

18. "Tiranía cultural" (homenaje a Gloria Anzaldúa), Mujeres Creando, http://www.mujerescreando.org/pag/articulos/2005/arti_tiraniacultural.htm.

19. As has been said before, extranjeras (foreigners) are part of Mujeres Creando description of the range of difference included in their discourse in terms of their construction of an alternative radical mestizo queer subjectivity. The "conversation" of Mujeres Creando and Anzaldúa can be imagined as a conversation between extranjeras creating a new space of community and dialogue; inventing a transnational complicity in poetry, ideas, and practice—surely very critical of each other, surely very creative; a kind of conspiratory communal discourse (in which Lorde would have been kindly invited as another extranjera) aiming at women's laughter and joy.

20. In the already mentioned book of Indian subaltern studies, compiled by Rivera Cusicanqui and Barragán (1997), there is a translation of Spivak's "Subaltern Studies: Deconstructing Historiography" by Silvia Rivera and me.

CHAPTER THREE/ *CRAVO CANELA BALA E FAVELA/*
LUSO-AFRO-BRAZILIAN FEMINIST POSTCOLONIALITIES

SIMONE PEREIRA SCHMIDT

Translated by Ramayana Lyra

Perhaps there is nothing "more Brazilian" than the classic association of the female body and male desire. Yet lurking behind this apparently harmless consensus lies what are in truth ceaseless practices of violence against women, who are thus constrained in their freedom of movement and initiatives or sold as seductive commodities—nothing better than the endless televised beer commercials invading our homes to illustrate the booming business that is increasingly dependent on the use of women's bodies. When other forms of prejudice, such as those of class and race, are added to those surrounding gender, violence against women becomes a monumental concern. A few years ago, Brazilians were sad witnesses to the assault of a domestic worker, Sirlei, who was the target of the misogynist rage of a band of young men from the wealthy Zona Sul district of Rio de Janeiro. On this occasion, in an article disseminated through the press, Brazilian Minister of Policies for Women Nilcéia Freire correctly observed that although society as a whole proclaimed its solidarity with the victim, greater reflection on what motivated this act of violence was needed. As she argued, the act of aggression constituted "an exacerbated version—and therefore so revolting to all—of a type of violence that has been naturalized, made banal and even authorized. This may seem excessive, but it is nonetheless the case of men's violence against women in Brazil and the world over—authorized by patriarchal society." Drawing these connections between women's bodies, violence, and patriarchal culture, Freire directs our attention to a fundamental debate that must be carried out with the greatest rigor in Brazil today: the tense and poorly resolved legacy of slavocratic patriarchy and how it unfolds and expresses itself in gender-, class-, and race-based forms of inequality and violence.

Edward Said once asserted that "to have been colonized was a fate with lasting, indeed grotesquely unfair results," which means being potentially "a great many different, but inferior, things, in many different places, at many different times" (Said 2001, 294–95). Thus, basing ourselves on Said's reflections, we may say that "to have once been colonized" is a past to which we continue, inevitably linked along a thread of historical continuity. Its starting point is constituted by the trauma of slavery, and it unfolds today into the violent urban space of Brazilian cities, finding its synthesis in the punching and kicking that Sirlei's body was forced to withstand. That is, the "dark-skinned" body of a woman, the body of a domestic worker whose assaulters "mistook" her for a prostitute (which, following the fascistic logic of prejudice of these bad boys, would have been their preferential target). Thus, it would not be overdrawn to emphasize here that the body that became the target of such violence was appropriately situated, in terms of gender, race, and class, in the unequal social order that prevails in contemporary Brazilian society and whose drama is nowhere played out more clearly than in the tensions of its major capital cities.

Freely circulating through the nation's imaginary, for domestic and foreign consumption, is the stereotype of the dark-skinned woman who is a facile object of male desire. If author Jorge Amado's fictional Gabriela comes immediately to mind as one of the most consecrated representations of this model, the most intractable reference can be found in the still polemic work of sociologist Gilberto Freyre. Obviously, discussion of his monumental work is not a task at hand here. Rather, I limit myself to emphasizing the originality of the reflections he made, within the context of the 1930s Brazilian modernist project of interpreting national culture. His pioneering work analyzed the complex relations between masters and slaves that were established through the constitution of Brazil's colonial society (Freyre 1954 [1998]). The body of the slave woman, appropriated by the plantation house master, is at the center of his analysis. The tense space that separates (and connects) the *casa grande* (plantation house) and the *senzala* (slave quarters) finds its expression in the body of the slave woman, sexually enslaved by the master. As Ria Lemaire (2000) has suggested, herein lies a strong metaphor for power relations in Brazilian society.

The interpretation that Freyre has developed through his central metaphor —that is, the way he interprets the role of this interracial sexual encounter in the formation of Brazilian culture—has, as we well know, stirred up an intense debate that is far from being exhausted. Many writers have argued that the author's eulogy of this particular form of interracial encounter can be considered one of the most well-constructed justifications that exists for the violence perpetrated by Portuguese colonizers. According to these authors (Barbeitos 1997; Almeida 2000; Lemaire 2000; Silva 2002; Thomaz 2002; Ribeiro 2004; Pinto 2007), Freyre's enthusiastic eulogy for the fraternal and egalitarian contact between the different cultures and races that formed the Brazilian nation can be seen as a powerful mystification, in the sense that Albert Memmi (1977) used this notion, that is, to refer to set of discursive constructions elaborated by the colonizers as a means of ideological justification for colonial acts. This topic suggests a wide range of analyses of the sexual and racial violence that are a consequence of the agrarian and slavocratic patriarchalism that founded Brazilian society, leaving an indelible mark on its worldview, as well as its social, political, cultural, and sexual practices. It is not my intention to go further into this debate at the present moment. What I would like to emphasize is the centrality of the metaphor that is provided by the encounter between master and slave woman, constantly reactivated in a society like our own, so strongly marked by gender and racial inequalities and yet so subtly constructing the discourse that provides cover for it.

Another aspect that deserves attention in our brief glance at Freyre's work is the way it constantly reconstructs the tense space between the casa grande and the senzala that shoots through Brazilian society. The dislocations between city and countryside, between center and periphery, between south and north (or, as Boaventura de Sousa Santos says, between the south of the north and the north of the south; Santos 2004a) are the ways the nation's founding spaces of racial, social, and gender inequality unfold and take shape. From the slave master's encounter with his slave, an encounter tainted with sexual violence, comes the colonized body in a double sense: first, as the body of the slave woman, appropriated by and subjected to the patriarchal, racial, and sexual power of the master; Second, as the mestiço body, fruit of interracial sexual contact, the mixed-race body that according to the testimony of the Angolan writer Arlindo Barbeitos (1997, 323–26) constitutes a veritable battleground where all the contradictions of the contact between blacks and whites in the colonial history of his country meet.

The subaltern woman's body, a stage of conflicts where the tensions resulting from Brazil's unequal gender, class, and race relations unfold, is a colonized body and veritable battleground where the casa grande and the senzala continue to confront each other. This body has been represented in recent fictional works that are my specific object of interest here. The narratives chosen for this reading are *Ponciá Vicêncio*, by Conceição Evaristo (2003); *As mulheres* de *Tijucopapo* (The Women of Tijucopapo), by Marilene Felinto (2004); and the film *O Céu de Suely* (Suely's Heaven), by Karin Aïnouz (2006). By tracing the way the three protagonists of these narratives are portrayed, we can discuss their bodies and the dislocations they effect, analyzing their motivations and the effects that such shifts produce. Taking the subaltern female body as a referent, located in accordance with the injunctions of gender and race in the context of Brazilian cultural discourses, we can think of three different moments, which make up a kind of typology of agency of women in subaltern conditions: denouncing subordination, rebellion, and reinvention.

My reading of several fictional works by Brazilian women writers belongs to such an endeavor. Their characters can be considered intensely representative of women's experiences situated within the space of tension I have already referred to, the space that separates and connects the master's house (casa grande) and the slave quarters (senzala). In the trajectory of the three characters, Rísia, Ponciá, and Hermila, the first milestone in their formation is the road. However, these characters each face the tension underlying the orders of gender, race, and other vectors of inequality that place their bodies in transit in different ways.

In *Ponciá Vicêncio* (Evaristo 2003), a novel by Conceição Evaristo that came out in 2003, we are able to identify the protagonist's passages, dislocations, and coming into her own. The character whose name becomes Evaristo's title is marked by a subjectivity that is firmly rooted in cherished memories of her family of origin. Raised by descendants of slaves whose old master gave them his own last name, Ponciá decides to leave the countryside and her family to try her luck in the big city. Alone, she sets out in search of the unknown, into which she is lost. Ponciá disappears in the anonymity of the city. The narrative unfolds in the passage from childhood to adult life, between city and country, and between the memories that keep her going and the emptiness of the present. The character is slowly submerged in her own recollections, her presence erased within the current moment, consumed by memories—whether the search for a past moment or for one that never really existed. As the narrative unfolds, Ponciá's story becomes one of growing absence and an intense desire to return.

When she leaves her small town and the comfort of her mother's home, Ponciá takes a train that will carry her to the big city, the promise of the city, the vertigo of the city:

> As the train slowed down and came to a halt at the platform, Ponciá
> Vicêncio pressed the small bundle of clothing she had been carrying
> throughout the trip closely to her chest. She stood up in anguish and

shot a desperate glare out the window in search of someone. There was no recognizable face. A deep sadness ran through her, even though she already knew no one would be waiting for her. She knew no one, she had never been to the city before. She had left all her relatives behind. No one else had dared such an adventure. (Evaristo 2003, 34)

It is important to note from this passage that Ponciá is the first of her people to dare to set out on this type of adventure. But in her contact with the threatening unknown of the city, she is alone, and finding herself alone is a reason for profound discomfort, or perhaps unbearable suffering, for someone who, like her, comes from a solid web of family relations, an identity-giving network based on ancestry, on family stories, on ranching and handcraft traditions. The city, where no one knows her, suspends in one stroke her contact with her deepest roots. The character dives into the darkness of a world populated only by memories. Oscillating between the desire to return to her homeland to rejoin her family, the increasing loss of consciousness and interest in life, and the ever deeper dive into her tormented subjectivity, the character Ponciá Vicêncio represents, in my reading of the role of the subaltern female body in transit, a gesture of condemnation by the authorial instance, in which the deep and painful motivations that characterized the experience of black women in Brazil's postabolition history are evident. However, the process experienced by the character signals in the opposite direction: crushed by her nonplace in the order of unequal relations in our society, the character does not move toward the realization of her projects and the motivations that drove her to the city, but instead appears to give in to a gesture of resignation and dispersion. It is as if by just reconnecting to her community of origin, the character could gain strength to replenish her faded subjectivity. However, as Stuart Hall points out in relation to diasporic communities, members of such communities (such as Ponciá) face enormous difficulties in reconnecting to their communities of origin, feeling that in their attempts to a return, even if symbolic, "the 'land' has become unrecognizable" because "history, somehow intervened irrevocably" (Hall 2003, 27). Unable to reinstate an old connection with her people and her homeland, the character's gesture of dismissal is all there is left.

In *As Mulheres de Tijucopapo* (Felinto 2004), a novel originally published in 1982, Marilene Felinto introduces us to the character Rísia, a young woman who, while walking obstinately toward the land where she supposes she will uncover her origins, delivers a brutal story of painful, shattering, and violent memories. Her story, as she narrates it, is marked by departures: from the sweltering Recife of her childhood to her search for a better life in São Paulo; from her frustration in São Paulo toward a utopia of a women warriors' revolution in

Tijucopapo, her mother's birthplace. The entire narrative thus transpires as a crossing: from her father's house to the outside world, from São Paulo toward Tijucopapo, from childhood to adulthood. In short, the entire novel describes a passage, and in this sense can be read as an initiation rite through which the protagonist seeks to understand her own history and confront the conditions of her existence.

In this account that in the present tense of the narrative unfolds in the mythical space of the Brazilian hinterland, Rísia is often reminded of what her mother once asked her, "So you really think heaven is near?," a query that comes back to the protagonist in a sweep of rage and impotence that she meets with a challenge:

Heaven. So that's it, mom. So the sky is the limit? Heaven . . . of course heaven would have been way too far away for the little girl I was. But look, heaven just doesn't exist, it's simple as that. The sky is just a place where a Varig airplane can take me somewhere. Heaven and its ironic blue looking down on me when here on earth I am dying in the gray rain of my suffering, from never having had a colorful Christmas stocking because heaven was just way too far away, an unreachable place. Heaven, mom, is no more than clouds I touch from the windows of the plane. (Felinto 2004, 133–34)

Rísia travels the backroads of the hinterlands, avoiding major highways; she makes her way through the backlands in search of a doubtful origin, in search of utopia and vengeance. Getting herself moving, heading toward the mystery and salvation represented by the women that are meant to avenge her past, hers and that of all those who, like her, are "the muddied children of poor parents," the ones that big cities are up in arms against, Rísia reminisces, "I almost lost my power to speak in São Paulo." To lose the ability to talk, this kind of imposed muteness in which her painful narrative stakes itself like a banner, we perceive the violence of the city as the protagonist is made to feel it: "I left São Paulo so I wouldn't become a whore"; "In downtown São Paulo, I was up against a concrete wall," "In São Paulo, I was no more than trash" (Felinto 2004, 137, 138, 141). This is why, in the final redemptive act of the women warriors of Tijucopapo, their weapons are pointed straight at São Paulo's Avenida Paulista, the major symbol of the opulence and grandiosity of the city as it contrasts with the dire need faced by those who live on the margins of the city, the world, and life, like Rísia:

I will come down from the wilderness in battle, marching, parading proudly for a just cause. . . . I will descend with my guerrilla band, we'll take over the highway that links Tijucopapo to Avenida Paulista in the city of São Paulo apples of Paradise and I will go out in search of so many lights so many light bulbs from Avenida Paulista to hang on the lightposts of my street on that day that the lights didn't go in Recife in 1969 in the late afternoon, Nema heading on toward Pedra Branca and leaving me unprotected almost nude in the middle of the street. You will come by. We'll be off and our banner will remain where we've left it. We're going to stake out our claim. (Felinto 2004, 185–86)

In her relentless march, Rísia seeks the roots that, in fact, she does not have and concludes that "I live alone in the world because there is nowhere else to live. Because the world, from São Paulo to Recife and to all those places where films are made, the world just hurts too much" (Felinto 2004, 155). Thus, we can understand the character's experience within a discursive construction in which revolt is imprinted, heavily marked by issues of gender and race, in a history of overt exclusions. The words of Donna Haraway, although in a different context, may help us understand the character's position within the authorial project: "it will be necessary to deal with power, privilege, exclusion, and past and present racial and sexual exploitation. I suspect that the nation will have to swallow the castor oil of sober responsibility for such a racialized sex" (1997, 264).

However, reading the novel leads us to see that the solution to the impasses lived by the protagonist do not transpose the boundaries of utopia, remaining in a state of revolt and outcry, without any concrete agency. That is why the solution to all the tragedies experienced by the character are resolved in the libertarian utopia of "women of Tijucopapo," a symbolic projection in which the fantastic supplants realistic language.

A film released in 2006, director Karim Aïnouz's *O Céu de Suely*, treats the same topics that characterize the novel described above with surprising sensitivity. The film's protagonist, Hermila, is a twenty-one-year-old woman who returns to her hometown in the drought-ridden *sertão* of the Brazilian northeast from the life she had been sharing with her boyfriend in São Paulo. Hermila returns to her hometown with her infant son in her arms and bearing a confused array of feelings about whether to stay or leave again for some other distant place. Regarding São Paulo, Hermila says, life "was good, but everything there just cost too much, there was no way to manage. So we decided to come back." She comes back ahead of her boyfriend, the father of her child, and returns to her grandmother's house in the town of Iguatu, where she awaits his promised return. As time goes by and the boyfriend fails to return, Hermila is gradually overcome by the desire to move on again. The scene in which the young woman, now thoroughly disenchanted with her boyfriend and unable to conceive of staying on as an option, goes to the local bus station to inquire about the price of a ticket to "somewhere as far away as possible" is one of the key moments revealing the process of her "sentimental education."

Suely's (this is the name that Hermila has chosen for herself in the scheme she has devised to obtain money for her journey) heaven is a distant place where she will perhaps be able to find her happiness. For Hermila, heaven is the place she is searching for. It is not an unreachable destiny, but one that serves to guide her sojourn, her obstinate faith that there is somewhere that life can be reinvented. When she takes the name Suely in her decision to raffle her own body to get money for her journey, she ironically promises those who buy a ticket a chance at "a night in paradise." Paradise: Suely's heaven.

In a testimony given during the "making of" sequence that accompanies his film, the director of *O Céu de Suely* identifies the challenge of imagining a woman leaving her place of origin as the starting point of his creative endeavor. Raised by the women of his family in an environment in which men were almost always absent (a situation common to many families, particularly so among the popular classes in Brazil), Karim Aïnouz recounts that this absence inspired him to imagine what the destiny of his own family would have been if one of those women so strongly connected to the plot of family life had decided to leave, to change her place of residence and her life. From this query, the underlying theme of the film was born. The director's question is based on a known Western tradition in which women are rooted in their places of origin, with strong ties to the home, children, care of others, and the perpetuation of kin. With rootedness and the provision of care connected to women's responsibilities, absence, nomadism, and comings and goings are expected of men. Thus, Hermila breaks with the expectation that women stay and men leave. She charts another course that begins when she and her boyfriend leave for São Paulo and continues with her return to Iguatu, nurturing the idea that she will soon depart again and this time get as far away as possible (the closest possible to Paradise?). Thus it is no coincidence that the first and last scenes of the film take place on the road, against a wide horizon and clear open sky, both promise of freedom and evocation of abandonment: the *sertão*, the small town in the middle of nowhere, the young woman at the roadside carrying her small child, arriving only to leave again. Furthermore, the entire town of Iguatu makes us conjure a highway or a place that one is merely passing through. Scenes take place on the streets of the town, on the highway, at the local gas station, at the bus station. In many of them, the town, crossed by car, motorcycle, bus, or truck, seems to be invoking departure, reminding its inhabitants that it has so little to offer to those who stay. Yet there are many who do stay. The women of Hermila's family stay. But she does not.

The character's trajectory thus refers to a third moment in the typology that mapped the journeys in the narratives made by the female subaltern body. Hermila/Suely represents an important change in the movements described by this body and subjectivity, because, refusing the subjection and repetition of the past, the character negotiates new places, reinventing gender and race positions and founding a new life project. To better explore the idea of negotiation to which I refer, it is interesting to cite Adriana Piscitelli's use of this concept, drawing on Gayatri Spivak, to discuss the intersections between gender, color, and location in her analysis on women's sexual tourism in northeastern Brazil. At such intersections, Piscitelli identifies the agency of these women in search of social mobility: "I think of negotiation in the sense ascribed by Spivak to this term: as the alternative to change something that one is forced to live with; to be effective in this undertaking it is necessary to preserve these structures, instead of destroying them. From the point of view of 'tropical sensuality,' presented in the notes, the successful Brazilian women are those who, by taking advantage of, and exploring, the close association between 'color' and 'native femininity' that they supposedly embody, are able to enter into prostitution abroad" (Piscitelli 1996, 33).

Just as Osmundo Pinho identified in the cultural "afro" movements in Bahia that resignified the cluster of race and gender stereotypes—and which have historically composed our repertoire of nationality—in *O Céu de Suely* we can read the character's performance as an act of subversion. This subversion, "in search of affirmation and cultural modernity," reveals "the body as a nonbeing, a variable and contentious boundary" (Pinho 2004, 107–8).

The debates about the modes of resignification of the subaltern female body in the discursive contexts shaping the national imaginary achieve a very particular meaning from the perspective of cultural translation. Focusing on recent Brazilian texts, placing them within the debate which I consider as a type of translation of the postcolonial agenda into Portuguese, I intend to examine two important issues. The first one has to do with the very task of translating, whereas the second one deals with the importance that such a task has for contemporary feminism. With regard to the need to translate postcolonial concerns into Portuguese, I take the notion of travel as my reference, particularly expressive within the transnational and globalized context in which we find ourselves today. As Claudia de Lima Costa suggests, "within the context of stories of travel, migration and other dislocations, always diverse and interconnected, and of the transnational circulation of theories and concepts, the issue of translation becomes pressing, constituting on the one hand, a unique space for the analysis of representation, of the power and asymmetry between languages, and on the other, for the examination of formations of language and the institutionalizations through which these theories and concepts travel" (Costa 2004, 187).

Analyzing the transnational and intercultural routes that modernity has traced through the African diaspora, Paul Gilroy (2001) has created the powerful metaphor of the black Atlantic. Taking the figure of the ship as one of the earliest modern chronotropes, Gilroy travels the route of its diverse meanings, beginning with its function as a cultural and political unit, a mobile element that, through its dislocations, linked and connected otherwise fixed and distant spaces. Through this figure he evokes the slave trade and its relationship to modernization projects. At the heart of his reflections, we find the leitmotif of the voyage and its historical results. Furthermore, the black Atlantic becomes the imaginary space of another voyage, not protagonized this time by the colonizers on their routes of expansion and conquest but becoming a way of rethinking the culture of travel through the experiences and cultural exchanges enacted by subaltern peoples.

Starting from this hybrid and transcultural space of the various routes of slave trade sea crossing, we are able to begin to think of other routes that have linked Africa, Europe, and the Americas, yet branch out in other directions. Here I refer specifically to the colonial project that was undertaken by the Portuguese beginning the fifteenth century, and which in anachronic, problematic, and ex-centric ways persisted until the end of the twentieth century. This other route, shaped in the time and space of what we can think of as the transnational territory where the Portuguese language is spoken, found its greatest utopian projection in the fascist project of the Salazar regime. Thus, the totalitarian Portuguese government that was in power from the 1930s to the 1970s reissued age-old imperial dreams, through the maxim that defined these territories as one country unto itself, "from Minho to Timor." At the root of this utopia were Freyre's theories, kept alive as a phantasmagoria of superb utility and thus put to the service of the Portuguese colonial project as a cordial, interracial mestiço and nonracist form of colonialism. Underlying the interpretations that were made of Freyre's ideas was the effort to legitimate the endeavors of Portuguese colonial power.

In more recent times, marked by the postcolonial experience, there are a number of different discourses that within the intellectual field of Portuguese-speaking nations are concerned with resignifying this transnational and intercultural space. The Portuguese anthropologist Miguel Vale de Almeida (2000) took inspiration from Gilroy's Black Atlantic (1993) for the creation of his image of the Atlântico Pardo (or "brown Atlantic") in which through the frictions between the two images, the ethnic, historical, and political differences between the postcolonial experiences of North and South become apparent. According to Almeida, if there is one aspect that integrates Brazil within the postcolonial experience that involves other Portuguese-speaking countries, particularly the African ones, it is the particular mixing of races or *mestiçagem* that is a consequence of slavery. Thus, the postcolonial task at hand, in the Brazilian case, would be to interpret the question of mestiçagem and its implications in terms of the social, racial, and gender inequalities that have persisted until the present.

Boaventura de Sousa Santos sheds considerable light on this task when he proposes that "Portuguese colonialism demands a dense articulation with the question of sexual discrimination and feminism," in an endeavor to "elucidate the sexist rules of sexuality that tend to lay a white man down on the bed with a black woman, and not a white woman and a Black man" (Santos 2002, 42). According to Santos, the mixed-race body in this context has been constituted as a locus of fluid and changing meanings, according to the historical moment and its interpretations. There were moments in which the mulatto body (especially that of the mulatto woman) was seen as degradation, a concrete display of the disgraceful aspects of racial mixing. At other times, quite the contrary: it was portrayed as the depository of the most celebrated expectations of the interracial project linked to the pliant and cordial nature of the Portuguese. Thus, in the name of interracial contact, the idea of an antiracism was promoted, or of a "racism without race, or at least a racism that was 'purer' than its racial base" and through it, a sexism of discourses and practices populated by ambiguous representations of the mulatta's body, as place of sin and desire, repulsion and pleasure. Thus, according to Santos, "the sexist and inter-racial bedplace became the basic unit through which the Empire was managed and racial democracy was used as an anti-racist trophy held up by the white, Brown and Black hands of racism and sexism" (Santos 2002, 43).

The critique of Portuguese colonialism's reading of Freyre's "luso-tropicalist" project and the analysis of its political effects and historical consequences for Brazilian culture has led us to a more specific reflection on the ways in which feminism, through practices of coalition and cultural translation, has appropriated the premises of postcolonial studies. Costa has pointed to the importance of the increasingly sought intersection of these two fields: "Many feminists, in seeking productive ways to establish dialogues for the articulation of transnational alliances between different feminist communities spread throughout a world of increasing movement and cultural contacts, have resorted to the practice of translation as a privileged place for negotiating difference" (Costa 2004, 191).

In spite of the many difficulties experienced in the complex connecting of feminism and the postcolonial, it has represented a theoretical encounter of the greatest importance, since both fields are concerned with tracking down and shedding light on the veritable "shady areas" on the map of inequalities that constitute the relationship between countries, groups, and subjects. For this reason, I would like to point, however succinctly, to some of the important contributions that postcolonialism has to offer for defining the course of contemporary feminist theory.

The first contribution is linked to Mary Louise Pratt's notion of the "contact zone." Dislocating the idea of the contact zone to render it useful for contemporary criticism, Pratt perceives the possibility of bringing borders to the center of discussion "while homogeneous centers are dislocated toward the margins." With her proposal, the author is not, as it may seem, merely slipping into a pure and facile eulogy of the margin. Rather, her "contact zone" perspective puts the autonomy of different identities into interaction, "as border strips, as sites of permanent critical and inventive interaction with the dominant culture, as permeable zones of contact through which meanings move in different directions" (Pratt 1999, 14).

The implications that this idea has for feminist theory are self-evident. If, as Teresa de Lauretis (1994) argues, we can never be "outside" technologies of gender, it seems to me that the constant movements of theory can only be enriched by the contact perspective. Gender becomes one more element that is constantly negotiated—together with class, ethnicity, race, nationality, and so on. Furthermore, here multiculturalism comes to enjoy significant participation. As Ella Shohat (2001) has argued, the idea of "relationality" must be resignified; in other words, rather than focusing on communities that resist a dominant center (which is, furthermore, one more way of privileging the center, at least as antagonist), we must seek to "establish horizontal and vertical links, connecting communities and histories in a conflict-laden network."

A second important contribution that postcolonial discourse makes to feminism comes from Shohat's formulation regarding our need to deconstruct the Euro-centrist history of feminism. Here I add my own brief personal testimony to the debate.

My becoming a feminist during the early 1980s occurred to a large extent through the definition of a feminist specificity that differentiated us from the so-called women's movements, that is, the movements that had sprung up as popular struggles spearheaded by women, in a country that at that time was undergoing a democratic rebirth after the harshest period of the dictatorship. Young intellectuals in training, we learned the meaning of the term *specificity* early on. It was a word through which we sought to define ourselves, moving away from those who held up the banners of broader social causes, using their condition as women to demand that which, in our opinion, was dictated to them by a leftist agenda that was historically masculine and patriarchal.

I was thus destined to take a long journey that on many occasions had me crossing the boundaries that separate theory from political action. In a movement of coming and going that was not unlike the numerous stitches that make up a seam, the seam itself became necessary for my personal and political trajectory. This led me to the understanding that I have today—that from a historical context different from the European and North American ones, I have been and am part of another history of feminism: one that is not always identified with modernity and that is always seen as situated on the periphery. As part of that other history located in Latin America, I witnessed the emergence of movements such as that of the *margaridas* in the Brazilian state of Paraíba, of landless peasants, and of the homeless. I witnessed the struggle of women who went out on the streets banging their pots and pans to protest hunger and the high cost of living and mothers who went out on the plazas to call out for their missing sons and daughters. Domestic workers, housewives, black, white, brown, *cholas*, indigenous women, mothers, guerrilla fighters, margaridas, Evitas, Beneditas, the history of feminism, in these parts, often runs against the grain of postmodernity, written into the history of painful struggles in which class and race necessarily intersect with gender, each putting its entire set of urgencies on the order of the day even before such elaborations come to figure on the agenda of metropolitan feminisms.

There is, in fact, no way to write the history of feminism through the demand for a specificity that has been constructed outside our own experience. This may be why the most urgent task for a feminist theory constructed from "outside the center" is to reread its history against the grain, establishing a contact zone in which the history of women's movements in Latin America and the theories produced within the academy, translated from their contexts in the major hegemonic centers, are placed in positions of dialogue.

To a large extent, a network of interactions of this type remains to be built in the many fields of our theoretical practice. This would mean to work within the lacuna produced by globalization, toward the building of other noncentralized spaces of knowledge and power.

In such spaces of transnational contact that link experiences horizontally and thus break with simple North–South dichotomies, creating other meanings and other routes for travel between cultures, it has been possible to put different experiences of confronting the violence that emanates more or less directly from colonial experience in touch with one another. Moving away, in historical and political terms, from the utopian project of Salazarist "lusophony," numerous authors writing in the Portuguese language have attempted to resignify the utopia of a transnational and intercultural space of interaction for countries emerging from the Portuguese colonial experience. The space where experiences intersect and memories of violence are shared, in search of current and situated answers for the dramas that are lived within these contexts, continues to be an important step taken by these authors in aesthetic and political fields.

An endeavor of this sort seems to put into practice some of the challenges that Santos (2004) proposes for those who have adopted an emancipatory perspective, intent on building a "counter-hegemonic globalization." According to the author, one of these challenges would specifically be "translating different partial projects for social emancipation" in an attempt to "transform the incommensurable into difference, a difference that enables intelligible reciprocity between different projects for social emancipation without one leading to the subordination or absorption of the other" (Santos 2004a, 35).

In other words, putting different Portuguese-language postcolonial experiences into speech is a project that only makes sense insofar as the latter represents an investment in a project that translates the historical, political, racial, ethnic, and gender meanings of the different modes of living out the consequences of colonial experience. On the other hand, it is also necessary to invest in the idea of situated postcolonialism marked by theoretical and political differences that distinguish it from the postcolonialism of the North, which has disseminated reflections based on its historical experience with much greater ease. The South, as Santos tells us, can be interpreted as a metaphor of human suffering linked to the violence of colonial experience. Learning through the South would thus be one of the major challenges for endeavors to translate postcolonial experiences.

If we return to the narratives analyzed, we can identify in the nation's large cities, considered an icon among the countries situated to the south (Rio de Janeiro in *Ponciá Vicêncio*, São Paulo in *Mulheres de Tijucopapo* and *O Céu de Suely*) the locus where one can trace the geography of poverty and anonymity that are so hurtful to these characters. The muteness that threatens them provides the most visible markings of the violence they suffer. Against it, Rísia imposes her incisive speech. To defend herself from it, Hermila invents Suely and puts her body up for sale. Hermila has inscribed in her own body her answer to the muteness imposed by the city she has had to leave and by the man who has left her. Hermila invents Suely and promises paradise to the men of Iguatu, buys a ticket to Porto Alegre, and once again leaves the little matriarchy that has protected her. She refuses this protection and, although it causes her suffering, prefers to move on, toward someplace she has never been and to which she heads off on her own. Her body put up for sale simultaneously incarnates the whole extension of her misery and her hope, because the body that she sells is at the same time degraded, exposed, an object that awakens the aversion of her grandmother and neighbors, and a gesture of appropriation on Hermila's part of that which is hers, the first site from which identity springs—remembering here Adrienne Rich's classic essay (2002) in which she defends a politics of location that is founded on the body as the first site of experience. If Rísia left São Paulo "to avoid becoming a whore," Hermila prostitutes herself to leave Iguatu and find somewhere else to live.

Women live their exclusion through their bodies. Ponciá takes leave of reality, her lost gaze out the window, the slowness of her gestures, provoking perplexity and, on occasions, a violent reaction from her husband, her inert body no longer responds to her husband's actions nor to her own command. In *As Mulheres de Tijucopapo*, Rísia's body becomes, according to Elódia Xavier, a violent body: "Here, violence becomes the springboard that pushes the character to make revolution, joining up with the warrior women of Tijucopapo. The language itself is impregnated with violent signs, an expression of embittered subjectivity that searches through its struggle to recover its lost dignity" (Xavier 2007, 120).

This body that has responded violently to the aggressions it has suffered, threatening attacks and revolution, as well as Hermila's body put up for sale or Ponciá's inertia—all of these bodies reveal different forms of the body-battlefield that Barbeitos (1997) has spoken of, not unlike the colonized body discussed by authors such as Gloria Anzaldúa (2005) and Chandra Talpade Mohanty (1991b). Yet this body is also a form of speech, a discourse. As Haraway (1994, 253) has pointed out, "we are painfully conscious of what it means to have a historically constructed body." In dealing with the struggle over the power to signify, in dealing with attributing meaning to the world and to themselves, there doesn't seem to be any other way less "warlike" to conceive of social relations. Haraway asserts that "contests for the meanings of writing are a major form of contemporary political struggle. Releasing the play of writing is deadly serious" (Haraway 1991, 175).

The characters in the narratives I consider here want to speak of their experience. They want to enter the arena of struggle around meaning, through self-representation. This is what propels their movement, why they take to the road, why they refuse to remain in one place but move on, return, continue to search. The question of identity that is at stake in this search is of vital importance for each one of them. Rísia, Ponciá, and Hermila build and remake themselves in this search for somewhere else, and their identity is built out of this movement. Their condition as transitory, as passersby, the incessant searching that sends them off to another place, is perhaps not unlike the condition of exile. Here is where I locate the characters in this narrative within a particularly meaningful field, identifying their experience with what I consider one of the most representative contemporary experiences: the loss of fixed points of reference, of a sense of origin, the imperative of change and movement as a constant that destabilizes and cuts across the vectors of identity.

In speaking of exile as a marker of the contemporary and postcolonial condition, we need to understand this lack of belonging, this inability to adapt or feeling of being "away from home" in a less metaphorical sense and one that is painfully impregnated with historicity. In speaking of exile as a marker of postcolonial experience, I refer to Edward Said, who viewed the condition of the exiled as a sort of counterpoint (2003, 46–60). The exiled, according to him, experience the pain of their condition but also reap its learnings; to live in exile means to live in counterpoint, to live two simultaneous experiences: suffering and wisdom, being here and there at the same time. Within postcolonial experience, there is also a two-sided inscription, that of the past lived in a subaltern condition and of the present. Following Mikhail Bakhtin (1988) we can speak of the chronotope of exile: time insinuated through space, turning the condition of exile into an experience in which translocations occur not only within geographic space but also within the distinct temporalities evoked by this experience.

For each of the characters analyzed here, leaving home represents the search for what they desire. The city, however frustrating, aggressive, or brutal, holds up the promise of the freedom of incessant searching and is but the beginning of the act of moving on. Each of them—Rísia, Ponciá, and Hermila—tries to find her own way home, whether this is the mythical maternal home represented by Tijucopapo or the hometown of Iguatu, in the devastated and hopeless sertão that Hermila comes from, or the home of her childhood to which Ponciá nurtures desperate and frustrated dreams of returning. Perhaps we should think of coming home as impossible, because home no longer exists. The road leaving home is one of no return. This makes us reflect on the experience of nomadism and territorial dislocation as significant experiences of contemporary existence. Exile, as Said pointed out, is a place where one experiences paradoxically both the pain of "a fracture that never heals" and the existential freedom of one who "crosses borders, breaking the barriers of thought and experience" (Said 2003, 58). This experience of freedom may be interpreted as the object of desire that moves characters from the beginning to the end of their narratives, turning them into warrior women who go beyond the prescriptions that bound them historically to their mother's home.

In the name of this freedom to cross borders, the characters move on, wander, lose their way, and start over again. Ponciá does so in her attempt to return to her village in search of her family; Rísia goes out to join the warrior women of Tijucopapo and begin the battle; Hermila, to move on, further, and ahead. These are particularly feminist ways of reading and interpreting the world and producing discourses that intervene in their particular contexts, initiating—through war or without it—a form of contemporary political struggle in which places of power are subverted, dislocated, or translocated.

One way or another, the characters' displacement reminds us that for all those who experience subalternity, territorial dislocation can be seen as a negative experience, as a desire to have a place, find one's roots, have a home to return to. This home is, for sure, a zone of security, in opposition to a "contact zone" (Pratt 1999, 7–30), where one encounters risk, freedom, and the minefield represented by others, always there to challenge the subject who is on the move. The desire that everything "end well" is the leitmotif for the characters' agency, who, as we have seen, perform their journeys and resignifications of their subaltern bodies at three different times and directions: in Ponciá's passive yet subaltern resistance; in Rísia's insurgency that only finds fulfillment in utopia; and in the case of Hermila in the assumed reinvention of existence, the result of negotiation and transgression of places and roles. Although these are three different narrative instances concerning the affirmation of these women's subjectivity, they undoubtedly indicate a process, begun a few decades ago, of transforming the meanings of race and gender in this enormous "discursive fortress" that is the "Brazilian national imaginary."

CHAPTER FOUR/*EL INCANSABLE JUEGO*/THE UNTIRING GAME/ DOMINICAN WOMEN WRITING AND TRANSLATING OURSELVES

ISABEL ESPINAL

The Untiring Game is my translation into English of Yrene Santos's book El incans-able juego (2002), a collection of poetry written in Spanish in the United States but published in the Dominican Republic. The context of the book's production and the factors surrounding its translation, and the reception of both, point to the tenuous position of Dominican women in a transnational and transcultural literary marketplace. The difference between how El incansable juego stands up in English versus the popularity of other translated poetry is a differential, to use Chela Sandoval's term, embedded in literary Latina political struggle, even as Santos's poetry generally eschews political themes per se. Sandoval defines and describes differential consciousness as operating "like the clutch of an automobile: the mechanism that permits the driver to select, engage, and disengage gears in a system for the transmission of power. Differential consciousness represents the variant, emerging out of correlations, intensities, junctures, crises. What is differential functions through hierarchy, location, and value—enacting the recovery, revenge, or reparation; its processes pro-duce justice" (Sandoval 1991, 14). Thus translation as a tactic can be differen-tially employed—at times highly engaged, at times not engaged at all, when the ultimate goal is social justice for Latina/os.

Following Sandoval's Third World feminist theory (1991, 2000b), we can say that Santos and I work from a "differential consciousness" and that writing and translating for us are a matter of politics and an act of faith. Just as San-doval finds European postmodern theories lacking for an understanding of

Latina women's lives, so are the Euro-centric translation theories (Bandia 1995; Gentzler 2001) insufficient to understand the position of a Dominican York woman translating the Spanish-language poems of another Dominican York woman.[1] A Latina translation "theory" can be created from the intersection of translation theory and Latina studies, à la recent calls for interdisciplinary approaches to translation (Gentzler 2003). In that vein, my analysis follows scholars of Latina/o literature who have specifically addressed translation theory vis-à-vis Latina/o literature and life (Alarcón 1989; Flores 1993; Foster 1994).

To fully critically assess El incansable juego and its translation, it is imperative to look at the production context of the original text and the translation, to address the motivation for translation, the social position of the translator, as well as questions of audience: to whom does the translator translate? Who does Santos reach by having her poems translated? Does she address different audiences, and if so, what are the differences? Who are her readers — supposed, imagined, and otherwise — and how does that figure into her work? In addition, how do changes in the lived experience affect her writing, including style, genre, and themes? Does Latina/o identity and Dominican identity as such figure into Santos's writing and its context? What are the social, political, and economic conditions of cultural production for the Spanish versus the English version of her work? It is illuminating to see how Santos is presented and/ or marketed. In this chapter, I begin to address some of these questions and join recent studies of literary translation that look at the social and economic context of translation (such as Venuti 1998; Apter 2001a, 2001b; Larkosh 2002).

My analysis uses elements of ethnography and autoethnography, as employed by scholars such as Bryant Keith Alexander (1999), because I am implicated in the questions as the translator of the work. Just as Alexander researches issues of African American male teachers in the college classroom and brings elements of his autobiography into the analysis, I will bring elements of autobiography into this analysis of translation. Autoethnography has been described as "the defining of one's subjective ethnicity as mediated through language, history and ethnographical analysis; in short . . . a kind of 'figural anthropology of the self'" (Lionnet, cited in Alexander 1999, 309). It has also been described as part autobiography and part cultural ethnography (Goodall, cited in Alexander 1999, 309). As in the work of anthropologist Ruth Behar (1993), I weave into my writing third person, first-person singular, and first-person plural. My analysis may seem rustic and raw at times, like the Cibao countryside where Yrene comes from and where a good part of my own personal culture comes from. It may also seem boldly tough, crude, and overconfident in an urban kind of way, reflecting another source of my cultural influence: Brooklyn, New York. It may at times seem self-indulgent, just like much of lyrical poetry can seem. I apologize for the rough edges here and I hope you, the reader, can indulge me and that you will be rewarded with some new knowledge, insight, or pleasure in this essay. I come from a culture of hospitality, brought over from Dominican campos[2] and transported and translated into working-class apartments in New York City. In these different places, when someone visits us, we tend to give our best offerings, knowing that they may seem unrefined to more sophisticated visitors. (Or to visitors who don't have the demands on their time that we do and who have many more material resources to draw on than we do.)

Yrene Santos is a Dominican poet who has made the United States her home since 1992.[3] She began publishing in the Dominican Republic and has continued to write and publish since residing in the United States. Thus, she joins a tradition of Dominican writers living in the United States who have been overlooked in literary histories and commentaries (Molina 1998; Torres-Saillant 1998).[4] She also has performed her poetry in a multitude of venues throughout the Northeast; her training as an actor, combined with her distinctly Cibaeña lyrical intonations, have given her oral readings an added dimension that cannot be transmitted on the written page. Santos has been a member of various writers' circles, including the Tertulia de Escritoras Dominicanas en Estados Unidos, and the prestigious Taller Literario César Vallejo in the Dominican Republic. Her first book of poetry, *Desnudez del silencio*, was written and published to critical acclaim in the Dominican Republic in 1988. In 1998, she published an unbound small collection of poems inserted into an envelope, *Reencuentro*, under the innovative Candelaria series edited by Puerto Rican writer Lourdes Vázquez out of New York. Santos's second bound book, *El incansable juego*, was written in the United States, but published in the Dominican Republic in 2002, also to critical acclaim. For example, the national magazine *Ahora* listed the book in the number one spot in its literary list of "Los más leídos" for November 4, 2002,[5] and featured her book as only one of two recommended reads for that issue, stating that "En *El incansable juego*, poemas de gran virtuosismo, Yrene Santos explora con gran lirismo el mundo interior y complejo de la mujer contemporánea. Poesía trabajada con desenfado y aires de absoluta libertad" (In *El incansable juego*, poems of great virtuosity, Yrene Santos explores, with much lyricism, the interior and complex world of the contemporary woman. Poetry crafted with self-assurance and an air of absolute freedom) ("Los más leídos" 2002).

One way to explore Santos in the context of audience is by looking at the language used in describing not just her texts but also the public performances and workshops in which she is involved. In the Dominican Republic and other Latin American settings, she is often identified as a "woman writer" even as her writing deals with "universal" themes (see Cepeda 1987; Taveras Hernández 1987; Rosario Candelier 1988; Martínez-Márquez n.d.; Aguasaco 2004; Comunicación e Información de la Mujer 2001; and "Los más leídos" 2002). In the foregoing quote, her poetry is said to explore the "mundo interior y complejo de la mujer" not the mundo del ser humano, which might give her a broader audience of identification. A Dominican critic wrote of her first book; "Como se siente mujer y sabe poeta, doble condición que se conjugan armoniosamente en Yrene Santos, en: 'Créenme' anhela 'un poema comulgando en nuestra cama'" (As she feels herself a woman and knows herself a poet, a double condition that comes together harmoniously in Yrene Santos, in: "Believe me" she longs for "a poem taking communion in our bed") (Rosario Candelier 1988, 5). This particular example, however, does not contain anything exclusively female, since the idea of a poem taking communion in bed can apply to a male voice as well as a female one. Thus, this critic presented the sexuality and eroticism of Santos's poetry as a reflection of her womanhood rather than a reflection of her humanity. This phenomenon does not limit itself to the Dominican critics. In a seemingly very favorable review, a New York–based Latino critic also frames Santos almost exclusively as a woman poet (and the reader as a male) when he writes: "Si usted se pregunta: Que siente el alma femenina después de hacer el amor? El Incansable Juego le dará una respuesta" (If you are asking yourself: What does the female soul feel after making love? The Untiring Game will give you an answer) (Aguasaco 2004). A woman-centered identification is not one that Santos totally rejects; on the contrary, she is aware and enters into a literary political battleground even as politics is not worked out extensively as a theme in her poetry; the politics comes from the context. The dedication to her 1988 book frames this political vision: "A la mujer: porque ella también puede y debe manifestar sus deseos, sus pasiones, su ternura; sin esperar, ni dejar que siempre sea el hombre quien se exprese verbal y emocionalmente" (To women: because they also can and should manifest their desires, their passions, their tenderness; without always waiting, nor allowing men to be the ones to express themselves verbally and emotionally) (Santos 1988, 4). However, neither of her books is limited to a female vision or aesthetics.

Santos is part of a tradition of women writers in the Dominican Republic who have fought sexism in poetry and through poetry. As documented by scholar Daisy Cocco de Filippis, the literary environment has been hostile to Dominican women in various aspects, including sexism, racism, and Eurocentrism (Cocco De Filippis 1988). In a personal conversation in 1994 with another Dominican poet, Marianela Medrano, I learned that Santos, along with Medrano, Aurora Arias, and other women of their generation, found the need to organize with others as women poets in the 1980s in Santo Domingo because there were few spaces where women writers were openly welcomed. In the literary spaces of Dominican writers writing in Spanish in the New York area in the early 1990s, Santos also encountered rampant sexism, which prompted her to join the Tertulia de Escritoras Dominicanas founded by Medrano, Cocco de Filippis, and others.

In recent years Santos has participated in the Writer's Workshop Series of the William Joiner Center for the Study of War and Social Consciousness at the University of Massachusetts, Boston, putting her in the company of such writers as Marjorie Agosín, Daisy Zamora, Rosario Ferré, Claribel Alegria, Martín Espada, Naomi Ayala, Tino Villanueva, Jack Agüeros, Leroy Quintana, and Raoul Ybarra. In this context, Santos represents a Dominican writer within the identity of "Latino" or "Hispanic," but also within a global identity of "oppressed" people:

> One primary goal of the workshops is to encourage Latino students to become comfortable and equally fluent in both languages, English and Spanish. Most writers who lead workshops come from places torn by war, conflict, and violence. . . . These are writers who have confronted experiences of war, terror or violence, and, in the classroom, work well with inner city students who have all too often been witnesses to or victims of violence. They are writers who offer students alternative and fresh ways of understanding and reacting to their experiences and can speak convincingly of the importance of language in expressing feelings and emotions and the power of the written word to communicate to others the important issues facing individuals and entire communities. Writers often come to serve as role models, committed individuals dedicated to the discipline that writing requires, writers who have learned the value of finding one's own voice and describing one's own history as a way of defusing and resolving conflicts, both internal and external. (Writers Workshop Model 2005)

Thus, by moving to the United States, Santos somehow ceases to be merely a woman poet and takes on some dimension of universality but still within new boxed categories: that of Latina and of coming "from places torn by war, conflict, and violence" (see also Suárez-Boulangger 1998). She comes to be paradoxically a universal Latina/o, a universal "other" for a North American white audience. Thus, in these other contexts, the identity of Santos and her supposed readers is presented differently, shifting with her migration. Yet there has been no place, neither the Dominican Republic nor Latin America more broadly nor the United States, where the range of the view of her writing and her readership has not somehow been curtailed by the narrowness of the categories into which she has been inserted.

Translation in Latina/o Literature and Lives

Translation itself is a theme used for the understanding of both Latina/o literature and Latina/o lives. Juliana de Zavalia asserts that for Latina/os, "translation is a way of life, a strategy for survival in the north" (Zavalia 2000, 199). For Latina/os living in the United States, translation itself is an untiring game, which comes to define our lives as Latina/os. As new waves of Latina/os follow us, the longer we are in the United States, we take on the role of cultural brokers for the incoming groups.

Additionally, for many Latina/os such as myself, born in the United States or immigrating as children with parents who do not speak English, translation starts practically in infancy. More and more attention is being placed in the political arena to the burden on Latina/o children who must literally as well as figuratively work as interpreters and brokers between the world of their Spanish-speaking parents and the English-speaking world of teachers and school administrators, the welfare bureaucracy, the medical system, utility companies, and so on. In particular, the use of child interpreters in medical settings has garnered enough attention to promote legislation in places such as California that would bar the use of child interpreters and force medical practitioners to hire professional interpreters. Many dramatic and traumatic situations are occurring, where Latina/o children get caught in the middle, as in New York, where it was recently reported that a Latina immigrant's rights advocate "overheard doctors at St. Vincent's telling a construction worker, through his 7-year-old cousin, that the worker needed an amputation. 'The child said, "I'm not sure if they said foot or said toe,"' Ms. Archila recalled. 'This worker, he was about to cry'" (Bernstein 2005, B1).

The Latina/o child translator appears with frequency in Latina/o literature as well, as in the case of Esmeralda Santiago of *When I Was Puerto Rican*. Santiago serves as her family's interpreter in New York. At times this is liberating, as when she is able to negotiate herself back up to eighth grade after the school principal had decided she would be sent to seventh. At other times, being a child interpreter is a scary burden, as in the following passages. "When Mami was laid off, we had to go on welfare. She took me with her because she needed someone to translate. . . . I was always afraid that if I said something wrong . . . the social workers would say no, and we might be evicted from our apartment" (Santiago 1994, 249). "Often I would be asked to translate for other women at the welfare office, since Mami told everyone I spoke good English" (250). "I didn't know what to do. To tell the interviewer that I knew the woman was lying seemed worse than translating what the woman said as accurately as I could and letting the interviewer figure it out" (250). "I never knew if my translations helped, but once an old jíbara took my hands and kissed them, which made me feel like the best person in the world" (251). Like Santiago, I came into translation under very similar circumstances, as a "natural" part of growing up in a city whose institutions did not speak the language of my parents and extended family. Likewise, my experience as translator was and is both scary and very rewarding. Like Santiago, and the many Latina/o children who are translating sensitive as well as mundane topics every day across the United States, I did not receive any formal training in the matter.

Although it often defines the Latina/o experience in the United States, translation is of course not unique to Latina/os. Translation constitutes a cultural practice that crosses linguistic/cultural borders. As Nigel Hall points out, worldwide, the "vast majority of translation and interpreting events . . . are mediated by non-professionals as part of their everyday family and community experience. By and large, it is the volunteers, friends, relatives and children who simply get on with the task of interpreting for those who need it" (Hall 2004, 286). Yet Hall also states that translation theory and research has neglected the role of these "natural" translators, particularly the children. No doubt many a professional or academic translator started out as a child interpreter or translator, but this coming into translation through childhood has not been explored or theorized adequately within translation studies, although it has made its way into the social sciences, the field of education, and the popular press.[6] Studies such as Hall's, which explored Pakistani children translating for adults in England, point to the international aspect of this phenomenon. Many of these studies focus on the issue of power—the enormous power that is placed in the hands (or mouths) of many Latina/o and other bilingual children in the United States, especially vis-à-vis their parents, teachers, and other adults in authority positions. Yet there is also a powerlessness in how children are put in this vulnerable position—at times coerced into translation by the sociopolitical context.

Translation is an intimate part of my own identity. I realized this when I found myself writing poetry about translation.

Translator-diplomat
Catching the words
As they
J
u
m
p
e
d
Out of her mouth
Saving them from crashing
On the hard surfaces
Of their faces
Saving their faces
From the hard surfaces
Of her words
Saving the words
For later. (1994)

Don't translate this!
Don't say these words in English
Teach them
Whisper them
Shout them
Learn them
Breath them in
Put your lips on his and blow them into his mind
Catch them back on your tongue
As they bubble out of his mouth (2002)

The second poem underscores the extent to which even as we have learned to "live in translation," as Latina/os we often refuse to translate and prefer to let the English and Spanish come out of our mouths or sit on the same page without translation. It can simply become tedious, and we become hartos of this role. The translation refusal may even come out of a deep-seated resentment that we've been thrust into the role prematurely and without our full consent, that as translators we've been repeatedly exploited and perhaps robbed of part of our childhood. Or we may refuse on other political grounds. Dominican American writer Junot Díaz once said that he intentionally does not take on the role of a "native informant" who explains Dominican cultural experience to white audiences (Céspedes and Torres-Saillant 2000, 900). Specifically, with regard to the appearance of Spanish in his texts, he, like other Latina/o writers, consciously does not set off the Spanish in italics, nor does he provide translations for the Spanish phrases. This line of thinking and writing has a rich tradition within Latina/o literature, as epitomized and theorized in Gloria Anzaldúa's foundational *Borderlands/La Frontera*[7] (1987) and in books such as *Yo-Yo Boing!* by Giannini Braschi (which has been called the first novel written entirely in Spanglish). I owe to Anzaldúa even the gumption it takes to include these poems in a scholarly essay. Presenting poetry in theory and theory in poetry, as Sandoval pointed out, was a differential move by U.S. Third World feminists, a move whose theoretical implications were repressed by hegemonic academic communities, both North American and European, male and female (Sandoval 1991, 5). Additionally, as Norma Alarcón points out, there is a history for Chicanos specifically, and I would argue for Latina/os in the United States more generally, to see the translator as also a possible betrayer of or traitor to the community to the extent that translation is used by dominant groups as a method to control the subordinate and subaltern linguistic "others." Like the young Esmeralda Santiago, when translating, we often ask ourselves, should we or shouldn't we translate, who benefits from our translation? We are also aware that an "honest" translation may not always be ethical in the final analysis. We are very aware of how our translations are received and of the power dynamics within and between our intended audiences. For this reason, we translate differentially.

In "The Task of the Translator," Walter Benjamin asserts that it is not fruitful to consider the receiver of a work of art because "no poem is intended for the reader" (1969, 69). This was published many years before the heyday of reader response criticism and of reading ethnographies such as those of Janice Radway (1984, 1997) and Jacqueline Bobo (1995) that specifically concerned themselves with the receivers of literature to better understand the phenomenon of literature. Benjamin goes on to say that "if the original does not exist for the reader's sake, how could the translation be understood on the basis of this premise?" (Benjamin 1969, 70).

As a translator, writer, and critic, I'm very interested in audience; I want to see readers taking an interest in Santos's work via my translations. I want to hear that someone, who did not know Spanish to read it in the original, has found Santos's poetry moving and beautiful via translation. I also want to hear from bilingual readers, as I have at a few public readings, that my translations are good. Even without any of this, I am still drawn to translate; ultimately the task of translation is something I do for myself, because there is no guarantee of any connection with any reader. So, yes, in this sense, Benjamin is correct—when it comes to translating literature, even the translation does not need to be overly preoccupied with the reader, because "the reader" always has an element of the unknown. Translation is also something I do for the writer, *for Yrene Santos* and *for her text*, my homage to her as a reader of her poetry, an act of appreciation and thanksgiving. It is a risky act and a risky relationship that requires trust on her part—the trust that I will do right by her work. I am fully aware of the risk of losing Yrene Santos altogether, as Maryse Condé states about translations that have been made of her writing: "In translation, the play of languages is destroyed. Of course, I recognize that my works have to be translated, but they are really not me. Only the original really counts for me. Some people say that translation adds to the original. For me, it is another work, perhaps an interesting one, but very distant from the original" (quoted in Apter 2001a, 92). Part of my work as a translator is also to become an advocate for Santos, an advocate for her as a writer but also an advocate for my reading of her and my judgment of her. With translation comes the need to justify—why translate *this*? Why translate *her*?

My immediate response to these questions is that I translated because Santos asked me to translate her book. But that response begs the question of how she came to know that she could ask me and how I came to translate literature. I first began to translate Dominican women's poetry after I had written some poetry myself, inspired by a community of Latina/o writers that was meeting in New Haven, Connecticut, at the time (early 1990s). That one of the "leaders" of this group was a Dominican woman writer made an enormous impact on me. I was encouraged by her example to seriously think of myself as a writer and get my work read and heard by others. After some initial small successes—winning first prize in a city poetry contest and getting some poems published in various venues—I had the confidence to take on someone else's writings in Spanish and convert them into English. Without my own small accomplishments and recognitions, I may not have felt I could trust myself to do well by them, just as Esmeralda Santiago may not have had the gumption to translate had she also not had some success negotiating with and negotiating in English (getting herself back up to eighth grade). Had I not had the example of Latina/o writers and theorists who are comfortable in Latina/o English, I might not have felt that my version of English, that my final translation product was okay. Indeed, I have learned to be comfortable with an English that may somehow still sound like the Spanish it is not supposed to be. At the same time, keeping in mind the realities of Latina/os and translation, I know that the stakes will not be as high as, for example, the seven-year-old who was not sure if it was a foot or a toe that the doctor wanted to amputate.

For the most part, Santos's poetry was not difficult for me to translate. Reading her poetry, I couldn't help but translate it. She plays with images, concepts, and psychology in ways that seem timeless and compelling. I feel I am saying something as I translate and make the translations as public as I can. Santos's words translate effortlessly and beautifully. For example, "los espejos ya no cuentan / . . . / se romperán para dejarme sin forma / sin ojos repetidos / sin sombra a que atenerme" (2002, 17), which I translated as "the mirrors no longer count / . . . / they'll break to leave me without form / without repeated eyes / without a shadow to hang onto." I found I had to do very little as a translator. Sure, I could have used "don't count anymore" instead of "no longer count," but either way would have been fine. Occasionally, there are wordplays in El incansable juego that are impossible to translate fully, as in the phrase "le dolía el dolor" (2002, 18) which can be translated as either "pain pained her" or "pain hurt her." Although "pain pained her" uses a similar word play as in the original, it is not as colloquial a phrase in English because the verb to pain is not as common as the verb to hurt. I chose the more colloquial construction so as to not create a distance by using elitist language, feeling that this was truer to the original poetry in Spanish. Another similar example is a short poem that uses a lot of l's and ll's: "Llanto en el llano de la luna llena / llega / llora / . . . / lluvia / llueve" (Santos 2002, 54). There was no way to translate the wordplay and the meaning intact. This is one I would have loved, as Latina/os often do, to have simply refused to translate! But as Latina/os also often do, I went ahead with what I knew was not a perfect translation, but that had at least a little word-playfulness to it: "A weeping in the full moon's plain / arrives / cries / . . . / rain / rains."

Benjamin's quote of Rudolf Pannwitz's ideas about translation is very close to what Latina/os in the United States do every day to the English and Spanish languages as we translate from one to the other. "Our translations, even the best ones, proceed from a wrong premise. They want to turn Hindi, Greek, English into German instead of turning German into Hindi, Greek, English. . . . The basic error of the translator is that he preserves the state in which his own language happens to be instead of allowing his language to be powerfully affected by the foreign tongue" (Pannwitz, quoted in Benjamin 1969, 80–81). However, for many Latina/os such as myself, it is not always just one side that is "our own" language. For many of us, neither language is really foreign, yet Pannwitz's precept still applies. Because Latina/os most definitely allow each of these languages to be affected by the other, ours is not a translation of preservation but, as Juan Flores (1993) points out with the use of the term trans-creation, ours is a translation of constant re-creation.

Notes

1. According to the *Urban Dictionary* (http://www.urbandictionary.com/define.php?term =dominicanpercent2oyork, accessed May 2012), *Dominican York* is a Dominican slang term defined as "1) A Dominican immigrant living and working in New York City. 2) An American-born person of Dominican descent who was raised in NYC." It is akin to the term *nuyorican*.

2. Throughout this essay I may use some Spanish words that I do not italicize or translate.

3. For more information about Santos and her poetic work, see Cepeda (1987); Fuertes (1987); Taveras Hernández (1987); Rosario Candelier (1988); Sosa (1988); Pla Benito (1990); González-Gimbernart (1996); Ruiz (1997); Cocco De Filippis (2000); Cocco De Filippis and Rivera Valdés (2000); Community Reading Series (2002); *Los más leídos* (2002); Circulará Nuevo Libro de Yrene Santos (2003); Pondrán a circular (2003); Aguasaco (2004); and Martínez-Márquez (n.d).

4. These writers include the poet Julio Alvarado, the fiction writer and poet Juan Rivero, the poet Héctor Rivera, the poet Alexis Gómez Rosa, the fiction writer Viriato Sención, the poet Marianela Medrano, and the fiction writer José Carvajal.

5. The label "Ficción" was used even though the book is poetry. There were only two categories, fiction and nonfiction, with no separate category for poetry.

6. As evidenced in articles such as Budge (1998); "Children Valuable as Cultural Interpreters" (2004); Cohen, Moran-Ellis, and Smaje (1999); Sanders (2003); Orellana, Dorner, and Pulido (2003); Pabst (2004); and Bernstein (2005).

7. The "white" reader (as a socioliterary category, not a biological reality) has caught on to this Latina/o refusal and subversion, as in Doris Sommer's (1999) warning to her fellow (would-be) hegemonic readers in *Proceed with Caution, When Engaged by Minority Writing in the Americas*.

CHAPTER FIVE/PEDAGOGICAL STRATEGIES FOR A TRANSNATIONAL
READING OF BORDER WRITERS/PAIRING A TRIANGLE

MARISA BELAUSTEGUIGOITIA RIUS

El Delito
se encontraba
doblado entre la tortilla
La Prieta
—"Lost and Found"

Claudia de Lima Costa, in the second introduction to this volume, opens with strategic questions: how can translation produce continuity across heterogeneous dimensions of signification? How can we think through the gap of translation and account for the multiple forces that overdetermine translation practices along with its strategies of containment? Rather than asking about loss, rupture, and discontinuity, this chapter underscores finding and continuity. I want to focus on what may be found in translation.

Invited to participate in the *Translocalidades* project, I was immediately attracted by the allure created by the possibility of finding what has been lost in varied transits, in an unexpected way, and in an unpredictable place. Translation is the place for "lost and found." Objects and relations immersed in translation may be reshaped inside texts that travel across national, linguistic, symbolic, and cultural borders.

More than "losses" this chapter explores "findings." The possibility of having a special "office," a place where you may find what you have lost ("Lost and Found") is not translatable into Spanish. In Spanish we would say "Office of Lost Objects"; the tension falls on the act of losing, not on the event of finding.

I remember the sense of completeness, of mouth-full sensation, the first time I read "Lost and Found," a place where lost objects could be recovered. I was on vacation with my three nieces, who were running wildly around the avenues of Universal Studios, a spectacle of simulation and memory. My sister-in-law and I made a big fuss of such a place and played with the possibility of finding there what we had lost "somewhere" else (youth, flexibility, love). My seven-year-old niece, Maite, asked: "Can I go and get my yellow sweater?" It was an angora sweater that she lost—in Mexico, of course—and over which she had wept many tears. Maria José followed with, "Please, let's go and get the coin you gave me on my birthday!" My father—their grandfather—used to give them *una moneda de diez pesos antigua*, which he polished until it glittered. I took over that tradition, and my niece took over the tradition of losing them. It had not taken long to remember their dearest losses. We made a long list of things lost: patience, time, wedding rings. Remembering details of the things-persons-affects lost gave way to the excitement of finding "there" what has been lost "somewhere else."

I did not tell them the rules of losing and finding things in such places. I did not tell them that they could never find there things that were lost somewhere else. I stood hypnotized by their excited walk to the "Lost and Found" office, by their animated lists of dear things lost.

This fiction was the best gift I could give them. Those lost objects and affects appeared in our memory and came back. We created a sort of redefinition of the act of losing and placed an accent on the possibility of finding. The art of finding relies specifically on recovering the loss, filling the vacuum with an idea of what was lost, reimagining and bringing it back. When this happens, more than finding, we would face a discovery: the re-covering of things lost. That is what this chapter talks about.

Pedagogical Maneuvers: Reading as Re-covering

This essay points to precise *movidas* (maneuvers) enabled by a pedagogy of reading border texts. What I seek to underscore is the way in which Chicana/o studies knowledge and cultural practices may travel "back" and be appropriated and taught in Mexican classrooms. I am particularly interested in the circulation-translation of Gloria Anzaldúa's work in Mexican graduate classrooms, specifically in the Gender Studies Program at the National Autonomous University of Mexico (UNAM).

I understand movidas in the way Chela Sandoval addressed them in "Love as a Hermeneutics of Social Change, a Decolonizing *Movida*" (Sandoval 2000a, 140), as the operations that situate and legitimate subaltern knowledge and articulate methodologies in the process of building by assembling texts from both sides of the border.

Two important questions emerge. How does this knowledge—produced on the other side of the border—make sense in Mexican pedagogical scenarios? In other words, through which pedagogical maneuvers do these transnational texts get appropriated, understood, translated? What is most interesting for me is to show how in the process of translation of Anzaldúa, a closed classroom may get transformed into an open, transnational one.

I figured out a way—a pedagogy—to read Anzaldúa transnationally. What I propose here is the reading of x through the reading of y. Read Anzaldúa through the writings of Subcomandante Marcos, another border writer, to read Anzaldúa's *Borderlands* (1987) and "La Prieta," through the other border of the Mexican nation, the southern one: to read Chicanas through the rebellious words of the Zapatistas.

The Return: Teaching Chicana Theory in Mexico

When I returned to Mexico City to UNAM after finishing my doctoral studies at the University of California, Berkeley, in 2001, a couple of years before Anzaldúa's death, I was looking forward to working with border thinkers like her, who may imagine the nation as a space caught between complex, dense, and painful borders. I experienced Anzaldúa's death as a loss, but also a challenge. A loss as an artist, intellectual, and writer, and a challenge related to the possibility of translating her work into Mexican academia where, especially in those days, her work and Chicana theory and literature were hardly (if ever) read.

I offered a graduate seminar: "The Indian and the Chicana as Excess of the Nation: Mexico's Southern and Northern Borders," including Anzaldúa's work as well as Subcomandante Marcos's writing as textual limits of the Mexican nation. Both could be considered spokespersons of migrants and Indians, respectively, both border writers, both creating at the limit of the nation's borders and discourse.

The purpose of the seminar was to analyze the tools of translation of this "inadequate" other—the Indian and the migrant—as the nation's excess on both borders. I placed Chicanas and Zapatistas face to face, mask to mask, ink to ink with one another. Indians and migrants are precisely two subjects that the nation refuses to fully integrate; they represent the unstranslatable, due to an excessive difference in color, tongue, and culture.

The reasons I decided to teach this course are diverse. The Zapatista rebellion in 1994 caused great expectations as they addressed the future not only of Indians but of other ex-centric groups and identities, such as migrants, workers, and women. The Indian narrative needed a translator. Subcomandante Marcos — part of the Indian resistance — offered his famous communiqués and more precisely his postscripts as narrations from below. The migrant and Mexican community in the United States also needed a spokesperson; Anzaldúa has translated their pain, their experience, and their memories without being formally assigned as such. Both built bridges and unveiled alliances to connect, understand, and mirror each other's national, international, and local similarities and differences.

Zapatistas and Chicanas form part of the Mexican "debris," outcasts along with other marginal groups — such as poor women, peasants, unemployed youth, workers, unions, and students — all of them addressed by Subcomandante Marcos's famous postscript writings.

Many things happened regarding the seminar I proposed. There were "no" students, there was "no" assigned space. Later I learned that my syllabus did not even reach the evaluation committee that decides which courses are going to be taught. Notwithstanding the importance of the Zapatista movement and the dire issue of migration and the consequences of more than approximately 12 to 14 million Mexicans living in the United States, the seminar was rejected.

Ten years later this academic gate control is beginning to change. Anzaldúa and other Chicanas such as Norma Alarcón, Sandra Cisneros, María Lugones, and Chela Sandoval are being taught mainly inside the gender studies program at UNAM and other sites as meaningful intellectuals.[1]

During my graduate studies and subsequent stages at the University of California, Berkeley, I understood the need to translate the production of cultural and political representations of Chicanas and other women of color. Their work has been of the utmost importance, mainly because of the difficulty in finding in Mexico accessible publications of "women of color," working-class writers, and thinkers.[2]

A significant percentage of my undergraduate and graduate students at UNAM, who travel on average three hours a day to reach the university, belong to working-class families and have at least one member of their family working (mostly illegally) in the United States. They relate strongly to Anzaldúa's work, especially *Borderlands / La Frontera* and also in "La Prieta" to *This Bridge Called My Back*, where this situation can be noticed.

Marcos and Anzaldúa constitute two border thinkers whose work deals with nationalism, citizenship, racism, and sexism, with a design of transnational readings for an intercultural nation. Their powerful textual production made me think of the limits/limitations of translation in a transnational frame and, moreover, about the bridges and networks that may recast those limits.

The circulation of Anzaldúa's work in Mexican academia becomes meaningful, especially today when the borderlands, North and South, are facing the real construction of walls and an insistent racist politics of immigration. Subcomandante Marcos's communiqués had gained popularity; they were read extensively and created a need to know and contact the Indian other in a way never before experienced. It is this passion and this desire to which I want to allude.

The transnational circulation of narratives that politically, historically, and critically unpack hate, disgust, and racism is important to the construction of a pedagogy that understands and resists forces of oppression. What I propose is then the reading of Anzaldúa in Mexico through Subcomandante Marcos's writings. In other words, I propose creating a pedagogy of *reading doubles*, "inadequate" writers, who refuse their originals, and seek new meaning. I propose a reading, as translation, that represents a way to connect northern and southern Mexico and the United States and the Mexican border, Chiapas and Texas, through two writers whose themes are precisely the subjects of Mexican exclusion: Indians and migrants, people of Mexican descent in the United States, and Indigenous subjects.

To consolidate this pairing I recur to a third writer, Rosario Castellanos. I incorporate some accents of *Balún Canán* (1989 [1958]) not only to enhance the reading in pairs but mainly to consolidate the Indian/migrant double reading. I pair Castellanos to facilitate the connection and profoundness of the indigenous imaginary in Anzaldúa's work by referring to another Mexican skillful depicter of Indigenous complex, contradictory, and meaningful life.

Found in Translation: Pedagogy of the Double as Transnational Reading Strategy

The reading of Anzaldúa paired with Subcomandante Marcos, supported by the narrative of Castellanos, functions as a triangle with capabilities of connecting to stories in the *Borderlands* and destabilizing national identities and disciplinary thinking. This triangle and its translation strategies emerge from reading *Borderlands / La Frontera* and "La Prieta" with a selection of communiqués by Subcomandante Marcos[3] and is supported by accents from Castellanos's *Balún Canán*. It departs from the pedagogical potential of the following questions. How may these texts be readable-translatable across borders? What may be the strategies that enhance and expand the reading in Mexican academic circles of a complex and eccentric writer such as Anzaldúa?

This analysis underscores what Mexican national narrative, on the other side of the border, is refusing to see and hear: the differences, the array of forms of discrimination, the possibilities and the abysmal failures in our politics of immigration and citizenship.

This refusal to see and to know the other—on both sides of the border—has been transformed into an absence in the nation's imaginary; this vacuum insists on being addressed. In Ricardo Piglia's words, "No es lo real lo que irrumpe, sino la ausencia, un texto que no se tiene, cuya busca lleva, como en un sueño, al encuentro con la realidad" (It is not what is real, what bursts in, it is the absence of an unavailable text, whose search takes you, like in a dream, towards the encounter with reality) (Piglia 2005, 27). In other words, it is precisely absence that produces the urge to search.

I analyze both border writers as transnational ones who emphasize the importance of translation, transdisciplinary thinking, and transnationality for the construction of intercultural identities, which could enhance knowledge and communication with the ultimate other (the Indian, the Indian woman, the migrant).

The politics of translation I propose constitutes a pedagogical approach I call *pedagogy of the double*, a maneuver that makes visible what is refused due to an excess of difference related to national, gendered, racial, and sexual identities. The central movida of this text is then the pairing of a triangle by the constructions of mirrors, of reading practices that may articulate Chicana-Mexican narratives through displacements of domesticated readings emerging from hegemonic narratives. Pedagogy of the double works on the construction of doubles as textual contiguities, as replicas. The idea is to design a strategy to read the U.S. and Mexican border through writers, women, artists, and critical thinkers who have revisited the notions of exclusion, alterity, and citizenship.

The notion of double is inspired in the fiction of defacement of the "original," as the possibility of resembling (mirroring) one another without being captured or measured as false by the original. Regular doubles, by which I mean replicas, travel within the domain of the original and constitute meaning by an operation of splitting, where the negative part of the equation is transferred to the "other." As Anzaldúa states, "To be close to another Chicana is like looking into the mirror. We are afraid of what we'll see there: Pena. Shame. Low estimation of self. In childhood we are told that our language is wrong. Repeated attacks on our native tongue diminish our sense of self" (Anzaldúa 1987, 58). These writers are critics of hegemonic narratives of nation and identity and center their arguments in the resignification of liminal (border) knowledge recovered through the revision of the Indigenous subject, the Indian women, and the Chicana writer. Our pedagogical approach views these texts mirroring each other to reproduce and augment their tones.

I use the notion of pedagogy as the administration of liminal knowledge, a management of intervals of rupture in the text that may influence practices of reading, which interrupts the seamless mirroring of original/copy, real/

false, north/south binaries. The management of intervals is proposed through a special arrangement of textual contiguity: the parallel reading of a triangle of writers (Anzaldúa, Marcos, and Castellanos). This triangle and its parallels foster not only a rereading of the nation's exclusions but the articulation of interrelated strategies of visibility and citizenship construction for women, Indians, and migrant communities, which may travel across national borders.

My central goal is to encourage a transnational reading of border thinkers through a pedagogical approach, a politics of reading. This maneuver constructs doubles not as negatives or shadows of representation but as correlative points of juncture and affiliation, as a strategy to induce the reading of intellectuals and writers unknown or neglected through more "legitimate" or original ones.

Anzaldúa inserts the category of the double in *Borderlands / La Frontera*. In her last chapter, "La Conciencia de la Mestiza/Towards a New Consciousness," we identify this notion as the administration of inadequacy in the other, to reify and return to the "original" as the measure of adequacy. We read:

> To say you've split yourself from minority groups, that you disown us, that your dual consciousness splits off parts of yourself, transferring the "negative" parts onto us . . . To say that you are afraid of us, that to put distance between us, you wear a mask of contempt. Admit that México is your double that she exists in the shadow of this country that we are irrevocably tied to. Gringo, accept the doppelganger in your psyche. By taking back your collective shadow the intracultural split will heal. And then finally, tell us what you need from us. (Anzaldúa 1987, 86)

The double is the one that exists only by the shadow of the original. What I am trying to convey with such a pedagogy that decomposes the double as passive copy is the possibility of the existence of the double outside the shadow of the original, through the light of another text that may illuminate its dark zones. What I want to convey is the possibility of inducing a split in the function of a "replica"; to call on Anzaldúa to displace the function of the double as the concept that absorbs negative residuals, and to conceive it as a *reply*, a way of "talking back." In other words: to be the faulty replica (copy) and to respond-replay, replicate at the same time.

The main maneuver is to transform the notion of replica as copy into replica as contestation, or "talking back," to master narratives. That means doubles, refusing their originals, talking to each other and talking back: Indians and migrants, Mexicans in the United States, Chicanas and Chicanos refusing essentialist "original" notions of nationality, language, culture, and citizenship and re-creating their experiences and their cultures.

The pedagogy of the double I propose represents the possibility of reading as breaking this process of transfer of the negative veil to the "other" and inducing a two-way circulation of significance: Chicana and Mexican, United States and Mexico, Marcos and Anzaldúa, recasting signification from one to another.

Pedagogical Maneuvers: Reading as Redefinition of Scales and Distances

Regarding the issue of reading as translating, as replica, as a copy with capabilities of independence of the original, Ricardo Piglia states: "Reading is an act of redesigning distances and scales" (Piglia 2005, 12). That means that reading —reproducing the text into one's frame of intelligibility—means imagining reality on another scale, repeating, constructing a simulacrum with other proportions. Reading means replying, replicating, constructing both a parallel world and an answer (a replica, a replay).

Interrupting the master/copy, original/double narrative does not mean ceasing to be a replica, a double, because reading—under this proposal of intervention of master narratives—means *replicating* (reproducing and replying) by altering the relations of representation, it means creating a "replica" with modified relations of representation where the original is unpacked and dismantled, to the point of transforming it from metaphor to metonym, from whole to part.

What I read is then a copy of what the author creates, a modified copy precisely to the measure, proportions, and scales of "my" world. The transit of a metanarrative, or of an author from metaphor to metonym, means an alteration in its function, from representing the whole to constituting a fragment of the whole, an alteration in scales, and a disruption in distances, because the reader may detach or approach herself to sections of the material read.[4]

Reading as translation then is related to an art of reengineering of scales and distances as an act of reappropriation. A transnational reading within this economy of signification means to reproduce, to copy, to create a replica (in both senses as "talking back" and as simulation, which may be perceived as more real than reality itself).

Here we encounter the foundational act of resisting: to replicate (to talk back), to respond, within the contradiction of doing so and being a replica, a copy, a double. To translate, then, would signify to read, to talk back from another perspective, another set of angles, distances, and scales, that constitutes the proper and the appropriated world at the same time.

In *Borderlands | La Frontera* Anzaldúa makes clear how Chicanas as failed doubles of Mexicans, as their faulty copies, are trying to generate a reply, as in talking back, that moves away from previously framed originals. She points particularly to women's practices framed by Mexican culture, as the norm and the original: "I remember one of the sins I'd recite to the priest in the confession box the few times I went to confession: talking back to my mother, *hablarpa'tras, repelar, hocicona, repelona, chismosa,* having a big mouth, questioning, carrying tales are all signs of being *malcriada.* In my culture they are all words that are derogatory if applied to women-I've never heard then applied to men" (Anzaldúa 1987, 54). Reading transnationally means mapping, reproducing, tracing borders between parallel worlds. Reading as replica, as a copy, parallel to reality, allows us to think, as Piglia states, that what we can imagine—what we read—exists always on another scale, in another time, sharp, clear, and far away, similar to being in a dream (Piglia 2005, 17).

Reading means then adding to parallel worlds. What I introduce here is a topography of reading, which means validating the under world, the replica beyond its function as shadow, as a "negative." In such way we may face the reconstruction of reality by simulating, replicating parallel worlds. A different perception of reality may develop from this act of simulation. In Piglia's words:

> La lectura, decía Ezra Pound, es un arte de la réplica. A veces los lectores viven en un mundo paralelo y a veces imaginan que ese mundo entra en la realidad. . . . Esta obra privada y clandestina anula la tensión entre objeto real y objeto imaginario, todo es real, todo está ahí, y uno se mueve entre los parques y las calles, deslumbrado por una presencia siempre distante. (Piglia 2005, 12–13)

> (Reading, according to Ezra Pound, is an art of replicating. Sometimes readers live in a parallel world, and imagine that this world enters reality. . . . This private and clandestine work cancels the tension between real and imaginary objects, everything is real, everything is there, and one moves inside parks and streets, dazzled by an ever distant presence.)

This kind of clandestine reading represents a strategy, an allegation against the political and cultural penetration of hegemonic economies of meaning.

The writings of Subcomandante Marcos and Gloria Anzaldúa, accentuated by Rosario Castellanos, represent this adding to parallel worlds, a reading of borders that does not rely on centers but on limits that mirror borders, in remote and nearby frontiers, that rub each other in a way that extracts new and restoring meaning. An example of the former could be stated by reading a scene, let's say the scene of war in the northern and southern borderlands. This implies redesigning scales and distances to relocate proportions and languages to understand the double effect of war inside our two borderlands. Let us exercise a parallel reading of this one concept, which has been foundational in the writing of both *Borderlands* and the communiqués: war. The situation in both national limits, the so-called low-intensity warfare, to repeat how the military addressed the tensions between Zapatista rebels and the military, and the situation of crossing and living in the borderlands, resembles — copies — real war.

Immersed inside a war zone, Zapatistas and Chicanas claim painful transformations and change based on blood, as an effect of the grating of two worlds. Blood is the common link, the ink of both texts. Subcomandante Marcos represents blood as the sacrifice for the possibility of justice and hope:

> En ese primer golpe a los muros sordos de los que todo tienen la sangre de los nuestros, nuestra sangre corrió generosa para lavar la injusticia que vivíamos. Para vivir morimos. Volvieron nuestros muertos a andar pasos de verdad. Con lodo y sangre se abonó nuestra esperanza. (EZLN 1994, 147)

> (In that first strike against the deaf walls of those who have everything, our people's blood, our blood, was generously spilled to wash away the injustices within our lives. To live, we died. Our dead ones returned to walk the steps of truth. Our hope was nurtured with mud and blood.)

Anzaldúa talks about rubbing and grating through the description of the borderlands as a wound: "The U.S. Mexican border *es una herida abierta* where the Third World grates against the first and bleeds. And before a scab forms it hemorrhages again, the lifeblood of two worlds merging to form a third country—a border culture . . . the prohibited and forbidden are its inhabitants. *Los atravesados* live here: the squint-eyed, the mongrel, the mulattos, the half-breed, the half dead; in short, those who cross over, pass over to go through the confines of the 'normal'" (Anzaldúa 1987, 3).

Sacrifice, blood, and open wounds constitute a narrative that explains life attached to war in the borderlands, at the northern and southern limits of the Mexican nation. The image of the wound constitutes a primordial frame for Anzaldúa, as quoted above. War is also the narrative exposed by Subcomandante Marcos; the war also as wound, an aperture, we read,

> Hoy como en 1993, cuando preparábamos la Guerra, como en 1992 cuando la decidimos, como en el 1984 cuando cumplimos el primer año, como en 1983 cuando se inició el despertar de la esperanza, el

plan zapatista es el mismo: cambiar al mundo, hacerlo mejor, más justo, más libre, más democrático, es decir, más humano. (EZLN 1995, 139)

(Today, the Zapatista project is the same as in 1993—when we were preparing the War, as in 1992—when we decided it, as in 1984—when we celebrated our first anniversary, and as in 1983—when hope was first awakened: we strive to change the world, to make it better, fairer, freer, more democratic, in other words, more humane.)

It is clear for both types of war that their reason is changing the world as we know it. Both border writers fight for the merging of a new world.

This form of contact produces doubles that mirror each other and transfigure the contours of the nation. Borders that separate Indian and others, men and women, migrant and citizen, güeras and prietas,[5] will mirror themselves departing from texts that visualize forms of oppression, particular strategies of representation, and narratives containing the slips and spells of the other, as Anzaldúa shows clearly in Borderlands / La Frontera, when she addresses the slits of her tongue: "'We are going to have to do something about your tongue,' I hear the anger rising in his voice. My tongue keeps pushing out the wads of cotton, pushing back the drills, the long thin needles, he says. And I think, how do you tame a wild tongue, train it to be quiet, how do you bridle and saddle it? How do you make it lie down?" (Anzaldúa 1987, 53).

Anzaldúa and Subcomandante Marcos address the issue of holding war (on words, power relations and a real one against the military's presence on both borders). Anzaldúa points at the border between the United States and Mexico as a war zone, and Subcomandante Marcos—by underlining the war held by women against some Indigenous cultural practices and poverty—points to a war for equity. Both texts give a profound idea of what is being faced when we talk about Chicana and Indian struggles. Let's follow some fragments of both writers on the issues of war, change, and equity.

Barefoot and uneducated, Mexicans with hands like boot soles gather at night by the river where two worlds merge creating what Reagan calls a frontline, a *war zone*. The convergence has created a shock culture, a border culture, a third country, a closed country. (Anzaldúa 1987, 11; emphasis added)

Escuchen a Ramona—que está aquí para recordarnos porque estamos en guerra, escuchen a Ramona decir cosas tan terrible como que las mujeres indígenas quieren vivir, quieren estudiar, quieren escuelas, quieren alimento, quieren respeto, quieren justicia, quieren dignidad. (EZLN 1994, 164)

(Listen to Ramona, who is here to remind us why we are at war. Listen to Ramona saying such terrible things such as Indian women wanting to live, wanting to study, wanting schools, food, respect, justice, dignity.)

Subcomandante Marcos and Anzaldúa enable strong criticism of actions centered on top-down processes. They are experts on the architecture of resistance and writing that allows transit, translation, transdisciplinary, and transnational reading across the borderlands.

Both narratives mirror each other, imagining reality on different scales, repeating and constructing textual simulacra. They intervene in the master/copy narrative by altering the relations of representation, where the "original" is unpacked and dismantled to the point of transforming it from metaphor to metonym, from being whole to being fragment. We read in Subcomandante Marcos's communiqué how he is inspired by the 1960s, '70s, and '80s, decades marked by student strikes, guerrilla movements, feminist growth, and the rise of liberation theology.

No tenemos de que avergonzarnos. Somos producto de la sabiduría y la resistencia indígena con la rebeldía y la valentía de la generación de la dignidad que alumbró con su sangre la oscura noche de las décadas de los sesenta, setenta y ochenta. De este encuentro aprendimos a ser firmes, hemos aprendido a ser mexicanos, a vivir luchando para ser dignos. (EZLN 1995, 434)

(We have nothing to feel ashamed of. We are the offspring of wisdom and Indian resistance, mixed with the rebelliousness and courage of a generation of dignity, a generation that lightened the dark nights of the decades of the sixties, seventies, and eighties with their blood. Since then we have learned to be firm, to be Mexican, to live and fight for our dignity.)

Anzaldúa focuses on the history of women, the Mexican precolonial history, and millenarian female protest: "My Chicana identity is grounded in the Indian women's history of resistance. The Aztec female rites of mourning were rites of defiance protesting the cultural changes which disrupted the equality and balance between female and male, and protesting their demotion to a lesser status, their denigration" (Anzaldúa 1987, 21).

Subcomandante Marcos and Anzaldúa represent two mechanisms of translation and mediation of the excessive other, the Indian, and the migrant. Why read them together, and why read them in academia? In the first instance, we can compare strategies and pedagogies of translation of what is considered other and foreign to the nation and what does belong to its core. Another level of reading may address the millions of Mexicans and those of Mexican descent who live in the United States as a derivation of the narrative of the double, quoted from the Freudian *Unheimlich*: the familiar made strange. In short, Marcos and Anzaldúa may be translated as the nation's foundational exclusions that may talk back, return, replay.

Anzaldúa and Marcos: Reading Doubles and Double Reading as Interruption of Master Narratives

The "master/double," "original/copy," "Western/other" economy is centered on the structure of colonialism. The relation between Europe, the United States, and Latin America is founded on the economy of original and copy, where the copy may be understood as a negative double, as a faulty reproduction of the original, whose culture, language, and existence is never quite right. This rendering of the colonized as inaccurate facilitates domination, as demonstrated by Mary Louise Pratt in *Imperial Eyes* (1992). Through the example of Guaman Poma's letters, Pratt elaborates a discussion around the tension between the hegemonic act of reading and the possibility of being readable, without being able to respond. The "imperial meaning-making" economy she defines as "contact zones" is interesting for developing the signification of the double in our proposal of translation as reading and reading as creating parallel worlds.

What we seek to interrupt is the idea of the double as the one that is not allowed to reply/translate back and is instructed mainly to reproduce the original signification. Pratt complicates the possibilities of reading, replying, as talking back, through the conceptualization of contact zones. She defined these zones as "social spaces where disparate cultures meet, clash and grapple with each other, often in highly asymmetrical relations of domination and subordination — like colonialism, slavery, or their aftermaths as they are lived out across the globe today" (Pratt 1992, 4). Pratt fosters a critique of ideology sustained by a foundational question: how has travel and exploration writing produced "the rest of the world" for European readerships at particular points in Europe's expansionist trajectory? A "contact" perspective in Pratt's words: "emphasizes how subjects are constituted in and by their relations to each other. It treats the relations among colonizers and colonized, or travelers and 'travelees,' not in terms of separateness or apartheid, but in terms of co-presence, interaction, interlocking understanding and practices, often within radically asymmetrical relations of power" (Pratt 1992, 7).

The issue of contiguity and contact in asymmetrical relations is very important for the kind of reading we are enabling, because reading is generated precisely in the midst of these cartographies of power. Our triangle of authors (Anzaldúa, Marcos, Castellanos) is an effect of the battle to make sense from below inside the borderlands or contact zones, subsumed in radically asymmetrical spaces of power. The only difference is that replicas—doubles immersed in triangles even inside contact zones—under our pedagogy may reply, talk back, and . . . speak.

The colonial double pattern alters the subaltern to the point of resembling the original at any cost. The pedagogy of the double is based on the possibility of pairing texts, making doubles visible, but replicating (with different distances and scales) and replying to "the" original. The model will be reached in the interchange of texts, concepts, voices, demands, histories, and historical accounts, from border to border, in a recasting of perspectives: setting scales and distances through the appropriation of the master's (colonizer's) discourse, of the master's own terms.

To make more comprehensible the pedagogy of the double I introduce as a reading strategy, let's briefly examine an intervention, a detachment, of the original by following the way Anzaldúa escapes Octavio Paz by talking back to his idea around the *Pachuco*, the *Pocho*, as a subject lost for the nation. According to Paz:

> El Pachuco ha perdido toda su herencia: lengua, religión, costumbres, creencias. Sólo le queda un cuerpo y un alma a la intemperie, inerme ante todas las miradas. Su disfraz lo protege y, al mismo tiempo, lo destaca y aísla: lo oculta y lo exhibe. (Paz 1994 [1983], 17)

> (The Pachuco has lost his whole heritage: language, religion, customs, beliefs. The only thing he is left with is a body and a soul in the open, defenseless on the eyes of everyone. His disguise is his protection, but it also makes him stand out and isolates him: it does both hide him and point him out.) (translation extracted from Paz 1985, 15)

Norma Alarcón states that Chicana writers are women who are not in search of an author, of "originals," but who are trying to get rid of the many authors that silence them (Alarcón 1990, 213). Anzaldúa quotes Alarcón and "talks back" to Paz; she writes about her tongue, about the *rebeldía* of her broken language. El Pachuco (pocho) represents for Paz somebody who has lost his tongue, his language, his identity. Anzaldúa demonstrates poignantly that instead of loss, there is a gain, something gained in this transition from losing a language to talking back in another language created in the borderlands.

She states: "*Pocho*, cultural traitor, you're speaking the oppressor's language by speaking English, you are ruining the Spanish language. But Chicano Spanish is a border tongue which developed naturally. *Change, evolución, enriquecimiento de palabras nuevas por invención o adopción* have created variants of Chicano Spanish, *un nuevo lenguaje. Un lenguaje que corresponde a un modo de vivir.* Chicano Spanish is not incorrect, it is a living language" (Anzaldúa 1987, 55).

In his famous postscripts, Subcomandante Marcos represents life at the borderlands and the multiple ways in which Indians talk back to a nation that undermines their languages. He writes to show the nation what is gained through Indian culture. His communiqués convey the many meanings, the uncountable voices and languages created by the indigenous cultures. In *México entre el dolor y la esperanza*, a communiqué delivered on September 22, 1994 (EZLN 1995, 77), Subcomandante Marcos translates—in a postcript—a portion of a story narrated by El Viejo Antonio, an Indian friend, a wise old man, that represents the language, culture, knowledge of Indian peoples not as copy, not as shadow of the West, but as a culture of its own:

> El Viejo Antonio separa con sus manos un tizón de la hoguera. Lo deja en el suelo. "Mira," me dice. Del rojo, el tizón sigue el camino inverso que el señor negro del cuento: naranja, amarillo, blanco, gris, negro. Aún caliente las manos callosas del viejo Antonio lo toman y me lo da. Yo trato de fingir que no me quema, pero lo suelto casi inmediatamente. El viejo Antonio sonríe y tose, lo vuelve a tomar del suelo y lo remoja en un charquito de agua de lluvia, de agua-noche. Ya frío me lo vuelve a dar. "Toma . . . recuerda que el rostro cubierto de negro esconde la luz y el calor que le harán falta a este mundo"; me dice y se me queda viendo. (EZLN 1995, 77)

> (El Viejo Antonio takes out a brand from the fire with his hands. He puts it on the floor and tells me, "Look." From red, the brand goes the opposite way than the black man in the story: orange, yellow, white, gray, black. The calloused hands of El Viejo Antonio pick up the brand, still hot, and hand it to me. I try to pretend that it does not burn me, but I let it fall almost immediately. El Viejo Antonio smiles and coughs. Once again, he picks it up from the floor and soaks it in a small puddle of rain water, of night water. When the brand finally cools down, he returns it to me. "Here" . . . he says, and stares at me . . . "remember that the face painted in black hides the light and the warmth that the world will need.")

It is blackness the color of the double, of the shadow which holds this other knowledge. Both Anzaldúa and Subcomandante Marcos use stories, jokes, songs, memories to illustrate the kind of knowledge and lifestyle in the borderlands.

This need to escape founding fathers, the master readings, or masters as authors represents a movida that Anzaldúa and Marcos produce to live apart from the foundational narratives that make them live as shadows. The double contesting—replicating—the original follows the contours of the master narrative by mirroring fear back onto the "original." Anzaldúa states, "Why do they fight us? Because they think we are dangerous beasts? Why *are* we dangerous beasts? Because we shake and often break the white's comfortable stereotypical images they have of us" (Anzaldúa 2002, 185).

Subcomandante Marcos in *Seven Winds* (2009) replicates the ways Indians are insulted and downplayed by writing a manual, which illustrates how an Indian "has to be treated." The text replicates a manual, an intervention on "what to do in the case of . . ."

> El folleto que resuelve lo que hay que hacer frente a un indígena, por ejemplo, diría: "mire de arriba a abajo, de modo que esa cosa que tiene enfrente sepa quién manda y sepa que no todos somos iguales, sonría burlonamente, haga chistes sobre la forma de hablar o de vestir de la cosa esa. ¿Su valor? Vale menos que un pollo." (Los Siete Vientos / Sexto viento una otra digna rabia, 2009)

> (The manual that can tell us what to do when we see an Indian, would read something like this: "Look at it from top to bottom, so that, that thing in front of you knows who is in charge, and that not everyone is equal. Sneer at it, make jokes about the way that thing speaks or dresses. How much is it worth? Less than a chicken.")

Worthless Indians and migrants may talk back. The challenge is being able to hear them, to read them, to translate them.

Ruptures of the Nation through Replicas of the Double

A way to understand this replica, this response, is addressed by Homi Bhabha as a double narrative specified through the intervention of two temporalities: the pedagogical and the performative (Bhabha 1994, 144). The pedagogical represents the process of construction of identity "as one," produced as an accumulative narrative of successive historical moments, "the monumental time of the nation." The performative represents an interval of lost identity in the signifying process of cultural identification, the distracting presence of another narrative, repetitious, recursive that disturbs the contemporaneity of the national. Through this rupture the performative introduces a temporality of the in-between. In Bhabha's words, "alienated from its eternal self-generation, 'the people as one,' become a liminal signifying space that is *internally* marked by discourses of minorities, the heterogeneous histories of contending peoples, antagonist authorities and tense locations of cultural difference" (Bhabha 1994, 155).

Anzaldúa addresses this need for rupture and inter(re)ference (the performative move) by referring to the repeated expulsion of the particular ways of loving, healing, and knowing in the borderlands. Here we appreciate a call for the intervention of the performative inside the pedagogic time and narrative. In Anzaldúa's words: "Let's stop importing Greek Myths and the Western Cartesian split point of view and root ourselves in the mythological soil and soul of this continent. Instead of surreptitiously ripping off the vital energy of people of color and putting it to commercial use, whites could allow themselves to share and exchange and learn from us in a respectful way. By taking up *curanderismo*, Santeria, shamanism, Taoism, Zen . . . Anglos would perhaps lose the white sterility they have in their kitchens, bathrooms, hospitals, mortuaries and missile bases" (Anzaldúa 1987, 68–69).

Subcomandante Marcos enables the performative to intervene in his narrative through the stories narrated by El Viejo Antonio (see Marcos and Pachecho 2004). Antonio represents the performative rupture in the Zapatistas' narrative. He articulates the other ways of knowing, thinking, and living that contradict the authors of the "white world." In January 2009, in the context of the Festival of Dignifying Rage (Primer Festival Mundial de la Digna Rabia, December 26, 2008–January 4, 2009), Subcomandante Marcos mirrors Anzaldúa and inscribes this knowledge dimension into the nation's pedagogy:

> Desde hace mucho tiempo, el problema de los calendarios y las geografías han desvelado y develado al Poder. . . . en su torpe truco que este festival ha develado, Grecia queda muy lejos de Chiapas y en las escuelas se enseña que México queda separado por un océano de Francia, el País Vasco, el Estado Español, Italia. Y si vemos un mapa, podemos notar que Nueva York queda muy al norte de la Chiapas indígena mexicana. . . . pero no arriba ni abajo hay esa separación. La brutal globalización neoliberal, la IV Guerra Mundial que le decimos los zapatistas, puso los lugares más distantes en simultaneidad espacial y temporal para el flujo de riquezas . . . y para su apropiación.[6]

> (For a long time, the problem with calendars and geographies has unveiled Power at the same that has kept it restless. . . . This festival has

revealed the truth of such a clumsy trick, and has showed us that Greece is far away from Chiapas. At schools it is taught that an ocean separates Mexico from France, the Basque Country, Spain, and Italy. And if we pay attention to a map, we can see that New York is located far up north of Mexican, Indian Chiapas. . . . But such separation is inexistent both up and down. Brutal, neoliberal globalization—what we, the Zapatistas, call the World War IV—has situated the farthest places in a position of temporal and spatial simultaneity only to increase the flow of wealth . . . and in order to seize it.)

Mapping as rereading scales and distances in a globalized world is clear in this example. Alluding to the rupture caused by this double movement, Bhabha states: "We have then a contested conceptual terrain where the nation's people must be thought in double-time; the people are the historical objects of nationalist pedagogy, giving the discourse an authority that is based in the pre-given, or constituted historical origin in the past; the people are also the subjects of a process of signification that must erase any prior or originary presence of the nation-people to demonstrate the prodigious, living principles of the people as contemporaneity" (Bhabha 1994, 145). Bhabha points out that it is precisely in reading between these borderlines of the nation space where the replica appears.

Anzaldúa and Marcos address this double articulation by pointing to the necessity of thinking in this double-time narrative and engendering dialogue between the hegemonic pedagogical world and the marginal performative one, as we can perceive in the following quotes:

Many feel that whites should help their own people rid themselves of race hatred and fear first. I, for one, choose to use some of my energy to serve as mediator. I think we need to allow whites to be our allies. Through our literature, art, corridos, and folktales we must share our history with them so when they set up committees to help Big Mountain Navajos or the Chicano farm workers or Los Nicaraguenses, they won't turn people away because of their racial fears and ignorance. They will come to see that they are not helping us but following our lead. (Anzaldúa 1987, 85)

Y entonces, según el acuerdo de la mayoría de esa gente que vamos a escuchar, pues hacemos una lucha con todos, con indígenas, obreros, campesinos, estudiantes, maestros, empleados, mujeres, niños, ancianos hombres y todo aquel que tenga bueno su corazón y tenga la gana de luchar para que no se acabe de destruir y vender nuestra patria que se llama México y que viene quedando entre el río Bravo y el Suchiate.[7]

(And then, according to a majority of those people whom we are going to listen to, we struggle with all of them, indigenous people, workers, peasants, students, teachers, employees, women, children, old men, and everyone with a good heart and with desire to fight so that our homeland is not sold or destroyed which is named Mexico and which is situated between the Bravo and the Suchiate rivers.)

Pairing a Triangle: Accents of Castellanos in the Reading of Anzaldúa

The pedagogy of the double referring to the pairing of Rosario Castellanos and Gloria Anzaldúa intends to reflect accents of the reading of a well-known middle-class, white, and critical writer—a so-called *Güera* (white woman) in Mexico—into another mainly unknown in Mexico, woman of color, working-class, and lesbian writer—a *Prieta* (a women of color).[8]

I want to refer to Anzaldúa's narrative, specifically her essay "La Prieta," through the narrative of a foundational binary: white/Indian. This binary is addressed in Mexico as Güera (white) and Prieta (brown). Chicana theory and literature has worked on that binary profusely; two essays are particularly important: "La Güera" by Cherríe Moraga and "La Prieta," by Anzaldúa, both from *This Bridge Called My Back*.

"La Güera," marked by whiteness, functions as the supplement to make women visible in appropriate sexual ways, and "La Prieta" marked by color, embodies various kinds of invisibility, illegitimacy, and queerness. Güeras and prietas grasp an oppositional binary, which represents the most visible and consistent asymmetrical divisions in Mexican society: gender, articulated with race and supplemented by class, as the privileged vectors of asymmetrical difference. In "La Prieta," Anzaldúa revises the sites of production of racial, sexual, and gender categories. She writes:

> Qué lastima que nació m'hijita morena, muy prieta, tan morena y distinta de sus propios hijos güeros. Pero quería a m'hijita como quiera. Lo que me faltaba de blancura, tenía de inteligencia. Pero sí fue una pena que fui oscura como una india. (Anzaldúa 1988, 157)

> (Such a shame that my daughter was born brown! Prieta, so different from her own sons, güeros all of them. But I still loved my daughter. What I lacked in whiteness, I made up for in intelligence. But, yes, it was a shame that I was born dark as an Indian.)

The binary Güera/Prieta points to the repudiated binary of the nation: the migrant and the Indian. Moraga "La Güera" and Anzaldúa "La Prieta" address one of the most flagrant Mexican polarities: the racial and gender division between güeros and prietos (whites and mestizos, Indian or black). "La Güera" and "La Prieta" are not only a pair of opposites, but are binaries constitutive of Mexican society. For every *güerita*, white, middle/upper-class woman, there is a *prietita*, mestiza, brown, Indian, poor woman. For every way of seeing, there is a way of veiling.

Güera means both the site of legitimation as white, and the site of delegitimation as women. Güera is what Mexican upper/middle-class women are called by the army of people who serve them. But *güera*, as a name given to women, also represents the site of a particular sexualization of womanhood in patriarchal frames. It may mean, in particular contexts of violence, the possibility of "fucking" (*chingar*) the West, the United States, or the *patrón* (master).[9]

The strategy for circulation of "La Prieta" relies on the deconstruction of a binary, in which the seams of the constitution of binaries—original and double—would be shown. This means reading güeras and prietas, these sexualized doubles, not as a representation of default but as constitutive outsiders.

Balún Canán's final line reads both the impossible and imaginary encounter between güeros and prietos, between Indians and whites. By the end of the novel, the Nanny—the central character—is thrown into the street. The girl, without a name, addresses her departure in the following way:

> Pero la india me mira correr, impasible, y no hace un ademán de bienvenida. Camino lentamente, más lentamente hasta detenerme. Dejo caer los brazos, desalentada. Nunca, aunque yo la encuentre, podré reconocer a mi nana. Hace tanto tiempo que nos separaron. Además, *todos los indios tienen la misma cara.* (Castellanos 1958, 227; emphasis added)

> (But the Indian watches me quite impassible, gesturing a welcoming sign. I slow up—slower and slower til I stop. I let my arms drop, altogether discouraged. Even if I see her, I'll never recognize her. It's so long since we parted. Besides, *all Indians look alike.*)

By the end of the novel, the prieta, the Nanny, is expelled from home. The girl will never recognize her again because "all Indians have the same face."

The Nanny and the girls (güera and prieta) created a parallel world full of love, knowledge, and amusement. The reading of this novel allows for the intrusion of their world inside the reader's "reality." Reality may be a mixture of parallel scenes, of copies, of worlds created by scales generated by a girl and her Nanny, by the broken distances in between them, by their replicas and their talking back in tongues to the world that separates them, the world that drastically distances whites and Indians.

The Nanny expelled from the "master's" home—in an extended journey undertaken by millions of Mexicans—could reach the United States. With her wisdom, her border knowledge and culture, could she unravel into Anzaldúa's new mestiza?

I propose that *Borderlands / La Frontera* begins where *Balún Canán* ends. With such a continuity and parallel narrative the Nanny could be read as *The New Mestiza*,[10] as one of the millions of Indians crossing the border to work as nannies in the United States or in search of work. What kind of reading would emerge when North and South, Chiapas and Texas, Güera and Prieta, Nanny and new mestiza, United States and Mexico, parallel worlds contact each other?[11]

What Anzaldúa provokes is the necessity of peeling her discourse like an onion, until the bare question of the text appears: "¿Cómo le vamos a hacer para vivir juntos sin herirnos? How are you going to deal with me: a prieta, queer, obrera, izquierdosa, lesbiana?" (Anzaldúa 1988, 53).

In the literary and cultural world of Mexico, Rosario Castellanos—the Güera, the site of visibility—could provide a bridging reading to the "the other side," but from the tongue, voice, and discourse of the Nanny, the place of excess in *Balún Canán*. The Nanny only talks to the girl in the novel; in *Borderlands / La Frontera*, she speaks in tongues and talks back to the world. In the narrative of *Balún Canán* and through our proposed pedagogy of the double, the Nanny could be read as the double of the new mestiza, pointing to the amount of culture, knowledge, and value accumulated in the language and in the body of a wetback: migrants and Indians together reflecting knowledge and replying.

A prieta may have problems in crossing a border when a passport is needed. A güera may not even need a passport, with her color, her assumed heterosexuality, and her class the most legitimate ones. But a güera may be the passport of the prieta in a racist world. What needed to happen to make a prieta "carry" a güera not on her back but inside her tongue? What narrative could invert the power positions and grant access to güeros only if accompanied by an Indian? The crossing of Anzaldúa's and Castellanos's narratives provides a bridge, this time not on the backs of so many women of color but through their tongues, their replicas, their words. Are we able to see or read Anzaldúa's new mestiza inside the Nanny, inside so many wetbacks that cross our world?

One of the varied founding stories of *Balún Canán* narrated by the Nanny to the girl has to do with the Indian version of the creation of the world. Around that narration the Nanny tells the girl that Heaven—according to the Indian gods, the Nine Guardians—could not be accessed by whites if not led by a poor person. Heaven can only be reached in doubles and led by a prieta. Here is a section of the story:

"And from that moment they called the man of gold rich and the men of flesh poor. And they ordered things in such a way that the rich man should care for the poor and shelter him, since it was the rich man who benefited by the poor man's acts. And the lords so ordered it that the poor should answer for the rich before the face of Truth. That is why our law says that no rich man can enter heaven if a poor man does not lead him by the hand." Nana falls silent. Carefully she folds the clothes she has been mending, picks up the calabash with the colored threads, and gets to her feet to be going away. But before her first step can take her from me, I ask her: "Who is my poor one, Nana?" She stops, and as she helps me to my feet she says: "You don't know yet. But if you watch carefully, when more years and understanding are upon you, you will recognize the poor one that is yours." (Castellanos 1958, 32)

Heaven cannot be reached individually. One of the outcomes of this proposal of translation, of this methodology of reading in pairs—in doubles—is to let the güeros know that their access is impossible if not with a poor mestiza, Indian, with a double that would make them see that they alone are not the way to a better world—another world is only possible in pairs—and to underscore the ways in which leadership must come from below.

Reading in triangles, translation as pedagogy, may constitute a threefold strategy: make prietas visible, recast the ways to "Heaven," and finally reedit knowledge production from below. Anzaldúa is the privileged prieta, who may provoke this displacement in Mexican academia. Let us imagine the ways in which this binary North and South, white and brown, queer and straight, güera and prieta may turn into a critique of knowledge production in a transnational, transdisciplinary, and transsexual way. Anzaldúa with Castellanos, mano a mano, and Anzaldúa, according to Castellanos, leading the way to Heaven.

Anzaldúa closes the narrative section on *Borderlands* with a reference to the "return." How can you return to a place you have never been? That is the challenge: to make Anzaldúa return to Mexico, where she was only in her imagination. Her narrative has the potential to develop consciousness and critique, enhanced by the contiguous reading of her doubles, Subcomandante Marcos and Rosario Castellanos.

If translation is reading, imagining other's realities in different scales and distances, replying, and pairing parallel worlds, *Borderlands | La Frontera* and "La Prieta," are invaluable texts for Mexican academics to understand and teach about scales and distances of our new mestizaje (our new mestizas) and about their strategic doubles. Subcomandante Marcos, Gloria Anzaldúa, and Rosario Castellanos constitute a triangle in doubles that may convey inside our class-

rooms a way of translating who we are today as Mexicans as Americans and—
better—who we could be. Hardly any other translation may achieve such an
intervention in distances and scales.

Notes

1. In a recently published chapter we expand on the academic departments that are incorporating Chicana theory. See Belausteguigoitia Rius and Magallanes (2013).

2. Ten years later we can find an increase in the self-representation of working class and
indigenous women due to the resistance vis-à-vis increasing violence across the nation.
Human rights activists and academia along with NGOs and social movements have articulated successful strategies to reproduce the writings, voices, and demands of these women.

3. I propose as reading material the communiqués written during the indigenous rebellion from 1994 to 2001. This period of time represents the beginning of dialogue between
rebels and government and the discussion of the accords signed in the House of Representatives in August 2001. Adding to this I include the last (sixth) Declaration of the Lacandona
Jungle (Sexta Declaración de la Selva Lacandona), made public in June 2005. See EZLN,
Documentos y Comunicados, vols. I–V (Mexico: ERA, 1995–2000).

4. The double as pedagogy intersects with the notion of mirror and mirroring with the
other. Subjects get constructed as fiction of the "original." Jacques Lacan states that subjectivity only starts when the "caretaker's" gaze is anticipating a complete and final form vis-
à-vis a fragmented body (the body of a six-month-old baby). This can only happen within
a surface, a mirror, which reflects the gaze of the mother into the child as "anticipated"
subject. See Lacan (1985).

5. In Mexico, güeras and prietas constitute the opposition between blonde and brown
women; the sexual, gender, and class dialectic of discrimination operates heavily in terms
of color within this dyad.

6. See Primer Festival Mundial de la Digna Rabia, http://dignarabia.ezln.org.mx.

7. Sexta Declaración in Belausteguigoitia and Leñero (2006), 392. See http://www.enlace
.com.mx.

8. To see more on the discourse of güeras and prietas in Mexico and in Mexican academia, see Belausteguigoitia 2009.

9. To see definitions of the Mexican expression "Chingar," see Paz (1994 [1983]).

10. I owe Norma Alarcón here: this connection emerged in one of her courses at the
University of California, Berkeley, during fall 1997.

11. This set of questions gave way to an editorial project at the Gender Studies Program at
UNAM, which could grant access to prietas publication and provide a rereading of foundational texts from below: *Las Güeras y las Prietas: A Bridge Called My Tongue*. This was a project
that could grant access to the nation's impossible subjects: the Indian, the Chicana, the
prieta, and could reread the texts of the güeras from below, only if accompanied by its
shadow, a text written by a prieta. This movida would unpack the hegemonic sites of theoretical and narrative production.

PART II

MEDIATIONS/NATIONAL/TRANSNATIONAL IDENTITIES/CIRCUITS

CHAPTER SIX/FEMINIST THEORIES, TRANSNATIONAL TRANSLATIONS, AND CULTURAL MEDIATIONS

CLAUDIA DE LIMA COSTA

Biographical (Dis)Locations

I begin my reflections on the politics of transnational translations by way of an autobiographical note. Much of my adult life for the past thirty years has been spent traveling across the North and South of the Americas while living in different localities: Rio de Janeiro, Brazil, my place of birth and where I grew up feeling out of place; Barquisimeto, Venezuela, a transitional stop point in my tumultuous passage through marriage and motherhood; and the North American Midwest, where I entered higher education, feminism, and a new sense of self. After completion of my U.S. doctorate, I left marriage behind in Venezuela to begin a long-distant, transnational partnership that to this day still shapes my travels North (United States) and back to the South (Brazil) of the continents, despite the increasing prices of airfare, the long sleepless hours in transit, the more acutely felt body discomfort in the decreasing size of airplane economy seats, and the more numerous and hostile migratory checkpoints in the aftermath of September 11, 2001. These three locations in the map, corresponding to critical stages in my intellectual journey and chronology, also constituted translation zones — places where I constantly had to translate myself to others and back to myself both literally and figuratively, always with an accent in the foreign and, by contamination, in the native language as well. As Doris Sommer's work on bilingualism shows, "words don't stay put; they wander into adjacent language fields, get lost in translation, pick up tics from foreign interference, and so can't quite mean what they say. Teaching bilinguals about deconstruction is almost redundant" (2004, xix).

Borrowing from Marianne Hirsch's poetic words, linguistic and geographic (dis)locations, accompanied by bilingualisms, "prepared me to conceive of identity as fractured and self-contradictory, as inflected by nationality, ethnicity, class, race, and history" (1994, 87), and also allowed me to find in feminism "a space of relation and relocation, a place from which I could think and speak and write, a home on the border" (1994, 88).

After a decade living in the United States as a "resident alien," and bringing in my luggage back to Brazil the theories and concepts formative of my academic self, I assumed a teaching position in a federal university in the south of the country (and south of my place of origin), just to begin the daunting task of reappraising and translating what appeared to be—to recall a renowned Brazilian literary critic—"ideas out of place" (Schwarz 2000, 9). Since then, and due to transnational partnership ties, I have continued keeping close ties to the U.S. academy and have learned more about the particular dynamics of the Brazilian academy. My scholarship, in light of my life trajectory and experiences, has been shaped from early on by a concern with the ways feminism as a geopolitical knowledge formation travels across different spaces, as well as with the processes of reception it encounters in its multiple (dis)locations.

Taking advantage of my position as a former coeditor of the foremost Brazilian academic publication, *Revista Estudos Feministas*, I want to explore the travels and translations of feminist theories across the North–South axis by examining the publishing practices of the journal vis-à-vis the larger academic institutional structures to which it is affiliated. More specifically, to approach the difficult task of unraveling the import/export of feminist ideas—and the institutionalities that oversee this process—is to develop an analysis of the circulation of feminist knowledges from their contexts of production to their reception.

As stated in my introduction to this volume, there is always a material apparatus that oversees the travels of theories and organizes their translation, publication, and circulation. This apparatus—at the same time constituted by and constitutive of the contexts of reception—influences in significant ways which theories/texts get translated and resignified for better fit with local agendas. Among the institutionalities controlling the circulation of texts in the symbolic networks are the *revistas culturales* and academic journals which, according to Nelly Richard (2001), play the role of cultural mediators between metropolitan theories and their peripheral translations.

My objective in this chapter is to examine all the volumes of *Revista Estudos Feministas*, published from its emergence in 1992 until recently, as a case study of the travels of feminist theories to scrutinize the ways the journal plays the role of cultural mediator in that process.[1] To do so, it is necessary to engage in an analysis of the editorials, the journal's thematic contents, citation practices, the journal's politics of financing, and, finally, the specificities of Brazilian academic feminism. In sum, as Richard (2001) suggests, to grasp the production and circulation of knowledge demands a scrutiny of the local academic and extra-academic networks and their relation to institutional fields, the inscription rules of epistemological repertoires, and the broader political-intellectual conjuncture.

I would like to stress that we already have incisive studies about the processes of cultural translation operating in the economy of symbolic and material exchanges. Such studies have traced the global circuits of theories and their dislocations across axes structured by the relations of power and marginality in diverse "translation zones."[2] However, the majority of these more recent studies focus on the circulation of signs and meanings across regions other than Latin America, and few of them offer a more in-depth inquiry into the travels of feminist theories and their analytical categories.[3]

In the context of the Americas, the overarching question I pose is as follows. How can feminists in the North and South (understood more as metaphorical spaces opened up by the frictions of power asymmetries, rather than concrete and delimited geographical regions), working in the gaps and silences of translation and underscoring unequal relations between regions, languages, and institutions, contribute to a counterpractice of translation (*traduttore, traditore*) that disrupts hegemonic narratives about gender, feminism, and the subaltern?

In what follows, I first elaborate some notorious instances of the travels of theories, emphasizing the complex circuitry of knowledge formations and their subsequent transmutations/appropriations. Then, I turn to the pages of *Revista Estudos Feministas* as illustrations of larger epistemological quandaries on the feminist politics of translation. Finally, I conclude by arguing that despite the geopolitical vectors overdetermining the journal's overall project, significant spaces were created to allow for disruption—however small and delimited—of the metropolitan theoretical scripts in countertranslation practices.

Theoretical (Dis)Locations: Some Instances

Instance 1: Pal Ahluwalia (2005), in his exploration of the African roots of poststructuralism, analyzes the autobiographies of Jacques Derrida (*Monolingualism of the Other*) and Hélène Cixous (*The Newly Born Woman*) to point out a curious proximity between French poststructuralism and colonial Africa, more specifically, Algeria. Ahluwalia argues that Derrida and Cixous, by being placed in between French and Algerian cultures, were deeply marked by the experience of colonization. This particular historical context of both thinkers—that of exile, of being in the margins—contributed in significant ways to their radical interrogation of Western theories. The same colonial experience, formative of perspectives critical of Western theories, finds resonance in the work of Edward Said, Frantz Fanon, Louis Althusser, and Pierre Bourdieu. In looking at these specific affiliations, Ahluwalia wants to show how poststructuralism does not recognize its African colonial roots. However, these thinkers are considered the ones who most challenged the epistemology of French colonialism and its idea of cultural superiority. The specter of Algeria continues to inhabit poststructuralist theories. In this sense Robert Stam (2001) argues that ignoring the influence of subaltern and anticolonial theorizing in the decentering of Eurocentric master narratives, thus obliterating the ways Third World thinking was codified by those affiliated with structuralism and poststructuralism, is to give this theoretical corpus a white coating and a French accent.

Instance 2: Henry Louis Gates (1989) observes that although France is usually associated with the birthplace of deconstruction—and Derrida is considered its most prominent talking head—Afro-American communities have been engaged in deconstruction in its rhetorical practices *avant la lettre* for over two centuries. Through what Gates calls signification—a practice in which the subject of enunciation (in this case, the slave) could indirectly contest his master by using humor, charade, and other figures of speech—the slave was able to subvert the master's discourse, thereby rhetorically undermining his power. Gates argues that the discursive tropes used then were not those characteristic of deconstruction (such as metaphor, metonym, metalepsis, catachresis, or hyperbole), but more akin to the tropes deployed in the Afro-American folkloric tradition that Zora Neale Hurston documented: loud-talking, specifying, testifying, rapping, and playing the dozens.

Instance 3: Néstor García Canclini, in assessing the different effects of globalization in the North and South of the Americas, points out that the Latin American canon—as we already know very well—is a complex articulation of myriad European influences (which in turn, I might add, are also articulations of influences from elsewhere). According to Canclini, "Latin American humanities and social science scholars, and more generally cultural producers, make critical appropriation of metropolitan canons and reconvert them, so to speak, responding to different national motivations" (2001, 10–11).

Instance 4: Joan Scott (2002), writing about the travels of the gender concept, argues that Julia Kristeva, frequently characterized as a French feminist (together with Cixous and Luce Irigaray), was born in Bulgaria, where she began her career as an interpreter of Mikhail Bakhtin, who, in turn, had developed a historicized version of structuralism as a way of critiquing Stalinism. Bakhtin's emphasis on the dialogical nature of meaning contradicted that communist state's idea that language could be policed and its signs controlled. As Scott tells us, Kristeva went to Paris, carrying along with her baggage the Bakhtinian notion of polyphony and introducing it to the structuralist debates in the mid-1960s. She translated the term *polyphony* as intertextuality so as to give some dynamism to structuralism. According to Scott, what came to be known as French feminism (which is, in fact, an American construct) was crucially influenced by the philosophical movements against communism in Eastern Europe, including a Bakhtinian theory that placed interaction and dialogue—and not the confrontation of difference—as the grounds for communication. However, in the U.S. feminist debates of the 1980s, French feminism is subsumed under poststructuralist theories of language with an emphasis on difference, whereas Anglo-Saxon feminism, anchored in social science's empirical research tradition, is represented as an advocate of equality.[4] Scott stresses that in the encounters and theoretical exchanges between Eastern European and Western feminism, the specificities of the historical context are erased. An emphasis on the difference between the East/West divide ends up placing theory on the West side, while the East supplies the case studies.

Echoing Scott, Chilean cultural critic Richard (2002), in reflecting about the interactions of North and Latin American feminisms, had also pointed out that in the North–South axis, feminists in the North are seen as the abstract mind for the concrete body of feminists in the South. In other words, despite such travels and dislocations, "theory" still continues to stand under the sign of the West (Bhabha 1988), which in turn remains to this day the archival source of information on non-Western locations (Niranjana 1992).

To conclude my discussion of the foregoing examples, Scott alerts us that with the pluralization of feminisms in contemporary times, we need to understand feminism itself as a process of translation (in the sense of faithless translation) signaling the mutability of words and concepts, connoting not only distorted repetition but movement in space and time as well. In the Brazilian academic scenario of the 1990s, two recently founded feminist journals, I argue, became the privileged site in the circulation of feminist knowledges,[5] playing the significant role of cultural mediators between, as Richard (2002) puts it, metropolitan theories and their peripheral translations.

As I maintain in the second introduction to this volume, much ink has been spilled about the travels of theories across different topographies and through itineraries that are ever more complex. One way to approach the difficult task of unraveling the import/export of feminist ideas and the institutionalities that oversee this whole process is to develop an analysis of the circulation of (feminist) knowledges from their contexts of production to their reception. By what means and through which routes do feminist concepts gain temporary (or even permanent) residence in different representational economies? It is well known that texts do not travel across linguistic contexts without a "visa." Their dislocation can only take place if there is also a material apparatus organizing their translation, publication, and circulation.

To scrutinize the ways journals become cultural mediators in the traffic of theories and discourses, it would be necessary to carry out tasks such as (here the list is of course only suggestive, not exhaustive) the analysis of journal's content and the transnational quotation market, appraisal of the knowledges being disseminated by the journal, analysis of the location of the journal vis-à-vis the disciplinary fields of the academy (and the field of feminism), assessment of the journal's editorial board and its representation in the larger discursive context, and consideration of the issue of canonicity and the silencing of other feminist genealogies in the practices of translation of foreign-language articles.[6]

Given space limitations, I pursue only some of these tasks, which a broader study with a more in-depth scope should certainly undertake.

Revista Estudos Feministas *as a Context of Reception*
in the Travels of Feminist Theories

Revista Estudos Feministas is the only refereed, interdisciplinary feminist academic journal in Brazil that is national in scope. That is to say, although it has been housed at two federal universities so far, it does not reflect the orientation of any particular graduate program or research center. It is published quarterly and is dedicated to enhancing the visibility of scholarly production in the vast field of feminist and gender studies in Brazil. A very interesting feature of this publication is its mix of academic articles and thematically focused "dossiers" (with shorter articles in either academic or essay format) on issues of current relevance for the public debate and which are geared to a feminist activist/nongovernmental organization reading formation.

The first issue of Revista Estudos Feministas appeared in 1992 (number 0) and, in 1999, its institutional home changed from the Federal University of Rio de Janeiro to the Federal University of Santa Catarina in Florianópolis.[7] For many years it received generous funding from the Ford Foundation and, later, from the Brazilian research council, CNPq. In 1998, the Ford Foundation ceased funding the journal and today it is dependent on CNPq resources, the university infrastructure, and individual subscriptions to continue publishing.[8]

THE EDITORIALS: SETTING GOALS

Revista Estudos Feministas's goals at launch were daring and innovative. According to the editorials of its first volumes (1992–94), it established the following objectives: first, to be a channel for the women's social movement; second, to disseminate feminist knowledge, thus contributing to the consolidation of gender studies as a multidisciplinary field; and third, to be attentive to women's social demands and serve as a space for feminist debates.

Having set such objectives, the journal had as its priority "the renewal of knowledge in the human and social sciences from the perspective of women's historically subordinate place in society." Hence the journal would emphasize the linkages between political practice and the academy, articulating a trenchant critique of established epistemologies. With the translation of previously published foreign-language articles by internationally renowned authors (mostly from English and French publications), the editors "would enable Brazilian readers' access to the most pressing theoretical and methodological issues in international feminist debates." As stated in its first editorial, the journal would also publish English, French, and Spanish versions of some of its original articles to facilitate the international circulation of Brazilian authors, thereby encouraging productive intellectual exchanges. In its special issue of 1994, which selectively published some debates from an international colloquium gathering Brazilian, French, and French Canadian scholars, the journal also signaled interest in a "comparative approach that would interrogate feminist perspectives in these three contexts."

However, in the following issues this comparative approach was not forthcoming. On the contrary, in the editorials the words *feminism* and *feminist* (feminist studies, feminist theories, feminist movement) became even more sparse, and in 1995, they were replaced by expressions such as *women's movement, gender studies,* and *gender relations* ("the journal is in the vanguard of academic discussion about gender, together with an attention to those topics that are of concern to the women's movement"). Beginning with the first issue of 1996, terms such as *feminist theories, feminist studies,* and *feminist movement* completely disappeared from the editorials, only reemerging after 1999, when they become a constant presence in all the editorials. It should be observed that this coincides with the change of the journal's publishing house from the Federal University of Rio de Janeiro to the Federal University of Santa Catarina—that is, a movement from center to periphery in terms of the academic cartography of power and influence of Brazilian universities (a point that is further elaborated ahead).

My intention in studying the editorials of *Revista Estudos Feministas* is not simply to catalog words and expressions but to examine the extent to which the presence or absence of certain terms are symptomatic of the journal's context of reception and the underlying factors and forces that play a crucial role in the travels and translations of feminist theories. About the latter, I advance two points. First, while claiming to be a vehicle for the debates on gender and feminism in Brazil, the journal in fact has had an important constitutive role in the field it usually claims to represent. Its editors and editorial committees have exerted (and inevitably exert) the function of gatekeepers of the feminist academic community, policing the many local appropriations/translations of theoretical debates in (mostly) English and French. This control is also in part wielded by the agendas of the journal's funding agencies — the Ford Foundation (from 1992 to 1998) and the Brazilian government research council/CNPq (from 1992 to the present) — and by peer reviewers located in different disciplinary terrains. These formative structures of a gender studies canon played a decisive influence on the circulation of theories, authors, and discursive practices. In the pages of the journal, the theories and authors who have high transit and who are most cited are those closest to the international circuits of academic prestige and are situated at privileged racial, geographical (Rio de Janeiro and São Paulo), and class sites.[9] With the assent of such institutions, agencies, and peer reviewers (given the particularities of the Brazilian academic system, they tend to work more in consonance than dissonance), feminist academic journals earning the seal of quality become the legislators for particular kinds of feminist discourses and knowledges. For example, despite positioning itself at the vanguard of feminist academic discussions, until 2000 the journal had published very few analyses of the intersections of race and gender. Only in 1995 was a dossier organized with a focus on black women. In relation to other subaltern groups, and despite the publication of a dossier on indigenous women in 1999, the journal did not disrupt asymmetrical practices of representation, given that all the articles in that dossier were written by white academics speaking for indigenous women. Current debates on non-Western epistemologies have not yet found echoes in the journal's pages or in other latitudes of the Brazilian academic landscape.[10]

Given the historically overwhelming presence of consolidated fields in the social sciences (anthropology and sociology) in the journal until 2000, and seeking legitimacy from the scientific community as a whole, *Revista Estudos Feministas* contributed more significantly to the dissemination of disciplinary discourses about gender, following "scientifically rigorous" theories and methodologies, than for interdisciplinary (or even antidisciplinary or, for that matter, postdisciplinary) innovative viewpoints that would question taken-for-granted disciplinary paradigms—a goal that has been the trademark of feminist theories.[11]

Second, despite the journal's commitment to heterogeneity, stated in the first editorials, discourses and practices do not happen in isolation but are mutually imbricated in the creation of a common effect. A scrutiny of several issues of the journal reveals that the articles addressing feminist theories and epistemologies are usually translations from English and French. Among the Brazilian authors published by the journal, very few have engaged exclusively in theoretical discussions or debates on the concept of gender and its semantic instabilities.[12] For Mary Castro and Lena Lavinas (1992), the empirical orientation of Brazilian contributors from the social sciences may be due, among other things, to a lack of practice with the essay form, unlike, I would add, the writings by feminist scholars working within the humanities. According to Castro and Lavinas, "the essay, following the tradition of the Frankfurt School, collaborates with the theoretical exploration of objects in process of formation, without commitment with the order of facts, but engaged with ideas, what potentially facilitates creativity" (1992, 217)

Theories and concepts are appropriated and resignified to better adapt to the case studies, and this is done through two venues that have been constitutive of Brazilian academic feminism. According to Lia Zanotta Machado (1997), one venue has taken us (until recently) to French structuralism with its emphasis on the ideal of equality and the denial of difference, whereas the other takes us to Anglo-American poststructuralism, stressing questions of otherness and politicizing the discourses about difference. It is interesting to observe that at this theoretical crossroads, *Revista Estudos Feministas* ended up (not intentionally) making invisible other feminist theoretical genealogies.[13] In this sense, until the last decade there has not been in the pages of the journal a significant presence of feminists theorizing from other parts of Latin America or even from the intersection of gender and postcolonialism in the articulation of a radical marginality.

THE TRANSNATIONAL CITATION MARKET

It is by now well known that citation practices not only are largely responsible for the formation of scholarly canons but are seen as the most objective measure of academic merit (Lutz 1995). There are a significant number of studies, mostly coming from the fields of applied linguistics/discourse analysis as well as bibliometrics, on the uses of citations as a core activity in knowledge production (Lillis et al. 2010). Who gets cited, where, and by whom—namely, the geolinguistics of citations—exposes the routes through which theories travel, and (masculine) intellectual lineages are constructed in a global context.[14]

Emphasizing the geopolitical dimensions of citations, Theresa Lillis and colleagues (2010), for instance, studied the link between these micro-practices to larger social practices of knowledge production, circulation, and evaluation globally. The Science Citation Index and the Social Sciences Citation Index (both managed by Thomson Scientific) are the dominant measures by way of impact factor of a journal's influence and what gauges its visibility. A journal's inclusion in such indexes also affects the authors' perceived value and, in some countries such as Brazil, affects financial allocation of resources for both the author (for his or her research) and the academic publication, among other things. One of the relevant but not surprising conclusions of the Lillis et al. study, whose research encompassed 240 published psychology articles in English-medium journals, is that "the global status of English is impacting not only on the linguistic medium of publications but on the linguistic medium of works that are considered *citable*—and hence on which/whose knowledge is being allowed to circulate" (2010, 121).

In light of this discussion, what are the citation practices in *Revista Estudos Feministas*?

Given that it is a Portuguese-medium publication, a survey of the articles that were published in the period of ten years (1992–2002) shows some reasonable equilibrium in citations of Brazilian and foreign authors.[15] Among foreign authors, there is a clear predominance of references to English-medium works, followed by French ones. Citations of authors writing in Spanish are very scarce in this period, only gaining visibility in the more current issues of the journal, which also coincided with an increase in publication of articles in Spanish from authors residing mostly in Latin America, a consequence of a clear attempt by the editors to establish more dialogue with their Spanish-speaking feminist counterparts, especially those from Argentina. However, it is interesting to note that a special issue of *Revista Estudos Feministas* in 1994 on race published articles on feminist epistemologies and methodologies that had no citation to either Portuguese- or Spanish-language articles.

Some preliminary conclusions can be drawn from this initial analysis. First, it is reasonable to expect that for a Brazilian academic publication with a focus on developing and strengthening the field of feminist and gender studies nationally, reference to Brazilian authors in the articles is directly linked to feminist concerns that respond to contextual specificities.[16] However, in an attempt to legitimate and consolidate this emerging field vis-à-vis the academy, one notices a very clear tendency by feminist authors in *Revista Estudos Feministas* to cite more frequently (white, Euro-centric) male scholars (Foucault, Giddens, Sahlins, Bourdieu, Lyotard, and so on) whenever theoretical questions were broached. This finding only corroborates a point that had already been made by Barbara Christian (1987) and Catherine Lutz (1995), who most eloquently highlighted the intellectual colonialism of canons of theory that usually leads to the suppression of marginal voices. According to Lutz, "theory has acquired a gender insofar as it is more frequently associated with male writing, with women's writing more often seen as description, data, case, personal, or, in the case of feminism, 'merely' setting the record straight" (1995, 251).[17] Second, whenever the balance tilted toward citation of English-medium works, the topic of the articles had a more transnational focus, particularly those exploring the contributions of theories and methodologies for feminist knowledge building, as well as discussions of the intersection of gender and race. Third, with the "arrival" and increasing influence of poststructuralism and queer theory in Brazilian feminism in the 2000s (particularly by way of the translation into Portuguese of Judith Butler's *Gender Trouble*), and followed by the slow waning of structuralist approaches so far predominant in feminist sociology and anthropology, English-medium texts from Anglophone centers, translated into Portuguese, largely supplanted the translation of French ones and became dominant in the pages of the journal. Interestingly, these theoretical tectonic changes coincided, on the one hand, with the proliferation in the journal of articles from other disciplinary fields, such as history, political science, education, philosophy, cultural studies, and film studies, to name a few, and the decrease in the number of articles from anthropological and sociological perspectives, which had until then been the prevailing locus of enunciation for Brazilian feminism.[18] On the other hand, such diversification of feminist analyses, opening them up to more trans- or postdisciplinary approaches, may also be viewed as a response to the institutional home change of the journal to a federal university[19] away from the São Paulo–Rio de Janeiro axis of academic power.[20]

Finally, attention to postcolonial theories is still lacking in feminist debates in Brazil, except in literary studies. Intersectional analyses (despite recent criticisms in the Anglophone academy) are also emerging as concerns with race/racism and ethnicity have held center stage in public debates and government policies to redress historically enduring social and economic inequalities.

Going back to the findings of Lillis et al. and their account of the current position of English as the global academic lingua franca (which partly echoes the citation—and translation—practices in *Revista Estudos Feministas*), "The highly stratified system that is in place which privileges English-medium texts from Anglophone centre contexts, including English-medium citations [must be acknowledged as a contradictory force]. English cannot be viewed as a transparent medium, simply 'translating' knowledge from one language to another; its status within global evaluation systems is actually shaping what gets counted as knowledge, illustrated in this paper by the privileging of English-medium citations and the exclusion of citations to work in other languages" (2010, 131).

I conclude this section by pointing out that despite *Revista Estudos Feministas*'s chief contribution to a change of direction from women's studies to gender studies in the Brazilian academy—hence opening the way to the study of the intersections of gender with other axes of difference and asymmetries of power—there is still a need for us to continue being vigilant (in Gayatri Spivak's sense of the term) about citation and translation practices so as not to lose sight of feminism's political and epistemological project.

In the Brazilian founding anthology of gender studies, *Uma Questão de Gênero* (Costa and Bruschini 1992), one can notice that the gender category threaded different routes according to disciplinary fields and their respective prevailing paradigms. The reading of several issues of *Revista Estudos Feministas*, tentatively explored here, suggests that the debates about gender studies were deeply marked by a sociological and anthropological perspective and strongly influenced by a structuralist paradigm with an empirical focus.[21] Other feminist discursive interventions (until recently) found little room in the pages of *Revista*.

I argue, following Richard's advice, that when examining the role feminist journals and cultural magazines play as critical mediators and productive (mis)translators in the traffic of theories, it is imperative that a space be created for heterogeneous textualities. This implies not only "the coexistence of diversity of intellectual affiliations, disciplinary and anti-disciplinary, but also of a variety of discursive tones and textual forms authorizing various sites of enunciation and representational registers" (Richard, 2001, my translation). Such heterogeneity potentially enables the articulation between academic reflections and other kinds of enunciatory practices and countertranslations in the feminist project of decolonizing knowledge.

Feminist Publications and Cultural Mediations:
Dislocating the Theoretical Sign

How, one asks, do we escape those epistemological economies that have institutionalized the Anglophone academic centers as the grids of intelligibility for theory and, more specifically, for feminist theory? I will of course avoid engaging here the most instigating debate on what "theory" is, together with its correlatives (the place, the object, and the subject of "theory"). However, what cannot be avoided is the issue of translation and its relation to both "theory" and power. As Iain Chambers remarks, citing Talal Asad, "both translator and the translated are exposed to unauthorized planetary processes and procedures that expose the 'conditions of power'" (Chambers 2010, 261–62). Trenchantly, Chambers continues,

> The assumed ethnographic authority of the West on the rest of the
> world is challenged in the very transit and translation of its languages
> elsewhere. The subtle lesson of Walter Benjamin's discussion of the task
> of the translator is that the sought-for transparency of an "original" text
> gives way to the mutation not only of the language of the translated but
> also that of the translator. Language is never a merely linguistic matter,
> Heidegger reminds us, and in the transitivity of translation clearly nei-
> ther language is untouched by the historical processes in which each is
> suspended and sustained. In opening up a process that is irreducible to
> the language of either the translator or the translated, the performativ-
> ity of the translation exposes itself to the arbitrary, that is, the violent
> exercise of worldly conditions. (2010, 262)

I appropriate Chambers's citation to contend that journals such as *Revista Estudos Feministas* have a crucial role to play in the transitivity of translation and the cultural turbulence it causes when entering different terrains. Rey Chow has cogently shown us that "genuine cultural translation is possible only when we move beyond the seemingly infinite but actually reductive permutations of the two terms — East and West, original and translation — and instead see both as full, materialist, and most likely equally corrupt, equally decadent participants in contemporary world culture" (1995, 195).

At this point let me return to the studies on citations explored earlier, which I tried to use as a way of mapping out the travels of theories and their directionalities. What such analyses, quantitative and qualitative, occlude about citations are the lessons that Roland Barthes and Jacques Derrida taught us and that are foundational for literary critics. According to Barthes, texts are always intertextual, echoing the voices of other texts, which in turn reverberate the voices of other texts and so forth, with no original point of departure. For Derrida discourses are citational, in that speakers are continually saying what has already been said, repeatedly copying and counterfeiting other discourses. Theories are evidently intertextual and citational, that is, they do not necessarily appear in the usual form of a scholarly citation. They are hidden in between the lines of the text or in its margins, in the presuppositions that are not spelled out by the author or in the complex systems of knowledge formations illustrated in the beginning of this chapter. This citationality of theory, residing in the near invisibility of the lower strata of texts, is what needs to be fleshed out—and translated, appropriated, redeployed—in the pages of feminist journals.[22]

Rosi Braidotti (2000), speaking of the export/import of ideas in the transatlantic divide and the commodification of the feminist academic and publishing market, in a Deleuzian vein, argues that a critical perception of the historical embeddedness and empirical embodiment of the concepts with which we work requires transversal alliances among different types of intellectuals, as well as a constant exercise in becoming-polyglots, becoming-transdisciplinary, becoming-nomads.

How can we, from the location/locution of a journal such as *Revista Estudos Feministas*, develop a practice of (cultural) translation/citation that responds simultaneously to local contingencies and to global flows of discourses on gender and feminism? Putting the question in other words, how do we expose the logics of hegemony?

As a present coeditor of the section of *Revista Estudos Feministas* titled "Debates," I and my colleagues have been translating and publishing cutting-edge feminist theoretical articles and inviting responses by feminists from Brazil and other Latin American countries in an attempt to provide a critical reception of the translated texts. Unfortunately, their responses do not travel back due to lack of resources for translation into the academic lingua franca, hence revealing one of the many occult factors that interfere in the practices of cultural translation and the articulation of transnational feminisms. As Emily Apter (2001b) rightly points out, these layers of invisible interventions are, in a very obvious way, crucial for giving a text access to translatability. This is the worldly terrain on which we must continuously and untiringly struggle to theoretically dislocate the sign (Chow 1998a) from the West toward new postcolonial geographies and languages—theoretical or otherwise. Nonetheless, this is a call that, not surprisingly, I am not heeding in this chapter.

Notes

1. The first issue of *Revista Estudos Feministas* came out in 1992. In 1999 I assumed editorship of the journal with anthropologist Miriam Pillar Grossi when it moved from the Federal University of Rio de Janeiro to the Federal University of Santa Catarina in Florianópolis, where I teach. In 2004 I stepped down from the general editorship to coedit the yearly "Debate" section of the journal.

2. This term was coined by Emily Apter (2006), after the notion of "contact zone" explored by Mary Louise Pratt (1992).

3. The writings by Nelly Richard in Chile and Francine Masiello and Jean Franco in the United States are notable exceptions.

4. Scott (2002) stresses that what this picture leaves out is the fact that there are a number of French feminist scholars/activists committed to empirical research and a number of Anglo-American feminists allied with poststructuralism.

5. I am referring to *Cadernos Pagu*, with its editorial home at Universidade Estadual de Campinas/Unicamp, and *Revista Estudos Feministas*, institutionally based at the Federal University of Rio de Janeiro and, from 1999 onward, at the Federal University of Santa Catarina. Both of these pioneering feminist peer-reviewed journals were founded in the early 1990s.

6. Similar concerns were also raised by Jeanne Frances Illo (2005) in her study of academic feminist theorizing in Asia. Maria Dolors Garcia Ramon, Kirsten Simonsen, and Dina Vaiou (2006) also address these issues in their study of the editorial practices in the journal *Gender, Place, and Culture*.

7. This is when I came on board as coeditor of the journal. I remained in this position until 2004. In 2006 I took on, with other two colleagues, the editorship of the journal's annual section, "Debate," where I have been active until now.

8. Because the journal is partly funded by the government through its research council, it is freely distributed to Brazilian university libraries, so institutional subscriptions are very limited.

9. It is indeed revealing of the class and racial structure of the Brazilian academy that only recently did an Afro-Brazilian scholar occupy a position in the chief editorial ranks of *Revista Estudos Feministas*.

10. Beginning in 2006, the journal inaugurated an annual special session, "Debate," with the objective of translating current feminist debates taking place in the global North and inviting respondents from Brazil and Spanish-speaking countries in Latin America to situate these theories vis-à-vis their contexts of reception. Gloria Anzaldúa's "La concienciamestiza" was one of the translated articles that stimulated discussion on race and the coloniality of knowledge in the pages of the journal.

11. In other articles (Costa 1998a, 2000) I explore how Brazilian appropriation/translation of gender has resulted—among other factors, such as the financing of research by the government and international foundations—in a growing depoliticization of feminist studies and the proliferation of research on masculinities (usually predicated on heterosexual men). On the same note, see also Adriana Piscitelli (1998). Of course, a decade later and under the influence and increasing academic visibility of queer studies, this picture has changed considerably.

12. For an illustration of this point, see Maria Luisa Heilborn and Bila Sorj's (1999) account of the formation and institutionalization of gender studies in Brazil. Doing a gender genealogy that has as its point of departure the Anglophone tradition, the authors end up reinscribing a tricky narrative of origin and reaffirming a canonic reading of the Northern trajectories of the concept, which reaches its culminating point—and perhaps the most interesting but unfortunately the least explored in the article—in the theorization of Judith Butler and her subversion of gender as a dichotomous category.

13. See Ella Shohat (2001) and, more recently, the Brazilian debates on narratives of feminism published in *Revista Estudos Feministas* 17, no. 1 (2009) in response to Clare Hemmings's (2005) article on telling feminist stories.

14. See Clare Hemmings (2011) for a politically enlightening analysis of how citation practices secure a dominant story of Western feminism, and for examples of how to deploy citation tactics of de-authorization to "bring into relief the political grammar at the heart of feminist narrative" (164).

15. This analysis was not carried out following any rigorous methodology—as in those studies from a more quantitative perspective—but was a result of ethnographic observations from the privileged position of being a coeditor of the journal for many years.

16. For a discussion of the consolidation of feminist and gender studies in the Brazilian academy, see Ana Alice Costa and Cecilia Sardenberg (1994), Albertina de Oliveira Costa (1996), and my own reflection situating this knowledge formation in relation to the postmodern debate in Latin America (Costa 2000).

17. Christian brings to this discussion the significance of the racial element, that is, how theory not only gains a gender but is always already racialized. For another empirical study of how journals construct scholarly canons, see Bonnie McElhinny (2003).

18. An exception to this list is the field of Brazilian feminist literary criticism, which very early on was under the influence of Lacanian psychoanalysis and Derridean deconstruction, on the one hand, and questions about identity and difference on the other (following the tendencies of Anglophone feminist criticism). For an insightful and historically important account of Brazilian feminist literary criticism, see Heloísa Buarque de Hollanda (1992). A more recent analysis of this field in the past twenty-five years can be found in Cristina Stevens (2010).

19. With a strong community of feminist academics, the Federal University of Santa Catarina has been housing for more than a decade what has become the largest academic feminist conference in the Americas, Fazendo Gênero Seminar. The last meeting of the seminar, in August 2010, gathered more than four thousand feminists, including participants from Latin America, the United States, Europe, and even Japan. No other Brazilian professional association has assembled similar numbers of attendees in its congresses.

20. The predominance of sociology and anthropology is also explained by the fact that these were the disciplines that first introduced feminism in the academy. However, its academic legitimacy came with a price: whereas in the United States feminist academics challenged the basic presuppositions of the scientific canon, Brazilian academics argued for the scientific rigor of feminist knowledge and methodology.

21. See Machado (1997) for a discussion on the structuralist influence in the Brazilian academy, particularly in the field of gender studies.

22. For a clever criticism of conventional studies of citations, see Diana Hicks and Jonathan Potter (1991).

CHAPTER SEVEN/POLITICS OF TRANSLATION IN CONTEMPORARY MEXICAN FEMINISM

MÁRGARA MILLÁN

In this chapter I focus on the analysis of three important feminist publications and publishing circuits that, in my view, play a crucial role in making visible a feminist politics in contemporary Mexico. I am referring to *Fem* (1976), *Debate Feminista* (1990), and *La Correa Feminista* (1991). I emphasize what I call these journals' "translation politics," that is, the concepts of feminism and/or gender they promote in light of the authors and critics they translate, nourishing a political standpoint. In this context, the notion of translation means two things: the choice of theory and authors to be translated, and the way these are aligned with the local political context. By envisioning translation as politics, I argue that this is one way feminist groups make alliances with social movements and political actors. The political moment I focus on to illustrate this is the Zapatista movement in Mexico and feminist representations of indigenous women who participate in the movement.

Constructing the Polyvalence of the Feminist Subject

In what sense is it pertinent to talk about *Mexican feminism*, if we consider feminism to be transnational, universal? I argue that it is essential for contemporary feminism to be able to see its unavoidable placement, its relationship to national and colonial/postcolonial legacies and geopolitics, its belonging to a political culture, as a means of deconstructing its universalistic view of itself.

Feminism has embraced poststructural critique of the universal subject, yet it is also implicated in the modern paradigm of a unitary, universal subject, which constructs its own individual life. This modern paradigm also draws on a belief in progress as evolution, as development and social change with a positivist accent. The subject of feminism has undergone a process of pluralization from one mainstream or hegemonic voice (white European or Anglo-American) to the recognition of class, cultural, and political differences among and between women. Recognizing power relations, subordination, and coloniality among women and constructing dialogues across differences have become theoretical and political necessities for feminism.

Woman as a global tale, a subject anchored merely in sexual difference, gave way to women as the interaction of body/culture/race/age/sexual orientation and other vectors, infusing the concept of gender with multiple meanings. Challenges to "the national" and local feminisms arise from the nation's internal contradictions, and the relationships of hegemony/coloniality among and within nations in the global system, issues that have been signaled by those calling for a multiracial, multicultural, intercultural, or decolonized feminism.

The place of enunciation is essential for a more complex understanding of feminisms and their subject(s). Magazines, journals, and editorial production can be hegemonic places and thus must be considered sites of cultural/political intervention. They bring together groups that enable public discussion of a set of topics while producing frameworks to understand them. Because feminism is a multilocated practice, feminist publications are especially relevant in shaping communication between different kinds of practices, as well as between local and global perspectives. Feminist magazines and journals are privileged sites from which to articulate the complexity of the relationship between feminism and national politics (Biron 1996), between the transnational character of the academic dissemination of theory and its local processes of translation/appropriation/reelaboration. Claudia de Lima Costa (2003) explores the tension between metropolitan theories and their peripheral translations/appropriations. Underlying this is the problem already established in Latin America (and Latino/America): does the South produce theory, or is it merely the inspiring element for the theory of the North? Nelly Richard (2001, cited in Costa 2003) calls attention to the organization of the phenomenon of translation, anchored in a "material-discursive apparatus." Serving as cultural mediators, feminist magazines and journals are part of such apparatuses as translators/disseminators of theories.

In what follows, I provide a brief periodization of the development of Mexican feminism over the past four decades as a basis for analyzing the development of the three publications on which I focus and their role as political translators.

Feminism as Vanguard: From Therapy to Politics

In the 1970s in Mexico, we had the confluence of the world boom of feminism together with the cultural revolution of that decade and the emergence of the guerrilla movements in Latin America as referents for a radical, militant, and avant-garde feminism. The awareness of the need for a movement for women's liberation was often parallel to the left socialist option. At the time, however, the main political parties and leftist groups only partially recognized feminist struggles, often considering feminism as "petit bourgeois" and connecting it— if not subordinating it—to revolutionary political change.

Mexican feminism in the 1970s was clearly fashioned as a vanguard politics, led by radical, middle-class academic and intellectual women seeking emancipation and understanding feminism as a change in their own lives.[1] This required both a consciousness of self, generated in the small group, and public, symbolic, exemplary action. Although political intervention was considered necessary, institutional and state participation was very controversial. The countercultural interventions of the feminism of the time, as well as the condemnation of violence against women and their sexual objectification, were central issues.

A review of the publications of that time clearly illustrates the spirit of the militant Left that nourished Mexican feminism and rapidly spread. They engaged in a dialogue with feminist theory, especially the canonic Simone de Beauvoir and the second wave of Anglo-American feminism, together with the irruption of Afro-American and Chicana interventions. This was localized in Mexican political culture and its specific referents: an authoritarian state that exerted its power through the double-sided coin of repression and cooptation.[2]

There were three main feminist publications in those years: La Revuelta (1976), Cihuat (1977), and Fem (1976). They appeared as a result of the atmosphere created by the official celebration of International Woman's Year in 1975, which favored, on the one hand, the development of a certain kind of feminism based in institutions, called "official feminism," and, on the other hand, the organization of groups of women who identified as independent feminists. Mexican feminism criticized the subordination of women's demands within Left political discourse and of women themselves in the everyday political practice of leftist organizations. Many times, however, they were reproducing within their own feminist groups the authoritarianism and concentration of power they were criticizing on the Left.

Groups of women burned brassieres, protested the celebration of Mother's Day, and demonstrated against the Miss Universe pageant in Mexico City in 1978. They published a series of foundational theoretical writings. Marta Acevedo's article "Women Fight for Their Liberation. Our Dream Is in a Steep Place," published on September 30, 1970, in the cultural supplement of the weekly ¡Siempre!,[3] reviewed the feminist gathering that had taken place in San Francisco that same year. This text had a significant influence on Mexican feminism of that era, making evident the effect of U.S. feminism. The other article, titled "Women's Liberation Here" and published on September 5, 1970, was from the pen of the renowned writer Rosario Castellanos.[4] The piece showed a feminism aware of the women's liberation movements in other countries and concerned with producing theory situated in the national context.

Fem was founded by the renowned Guatemalan art and literary critic Alaíde Foppa, who was disappeared in her own country in 1980, and Margarita García Flores, journalist and chief editor of Los Universitarios, the journal of cultural critique of the National University. They put together a talented team of women writers and artists. Their first issue featured Elena Poniatowska, Elena Urrutia, Margo Glantz, Nancy Cárdenas, and Marta Lamas, among others—women who became the avant-garde of Mexican feminist thought.

Fem is the oldest feminist magazine in Latin America. Its format, like its contents, defined it from the beginning as a magazine addressing a broad readership, with a poetic-literary leaning, cultural analysis, and reviews of films, theater, and such. Its editorial policy was inclusive, opening space for writing by men, such as Carlos Monsiváis and Tomás Mojarro, among others. It published essays by Latin American women as well as a few translations as leading articles.

The newspaper La Revuelta, by contrast, was produced by young activist women with a radical and social feminist perspective. Its theoretical approach was rooted in a basic principle of feminism: the personal is political. A small group produced the material for the articles published. Distributed outside factories, La Revuelta was an effort by an erudite middle-class feminism to get beyond their own experiences and become involved with social struggles. The Collective La Revuelta published nine issues between 1976 and 1978 and then began collaboration with the newspaper Unomásuno, which lasted until 1982.

Cihuat was a political bulletin published by the Coalición de Mujeres Feministas (Feminist Women's Coalition), which repeatedly denounced the situation of oppression and exploitation of Mexican women and sought to persuade women to form part of the feminist struggle. There were only six issues; the last appeared in 1978.

Fem has been an ongoing and consistent nucleus of Latin American cultural criticism, which survived until 2005 in paper edition. During its first fifteen years, it brought together a large group of women's voices. Because of the length of its publishing life, it offers a broad and ambitious vision of feminism in Latin America. Polyvalent, it maintains a clear political definition without being affiliated with a specific group and a theoretical orientation without locking itself in the academic world. The magazine maintains relations with women authors and feminist movements of its time. It publishes few translations and focuses more on unpublished original essays, including a large number of personal testimonies and interviews. *Fem* has also translated feminist texts that have left their mark on contemporary cultural criticism, like its issue on Chicanas in 1984, with a text by Cherríe Moraga and a text by Italian post-structuralist feminist theorist Rosi Braidotti in 1985.

The 1970s was also a time of great politicization in Mexico: the ascent of independent social movements — critics of state corporatism — and the emergence of military challenges from armed guerrillas. The feminist movement of those times was discussing its relationship to leftist groups and the "wider popular movement" of women. In this process of feminist self-definition, there were two somewhat contradictory developments: the shift away from one's own immediate experience, moving the personal to the terrain of politics, and the effort to legitimate feminism in institutional terms.

The "subject" of this feminism was thus constructed on various fronts: the small group, partisan militancy, the struggles of the independent union movement, the academic world, the mass media, the art world, and the institutional sphere. A multiplicity of groups and people were opening spaces, doing the hard, subterranean work, which became the basis for cultural transformation in the long run.

The interaction between the global and the local was clear in this decade. Many testimonials refer to the organizing impetus provided by the first of four UN women's conferences, held in Mexico City in 1975. Official institutional spaces and antiestablishment independent ones were opening, all disputing the same constituency, that of "women."

The local referents of Mexican feminism in the 1970s were multiple. First, there was the Left, which did not take on feminism as a central aspect of its project and which viewed women as a subordinate "sector" in the strategic struggle. Second, there was the authoritarian state, which also treated women as a sector, imposing the discourse of development and assigning gender tasks on behalf of the nation, thus constructing gender: family, reproduction, moral values. Finally, feminism walked hand in hand with the lesbian and gay movement, which emerged in the following decade as an autonomous movement in an often-conflicting dialogue with heterosexual feminism.

The authoritarian Mexican state developed a political system that was nourished by revolutionary and populist discourse, hegemonizing the historical and symbolic process of the Mexican Revolution to define the mestizo nation, excluding anything that did not fit with the "institutional revolutionary" project of development. Facing such a state, Mexican feminists decided (just as their counterparts on the Left did) to define their movement as independent of formal political institutions. At the same time, feminism declared its autonomy of the leftist political parties, with the possible exception of Trotskyism, which was also marginal within the Left. Feminist groups, like leftist ones, divided and rearticulated themselves in relationship to the state, prefiguring the differences between the official and independent, institutional and autonomous feminist movements. Later on, these debates became even more complex, with the spread of international funding and the proliferation of nongovernmental organizations (NGOs) in the 1990s.

Feminism as Politics

Over the past two decades, Mexican feminism transformed current policies at the federal and state levels, constructing a strategy of alliances for its public interventions. Particularly in the 1980s, what we observe is a significant organization of women through civil associations and NGOs. In both urban and peasant rural contexts, women acquired visibility, expressing specific demands within the organizations of unionized women. Women in the education field, maquila workers, domestic workers, and those belonging to the popular urban movement all discussed and articulated their standpoints while working against violence and for health benefits. A plural subject of feminism became visible through the organization of women in these diverse locations, at the same time that NGOs emerged as a new expression of feminism.

The strategies of alliances and the relationship to political participation were also modified in the 1980s: the national women's movement demanded that the state participate by assisting female victims of sexual and domestic violence. The Center for Guidance and Support for Rape Victims was created in 1987. As a result, organized women in public institutions started to open spaces for the development of policies relevant to women. Feminism moved from vanguard positions to social responsibility actions, negotiating with the state for spaces and broadening feminism's political arena. The 1985 earthquake and the civil social mobilization that followed promoted women's organization. The seamstresses' movement had a very strong effect on women's and feminist organizations. A group of feminists advised and supported the seamstresses' legal and union struggles.[5] In the words of Marta Lamas, the need for a new form of doing politics was evident (Lamas 1986a).[6] Not only was society organized from below, but feminist demands took form in the state. The presidential elections of 1988 were another milestone in the organization of civil society: the electoral fraud carried out by the Partido Revolucionario Institucional, which brought Carlos Salinas de Gortari to power in the face of a citizens' movement around opposition candidate Cuauhtémoc Cárdenas Solórzano, had consequences in terms of citizen consciousness. Salinas de Gortari began his term appropriating the word that marked civil organization in the wake of the 1985 earthquake: *solidarity*. This regime implemented neoliberalism—what it called "social neoliberalism"—decisively, promoting deregulation of working conditions and threats to the land of the *ejidos*, even while launching social programs. Of course, women were part of social programs like Mujeres en Solidaridad (Women in Solidarity) of the Programa Nacional de Solidaridad (PRONASOL), which was the official program for social development during the Salinismo period.[7] The NGOization of feminism (Alvarez 1998c) and civil society in general became more widespread during the next decade of the 1990s, but only because of what had begun in the 1980s. Poverty, citizenship, equality, legal advice, and civil rights were added to the issues of violence and health already on the feminist agenda.

Feminist activism during the 1990s showed growing complexity: there were conferences for the valorization of domestic labor, but also campaigns like Taking Back Spaces, Access to Justice for Women, and the founding in 1999 of the first feminist political association, DIVERSA, which requested its electoral register as a political party.[8] The Law for Assistance and Prevention of Family Violence was implemented in 1997; in 1999 the Instituto de la Mujer (Institute of Women's Affairs) for the Mexico City government was founded; in 2000, the First National Consultation on Women's Rights was launched. NGOization emerged along with the transnationalization of feminism, as analyzed by Sonia Alvarez (1998c), who argues that the field of action for organized feminism in NGOs and participation in the institutional settings of politics, such as parties, states, and multilateral organisms, helped put gender on the global agenda. After the NGO boom, however, critique followed. Analysts pointed to the dangers of local feminist agendas being made to fit the requirements of the global agenda via funding priorities of international agencies. Moreover, the distance between the global and local becomes visible, as Alvarez states: "the decentering of the Latin American feminist field" in the 1990s "was accompanied by an intensification of power imbalances among women" (Alvarez 1998c, 317).

The 1990s were also the period of discursive hegemony of gender studies in the academy and of the gender perspective in politics. But the event of the 1990s for Mexico, and somehow the world, was the Zapatista uprising. After 1989 and the fall of socialism, 1994 in Mexico was the aftermath of conservative neoliberal politics: a disoriented Left without alternative programs and disillusionment of civil society movements accompanied Salinismo's "social neoliberalism." Earlier critics of the Mexican state were captivated by the personality of Salinas.[9] The Mexican feminist movement was not excluded from the general disorientation of the Left or from its dispiritedness after the electoral fraud of 1988 and in the face of the corrosive action of the Salinista state.

A new phenomenon seems to develop in these years, accompanying the emergence of the Zapatista movement, that defies dualistic notions like theoretical feminism and popular feminism and leads to more complex discussions within feminism and among feminist groups from different political tendencies. The practices of feminist NGOs in rural Mexico have followed two paths: one dominated by the aim of bringing "development" to the rural and poor areas, which are also the indigenous regions, and the other seeking to break through the class and cultural barriers separating mestiza from indigenous women, and redefining, up to a certain point, the meaning of mestiza feminism. Whereas the first tendency takes an assimilationist approach to poor and indigenous women, the second starts to recognize cultural differences and the critique of the capitalist model implicit in indigenous cultural forms.

Feminist Magazines from the 1990s

In 1986, a group of feminists summoned by Marta Lamas presented a proposal to the newspaper La Jornada, with the intention of creating a supplement that would be a vehicle for debate within feminism as well as for bringing feminism to the rest of society. The newspaper took on the project, but as it was being set up, differences arose between a more journalistic faction and a more intellectual one. In the end, the supplement maintained an informational profile. In March 1990, an independent magazine, Debate Feminista, was launched with a more critical, intellectual perspective.

Debate Feminista is, by far, the most important theoretical journal of Mexican feminism. Building on the previous experience of its editor, anthropologist and activist Marta Lamas, Debate Feminista became the main translator of feminist theory produced in English, French, and Italian. Lamas had already published an important article in the academic journal Nueva Antropología, in 1986, along with a translation of the influential text by Gayle Rubin (1978), "The Traffic in Women: Notes on the 'Political Economy' of Sex."

Debate Feminista appears twice a year as a booklike publication of some three hundred pages, which presents state-of-the-art monographic essays on feminist topics. In the issues published during the two decades since its founding, the journal has consolidated a theoretical profile that seeks to foster open reflections on certain local and transnational issues: democracy, otherness, law, body and subject, cities, writing, politics, and queerness, among others.

Debate Feminista was the journal that introduced contemporary feminist authors from abroad—such as Teresa de Lauretis, Judith Butler, Adriana Cavarero, Lia Cigarini, Nancy Fraser, Julia Kristeva, Gayatri Spivak, and Luce Irigaray—to academia and the leadership of the movement. It presents an open structure in the sense of constantly offering a space "from another place," dedicated to views that are not always openly feminist, and publishing some male authors in most of its issues.

It maintains an organized yet flexible structure, leaving room for sections such as "From the Couch," reflecting the interest in a psychoanalytical perspective. Some texts that appear in "From the Left," "From the Everyday," or "From Another Place," provide a space for interviews, testimonials, or denunciations. There is a space for photography, called "From the Glance," another called the *"Argüende"* (Mexican expression for gossip and/or argument), and a space traditionally dedicated to political satire edited by Jesusa Rodríguez and Liliana Felipe, directors (until 2004) of an important lesbian critical cultural theater named El Hábito and renowned Left activists. All this accompanies the "hard nucleus" of the journal, which organizes texts around a selected subject matter in every issue.

We could characterize *Debate Feminista* as a journal of intellectual feminism, which addresses a strongly theoretically informed audience, already "initiated" into feminism; in political terms, it takes a liberal Left perspective. The activism of its editor, Marta Lamas, has centered on reproductive rights, the legalization of abortion, and advocacy for a secular state. She is also the director of the Information Group on Reproductive Choice.

For its part, *La Correa Feminista*, created in 1991, brought together a radical and autonomous feminism around the journalists Ximena Bedregal and Rosa Rojas. It was published by CICAM (Center for Research and Training of Women). The original objective of CICAM was to constitute a kind of chain or belt, as the name *Correa* implies, made up of feminisms existing in the different states of the country, which resist the centralization of information in the nation's capital.

Correa Feminista's nineteenth issue, for fall and winter 1998, was a self-assessment. In that issue, they revisited their original desire and the contradictions of positing an autonomous and radical kind of feminism that recognized "social needs" to broaden democracy and opposed the efforts of the state to make functional its neoliberal project by "incorporating aspects of the demands that feminism had developed" ("7 years of *La Correa Feminista*"). *La Correa* reestablished its project in 1998 after asserting that "Mexican women" is not a homogeneous collective and moreover, that it contains irreconcilable positions, by stating that "the voice of the majority sectors with more material and economic power, tended toward the practice of silencing discrepant voices." In this issue CICAM announced the advent of *Creatividad Feminista* (Feminist Creativity), published online. The themes in the following issues centered on feminism and politics, democracy, war, autonomy, and development. The e-magazine joined a sector of Chilean feminism represented by the writer Margarita Pisano, first calling themselves the *feministas cómplices* and later identifying with a broader "current" of the movement of self-proclaimed "autonomous feminists."[10] This site gave life to a new cybernetic project, Mamametal, driven more toward artist expression, mainly through photographs and videos.

Fem continued to appear regularly throughout the 1990s, representing what Lamas called *mujerismo* (or "womanism"), committed to feminist writing, interviews, and documenting women's movements and publishing women's literature and poetry.

To complete this panorama of forces and feminisms, we should also trace the trajectory of *La Doble Jornada*, the feminist supplement to Mexico's leading leftist newspaper, *La Jornada*. From 1986 until 1998, *La Doble Jornada* (Double Workday) was led by Sara Lovera. During this time, it circulated widely, fulfilling its mission as a space for women's networking. Beginning in 1998, the supplement became *Triple Jornada* (or Triple Workday), under the editorship of Ximena Bedregal and Rosa Rojas, both from *La Correa*'s team.

The transition from the 1970s to the 1990s is marked by the multiplication of social movements and the growth of civil society; the proliferation of NGOs working with peasant, working-class, and indigenous women; the destructuring of the classic leftist paradigm; the end of "actually existing socialism," the cold war, and guerrilla warfare as a means to confront state power. The preoccupation with democracy grew after the electoral process of 1988. The relationship with the state and political institutions became one of the most controversial issues within social movements, including feminism.

Zapatismo and the Difficulty of Mexican Feminisms in Dealing with Indigeneity

The Zapatista movement, which emerged dramatically onto the national and global stage in an armed uprising on January 1, 1994, questioned the whole notion of an independent and mestizo nation and nourished critical and leftist discourses. The uprising provoked different reactions and opinions. While other political currents on the Left were endorsing and recognizing the Ejercito Zapatista de Liberación Nacional (EZLN, the Zapatista National Liberation Army), Zapatismo opened a controversial space for Mexican feminism. Although the movement could not avoid recognizing the importance of the emblematic actions of indigenous Zapatismo—like the Women's Revolutionary Law, the presence of women commanders (*comandantas*), and the progressive words of the insurgents, feminists questioned the articulation of indigenous women's voices and the discourse around indigenous women, especially because of the central male figure and spokesperson of the rebellion, Subcomandante Marcos.

The reception/discussion that Zapatismo generated in the different fields of Mexican feminism has provided a key horizon of visibility for indigenous women. I only consider *La Correa Feminista* and *Debate Feminista*, because these two publications generated the most writings about feminism and its relationship to Zapatismo, whereas *Fem* continued with a policy of presenting the voices of the women in the movement. *La Correa Feminista* published a compilation of materials and position papers in a volume titled *Chiapas: and what about the women?* in December 1994. That first volume already proposed an agenda for an "autonomous feminism": opposition to violence against women, advocacy of the decriminalization of abortion, and the insertion of indigenous women in the debate around political and territorial autonomies. However, in the introduction to the issue by Rosa Rojas (1994) and in Ximena Bedregal's article (titled "Chiapas, reflections from our feminism"), the editorial group assumes a critical position toward the Zapatista insurgency, particularly in relation to the EZLN's "Revolutionary Women's Law," issued publicly on the first day of the uprising and heralded by many, locally and globally, as an unprecedented proclamation of indigenous women's rights.

Based on considerations of principle, *La Correa* declares that feminism is a pacifist movement, which cannot support a project that "liberates" through a military approach, given that such structures are in themselves patriarchal, vertical, and authoritarian. Feminism must question the war machine and its patriarchal logic, as illustrated by the guerrilla in Central and South America. The magazine distinguishes the feminist critique of violence from that made by conservatives and liberals, arguing that the latter is hypocritical because it recognizes the violence in the other but not in its own logic (the violence embedded in the state). The discourse and practice of the Zapatistas "strengthens the idea that violence can only be fought with violence and that it is valid if it comes from the forsaken, the dispossessed, the oppressed" (Bedregal 1995, 47).

They also take distance from the Women's Revolutionary Law because it falls short in terms of their feminist goals.

It gives no guarantee of the subversion of the patriarchal order that prevails in the communities of the Zapatista territory, in Chiapas and the rest of the country. It will not be more than a partial declaration of good intentions, as long as women remain as second class humans, precluded by masculine authoritarianism—which women also help reproduce—from being owners of their bodies, . . . as long as their wishes for a good life remain a secondary issue for some future point in time, as long as they are not the real owners, materially, politically, socially and symbolically, of their lives, as long as their voice is not a vertebral element in the construction of daily life. (Bedregal 1995, xi)

Further ahead in the text:

In general terms it is evident that it is not feminist in as much as it only proposes a few claims for women and not a proposal for community based on the experience of the feminine, critical and conscious, criticized and reconstructed. . . . From our occidental and enlightened urban perspective, if indigenous women are generally invisible, and with the barrier of war they are directly inaccessible, it is practically impossible to know if [the Revolutionary Women's] law is a real product of a women's process opposing patriarchal and violent customs, or if it is a product of the leaders facing the need to incorporate women into traditionally male tasks and/or to give the idea of a larger democracy. (Bedregal 1995, 54–55)

Were women the ones who promoted the law, or was it a strategy of the male and patriarchal leadership? Women are left trapped in this nonvisibility that causes them to be represented as victims.

However, Bedregal notes that there are certain analogies that bring together "critical feminism" and the rebellious movement. The first one is the analogy between "natives" (*Indios*) and "women," both rendered invisible and marginal in dominant discourses. The second convergence appears in the "particular" aspects of the Zapatista discourse, when revealing the fallacy of the neoliberal model and its promises and, above all, by claiming the validity of rebellion, which "has installed hope for difference and diversity, [e]lements that should be, for feminists, nourishment for their imaginations" (Bedregal 1995, 49).

The editorial values other dimensions of the EZLN, such as the fact that its leaders recognize that they are talking from a specific location, without pretending to impose one "truth" for all. The wisdom present in the communiqués by both the Indigenous Revolutionary Clandestine Committee and Subcomandante Marcos is praised by its successful communication strategies, which feminists have not yet developed. A second volume on *Chiapas ¿and what about the women?*, published in December 1995, offered an account of the political climate and the great civil society mobilization following the Mexican army's February incursion into the Zapatista zone, searching for the Subcomandante. The invasion destroyed a series of communities, cut off communication with the area for over a month, and drove the population to seek refuge in the mountains. This was the second great military offensive[11] after the first twelve days of open war following the onset of the rebellion. The organized local mestiza women's movement in Chiapas was very active during this period. In February 1995, the First National Women's Convention was held. The State Women's Convention in Chiapas had occurred seven months earlier, in July 1994. The course of the Zapatista movement in 1995 and 1996 was toward a reform of the Mexican state. Women's issues were on their agenda. In the mesas of San Andres there were several topics: indigenous rights and culture, democracy and justice, well-being and development, Chiapas conciliation, and women's rights in Chiapas. In this discussion, some mestiza feminists were invited, and during the Zapatistas National Consultation for Peace and Democracy in August 1995 a specific question was included concerning women's political participation—the "sixth question." This was a result of a demand made by feminist anthropologist and activist Marcela Lagarde.

The second volume features a reaction to *La Correa*'s position on autonomous feminism vis-à-vis Zapatismo from Mercedes Olivera (1995) titled "Feminist Practice in the Zapatista National Liberation Movement," and a response by Bedregal titled "A Dialogue with Mercedes Olivera: Memory and Utopia in Feminist Practice." The first is a vision from Chiapas that analyzes the organizational environment around Zapatismo and the progress achieved within Zapatismo in relation to indigenous women's participation and the recognition of their voices and labor, as well as the advances represented by the mobilization against the colonial model imposed on both indigenous men and women. For Olivera, inside Zapatismo and its context, "the possibility of turning feminism into a larger social practice" (Bedregal 1995, 176) is at stake: "We feminists . . . who have worked in Chiapas value the progress obtained by women in deconstructing and reconstructing their identities as indigenous women and poor peasants" (Bedregal 1995, 177).

Differentiated shades of feminism began to emerge. On one side, we have a feminism that is urban and radical yet sectarian and dogmatic, paradoxically interested in feminism of difference, yet uninterested in the differences among women themselves, a sisterhood of patriarchy's radical criticism. On the other side, a "peasant" feminism gains a sharper profile, identifying with the denied culture of forbidden diversity, that of indigenous ethnic groups, and concerned with the issue of identities. The latter, even though it recognized patriarchal structures, prioritized "the practice of a broader feminism," making indigenous women visible as subjects with social agency: "In any case, they themselves (the Indigenous women) will be the ones to decide whether to promote or not the feminist character of their organizations and their movement" (Olivera 1995, 184).

Bedregal's response reaffirms the criticism of armed action, even when coming from the poor. In effect, she prioritizes a radical and radicalizing (liberal) subject, over other ways of building agency and self-validation, including indigenous ones.

Debate Feminista as an editorial group declared its position on the Zapatista movement in its editorial section in issue number 9, March 1994: "When the war exploded in Chiapas, many of us asked ourselves what the feminist perspective was on the conflict. There were those who felt sympathy for the movement, but felt conflicted by their pacifist inclinations; those who were more concerned about the situation of the women in Chiapas who were being displaced by the conflict; those who were more worried about the risk to the democratic project; those who were enthusiastic about the Women's Law, and those who were worried by the political strength of the Catholic Church within the Zapatista movement." The editorial also mentions that those who traveled to Chiapas were able to check, after talking to local feminists, that "one thing was the idealizing *chilanga* [meaning from Mexico City] view and another the harsh social reality." The existence of internal divisions, the rejection of many communities toward the armed path, the patriarchal and authoritarian attitudes of the Catholic Church and of some members of the Zapatista army all spoke of a messianic posture that was the opposite of "the work of the masses."

In this issue, *Debate Feminista* published the Women's Revolutionary Law with a fragment of Subcomandante Marcos's letter in which he refers to the way the law was elaborated in March 1993; it also published a document sent by the San Cristóbal Women's group on reproductive rights. The editorial in *Debate Feminista* exposed here one of the main points of the group's feminist political agenda: the criticism of a religious conception of maternity, wherein a woman's body is considered a "divine instrument" and "from the moment of conception, the human being in formation has complete autonomy from the mother." Regarding this, *Debate Feminista* highlighted the secular tradition of the Mexican state. By publishing the whole text of the "Pastoral Document on Abortion," written by Don Samuel Ruiz, and an article of Michel Bovero on secular thought, the editorial emphasized the journal's democratic secular affiliation, pointing to a critical tension with Zapatismo.

In issue number 24 (October 2001), seven years later, we find the result of the reflection provoked among a sector of Mexican feminism by the indigenous uprising and its meanings. "Racism and Mestizaje" is the title of the issue, presenting a special section with various articles that question racism in Mexico and its role in the construction of the nation. Articles like Ruiz's, "The Pretty India: Nation, Race and Gender in Revolutionary Mexico," and Marisa Belausteguigoitia's, "Without Face and without Tongue, Body and Language at the Threshold of the Nation," explored nationalism and the construction of the indigenous feminine. The volume gathered several articles on Zapatismo, included poetry in the Tseltal and Tzotzil languages, Comandanta Esther's intervention at the Mexican parliament, and a photographic testimonial.

In Rosalva Aída Hernández Castillo's article, "Indigenous Women and Their Gender Demands, between Feminist Ethnocentrism and Ethnic Essentialism," we find a critical stance toward Mexican feminism for its ethnocentrism. For Hernández Castillo, the main point is the articulation of indigenous women on gender-related demands, together with the demands for autonomy of their pueblos, "as a struggle with many fronts," in which "hegemonic feminism" does not build bridges. She defines "hegemonic feminism" as one that "emerged in the center of the country, and was theorized from academia where the struggle in favor of abortion rights and women's reproductive rights has been central" (Hernández Castillo 2001, 207n4). The "centering" of this hegemonic feminism impeded it from building bridges with religious sectors that have been reflecting on women's issues and organizing them based on their social conditions. The result was an exclusionary hegemonic feminist agenda that privileges the demands of the educated urban experience and is linked to a notion of individual rights that doesn't attend to the idea—maybe forever lost—of community.

Marta Lamas and Subcomandante Marcos had exchanged letters about the legalization of abortion, published in La Jornada, on April 29 and May 11, 1994. The discussion occurred because of an alleged demand by the EZLN that abortion would be criminalized in the reform of the penal code in Chiapas. Lamas pointed out that decriminalizing abortion was a central question in a truly democratic project, in the sense of "the respect towards plurality and individual guarantees" (Lamas 1994, 141). She also clarified that in our countries, women with economic means can have sanitary abortions, whereas poor women have to resort to interrupting their pregnancy in ways that put them at high risk of death, which means that the "individual guarantees" are delimited by one belonging to a certain social class. On May 11, 1994, Marcos denied that the EZLN was asking for the criminalization of abortion or the reformulation of the penal code, and he transcribed the twenty-seventh item in the EZLN's demands, where what was being asked was "To remove the Penal Code from the State of Chiapas because it doesn't allow us to organize ourselves, except with weapons."

In his response, Subcomandante Marcos made an affirmation that he repeated in a number of communiqués: the idea that the Women's Law was imposed by the Zapatista women within the EZLN, the idea that the changes that women were making were happening "in spite of the newspapers, churches, penal codes and, it is fair to recognize, our own resistance as males to be thrown from the comfortable space of domination, which we've inherited" (Subcomandante Marcos in Rojas 1994, 145). Finally, in postscript style, there are some strong affirmations: that indigenous women have abortions and not by their own choice but because of chronic malnutrition; that they are not asking for abortion clinics because they don't even have childbirth clinics; and that "carrying firewood up the hills is something that no penal code considers" (Subcomandante Marcos in Rojas 1994, 145).

This polemic around abortion rights took shape again years later, between December 2002 and January 2003, from issues number 1362 to 1367 of the weekly *Proceso*, an independent and critical political journal. In this polemic, renowned critic Carlos Monsiváis and Marta Lamas spoke from one side, and the poet Javier Sicilia, the intellectual and communitarian theorist Gustavo Esteva, and the feminist activist and specialist on Meso-American religious culture Sylvia Marcos spoke from the other.[12] The controversy started with Monsiváis's article titled "On Bishops and Social Geology" (*Proceso* no. 1362, December 2002), written in reaction to the bishops' "recommendation" after the declaration of the First Summit of Indigenous Women from the Americas. The recommendation was not to use the word *gender* because indigenous women would consider it "external" to their culture.

The discussion revolved around reproductive rights. In *Proceso* (no. 1366, January 5, 2003, 59), Lamas defined her position as "In this debate about gender, which is also about essentialism, it would be interesting to enter and define the contours of this fair and free world we think possible, which for me, is not the world from the past nor the one from the present. It is a world that recognizes sexual differences without imposing false complementarities and that favors the development of human potentialities. . . . In a utopia of a world without economic exploitation, sexual and reproductive rights are a fundamental axis." From a Christian viewpoint critical of modernity, Sicilia (2003) approached gender as a vernacular ordinance, versus the modern ordinance, where "the Roman right is the only measure of it all." The vernacular orders the human universe in a proportional manner, through a guide that moderates man's actions in of the face of physical and human nature: "This proportion implies, among many other things, the understanding of maternity as a gift, not as a right." For Sicilia, the loss of such proportionality occurs when social (capitalist) development is centered on the economic as the absolute value, "where human beings have evicted sacred order from their lives," and there the modern debate on reproductive rights is generated.

Sylvia Marcos intervened in *Proceso* no. 1365 to point out the importance of listening to what the indigenous women were saying, from their spiritual and practical location, quoting María Estela Jocón, a Mayan from Guatemala, who states: "What is understood [or 'what we understand'] from the practice of a gender[ed] approach is a respectful relationship . . . of balance, equilibrium— what in the West would be called equality" (2002). For Sylvia Marcos: "The concern is that the feminist discourse, located in the urban elite, acts as a colonizing and 'involuntarily' hegemonic element" (2002). For Sicilia, women "have all the right to defend . . . their reproductive rights and apply them in their bodies, what they have no right to do is to erect them as a supreme value for women that is why I've said that [Lamas's] discourse is colonialist, as it pretends to make the indigenous women say what they never said" (Sicilia 2003, 59).

These debates refer us to a pressing need among diverse feminisms in Mexico: to develop a position dealing with indigenous women outside "*indigenismo*," the paternalistic and colonialist discourse toward the indigenous that the Mexican state developed in the twentieth century. Leaving behind indigenismo implies a series of theoretical destabilizations of feminism as a critical apparatus. As a condition of openness to the diversity of the feminine and feminist subject, part of the process is to decolonize our own assumptions. This observation is an appeal to recognize that class and ethnic segregation by the Mexican state through nationalism/indigenismo has created great divisions among women. These divisions are shifting and redefining themselves. Indigenous women's voices are already being heard in other spaces, the ones that the local and international feminist Zapatista movement has been opening—fields of enunciation for a voice of their own. By "their own" I do not mean untouched by various discourses. Precisely the opposite—a voice that appropriates a multiplicity of discourses so as to *be in the world*, and *make the world be born*, yet not necessarily coinciding with mainstream feminism's political agenda, but generating its own agenda, anchored in indigenous life experience and cultural and cosmogonic horizons.

Debates surrounding neo-Zapatismo elucidate the located meanings of *emancipation* for indigenous women, destabilizing univocal and universalistic claims of "women's liberation." These are other kinds of translations, transits between cultures and cosmogonic belongings. The debates do not abdicate such concepts but fill them with diverse, localized, and useful content for a concrete subject. As a whole, indigenous Zapatismo revealed to Mexican mainstream feminism a vision of indigenous women less attached to silences and shadows, casting them as more political players, whole and differential subjects, conscious of identity politics. The debates around Zapatismo provoked within hegemonic feminism a broader self-reflection in the nation's classist and racist mirror. The nation appears as an object of feminist critique, not exhausted in its characterization as "patriarchal," and instead recognizing the complex heteroglossia that constitutes it and of which we women, white and of color, are part. Most important, in this intercultural dialogue, mainstream feminism has turned to look at itself, expanding the borders of its own self-imposed location, thus advancing toward a more inclusive and plurivocal conviviality.

Notes

1. We must mention four women's organizations: Mujeres en Acción Solidaria (MAS, 1970), Movimiento Nacional de Mujeres (MNM, 1973), Colectivo La Revuelta (1975), and Cihuat (1977), called the "seed groups," as they were spreading the feminist seed within social movements.

2. Mexico was at the end of a political crisis after the 1968 student movement, toward which the state's reaction had been brutal. The Partido Revolucionario Institucional had been in power for fifty years. The institutionalization of the Mexican revolution made it possible for a nationalist and revolutionary rhetoric to coexist with repressive and authoritarian practice. During Luis Echeverría's six-year term as president, he tried to reconfigure the political scene through a "democratic opening," which was characterized by a method that combined cooptation with repression of the opposition.

3. The magazine *¡Siempre!*, edited by the journalist José Pages Llergo, was one of the most important spaces for information and opinion in those years (1960–80). Its cultural supplement, called *La Cultura en México*, was edited by Carlos Monsiváis, an intellectual sensitive to the feminist and lesbian movements. It was a cultural supplement that disseminated the best of national and international cultural criticism. In the authoritarian and presidentialist environment of Mexico from 1960 to 1980, this supplement was a breath of fresh air.

4. Rosario Castellanos, "Liberacion de la Mujer aquí," *Excelsior*, September 5, 1970, cited in Ludec (1999).

5. In 1987, the state of Guerrero established the first Ministry of Women's Affairs in the country. In 1989, the Mexican state created the Specialized Agencies on Sexual Crimes and the Center for Support of Victims of Sexual Violence.

6. See Patricia Ravelo Blancas, "Protagonismo y Poder: El sindicato de costureras 19 de septiembre," http://www.juridicas.unam.mx/publica/librev/rev/nuant/cont/49/cnt/cnt1.pdf.

7. *Salinismo* refers to Carlos Salinas de Gortari's six-year presidency. Salinas "won" the 1988 elections against Cuauhtémoc Cárdenas through electoral fraud. His government applied a strong neoliberal policy, called social neoliberalism. An important part of these social politics were expressed through PRONASOL, and in the countryside, PROCAMPO and PROGRESA, where specific social welfare programs were developed for peasant women.

8. This was an antecedent of the first feminist political party, México Posible, led by Patricia Mercado.

9. *Nexos* magazine is the product of a group of progressive intellectuals who move to the right as they coincide with the policies of Salinismo. Among them was Héctor Aguilar Camin. In that period, the magazine *Vuelta*, founded by Octavio Paz and long considered more center-right than *Nexos*, was still being published. *Vuelta* ceased publication after Paz's death in 1998. The editorial project that succeeded it is *Letras Libres*, edited by the historian Enrique Krauze.

10. In the 1970s and 1980s, the tension between official and independent feminism was expressed above all in relation to participation in the state; in the 1990s, the tension between autonomous and institutional feminism emerged above all in the feminist Encuentros, in which the autonomous feminists critiqued the funding of NGOs and the role of these institutions in determining feminist agendas.

11. The first military offensive, in January 1994, followed the uprising and lasted twelve days; the second was the one launched in February 1995 by Ernesto Zedillo, after publicizing the identity of Subcomandante Marcos in a televised event in which Subcomandante Marcos "was unmasked." See the interesting essay by Michael Taussig (1999) about the metaphor of unmasking the Subcomandante.

12. To follow the whole polemic, see Lamas (2002, 2003), Monsiváis (2002a, 2002b), Sicilia (2002a, 2002b, 2003), Esteva (2002, 2003), and Marcos (2002).

CHAPTER EIGHT/BODIES IN TRANSLATION/HEALTH PROMOTION IN INDIGENOUS MEXICAN MIGRANT COMMUNITIES IN CALIFORNIA

REBECCA J. HESTER

> Health promotion is not apolitical, rather it is
> an explicitly, politically orientated activity.
> —Theodore H. Macdonald, *Rethinking Health Promotion*

In her essay "The Politics of Location as Transnational Feminist Critical Practice," Caren Kaplan (1994) suggests that "in a transnational world where cultural asymmetries and linkages continue to be mystified by economic and political interests at multiple levels, feminists need detailed, historicized maps of the circuits of power" (148). Building on her suggestion, in this chapter I track two moving subjects as they intersect, produce, and reproduce each other. The first is the theory of health promotion, which is currently driving global, national, and local health agendas. The second is the female indigenous migrant population from Oaxaca, Mexico, who participates in health promotion programs in California.

I focus on the ways women's understandings of their bodies and their selves are informed at the interface of a global health agenda and translocal social forces, both of which propose to secure women's well-being, albeit through very different and often competing strategies. As transnational subjects "in translation" between Mexican and U.S. norms, indigenous Mexican women in California must negotiate the political, economic, cultural, and social forces which at once undermine their health while also actively promoting it so they can continue to be/have healthy (re)productive bodies. If, as feminist scholars have argued, the body is a discursive construction, then the goal of this essay is to show the way women's bodies are written by and through the forces with which they engage in their daily lives (Price and Shildrick 1999).

As Janet Price and Margaret Shildrick (1999, 7) point out, "to say that the body is a discursive construction is not to deny a substantial corpus, but to insist that our apprehension of it, our understanding of it, is necessarily mediated by the contexts in which we speak." Insofar as the context provides the terms and terrain for action, women respond to and through the discourses they encounter in a particular physical (geographic and corporeal) location. Mindful of this, I begin by tracing the global emergence of health promotion as a discursive construct informing local spaces for action (Velasco Ortiz 2004) for indigenous women in California. I caution against the uncritical adoption of this health strategy for indigenous Mexican migrant women because of the epistemological baggage it brings with it.

In the second section, I discuss the extent to which Triqui and Mixtec migrant women are not only written by the health discourses they encounter but become agents in that writing. I argue that it is in their responsiveness to the forces they encounter in a rural California town that indigenous women express their agency, and through it their understanding of their "bodies" and their "selves" is produced. Understanding women's embodied experiences as interactive and processual provides a lens through which to conceptualize women's agency in terms that do not set up an oversimplified or overdetermined binary of acceptance of/resistance to the forces they confront, while at the same time it points to the historical, social, economic, and cultural disciplines through which their subject formation takes place. This has particular relevance to migrant populations, who are often "essentialized" and whose subject formation is perceived to be not only pathological but also static and unchangeable.

This research is informed by the idea that women's bodies are a key site for the negotiation of power relations in "modern" society. As such, they are inherently political. In a note taken from the Diálogos Feministas at the World Social Forum, Virgina Vargas describes how women's bodies are transformed into symbolic expressions of power relations: "Conscious, as feminists, that our bodies are full of cultural and social meanings, we also see that women's bodies are key places where many political and moral battles are waged. It is through the bodies of women that the community, the State, the family, the fundamentalist forces (state and non-state), religions, and the Market seek to define themselves. These forces and institutions, through a plethora of patriarchal controls, transform women's bodies into expressions of power relations" (Vargas 2006, 35). In addition to the forces Vargas outlines, indigenous Mexican migrant women in the United States must contend with the specter of immigration policy, which keeps them in a constant state of insecurity and which in California limits their access to health services.

A Brief History

The first global conference on health promotion was held in Ottawa, Canada, in 1986. Thirty-nine countries came together to discuss the growing need for primary health care. Organized "as a response to growing expectations for a new public health movement around the world," the Ottawa conference proposed health promotion as the answer to global health issues (*Ottawa Charter of Health Promotion* 1986). This gathering resulted in the Ottawa Charter, which has been characterized as the "Bible" of health promotion because it represented "the ultimate ideal and vision of how the goal of health should be obtained through actions at various levels: global, national, community and individual" (Fosse and Roeiseland 1999). The Ottawa Charter defines health promotion as "the process of enabling people to increase control over, and to improve their health." It states that "to reach a state of complete, physical, mental, and social well-being, an individual or group must be able to identify and realize aspirations, to satisfy needs, and to change or cope with the environment. . . . People cannot achieve their fullest health potential unless they are able to take control of those things which determine their health. This must apply equally to men and women."

According to the charter, health promotion was conceptualized as a strategy for ensuring "Health for All by the Year 2000." This proposition built on the progress made through the Declaration on Primary Health Care developed at the International Conference on Primary Health Care held in Alma Ata, Soviet Union, in 1978, the World Health Organization's Targets for All document, and the debate at the World Health Assembly on intersectoral action for health (*Ottawa Charter of Health Promotion* 1986). Also influential was the Lalonde Report, written by Marc Lalonde, then minister for Health in Canada, in 1974. The Lalonde Report outlined a strategy for reducing health care costs "by empowering everyone in the community to identify their health agenda, and to develop agencies by which these could be 'advocated' at the neighborhood level, and then mediated by open access to government agencies" (Bell 2003, 23). This model informed the subsequent development of health promotion strategies across the globe.

Although health promotion as outlined in the Ottawa Charter is informed by social democratic ideals in that it supports gender equity and aims to "empower" communities to participate in their own health, many scholars have pointed out the flaws of health promotion as it has been implemented in the

United States. Critics have pointed out that insofar as it overemphasizes individual responsibility for the state of one's body or health it may inadvertently contribute to messages that reinforce prejudice toward the elderly, handicapped, and other socially vulnerable subjects and "blame the victim" (Minkler 2000, 10).[1] Related to this is the idea that health is influenced by the material and cultural environment within which people live, and therefore a focus on lifestyle "choices" oversimplifies the issue (Daykin and Naidoo 1995, 61). The idea that lifestyle is a choice has been identified as a flawed assumption of market society, wherein citizens are synonymous with consumers (Nettleton and Bunton 1995, 48–50). Furthermore, given that women are frequently targeted as care providers in conventional health promotion campaigns, they are expected to shoulder the burden for their ill health and that of their families. Norma Daykin and Jennie Naidoo (1995, 63) call this the paradox of "responsibility without power." In other accounts, individuals have power, but it is the power of self-regulation and self-surveillance used to manage individual and social bodies from afar (see Petersen 1996; Rose 1996; Inda 2006).

One of the primary factors contributing to these critiques is the shift in government rationalities beginning in the 1970s away from government provision for the social body to one in which individuals were not only encouraged, but were obligated to assume responsibility for the health and care of their bodies. This shift represents a move away from the social democratic postwar ideals that informed the development of the Ottawa Charter to a neoliberal global agenda in which individualism, free markets, and deregulation or decentralization became hegemonic (McGregor 2001). In so doing it responds to critiques that the welfare state was fostering dependence and that people not only could but should care for themselves, hence the focus on empowerment.

The consequences of this transformation in political and economic policy have resulted in the rewriting of the social contract. Where formerly the state had a responsibility to provide for the well-being of its citizens and each citizen had a responsibility to ensure the well-being of the state and each other, under neoliberalism the state's responsibility is to guarantee that opportunities are available in the market for citizens to care for their well-being, and in return each citizen is responsible for guaranteeing that the market can operate. The direct relationship between the well-being of the state and its citizens under neoliberalism is therefore mediated through and on behalf of the market. This latter rationality has subsequently informed health promotion's implementation at all levels. Succinctly, "this means that whereas the achievement of health as a human right as envisaged at Alma Ata required health to be seen as a public good, . . . [the neoliberal development orthodoxy] — based on the promotion of economic growth through structural adjustment of national economies and the liberalization of trade, investment and finance—was to provide the context for the development of global and national health care policies" that redefined health care as a private responsibility (Thomas and Weber 2004, 192–93).

Making Responsible Health Subjects

As responsibility for health care has shifted, so has the perception of political subjectivity. Jonathan Inda explains, "For post-social regimes of government, the political subject is less a social citizen whose security is guaranteed through the bonds of collective life and the receipt of public largess than an individual whose citizenship is derived from active self-promotion and the free exercise of personal choice" (Inda 2006, 14–15). Prior to the implementation of neoliberalism, "the subject of government was conceptualized . . . as a social citizen—a social being whose security was guaranteed through collective dependencies and solidarities. The individual was ordained into society in the figure of a citizen with social rights and needs" (Inda 2006, 11). Eschewing the security of collective solidarity, neoliberal health care requires that the individual perceive her "self" as a reflexive project "that involves the abandonment of a concept of the life course being shaped by tradition and certainty in favor of one that is a series of passages involving at each stage the calculation of risks and opportunities" (Petersen 1996, 46; see also Giddens 1991, 74–88). Alan Petersen describes it thus: "Neo-liberalism calls upon the individual to enter into the process of their own self-governance through processes of endless self-examination, self-care, and self-improvement" (1996, 49). As Kathryn Ellis explains, "the emphasis has shifted from sharing the risks of dependency to protecting the state from dependency—or preventing states of dependency from ever arising" (Ellis 2000, 18).

The transition from welfarism to neoliberalism thus represents a change in the way political subjects are perceived and in the way they perceive themselves. Importantly, these changes in perception have been brought about through increased attention to individual bodies as the site of social pathology. Insofar as health promotion is concerned with the practices, techniques, and discourses through which a subject transforms herself to achieve a particular state of being, it is a political project whose goal is to create a particular kind of ethical subject through a focus on the body.[2] According to Michel Foucault (1997, 225), "ethics is a modality of power that permits individuals to effect, by their own means or with the help of others, a certain number of operations on their own bodies and souls, thoughts, conduct, and way of being." One of the primary changes signaled by health promotion scholars is that the individual now perceives herself as having a moral "duty to be well" to continue to live a productive life. In a reversal from previous health models in which socio-economic status was a primary determinant of health and therefore one needed to be productive to have good health, under neoliberalism, one first needs to have health to be productive.

In the United States, the moral and financial burden imposed by neoliberal health promotion regimes weighs particularly heavily on Mexican migrants, whose primary reason for migrating is often economic. In this context, the duty to be well and the duty to provide overlap. Therefore, the need for a healthy body is paramount given that the migrant worker is generally providing economic support to a large kin network both within the United States and in Mexico. Migrant women feel this burden acutely due to the fact that they are seen as the care providers for their families in the United States and a source of economic and moral support for their families in Mexico. In the United States, they often have to assume health care responsibilities for the entire family, which include overseeing clinical and social service appointments and completing the cumbersome amount of paperwork that participation in these services requires, as well as taking time off to nurse sick children. Women who work full-time are often expected to take care of all the domestic duties as well.

In light of these changes, it is imperative to ask just what are health promotion programs promoting? As much of the sociological literature on health promotion has pointed out, the sociocultural and political conditions of contemporary society are informed by a new risk climate, "characterized by the existence of 'high-consequence risks' linked to processes of industrialization and globalization, for the self-creation of identity and a personal sense of security" (Petersen 1996, 46; see also Giddens 1991; Beck 1992). In this context, individuals are obligated to avoid health risks by using available biomedical information and services. Health promotion therefore operates through the assumption that the mind controls the body, a distinctly gendered and Western mode of thinking.[3] It is assumed that by targeting minds through health education efforts, the information will be used to create healthy bodies, that is, that one's mind will control one's matter. When one does not (or cannot), her moral and physical worth is called into question (Petersen 1996, 53; see also Inda 2006). Given this, a focus on individual health can actually be counterproductive to a sense of personal well-being. Taken to a national scale it can also be used to justify the political and social exclusion of those bodies deemed deviant or pathological (see Terry and Urla 1995).

The effects of neoliberal health promotion—moral and physical uncertainty, individual autonomy rather than collective support, and the moral duty to be well—are in direct contradiction of the social democratic goals of empowerment and community participation outlined in the Ottawa Charter. It is important to point out that insofar as health promotion is a global strategy for providing targeted primary health care often tied to development agendas, and insofar as women are seen as the guarantors for individual and family health, the political logic underlying contemporary health promotion has serious repercussions for poor, rural women all over the world, who are most often the targets of development policies. As I have argued, health promotion has changed as the global political economy has shifted, and therefore caution should be exercised when translating it as an empowerment strategy through which to address health care issues for socially marginalized and vulnerable populations. This cautionary note is especially relevant for the women's health movement, which has held up health promotion as an empowerment strategy for more than thirty years, and for indigenous movements, whose struggles for social justice often concentrate on rural communities where health promotion programs are central components of rural "development."[4]

Rewriting Corporeographies

In order to make a particular theoretical formulation travel across cultural and historical specificities, one needs to rethink the structure of assumptions that underlies a theoretical formulation and perform the difficult task of translation and reformulation.—Saba Mahmood, The Politics of Piety (paraphrasing Butler)

Considering that health promotion is a global political project aimed at promoting an ethic amenable to neoliberal political objectives, it is important to understand its implications for migrant women's embodied understandings in a transnational context. To discuss these implications, I draw from fieldwork conducted with two indigenous *promotoras* working for the California-based nonprofit Centro Binacional para el Desarrollo Indígena Oaxaqueño's (CBDIO). CBDIO's Proyecto de Salud Indígena (Indigenous Health Project) links Mixtec and Triqui migrants with local health services and educates them about health risks affecting the Mexican migrant population in the United States. I suggest that within the context of CBDIO's program, the neoliberal health promotion imperatives already outlined, which both assume and attempt to produce an autonomous and independent health subject, compete with gendered norms carried over from Oaxaca to secure women's well-being. These gendered norms, which in some cases require that women play a more passive, silent, and invisible role in the public sphere, are also overlaid with political and economic concerns, which inform women's self-understandings and perceived needs. My argument is that indigenous women's embodied subjectivity exceeds that posited by the neoliberal health model, and consequently indigenous women draw from a variety of forces, which contribute in sometimes contradictory ways to their health and well-being. Specifically, I argue that both neoliberal health promotion and translocal patriarchy provide a means through which indigenous women in Greenfield, California, can exercise their health citizenship.

Traveling Bodies

The services CBDIO provides have become vital as the indigenous population in California has grown over the past few decades. Political and economic changes in Mexico and the United States have affected migration patterns in such a way that Mexican states with large indigenous populations, which formerly had very little out-migration, are now seeing whole communities moving to the larger cities within the nation or migrating to the United States (Fox and Rivera-Saldago 2004, 3). Although Mixtecos have a long history of migration within Mexico, the number of them migrating to the United States has increased significantly since the 1940s with the Bracero program (Velasco Ortiz 2005, 31).[5] "Many [Mixtecos] were braceros during that program's 22-year run from 1942 to 1964" (Bacon n.d.). This number increased again in the 1970s when many of the migrants working in the fields in Baja California pushed further north. Prior to the 1970s, most of the out-going migration was to other regions in Mexico, such as Veracruz, the Federal District (Distrito Federal), and Sinaloa. This trend was mirrored by the Triqui migrants starting in the 1980s.[6] The Mexican economic crisis in the 1980s, the 1986 Immigration Reform and Control Act, the implementation of the North American Free Trade Agreement in 1994, and increasingly conservative immigration policies in the United States, among other things, have all ensured that this trend will continue.[7]

Because conservative immigration policies in the United States have made it harder to cross the border, male migrants have increasingly opted to bring their spouses and families to live in the United States rather than risk the danger and economic hardship of multiple border crossings for return visits to Mexico. In consequence, "the parallel process of long-term settlement and geographic concentration has led to the creation of a 'critical mass' of indigenous Oaxacans, especially in California" (Fox and Rivera-Salgado 2004, 11). Regardless of what side of the border they live on, however, indigenous migrants suffer from racial prejudice. Jonathan Fox and Gaspar Rivera-Salgado explain that "both in the United States and in Mexico, indigenous migrants are subordinated both as migrants and as indigenous people, economically, socially and politically," and as a result, "are excluded from citizenship rights in either country" (Fox and Rivera Salgado 2004, 4). Related to this discrimination is their low socioeconomic position in labor markets, which are stratified by both ethnicity and gender on both sides of the border. Indigenous women also experience gender subordination throughout their migration trajectory from within the indigenous community (Velasco Ortiz 2004).[8]

Given these factors, health promotion is perceived as a welcome source of information and support for indigenous women in California. As they adjust to life in the United States, they seek information in their own language that will help them understand the cultural and social norms in their transnational community. Information exchange is no easy task for them or for the health care providers they encounter, however, because many indigenous Mexicans have little formal education and speak little Spanish; often, the languages they do speak are not written. They must therefore engage in the difficult exercise of adapting to a culture that operates on paper without having strong reading or writing skills as well as contend with the pervasive assumption that all Mexicans speak Spanish.[9] Given this, the knowledge and support provided by CBDIO's health promotion program facilitates their survival and that of their families, while also helping them avoid negative interactions with authorities that could lead to their deportation. CBDIO's programs often provide information on legal issues, such as workers' rights in pesticide exposure, in addition to health education and information and help with written and spoken interpretations. The provision of these services is the primary job of the promotoras.

Teresa (Triqui) and María (Mixteca) both work as health promotoras for CBDIO in Greenfield, California.[10] The stated goals of their health project are "to offer education on health themes and to help farmworkers and indigenous people access health and social services in Merced, Fresno, Tulare, Kern and Monterey Counties." This program was created because, as CBDIO's brochure explains, their staff is aware of the additional barriers indigenous and Mexican migrant farmworkers experience in relation to health and medical services. It states, "Conscious of the language and cultural differences that exist between Mexico and the United States and of the barriers to medical attention that they represent, we are concerned to give help and information in their own language whether that is in Spanish or an indigenous language."[11] The primary job of the promotoras, then, is to translate not only between languages—indigenous, Spanish, and to some extent English—but also between medical and social systems to facilitate access to health information and care for indigenous migrants in California. One way of understanding their complex role is that of cultural brokers or translators.

For seven months, from January to July 2007, I actively participated with Teresa and María as a volunteer promotora in the health promotion program of CBDIO in Greenfield. CBDIO's main office is located in Fresno, California; however, they also have offices in Los Angeles and Santa Maria. Their mission to promote the economic, social, and cultural development of Mexican indigenous groups in California takes them wherever indigenous migrants reside in the state. As a volunteer, I also participated in health-related events and trainings that CBDIO held in rural communities throughout California. In addition to participant observation, I held one focus group with members from each indigenous community and conducted semi-structured interviews with many program participants, local leaders and politicians, as well as with CBDIO staff, including the two indigenous health promotoras working in Greenfield and two others in Fresno. During this period I also made several trips to Mexico City and Oaxaca, Mexico, to conduct interviews and participant observation with health promotion staff working for the Instituto Mexicano de Seguro Social (IMSS) which has health education programs targeted at the rural poor.

I chose CBDIO because it actively supports gender equity and because the staff is acutely aware of the devastating effects of neoliberal development policies on indigenous communities in Mexico. Indeed, CBDIO is closely linked to the Frente Indígena de Organizaciones Binacionales, which fights unfair economic and social policies in Mexican indigenous communities on both sides of the border. Given this, it seemed paradoxical that they should choose a neoliberal health strategy to work with indigenous migrants in California. According to the CBDIO director, Rufino Domínguez Santos, the promotora model was chosen because "it is the model they use in Mexico and people are familiar with it" (personal communication 2006). Indeed, health promotion has a long history in Mexico through the IMSS, which first began using promotoras in rural communities in the 1980s.[12]

According to a staff member at the IMSS office in Mexico City who has worked on the program since its inception, the idea for the promotoras came from Mao Zedong's barefoot doctors in rural China. Mao's plan to turn peasants into barefoot doctors was implemented in 1956 as part of the Great Leap Forward meant to increase agricultural production by ensuring a healthy workforce. Part of his platform was a backlash against Western-style "elite" medicine and its "bourgeois" policies. Under his rule, "self-interested" physicians who only treated rare and difficult diseases rather than addressing the common parasites plaguing the Chinese peasantry, were denounced as "disregarding the masses" (Valentine 2005). Although the idea for the rural promotoras came from China, the driving force behind its adoption as a national strategy in Mexico came out of the Primary Health Care agenda developed at Alma Ata.[13]

CBDIO's health promotion program in California is therefore a translated version of a communist Chinese model that was reformulated at the international meeting on Primary Health Care held in the Soviet Union, adopted at the national level in Mexico, and then brought to California through nonprofits and private foundations. As already outlined, its current manifestation serves a neoliberal agenda; however, its goal of keeping a healthy agricultural work-force has not changed since its beginnings in China. In California, CBDIO is not alone in adopting the "Mexican model" of health promotion. The California Endowment and the Health Initiative of the Américas (formerly the California-México Health Initiative), both of which are influential in setting the agenda for migrant health services in California, favor the promotora model based on their field research and experience with the programs implemented by the federal government in Mexico.[14] Indeed, their interest in this model often drives the funding process for nonprofits working with Mexican migrants in California. As a result of the interest and influence of major health funders and the increased cross-border migration of people and ideas, this strategy has spread across California as the model for working with Mexican migrant farmworker populations.[15]

Negotiating Competing Forces

The tension between the moral imperatives of neoliberal health promotion and the pressure to adhere to gendered norms dominant in indigenous Oaxacan communities is palpable in many aspects of the Proyecto de Salud Indígena. The promotoras, as well as the female program participants, must negotiate the implications of assuming the risk and responsibility for their own health and that of their families and communities by scouring the local institutional and social environment for information and services, while at the same time respecting their husbands' wishes and desires for them to perform the role of "decent" women who do not actively occupy the public sphere or interact with unknown men and women.[16] For Mexican indigenous women in Greenfield, there are incentives to respond to both moral imperatives.

Responding to neoliberal health promotion regimes means that one will learn where and how to take care of one's needs should one need the information or services. This does not mean the health subject will necessarily become more empowered or even take the kind of action encouraged by the health promotion program. Nonetheless, although program participants may not always retain the medical information or even use it as intended, they will have been provided it, and they walk away with the knowledge of where to go should the need arise. These things give them a greater sense of security and provide increased choices in how and where to engage in self-care.

Other incentives to become an active health citizen include free food at the workshops and, in the case of prenatal classes given by the local clinic, free items for a baby, such as a stroller, diapers, or a car seat. Finally, a very important incentive for attending the health promotion program and one that is not premised on individual action, is that it guarantees continued help from the promotoras. This can mean a phone call when the Salvation Army is giving out vouchers for groceries, help with filling out an application for food stamps, or help with acquiring a restraining order when an abusive husband has gone too far. Keeping a good relationship with the promotoras is tantamount to having an extra level of security in a difficult and uncertain environment.

On the other hand, incentives to follow patriarchal desires include keeping a breadwinner in the house despite the subordination and possible violence his presence engenders, both of which can negatively affect women's health.[17] In addition, community pressure to be a decent woman also provides a strong incentive to adhere to gendered norms. One interviewee expressed the constant pressure to uphold gendered social norms and not exercise an "active" citizenship by saying, "You can't walk outside in the street because there are a lot of people who gossip" (interview with Triqui woman, April 2007). In this small town of sixteen thousand people, where the main street is about six blocks long, autonomy in the public sphere is difficult for women. This difficulty is exacerbated by the constant threat of immigration raids, threats that existed even prior to the implementation of Secure Communities and could result in separation from their families and deportation.[18] More recently, a backlash against the indigenous community in Greenfield has increased scrutiny of their public and private behaviors by nonindigenous residents. The "Save Greenfield" and "Beautify Greenfield" movements, promoted largely by nonindigenous Mexican-origin residents, have condemned indigenous behaviors (noisy parties, frequent pregnancies, marriage arrangements) and the seeming preference given to indigenous residents by the local police department.[19] In addition, despite the geographic distance between Oaxaca and California, telephone, Internet, and constant migration carries news back and forth between the two states, and any social misstep in either place becomes grounds for public and private reprimand coming from the other side of the border. Indeed, indigenous women in Greenfield have experienced the rejection of their community for transgressing their socially prescribed roles (see Paris Pombo 2006a).

For indigenous women, the duty to be an active health citizen in the United States often clashes with the duty to be a "good" wife and mother as defined by social and cultural norms in Oaxaca. Indigenous women in Greenfield draw from both to care for themselves and their families. Although these standards vary by community of origin and ethnicity, generally a decent woman does not occupy the public sphere, and if she does it is only on the way to take care of business. She does not linger to talk with men she does not know, nor does she take an active role in community politics. Although these norms are challenged by some migrant women in California, they nonetheless continue to be a structuring force informing women's roles and health status in Greenfield. Given this, becoming an active citizen who participates unaccompanied in the CBDIO health workshops at the public library, where men she does not know also attend, who actively seeks resources by talking with anyone who might have pertinent health information, and who becomes involved in community initiatives concerned with health issues (of which there are many in Greenfield) are all taboo for decent women.[20] This is as much the case for the promotoras as it is for program participants.

Although these norms generally apply for both indigenous groups I worked with in Greenfield, they are especially true for Triqui women whose husbands are reputedly very jealous and violent.[21] In the case of the Triqui promotora, her husband would refuse to pick her up after a late-night health class, or he would leave her waiting for excessively long periods after a community meeting to show his discontent with her job. He also repeatedly encouraged her to come work with him in the fields, where he could keep an eye on her. This kind of jealousy extends into the clinical environment, where wives must be seen by a female doctor because, as I was told by indigenous men and women alike, "no other man has the right to see her private parts."[22]

Neoliberal health imperatives and gendered norms come into direct competition within the space of the health workshops. One example of this occurred during a workshop I conducted to assess the health needs of the Triqui community. Many of the women participants brought their spouses, who did all of the talking while none of the women in the room spoke during the whole hour. When I brought this up in an interview I conducted with two of the female participants after the workshop, they said it is because "the men are jealous and they don't let their wives speak." Both of my interviewees are single mothers whose husbands had been deported to Mexico, so neither husband was in the room. When I pointed out that they did not attend the meeting with their husbands, one of them responded, "What happens is that one doesn't know how to talk and then the husbands are very jealous." Clearly, in this context, active citizenship comes into direct conflict with gendered norms in the indigenous community. These norms dictate who can speak in public. This comment leads me to conclude that either women do not have the permission and therefore don't have the experience to conduct public speaking, or in a related interpretation, health workshops are conducted in a way that marginalizes some of the participants even as they are attempting to involve them. This realization raises questions about health promotion strategies that rely on active audience participation or interactive "classroom-like" behavior to relay health information.[23]

As was apparent in the workshop, the Triqui men clearly assume the public speaking role on behalf of the women. For example, during the same meeting when I explicitly asked the *women* if life was better here or in Mexico, one *man* answered that "it was better here because in Mexico the women have to cook with wood and when the wood is wet it makes a lot of smoke in the house. In the United States they have a stove and electricity so it is better here." Then he added, "at least I imagine that's what they would say if they talked." Although this comment is important for what it reveals about the differences between rural California and rural Oaxaca, it is also significant for what it reveals about the gender dynamics in the Triqui community.[24] "Empowerment" strategies are meant to help people make the information their own so they can use it to improve their health. In this context, however, the answer to the questions did not "belong" to the women in the room in the sense that they could describe their lived realities; these daily experiences were translated for them by the men in the focus group. An obvious solution to this problem would be to conduct a focus group with only women—in this case, only women had been invited. Yet because of the same gender dynamics informing public participation in general, many husbands accompanied their wives. The trade-off for the Triqui women in this workshop was that although they didn't or couldn't speak because men were present, by adhering to gendered community norms they were at least able to attend and hear the information presented. Attendance at the workshops does not mean, however, that participants use the information they receive in prescribed ways. Indeed, competing social and economic concerns often disrupt the linear translation of health information into action.

Several times a month the promotoras organize health education workshops where they cover topics such as asthma, children's oral care, diabetes, pesticides, and other relevant health issues. The goal of these workshops is to inform indigenous migrants of health risks so that they will take preventive action to avoid or eliminate illness and disease in their bodies and those of their family members. In some cases, the information is accompanied by a screening of some sort. For example, on one occasion we did a workshop on diabetes where, after explaining what diabetes is in medical and biological terms, María and I spent over an hour pricking fingers to get blood sugar readings on many members of the Mixteco community. The health workshops operate on the premise that people will take preventive action to avoid health risks. In the case of this workshop, only one woman was identified as having extremely high blood sugar. She was encouraged during the workshop by the Mixtec promotora, as well as by a local Mixtec leader who was the woman's nephew, to make an appointment with the doctor to have her blood sugar rechecked. When she still hadn't gone to the clinic after several weeks, María offered to meet her at the office on a Sunday to do another screening. The woman never did do a screening either at CBDIO's office or at the doctor's office. As this example shows, the translation from information into preventive action is not always linear. Indeed, it was not uncommon in my interviews to hear that people did not want to go to the doctor or get screened for health problems because they were scared to find out what illness, if any, they had. This concern was often fueled by reluctance to see a doctor who would make them undress, run tests on them, and touch them only to conclude that "there was nothing wrong." In deciding whether to follow up on an identified problem with a doctor's appointment, some women concluded that it was better to keep their clothes on and their reputation intact than be a proactive health consumer. That is, many women preferred the security of maintaining good relations with their spouse and their community to the security of knowing if they had a disease that was not immediately affecting their lives.

Adherence to gendered norms was not the only reason women didn't follow through with the health information they received in CBDIO's workshops, however. In an interview with two Triqui women, I asked which workshops they had attended. One of them responded for both saying that they had been to the workshops on children's oral care and diabetes. I then asked, "Do you remember what you learned about diabetes?" The same woman responded, "She [the promotora] said if someone has diabetes they can get help for free." I asked the other woman if she remembered anything from the workshop and she shook her head "no." I asked if they remembered anything about children's oral health. The same woman responded, "We learned that if you have bad teeth you can get them pulled out for free, too." I turned to the other woman and asked if she had taken her three-year-old daughter, who has several visible black spots on her front top and bottom teeth, to the dentist as a result of the workshop. She responded, "No because my daughter doesn't have a lot of stains. Well, she does, but not a lot." These comments clearly indicate that although women are attending the workshops, their active citizenship takes on a different form. Rather than use the information to get preventive care, they are storing it away so when they need an intervention, like getting rotten teeth pulled, they know where to go to get free or low-cost health services. In the interim, they are taking care of more financially and physically pressing needs like putting food on the table and keeping a roof over their families' heads.[25] This was certainly the case for my interviewees, who were both single mothers.

Although the workshops are meant to enlighten program participants so they will assume individual responsibility for their health, and therefore take an active role in preventing their bodies from becoming ill or diseased, my research shows that they do not always have this productive effect, as the stories demonstrate. In a few cases I observed, they completely missed their mark by assuming that participants had universal consumption practices. This occurred in a workshop conducted in Fresno on car seat safety. After listening attentively for an hour on how to properly install and use a car seat, one woman turned to her neighbor whispering, "Ni tengo carro!" (I don't even have a car!).

On occasion, the workshops actually had the opposite effect insofar as participants used the information to reaffirm their own embodied understandings in contrast to those being presented. For example, in an educational workshop with the Mixteco community, the promotora and I were presenting on asthma. I read the information in Spanish and she translated it into Mixteco. As I was reading the possible ways to control asthma according to a guide the promotoras had been given by the local clinic, one of the women in the audience raised her hand and said, "We don't think like that. If someone has a problem with breathing we take them to a traditional medicine doctor for an egg cleansing ritual. We know that there must be an emotional problem and the doctors at the clinic will not understand that. They will only look at his body and not at the real problem."

This woman was using the workshop to contest the hegemonic biomedical system and challenge the assumption that all illnesses could be cured by allopathic doctors who only focus on the physical aspects of illness. Rather than becoming empowered by the knowledge being presented, she used the information to reinforce her own beliefs and those of others in the room whose health paradigm was being ignored in the biomedical information provided during the presentation. By critiquing biomedicine, this participant was also invoking and, in so doing, reaffirming a healing system that is not based on individual bodies and selves but takes a more holistic and social approach to embodiment and health. Indeed, this social approach to health is one of the reasons indigenous women adhere to community norms that appear to be unhealthy within an individualized neoliberal framework (i.e., patriarchal norms that impede "active" citizenship) but which, according to indigenous healing paradigms, can be the source of health as well as illness.

When we did this same presentation with the Triqui community, we were confronted with a different challenge, which forced us to once again rethink the assumptions about the subjectivities of the participants underlying our presentation. On this occasion, we spent the first twenty minutes of the presentation explaining that asthma affects the body by constricting the passage of air to the lungs. After we finished describing this process and the elements that can cause an asthma attack (dust, mold, cockroaches, etc.), one woman raised her hand and asked, "What are lungs?" This woman's comment was partly fueled by the fact that the promotora was inserting the Spanish word for lungs (*pulmones*) into her Triqui translation because she didn't know the word in Triqui. Even when the Triqui word for lungs was offered by another participant, however, she said she still didn't know what or where they were.[26] We found ourselves sketching the human body and offering lay explanations of what the lungs were used for. It was clear from this discussion that the woman who asked the question was not able to follow along or absorb the information presented in the workshop because we, the presenters, assumed that everyone had the same understanding of their bodies, an assumption that was clearly erroneous. Indeed, the very atomized and mechanistic approach to health and the body proposed in our workshop, which was based on biomedicine, was called into question by this participant who had not learned to look at her body in this way. As we learned, the description of lungs she was asking for would necessarily require more than a linguistic translation; it would also necessitate a cultural translation between indigenous and neoliberal worldviews.

Trust and Translations

One very important aspect of the CBDIO health promotion model is that they use promotoras from the same ethnolinguistic background as the people they serve. In this case, the CBDIO office in Greenfield has one Triqui from Constancio del Rosario and one Mixtec promotora from San Jose de Las Flores, two pueblos located very near Putla, Oaxaca. Many of the indigenous migrants that use CBDIO's services are from the same region and often the same pueblo as the promotoras. The fact that they have many commonalities with the communities they serve is meant to instill a sense of trust in the services of CBDIO. As Teresa repeatedly explained, however, trust didn't come easily. She spoke of her first workshops, which only men attended. She described it as "very difficult," especially when there were a lot of young men. This is so because, as indigenous women, she and María are subjected to the same gendered paradigms in California that they experience in Mexico by indigenous men.

These gendered paradigms have influenced the themes they give in the workshops, as well as the way they translate the information given. For example, neither of the promotoras wants to give a workshop on prostate cancer, although they know it is a very important health issue for men. As Teresa said, "Sometimes I read about the prostate, but then I ask myself, how am I going to explain this?" She added that even the female health educator from the local clinic who is not indigenous won't give the workshop because, as she says, "it should be a man who gives this workshop." As this example demonstrates, it is not only women's health that is jeopardized due to the gendered norms of the indigenous community. This inability to talk to men about certain aspects of their bodies was also apparent in a workshop on diabetes. At one point I was explaining in Spanish that diabetes can cause impotence. After finishing, I turned to María so she could translate and she just looked at me and said, "keep going," without interpreting what I had just said. Apparently, talking about men's reproductive organs in public is not something a decent woman would do. Yet because health is seen as women's work, there are few men who seek employment as health promoters.

These translation exercises are also difficult for the promotoras because they don't always have the words to express their ideas. This is so for Teresa because, although she learned Triqui growing up, she didn't speak it much until coming to California. For this reason she didn't know the Triqui word for lungs. She says her Triqui has improved significantly since she got the job with CBDIO. María, on the other hand, speaks fluent Mixteco but only learned Spanish well while working in the fields in California. The fact that neither of them is fully bilingual makes it difficult to discuss delicate health issues in public in both languages. This difficulty is further complicated by the assumptions about bodies, selves, health, and healing inherent in each linguistic and cultural system.

Conclusion

On the face of it, health promotion has been touted as an excellent global and national strategy for working with "hard-to-reach," underserved, and marginalized populations who experience additional barriers to health care. However, I have argued that caution should be exercised when adopting it as an empowerment strategy for indigenous migrant women because of the epistemological baggage with which it travels. Neoliberal health promotion's focus on risk is not attentive to indigenous cultural norms and beliefs that many illnesses have social rather than physical causes, nor does it take into account the patriarchal forces shaping the ways women exercise their health citizenship. Another shortcoming of this model is that much of the information given in the health workshops is meant to increase interactions between women and the local clinic to detect any health problems early. By advocating increased clinical interactions, the promotoras are also advocating increased medicalization of women's bodies and their lives. Increased subjection to "the medical gaze" is quite the opposite of the antiauthoritarian, community-based empowerment model that health promotion programs traffic under and that was central to the women's health movement.[27]

Although health promotion aims to produce an ethical subject who fulfills his or her obligation to the national polity, not through relations of dependency but through seeking to realize him- or herself as a free, self-reliant subject (see Rose 1996; Inda 2006), cultural norms in the indigenous community do not give primacy to individual "independence" and "autonomy." Rather, the emphasis is placed on the social body over the individual. In a cultural sensitivity training offered by CBDIO, one of the presenters explained that "the primary identity in the indigenous community is communal and collective" and that "the United States is very individualistic in comparison."[28] Indeed, women in my study often had to negotiate between social forces that assumed either a collective or individual subjectivity to secure their health and well-being. In terms of the former, women had to adhere to the gendered norms of the community. As for the latter, they were expected to act as individualized citizens apart from social, political, economic, and cultural pressures coming from either side of the border. This research demonstrates that Mexican indigenous women in transnational contexts are continually translating a series of cultural dichotomies (individual/social, subject/object, mind/body) at the level of their bodies. In so doing, they are continually rewriting their corporeographies, albeit under constrained conditions.

Notes

1. For a review of work that discusses victim blaming, see Rose Galvin (2002).

2. This definition of ethics comes from Michel Foucault (1990). See also Mahmood (2005, 28) for a discussion of Foucault's distinction between morals and ethics.

3. For a critique of the mind/body separation and its assumptions, see Grosz (1994).

4. The Boston Women's Health Book Collective began using this approach in the 1970s. See their publication, *Our Bodies, Ourselves* (1998 [2005]). For a critique of development policies in rural communities in Latin America see Arturo Escobar (1995).

5. For a discussion of Mixteco migration, see Sylvia Escárcega and Stefano Varese (2004).

6. Currently, there are numerous communities of Triqui and Mixteco migrants working in the fruit and vegetable fields in the southern and central coast of California and in the Central Valley. Although most of these agricultural workers are men, women are becoming more numerous (Paris Pombo 2006a). Researchers estimate that in the 1990s between 45,000 and 55,000 Mixtecs worked in agriculture in California's Central Valley and that indigenous migrants were expected to represent more than 20 percent of California's farmworkers by 2010. In 2007, estimates put the indigenous Oaxacan population in California at between 100,000 and 150,000 (Kresge 2007).

7. The coffee crisis is one additional factor, as is the fact that much of the agricultural land in Oaxaca is fallow.

8. Laura Velasco Ortiz (2007) has discussed this in relation to the domain of male authority over women's spaces of action in Baja California, an important stop for indigenous migrants on their way further north.

9. Although it is beyond the scope of this chapter to discuss the historic exclusion of indigenous communities from formal education through government neglect and as a result of profound racism, it is important to signal that many indigenous people believe that

literacy is a valuable and important skill and the desire for their children to acquire this powerful tool often contributes to their decision to migrate. The teacher's strike in Oaxaca and the Zapatista uprising in Chiapas — social movements in two of the poorest states in Mexico, which are also primarily indigenous — are responses to this historic racism and neglect.

10. Both names are pseudonyms.

11. All translations from Spanish to English are mine.

12. There are other federal and regional health promotion programs in Oaxaca, however, the IMSS promotora program is the most well recognized by the rural populations and is the one that is often visited by U.S. nonprofits and private foundations working with Mexican migrants in California.

13. Personal interview conducted in Mexico City, March 20, 2007.

14. Personal interviews with a former staff member of the California Endowment who participated in the information gathering trip on health promotion in Oaxaca, Mexico, conducted February 10, 2007, and a staff member from the Health Initiative of the Américas conducted April 19, 2007. Interview with Mario Gutierrez, director of Rural and Agricultural Worker Health Programs at the California Endowment, conducted July 10, 2007, Puebla, Mexico.

15. On the surface the choice to draw from a Mexican model of health promotion appears "culturally sensitive," but the historic exclusion of indigenous groups from social services in rural Mexico and the profound racism they experience when they do access clinical services coupled with the highly gendered nature of social and medical services for all Mexican women belie its well-intentioned adoption for working with indigenous Mexicans in California. As one of the researchers in a binational project looking at the work of promotoras in indigenous communities in Oaxaca and California, I witnessed firsthand the outright racism of the medical staff in one of the primary sending regions in Oaxaca. Interviews with participants in the promotoras program and with rural medical staff, as well as participant observation in rural indigenous communities in Mexico, highlighted the gendered nature of clinical services and health promotion, which are almost exclusively targeted to women who are expected to be the care providers for the whole family. Given the fact that health promotion in these communities is more often experienced as onerous and oppressive (rather than empowering) for rural Mexicans in Mexico, it seems an unfortunate choice for working with them in California. Yet women use these programs in strategic ways that do not always correspond to the health imperatives they promote.

16. See Xochitl Castañeda and Patricia Zavella (2003) for a discussion of the role of "decent women."

17. A report on violence in indigenous communities outlines the abuses that indigenous women experience from birth and throughout their lives at the hands of loved ones, as well as strangers. See Instituto Nacional de Salud Pública (2008).

18. While I was conducting my research, the threat of immigration raids was ever-present. The fears this threat engendered were not unfounded — there had been raids in Greenfield that resulted in the arrest and deportation of many local residents. See Paul Johnston (2004).

19. Kimber Solana, "In Greenfield, Oaxacans see Hostility Grow: Indigenous Groups'

Request for Support from City Leaders Largely Ignored," *Californian*, June 10, 2011, http://www.thecalifornian.com/article/99999999/NEWS01/101080321/In-Greenfield-Oaxacans-see-hostility-grow.

20. It is important to point out that indigenous women in other California communities do not experience these norms in the same way and in many ways are more successful at outwardly challenging them. I thank Nayamin Martínez Cossio for pointing this out.

21. This information was provided through interviews with Triqui and Mixtec women in California and was confirmed in interviews with health promotion program staff in Oaxaca and Mexico City conducted in March 2007.

22. This point was brought to my attention in the interviews with CBDIO staff in Fresno, as well as with the IMSS staff in Oaxaca. It is important to note the assumption that the doctor will be male.

23. The phrase "classroom-like" behavior was discussed by a panelist who teaches English as a second language for teachers at a conference on transnational health in Berkeley, California, on April 18, 2007. She pointed out that many of these teachers are challenged to come up with different strategies for working with adults who have had very little formal education and consequently aren't familiar with "classroom-like" behavior.

24. My thanks to Jonathan Fox for pointing this out.

25. I thank Pat Zavella for pointing this out.

26. The fact that many of the women did not have basic knowledge of their bodies has to do with the fact that most indigenous women in Oaxaca do not have more than a fourth-grade education. This fact is linked to perceptions within some indigenous communities that women don't need more education than that to prepare them for their domestic responsibilities. It is also linked to the historic neglect of the Mexican government in providing anything beyond basic education services in largely indigenous areas of Mexico.

27. Because it is "common knowledge" that men do not seek health services, only women are pressured to increase their clinical interactions. When asked why pressure is not put on men to take an active role in disease and illness prevention, the response from all sectors has been that men simply don't go to the doctor. This "fact" means that women are also asked to become educated on health risks for men and communicate this information to their partners, making them responsible for male and female health care. The gendered assumptions in health promotion strategies in the United States are a carryover from those in Mexico, which also explicitly target women. To incorporate men in the United States would therefore deviate from their customary and familiar practice.

28. Quote taken from a training conducted by Nayamin Martinez Cossio, an employee of CBDIO, at the Department of Health in Salinas, California, June 29, 2007.

KIRAN ASHER

The task of the feminist translator is to consider
language as a clue to the workings of gendered agency.
—Gayatri Spivak, "The Politics of Translation"

In the Introduction to Debates about Translation, laying the conceptual ground-work for this project, Claudia de Lima Costa begins with a review of the trans-national travels of theories, including feminist theories. She notes that it is often the most abstract and decontextualized theories that "cross borders" best and gain scholarly traction. In contrast to Costa, social scientists working in the field of women, gender, and Third World development (hereafter referred to as gender professionals or development feminists) tend to find theories, especially of the postmodern and postcolonial ilk, untranslatable precisely because of their abstraction. Gender experts claim that postcolonial feminist analyses of discourse and representation are too textual and do not help to improve Third World women's deteriorating material conditions. In the 1990s I was a biologist turning social scientist, and my knowledge of development and feminism was nascent. As I began research on Afro-Colombian struggles for ethnic and territorial rights in the biodiversity and natural resource–rich Pacific lowlands (about which more later), I, too, shared development femi-nists' skepticism about the applicability of "theory" for praxis. After almost two decades of crossing continents and linguistic and disciplinary boundaries, I am learning to read.

Reading in this context does not refer *sensu stricto* to literacy nor yet to a simple revelation of Third World women's "gendered agency." As with Costa's call to scrutinize the cultural translation/travels of theories, by "learning to read" I mean being self-reflexive about the geopolitics, objectives, and subjects of our investigations. Lest self-reflexivity be misunderstood as self-narration or biography before business-as-usual (representing the "reality" of Third World women so as to "help" them), let me spell out the postcolonial feminist lesson that undergirds this essay, which I elaborate later: clarifying the contexts in and forms through which Third World women are discursively constituted as the subjects and objects of knowledge and intervention. In the analytical language of this volume, this might mean asking: who or what is being translated or made legible, by whom, for whom, and for what purposes? But translation is not an unmediated act, discourses are textual as well as tactile, and clues have to be actively unraveled. In this essay I consider the work and words of Matamba y Guasá, a network of black women's organizations from the department of Cauca in the Pacific lowlands of Colombia, to trace how black women's activism is shaped differentially, unequally, and discursively within the complexities and contradictions of development discourses and local struggles. I locate black women's struggles in the context of broader political-economic and cultural struggles and question some of the binaries (theory versus practice, power versus resistance, discourse versus materiality, victims versus guardians, and so on) that plague and limit so much thinking in the field of Third World women, gender, and development.

I begin with a sketch of how Third World women and gender become part of the constituency of economic development in what have come to be known as the "women-in-development" (WID), and "gender and development" (GAD) approaches. Then I outline postcolonial feminist critiques of WID and GAD and counter critiques by gender experts. Rather than a comprehensive review of the women, gender, and development literature or of postcolonial feminism, this section is a necessarily cursory discussion of the insights of the latter and their relevance for my reading of black women's activism.[1] I conclude with an invitation to us—researchers, scholars, activists, and gender experts from the North and South—to examine our desires and methods to better the lives of Third World women in an attempt to inhabit what Costa calls the "vexing linkages between feminisms and transnationalisms in the translation zone."

Third World Women and Gender in Development Discourses

Debates about women's "oppression" and inequality and gender relations of power parallel broader political and theoretical debates about modernity, development, and globalization. In the first decades of the post–World War II development project the new independent, "underdeveloped" nations of the Third World launched ambitious industrialization and large-scale agriculture projects to foster economic growth and "catch up" with the developed countries of the First World. During this time, little or no specific attention was paid to domestic and subsistence sectors—which ostensibly did not contribute to the productive and economic activities of these nations. Naila Kabeer (1994, 5) notes that whereas men entered the development process as heads of households and "productive" agents, women were seen primarily in their roles as housewives, mothers, and "reproducers" and were relegated to the "welfare" sector. Thus, during the first UN Decade of Development (1961–70), Third World women were primarily targets of population control, food aid, and poverty reduction policies (Braidotti et al. 1994).

Since the 1970s, Third World women began making active appearances in the lexicons of economic development thanks to the efforts of a broad spectrum of feminist scholars, activists, and gender professionals from the North and South.[2] Danish economist Ester Boserup's book *Women's Role in Economic Development* (1970) played a key role in demonstrating that Third World women make a considerable contribution to productive sectors, especially in agriculture. Boserup's research also flagged the negative social and economic effects of development projects on women, showing that the first generation of development projects denied women access to the credit, technology, and training to enter the modern sector (Braidotti et al. 1994, 78). Thus, Boserup challenged the assumption that the benefits of economic growth trickle down to the poor. However, she did not reject economic modernization but rather advocated that women be better integrated into the modern sector to become equal beneficiaries. Boserup's work laid the foundation for WID approaches. These approaches have de facto roots in Western, liberal feminism, which locates the cause of women's oppression in public and private patriarchy. By the tenets of liberal feminism, modernity and progress are the antidotes to sexism and other sources of inequality and exclusion.

During the second UN Decade of Development (1971–80), a cadre of professional women from the non-Western world and Western-based feminists focused attention and resources for "growth with equity" programs for women. In 1975, at the first UN Conference on Women held in Mexico City, the decade 1976 to 1985 was declared the UN Decade for Women. In Mexico, the original WID demand for equity was reformulated as the need to alleviate poverty among women because governments and development agencies felt that the demand for sex equity was associated with Western feminism. The demand for equity also became linked to the argument of economic efficiency and women were labeled a valuable "resource" to be "harnessed" for efficient economic growth (Braidotti et al. 1994, 80). In the annals of development, poor women began appearing as potentially key players and economic producers.[3]

This shift occurred at a time when the Third World economic development arena was characterized by economic liberalization policies, such as "structural adjustment" programs designed to ameliorate problems of escalating debt, poverty, and social upheaval. Women in many parts of the Third World were incorporated as low-wage, unskilled laborers in the new export-oriented productive sectors and also bore the brunt of reductions in social spending.[4] With the development emphasis on market-driven growth, government resources earmarked for special women's programs dried up, and the policy spotlight shifted to gender.

The term *gender* appeared in development debates through the work of Marxist and socialist feminists (Beneria and Sen 1981; Mies 1982; Sen and Grown 1987; Kabeer 1994). Influenced by and extending structural and dependency critiques of modernization from Southern perspectives, Marxist and socialist feminists understand the inequities between women and men (gender relations of power) as part of a continuum of inequalities between countries, social classes, regions, and ethnic groups. For example, in *The Lace Makers of Narsapur*, a book that deserves to be at least as well recognized as Boserup's, Maria Mies (1982) traces how capitalism (class) and patriarchy (sexism) interact to exacerbate the unequal social and economic status of poor women working in a household industry in rural Andhra Pradesh, India. Though there is no consensus among Marxist and socialist feminists on the causes of gender inequality, there is a broad agreement on the need to reassess development and modernization enterprises and how women and men are incorporated into them (Sen and Grown 1987).[5] Gender experts developed a working definition of gender relations as a subset of the social relations of power and dominance at household, community, regional, local, national, or international level that shape and limit women's "productive" and "reproductive" labor. But the structural critiques of development were largely lost when gender analysis was translated into policy and took the depoliticized and institutionalized form of GAD approaches. These approaches focus on addressing women's everyday, practical needs by empowering women to become key decision makers in the household and community.

From the 1990s onward, *women* and *gender* have become key words in the diverse disciplinary and discursive realms concerned with economic development and globalization.[6] By the beginning of the twenty-first century, organizations ranging from states, nongovernmental organizations (NGOs), and multilateral institutions were engaged in some way with women's empowerment and gender mainstreaming.

Critiques and Countercritiques of WID and GAD

In recent years, feminists from the South and North have called into question the assumptions about Third World women and modernity underlying WID and GAD approaches. For example, Kriemild Saunders critiques both WID and GAD for being equally "gynocentric," that is, for being principally focused on women's positions vis-à-vis men, and therefore paying inadequate attention to how other vertical social relations affect women's lives (2002, 7, 11). She further notes that like their liberal Western sisters, Marxist/socialist feminists from the South "continue to be bound by an unquestioned commitment to an enlightened vision of socialistic development, entailing industrialization and modernity for the South" (2002, 11). Grassroots activists also question gender professionals and feminists associated with development institutions for not being in touch with the concerns of the poor women whose voices they claim to represent (Alvarez 1998b, first introduction in this volume).

The issue of representation is at the heart of postcolonial feminist critiques of WID and GAD (Ong 1988; Spivak 1989, 1999; Mohanty 1991b, 1997; Kandiyoti 1998). The term *postcolonial* does not refer to the period after the end of formal colonialism but to a set of theoretical and political positions. In brief, the postcolonial problematic draws attention to the forms of knowledge (scholarship) that were brought into being during the longue durée of colonial rule and continue into the present. Colonial scholarship or discourses (texts, practices, and institutions) represents colonial subjects as "backward," and the world in simple binaries such as "West/the rest," "modernity/tradition," "civilized/barbaric."[7] These representations are seen as always already existing as such (universal, essential) and thus erase any traces of colonial presence and intervention (ethnocentrism/Euro-centrism). Postcolonial scholarship draws analytically on poststructural insights, but it differs from the latter in that colonial power and practices are seen as constitutive of "Western" modernity. Of the various and debated lessons of the postcolonial critiques, I draw on two specific, interrelated meanings of representation to bear on the preceding discussion of WID and GAD and that of Matamba y Guasá that follows.[8] The first refers to representation as the constitution or production of the subjects and objects of intervention; the second refers to representation as *speaking for* or on behalf of marginalized or subaltern subjects.[9]

In her often cited essay "Under Western Eyes," Chandra Mohanty (1991b) analyzes Western feminist writings on so-called Third World women and suggests that they "discursively colonize the material and historical heterogeneities of the lives of women in the third world, thereby producing/re-presenting a composite, singular 'third world woman'" (1991b, 53). According to Mohanty, portrayals of Third World women as monolithic impoverished victims of patriarchy and/or capitalist development minimize the fact that women become women not just vis-à-vis men but also vis-à-vis particular class, religious, racial, colonial, national, and other historical and political locations. This is not a point about the plurality among women or heterogeneity of women's identities as is commonly misunderstood. Rather, Mohanty's argument is that there is no a priori Third World woman, but she is *discursively* produced as such by recent Western feminism in a manner reminiscent of colonial practices. The highlighted terms are commonly misread, so let me clarify that discourses are not merely textual, "the West" does not refer to a geographic location, and colonialism is not a time or an event of the past. Mohanty carefully parses out how representing Third World women through such binaries as "domination/resistance," "developed/underdeveloped," "victims/agents," replicates the universalism, ethnocentrism/Euro-centrism, and essentialism of colonial discourses. What is problematic about these representations is that like colonial discourses, they occlude the complex, contradictory, incomplete, and power-laden processes and practices against and within which women emerge and act. This argument does not deny the existence of "real" people and the "material" problems of poverty, hunger, inequality, and so on. It does, however, call into question practices — scholarly, developmental, or otherwise — that claim to know the unmediated reality or present a nondiscursive truth.

Gender experts counter these critiques for being untranslatable into action and for their textual and theoretical density. Their countercritiques can be summarized as follows (in no particular order). First, analyses of discourse and representation are too textual and have limited utility for pragmatic policy actions in development. Second, the focus on differences and heterogeneity can undermine the need for solidarity and collective struggles for democratic rights and greater inclusion in development (Nzomo 1995; Udayagiri 1995). Third, the warnings against essentialism and universalism can render the counterdiscourses and resistances of Third World women invisible, and thus leave no room for coalition building and political action. Finally, the "dense, theoretical language" of these critiques is not accessible to the large majority of Third World women who are "mired in widespread illiteracy and economic crisis" (Parpart and Marchand 1995, 19).

In response to these critiques, let me say that we might share Mohanty's concerns about Western feminist writings on Third World women because of our "own implication and investment in contemporary debates in feminist theory, and the urgent political necessity . . . of forming strategic coalitions across, class, race, and national boundaries" (Mohanty 1991b, 52–53). Yet we might want to be wary of pragmatic policies and development solutions. After all, despite the institutionalization of Third World development and of women's concerns through WID and GAD, the material conditions of poor women have only worsened. But such a response, and the other critiques of postcolonial feminism sketched here, overlook its key lesson: that the ostensibly nonideological concerns over women's development rest on and replicate colonial discourses about the Third World in general and women in particular. This lesson should not be confused with a postdevelopmentalist critique that posits development discourses as an extension of colonial practices and proposes retrieving subaltern voices and "counterdiscourses" of resistance as a solution (Escobar 1995). Postdevelopmentalist critiques are not postcolonial because they neglect that the "West" and the "rest" emerge relationally and constitute each other, albeit in uneven and contradictory ways (Asher 2012). The postdevelopmentalist focus on alternatives, then, is different from the postcolonial feminist insight that the relation between domination and resistance is dynamic, and women act *through* their active engagement *with* (not just *against*) multiple relations of power.

This last point leads me to the second meaning of representation and Gayatri Spivak's caution about the need to be persistently skeptical about representing subaltern voices (Spivak 1999). Among feminists struggling to mobilize postcolonial insights constructively, Spivak's remarks about "strategic essentialism" have gained much traction. But she warns, "the idea of the disenfranchised speaking for themselves, or the radical critics speaking for them; this question of representation, self-representation, representing others, is a problem" (1990, 63). That is, "strategic essentialism" cannot be translated as a license for scholars and advocates "to represent" or "speak on behalf of" someone. Rather, Spivak urges us to keep alive the question of representation—as an impossibility and a necessity—as part of the struggle to address the "real" problems of poverty and inequality. I believe the postcolonial feminist lesson here is that we need to think historically, politically, and analytically about ourselves as investigating subjects and Third World women as the subjects of intervention and action. I turn to this task next.

Matamba y Guasá: The Network of Black Women of Cauca

The Colombian Pacific lowlands are part of the natural resource–rich Chocó Department biogeographic region extending from southern Panama to northern Ecuador along the Pacific Coast. A global biodiversity hot spot, the region is home to a variety of ecosystems and myriad plant and animal species, many endemic to the area. In the early 1990s most of this region was yet to be overrun by drug cultivators and traffickers, guerrillas, or paramilitary forces. It was better known as a supplier of natural resources: timber, gold, platinum, silver, oil, and natural gas. Ninety percent of its population is Afro-Colombian. In 1993 the Colombian government passed a law (Law 70), based on Article 55 of the 1991 constitution, that recognizes Afro-Colombians as a separate ethnic minority and accords them various rights, including collective titles to their lands. The 1991 constitution also introduced widespread neoliberal reforms to generate economic development and extensive environmental conservation measures to preserve Colombian biodiversity. To implement these laws, the Colombian state launched numerous sustainable development initiatives to promote economic growth, conserve the environment, and improve local living standards in the Pacific region.

I initially went to Colombia to study collective land use among Afro-Colombians and their effects on the biodiverse environment.[10] However, the situation in the region was marked by paradoxes. State officials and Afro-Colombian activists seemed to agree that Chocó was rich in both biodiversity and cultural diversity and that these diversities were interrelated and needed to be protected. But there was little consensus on who was really Afro-Colombian, what constituted traditional or culturally appropriate practices, and the boundaries of black collective lands. Within this context, there was a burgeoning of grassroots organizing, including by black women at the local and regional levels. In their turn, Colombian state entities working in the region sought the participation of Afro-Colombian communities, especially that of black women, in its interventions. The state's apparent interest in local needs and gender concerns was related to the mandates of decentralization and participation outlined in the 1991 constitution and to the terms of international funding.

In light of this traffic, my research project changed and in 1995 I returned to Colombia to examine the multiple and contested struggles for black ethnic and territorial rights in the Pacific lowlands of Colombia.[11] Part of my task was to trace the heterogeneity of these struggles and differences in how blackness and black rights were constituted by various Afro-Colombian groups, including women's organizations.

From the outset, I faced a series of methodological and epistemological dilemmas. My training as a natural and social scientist stressed that my identity, my political beliefs and prior knowledge, the context within which the research was done—none of these were supposed to have any bearing on my research. However, in the 1990s, an unusual constellation of circumstances allowed me to gain unique insights into how Afro-Colombian struggles, including black women's activisms, were unfolding. On the one hand, as an Indian fluent in Spanish who lived in the southern United States and had done extensive fieldwork in Latin America, I was often treated as a privileged insider in black struggles. I was invited to observe and expected to attend the many meetings held by and for Afro-Colombian groups. In return I had to satisfy their curiosity about my identity (as an Indian woman) and my politics (concerning black movements, Indian independence struggles, Gandhian nonviolence, etc.). On the other hand, as a nonblack I was not allowed to participate fully in black ethnocultural politics. For instance, I was invited to one retreat to teach yoga to black activists to help them relax after long, frustrating workshops on developing political strategies. But I was not allowed to attend the workshops.

In addition to my ambiguous insider-outsider status, the multiplicity of gender, region, and ideology that marked the ethnocultural politics in the Pacific region also enabled these conversations. For example, some black women's groups struggled with their crucial yet unacknowledged role in black political struggles (Asher 1997). Nor did black women always agree with their *compañeros* about who was and was not an insider. Among some Afro-Colombian women's groups I was treated as a double insider—as a woman and as an Indian who was not black but who was not white either. Many black women were especially keen to discuss their experiences with ethnic and gender struggles and asked me to share my knowledge of Indian women's struggles.

Within the context of this research, I learned that Afro-Colombian women have always been active and visible in Pacific life. Their roles and activism were taking on new forms and significance in the 1990s in the context of the changing political economy and cultural politics in the region.[12] The Red de Organizaciones Femeninas del Pacífico Caucano Matamba y Guasá (Matamba y Guasá Network of Women's Organizations of Cauca) was one such network of black women's organizations from the department of Cauca in the Pacific lowlands of Colombia. It was established in 1996 to "consolidate their [black women's] struggles and to help them communicate with each other" (Red Matamba y Guasá 1997). Matamba y Guasá members are engaged in a number of activities— growing food and medicinal plants, promoting informal and formal education, establishing health care and housing projects, helping implement the law that recognizes the ethnic rights of black communities. Afro-Colombianas claim that through these tasks they fundamentally support the cultural and development politics in the Pacific region as black women.

Like rural women in many parts of the world, black women in the Colombian Pacific lowlands work within and beyond the household. Black women's domestic and community chores include subsistence farming, taking goods for sale to the market, making *guarapo* and *viche* from sugarcane, and many other tasks.[13] Luisa, a woman from the Grupo María Auxiliadora del Río Saija, describes the work of black women in a *copla* called "Trabajo de la Caña" (Sugarcane Work):[14]

Son las cinco de la mañana
Me levanto a cocinar
Voy a filar mi machete
Para irme a trabajar.

Coro
Ay! pobre mujer,
Qué bonita estás (bis)

Llegando al cañaveral
Me encomienzo a rociar
Y recojo mi cañita
Para irla a cargar.

Yo le digo a mi comadre
Que me venga ayudar
Llamando nuestro hijos
Y mi esposo dónde está!

Lo mando a cortar la leña
Pal' guarapo cocinar
Ay! Marido, yo le digo
Al tonel lo vamos a echar

Ya el guarapo está fuerte
Lo vamos a destilar
Voy a arreglar mi cochito
Y el viche sacando ya.

A mi comadre una botella
Que me vino ayudar
Y el resto que nos queda
Lo vamos a negociar.

Este es nuestro proceso
Para el viche sacar
Si ustedes lo quieren
Pal' Saija a trabajar.

It is five a.m.
I wake up to cook
I go to sharpen my machete
And go to work.

Chorus
Ay! poor woman
You are so beautiful

On reaching the sugarcane field
I begin to weed
And collect my cane
To take it with me.

I ask my comadre/girl friend
To come and work with me
Calling our children
But my husband, where is he!

I send him to cut firewood
To make guarapo
Ay! husband, I tell him
We will put it in the barrel.

Now that the guarapo is strong
We will distill it
I am going to fix my vessel
And we will brew viche.

A bottle for my girl friend
Who came to help me
Whatever is left
We will sell.

This is our process
To distill viche
If you want it
Come to Saija to work.

Members of Fundación Chiyangua, a group from Río Guapi, note that it is around such work that women organize:

> The organizational force of black women comes from work, from life itself. When women go in search of el chocolatillo or to fish, they often leave for up to five days.[15] Others stay in the house. For example, ones who are pregnant or unwell stay back with all the children: If I go, I leave the children with the neighbor and she takes care of them. If I have an older daughter she takes care of all the children, including the neighbors' children. That is the tradition and it becomes a form of work. (El Hilero 1998, 16)

In the 1980s, women in several Pacific towns formed small groups around their productive activities (such as baking, sewing, selling fish and produce). Colombian state programs of the time encouraged these groups to form cooperatives to facilitate development efforts, such as microcredit lending.[16] However, many women, especially from rural areas along the extensive network of Caucan rivers, could not participate in state programs because of the remote locations of their homes. Thus, in the 1990s they formed self-help groups, such as Promoción de la Mujer from Río Saija and Grupo de Apoyo a la Mujer from Río Timbiquí. Referring to how Fundación Chiyangua began, members note that it "emerges from a long history. It has some specific objectives: the recuperation of food and medicinal plants to ensure the subsistence and health needs of their community, and also to conserve biodiversity. The other aim is to strengthen organizational skills and training, especially among rural women" (El Hilero 1998, 16). During several conversations, Teófila Betancourt (a member of Chiyangua and now regional coordinator of Matamba y Guasá) mentioned to me that rural and urban black women wanted to get together to share their experiences and broaden the organizational base. This desire led them to establish Matamba y Guasá in 1996 to bring together "women defending their ethnic and territorial rights, and working for the welfare of their families and their communities" (Red Matamba y Guasá 1997).

By 1999, Matamba y Guasá consisted of seventy-four groups. Each group undertook activities based on its members' needs and experiences. The groups from Río Guapi promoted the use of plants from their *azoteas* and developed menus of traditional dishes; the groups in the Río Timbiquí region concentrated on raising pigs and chickens for food and sale; the groups in Río Saija focused on extracting traditional products from local food crops (such as molasses from sugarcane). Other groups in the network formulated projects to build houses, promote primary health care, find better transportation to and from regional markets, and obtain basic education for black women and their children.

Matamba y Guasá drew the attention of state agencies and NGOs to the key role Afro-Colombianas could play in sustainable development and conservation enterprises. Subsequently, several Matamba y Guasá undertakings began receiving varying degrees of logistical and financial support from these entities. For example, "productive" activities, such as raising chickens or processing food crops for sale, were sponsored by local development efforts. Under their mandates to conserve the region's biodiversity, national and international conservation projects supported Afro-Colombiana attempts to recuperate native food and medicinal plants. Because of their initiatives and efforts, Matamba y

Guasá members were also called on to participate in two key efforts to implement Law 70: a project to demarcate property boundaries and confer collective land rights, and another to outline community development plans in consultation with the local populace. In these ways, black women become key players in many regional organizations and activities, such as forming community councils, leading ethnic rights workshops, and calling meetings to recognize and preserve ethnic diversity.

Reading Afro-Colombian Activism: Differences, Discourses, and Dialogues

As I have discussed, WID/GAD efforts are responsible for the institutionalization of women and gender issues within development concerns based on two interrelated premises: first, that effective and efficient development depends on women's labor; second, that women's empowerment and welfare depends on their inclusion and recognition within existing development frameworks. Thus, WID and GAD readings of Matamba y Guasá activities highlight how Afro-Colombianas contest social relations of power and dominance by organizing around their "productive" and "reproductive" work. These approaches also contend that Afro-Colombianas are empowering themselves to become participants and decision makers in the development processes that affect them and their communities.

The copla below (presented during the Second Working Meeting of Matamba and Guasá) elucidates WID/GAD approaches.

La Biodiversidad es parte
De nuestra preocupación
Y por eso en el evento
Fue un tema de atención

Y en los tiempos de ahora
Nadie se puede quejar
Pues organizaditas
Mucho podemos lograr

Capacitación queremos
En técnica agropecuaria
Formación social
Y lideres comunitarios

Fue un tema de atención
Para invitarlos a todos

A seguir con los cultivos
En los tiempos de ahora

Las mujeres de estas tierras
Nos estamos preocupando
Por el progreso, el cultivo
Y por seguir organizando

Es un trabajo muy duro
No hay quien diga no es verdad
Con sacrificios y esfuerzos
Se llega a un buen final

Biodiversity is part
Of our concern
That is why it was
A theme of our meeting

In these times
We cannot complain
Because organized
We can gain much

We want to train ourselves
In agricultural technologies
Social formation
And community leadership

It was a theme today
To invite all
To continue with our cultivations
Today

The women of these lands
Are concerned
About progress, about culture
And about being organized

It is hard work
Nobody can deny it
With sacrifices and strength
We can reach a good end

The reference to terms such as *training, agricultural technologies,* and *progress* indicate that Afro-Colombianas are engaged with the concepts and activities of mainstream economic development. The juxtaposition of conservation, development, and women's sacrifices alerts us to the limitations of thinking of Afro-Colombiana organizing as simply resistance to power relations or as struggles for inclusion. That is, a binary representation of black women's subjectivities does little to help us understand the differences among them or the contradictions and unevenness of their struggles.

Black women understand these complexities without recourse to the language of postcolonial feminism or WID/GAD tools. This is evident in their texts—interviews, statements, poetry, stories, and songs. Issues of common concern, complaints, conflicts, news, and more are expressed through coplas such as the two quoted herein (Proyecto Ríos Vivos 2000). Indeed, wordplay is a central feature of Afro-Colombian culture and is reflected in the name of the network: *Matamba* is the name of a very strong vine and *Guasá* is a name of a musical instrument that is traditionally played by women. Here the terms are used to denote the strength of black women and a call to collective action. This oral culture is the fulcrum of the communication strategy of the women of Matamba y Guasá.

Black women are also cognizant of the multiple networks of social and political relations within which they live. For instance, women's struggles are not always against men, especially because many of the women are heads of their households. In Luisa's copla, "Sugarcane Work," the narrator calls on both her husband and her girl friend to work with her. Matamba y Guasá members also noted that they neither think of themselves as subordinate nor consider their work antagonistic to that of their menfolk. Yet during my interview with coordinating committee members, Eden said, "it took a lot of work, especially for those who have men in their household." Of the seventy-four groups linked to Matamba y Guasá, seventy are for women only. Men are welcomed to these groups, noted the compañeras, as long as they "behaved themselves." Although men are allowed to participate in group activities and meetings, only women make decisions.

Similarly, Afro-Colombianas note that as women and as blacks, their struggles are a key part of broader ethnic and territorial struggles. Members of the coordinating committee reflect their astute understanding of power relations within these struggles in the following statement about Matamba y Guasá's relations with black organizations in the region: "We meet them in public spaces but we maintain our characteristics. We interact and reach a consensus but we do not want to get involved in clientelist networks. Rather than obtaining representation and power, we look for spaces of participation for black women."

Afro-Colombianas maintain black solidarity in public. However, they maintain organizational autonomy and remain critical of "obtaining power and representation" through the clientelist networks of mainstream party politics in Colombia.

Matamba y Guasá members also understand that their alliances with state and nongovernmental entities are similarly fraught with tension. As a member of Fundación Chiyangua, Teófila Betancourt participated in state-sponsored "ethnoscience" workshops. Although she spoke positively of the information and knowledge exchanged during these workshops during a conversation in July 1999, she expressed skepticism about the utility of national "biodiversity databanks" for local communities. She continued, "We do not trust too many institutions and agencies. We speak with you because we know you especially through Fundación HablaScribe [a regional NGO]. But we prefer not to get involved in things we do not understand or with people and groups that we do not care about." Recognizing that there are differences of needs and strategies among the groups linked to the network, each group made its own decisions about seeking funds for its activities.

There are differences among Afro-Colombian women, they are aware of them, they have chosen to identify commonalities among themselves and form alliances across them, they reject that black women are primarily "victims" who need aid from the outside, they have a strong understanding of their self-worth, and they are keenly aware of the power of words, discourses, and representation. These issues are underscored in the vision and political perspective of the organizations of the network published in the 1997–98 annual bulletin:

> It is important to clarify that the meeting spaces [of the network] are generated and constructed by us, with our own initiatives. We have been struggling for recognition of women in our region and to overcome [the obstacles to recognition]. Activities such as ours, imply sacrifices, imply surrender to make our dreams come true and to achieve the proposed objectives. Beginning from these principles today we are ready to identify ourselves as women and come together as a gender, to recognize our similarities and differences.
>
> We do not want to be represented "by" anyone. We want to be considered protagonists of our lives and of our world. (Red Matamba y Guasá 1997–98, 15–16).

Attention to black women's words, texts, and discourses could lead to romantic assertions about their resistance and political activism. Yet viewed in the political economic and sociocultural context of the Colombian Pacific, they serve to interrupt activists' and scholars' tendencies to generalize about black women's identities and activism. Attention to texts in contexts serves to complicate our understanding of black women's activism, highlighting how it is shaped differentially, unequally, and discursively.

Postcolonial feminists and feminists of color in the West (see chapters 8, 15, 16, and 17 in this volume) have repeatedly pointed out that for women of color in the West as for Third World women, struggles for gender rights are intertwined with issues of racism, capitalism, and nationalism (and now globalization). This insight helps flag how black women's concerns and the responses of Afro-Colombiana networks emerged within the context of multifaceted, intertwined, and mutually constitutive relations of power—of gender (as women), of race or culture (as blacks), of class (as poor people), and of location (as rural, Pacific residents) at a time when blacks were granted special rights and black social movements were in the process of ethnicization to translate new laws into concrete results. Not surprisingly, each struggle affected the others: meeting basic needs remained a central concern of black women's cooperatives because prevalent economic models destroyed or failed to provide adequate livelihoods. Nor had the broader black struggles yet provided concrete economic alternatives; productive activities therefore remained central to women's concerns. At the same time, as local leaders of the network such as Teófila Betancourt noted, these political economic concerns were linked to the marginalization and exploitation of Afro-Colombians. That Afro-Colombianas were aware of the multiplicity and complexities of these realities and were negotiating them skillfully is evident from the astute remarks of network members. Stressing that the primary aim of the Black Women's Network was "revindication of ethnicity, gender, and appropriation of territory," black women's groups attempted to strengthen the organizational links between and among black communities and establish political alliances beyond the region (El Hilero 1998; Red Matamba y Guasá 1997, 1997–98). Afro-Colombianas were also keenly aware of their audiences, knowing well what could and could not be articulated within the fractured political economy and cultural politics of the Pacific.

Concluding Remarks

Since the 1970s, concerns over the global environmental crisis and the future availability of natural resources for continued economic growth have led to alliances among academics, government agencies, national and international NGOs, and multilateral banks. Asserting the importance of biodiversity for global human welfare, these alliances focus on generating plans to conserve biodiversity efficiently and effectively and promote sustainable economic development in the Third World. As large-scale, externally imposed development projects fail in Colombia, as in other parts of the Third World, discourses on sustainable management of the environment emphasize participatory and decentralized forms of development and conservation. This focus on the capacities of heretofore marginalized entities, such as women, indigenous communities, and grassroots groups, occurs at a time when Third World states are in the process of redefining their roles and reformulating the relationship between themselves and civil society. Afro-Colombian women's activities and organizations emerge and function within this context of globalization.

Since the end of the 1990s, the political and economic realities of the Pacific lowlands (as of other parts of Colombia) have taken a turn for the worse. Local people are increasingly caught in the crossfire of violence unleashed by the increased presence of armed forces (guerrillas, paramilitary, and military) and drug dealers in the region. Since 1999 an estimated four million Afro-Colombians have been involuntarily displaced from their homes. In the context of escalating violence (supported in good part by U.S. funding for the War on Terror), binaries such as theory versus praxis are inadequate for explaining how the Colombian state's inability (or unwillingness) to address the basic human rights of its citizens is linked to intertwined local, national, and global processes of power. They are also problematic because they rest on apolitical explanations of development and promote benevolence rather than a critical solidarity with black women's struggles. In short, they replicate colonial discourses.

In this chapter, I have argued that a postcolonial feminist reading of black women's activism suggests situating black struggles geopolitically to understand the dynamic nature of domination and resistance and the uneven and multiple power relations within which women act. In keeping with the contributions to this volume, I stress the heterogeneity of women's and feminist movements and trace how race and ethnicity intersect with gender, class, and other factors to shape Latin American women's subjectivities, needs, and activism. I invoke postcolonial feminist theories to remind us—scholars and gender experts—to reflect critically on our desires and methods to better the lives of Third World women, question our locations and translations/interpretations, and remind us that our feminist political projects are implicated and embedded within complex and uneven networks of power relations.

Notes

This chapter was originally published as "'Texts in Context': Afro-Colombian Women's Activism in the Pacific Lowlands of Colombia," *Feminist Review* 78 (2004): 1–18.

1. For detailed overviews and critiques of the WID and GAD approaches, see Braidotti et al. (1994), Kabeer (1994), Saunders (2002), and Tinker (1990). For a succinct but thorough overview of the lessons of postcolonial literature see Wainwright (2008).

2. Elsewhere (Asher 2000) I discuss how the concerns over economic growth become linked to environmental ones in the search for "sustainable development." Although I acknowledge that the debate about these linkages and about sustainable development is important and ongoing (currently connected with discussions about climate change), a satisfactory engagement with it is beyond the scope of this chapter.

3. There were broadly parallel discussions about women and gender within natural resource management and environmental discourses. For instance, in the 1980s Third World women began being characterized as "resource guardians" and "stewards of nature," rather than "resource degraders" and "victims." Ecofeminists such Vandana Shiva from India and Wangari Maathai from Kenya were instrumental in highlighting Third World women's dependence on nature for their survival. Development agencies began to describe women as key players in sustainable natural resource development and environmental management (Dankelman and Davidson 1988). For reasons of space I do not engage with gender and environment debates here.

4. There is by now a large body of literature examining the impact of structural adjustment policies on women in the developing world. For an early discussion on these impacts see Sparr (1994).

5. Development with Women in a New Era (DAWN), formed in 1984, is foremost among women's groups from the South that are critical of Western development models and especially WID approaches. See Sen and Grown (1987) for detailed discussions of DAWN's positions on women, gender, and development. Also see Braidotti et al. (1994) and Saunders (2002) for critical perspectives on DAWN.

6. Terms such as the environment and biodiversity also become part of these realms (Asher 2000). For example, the UN Conference on Environment and Development in Rio de Janeiro in 1992 and the UN Women's Conference in Beijing in 1995 both emphasized the important role of women in environmental management and biodiversity conservation.

7. See Hall (1996) for an accessible and clear discussion of the discourses of "the West and the rest."

8. See Williams and Chrisman (1994) for a discussion about the relations between colonialism, imperialism, and capitalism, an overview and debates about the origins and theoretical foundations of postcolonial thought, and excerpts from postcolonial writings.

9. Although many postcolonial feminists have developed these arguments, I draw on the works of Chandra Mohanty and Gayatri Spivak because their work is among the most cited and also most misread in the development feminist literature.

10. In the Pacific lowlands, people of African descent refer to themselves in various ways. Following the passing of a law that recognizes "Afro-Colombians" as a separate ethnic minority, the term Afro-Colombian became a commonly used self-descriptor along with the term black. The latter is not considered a derogatory term. On the contrary, it is claimed with much pride for it denotes a linkage with a rich cultural and political history. In recent years, the term Afro-descendant has gained currency in the region. However, it was not in use during the time of my fieldwork.

11. For details of the black struggle in Colombia see Asher (2009), Grueso, Rosero, and Escobar (1998), and Wade (1995) among others.

12. My discussion of Afro-Colombiana activism is based on my ethnographic research in the region (a total of sixteen months from 1993 to 1999) including conversations with members of women's networks such as Matamba y Guasá. I also draw on published and unpublished manuscripts about and by the women's network to inform this discussion.

13. Guarapo and viche are types of liquor from sugarcane usually brewed by women.

14. A copla is a type of poem or popular song mostly composed and sung by women in the Chocó region.

15. Chocolatillo is a plant used in basket making.

16. See Asher (2007), Escobar (1995), and Rojas (1996) for detailed discussions of the emergence and development of women's cooperatives during the development initiatives of the 1980s in the Pacific region of Colombia.

CHAPTER TEN/ *EL FRUTO DE LA VOZ/*THE "DIFFERENCE" OF MOYENEÍ VALDÉS'S SOUND BREAK POLITICS

MACARENA GÓMEZ-BARRIS

In June 2002, the Chilean feminist nonprofit *La Morada* sponsored a free street concert by the ocean in the tourist destination Viña del Mar to showcase its community work and health campaigns.[1] The objective of the event was to publicize a new study that had found an increased incidence of HIV contraction among Chilean youth. Vocalist and composer Moyeneí Valdés was the event's spokesperson and main attraction, in addition to the six other band members of the former jazz fusion group Mamma Soul. At the time, Valdés was still with the group that had ruptured the masculinist rock-oriented scene during the late 1990s with its "all-female" musical presence. Mamma Soul had also broken new sonic ground with its hybrid jazz/funk/hip-hop musical *alcances* and its thoughtful integration of female folk musical histories into its repertoire. When Valdés stepped onto the stage during the first sound check of the early afternoon rehearsal, I knew this would be a unique and unforgettable experience. I quickly regretted leaving the camcorder behind; my desire to disappear amid the crowd had wrongly led me to opt for a notebook and pen.

By the late afternoon a sizable group of about two hundred had gathered around the makeshift stage, awaiting the band but mostly anticipating Valdés's arrival, a vast on-stage presence in any condition. Dressed in tautly drawn Yoruba patterned clothing, a headdress, and mile-high spiked heels, Valdés strode to the front of the stage a few minutes later, proudly displaying the silhouette of her eight months' pregnant belly. As in the many performances that I've seen of hers since, Valdés offered a sublime concert that showcased her multiple talents as singer, dancer, and songwriter, all delivered with a force that can only be described as otherworldly. She rapped a series of complicated but seamlessly delivered lyrics into the microphone, performed a fiery solo on the conga, and at the end of the concert was moved to bless the stage in gratitude to Pachamama (the Aymara word for Mother Earth). In the final moments of the performance, Valdés made a fierce denunciation of the legacies of Augusto Pinochet's violence and damned the absence of political and judicial will to prosecute human rights violators during the transition to democracy. In less doctrinaire format, she marked her personal history as someone who experienced homelessness after the turmoil of her father's political execution. This semi-rant, semi–personal testimonial provided an entree into what unfolded as a disturbing yet beautiful rendition of "Gracias a la Vida," Violeta Parra's famous song.

Throughout the two-hour performance, I had barely noticed that anyone else was on stage beside her. Through sheer will Valdés seemed to whip up the clouds above into a menacing storm that threatened to pour down on the audience at any moment. When her haunting rendition of the folk song was over, I was too breathless to move. Even after the remains of the equipment had been cleared off stage and the rain had begun to come down, I remained motionless. It took me a few minutes to raise myself out of this stupor. When I did, I noticed my notebook poking out of the muddy waters of the street gutter.

Perhaps only in Valdés's skillful hands could this particular layered sequence of narrative, sound, and lyrics produce political and aesthetic possibility through a form of cultural translation. The stupor I experienced as researcher was the sheer force of the multiple embodied feminist translations that Valdés made on stage; as Claudia de Lima Costa (2006) deftly argues, translation can be a nexus of discourses and practices that have a genealogy in feminist practices. In this case, the productive encounter is routed through musicality, her body, and her very subjectivity.

Postmarket, Postenchantment

Reflecting on that uncanny performance, it seems that alongside great musical and performance talent, Valdés's crowning achievement that night was her ability to produce multiple affective modes and conjurings as forms of audience engagement that successfully crossed the exclusionary and dominant borders put up by moral, conservative, and religious discourses that police the female body and sexual practices. Through an emotional exchange between performer and audience that alternately produced rapture, pleasure, anger, melancholia, and appreciation, Valdés was able to articulate a politics in what amounted to an unmooring of sex practices, feminism, and the body, on the one hand, with state violence, militarization, and hegemonic masculinity on the other. By crafting social and emotive meaning for her audience, Valdés literally broke through the "structure of feeling" of postdictatorship Chile, where the combination of violence and commodity culture had produced social anomie, as well as an amnesiac national political culture, despite numerous important efforts to produce social justice in the aftermath of authoritarianism. Instead, Valdés's cultural politics, sound and movement had the effect of creating adhesion and collective reflection about pressing social issues, changing the terms of power through the epistemology of sound.

Much has been made of Chile's "economic miracle," the supposed result of the neoliberalization framework first put in motion by Milton Friedman and the Chicago Boys during Pinochet's regime. Sheer brutality and necropolitics were the basis for this economic restructuring. In the post-Pinochet, democratization era, market logics seemed to erase, transform, and otherwise tame the Left-political history of the nation that had combined cultural efforts at aesthetic rupture with the emergence of social movements for material equity toward a radical cross-class coalitional politics that incorporated millions (Gómez-Barris 2009). Given these developments, I raise the following set of questions. What political and aesthetic options were left in the wake of mass commodity culture that produced willing forgetting about those excluded from market miracles? Where did Chile's disenchanted youth population fit into this puzzle? The recent student protests against further privatization of public university education are one important route for new forms of social expression in the era of neoliberalism. However, that night, Valdés seemed to offer a response to the complex nexus of historical and social circumstances that sutured state violence to economic globalization resulting in rampant consumerism.

Several meaningful moments during Valdés's performance attest to a feminist politics as the basis for dialogue with her audience, who were and continue to be mostly young people. Rather than staging a set of already rehearsed political convictions, dead ends, and words without meanings, Valdés took the opportunity of the momentary silences between songs to discuss heterosexual and same-sex intimacy and the importance of the body as a site of autonomy. In a nation that has been governed by Catholic morality, heteropatriarchy, and authoritarian strains, Valdés's outspokenness on such matters ruptured the dominant cultural scripts. As this volume suggests, part of the work of the practice of translation is its ability to exceed the multiple structural containments and asymmetrical power relations embedded within any given scalar locale, precisely the work that Valdés did with her sound break political engagements.

Sound break politics are cultural efforts that rupture the hegemonic drone of economic neoliberalism that produce a visual and sound economy of commercialization, white noise, and an endless barrage of products. In the overly stimulated society that is late capitalism, Valdés mobilizes the capaciousness of sound and rhythm to open a space for the narration of a politics of social awareness. In my interviews with her and in multiple performances in public venues in Santiago, Valdés places such a rupture within a genealogy that links back to female folk singing, the Allende years, socialism, and feminist movements of the 1970s and 1980s. As she spoke about desire and responsibility, the mostly under-twenty crowd reacted, silently listening, linking arms, and seemingly learning from her pedagogical modes. At the La Morada event Valdés coached young people on the pleasures of sex, the importance of awareness about the AIDS crisis and its disproportionate effect on women, and the global unequal access to HIV/AIDS drug medicine, all of which were followed up by a soulful battery of lyrics.

In a nation where personal and social conformity is rampant, and within a predominantly male music scene, female vocalist and musician Valdés is unique. In part this uniqueness is about a consciously produced pan-Africanist fashion aesthetics, which at the time stood out in the Chilean public sphere, where gray and dark blue tones are every young person's daily school uniform and formal business suits the attire of hegemonic middle-class urban dwellers. How is Valdés's difference both constructed and revelatory of deeper problems within homogeneous discourses of society and culture?

Possessing Uniqueness

As she walked down the street with long locks and African print dresses, Valdés's pan-Africanist fashioning stood in stark contrast to the racial landscape, whereby the representation and creation of whiteness — on television, on census responses, and as a "possessive investment" (Lipsitz 1993) erased the admittedly small but historically present Black population. George Lipsitz argues that white people have material, social, and cultural investments in possessing white identity that get continually remade unless they are involved in the process of antiracist work. Although certainly the ethnic and racial legacies of Chile depart drastically from the U.S. context, I argue that there is a particular Chilean investment in "white" identity that shows up in decisions about personal security, in residential patterns, in symbolic absences of darker-skin people from the media, in desire for lighter physiognomy, and so forth. Many scholars have been remiss to bring categories and concepts of racial analysis to bear on places like Chile, instead favoring class-based or reconstructed

Marxist approaches. My point here is to bring to bear a concept like "possessive investment in whiteness" to a place and history like neoliberal Chile, if even only suggestively. For instance, despite a marked increase in Cuban, Peruvian, and African Black migration to the country over the past ten years, contemporary Black visibility as style, presence, and legibility, is hardly recognizable in dominant public spheres.[2] In many ways, this erasure works through the history of Chile's particular notion of exceptionalism in Latin America or, to rework Lipsitz's concept as a possessive investment in colonialism, where during the colonial period the elite historically looked toward Europe, especially "white" France, as a site of insatiable material consumption, as a way to devour a whiteness of being. In the aftermath of Salvador Allende's demise in 1973, Pinochet's neoliberalization of the economic, political, and cultural spheres in Chile linked the nation to the Washington Consensus. For Chile, the United States was a kind of hegemonic paternal figure that, despite its logic of empire, the neoliberal nation wanted to mimic its liberalization policies and global "successes."

During the 1960s and 1970s, among most young people the tendency was to critique and shun, like in most Latin American nations, the developmental interventions of the United States as "imperialist," producing a cultural decolonizing shift away from those things European and U.S. toward Andean musicality and spiritual practices. Of course, it would be unfair to characterize the whole of the Chilean population and youth population as similarly invested in the imaginaries and logics of empire and whiteness today. One measure of this was the large-scale antiglobalization marches that happened in 2004 during George W. Bush's visit to Santiago. Although the political Left may be more enlightened on questions of empire, there remains an investment in whiteness by the majority population. Another way to put this is that empire and whiteness have yet to be disentangled in ideological and practical ways in the context of Chile.

Specifically in the aftermath of the military coup rupture of September 11, 1973, the subsequent dual project of nation-making and neoliberalism resulted in a conservative backlash of homogeneity over the multifaceted expression of difference.[3] One instance of this is the degree to which the wide and rapid import of U.S. and European clothing and tastes were quickly incorporated in the mass clothing choices of the youth population, not dissimilar from the U.S. market place. As both an economic project and cultural determinant, neoliberalism operated to erase meaningful "individual" and collective distinctions in the project of making one's life or making a life for oneself. Furthermore, although increasing class inequality existed as a result of the market-oriented reforms, used clothes from the United States appeared en masse to smooth out these external class markers.[4] The cultural significance of the neo-liberal model is that rather than enhance distinctions and life choices, it serves to narrow the social imagination of possibility.

Thus, the desire to imitate the North within a neocolonial structural context further produced difference as a negative attribute. Given the legacies of racism and discrimination within the nation, exacerbated by xenophobia to incoming Afro-Peruvians and Cuban immigrants, Valdés's cultural response has been to produce ever more enhanced versions of uniqueness and excessiveness. Her cultural and racial politics mobilize Africanist sensibilities, political connec-tions, and purposefully "colorful" aesthetics to break through the homogeniz-ing national landscape. An awareness of the vast cultural horizon of both the richness of her distinction and the incommensurable space of difference she occupies, Valdés marks her gender, class, and race location beyond the confines of nation as a process of translation. Since witnessing that striking perfor-mance and her cultural political work as singer/dancer/musician and popular sex educator, I would describe her uniqueness not as a tropicalized object but as an agent that puts pressure on conformity by finding routes out of dominant logics. She breaks through Western-defined universality through disidentifica-tion and finds aesthetic forms of identification with cultural historical traces. Culture continues to be an important arena in a postauthoritarian transition, where discourses over the past were struggled over and rearticulated. Particu-larly feminist and antiracist politics have been routes out of conservative forces and their national ideologies. However, the difference is not solely structured around Valdés's aesthetic sensibilities, which does an important kind of cul-tural work in the neoliberal European white imagination and dominant cul-ture of the nation. Her sound break politics, on stage or elsewhere, are closely linked to feminism, human rights, and transnational racial politics that cross geographic borders in their social imaginaries that recognize difference. The history of revolutionary gender, race, and class politics has helped produce her political education and persona, while also situating the performance of her individual uniqueness within a transnational social sphere of political affini-ties like anticolonial struggle, transnational feminist politics, women of color feminisms, and the radical Black tradition

Following Puerto Rican poet Víctor Hernández Cruz's first use of the term, Susana Chávez-Silverman and Frances Aparicio coined *tropicalization* to de-scribe those tropes of European modernity that essentialize, reify, and fix forms of cultural identity and production in a variety of ways, often to repro-duce U.S. hegemony (Chávez-Silverman and Aparicio 1997). Of course, there is a way in which Valdés's difference could be read as such. However, her embrace of her multiracial identity, her political positionality as a communist youth, her belonging to hip-hop traditions, and her identification with the grassroots organization HIJOS (Hijos por la Identidad y la Justicia contra el Olvido y el Silencio), as a daughter of those who were killed during the dictatorship, mark her as uniquely Leftist, located within an Afro-diasporic arc of cultural production. In this way she literally embodies the South–North, North–South cultural flows exemplified in what Claudia de Lima Costa refers to as critical translation (chapter 6 in this volume).

Furthermore, the powerful presence of Valdés's cultural translation works on the terrain of her performance, both on and off stage. In this way, she fits into a long history of female cultural icons in the Americas—those who did not easily assemble to the machinations of masculinist reproduction of power relations and norms, such as the iconic figures of La Malinche, La Quintrala, Sor Juana Inés de la Cruz, and many others. These female subjects uniquely used their bodies and voices to intervene, and otherwise produce, gendered and racial difference with various social outcomes. Thus, Valdés is not only an object of othering fascination but a cultural producer whose politics and sound embody particular national and international political histories and sprout branches toward a feminist/racial/class translocal cultural politics of possibility.

Postmemory Loss

In the opening sequences of the film *La Cueca Sola*, novelist and radio personality Pedro Lemebel observes that Valdés exudes difference by merely walking down the block in La Florida, the neighborhood they share: her bright pink, alternately blue, alternately green locks, her multiple piercings, and tall platform shoes are enough to turn more than one head.[5] As a cultural symbol of contemporary feminist politics, and as members of the "postmemory" generation, the ones that followed those who directly experienced trauma (Hirsch 2001; Kaiser 2005), Moyeneí Valdés is featured in the striking documentary *La Cueca Sola* (2003).[6] The film weaves together a genealogy of feminist and human rights movements in the nation's recent history. It accomplishes this by using footage of women's street protests and the ever-present *guanaco* threat, the commonly deployed tank whose water cannon is often strong enough to throw activists to the ground.[7] Here, the voices of female subjects, notably Salvador Allende's daughter and former congress member Isabel Allende (not to be confused with the U.S.-based writer of the same name) are central to the filmic narrative of testimonial. One of the film's main intents is to interweave and make explicit the links between the feminist movement of the 1980s and the antiauthoritarian, rising human rights movement of the same period. Put differently, three of the four women featured in the documentary have gained national political stature and recognition,[8] and are icons of both the feminist movement and the human rights movement. As survivors with emotional, psychic, and physical scars, they share the life experience of having had a close male family member disappeared or executed by the military regime.

As a member of a younger generation, Valdés is equally iconic as these well-known women, representing the postmemory generation.[9] In the opening scenes of the film, Valdés offers her story: Her father, Sergio Valdés, was a Communist Party member and mural brigadista. While painting a political mural in the streets of Santiago, Sergio had been gunned down by the Central Nacional de Inteligencia, a branch of Pinochet's secret police. As the film unfolds, we encounter Valdés again, this time in her arrival to a meeting with a group of women in their twenties and thirties from HIJOS, the organization of sons and daughters of those whose relatives had been murdered or disappeared by the authoritarian regime or those whose family members had been tortured without having legal closure over the case.[10] Striking in the conversation is the degree to which Valdés shares common ground with these hijos despite her notoriety. As one young woman intones, "We couldn't believe it when we saw your story published in El Clinic," and another answers, "Yeah public figures usually don't admit it," referring to the silence and stigma around disclosing one's identity of dictatorship loss.

Returning to Valdés's biography, the authoritarian regime indeed produced her identity as a survivor. At the age of fifteen, in an aimless quest to deal with the misery of reality, music saved her. As she discussed one afternoon in 2003 while nursing her newborn baby in her small apartment, drugs and music "on the streets" were ways for her to survive the politically motivated execution of her father, whose persona and world she emulated and dearly loved. She spent time on the streets inhaling glue, scrounging through garbage bins for bits of food, and learning how to play drums, a school for which she is grateful and that offered her the possibility of rising from the ashes of the rupture her father's murder signified. As in most conversations with Valdés, her father's presence floats silently in the room. His bearded image hangs on the wall alongside posters of Bob Marley, Salvador Allende, Walter Rodney, and her own photograph as African queen.

In the several dozen times I have heard her testimonial, whether in public or semi-private settings, the death of her revolutionary artist father and the death of Allende's social dreams are continuously figured as primary moments of artistic loss and later recuperation. "Music," she has said, "enabled [my] survival." Through music, and later taking voice classes with a respected teacher, she initiated her journey to find voice in similar arts. Some of these cultural practices, like dyeing clothes, creating Yoruba patterns, and continuously new hairstyles, were passed down to her through the Black women of her family; others, like sampling and rapping, she learned from the hip-hop community in Santiago. Members of what was often referred to as "the conscious hip-hop world" were always stopping by at Valdés's house. In these various visits, I got a glimpse of the kinds of political investments and connections that surfaced in between improvisation, and between musical breaks, as I describe in the next section.

Cultural Memories of Trans(nation)

Valdés's small split-level apartment was a space of convergence and a hub of activity. Music was always in the background, dye bubbling up from the stove, kids running around, and piles of clothes perpetually being moved to make space to put headphones on and practice some lyrics or beats. In conversations with Valdés and members of her musical community, linking a diasporic memory of transnational activism through figures such as Marcus Garvey and Walter Rodney and anticolonial movements during the 1960s and 1970s in the Caribbean was as important as acknowledging the contributions of Salvador Allende and other revolutionary figures. One pan-Africanist identified male MC referred to this understanding of history as "the necessary project of human consciousness and evolution." This was a striking phrase to me, because one could image a similar kind of statement from those that practice new thought spirituality in California.[11] It seems to me the difference between his view and the new thought movement turned on the pivotal linkage to and definitions of struggles of social justice.[12] An older MC registered, "we're connected to the past and to the future," in "the project of working towards greater collective states of awareness through social change." Thus, composing, writing, rapping, singing, dyeing her own clothes, and creating beats are for Valdés and the Afro-centered community she's a part of a way to recuperate the memory.

The project of cultural memory here is doubly informed. First, it works through a translation of transnational Afro-diasporic histories and continuities (Black pride, Caribbean anticolonialism, musical genealogies, Afro-arts that are passed down maternally). Second, it works by living through and continuing to make live the cultural and political explosion during Allende's social dream, which includes the intertwined genealogies of human rights and feminist struggle, as discussed earlier. Even though female subjects were not often part of the roll call of names that entered into the hip-hop dialogical imagination, Valdés, in more private moments, returned over and over again to Violeta Parra (as music based in popular culture and as a tremendous female presence) as a singular influence. In an interview she said: "She changed the history of Chilean music. She's a genius. At the end of the 1950s she went with her guitar to tour Europe. She was ahead of her time" (Ella cambió la historia de la música en Chile, ¡es una grosa! Al final de los años 50 se iba con su guitarra en barco de gira a Europa. Era una adelantada a su época). Valdés also has plans in the works to produce a CD that would incorporate many Parra songs as reinterpreted tracks. Thus, for Valdés, cultural forms of being, possibility, and alternative political cultures, including feminism, socialism, and pan-Africanist politics, provided ways for her, as she puts it, "to piece out an existence for herself" in the rupture of her father's murder and the wider contextual terrain of slavery, colonialism, imperialism, and state terror.

Though there are many examples of her connection to Afro-based sound, Valdés's song "La Chimba" is one of the finest, because it starts out by lyrically locating her as representing Santiago de Chile, in groove with a global South hip-hop community:

> One more time representin' Santiago de Chile,
> Directly from the Third World flow.
> I come directly from *La Chima*. It's the Black barrio
> of Santiago.
> In my heart I'm agitating
> That body that will keep on enjoying.
> Where there are drums, there is also la guayara
> And el contrú, la zampoña del indio, with the cueca,
> And el bongó.

In these lines and musically, indigenous, African, and *criollo* instruments are intermixed in ways that underscore and enhance the history of Latin American racial and cultural transculturation. The barrio La Chima is figured as central to the urban space of Black cultural survival.

In the past few years, Valdés has moved to Mexico City permanently and been involved in organizing young rapper women into a collective project. In YouTube videos one can watch her with young women who are perhaps ten or more years younger than she and clearly see Valdés as a role model of sorts for their hip-hop work. In a Mexico City radio interview in 2007, Valdés describes how in some ways Chile restricted her ability to grow in musicality and restricted her access to a larger Latin American audience. In many ways, I read this comment as part of her critique of racism in the nation whose homogeneous hegemony again limits the creative capacity of difference and uniqueness. Of course, Chile's relative isolation in the global market, in terms of its distance from important Latin American music recording centers like Mexico City, Miami, and New York, surely contributed to this decision. In either case, Valdés's work with the Mexico City female rapper collective further illustrates her trajectory in sonic and activist cultural politics and the politics of translation.

Matters of Culture

From my point of view as a trained sociologist, analyzing one cultural icon and the accompanying effects or entanglements of that icon's production, like Moyeneí Valdés (in disciplinary terms an n of one), can be constructed as a nonrigorous, tangential, and unconvincing methodology. The assumption is that for social realities to exist as such they must be quantifiable, rather than a mere blip on the radar screen. In this piece, I am interested in pursuing a line of inquiry that centers a female Afro-Andean cultural producer and the embedded quality of her cultural moves. By *cultural moves*, I'm referring to what the sociologist Herman Gray describes as "cultural strategies [that] emphasize struggles for black recognition" and "cultural tactics and organizations that move beyond mere recognition to challenge, disrupt, and unsettle dominant cultural representations and institutions" (2005, 3).

Although cultural studies has made important tracks in this terrain, a focus on cultural icons like Valdés as a unique subject whose production literally "turns heads" and expands the realm of possibilities through racial and feminist politics seems to be impactful enough that it is worthy of sustained inquiry. What does Valdés understand about cultural memory and history that is often gleaned out of official stories of the Chilean nation? How does her difference and uniqueness promote opportunities for critical and social responsibility?

Valdés positions herself and her history within multiple identities and political commitments: as a multiracial (Afro, Mapuche, mestiza) feminist composer, rapper, and conga drummer whose father was a *brigadista*, shot dead by Pinochet's military police. She was already well known in the country as Mamma Soul's lead singer, composer, and conga drummer, an unusual group in the music scene in the nation, as I mentioned earlier, because its seven members were all female, explicitly feminist in their lyrics and interviews, and enormously popular on the charts. In such instances, Valdés embodies and articulates a transnational feminist and raced identity to Chilean audiences. Using interviews, song lyrics, rhythms, and performances, I analyzed how Valdés's hip-hop/jazz cultural productions, dance performances, and politics are dually framed within a tradition of Chilean women singers and a transnational framework of Afro-diasporic music, feminism, and performance.

Questions of identity have conventionally been examined within a national (and modern) framework that often does not consider how transnational ideas and flows influence the making of national social and cultural identities. Well-known Afro-Chilean singer Valdés's cultural work and on-stage persona challenge the assumptions of a nationally bound identity, social formation, and political orientation. Through her individual and social difference—produced out of a community of artistic and political struggle—Valdés offers a future-oriented politics that breaks and challenges the erasure of "difference."

Notes

1. Casa de la Mujer La Morada is a national feminist organization based in Santiago, which began in 1983 as part of the feminist movement in Chile that was spawned during the Pinochet dictatorship. Members played an active role in the downfall of the dictatorship as well as the transition to political democracy. It has broken ground on several issues in the nation, including sex education, queer support groups, and women's community health work and is host to the independent community radio station Radio Tierra.

2. Another instance of the erasure of difference shows up in the struggle for land in the South by a strong and militant Mapuche social movement, which has worked tirelessly for social justice around land, language rights, self-determination, and cultural visibility. Mapuche, Pehuenche, and other indigenous populations are continually constructed in modernity's frame, as in many other Latin American nations, as a residual population that will eventually be seamlessly assimilated into the fold of the nation-state and national homogeneous identity.

3. Given that the nation-state is always about the production of smoothing out meaningful differences, I don't want to overstate the point that this began with the military dictatorship and the political transition. In fact, glossing over, incorporating, or further demarcating ethnic/racial, religious, gender, and sexual difference operates to produce "difference" and the constitution of nation and national subjects (see Gray and Gómez-Barris forthcoming).

4. See Nelly Richard (1998) on the introduction of used clothes from the United States, which effectively homogenizes and disciplines the collective body, "erasing" class differences.

5. Lemebel interviews Valdés for community station Radio Tierra, a piece of which is shown in director Marilú Mallet's *La Cueca Sola* (2003), which features Valdés, as I discuss later.

6. The film is directed by Chilean exile and Canadian resident Marilú Mallet, who also made the 1983 autobiographical film *Journal Inachevé* (*Unfinished Diary*).

7. The term *guanaco* refers to the large military tanks that sprayed enormous amounts of water at peaceful protestors during and after the dictatorship. The name refers to undomesticated llamas whose spitting is characteristic.

8. The women featured in the film are Senator Isabel Allende, Carolina Tohá, Estela Ortiz, and activist Monique Hermosilla.

9. In her important book on the gray zones of memory of this generation, Susana Kaiser (2005) builds on Hirsch's concept of postmemory to describe the particularities of this terrain for the Argentinean dirty war.

10. Impatient with the slow judicial proceedings to prosecute criminals of state terror, HIJOS often takes justice into its own hands by outing torturers in the barrios where they live. Throwing red paint on houses, sticking posters up on street posts with the name of known torturers in the neighborhood, gathering in front of the house for rallies with bullhorns that denounce torture and its practitioners, and so forth.

11. The *new thought spiritual movement* is a better term than *new age*, because the latter evokes facile individualist and consumer religiosity, whereas the former is grounded in communities of spiritual practice.

12. I don't want to stress this difference too much though, because there is a branch of new thought or new consciousness movements in California that take social activism quite seriously, invoking the term *sacred activism*, among others.

CHAPTER ELEVEN/TRANSLATION AND TRANSNATIONALIZATION OF DOMESTIC SERVICE

TERESA CARRILLO

Translations between English-speaking and Spanish-speaking women occur on a daily basis across the United States within the employer–employee relationship of domestic service. Private homes become the meeting ground between immigrant women and employers who have enough disposable income to hire maids, nannies, house cleaners, and caregivers to perform domestic service in their homes. In the exchange of domestic service for an hourly wage, an ongoing process of translation takes place on multiple levels between the employee, her employer, and the increasingly transnational industry of domestic service.

On an individual level, the employee and family she serves contend with language and cultural differences to communicate instructions, preferences, and expectations. The worker is challenged to perform her duties in a way that corresponds to the employer's concept of good homemaking by translating her culture-bound socialization regarding home and family life to what she understands as the norms and expectations of her employer's household. The employer, in turn, converts housekeeping and care-giving chores into a commodity, delegating various tasks to the employee and taking on the role of supervisor of those tasks. Together, both parties engage in a complex reconfiguration of what has been called "women's work," translating nurturance and care into paid labor.

These personalized aspects of translation take place within a larger context of a global market for domestic service and an increasingly transnational division of social reproductive labor. In global cities like Los Angeles and San Francisco, the practice of employing immigrant women from Latin America is widespread. Pierrette Hondagneu-Sotelo studied Mexican and Central American domestic workers in Los Angeles and notes a growing demand for female labor devoted to "commodified social reproduction" combined with a "laissez-faire approach to the incorporation of immigrant women into paid domestic work. No formal government system of policy exists to legally contract foreign domestic workers in the United States" (Hondagneu-Sotelo 2002, 265). Although no formal policies that would allow for work visas for the vast majority of domestic service workers in the United States exist, the norms and policies that do exist have created a uniform and widespread use of undocumented labor in domestic service. The resulting regime of commodified social reproduction creates exploitive conditions for domestic service workers based on their lack of legal immigration status, their exclusion from labor law, and the devaluation of their work within a patriarchal, sexual, and racialized division of labor (Parreñas 2008).

Although patriarchal and racialized norms of domestic servitude are codified and reproduced in the intimate spaces of the home within a context of the transnational domestic service industry, they have not gone unchallenged. In an emerging domestic workers' rights movement, immigrant workers are demanding that their rights be recognized and that their labor be regulated and fairly compensated. In New York and California domestic workers have pushed for legislative changes that would bring domestic service under the purview of labor law, in most cases for the first time. Their efforts have remained somewhat isolated, with a notable absence of mainstream feminist participation in the movement. Feminist organizations may be reluctant to get involved in domestic service worker organizing and advocacy because they understand the issues as labor issues and not issues of gender justice or structural patriarchy. This situation demonstrates how translation on many levels is indispensable to forge the feminist and antiracist alliances imagined in the introductions to this collected volume.

Drawing on the framework of conceptual translation applied to the study of transnational migration by Ewa Morawska and Jonathan Fox, this chapter focuses on the multiple levels of translation needed for feminist coalition building in the face of the transnational domestic service industry. Beyond the translational challenges involved in interpersonal communication, there is a deeper need for translation in the realm of domestic service. The intimate space of the home becomes a workplace, and the profoundly human activities of nurturance and care become commodities. Domestic workers and their employers meet on a completely unequal plane within the sanctity of the employer's home. The employee is perceived as the outsider who is foreign to the language, legal, and labor systems of the employer's community and nation-state. At the same time, nannies, caregivers, and domestic service workers become integrated into the households, families, and communities in which they work. This creates a situation of mutual dependence between employers, employees, and the domestic service industry, yet there is a growing reluctance to acknowledge domestic service work, workers, and their rights. For employer and employee to live and work within this contradiction, a delicate translation is required that can mollify and reconcile two contradictory stories into one. For too long this has been a one-way translation directed from the more powerful of the two parties—the employer. On a larger scale there has been a lack of conceptual translation between feminist movements and the intersectional movements of immigrant domestic service workers. Domestic service workers have not enjoyed the support of mainstream feminist organizations in their resistance to the way immigration and labor policies have codified the racialized and patriarchal structures that uphold the feminist contradictions of the domestic service industry. Morawska wrote, "for our interdisciplinary conversations to allow meaningful 'translations' of concepts and approaches used in different disciplines," we need to expose some of the presuppositions of our particular academic field. She advocates that we become "interdisciplinary polylogues, conversant in many languages and, thus, capable of 'translating' into and in-between disciplines" (Morawska 2003, 612). A critical discussion of the domestic service industry calls for conceptual translation between the language of feminism, transnationalism, and labor to explore the use and exploitation of domestic work in the receiving countries, the exclusion of domestic work from labor laws, and especially the problematic way domestic work is devalued within patriarchal and nativist discourse about domestic service.

In this discourse, domestic workers are illegal aliens performing unskilled labor that housewives used to do "for free." The influences of patriarchy combine with the disempowering effects of an immigrant's undocumented status to erode prestige and value assigned to domestic service and caregiving work. Exclusion of domestic workers from most labor law allows practices that also contribute to the exploitive nature of domestic work. These practices and perceptions have many results. On an individual level domestic service workers remain underpaid, overworked, uninsured, unheard, unrepresented, and unappreciated. Their work is not regulated, gauged, or visible and is exempted from key legislation including U.S. labor law and health and safety laws. Domestic workers are excluded from contributory social safety net programs such as Social Security, Medicare, and unemployment insurance. Consequently, at the end of their working lives domestic workers become old without gaining access to old-age pensions and health insurance. Domestic service work remains afford-able, accessible, and convenient for the employer, who is largely immune from penalties if they neglect to pay payroll taxes or provide benefits for their maids and nannies. (President Bill Clinton's first two female nominees for attorney general in 1993 present notable exceptions.)[1] On the level of the nation-state, the sending country benefits from remittances but provides very limited social welfare functions to migrant workers before they leave or once they return and to families and dependents of workers abroad while they are gone. The United States evades the costs of the social safety net for the bulk of domestic service workers and their families by highlighting their documentation status, thereby disassociating any obligation to the informal workforce. U.S. employers benefit from the labor of the worker without having to worry about or pay for their so-cial welfare needs. These inequitable arrangements are rooted in a patriarchal and anti-immigrant discourse that casts female migrants as unentitled, unde-serving, and illegal. Domestic service workers experience a need for translocal translation that grows out of their complex interactions with local, national, regional, and global power. They experience a need for multiple translations based on their intersectional identity and positionality. Most of all, they expe-rience a mutual need for translation with feminists that will allow for coalition building to create new affiliations, solidarities, and movements for the benefit of all.

Caregivers and Domestic Service Workers in the United States

Today more women are crossing borders to live and work abroad than at any other time in history. The feminization of migration is a worldwide trend that began in the 1960s and continues to the present day. Latin America and the Caribbean have a higher proportion of female to male migration than other regions of the world, with slightly more than half of the migrants from this area being female (Zlotnik 2003). In an earlier article (Carrillo 2007), I argue that the feminization of migration is fueled partly by the transnationalization of domestic service and that a growing number of women from Latin America are making that difficult and dangerous decision to leave their home and come to the United States in search of a job in domestic service.[2] Immigration pol-icies have tracked immigrant women into domestic service, starting with the "public charge" exclusion in the late 1800s and continuing through the many reformulations of policy through the Immigration Reform and Control Act of 1986, Proposition 187 in California in 1994, and the major reforms of immi-gration and welfare policies in 1996 (Carrillo 2007). The fact that women are the most faithful remitters and send home a larger portion of their earnings than men do only feeds the trend toward growing female migration (Ehrenreich and Hochschild 2002). Even though a combination of patriarchal and racist immigration and labor policies have worked against the interests of immigrant women, most of the advocacy work done by domestic service workers has focused solely on changing labor laws.

In the refrain "The hand that rocks the cradle rules the world" a kernel of truth may lie in the idea that some kind of exchange takes place when Latin American immigrants come into U.S. households and engage in homemaking.[3] Hour by hour, day by day, nannies, caregivers, and domestic service workers become integrated into the households, families, and communities in which they work. This integration proceeds in the face of anti-immigrant rhetoric and policies, building the central contradiction of transnational domestic service in the United States of a growing dependence on immigrant domestic service along with a growing reluctance to acknowledge domestic service workers and their rights. The weight of this contradiction bogs down every interaction as women from the United States and those from Latin America engage in communication and exchange within the employer–employee relationship of domestic service. The contradiction is even more stark when considering the political culture and context of the women who migrate from Latin America, more and more of whom come from Mexico.[4]

In 1987 I lived in Mexico City and worked with the Nineteenth of September Garment Workers Union (NSGWU).[5] During that year, I was surrounded by activist women—leaders of the union and of the many independent neighborhood organizations that constituted the popular urban movements. The NSGWU offices were set up in temporary structures around the periphery of what had been a parking lot in the heart of the San Antonio Abad garment district, and women from the growing popular urban movements met on a regular basis at the union locale. The NSGWU offered a free meal to activists on a daily basis, so the union offices became a central meeting place for garment workers and women from the neighborhood associations that formed the two large umbrella organizations of popular urban movements, the Coordinadora Nacional del Movimiento Urbano Popular (National Coordinating Committee of the Popular Urban Movement) and the Asamblea de Barrios. From my position within the NSGWU I was privileged to witness firsthand the emergence of a popular women's movement with an agenda centered around issues that have a great effect on so-called women's work within a traditional division of labor, such as housing, basic needs, and public services. The movement was based on the politicization of women's work and the everyday lives of the poorest urban Mexican families (Carrillo 1998). From the midst of that movement, it seemed that poor women had stretched the boundaries of feminism by making their claims based on their identity as women and their responsibilities within a traditional gendered division of labor. Instead of rejecting their role as primary caretakers of the house and home, poor women in the popular urban movements embraced their role and built a feminist political project around the politicization of women's work (Rodriguez 1994). But when I returned to the United States, I hardly heard one word about the popular women's movement in Mexico. I wonder what happened to that large, vibrant movement and the hundreds of thousands of women who marched, chanted, and made demands to local authorities to put in streets, clinics, and water, gas, and public transportation lines to serve the popular neighborhoods and alleviate some of the burden of women's daily work. A unique form of popular feminism manifested itself in the collective spirit among women in Mexico to politicize their role as caretakers of their families, homes, and communities. But the politicization of women's work did not translate as a feminist demand in the political projects of domestic workers in the United States. When focusing on the setting of domestic service and the politics of domestic work in the United States, what is notable is the absence of feminist ideals and practices that challenge the devaluation of women's work. In its place we see a redefinition of domestic work and domestic service worker issues as labor issues.

Feminist Silence around the Politicization of Domestic Work in the United States

From the earliest articulations of federal labor law in the United States, domestic service work has been exempted or excluded. In the National Labor Relations Act (also called the Wagner Act) of 1935, domestic workers are excluded from the definition of *employee* and thereby limited in their rights to form labor unions and collectively organize. The act's definition of *employee* "shall not include any individual employed . . . in the domestic service of any family or person at his home."[6] Specific exemptions for domestic workers are also found in the Civil Rights Acts in 1964 and 1965, the Occupational Safety and Health Act (1970), and Title VII, which prohibits employment discrimination on the basis of race, color, religion, sex, national origin, disability, or age. The Fair Labor Standards Act (FLSA) of 1938 sets federal minimum wage rates and regulates wages in conjunction with varied state laws. The FLSA does not exclude domestic workers outright but does outline exclusions and exemptions that curtail the applicability of the law for casual employees, including babysitters and caretakers, and for live-in domestic workers who cannot receive overtime wages.

The U.S. Department of Labor enforces laws that offer targeted protections for specific sectors of the workforce. For example, the Migrant and Seasonal Agricultural Worker Protection Act provides employment-related protections to migrant and seasonal agricultural workers and the FLSA includes provisions against the use of child labor. The Americans with Disabilities Act of 1990 is designed to eliminate discrimination against people with disabilities by providing enforceable standards. There is no federal law that provides specific protections for domestic service workers. In fact, domestic workers are often excluded or exempted from laws due to the number of employees or the presumed intermittent nature of employment. Both the Americans with Disabilities Act and Title VII, for example, apply only to employers with fifteen or more employees, and the Age Discrimination in Employment Act applies only to employers with twenty or more employees. Employer sanctions for hiring undocumented workers laid out in the Immigration Reform and Control Act (1986) can be applied only to employers with five or more employees and are not applicable to intermittent employment. These examples of exemptions and exclusions in labor laws illustrate how domestic service work and workers have not been allowed into the realm of protected and regulated labor.

On the whole, domestic workers are not recognized as a legitimate sector of the labor force deserving of the protections and guarantees of U.S. labor law but as an informal labor force operating in the shadows of the service sector. There are a number of important exceptions to this characterization—state initiatives to create domestic service labor laws. The New York Domestic Workers' Bill of Rights from 2010 guarantees basic work standards and protections for nannies, caregivers, and housekeepers in the state of New York. The law counteracts prior exclusions and exemptions for domestic workers, including extending the right to overtime pay for live-in workers and removing the domestic worker exemptions of the New York Human Rights Law and the Workers' Compensation Law so that domestic workers can access disability benefits and sue for sexual harassment and harassment on the basis of race, religion, gender, and/or national origin. The New York law defines a domestic worker as "a person employed in a home or residence for the purpose of: caring for a child, serving as a companion to a sick, convalescing or elderly person, housekeeping, or for any other domestic service purpose."[7] The law excludes "casual" workers, companions as defined by the FLSA, relatives, and caregivers funded by a government program.

The New York law represents a substantial victory for Domestic Workers United, an organization of Caribbean, Latina, and African nannies, housekeepers, and caregivers in New York. According to Joycelynn Campbell, organizing coordinator for Domestic Workers United, in New York 93 percent of domestic workers are women, 95 percent are women of color, and 99 percent are immigrants, mostly from Caribbean and Latin American countries. In a critical review of the campaign to pass the Domestic Workers Bill of Rights in New York, Campbell emphasized that grassroots organizing by domestic workers themselves was key, as was support from labor unions, immigrant rights groups, clergy, and students. In a glaring absence, support from feminist organizations was not even mentioned (Goodman 2010). In contemporary feminist movements in the United States, there is no sector that corresponds to the women-led popular urban movements in Mexico that collectively advocated for government services and infrastructure to alleviate the burden of poor women's work. The closest approximation in the past would be the feminist Wages for Housework campaign of the 1970s,[8] which called for assigning a wage to unpaid women's work as a way of valuing the work. Fairbairns later argued that this campaign was a sad indictment of the women's movement because it demonstrated that feminists have lost the battle to force men to do their share of the cleaning (Fairbairns 1988, 1). I consider the advances of the popular women's movements in Mexico to be one of the most significant outcomes of Mexican feminism in the 1980s, but the impetus to politicize the social reproductive work of women gained little traction as a feminist issue and did not translate into contemporary domestic worker movements in the United States.

In an extended analysis of the struggle to pass the Domestic Workers' Bill of Rights in New York, Premilla Nadasen and Tiffany Williams review the history of domestic work in the United States and in the global economy. They include a history of organizing and legislation for domestic work and place domestic workers along with farmworkers and others into a category called "excluded workers" because of their lack of coverage by most labor laws. They suggest that collaboration between domestic workers and other organized excluded workers signals a new direction for the labor movement and labor laws (Nadasen and Williams 2010, 20). Excluded workers demand labor rights based on human rights, dignity, and formalization and regulation of labor. In one instance of collaboration, domestic workers and day laborers created the Excluded Workers Congress at the second U.S. Social Forum in Detroit in June 2010, asking for formalization of their work and equality under the labor law. Nadasen and Williams's analysis, like many that focus on domestic work, conceptualizes the struggle primarily as a labor movement and not necessarily a feminist movement. They conclude by saying, "Over the past two decades, domestic workers have built a movement that transcends racial barriers, cultural differences, national identity, and legal status, with the goal of improving the lot of some of the nation's most vulnerable workers. The multiracial, transnational, feminist nature of contemporary domestic worker organizing may help chart a new political framework for social justice advocates in the 21st century" (Nadasen and Williams 2010, 21). What is striking is that the modifier *feminist* appears only once among numerous repeated references to multiracial, transnational, and labor-based models of organizing. The intersectionality of domestic worker identity/location provides a framework for coalitional politics between feminist, labor, and immigrant rights movements, and there is a need for conceptual translation between movements for this to happen. Feminists need to reconceptualize the issues of domestic service, taking a narrow focus on labor relations between employee and employer and broadening it to create a more inclusive framework. By keeping the issue in the frame of labor, the interests of female employees are pitted against (often female) employers. Although the entire household employs and benefits from the labor of domestic service workers, it is often a woman who is delegated the primary responsibility of supervising the domestic worker. When pitted against one another, women find it difficult to work in solidarity to mobilize for structural changes that could improve the lives of all involved.

Up until 2013, New York was the only state that had passed a Domestic Workers' Bill of Rights, but on July 1, 2013, Hawaii became the second state to pass a law with specific protections for domestic workers, and there are calls for new legislation in other states. In California, Assembly members Tom Ammiano and V. Manuel Perez sponsored AB 889, a California Domestic Workers Bill of Rights, which was passed by the California Assembly and Senate, only to then be vetoed by Governor Brown in 2012. In his veto message Governor Brown said that it would be more prudent to do the studies to answer questions about costs and consequences before enacting the new law and cited an estimated increased cost to the state of California of $200 million per year due to a drafting error that leaves most In Home Supportive Service workers subject to the measure. In 2013 a new bill, AB 241, was passed by the Assembly in May, made it through the Senate Labor Committee in June, and was scheduled to be heard by the Senate Appropriations Committee in August. AB 241 is similar to the New York law but goes a bit further to remove all exclusions for domestic workers in California's Wage Order 15 and extend overtime pay and workers compensation to domestic workers. The proposed law stipulates industry-specific protections to use kitchen facilities and to cook their own food and creates standards for sleep that would apply to live-in caregivers, but specifically excludes In Home Supportive Service workers paid by the state. Analysts estimate that about 200,000 domestic workers in California would benefit from the passage of the law. The vast majority are immigrant women who earn wages well below the poverty line and are vulnerable to exploitation due to their immigration status and exclusion from fundamental labor protections. The list of supporters of AB 241 is quite varied, including immigrant advocate groups as well as some women's groups and labor unions, with the most consistent support coming from small collectives of immigrant women such as CHIRLA (Coalition for Humane Immigrant Rights of Los Angeles) and MUA (Mujeres Unidas y Activas [Active Women United]) in San Francisco. Four other states—Colorado, Illinois, Massachusetts, and Oregon—are considering similar bills. The campaigns to pass new domestic worker laws in New York and California were dominated by labor organizations; where there is feminist advocacy, it comes primarily from small organizations of immigrant women. In the materials produced by the domestic workers' rights movement, there are few explicitly gender-based critiques of the sexual division of labor or the undervaluation of domestic work; calls for reform are subsumed within a transnational, multiracial, and class-based framework that focuses on the need for regulation of labor.

In reviewing the limits of labor and immigration law for domestic workers, it is clear that the doors of opportunity did not swing open for Latin American immigrants coming to do domestic work in the United States. Like Chinese female immigrants before them,[9] Mexican and other Latin American female immigrants are associated with undesirable permanent settlement of Latino families and a fuller, more costly incorporation of immigrants as communities rather than lone workers without family obligations. Female immigrants used to be cast as likely to be "immoral" or to become a "public charge" in an effort to broadcast an unwelcoming message. More recently, female immigrants are associated with childbearing and demographic growth of the foreign-born population. In this updated version, female immigrants are still cast as unscrupulous and immoral; their choice to become a parent is seen as irresponsible as evidenced in the phrase "anchor baby" in reference to their children. In the past, legalization and work permit programs consistently favored male immigrants by focusing attention onto male-dominated realms of work while simultaneously neglecting the jobs in domestic service that are traditionally filled by women. Even while the demand for low-cost domestic service steadily rises in response to the care deficit in the United States, the prospects for female immigrants working in this sector to acquire legal status remain dismally low. As Mexico and the United States engage in dialogue over immigration, there are no indications that the needs of female immigrants will be addressed. If nothing is done, domestic service will remain an informal, undocumented, unregulated, and exploited domain of work. This is a clear instance in which translocal translation is indispensable for confronting the issues of the domestic service industry and developing a feminist critique that cuts across the intersections of location and subject positioning of immigrant domestic service workers.

Some of the effects of confining domestic service work to the informal, unregulated sector include devaluing the work and ensuring that these paid services will remain affordable to middle-class families in the United States. Like the policies that discourage immigrants from migrating with their dependents, the policies that isolate domestic service work to the informal sector contain the costs of social reproduction: raising, caring for, and socializing the next generation. Diasporic populations bear the weight of these contradictions while presenting advantages to both the sending and receiving countries. In the United States, undocumented domestic workers work long hours for little pay, use public services at a disproportionately low rate due to a lack of eligibility and a lack of a sense of entitlement, and are subject to a high level of social control under the constant threat of deportation. Sending and receiving countries lack responsiveness to the social welfare needs of domestic service workers, amplifying the bargain that this population represents to both systems: faithful remittances to the sending country and low-cost, controllable labor to the receiving country and the families and communities that benefit from the work. Domestic service workers are hit with the devaluation of social reproductive work from all sides. Governmental policies—including those on immigration, labor, welfare, and even education—push immigrant domestic workers into the most exploitable corners of the workforce. Anti-immigrant campaigns cast immigrant women as unworthy of the right to raise their own children in the United States, despite the fact that they are hard-working participants in the workforce and provide valuable loving care to children. Even liberal feminists in the United States fail to acknowledge the value of domestic service work for fear of pricing themselves out of their own liberation. But in the long run, this exploitive arrangement is not in the interest of any woman, regardless of her location, because it codifies and allows for the perpetuation of an inequitable division of labor along gender lines.

Migrant women crossing borders to fill the care deficit in the United States and other receiving countries are living the contradictions of transnational motherhood, illegal documentation status, invisibility, lack of regulation in the realm of domestic labor, and lack of representation and voice. These disempowering trends that are rooted in a fundamental devaluation of domestic work (so-called women's work) have not translated into feminist discourse in the North or South. Instead, we are left with a resounding silence around the issues of domestic service and the transnationalization of domestic work. Verónica Feliu (chapter 12 in this volume), comments on the difficulty of translating "the silence around the labor women perform for other women" due in part to the obscure realms to which the analysis leads as feminists "have to deal with our own ghosts" in reference to domestic work and service. Feliu situates the use of domestic workers in Chile, a growing number of whom are Peruvian immigrant *domésticas*, within a patriarchal and racialized frame that mirrors the context of transnational domestic service in the United States. She calls for a "profound transnational commitment among feminists" to debate questions of race and racism between women "parallel to the issues of immigration and xenophobia." Both Feliu's analysis of domestic workers in Chile and my analysis of domestic workers and the lack of regulation of domestic work in the United States support the contention that there is a lack of will on the part of mainstream feminist movements to hear and translate popular feminist messages from Latin America. The critique also signals a way out of this problematic for feminists and feminist movements by engaging in a conceptual and translocal translation and reinscribing the issues of domestic work and domestic service as both feminist and labor issues.

In the United States there is a great reliance and interdependence between employers and domestic service workers as they engage in daily contact within the intimate spaces of private homes and family life. Yet the two groups remain distinctly separate and separated in a relationship shrouded in denial and evasion due to an inability on the employer's part to openly acknowledge the value of the services being delivered and the vital role domestic service workers play in their family's daily life. Barbara Ehrenreich comments that the contradictions of housework arouse a "special angst" in feminists because there is no getting around the fact that "someone is working in your home at a job she would almost certainly never have chosen for herself" if she had a choice, and that the "implicit lesson for the household's children is that anyone female with dark skin and broken English is a person of inferior status." Ehrenreich challenges feminists to make work visible again; to translate the feminist ideal of valuing all the work that goes into "creating and maintaining a livable habitat" into daily practice (Ehrenreich 2002, 103).

Unfolding alongside the global restructuring of production is the global restructuring of reproductive work. This reality presents a formidable challenge for translating feminist ideals into practice. I have already reviewed a number of noteworthy attempts to do this. For example, Domestic Workers United successfully campaigned for comprehensive legislation to protect the rights of domestic workers in the state of New York. The Domestic Workers' Bill of Rights became law in New York in November 2010, mandating labor rights and protections for domestic workers, including a living wage, health benefits and leave, prohibition of trafficking, and elimination of exclusions for domestic work. In Los Angeles, CHIRLA organized a Household Workers Committee that pushed for new legislation to give labor rights recognition for household workers in California. CHIRLA allied themselves with the immigrant women's organization MUA in San Francisco to lobby for the passage of the California Domestic Workers Bill of Rights. These two examples of local initiatives based on the regulation of labor create a contrast to initiatives at the international level to mine the UN Universal Declaration of Human Rights for articles supporting domestic workers on the basis of their human rights, including Article 4 (Freedom from Slavery and Servitude), Article 12 (Freedom from Interference with Privacy, Family, and Home), Article 13 (Right to Free Movement in and out of the Country), Article 23 (Right to Desirable Work with Equal Pay), Article 24 (Right to Rest and Leisure), and Article 25 (Right to Adequate Living Standard). Drawing on rights outlined in the declaration, the International Labour Organization recently adopted a new treaty to extend labor protections for domestic workers. The new Convention Concerning Decent Work for Domestic Workers establishes global standards for the estimated 50 to 100 million domestic workers worldwide, including labor protections with provisions for days off, limits to hours of work, and a minimum wage. "Key elements of the convention require governments to provide domestic workers with labor protections equivalent to those of other workers, including for working hours, minimum wage coverage, overtime compensation, daily and weekly rest periods, social security, and maternity protection. The new standards also oblige governments to protect domestic workers from violence and abuse, and to ensure effective monitoring and enforcement" (Human Rights Watch 2011). Advocates for domestic worker rights are now pushing for national governments to bring their laws in line with the treaty and ratify it. This, like many international conventions, outlines overarching global standards and leaves it to individual national governments to implement the goals by enacting legislation.

The most compelling need for domestic workers is for comprehensive legislative reform at the national level that would eliminate exclusions and exemptions for domestic work in labor laws and would create a pathway to citizenship for the predominantly undocumented sector of household workers in the United States. Lawmakers might choose to follow the Canadian example of the Live-in Caregiver Program, which issues work permits and offers permanent residency after two years. The United Kingdom provides another example with a visa known as the INF-17 for already employed domestic workers with no live-in requirement. Existing U.S. visas, such as the J-1 au pair visa or the A-3 and G-5 "nanny" visas for foreign diplomats and business managers, could also be modified to encompass domestic workers and include a pathway to citizenship. Any reform that provides legal status to undocumented domestic workers along with labor regulation of the domestic work sector would offer recognition and value to reproductive labor, lessen worker abuse and exploitation, and greatly improve the work lives of domestic service workers and their families.

Feminist voices in the North have been largely silent around issues of domestic work. When the Immigration Reform and Control Act was passed in 1986, not a single feminist organization offered testimony in Congress, and the resulting amnesty provision (pathway to citizenship) favored men to women four to one; only 20 percent of those who were granted amnesty leading to legal permanent residence were women. This gender inequity resulted partly from the way work was defined and documented in the amnesty provision of the law (Arp, Dantico, and Zatz 1990).[10] This is one of many examples of how legislation based on patriarchal ideologies has worked to retain patriarchal aspects of the sexual/global division of reproductive labor and disempower women. In a careful examination of gender and globalization in the case of Filipina domestic workers, Rhacel Salazar Parreñas writes, "Forces of patriarchy encourage the feminization of labor and migration, as it is the demand for women's work, low-wage labor, and a docile workforce that pushes the labor and migration of women in globalization" (Parreñas 2008, 17). In today's environment of a growing feminization of migration combined with the commodification of domestic work, there is a great need for conceptual and translocal translations of feminisms across the Americas.

Notes

I express my appreciation and gratitude to Rebecca Hester, who gave me lots of helpful and substantive editorial feedback on this chapter. Gracias, Rebecca!

1. The 1993 Clinton-era scandal involving Zoë Baird and Kimba Wood was dubbed "Nannygate." At issue was whether the female nominees for attorney general had hired or paid payroll taxes for immigrant domestic service workers they had formerly employed. Neither Baird nor Wood gained confirmation approval from the Senate.

2. Work that points out the gendered and sexual nature of violence and state violence on the border and in immigration control includes Sylvanna Falcon (2006), Fregoso (2006b), and Saucedo (2006) all found in the volume compiled by the organization Incite! Women of Color against Violence.

3. In an 1865 poem by William Ross Wallace titled "The Hand That Rocks the Cradle Is the Hand That Rules the World," the cited refrain emphasizes the importance of motherhood as a force of change. It is interesting to consider Wallace's poem in the context of transnational domestic service in which it is not necessarily the mother who rocks the cradle.

4. According to Jeffrey Passel and D'Vera Cohn of the PEW Hispanic Center, 58 percent of the undocumented population in the United States is Mexican. Another 23 percent originate

from Central or South America. A full 81 percent of the total undocumented population comes from Latin America. Among Mexican migrants there has been a growing trend toward feminization of migration beginning in the early 1990s (Passel and Cohn 2011).

5. The Nineteenth of September Garment Workers Union is named after the 1985 earthquakes that devastated the garment district in Mexico City and prompted the formation of a very visible women-led union, the first independent union to gain recognition from the National Labor Relations Board in the 1980s. For more on the NSGWU, see Carrillo 1998.

6. U.S. National Labor Relations Act, 29 U.S.C. §§ 151–69, Title 29, Chapter 7, Subchapter II, 1935.

7. The New York Domestic Workers' Bill of Rights (A 1470B/ S2311E) went into effect on November 29, 2010. New York was the first state to enact a labor law offering specific protections and provisions for domestic workers. See "Domestic Workers' Bill of Rights," Department of Labor, http://www.labor.ny.gov/legal/domestic-workers-bill-of-rights.shtm.

8. On the Wages for Housework Campaign see Mainardi (1970) and Fairbairns (1988).

9. The Forty-Third Congress signed into effect the Page Act on March 3, 1875, which prohibited immigration of Chinese and Asian women to the United States for the purpose of prostitution. The law read that "in determining whether the immigration of any subject of China, Japan, or any Oriental country, to the United States, is . . . for lewd and immoral purposes; . . . said consul-general or consul shall not deliver the required permit or certificate. . . . SEC.3. That the importation into the United States of women for the purposes of prostitution is hereby forbidden" (43rd Congress, session II, Ch. 141, March 3, 1875, chapter 141). The Page Act called on individual officers to ascertain whether an immigrant is of a class whose importation is forbidden. The Page Act functioned as a mechanism of exclusion for Chinese female immigrants.

10. The amnesty provision in the 1986 Immigration Reform and Control Act (IRCA) allowed for 1.9 million immigrants to regularize their documentation status and become legal permanent residents (LPR) if they could prove, among other things, that they had been living and working in the United States for a five-year period. Female immigrants found it more difficult than male immigrants to produce the documentation that the INS required to be granted amnesty, partly because of the informal nature of employment in domestic service. An additional 1.1 million immigrants became LPRs through the Special Agricultural Worker provision of the IRCA, but very few women benefited from this provision as well, due to, among other factors, the jobs that were included or excluded. For example, field workers (majority male) could apply for LPR but cannery workers (majority female) could not. Among the 3 million immigrants who gained legal status through the IRCA, only one in five were female. For more on the IRCA see Arp, Dantico, and Zatz 1990.

VERÓNICA FELIU

María was nineteen years old when she first arrived at my house on the same day I came home from the hospital. She was the first and only "nana" I ever had. The last time I saw her was at the Santiago airport in 1973, when my family and I were going to Spain for an undetermined period of time. I never saw her again, nor did I know of her whereabouts until recently. A few years ago, María went to my father's law office in Santiago (where my family resides again) to ask him for help to improve her slim retirement benefits. My father said he couldn't do much for her, because the laws that protect and regulate domestic work in Chile came into effect after María had stopped working. I believe she now lives with her father in the countryside in the town of Catemu, where she is from.

María's ancestors were Mapuche, the most numerous indigenous people in Chile. At least, that is what I was told by my family. I never asked María about her origins, probably because I was never really interested in knowing about them. Like the majority of Chileans at the time, I knew very little about the indigenous cultures that form part of my country, except for the clichés that were part of our school education, most of them based on the Europeanizing views of the Spanish poet and soldier Ercilla. Like most of my generation, I never learned at school that the Mapuche are actually a people, a nation within the nation. I also ignored that they enjoyed an autonomy that was only taken from them at the beginning of the nineteenth century, after Chilean independence, when the newly created nation-state declared itself a homogeneous "patria" for all the people living in the territory (Tricot 2006). I only learned much later that the Mapuche refer to the rest of the citizens who do not belong to their community as chilenos, or huincas in Mapudungun, their language. Indeed, the Mapuche have never fully considered themselves chilenos, much the same as the other indigenous peoples in Latin America do not embrace the nationality of the country in which they live. Chileans, on the other hand, grow up without acknowledging the existence of another people with its own culture, traditions, leaders, and ways of conceptualizing life that actually lives among them, invisibly, mostly silenced.

In the house where I grew up, I always heard that María had learned everything she knew (from cooking and cleaning habits to her ways of reasoning) while living with us. Apparently, she had arrived to our house without any knowledge, and there was nothing we could learn from her. After all, she was just "una india." Yet my relationship with her, developed throughout my formative years, has had a strong influence on my views thereafter about domestic labor and the inequalities in my country based on race, class, and gender. I am certain I am not alone in this, as many of the feminists growing up in Chile have dealt with the fact of having a woman serving in their house at some point in their lives, if not throughout their whole life from the earliest time they can remember. Like many of them, I grew up with pieces of a different culture inside me, of which I am not aware. Invisible threads forming "mis nudos," as Julieta Kirkwood (1986) called the numerous contradictions within feminism, the most prevalent of which is the contradiction between theory and practice. Kirkwood's approach to the contradictions within feminism was to untangle them. She stressed the need to travel through them to find the origin of the thread, so as to understand and generate debate and thinking. In her view, this was the way to politicize practice, because for her, feminism was the development of both practice and theory.

As you may have already guessed, my writing about domestic service in Chile is directly linked to all the years in which I have tried to overcome my own sense of guilt for not having truly understood María. But there's something else. Despite the fact that I erased María's indigenous and cultural identity while she was living with us, at the same time I developed a deep and very emotional connection with her—which is related to her being, in many ways, my second mother and, as I grew up, my confidant. Many years later, as a Latin American scholar in the United States, I came to understand that one of the consequences of that intense relationship is the fact that in my adult life I have never been able to hire someone to do my household chores.

While I struggle to translate this personal experience buried so deeply inside me, I have come across various other axes of translation that complicate every aspect of this intricate net. In the words that follow, I try to untangle some of these nudos, while I carry out the difficult task of translating silences.

It is one thing to try to translate concepts and terms that do not find their way through words, which cannot do them justice. It is quite another matter to attempt bringing the unsaid to the surface, to give language to realities that subjects have not been able to tell themselves. The silence around the labor women perform for other women, in the writing of Chilean feminists, is a very difficult concept to translate.[1] This is not so because it is a complex idea. As a matter of fact, there are simple answers, but all of them lead us to obscure realms, where feminists (including myself) have to deal with our own ghosts, with our own repressed memories, and as Cherríe Moraga so poignantly said, with that racism we have internalized, the one we aimed at ourselves. "For each of us in some way has been both oppressed and the oppressor. We are afraid to look at how we have failed each other. We are afraid to see how we have taken the values of our oppressor into our hearts and turned them against ourselves and one another" (2002, 30).

In Chile the silence in relation to domestic labor has been partially broken in recent years, and this has been possible only after the practice has undergone an important transformation. After centuries of indigenous and mestiza women emigrating from the South to the big cities to clean, cook, and raise children for others, the reality of the market in the past ten years or so has started to open other job possibilities for them. As the number of Chilean women willing to live in the homes of their employers has decreased, Chile has become a recipient of immigrant labor, mostly from Peru.[2] This fact has created a whole new area of research for feminists and social scientists in general, who are increasingly becoming concerned about the treatment Peruvians get when living in their neighboring country.

Of all the Peruvians who have immigrated to Chile since 1993 (more than eighty thousand), it is estimated that 55.6 percent are women (Stefoni 2004). Most of these women go alone to Chile, to find a job to support the family left in Peru. In the context of this transnational motherhood that has been widely studied in the case of women migrating from Central and Latin America to work in the United States, according to Pierrette Hondagneu-Sotelo, "historically and in the contemporary period, paid domestic workers have had to limit or forfeit primary care of their families and homes to earn income by providing primary care to the families and homes of employers, who are privileged by race and class" (2007, 394).

Thus, as is the case in all the female diasporas throughout the Americas, these women face gender and race discrimination not only in the salaries they receive but also in the ways they are treated by their employers and the society as a whole. In the case of Chile, studies have shown that 94 percent of the women coming from Peru to perform domestic work have finished high school, and a significant number of them (25 percent) also have college degrees.[3]

This demographic phenomenon, in a country with relatively low levels of immigration throughout its history, has aroused all sorts of comments in the media and inspired research developed by several nongovernmental organizations (NGOs) such as FLACSO (Facultad Latinoamericana de Ciencias Sociales), CEPAL (Comisión Económica para América Latina y el Caribe), and the Instituto de la Mujer. The first public evidence of the recent increase in immigration was the numbers provided by the census of 2002. According to the National Institute of Statistics the percentage of foreign population living in Chile went from 0.86 percent in 1992 to 1.22 percent in 2002 (Zavala San Martín and Rojas Venegas 2005, 159). Even though these are small percentages compared to the number of Chileans living abroad, mainly in Argentina and the United States,[4] they nonetheless represent a relevant growing tendency to many observers (Zavala San Martín and Rojas Venegas 2005, 159).

In addition, immigration has become a hot topic in Chile due to the fact that a large majority of Peruvian immigrants (78 percent) is concentrated in Santiago. As citizens of a very centralized country, Chileans have traditionally given special consideration to anything that has to do to with their capital, almost as if the other regions did not exist (Stefoni 2004, 322). This is reflected in the way research is conducted and funded throughout the country, as most of the influential research and academic organizations are situated in the capital. It also affects the interests of the media and public opinion.

Many observers have asked themselves why, to the collective perception, Peruvian immigrants appear to be the most numerous in Chile, even though the number of Argentineans is (and has always been) larger. They also wonder why the Peruvian presence (among other groups) generates considerably more xenophobic and racist sentiments among Chilean citizens. Many have concluded that the Peruvian presence is "more obvious" because of their darker skin color.[5] They are, then, perceived as indios and therefore linked to underdevelopment and backwardness (Stefoni 2004).

Wilfredo Ardito Vega, a lawyer for the Peruvian Legal Defense Institute who has studied and documented the phenomenon of Peruvian immigrants in Chile, quotes someone telling him, "For many years, we Chileans did not believe we were racists, until the arrival of your countrymen" (Ardito Vega 2001). Comments such as this, accompanied by all sorts of pejorative epithets, are common throughout the media, as well as on the Internet, in chat groups, or street graffiti.[6] They all indicate a remarkable detachment between Chileans and their own identity, as well as an unquestioned positioning as individuals in relation to the others and the self. As Silvia Rivera Cusicanqui has explained it, in relation to the Bolivian society: "In postcolonial societies . . . the process of ethnic plunder or imposed (and self-imposed) acculturation has created situations of self-negation which themselves constitute marks of ethnicity that nonetheless evoke also the aspiration to possess someone else's ethnicity. In that sense . . . ethnicity is defined also by its borders, that is, by those spaces of interaction with 'others,' which obligate or induce the subject to affirm (or hide) his/her own difference" (1991, 3). The sudden interest among researchers to understand the phenomenon of immigration comes at a time when Chile is perceived by many as a country that has left behind its underdevelopment and is now economically more stable than its neighbors. The counterpart to this perception, however, is the fact that Chile has one of the worst distributions of income per capita in the region. Even though the percentage of people living under the poverty line decreased in the late 1990s to 18.8 percent of the total population in 2003,[7] the richest portion of society (10 percent of the total population) still accumulates 41 percent of total income. Moreover, 60 percent of all households receive an estimated income of only US$160 monthly per person (Caro and Kremerman 2005). Despite this, Chile forms part of a globalized world that observes Chilean macroeconomic growth with great interest due to its consistent neoliberal politics and free trade agreements with the United States, Europe, and some Asian countries. In this context, it is evident from the social sciences perspective that a country that attracts immigration is an interesting place for international recognition and investment. That alone is an important reason to dedicate research to the topic. Now more than ever, Chile can be compared with the great model of the North and used as an example in the South for its achievements.

Within this realm, feminists have also found something important to say because the percentage of women migrating is so significant. The concern about domestic service, practically nonexistent during the past thirty years, has arisen now when the number of servants who are non-Chilean citizens grows every day. These immigrants are also women who, for the most part, are educated and—as is widely known—cook extremely well and speak in a very clear Castilian mode.[8]

Immigrants form part of the global exchange of goods among nations, and women, in particular, are fundamental contributors to world economies. As such they accept lower salaries than nationals and send an important portion of the money they make to families left at home. Hence, the big beneficiaries of their labor are ultimately the country of origin, as well as the country to which they migrate.[9] In this double arrangement, as Carrillo explains, the receiving country "evades the costs of the social safety net for the bulk of domestic service workers and their families by highlighting their documentation status, thereby disassociating any obligation to the informal workforce" (chapter 11 in this volume).

From the official perspective, though, immigration does not seem to have become an issue in Chile yet. In a personal interview, Carolina Stefoni, a sociologist who has widely studied the subject, told me that none of the Chilean governments of the past decade or so have designed clear lines of action in relation to immigrants. Consequently, there are no specific educational programs addressing xenophobia in schools and society in general. This is so because it is still uncertain whether immigration is positive for the nation, and therefore regulations have been fluctuating and inconsistent. Up to now, the only official institution that deals with the issue are the immigration officers at the border posts or in airports who ask travelers from Peru—exclusively—to show a certain arbitrary amount of money before entering the country. At the other end of the spectrum there is the Catholic Church, as the only nonprofit institution helping Peruvians in Chile through the Catholic Chilean Institute of Migration (INCAMI), an organization founded in 1955. Commanded by a priest and three Peruvian religious nuns, the institute uses a house in Santiago as its headquarters, where hundreds of Peruvian women come every day looking for domestic jobs or seeking labor protection against mistreatment from their employers.[10]

In my attempt to translate silences, I should put this in contrast with a country that, with the enthusiastic participation of feminists, has recently created around itself the aura of a not only progressive nation but one where gender issues are in the foreground with several successful stories to celebrate. As feminists have extensively written about it, two important factors contribute to the jubilee. One is that during the 1970s and 1980s, during Augusto Pinochet's dictatorship, one of the most significant and massive women's movements in Latin America took place. The second is the 2006 presidential election in which a majority elected Michelle Bachelet, a divorced woman with three children. However, even though both realities should be understood as the outcomes of incessant battles by feminists to gain power against masculine hegemony, they should not be viewed yet as symptoms of profound transformations of civil society.

In relation to the first factor, a fundamental achievement of the women's movement was the creation of a powerful discourse to contest patriarchal structures in public and private spaces. The utterance of this discourse, based on a consensual identity of "women," was possible during dictatorship due to the creation of various NGOs, funded mostly by foreign monies. Right after democracy was reinstated, the opening of gender studies in some academic institutions provided another channel for this discourse. Despite the empowering dimension of this identity politics, the use of "women" as an uncontested homogeneous reality ended up excluding not only key subjects from mainstream discussions but also concepts that remain untouched until today. Dominant Chilean feminist discourse of the past decades has tended to be local and centralized in Santiago (Tobar, Gody, and Guerrero 2003), self-referential, and exclusive of certain perspectives that question the very notion of women as a collective identity. In doing so, race and class (and in certain circles, sexual preferences) have become taboo topics, which is a potential impediment for further social change.

Despite the arrival of Peruvian women in the past decade, there are still an estimated 16 percent of Chilean women employed in domestic service (CLADEM 2004, 6). As Ruth Díaz, president of the House Workers Union (SINTRACAP), told me in an interview, at the present time Chilean "nanas" are as much appreciated as their Peruvian counterparts. According to her, the demand for domestic service has not decreased, and the number of Chilean women willing to do it remains very high. More middle-class women have access to jobs, and they increasingly need the presence of an assistant in their homes most of the day on a weekly basis. Even though this incorporation to the labor force does not necessarily mean an increase in economic living standards for middle-class women, it nonetheless "results in a labor shortfall in many homes where men's participation in household work has not kept pace with women's employment" (Ibarra 2007, 289). As Díaz explains it, as opposed to commonly held beliefs, Peruvians are not usurping the household jobs of Chileans. What has happened is that in the past fifteen years better educated Chilean domestic workers have become less inclined to live in the home of their employers. Therefore, what the immigrants are doing is performing a job (live-in nanas) that increases in demand, while Chileans find it hard to work puertas afuera due to a lack of offerings.

The fact that middle-class women continue to need the assistance of other women in their homes to be able to participate in the public space raises two main issues. One is that the basic inequality on which patriarchal society is based has not yet disappeared insofar as men continue to not acknowledge their part in domestic duties. Even with the increase of women in paid occupations, many studies produced by SERNAM (the National Office of Women's Affairs) and other research by feminist NGOs have demonstrated that labor distribution has yet to become equal. According to the 2002 census, only 35.0 percent of women were employed in a remunerated job (CLADEM 2004, 6). This percentage—only higher than Mexico and Costa Rica in Latin America—shows that many women in their active ages are staying at home because they are still attached to the traditional division of labor as the man provides the main income in the house. But it is also a consequence of the fact that in the workplace women receive considerably lower salaries than men do. This reality discourages women in Chile from becoming an active part of the workforce, on top of the imposed forty-five-hour work week (SERNAM 2002).[11] To make matters worse, according to Ximena Díaz, sociologist at the Center for Women's Studies (CEM), Chileans not only have very irregular work time contracts, they also work the most hours per week in the world (Díaz 2004, 159). This, together with the many abnormal employers' working demands, plus the long distances many have to travel to get to work in big cities like Santiago, makes the whole labor situation an exhausting and frustrating experience, especially for the middle and lower-middle classes.

The second important factor is that the state has not yet recognized the necessity of developing policies to help women become active in the job market, such as providing public child care, after-school programs, paternity leaves, reduction of working hours, a more democratic and accessible social security system, and paid family and medical leave, among others.

The lack of acknowledgment by male partners and the state are two faces of the same coin. They are obviously symptoms of a society still based on a patriarchal structure, but they also respond to the same condition: domestic service has conveniently been a "solution" that has excused both the state and male partners from becoming involved in incorporating women into the labor force.[12]

But women, and feminists in particular, have played an important role in this as well. They are accomplices of an order that paradoxically favors them and harms them at the same time. Because they have silently approved the presence of other women in their homes to perform domestic chores, they have permitted men, and also children, to become unaware of the necessity of sharing those chores.

According to Barbara Ehrenreich—in the context of U.S. society—"there is no reason to expect that men will voluntarily take on a greater share of the burden, and much of the need for paid help arises from their abdication." What the future seems to hold for the younger generations is that "without constant assistance [they will] suffocate in their own detritus" (Ehrenreich 2002, 100). Interestingly enough, Ehrenreich envisions the issue of domestic servants in the United States as an increasing reality, due to the growing insertion of women in the labor market. As she points out, "most Americans, more than 80 percent, still clean their homes, but the minority who do not include a sizeable fraction of the nation's opinion makers and culture producers: professors, writers, editors, media decision makers, political figures, talking heads and celebrities of all sorts" (Ehrenreich 2002, 91).

In Chile, on the contrary (although we lack further studies about it), the common knowledge is that domestic service is something quite widespread, not limited to use by the most privileged classes. This relies on the fact that Chile, like other Latin American countries, founded its nation-state without truly erasing most of the colonial practices, thus developing a relationship with domestic service based on a "natural" order of things. Before and after independence, criollos filled their homes with indigenous servants who performed all sorts of duties for them, underestimating the value and certainly the difficulty of such tasks. As Aída Moreno, a leader of domestic workers throughout Latin America, has stated: "From the mixture of Spanish and aborigines emerged the Chilean race, and the poor of the New World continued to carry out the same work as their ancestors, though now recognized as personas and as workers under the name of inquilinos. The dependence of the inquilino on the landowner is maintained to this day. The daughters of the peasants go to serve in the house of the patron, first in the house of the country estate and then in the city house" (quoted in Chaney and Castro 1989, 407). Generation after generation, the tradition of having a poor and uneducated woman at home has been an invisible and unquestioned reality for Chileans that is hardly ever linked to racism or exploitation, since it is a given, un mal menor, something that has always been there. Thus, poor women continue to leave their homes and families to help another woman who apparently "needs it more."[13] That is the case of Ruth Díaz, a middle-aged woman I interviewed in Santiago in 2006, who dedicated sixteen years of her life to serve in a house raising the children of another woman. Meanwhile, as she explained it to me with obvious remorse, her own children were on the streets without supervision, experimenting with gangs and drugs.

The tremendous contradiction behind an experience like Ruth's touches all the nudos of domestic service, which is one of the most complex social realities of all. When analyzed from a feminist perspective, trying to untangle and translate these nudos, and, as Kirkwood suggested, undo the thread to find its origin, the question of class (totally entwined with race) is unavoidable. Could someone think that poor women need child and domestic care less than rich women do? Are there arguments to justify that while a poor woman raises the children of someone who can afford to pay domestic service, her own children are abandoned to their own fate? In cases less radical than Ruth's, domestic workers rely on the grandmother, other members of the extended family, or a neighbor to take care of their children.[14] These are the available solutions for working-class women whose productive work is as undervalued as their reproductive labor. As Rhacel Salazar Parreñas explains it in the case of Filipina women working in the United States, "women pass down their care responsibilities to less and less privileged women in a global terrain. However, this process of the 'care chain' not only frees men of household work but also results in tensions and strains between women. . . . While the women in the middle of the care chain suffer from having to raise their children from a distance, the women at the end of this chain have to endure the hardship of overwork" (Parreñas 2005, 113).

Despite this, it is striking to realize the enormous responsibility that in the middle of the chain, the nana has in Chile nowadays. In the interviews I have conducted in this respect, I found it to be common sense that having a house helper is an unavoidable necessity (from both the perspective of the employer and the employee), without which life would be almost intolerable. Thus, there are cases in which the employers teach the empleada how to drive a car to drop off and pick up children at school or how to deposit a check in the bank or pay bills, among an extensive range of duties.[15] What this means is that the expectations about the service are progressively higher, as middle-class homes are left alone more and more hours a day and contemporary ways of living are increasingly more complicated and stressful. Therefore, the qualifications requested at the time of contracting a house worker are consistently becoming a vague terrain, subject to the most ample variety of demands on the part of the employer.

Interestingly, this revives an idea that feminists strongly claimed during the 1980s in Chile, which is that private is political, insofar as the domestic is the realm of both reproduction and production. Thus, the work of la nana should be understood as the pillar on which a whole society rests, which in practical terms implies that a domestic worker may have more power in the household than the actual employers have. Paradoxically enough, this power is far from being recognized by the whole society (including the workers who perform the task), as the domestic continues to be an invisible realm of production, and the domestic work is still the most unwanted and discreditable of all jobs.[16] Moreno synthesizes it very clearly:

Society does not value this work because it is not considered productive, nor that it contributes to the nation's development. But, even sadder it is the mentality of the house workers themselves, who feel inferior to the people who perform other kinds of jobs. We never talk about the fact that these people — professionals, government staff, business men, and, yes, even militants of the feminist movements — wouldn't be able to carry out their activities if we were not in their houses taking care of their children and performing the essential domestic tasks that allow their homes to function adequately. (quoted in Chaney 1998, 264)

Despite optimistic predictions made by some Chilean feminists in the 1980s that domestic service would increasingly become a more professionalized service contracted through a company only for certain hours and with specific demands, the reality is that it remains close to its colonial origin, when the servant was an indispensable element in the household. As it used to be in the past, domestic workers tend to stay with the same employers for long periods, establishing symbiotic relationships of mutual dependency, even when bosses find themselves in an insolvent position (Salazar and Pinto 2002, 212).

The generation that participated (directly or indirectly) in the women's social movement of the 1980s during the military regime, and were later part of the coalition of center-left parties that ruled the country between 1990 and 2010, have not renounced the comforts of domestic service. They have accepted this "indispensable company" even if they opposed other bourgeois goods when young. As adults they have prolonged, through their children, a patriarchal order in which the newer generational group ignores domestic work completely, having inherited a system based on the racist assumption that poor women do the work in their homes because they have nothing better to do, because they are intrinsically inferior.[17] In the words of Ehrenreich,

> what [children] learn pretty quickly is that some people are less worthy than others. Even better wages and working conditions won't erase the hierarchy between an employer and his or her domestic help, since the help is usually there only because the employer has "something better" to do with her time . . . not noticing the obvious implication that the cleaning person herself has *nothing* better to do with her time. In a merely middle-class home, the message may be reinforced by a warning to the children that that's what they'll end up doing if they don't try harder in school. (2002, 101–2)

Moreover, these newer generations will probably ignore (as their parents did before them) that part of their basic education was acquired from an adult that was not the parent, did not belong to the family, and in many cases did not share the parents' values and/or ideologies. The paradox is that this person represented and continues to represent a central figure with serious responsibilities and yet no real authority. Even though la nana takes care of the most essential needs of the children, she is still viewed as a stranger, and in some cases a potential danger for the family's well-being. She might also be the suspect of any disruption of what it is considered normal or any object disappearance in the house. Her acquaintances — either known or unknown by the family — can be subjects of distrust at any time; her manners, being different from those of the family, may become targets of jokes, comments, and, in some cases, reprimand, for she tends to be seen as the embodiment of an essential childishness, which ultimately erases her authority. Nevertheless, the fact that despite all of this, she is such an important piece in the education of the children—in some cases more so than the parents or other family members—leaves several questions for the future of feminism. One of them would be whether the newer generations are going to embrace their mothers' and grandmothers' gender battles, and also what kind of families and household structures they are going to build when they become household heads.

In relation to the election of President Bachelet—the other important issue of public content among feminists and women in general—an analysis of the contradictions around domestic service is also at stake. In 2005, still a candidate, Bachelet responded in several interviews that she did not have someone puertas adentro (a live-in house worker) when she was raising her kids.[18] Such a statement immediately defines the profile of a public woman in the Chilean collective imaginary. To the majority, it means that she was capable of arriving to such a position of power basically due to her own strength, even though she did not say she didn't have house workers, just that they did not sleep in her house. It is fundamental to notice, though, that the question about her having or not having a female worker erases the other one, which would be more crucial for the sake of feminism, which is, if during her child-raising years she shared equal responsibility with the fathers of her children (either before or after separation). For, as Barbara Ehrenreich and Arlie Hochschild say, the presence of domestic service not only enables affluent women to enter the workplace, "it enables affluent men to continue avoiding the second shift" (2002, 9).[19]

In relation to this, it is important to stress that a puertas afuera type of work does not translate into the kind of services provided in some First World countries, such as the United States, where the employee goes to one or several houses just to clean and in some cases cook a meal for the family while the family is usually out. The obligation of a woman who works puertas afuera in Chile may well imply eight to twelve hours of work in one house, performing all sorts of duties (including cooking, child care, and shopping for the family), with the common understanding that these services could be extended to weekends and nights in case of special requests from the employer.

Due to the gendered division of social life in Chile—a state that has not yet assumed its role in supporting women who work and divorce having only been legalized in 2004[20]—it is totally unthinkable that a single mother would have been able to ascend to the presidential office without the assistance of some kind of domestic service. This very fact is what makes it so obvious what an essential role the empleadas have played in the development of feminism and gender liberation. Does it make sense, then, to silence their very existence when talking about women's rights? Is it possible to obliterate their productive and reproductive role in society? Is it justifiable to avoid the issue of the mistreatment they sometimes suffer and the incongruence of making a woman renounce her dreams and needs for the sake of another woman's future?

Rosalba Todaro and Thelma Gálvez conducted a study on domestic service in Santiago, which was first published by the Center for Women's Studies (CEM) in 1984 and then, in a revised version, in 1987. In 1989, it appeared as an article in a volume in English, among several other studies on different parts of the region, titled Muchachas No More: Household Workers in Latin America and the Caribbean, edited by Elsa Chaney and Mary G. Castro.[21] The research is one of the very few works on this matter ever published in Chile. Thus, it has the merit of bringing to the surface, from a feminist perspective, a reality that a vast majority pretended to ignore. One of its main theses is that the work relation between worker and patron (employer) is "servile in nature," and that "domestic work will begin to lose its servile characteristic only when it becomes work contracted for defined services, not while it constitutes the consumption of someone else's time and labor" (Gálvez and Todaro 1989, 307). As a way to arrive at that goal, they propose "the possibility of short-term gains and middle-term alternatives within the system as we progress toward a more just and equal society, and the search for ways of working within labor organizations that would lead to strong unions by changing the fatalistic behavior and submissiveness of household workers" (Gálvez and Todaro 1989, 318).

In relation to the first goal, legislation (2003, 2008, and 2011) has progressively humanized domestic service, regulating it in terms of hours of work, contracts, and salaries.[22] In that respect, according to SERNAM, domestic workers have the same rights as any other employee. The employer, on the other hand, has the obligation to establish a written contract and protect the worker with health and retirement plans.[23] However, SERNAM also recommends that for these requisites to be respected, women should be organized and thus informed and periodically updated about their rights. This is, indeed, the second recommendation that Gálvez and Todaro made more than twenty years ago.

Domestic workers actually have a couple of organizations in Chile. One of them is the National Association of House Workers (ANECAP), founded with Catholic Church sponsorship in 1948 and obtaining legal status in 1965, and the other is the House Workers Union (SINTRACAP), created in 1947.

Elena Urrutia, former president of SINTRACAP, observes that the association keeps losing affiliates because the employers do not want their workers to be unionized and perceive the organization as a disguise for political activism. They also do not want their nanas to participate because of the irregularities they are incurring as employers. If they were discovered, they would have to pay high compensations, which all—regardless of their social status or political affiliation—want to avoid. According to Urrutia, during Bachelet's government, "It's the same with all kinds of employers, from the government or from the other side, rich and middle class. In fact, this is one of our main problems, that is when their contributions to our pensions get accumulated without payment for many years, fines are high and everybody tries to avoid the payment."[24]

Besides these organizations, there was also a university program for domestic workers, offered by the Catholic University Silva Henriquez, and organized by PRODEMU (Foundation for Women's Promotion and Development), a state institution created by the first Christian Democratic postdictatorship government targeted to working-class women, with the support of SERNAM and other institutions. The initiative was a response to the union's demands expressed in the Primer Congreso de Trabajadoras de Casa Particular, held in Santiago in 2002, and it aimed at "professionalizing" the labor performed by women in domestic jobs, promoting "self-esteem and dignity of the job performed."

Praxedes Peña, one of the promoters at PRODEMU of this university program, told me in an interview in Santiago in 2006 that although the initiative was a success for three years after its opening in 2003 with ample publicity in the media, its recruitment capacity in 2006 was in considerable decline. There was no media coverage for the program, and other priorities diverted the government from efforts such as professionalizing domestic service. According to Peña, the program already needed revisions of its principles and goals, but PRODEMU did not have the resources to carry them out. After a couple of years the program was canceled, and no other government-funded programs have since been created for domestic workers.

Although well intended, these initiatives and organizational efforts highlight the very contradiction between such practices and what Elizabeth Kuznesof calls the essential anachronism of the "continued importance of domestic labor . . . in the modern age, a continuation of patriarchal employment practices and paternalistic educational methods" (Kuznesof 1989, 32). Actions oriented to make this job more efficient just help prolong a system that maintains reproduction separated from production, relegating it to a female private domain. Real efforts should be made instead to bring to the surface the need for profound labor reforms, which will leave domestic work only—as Ehrenreich suggests—as housekeeping services "subsidized for those who have health-related reasons to need them–a measure that would generate a surfeit of jobs for the entry-level workers who now clean the homes of the affluent" (Ehrenreich 2002, 103). Moreover, attempts should not so much be aimed at unionizing the domestic workers but at implementing public policies to regulate service, based on the needs of the most disadvantaged sectors of society and not on those of the privileged. In the realm of transnational feminisms after the Fourth World Conference on Women in Beijing in 1995, an integral collaboration around these issues should be one of the priorities among feminists in the region, as has been the case of domestic violence and feminicide in past years.

I believe that eliminating domestic service as a servile colonial practice will require a profound transnational commitment among feminists throughout the region. Among Chilean feminists, a debate about questions of race and racism would have to take place parallel to the discussion about immigration and xenophobia. To achieve this, feminist discourses would have to avoid the comfortable category of women (and, by extension, the abstract use of the concept of gender) as a collective identity that does not represent class, social, and cultural specificities, acknowledging that the dichotomies women-men or women-patriarchy are not the only ones to analyze gender relations in society. This commitment would be highly enriched with the internal recognition of what Sonia Montecino has depicted as our hidden condition of mestizos (Montecino 1993). Doing that would lead us to accept the fact that we Chileans are the offspring of a union (many times polygamous) between un criollo and una india (almost certainly the house servant), and that "feeling white" is nothing but the erasure of our color and the expression of an inherited shame that impedes us from recognizing ourselves, as much as others. As such, this could be a productive step toward the end of those remains of slavery and a real transnational understanding with other feminists in the region. An approach that is "contextually appropriate," as Sonia Alvarez suggests, should "seek to recover those cultural-symbolic dimensions" that are often left aside in "policy-centered activism" (Alvarez 2000, 34). With this type of advocacy, feminists could design policies that "help (re)shape cultural understandings of particular social problems" (Alvarez 2000, 32), such as domestic labor.

In the context of Chilean feminism, the effort should first be aimed at recognizing the Mapuche culture as one living in daily interaction with the huincas. Second, advocacy should pursue a cultural embrace of the knowledge Mapuche women bring to the Chilean community when they leave their own. For, as Andrea Manqui, from the governmental National Indigenous Development Corporation (CONADI), told me in an interview, contrary to the common belief that Mapuche people live mainly in the countryside south of the Biobío river, 50 percent of them actually live in Santiago, segregated from their original communities. The majority of them are women who leave their families to perform services in the capital with few (if any) nets of support. According to her, there are no significant efforts from the official institutions to work with these displaced Mapuche women, working in isolation in private houses.[25]

The displacement of Mapuche women from their communities of origin — sometimes promoted by their own families — is understood by them as the main factor of the disappearance of their culture and traditions. It is also the main reason for the gender discrimination they suffer among their own people and their eventual lack of identity. In their own words,

> We, migrant indigenous women, are the ones who live and suffer in our own flesh the issue of gender and ethnic discrimination. . . . We start as adolescents, almost girls, forced by the economic urgency of our families, and why not say it, a bit pushed by our fathers and brothers. Then, we get ourselves to work in someone else's home . . . [and] days go by and our work doesn't change, always doing the same thing without any personal growth, without friends, without the social interaction that is indispensable to get to know people, to make friends, to date, to start our own families, etc. . . . When we return to our original families in the rural areas, we are strangers, we have other customs, other kindness and sensitivity. They make us feel this difference which becomes very dramatic when we finish our working life. Our destiny is of uprooting and solitude. (Centro Cultural Indígena 2002, 3)

Because discrimination toward the Mapuche (and generally all indigenous people in Chile) is so akin to that experienced by immigrants from Peru, it is necessary for feminists to address the connection between women coming as servants to the country and the internal migration that brings indigenous women to the capital. Both issues are socially accepted because of the racist assumption that women of color are naturally suited to perform domestic chores for others. Moreover, we need to denounce the fact that Mapuche workers, of whom 26.48 percent perform domestic work, receive lower salaries and hold more irregular contracts than their Chilean counterparts (Centro Cultural Indígena 2002, 6, 9). In a parallel gesture, feminists must connect the national situation of domestic service to the reality of the rest of the region, because in all Latin America — just as in Chile — 16 percent of the female workforce is in domestic service, and the conditions in which it is performed do not differ much among countries.[26]

In closing, I want to stress that domestic labor is a matter of international human rights (and the Organización Internacional del Trabajo [OIT] has already recognized that), and as such it should receive similar attention to that which other human rights abuses have gotten. To do so, women (who are the typical employers of maids) are the ones who need to raise it as a priority, removing it from that imprecise and abstract arena of a colonial practice that lives among us, as un mal menor. Feminists should acknowledge our fundamental responsibility in the perpetuation of such practices and that our role is not to dignify it, but to work toward its eventual eradication.

Notes

All translations to English are mine.

1. As opposed to the case of Chile, there is an important body of feminist research devoted to domestic labor in countries such as Bolivia (with a strong domestic workers' union since 1984), Mexico, Argentina, Peru, Costa Rica, and the United States.

2. Statistics show that immigration from Argentina is larger than the one from Peru. However, between 1992 and 2002, Peruvian immigration experienced a rise of 394 percent. Argentineans, perceived as equals or even superior by Chileans, do not perform low-income work.

3. These data are based on a study by the Organización Internacional del Trabajo (OIT), commented in the *Diario El Mercurio*, August 5, 2005. See also Stefoni (2004, 333).

4. In 1990 close to 5 percent of the total Chilean population was living outside the country. Throughout its history Chile has had a more consistent tendency to send people to other countries than to receive immigrants. An important contributing factor was the exodus during the 1970s and 1980s produced by exile during Pinochet's dictatorship (Martínez Pizarro 2003, 15–21).

5. Immigration from Ecuador and Bolivia represents 5 percent and 6 percent, respectively, of the whole immigration in Chile. Argentineans represent 26 percent and Peruvians 21 percent (Martínez Pizarro 2003, 26).

6. Regarding the xenophobia provoked by the "visibility" of Peruvians in Plaza de Armas, a traditional gathering place for locals, see Stefoni (2003, 111–12).

7. A big percentage of the population living in poverty corresponds to female-headed households (Márquez 2002).

8. Within the tradition of the bourgeois "novela de costumbres," Elizabeth Subercaseaux (2000) depicts these common characteristics of Peruvian domestic workers.

9. Santiago's downtown displays all sorts of publicity aimed at Peruvians from banks and other institutions to facilitate the transaction of remittances.

10. Despite my insistence, in September 2006 I was unable to interview Padre Algacir Munhak or the sisters, who told me they did not have time for interviews.

11. The change from forty-eight- to forty-five-hour workweek came into effect in December 2005.

12. I refer to partners who live in the house as well as the ones who do not. Even though divorce legislation is somewhat recent in Chile, marriage annulments were common practices (based on legal falsehoods by mutual consensus) during the 1980s and 1990s. Statistics show that 26.2 percent of houses in 2003 had a woman as head of household (Casen 2003, 16).

13. According to Praxedes Peña from PRODEMU, employers still travel from Santiago to the South looking for a young woman to bring home as a domestic live-in worker.

14. I thank Rosalba Todaro for her insight on the help of the neighbor, who usually receives a small monetary compensation for her work. This informal employment is rarely considered domestic work, either by the employer or the employee.

15. I thank Carolina Stefoni for pointing this out to me.

16. The last two censuses in Santiago registered a relatively small percentage of women performing paid domestic work. As Elsa Chaney explains it, "The numbers that appear on the Censuses are frequently not very reliable. . . . In those countries where people are asked to remain at home the Census day, it is probable that the number of domestic workers registered is inferior to the real one, for they go to spend the day with their families, and they are not usually interested in being identified as domestic servants" (Chaney 1998, 263).

17. The newspaper *La Segunda* (April 12, 2006) published an article in which the nanas were the actual informants about the characteristics and habits of President Bachelet's new secretaries of state.

18. See, for example, the interview by Margarita Serrano, published in *Diario El Mercurio*, July 2005.

19. In the quote, they are actually referring to "the presence of immigrant nannies." I have deliberately extended their comment to all domestic service.

20. Before the legalization of divorce, since marriages were nullified, wives had no legal recourse against their husbands. In many cases women had to go through intense battles to obtain some compensation or custody arrangements.

21. The volume was reedited in Spanish by Nueva Sociedad, Caracas, in 1993, under the title *Muchacha, cachifa, criada, empleada, empregadinha, sirvienta y . . . nada más: Trabajadoras domésticas en América Latina y el Caribe.*

22. Domestic workers' basic salary was 75 percent of minimum wage until March 2011, when the law established the minimum wage for them.

23. SERNAM, "Derechos de trabajadores de casa particular en Magallanes," http://www .sernam.cl/. In some of the interviews I conducted, I found out that many employees prefer not to make use of their retirement benefits so as to obtain a bigger salary every month.

24. SERNAM, "Trabajo doméstico, legalmente subvalorado and trabajadoras de casa particular: Que nos valoren y respeten," http://www.mujereschile.cl.

25. A seminar carried out in 2003 by the Mujer y Familia, hosted by the National Indigenous Development Corporation, was a successful initiative that ended up in one of the very few publications about Mapuche domestic workers, called "Nos hemos encontrado en el caminar de las mujeres mapuches" (On our way, we have encountered the Mapuche women), with revelatory testimonials. This initiative, though, has not been repeated, since the corporation has not received funds to do it again, according to Manqui.

26. See the article "Día Internacional de la Mujer 2006: Hay más pero no siempre mejores trabajos para las mujeres en América Latina," prepared by the Organización Internacional del Trabajo Department of Communication, available at http://www.ilo.org/public/spanish /region/ampro/cinterfor/temas/gender/nov/prensa08/masnom.htm.

CHAPTER THIRTEEN/PERFORMING SEDUCTION AND NATIONAL IDENTITY/ BRAZILIAN EROTIC DANCERS IN NEW YORK

SUZANA MAIA

Welcome to Brazil, the land of Carnival, beautiful women, and unrestrained sexuality. Internet sites promoting tourism in Brazil don't spare branding the nation with the body of its women. *Brazilian night with Hot Brazilian dancers,* announces a topless club in the outskirts of Queens, New York, appealing to one of the strongest stereotypes about Brazil in international arenas. But what are stereotypes, and what do they do to people engaged in their production? How do women who move transnationally experience them in their bodies and everyday lives? What are the interpretive clashes and the material conditions on which these stereotypes become translated from one context to another? What is, as Claudia de Lima Costa puts it in this volume, lost and gained in translations?

As a number of studies of colonial and postcolonial configurations have eloquently argued (Bhabha 1994; McClintock 1995; Stoler 1995, 2006), a stereotype is a discursive strategy predicated on historical relations and contexts of domination in which the Other is identified and categorized according to racial and sexual discriminations. More than just superficial constructs, stereotypes are generalizations and simplifications of much deeper processes of national identity formations, fractured as they are by lines of gender, class, sex, and race. This scholarship has also stressed that identifications with the nation do not occur only in public spaces or conscious levels. Rather, they are intimately connected to structures of feeling and behavior, fantasies, aesthetic sensibilities, ideals of femininity, masculinity, and beauty, and they often define the very possibilities of erotic interest.

Within contemporary border-crossing contexts, images of Brazilian women are delineated by stereotypical discourses, which have been forged through a long history of colonial and post- and neocolonial encounters. In those encounters different parts of the world are evoked according to collective representations that associate ways of dealing with the body and sexuality with geopolitical locations. Brazilian women have been represented as being of "mixed race," a view that attaches a not only racialized but sexualized value to them in global arenas. As scholarship on the intersection between sexuality, gender, and national formation in Brazil has argued (Parker 1991; Corrêa 1996; O. Pinho 2004), the desire and desirability of Brazilian women have been functional to early projects of Brazilian nation-building. In Brazil the ideology of racial mixture has been crucial to the construction of Brazilian national identity.

Particularly after the abolition of slavery (in 1888), and at a time when European evolutionist theories of race became prevalent, Brazilians had to come to terms with this perceived unique racial mixture, as compared with Europe and North America. By reappropriating colonial categories, Brazilian foundational authors interconnected the idea of racial mixture with notions of race and representations of tropical sexuality as defined by early European travelers and writers. For the different authors, racial mixture was conceived through the contact between native and, especially, African slave women and white colonizers in an atmosphere of excessive sexual license. However, whereas in earlier writings racial mixture was a source of degeneracy, in the seminal work of Gilberto Freyre it became a source of national pride: Brazil lived a "racial democracy," in comparison to German Nazism and racial segregation in North America. From being a characteristic that would impair the development of the country vis-à-vis European nations, racial mixture became a symbol of modernity, a proof of Brazilian malleability and ability to adapt to the complexities of a new world order (Vianna 1999; O. Pinho 2004).

In this formative period of the nation, Carnival and the image of the mulata, the mixed oversexualized woman, came to epitomize the festive and sexualized essence of the Brazilian nation (Parker 1991). As largely argued in studies of race in Brazil (Marx 1998; Hanchard 1999; Guimarães 2002), the discourse of racial democracy not only left unresolved but may have aggravated social inequality within the country to the disadvantage of the African-descended population. In Brazil, lighter shades of skin color still correspond to the privileged groups, whereas the darker shades correspond to the less advantaged. Yet the construct of an idealized mixed body, particularly as embedded in women's bodies, remains the ultimate symbol of the nation.

How do Brazilian women, belonging to different social locations in Brazilian class and racial configurations, experience their bodies as symbols of the nation as they move from one national context to another?[1] For the past few years, I pursued this question by examining the lives of Brazilian women who work as erotic dancers in New York's nightclubs, particularly the ones located in the borough of Queens (Maia 2009, 2010, 2012b). In those bars, Brazilians constitute the majority of dancers, followed in numbers by women from Colombia. Since the beginning of my fieldwork, the presence of middle-class, mostly professional and university graduate women has caught my attention as a subject for research. I was often struck with the disjuncture between the stereotypical images of the mulata represented in history and contemporary media as a Brazilian national symbol and the reality of these much lighter bodies dancing in the bars.

To understand this apparent paradox, I needed to think how national identity intersects with other kinds of identifications that are not necessarily bounded to the nation-state. Research on transnationalism and the predicament of the middle classes from other peripheral or semi-peripheral locations (Fernandes 2000; Guano 2002; De Kooning 2005) was helpful for guiding me through thinking how these women experienced the duality between the local and the global and how ultimately this duality is reconfigured with their migration to the United States. In particular, the considerations of Arjun Appadurai (1990) and Akhil Gupta and James Ferguson (1992) regarding the relationship between space, place, identity, and nation proved to be relevant. In their assessment of Benedict Anderson's seminal work (1991) they point out that the elite and middle class of peripheral countries do not necessarily identify horizontally with the other constituencies — that is, the working class, which in Brazil corresponds to racialized others of darker skin color.[2] Rather, the peripheral elite and middle class in the global South are more likely to identify with the elite and middle class of the First World centers of power.

This identification, however, can never be complete. If, on the one hand, their location as middle-class of lighter skin color puts them in a position of relative privilege within Brazil, on the other hand, their participation in a global middle-class identity is impaired by their disadvantaged location in the global hierarchy of nations. Inhabiting this dual frame of reference, Brazilian middle-class women have come to represent two somewhat contradictory and antithetical views of the nation. One is modern, clean, technologically advanced, in tune with First World consumption practices and fashion, educated, and white. The other, darker in skin color, is represented as politically and economically backward, chaotic, and unmanageable. Yet the latter carries the signifiers of a more "authentic" bodily culture, as manifest in public celebrations of sexuality.

In this chapter I argue that this apparent paradox is somewhat discursively "resolved" by a particular deployment of the language of racial mixture, which has historically been central to the definition of Brazil as a nation. *Morena* is a term that describes more than skin color, but as for other racial categories in Brazil, it adheres to different contexts, meaning different things in different moments and situations.[3] Historically dismissed by most researchers or clustered with mulata in references to the nonwhite population of Brazil, morena as a racial category has increasingly caught the attention of researchers (Norvell 2001; Guimarães 2002; McCallum 2005; and see chapter 14 in this volume). Here, I explore the ways in which middle-class women who work as erotic dancers in New York deploy racial categories such as morena to articulate the tensions in their shifting identity as they move across nation-states.

Building on scholarship that looks at identity as it is constructed in space and place, I adopt a transnational framework to look at how race and identity are performed as these women move across nation-states. To accomplish that, I adopt the concept of "nomadic subject," as developed by Rosi Braidotti (1994). Nomadism, according to Braidotti, is not just a theoretical and methodological option; it is also a style of thinking and an existential condition. To her, in a time when subjects have become highly mobile, the researcher must look at identity as no longer bounded to specific places and time. Moreover, the researcher herself must adapt to these changing configurations by adopting an equally unstable and empathetic relation to her subjects. To develop this nomadic identification between subject and object, it was necessary to have an empathetic relationship to these women, which is why I opted to work with a small number of them. It is my assumption that the life trajectories of Clara, Teresa, and Nana, the three women I present here, exemplify some of the experiences and constraints that other Brazilian women, sharing a similar social location, live through their bodies. I approach these women's experiences as they move back and forth between Brazil and the United States as moments and spaces inhabited in their life trajectory. Therefore, my work is not concerned about these women solely as so-called sex workers—a definition that was never used by them to refer to their own identity. Rather, I see their work as erotic dancers as a moment in the complex web of identification and disidentifications, of translations, as they cross national, class, racial, and gender borders.

Middle-Class Women: The Race and Sex of the Nation

Clara is one of the eighteen women from her extended family to migrate to New York from the northeast of Brazil. She is thirty-two years old and was born in a midsize town in the state of Bahia. When I asked Clara about her race in an interview, she said: "Branca, mas eu sou mesmo é morena, brasileira, morena" (white, but what I really am is morena—Brazilian, morena). As Robin E. Sheriff (2001) found for middle-class Brazilians of lighter colors in her research, Clara was not interested in discussing race and racial classifications. For her, race was a given, an unmarked social position in reference to Brazil. At no point in our conversations did she touch on the issue of racism in Brazil, except once when I confronted her with a direct question: "Is there racism in Brazil?" She answered: "Yes, there is a lot of racism in Brazil." Then she moved on to talk about something else. The only other time that she referred to racism was in reference to the United States. In her perspective, the lack of racially mixed people and the visual separation between blacks and whites was proof that the United States had only to learn from Brazilian models of racial contact and mixing. Even that was a remark she did not elaborate on.

When Clara answered "branca" (white) to my question about her race, she was giving me a category of the Brazilian census, which offers only five choices for defining race: branca, *parda*, black, indigenous, or yellow (for Asians). Parda is the only category in which morena as well as mulata could fit. But Clara could not put herself in the same box as mulata. By answering branca, she positioned herself in opposition to the other categories in the Brazilian classification system. Immediately afterward, however, she said: "morena, brasileira, morena." *Morena* in this case is directly associated to her transnational position and consciousness: brasileira. The movement that coupled *white* and *morena, brasileira* in the same speech act is the movement of calling on frames of reference that cross the borders of nation-states. Adopting the approach that race is not a fixed marker of identity but one that varies as people inhabit particular spaces, I focus on other discursive details of Clara's speech and on the semantic contexts in which her racial identity is defined. Next, I look at her life history in the Brazilian context and examine the social location of relative privilege, in reference to which she identified herself as white.

The trajectory of Clara's life exemplifies one common of the other Brazilian dancers, mostly from the middle and upper middle classes, who are part of my research. For most of them, their parents' generation was part of the expansion of the Brazilian middle classes, financed by the heavy influx of capital that flooded Third World countries in the 1960s and 1970s. As in the case of middle classes located elsewhere in the global South, these women are immersed in the "project of modernity" that Brazil has engaged in since the years following World War II. Among other things, "modernity" as the discourse that accompanied the efforts of "developing" the country following U.S. models also meant the massive entrance of women into the educational system and the labor market and the gender transformations that resulted, particularly for women from the middle classes. Freed from domestic work thanks to the availability of cheap labor by Afro-Brazilian women, middle-class women (most of them occupying the whiter spectrum of the Brazilian configuration) experimented with new gender roles and leisure. Divorce skyrocketed, and many women delayed marriage to pursue their own careers and to travel nationally and internationally.

Clara grew up in a family that identified itself with the markers of modernity, expressed by investment in education, a consumerist lifestyle, and access to foreign travel (O'Dougherty 2002). Her mother is a dentist and always encouraged her to have a career of her own. Clara, as well as other women in this research, went to private schools and college. When she was thirteen years old her parents divorced, and she moved with her mother and her sister to the capital, although she also spent a lot of time in a smaller city where her grandfather was the mayor. For her fifteenth birthday, her mother sent her to Walt Disney World for a holiday. In the 1980s she went to law school in the state of Minas Gerais, financed by her parents. Clara graduated from law school in 1995, passed the bar exam, and started working as an assistant lawyer for a private company. Still, she could not afford to live on her own, and her mother continued supporting her financially. Despite the promise of a bright future, in the 1980s, Brazil, like other so-called semi-peripheral and peripheral regions, was hit by an economic downturn and a sudden rise in international interest rates, resulting from the new alignment in the world economy. As inflation skyrocketed in the country and her salary was devalued, Clara's mother began renting an extra room of their apartment to foreign students to help with Clara's expenses.

Although I cannot know with exactitude the details of Clara's life, I know from my own experience as a member of a similar class that in spaces such as schools, parties, and vacations, middle-class people, mostly of light skin color, are more likely to relate on equal terms only to other light-skinned people. As documented in recent scholarship on the persistence of racial and class inequality in Brazil (Twine 1998; Sheriff 2001; Goldstein 2003), people from the middle classes, constituting a somewhat small elite, are invariably serviced by people of darker skin color. In their homes, domestic servants cook, clean, and take care of the children; at school and at parties, doormen, drivers, and waiters of darker skin color make salient the markers of being middle class. In these spaces of privilege, the *morenidade* of the middle classes is closer to values of whiteness and leisure time. On those occasions, *morena* does not indicate a result of racial mixture but of a tan acquired through the exposure to the sun. As John A. Norvell (2001) argues in the case of Rio de Janeiro, morenidade might in fact be a marker of class, because it indicates the amount of leisure time spent on the beach.

In her research on race among middle-class people in Salvador, Cecilia McCallum (2005) finds that, on the one hand, in the contexts just mentioned, whiteness is the most valued attribute as embedded in the practices and aesthetic preferences of the participants. On the other hand, as McCallum also points out, racial identifications change as one moves from one place to another in a city, or from one moment to another in the span of a day. In Salvador, a city that is estimated to have the largest African-descent population in Brazil, the contact between races happens at nearly all times, and there are other occasions when whiteness is not the hegemonic ideal. In cities like Salvador, Bahia, a tourist center, people from diverse backgrounds very often meet in public celebrations where blackness is the most valued color as a signifier of a more authentic race and culture. On occasions such as Carnival and the numerous street parties that take place in Bahia, people from the middle classes and of light skin color incorporate attributes that approximate them to blackness, as the genuine symbol of the nation. In these contexts, the category morena comes to signify not just a tan color but an ability to embody the sensuality resultant from the literal or symbolic mixing of races. The proximity of different bodies in this latter context is desirable as far as it does not threaten the hierarchies of privilege that are characteristic in the daily life of the participants.

With the economic crisis in Brazil in the 1990s, however, the ability of the middle classes to sustain the markers of social distance between classes and races was greatly affected. In 1995, after passing the bar exam and getting her permit to work as a lawyer, Clara's reality fell short of her expectations. The hardship was colossal, and at the end of each month, she hardly had any money at all. In total she made less than US$500 a month, and apart from paying all the bills, she still had to purchase outfits that would be suitable for a lawyer's status. Clara particularly remembers how dreadful it was when she had to take a bus to go to her office, in which case her whiteness was threatened by the proximity of other people of darker skin color, not in a separate atmosphere of celebration but in everyday life and work. After two years of struggling with her financial instability and lack of prospects for advancing her career, she decided to follow the path of her aunts and cousins who had already moved to the United States and worked as erotic dancers.

Clara decided to dance in Queens's clubs for a variety of reasons. First, most of her eighteen aunts and cousins were already working as dancers in New York, and they could introduce her to the bar scene. With their help, she could communicate not only with employers but, more important, with clients. Clara also felt safer working in a bar that was located in a more residential area and where, because of city regulations, the women are not allowed to be topless and do not have to perform lap dances and table dances.[4] To start dancing, it is necessary to book an audition beforehand, which a dancer friend could do by asking the manager of the bar. Managers are often willing to have new dancers because the clients are sustained by the allure of a variety of bodies and faces. As in other cases in the informal economy of world cities, managers prefer to work with networks of employees, due to their reliability when the older workers become responsible for the new ones. As Clara also puts it, the environment was familiar and festive, as opposed to Manhattan bars, which she perceived as overtly competitive and sexualized.

New York City's gentlemen's bar scene is hierarchically differentiated between the upscale bars located mainly in Manhattan and the local or neighborhood bars of the outer boroughs of Queens, Brooklyn, Staten Island, and the Bronx. The stereotypical glamorized bars correspond to the upscale bars of Midtown Manhattan, which serve a clientele of tourists, businessmen, financial executives, and politicians and are located near convention centers and hotels. They employ mostly white American women as well as women from Western Europe, such as Spain, Italy, England, and Denmark. Given the global preference for and value on light skin color, there is a significant presence of women from Eastern Europe and the former Soviet bloc. Adding to the aura of exoticism, there are also women from Asia, such as Thailand and the Philippines, as well as from Latin America.

In Queens's bars, the clientele consists mainly of immigrant men and American men from the working classes.[5] They include older Greek construction subcontractors, Italian restaurant managers or owners, and a new generation of Albanian men. There is also a Hispanic migrant clientele, particularly men from Colombia, Mexico, and Ecuador. "Whitish" Irish or second-generation Italian working-class Americans, usually electricians, firemen, or other unionized professions, also frequent the bars. In Queens, during their shift the women dance for about twenty minutes and socialize in the bar for forty minutes until their next set. The stage, where typically three women will dance at one time, consists of a long platform surrounded by the bar counter, which separates clients from dancers. Dancers make their tips mostly in the form of dollar bills when dancing on the stage, or when socializing with clients and encouraging them to buy drinks, from which the dancers receive a small percentage. Besides performing on the stage, an important part of a dancer's work is to socialize and to drink with clients when "on the floor." It is also on the floor as well as in the dressing rooms that dancers socialize with each other and where Brazilian women from the middle classes and other migrant women from various classes, racial and ethnic backgrounds, educational levels, and place of origin work side by side. It is also in these spaces that differences are reinforced and new, transnational hierarchies are created.

In Queens's bars, where anywhere from twelve to twenty women work each night, it is common to form cliques of dancers who socialize among themselves while analyzing the behavior of other dancers. Gossiping—a form of social organizing traditionally associated with women's forms of knowledge—is widely practiced among dancers. While sipping their beers around the counter or when counting money, redoing make-up, or resting in the dressing rooms, women comment on other women's behavior while asserting their own position of difference. In Queens, dancers make most of their money when dancing on the stage in the form of tips.[6] Clients give them dollar bills by handing it over in their hand or by placing it between their breasts or under the string of the bikini. The details of these negotiations are a crucial part of the performance and define the exchanges between client and dancer, which continues on the floor when she is not dancing.

The appropriate ways of performing the identity of an erotic dancer are a source of controversy and reveal the ways dancers define class and racial differences by using the language of morality. For Clara, for example, dancing is fine and fits with her ideas about partying and national celebration. However, touching or being touched by clients is unacceptable to her. For others, some touches are fine but not rubbing their bodies against clients' genitals. For still others, this is fine as long as they do not have go out with clients. The limits might shift depending on the relationship a dancer has with the client, on bar regulations, and on the increasing competition between dancers as more women, particularly immigrant women, search for work in bars. Thus, I often saw women acting in a way that they would not consider appropriate in some other context. Nevertheless, the allegation that "other" women are behaving inappropriately serves as a symbolic separation of these bodies, otherwise unlikely to be in such proximity. Through a moral discourse about the appropriate display of body and sexuality, Brazilian women from the middle class separate themselves from two other groups of women: the "Hispanics" and the other Brazilians from the working and lower classes, some of whom have darker skin. Excerpts from an interview with Clara are revealing of this process of "distinction" within the bar:

S: So, what is the difference between Hispanics and Brazilians? Do you think we are all part of the same culture?

C: In no way, I think that the Hispanics are *povinho* [little people], they are much more underdeveloped than Brazilians.

S: And who are the Hispanics, anyone who speaks Spanish?

C: No, not really. To me Hispanics are Colombians, Ecuadorians, Mexicans, that part of the world. You know by the way they walk, in the bars you know by the way they talk, they are fraudulent; they are repulsive, with exceptions.

Referring to a Brazilian woman who used to date a Greek man with whom she came to have a relationship, Clara tells me:

I met him in the bar, he is friends with the owner. He had just broken up with this other Brazilian dancer. I could never understand that relationship because I knew the woman, a girl from the Rio shantytowns, she used to do coke, smoke pot, and had a child with an unknown father. She left the child with her mother in Rio. *Gentinha mesmo*, little people. She wasn't a bad person, just low level, couldn't speak for two minutes without cursing. And he did a lot for her; he knew what kind of person she was. She was twenty-one and he, forty-eight. And she couldn't speak English, how did they communicate? I never understood that.

Historically, race in Brazil and in the United States were seen as two opposite and contrasting systems. In Brazil, segregation was never an official policy, and race classifications followed a color continuum, whereas in the United States the "one-drop rule" established a rigid color line and segregation between blacks and whites. Both morena and mulata, for example, would be categories that presuppose the existence of mixed races in Brazil, while in the United States there had been no such variations in color classification. The result was that in Brazil, racial identity is more malleable and depends on other physical and social determinants, such as hair, facial features, and, more important, one's position in the class hierarchy. In Brazil, as the saying goes, "money whitens." In the United States, there were no such nuances, and the relationship between races has been more confrontational.

However, as scholarship comparing the two countries has pointed out (Marx 1998; Winant 1999), the racial formations in the two countries have significantly changed in the past few decades. In Brazil, despite the large acceptance of an idealized form of racial democracy and the denial of racism, there is an increasing polarization of race and a growing sector of race-based organizations and consciousness, and racial identities have become more "polarized." In the United States, on the other hand, two parallel processes contributed to the displacement of the black–white polarity (Winant 1999): the civil rights movement and the massive entrance of diverse immigrant groups into the country. Desegregation between the black–white divide was accompanied by affirmative action and other compensatory policies toward African Americans, minorities, and immigrants. As Howard Winant (1999, 108) argues, in tune with the North American "racial lumping," identity politics encouraged the pan-ethnicizing or racializing of people from different backgrounds, thus creating broad categories such as Latino (or Hispanic) and Asian.

In the U.S. context, Brazilian women must enter one or another of these historically defined racial categories. Factors such as class and race locations as defined in the country of origin greatly affect the ways migrants are incorporated. A Brazilian woman will be classified as Latina (or Hispanic, the most common category in the bars), remain in the differentiated category of Brazilian, or even be classified as white depending not only on her color/race but also on the labor market she enters.

In the case of the exotic dancers examined here, when women from different racial and class locations in Brazil work side by side, the articulation of distinction functions in yet other ways. When Clara uses the expression *gentinha* to refer to Hispanics and Brazilian women from the working and lower-middle classes, she is in fact deploying a language of morality to distance herself from the racial lumping that would put her together with people she does not consider her equals in terms of race and class.

This process of social differentiation within the bar scene can be further illustrated by comparing the case of Clara with that of Teresa, whom I met through Clara and from whom she is careful to keep certain distance. I was talking to a few dancers in the dressing room in the basement of Highway gentlemen's club when Teresa came in, carrying her suitcase with string bikinis, small skirts, and dresses. The women gathered around her during their breaks and took turns trying on the outfits and commenting on how they looked. My presence immediately caught her attention, since I was the only one wearing street clothes. Why didn't I try on some outfits? Although I explained that I was not a dancer, she insisted I should give it a try. On this and all the other occasions when we met, she tried to convince me that studying dancers was not enough, I should also try to make some money by dancing and investigating the possibilities of my own seductive power.

A forty-five-year-old woman, Teresa has a degree in psychology and held a somewhat privileged position in the state government in Recife. In 1994, facing economic hardship due to the successive devaluation of her salary, Teresa decided to open a small clothing factory with her boyfriend. The love and the business partnership failed after a couple of years, after which she decided to come to the United States. In New York, Teresa worked as a house cleaner, the other most common job available for migrant women, until she heard about the work of go-go dancing. She said that even though she never thought of being a go-go dancer before, cleaning houses was insufferable to her.[7] Teresa said she had never cleaned her own house before and dreaded what the cleaning products did to her hands as much as the isolation of domestic work. Nevertheless, it took her nearly a year to start dancing. As a psychologist, she inquired into the nature of men's and women's sexual mores. Knowledgeable about the effects of dress and self-presentation in the production of desire, she started doing research on what outfits would play to men's fantasies. She explained the process of becoming a dancer to me in this way:

> First, I needed to do research about what it meant to be sexy to me, what it meant to be a woman who worked with her sexuality. I would put on a G-string and high heels and just spend a lot of time in front of the mirror, walking up and down in my place, hours in a row, until I felt like I knew how to do it right. I bought many different kinds of outfits. I had to learn how to be that kind of a woman. I was already a normal woman, but now I was a performer, a woman who seduces for money. Because when a woman is beautiful, you know, with blue eyes, that's fine, but that's not what dancing is about. The important thing in dancing is to arouse men's fantasies. Then you have to put some high heels on, corset, stockings, all that. My idea is that I was a *vedete*, like in Sargentelli shows, do you remember, these mulatas with beautiful clothes? I knew that I could not be just a normal person—a normal person I already was. I needed to have another persona there.

To Teresa, dressing the exterior body was not all she needed to do to transform her *self*. Along with the work of presenting herself to the gaze of others, she had to work on the level of imagination and fantasy. Although she usually referred to herself as a morena, to arouse men's fantasy she felt the need to define herself as a mulata in the context of the bar. To be a mulata requires more than a certain skin color or hair type. Mulata also implies a certain voluptuousness of the body and the feeling of "abandonment" that one experiences through the movement of the body in events such as Carnival (Norvell 2001; Giacomini 2006). Teresa's evocation of the image of Osvaldo Sargentelli's vedetes, who were mostly mulatas, relates to the deep-rooted representations that intersect in the formation of the Brazilian racial configuration as spectacle.

Sargentelli was the owner of a famous nightclub in Rio de Janeiro. In the 1970s and early 1980s, he became a celebrity. In his nightclubs, capitalizing on the allure of Carnival, Sargentelli put on spectacles of mostly topless mulatas wearing G-strings, which became icons of the Brazilian sex tourism industry. Teresa's reference to the body and sexuality of the mulata and to Sargentelli is part of the process of her translation of symbols and images excavated in the imaginary of the nation to fashion her new self across national borders, mimetically incorporating icons of Brazilian sexuality and race.

The approximation of Teresa's morenidade with the body of the mulata in this context also echoes her own particular location with reference to Brazil. Two elements may contribute to this approximation. First, Teresa's skin color is darker than that of most of the women in my research, and her hair type reveals (according to Brazilian standards) that her color is a result not of tanning but of racial mixture. This would not have much importance if her class location were not also slightly but significantly lower than that of Clara and her network of friends and family. The fact that Teresa sells outfits to other dancers in the bars puts her in a position of serving them—an inferior position in the social hierarchy of the bars. None of the other women in this project—and Clara certainly not—used the category "mulata" to classify themselves or describe the kind of persona they assumed in their performances.

For a dancer, assuming a persona that conflicts with her other subject locations is highly problematic in terms of her morals and her location within the larger society. The clash between what is considered morally acceptable and what is invested with extrasexualized performance and the boundaries of what is and is not acceptable are articulated through a language of race and class. More than once I heard dancers thoughtfully describing their situation as "living on the edge." Living on the edge of what? The differences between the kind of product they sell and the boundary between what can be considered prostitution is constantly in question and functions as a marker of social differentiations manifest through racialized representations within the bar. This process happens not just among dancers but also, as we will see, between dancers and men, inside and outside of the bar.

Ambivalent Relationships: Beyond the Bar Scene

Because their busy night schedules limit their social lives beyond the bar scene, Brazilian dancers end up relating mostly to clients and other dancers, and the bars constitute their main space of socialization. It is in gentlemen's bars that most dancers meet men with whom they develop important relationships and who represent their link to society at large. The kinds of relationships dancers have with clients are hierarchically organized within the structure of U.S. society in terms of race and class, and they represent different access to legal and cultural citizenship. Dancers' relationships to bar customers beyond the bar are a crucial arena in which dancers become incorporated into racial and class configurations in the United States. Marriage to a U.S. citizen is, for most migrant dancers, the only way to achieve or maintain their legal status. Only if they are legal can they think of moving to other job markets or, equally important, move freely between Brazil and the United States.[8] Depending on the conditions under which the women enter the country and their social location within the bar scene, their chances to meet people are more or less restricted to gentlemen's bars and people associated with them.

Establishing a relationship is an occasion in which stereotypes become highly ambivalent, regarding not just the dancers but also the clients. Just as Brazilian women differ in terms of race and social class, clients are not always white, are not always American, do not always have blue eyes, and are not as educated. Neither do they have the good habits that Brazilian middle-class women imagine them to have as ideal types. They are also divided by class, race, and educational level and are encountered in a variety of bars, which are in turn hierarchically organized in the geography of the city. In Queens, single youngish and whitish working-class American men are considered the most desirable by Brazilian dancers. The Americans present them with not only the possibility of becoming a legal citizen of this country but also, in anthropologist Aihwa Ong's (1996) definition, with achieving "cultural citizenship" through immersion in the cultural and social network to which the American prospects belong. Creating their own hierarchical classification and stereotypical categories, Brazilian dancers call Hispanic clients *bagaceiros*, or people who eat *bagaços*. In Brazil, the latter expression refers to a person who removes the sugarcane residue after the liquid is extracted; it can also refer to an animal that eats *bagaços* or leftovers. For dancers, this category implies an activity associated with the lower class, revealing the ways class intersects with racial perceptions in defining people's interactions, literally leftovers. From their point of view, Hispanics are depicted as "low-class" people because of their supposed inability to speak the language, the low status of their jobs, and their illegal residency status. Very few Brazilian men go to bars, and Brazilian dancers perceive them as cheap. Because they are compatriots, these men do not feel obliged to give as much in tips, and the dancers feel intimidated in their presence. Like the Hispanics, Brazilian men are believed to be unable to integrate in the United States and are not preferred by the dancers. Most Brazilian dancers avoid working in bars where the majority of clients are black, for, besides their own discriminatory preferences, they believe that blacks have reverse prejudice against them, not giving as many tips as others do.

A relationship that is common in some bars is that between dancers and "sponsors." A sponsor as they define it is usually an older man who supports a girl with money, gifts, and attention. Because most of the clubs in Astoria are owned and frequented by Greek clients, it is not uncommon to find an older Greek man who has one or more "girlfriends" whom he helps financially and goes out with. This was the case for Clara and Demetris. Demetris, twenty years her senior, was a regular patron for more than ten years of a bar where Clara worked and had been previously involved with other Brazilian dancers. In common with other Greek patrons in Queens, Demetris had his own subcontracting construction firm and a reasonable yearly income. When Demetris saw Clara, a young dancer fresh on the bar scene, he started the game of seduction by tipping her generously. Accepting this to be part of the game, Clara told him the nights when she would be working, and Demetris started going to bars more often when he knew she would be there. In exchange for her beautiful and young company, Clara began to accept generous tips and gifts from Demetris. With his help, she rented a basement apartment in Astoria on her own, a significant move in their relationship. When Demetris started frequenting Clara's apartment and began to pay some of her expenses, there was a shift in the fine balance between what occurred in the bar scene and outside it. Demetris became more than just her client. Now he became her sponsor. Clara was also supposed to be his exclusive dancer when he was in the bars, go out with him, and have him as her main company, even if she was not quite attracted to him as a boyfriend or lover. Although Clara, as much as other dancers who engage in these kinds of relationships, was seduced by the comfort, the constant gifts, and emotional support, the inequality of the relationship was a constant source of tensions. Dancers have to continually negotiate between what is demanded of them and what their own desire tells them to perform. Even if Clara had a somewhat privileged social position in Brazil and compared to other dancers, she still occupied a subaltern position in U.S. society at large and at that point continued to engage with men of somewhat subaltern status, like herself.

Very few women develop relationships outside of the bar scene, and, as we will see for the case of Nana, when they do so their chances for a better integration into the U.S. mainstream are greatly improved. Nana is a thirty-four-year-old woman who has been in my life since our college days in Bahia. Although she has a very white skin, when asked about the racial category that would most fit her, she considers herself mixed. She has a degree in sociology from the same university I attended, but our paths had not crossed since our undergraduate days. I moved to New York when I was twenty-five and met her once in a while during my trips home. One year, in the middle of a street party when we were both already drunk, she asked me, "is it true that a woman can make lots of money dancing in bars in New York?" Next thing I knew, in August 2003, Nana called me from Astoria. I am dancing, she said, and living with Clara. The next day I took the subway to Astoria. I was one of the few people she knew in New York, besides Clara and her family, and we became closer friends than we had ever been in Brazil.

Throughout her life, Nana has experienced the lifestyle of a modern single woman, living first with female roommates and then moving out on her own. The project of buying her own apartment along with the desire to travel and pay off some old debts were the immediate reasons she gave for deciding to leave Brazil. Despite her relative success in her profession as a state sociologist, the salary that she received there (about $500 a month) was incompatible with her lifestyle and ambitions. Besides economic and professional frustrations, Nana particularly expressed a profound dissatisfaction with gender roles in Brazil and the lack of what she considers desirable and available men. Through her friendship with Barbara, a friend of Clara, she learned about the work of go-go dancers in New York and about the kind of income she would be able to earn. She started working as a dancer in the same week that she moved to New York and did that for about a year and half. Periodically, I accompanied her to the bars and sipped a beer with a client or other dancers while she danced or while she sat compulsively talking about Brazil and what it meant to be dancing in New York. Nana came of age listening to Brazilian rock and roll, and she imagined a more noir, movie-like New York night underground scene. She paid attention to the illegal activities, complained of exploitation, called the bars brothels, and spoke clearly of sexual labor. To her, this was a kind of prostitution, and the discourse of Brazilian celebratory sexual culture did not fit.

From the start Nana knew that she did not want to stay in the nightclub scene for long. Immediately on her arrival in the United States, she enrolled in English classes in a state university and started auditing a few classes in international relations. She also knew that she did not want to overstay her six-month tourist visa and risk not being able to move freely in and out of the country. The second decision she made was that she wanted to get married and regularize her immigration status as soon as possible. She considered getting engaged in a paid marriage, as many women in Clara's network of family and friends did. Before she did that, though, she kept an eye open for more desirable options and started searching inside and outside of the bar scene for possible prospects.

Nana met Jimmy in a Greek café on a summer afternoon in 2004, just three months after she had moved to New York. They talked by the counter while sipping iced coffee and exchanged telephone numbers. Jimmy is a young white man from a working middle-class family from Pennsylvania.[9] His father worked in the car sales business and his mother worked as a secretary, and he and his brothers grew up in a suburban house and went to college for a few years. During his college years, Jimmy grew weary of suburban life and started feeding the dream of coming to New York. Even before graduating, he moved to Queens, at a time when Astoria was becoming desirable to adventurous suburban American youths who enjoy the edge of the ethnic mix and the affordable rents in what can be seen as the new style of a New York neighborhood.

Jimmy and Nana married just before her six-month visa expired. After that Nana continued working as a dancer, although they agreed that this would be temporary until she regularized her legal situation and learned more English. Later she found a job as the personal secretary of a designer and enrolled in the master's program in international relations at City College. "That is what happens to immigrants in the U.S.," Jimmy's mother said to me; he and his family have a positive view of a country that is willing to integrate those who work hard enough and do the right thing. According to them, Nana was doing the right thing by marrying a U.S. citizen, and this was a legitimate form of immigrants' integration. There was another case like this in the family, and all agreed that Nana and Jimmy were on the right path to becoming a modern transnational couple. His family paid for a generous wedding ceremony for about five hundred guests in a party house in the suburbs of Pennsylvania. Through strategically choosing between her marriage and professional options, Nana managed to leave the bar scene and incorporate into what can be considered a more white North America.

Uneasy Translations

The trajectory of three women presented in this chapter illustrates how, despite the attractions that motivate Brazilian women to move to the United States and engage in a labor market and in relationships that are mediated by the sexualization of their bodies, this process is permeated by a series of misunderstandings, ambivalences, and slippages, as is common of stereotypical formations. To some extent, the women who migrate are able to manipulate national symbols and use them in their favor—consciously or unconsciously—but in their daily lives, there is a disjuncture between idealized representations and their particular location in the class and racial configurations of both Brazil and the United States. The ways Brazilian women from the middle classes, most of whom have lighter skin color, articulate their identity reveals how a language of racial mixture is crucial to Brazilians' sense of self, how it is embedded in the ways Brazilians think of themselves and establish their relationships to others as they cross the borders of nation-states.

The use of the category morena tells well the transnational frame of reference occupied by Brazilian dancers. On one hand, they identify with the values of whiteness and distance themselves from the less privileged population of Brazil, of darker skin color/race. On the other hand, this identification is impaired by their subaltern position in regard to a global hierarchy of nations. White, but not quite (Pinho 2009), when crossing borders of nation-states Brazilian women from the middle class incorporate the values associated with racial mixture as signifiers of "authenticity" and valued as exoticism. At the same time, within the bar scene this apparent homogeneous and indistinct category morena becomes complicated as women from different class backgrounds working side by side differentiate themselves from women of other classes and/or perceived different races, national groups, and educational backgrounds, among other significant social markers.

The women presented herein do not correspond to the traditional academic subject, defined as an "other," socially, economically, and geographically distant from the researcher. They are middle-class Brazilian women who, moving across multiple borders, come to occupy various social locations in the United States. As nomadic subjects (Braidotti 1994), their identity as they cross borders is fragmented between two spaces, two nations. Not just victims here, not just perpetrators there, these women, like all of us, inherit a structure of inequality, local and global, with which we must grapple. By evoking an empathetic/nomadic perception of these women, this chapter tried to deconstruct stereotypical images of an apparent homogeneous category of Brazilian women and examine how social categories and identifications are delineated according to different contexts. The trajectory of these women manifests many of the ambiguities, moral dilemmas, conceptions of race and class, privileges, desires, and translations that are in play in the definition of identities that, crossing the borders of nation-states, delineate new social configurations in transnational spaces.

Notes

1. For an extensive list of studies on Brazilian emigration, see the bibliography organized by Maxine Margolis, http://www.brasa.org/portuguese/novidades.

2. See Maia (2012a) for an understanding of contemporary whiteness among Brazilians in a transnational framework.

3. Compare the study presented here with the case presented by Adriana Piscitelli (chapter 14 in this volume) on middle-class women who engage in sex tourism in Fortaleza, capital of Ceará, in the northeast of Brazil.

4. Because of the zoning regulations, toplessness is not allowed in these bars. To obtain a license for topless performances, the bar must be located in a distance over five hundred meters from schools, houses of worship, residences, and hospitals. In the densely populated neighborhoods of immigrant Queens, this means that the women basically wear bikinis and there are certain rules defining what they can do in their performances.

5. In 1990, Brooklyn and Queens accounted for 60 percent of the population of New York City and housed two-thirds of migrants. By the 2000 U.S. census, Queens, where most Brazilian erotic dancers live and work, had experienced the largest absolute population increase: 277,781 people, a growth rate of 14.2 percent. White non-Hispanics made up 32 percent of the borough's population, and Hispanics accounted for 25 percent, black non-Hispanics 19 percent, and Asian non-Hispanics 17.5 percent.

6. In the more upscale bars of Manhattan, depending on city regulations, dancers make their money mostly from table dances or lap dances. Those are more intimate dances that women offer to clients, commonly on a one-on-one basis. They can be performed in the bar area (table dances) or in a separated area called champagne rooms (lap dances).

7. As Nicole Constable (2006) argues, although there is a tendency in academic and activist literature in blurring the experiences of domestic workers, brides, and sex workers, it is also necessary to look at the differences among these categories of gendered migration.

8. Most Brazilian women come to New York with a tourist visa that allows them to stay legally for a period of six months, but with no permit to work. If they decide to overstay their visa, they have essentially two options. One is to stay in the country illegally as long as they can and make the most money possible and then go back to their country never to reenter the United States. In the other scenario, they get married and regain legal status. For those who decide to stay in the country and want to be able to move back and forth between Brazil and the United States, marriage becomes a consideration.

9. See Ruth Frankenberg (1997) for a study of the construction of whiteness in the United States.

CHAPTER FOURTEEN/TRANSNATIONAL SEX TRAVELS/
NEGOTIATING IDENTITIES IN A BRAZILIAN "TROPICAL PARADISE"

ADRIANA PISCITELLI

Discussions about cultural translation are premised on the view that any process of description, interpretation, and dissemination of ideas is always already caught up in relations of power and asymmetries between languages, regions, and peoples (Costa 2006 and chapter 6 in this volume). They also argue that translation terms, built from imperfect equivalences and privileging certain "originals," are made for specific audiences (Clifford 1997). This debate has evolved based on reflections about how cultural analysis constitutes its objects, with particular attention to the anthropological encounter, and also how theories "move" across contexts (Kaplan 1996). The premises of this debate are relevant to understanding the processes involved in any travel encounter.

In this chapter I consider how cultural translations work in the dynamics of a particular type of travels: sex travels. Taking as reference a specific modality of "sex tourism,"[1] I analyze how the "writings," readings, and reconfigurations of sexualized notions about Brazil play a part in the recent integration of Fortaleza, a city on the northeastern coast, in the global sex travelers' circuits.

Posing a discussion about the changing geography of sex travels in cultural terms might appear awkward to some readers. Yet a considerable amount of work (my own, among others) points to the fact that analyses exclusively grounded on economic aspects are unable to explain how "desirable" places are created in global sex circuits (Kempadoo 2004; Piscitelli 2007). In the universe of this type of travels, sought-after places are produced in the intertwining of economic, political, and cultural aspects. International sex circuits are intensely commodified, but poverty is not a sufficient factor to promote adding new spaces in those circuits. Economic aspects that make sexual services a relevant source of income for impoverished native populations are combined with the intensely sexualized images of certain places, mainly of the South. I am not simply alluding to the anthropological argument that commodity values can only be apprehended by understanding the place they have in a larger code of meaning (Sahlins 1976). My point is that those images are constitutive aspects of these particular commodification processes.

The discussions that take place in the World Sex Archives, one of the most popular websites aimed at heterosexual male sex travelers, illustrate this aspect. Poverty catches the attention of these men, particularly when it is connected to recent economic crises. However, in South America, countries that suffer extreme poverty, such as Paraguay (in the words of those sex consumers, "real Third World"), do not necessarily succeed in terms of enticing those tourists, in spite of the fact of being seen as offering the cheapest sex and allowing almost any kind of sexual practice. The alleged reason is that women of that country are perceived as not at all sensuous. The same happens with the highlands of Peru and Bolivia, where women are considered excessively indigenous and therefore, scarcely hot (Piscitelli 2005). On the other hand, Brazil, which in this website appears as the leading country in terms of its appeal to sex tourists in South America, is considered a nation where sexual services are relatively more expensive and women are seen as strict in terms of acceptable practices. Even so, it is highly desirable because it is perceived to be inhabited by a population that embodies a racialized, intense tropical sexuality.

Such notions about Brazil certainly go far beyond this website's scope. Understanding how these concepts have been produced and disseminated defies one-dimensional approaches to the transnational travel of ideas. Anthropological reflections about tourism state that the tours organized in industrial countries say more about the representations that the tourists have of the Others than they do about the societies visited (Bruner 1989). In sex tourism contexts, the native population seeking relationships with sex travelers translate themselves to suit sex travelers' expectations. But associating sexualized notions of Brazil exclusively or mainly with ideas produced in foreign countries would be a mistake.

Social scientists believe that a sexualized perception of Brazilianness constitutes part of the values in terms of which Brazilians see themselves (Parker 1991; Heilborn and Barbosa 2003). This construct is seen as largely dependent on the literary and scientific writings of European travelers, who have visited the country since the eighteenth century. Maria Luisa Heilborn and Regina Barbosa (2003) synthesize the ideas of diverse authors who wrote about this subject. According to them, the notion that the Portuguese colonizers found here in the tropics "a land with no king and no law" played a significant role in the emergence of Brazil's sexual imagery. Notions current in those writings, re-created in different historical periods, would have been incorporated by the native population, including leading social thinkers who discussed the constitution of the nation in the 1930s. In recent decades, the flows of ideas about Brazil took a different path. An example is offered by the official advertisements produced by governmental agencies since the 1960s, officially publicizing the country in the international tourist market by means of sexualized images of women (Alfonso 2006).

Understanding the dissemination of sexualized notions about the country, however, entails a historical analysis that distances itself from tracing linear flows of ideas. It demands paying attention to how national and transnational levels interact. It also entails—this is my main argument—considering how regional and local levels are entangled in those intersections.

In Brazil, diversified regional constructions associate the sexualized imaginary that stands for Brazilianness with specific places, particularly cities that have played an important role in Brazil's economic and political history and, deeply related to the slave labor system, are seen as racially marked places with a high percentage of black people and mulattos. This is definitely not the case of Fortaleza, capital of the Ceará, in one of the poorest regions of the country, nowadays seen as a foremost city attracting sex tourists in Brazil. Ceará, characterized by a relatively low percentage of population with African traits,[2] is distant from the perceptions of an exacerbated and frequently aesthetized sensuality that mark other cities, such as Rio or Salvador. On the contrary, an idea of harshness and even ugliness expresses the place this state and its capital city have had in national hierarchical constructions of identity.

Explaining how cultural translation works in the integration of a new place in the global sex travelers' circuits involves taking into account interpretations (of the visitors and the host population) that take place in highly unequal arenas. The versions permeating Fortaleza's assimilation into these routes allow us to perceive an intense contest of ideas expressed in disagreements among views of diversely positioned agents. The activation of imaginaries linked to regional and local constructions of gendered identities is a relevant aspect in this dispute.

I develop this argument on the basis of an analysis of how these visions work in a style of heterosexual sex travels named by some locals of Ceará as "middle-class sex tourism," by which they mean that visitors from various countries form relationships with local women from the lower and lower middle classes, most of whom are native to this state. As other states of the northeast, Ceará has sent internal migrants toward the richest states of the south of Brazil for several decades. But this flux has been altered. Ceará's inhabitants have joined the increasing number of Brazilians since the 1980s who seek to improve their lives by migrating to countries of the North (Piscitelli 2008). Middle-class sex tourism is linked to the desire for social mobility for a section of the local population and also to the concrete migration of some women to those countries.

I base these conclusions on the results of an ethnographic study. The main data were collected during eighteen months of ethnographic field work carried out between October 1999 and December 2008 in Fortaleza's "sex tourism" circuits.[3] These are touristy places in which mainly foreign and Brazilian tourists socialize together, alongside the local middle class and young women of the lower classes, some of whom go on *programas* (the local term for any act related to prostitution).[4]

In the next section I comment on how transnational flows of ideas are connected to the construction of a sexualized notion of Brazilianness and consider its relationships with regional and local constructions of identity. Then, I examine the economic, political, and cultural aspects related to sex travels in this context, exploring how the unequal positions of locals and international tourists are expressed in conceptualizations by which means native women are intensely sexualized and men of the countries of the North are depicted as embodying the best styles of masculinity. Finally, keeping in mind how gender, race, class, region, and nationality are written, translated, and incorporated in this context, I show how views of regional and local identity are intermittently and strategically recalled and effaced. In this universe, the local women who form relationships with sex travelers allocate the less valued (regional and local) traits to native styles of masculinity, thus justifying their choice of certain foreigners as ideal partners. Performing "national identity," these women attract those tourists, negotiate their positioning in relationships with them, and through these relationships, some cross severe local barriers, even migrating to countries of the North.

Thinking Region, Producing Nation

The production of the idea of a so-called Brazilian sexual culture allows us to perceive an intriguing aspect. The notion of a sexualized Brazilianness, a view that appears as a synthesis of the national character, has been recurrently produced with reference to specific Brazilian regions and cities.

The historian Margareth Rago (1998) states that, vastly integrated into Brazilian society, this view marked the writings of important social thinkers. In the 1930s, Gilberto Freyre (1954 [1998]) integrated new concepts in the Brazilian debate about the constitution of the nation. He included the discussion about the centrality of the family, paying considerable attention to sexual behavior. The author considered sexual life in Brazil to be a positive aspect,[5] responsible for the "racial democracy" that supposedly characterized the nation.[6] According to Rago's (1998) interpretation, in Freyre's writings the Brazilian people are considered the outcome of the miscegenation of three races (Portuguese, native Indians, and Africans) that in Brazil had no major problems in terms of mixing because sexual attraction was stronger than legal and rational requirements against the unions between different kinds of people. This sexual aspect was responsible for several traits of Brazilian culture: instinct, bodily games, lightness of manner, tolerance, and cordiality. Rago underscores the centrality that the sexual dimension has in Freyre's historical interpretation of Brazil, because it appears as a fundamental aspect that determines relationships in the private and public spheres in a nation where the public sphere is shaped by models borrowed from the private world.

Freyre's analysis is based on the social relationships linked to a specific model of economic production of the utmost importance during the colonial period: the sugarcane plantation cycle, in the northeast of Brazil, which relied on slave labor. But his explanation of Brazilianness is outlined with reference to a specific state and period: Pernambuco, during the sixteenth and seventeenth centuries. Based on this particular case, Freyre delineated the contours of a Brazilian patriarchal family as a root from which all the other relationships developed, which lasted up to the industrialization period and the subsequent decadence of large rural estates. The procedure of generalizing this type of family, connected to a specific regional model, to the entire country aroused relevant criticism (Corrêa 1982). My interest is in highlighting the fact that by thinking about a particular region, the author produced an idea of nation and Brazilianness that was vastly accepted.

In the contemporary period, a sexualized notion of Brazilianness has been re-created with reference to different regions or cities. Pernambuco did not disappear entirely, but Bahia and above all Rio de Janeiro acquired supreme importance. Salvador, capital city of the state of Bahia, and Rio were, in different moments, the country's capital cities. In present-day thought, however, most of the major associations of these cities with Brazilianness are related to racialized and gendered aspects that evoke sexualized African traits and are expressed in music, in popular feasts, and in the image of the dark-skinned woman. Thus, samba and later afoxês, Carnival and anesthetized mulattas regularly appear as symbols of national identity.

In the first half of the 1990s, the North American anthropologist Richard Parker (1991, 244) depicted the system by means of which "Brazilian society interprets itself, through the languages of sexuality and sensuality." During the 1950s, Sérgio Buarque de Holanda (1959), a leading social thinker, analyzed the connections between notions of national identity and a strong and primitive sexuality. He explored the Portuguese colonizers' imagery in a comparative perspective, taking as reference notions that permeated other colonizing processes, such as those that took place in North America. According to him, these Portuguese travelers linked Brazil to a particular idea of Eden, the lost Paradise, where the vegetation was abundant and the climate wonderful, there were no laws, man was free, and there was no sin (Rago 2001). This idea, recreated in popular national music during the 1970s,[7] is incorporated by Parker. In line with his thinking, in Brazil's imaginary there is no sin below the Equator. Sensuality is celebrated and, at the deepest level, is related to the meaning of being Brazilian.

According to this author, in Brazil, Carnival, with its sexual symbolism and its mixture of European, Indian, and African traits, is seen as the most authentic expression of the basic ethos of Brazilian life. Despite the apparent relevance given to native Indians, Parker considers that the typical characteristics of Brazilian Carnival are associated with African music and dances. Batucadas and sambas are interpreted in terms of their sensuous African roots. The two central characters of Carnival: the malandro and the mulatta, synthesize the association of Carnival with pleasure and sensuality. Particularly the mulatta, center of attention in this festivity, is considered an erotic ideal in Brazilian culture, the perfect embodiment of the tropical heat and sensuality.

Parker's interpretations (and those of some Brazilian social scientists) lead us to question whether sexuality is, in fact, a structuring principle in Brazilian society (O. Pinho 2004). Far from agreeing with this idea, my interest is to underscore that, while referring to a Brazilian sexual system, Parker is mostly focused on the imagery linked to three particular (racialized) cities, famous for their Carnivals, but mainly Rio de Janeiro and interviews done in that city for the most part. Thus, an explanation that privileges Rio seems to nourish the idea of a national cultural system.

The practice of drawing on sexual imagery connected to Rio de Janeiro to "talk" about Brazil was also evident in the government campaigns destined to advertise the country in the international tourist market. Presently, feminists and other human rights activists, struggling against the integration of Brazil into sex tourism global circuits, discuss and reject the traveling notions of a sexualized Brazilianness produced in Brazil that are exported to foreign countries. Nonetheless, since its early years in the beginning of the 1970s up to the end of the 1990s, the Empresa Brasileira de Turismo (EMBRATUR, the governmental body responsible for the regulation of the national tourist sector) disseminated images of almost naked women, mostly in Rio de Janeiro, in leaf-lets and banners. This city and symbols like the mulatta and samba, represent-ing the beauties of Brazilian beaches and the national Carnival, were chosen to structure Brazil's image in the international tourist market (Alfonso 2006).

The specific cities and regions by means of which Brazilians appear to re-create and disseminate a sexualized and gendered image of the nation are thus racialized spaces that mostly evoke the population's African ancestry. Even so, identities related to different parts of the country diverge from this representation. The notions linked to Ceará allow us to draw a remarkable counterpoint with that image of nation. In national terms the northeast, as a whole, is perceived as stricken by intense poverty. But as far as constructions of identity are concerned, the region is not considered a single entity. Ceará, which has a specific economic history in the region and is seen as scarcely marked by African roots, acquires singular traits.

This state's economy is depicted as distant from the sugarcane plantation system. During the sixteenth and seventeenth centuries, in the *sertão* (the hin-terland affected by extremely dry weather), the economy developed on the basis of cattle raising and, later, in the manufacture of jerked beef. The typical re-gional character of the tough cattle raiser (*vaqueiro*) is linked to this process. According to regional narratives, the indigenous population was progressively exterminated or absorbed by miscegenation. African slave labor use was mini-mal compared to the many slaves working in sugarcane, cotton, or coffee plan-tations (Abreu 1975 [1899]). It is important to observe that Ceará abolished slav-ery in 1884, four years before the Brazilian abolition, in a movement supported by one of the first feminist organizations created in Brazil, the Cearenses Lib-ertadoras (Shumaher 2003).

Contemporary authors highlight that what appears as a paradigm in histor-ical and literary writings about Ceará is not the mixture of three races but the blending of only two: between the Catholic Portuguese colonizer and the indig-enous population. This idea is somehow synthetized in *Iracema*, a novel by José de Alencar (1865), a writer born in Ceará. Iracema, a young indigenous woman, a *morena* (brown-skinned woman) with long black hair, falls in love with a blue-eyed Portuguese colonizer. Those writings are marked by the idea that there were (almost) no blacks in the state and the sparse (cultural) traces left by the African population can only be found in popular feasts (Pordeus 2006).

In this frame, diverse identity icons were created: in addition to the vaque-iro, the *jangadeiro* (fisherman), the *retirante* (who leaves the devastated coun-tryside during the droughts), and the *rendeira* (female lace-maker). The latter, vastly incorporated in regional music,[8] is probably the most disseminated of Ceará's images of women. These icons, albeit gendered, are distant from the sexualization and style of racialization that characterize the mulatta and the malandro. Far from being aesthetized in terms of their physical appearance, Ceará's typical characters, seen as *caboclos* (mixture of whites and indigenous) are considered to be the expression of the toughness and strength of the people from the sertão, embodying the harsh conditions of the land and the weather.[9] They are seen as short people with skin wrinkled and darkened by an unrelenting sun. A long way from the sensuality of the women with African traits, in the state's folklore and in tourist advertisements, the rendeira is cherished as a stout, intense worker. The beauty attributed to her is connected with qualities that are not physical. Rather, she is the bearer of a style of femininity marked by patience, honesty, and dignity.

Given the fact that Ceará's population does not fit the sexual image associated with Brazilianness, the journeys of sex travelers attracted by the idea of a population embodying an intense tropical sexuality in the shape of sensuous mulattas is intriguing. How, therefore, does the native population translate these expectations in the context of those transnational encounters? Before proceeding to answer, it is necessary to present the universe of sex tourism that I analyzed in that city.

A "Tropical Paradise"

At present, Fortaleza is considered to be a center of industry and tourism, because of its beautiful beaches and busy nightlife. With 2.1 million inhabitants, it is one of the fastest growing cities in the Northeast and is also one of the poorest metropolitan regions in the country (Instituto Brasileiro de Geografia Estatística 2000, 2001).[10] The social indicators of this region express the acute regional gendered inequalities in Brazil.[11]

Like other countries in the global South, Brazil is investing heavily in tourism.[12] In Fortaleza, the dramatic intensification of tourism is evident in the transformations of deserted beaches into resorts and in the increase in the number of hotels. In this context, there is a remarkable rise of international tourism, constantly increasing since the 1990s, connected to the arrival of direct international flights to the city. International tourism, which is predominantly male, represents little more than 10 percent of domestic tourism,[13] but is extremely visible in the touristy places of the city, where white foreign visitors are usually found in the company of darker local girls. Although tourism is considered to be the fastest growing source of employment in Ceará (Coriolano 1998), international tourism is regarded with both hope and concern because it is associated with sex tourism.

In Brazil, this type of tourism has attracted public attention since the end of the 1980s. Mainly conceptualized as prostitution, predominantly directed toward children and adolescents, it has become a source of national alarm. Prostitution involving women above the age of eighteen does not constitute a crime in Brazil; only exploiting or promoting prostitution is criminalized by the National Penal Code (articles 227, 228, 229, 230). But sex tourism involving young adults has also come under fire due to the fact that it is so often associated with international trafficking of persons.

The women of Fortaleza who form relationships with sex travelers have their own views about this issue. Among these women, those who are involved in what the locals call middle-class sex tourism or "elegant prostitution of Iracema beach" exchange sex for material benefits and goods, forming relationships with foreign visitors, which do not always incorporate direct financial payment.[14] They are mostly in their twenties and integrate the low and lower middle strata of the city. However, they are far from being extremely poor and/or illiterate.

These women's skin colors are locally regarded as being between *moreno* (brown) and *moreno claro* (very light brown). But moreno is not necessarily equivalent to mulatto. Although this latter term always alludes to African traits, *moreno* is also connected to the population of indigenous traits. Most morenas of Fortaleza are seen as caboclas and not as mulattas. From the local viewpoint, girls of those social classes who form relationships with foreign tourists, particularly when they are considered morenas, are usually perceived as prostitutes. Explaining this aspect requires a comment on racial categories.

In Brazil race is usually defined in terms of the relationships between African descendants and "whites" but was not traditionally defined by the bipolar, blood-based, black–white distinction common in the United States. I speak in the past tense because, as an effect of the globalization of black movements, currently bipolar classification coexists with the complex traditional classification (Fry 1995–96). The latter is a phenotype-based color continuum from black to white that integrates mixed race categories, such as mulatta. The racial classifications differ according to situation and context. Colors and phenotypes alone do not define people, whose social positions also depend on class, education, and income (Kofes 1976). To a certain extent, racial classifications are fluid—for example, when a dominant symbol of Europeanness such as education signifies whiteness and takes priority over phenotype (Guimarães 1999). Thus, a middle-class person with a college education, good salary, and elevated level of consumption whose appearance is mixed race can be seen as white, whereas a person with the same phenotype, looking poorer or involved in a robbery, will be perceived as black. To some degree money can whiten (Guimarães 1999), while poverty and or socially sanctioned behavior can darken (Piscitelli 2007)

Analogous racialization processes are evident in Fortaleza. Sexual relationships with foreign tourists, as sanctioned behavior, tend to stigmatize native women. But middle-class women, seen as light-skinned, mostly avoid the label of prostitution, which recurrently affects lower strata caboclas who accompany international visitors. The latter are placed in inferior racialized positions. In this city, the color continuum mostly alludes to mixed-race indigenous descendants. Although mixed raced Brazilians with African traits are marked by a certain sensuality, those with indigenous traits are barely connected to sensuality. Therefore, low-strata caboclas have little value in the local sex market, where the most valued women tend to be blond, perceived as light-skinned, and frequently from the states of the south. Local caboclas also have few opportunities of social mobility by means of marrying local men of higher classes.

Although some of the women interviewed think of themselves as sex workers, many do not consider themselves in those terms. The latter are young women who have stable jobs, sometimes in the tourist sectors, with low salaries (maximum US$200 a month) that do not go on programas. Notwithstanding, they accept and usually ask for presents and financial contributions to their medium- and long-term needs: clothes, watches, perfumes, mobile phones, payment of medical treatment or rent, monthly allowances, and even the necessary resources to start a small business.

Not all these young women intend to migrate. Some do not want to leave their families, for whom they provide (several were mothers at the age of fifteen or sixteen). Others fear the mistreatment and even slavery to which they have heard some Brazilian women are subjected abroad. Nevertheless, in this universe, some of the girls who consider themselves sex workers, and most of those who do not, dream of a better future in certain foreign countries. These young women yearn for diverse countries, mostly in Europe.

Middlemen and pimps exist in the somewhat loosely organized context of middle-class sex tourism. However, there are independent sex workers who pride themselves on their autonomy. Furthermore, from the viewpoint of women who consider themselves as sex workers as well as girls who refuse any connection with programas, relationships with foreign "boyfriends" constitute the simplest and safest path toward fulfilling their dream of migration. The idea is that such relationships provide the means to travel abroad without indebting or engaging themselves to middlemen. The local narratives highlight successful transnational marriages and affairs, with particular emphasis on the acquisition of apartments, bars, or restaurants in Fortaleza. These stories stimulate the girls who face the risks of leaving the country with or invited by those boyfriends.

Although it is not abject poverty that leads these young women into migration, economic aspects play an important role in the construction of their desire to leave. But as Kamala Kempadoo (1998) states when analyzing the motives that lead Caribbean sex workers to migrate, in Fortaleza, economic aspects linked to migration must be considered within the broader gendered patterns that affect these girls. These include divisions of labor, income-generating traditions, existing job opportunities, places they occupy in relationships with native men, and their position according to local racialized and classist conceptualizations. The women interviewed are affected by an extreme lack of educational and employment opportunities and by what they consider to be very strong local machismo. According to them, they are trapped in local class and racial barriers, which they feel are almost impossible to cross. In this context, offering sexual services for financial reward is an alternative. However, the preferred options are those that, establishing distances in relation to the traditional images of local and foreign prostitution, help create the climate of uncertainty shading these international encounters, stimulating the spread of "romances," and opening the way for the eventual departure abroad.

Caren Kaplan (1996) states that in the frame of tourism, the visited places and people are commodified, but so are the tourists. In the context of middle-class sex tourism, romantic attachment is not unusual. Concurrently, women deploy practices through which they obtain financial benefits from their foreign partners, which sometimes involve distancing themselves in behavior from sex tourists' preconceived notions of sex work. In the words of a twenty-eight-year-old hairdresser:

> He's fifty-two years old, an Italian. . . . Those things are like a game, you have to act, showing that you are not an easy girl. . . . Ninety percent of those foreigners don't want to form relationships with Brazilian women. . . . They think of Brazil as a sexual thing, where they find easy and cheap sex. If you want a relationship . . . you cannot say that you go on programas. . . . I told him that I worked at a friend's beauty parlor. He asked if I did not want to have my own business. And I said how, earning the minimum wage? When he went back he sent me an international payment order of R$ 4,000. . . . He's already sent me around R$10,000. . . . Whenever he called I asked for money. For the beauty parlor's furniture, for a course, "Oh, I'm sick! I broke my leg! I've got something in my breast!" I almost exhausted all potential sicknesses. It's the only way you have to gather money. (Fortaleza, November 2002)

This universe shelters a diversity of foreigners. Men from Europe and North and South America circulate on this beach. Among them there are bachelors or those who are separated, as well as married men, ranging in age from their twenties up to sixty years old and working in a variety of professions. Of the tourists I interviewed, the monthly income varied between US$1,000 (an Argentinean) and US$10,000 (a U.S. citizen). Although most of the interviewed travelers in search of sex had merely concluded secondary studies, a third of them had finished college.

From the viewpoint of the local women who form relationships with them, however, one of the main differences among the tourists is established by nationality. Although they can enjoy the company of South American men, these women overtly prefer men of the countries of the North. The other relevant differentiation is associated with the type of relationships for which these visitors look. Some men exclusively look for sex relations entirely divested of affection. Several see the city as a large, diversified brothel. Other sex travelers are in search of women who might enlarge the range of possibilities regarding long-term affective relationships. Married men might form relationships with native women that perform the role of overseas extramarital lovers visited three or four times a year and to whom they send monthly allowances. Bachelors might look for potential wives that, in their view, can re-create traditional patterns of femininity, including motherhood.[15] The low-strata girls who exclusively date foreigners prefer these last two categories of sex travelers. How are identities written, translated, and incorporated in this context?

Translations

Witnessing these sexual encounters, natives from other states of Brazil and from Ceará express their perplexity regarding the sexualization that permeates the sex travelers' circuits of Fortaleza. Highlighting the artificiality of a process that puzzles them because it does not seem to be consistent with identity notions associated with that state, they point to the inferior place those natives have in a "national" ranking of sensuality. A thirty-two-year-old teacher from Rio de Janeiro depicts the limits she perceives in Ceará's females and the "fake" character of constructions of sensuality that, according to her, are promoted by the circulation of images linked to other Brazilian cities:

> People here are full of restrictions. You see it in their clothes. Here it is summer all year round, but they use long sleeves, pants, shoes instead of sandals. In Rio it is normal to wear shorts: a pair of shorts, a small top, you are ready to go shopping. Here only tourists wear shorts. And today,

the sensuality here, it is not natural, it is copied, produced, brought by the media. It is something that has happened in the last eight years. It comes from Bahia, it comes from Rio. I think that even the foreigners might feel deceived. [Here] you do not find that natural sensuality of dark, long-haired women. What you see here is . . . unnatural sensuality. (Fortaleza, December 2001)

In a comparative perspective that draws counterpoints among different countries and also different regions of Brazil, the perception of the sexual restrictions of women from Ceará is somehow reiterated by native men of different ages. Re-creating the hierarchies that situate Ceará on an inferior level in international and national terms, native women appear as "deprived" regarding sexual freedom and determination compared with the women of European and North American countries and of the south of Brazil.

International sex travelers' views differ, however. Experienced foreign tourists are aware of the Brazilian regional inequalities that favor their sexual access to women in poorer cities, such as Fortaleza. However, national rankings of sensuality are irrelevant for most of the sex tourists I interviewed. They read native women's corporeal and sexual styles as the embodiment of the "authentic" Brazilian traits, which include a friendly character, an open spirit, happiness, and being easygoing together with a passionate temperament. In these men's impressions, Fortaleza stands for Brazil, a country that is associated with a hot climate and an exuberant sexuality and is connected to a high level of prostitution.

Those foreigners tend to draw relations between countries and nationalities cut across by gender. In their versions, the attributes allocated to Brazil, embodied in the blood, characterize native masculinity with an explosive and dangerous temper, in opposition to the "cold" blood of Europeans of one nationality or another. In these visions, native masculinity is associated with a certain indolence, which is in proportion to an excessive consumption of alcohol, a "stupidity" expressed by a bellicose temperament, and above all the attribution of an exacerbated sexuality, which is basic and not at all sophisticated.

Their own masculinities, on the other hand, are read as displaying signs of romanticism and delicateness. These travelers also insist on highlighting the dedication to work and the appreciation of responsibility in relation to the family, particularly fatherhood, as central elements in the constitution of positively appraised masculinities. On these points, these notions of masculinity reiterate those present in other (Western) contexts (Vale de Almeida 1995). But these formulations integrate themselves into a game in which no trace of personality or temperament escapes the relations between nationalities.

The readings of these interviewees apparently point to a positive appreciation of the local women. The traits linked to native femininity are delineated by their contrast with those qualities associated with the women from the respective countries of those interviewed. The qualities "written" on native girls are thus contrasted with the arrogance of the Germans, the closed nature of Portuguese women and the exaggeratedly positive self-appreciation of the English girls, the coldness and calculating nature of women from North America, and the haughtiness of Italian women.

In these views, on the one hand, women of countries of the North—perceived as persons who are independent, prioritize professional success, career, money, and also enjoy paid and/or exotic sex—are seen as spoiled by "feminist ideas" expressed in high levels of demands on the men and a certain masculinization. On the other hand, the tender temperament, the warmth, simplicity, and submission they attribute to the natives are incorporated into the idea of a femininity which, coated in traits of authenticity, fulfills a submissiveness, now perceived as long gone in Europe. The local attributes of womanliness are perceived as being characterized by a singular sensuality, coated in simplicity, which is also associated with a lack of intelligence: "They just think of making love and dancing *forró*," says a sixty-year-old retired Italian, giving me the example of a girlfriend. Demonstrating with his hands the accentuated feminine curves that sway from one side to the other, he adds, establishing a causal relationship: "She doesn't have much upstairs, she can't learn. I paid her school fees for two years but she doesn't even know her times table."

The intersection between gender and nationality is central in the sexualization through which natives are rendered inferior: the "heat" of the native girls, attributed to the women who go on *programas* and also those who don't, is linked to the propensity to (more or less) open forms of prostitution.

James Clifford (1997) observes that there is no political innocence for intercultural interpretation. This aspect is obvious in sex travelers' rewriting Brazilian notions of national sensuality as a natural propensity to prostitution. But the lack of political innocence is also evident in the procedures whereby native women who long to obtain benefits from those tourists translate these men's attributes. Among them, foreigners are frequently idealized, depicted as embodying the best styles of masculinity, in counterpoint to local styles of masculinity, which are invariably read as inferior.

In these relations, the local masculinities are rendered inferior, setting in motion regional constructions of identity. In a rereading of the toughness linked to Ceará's identity icons, invariably translated as macho, these styles are characterized by traits of aggression, intense possessiveness, affective remoteness, lack of respect, and infidelity. The attribution of these distinctive traits to the male natives was used by female interviewees to explain their choice of men from "the outside." In contrast, the foreigners appear to be embodying styles of masculinity linked to a certain openness and higher level of equality. These attributes may be allocated to one or another nationality regarding visitors from countries from the North.

Regional attributes are, however, effaced when these women muse about their own styles of femininity. In their readings, European femininities are marked by autonomy and in an analogous manner to the climate associated with the respective countries, to "coldness." In opposition to these styles of femininity, native womanliness is cherished, connected as it is to the "national" qualities the international visitors attribute to those girls. A caring temperament is part of these attributes, associated by some of the interviewees with the idea of dependence, based on economic necessity. In the words of a twenty-four-year-old waitress: "The women from their countries are not dependent on them, they have their own money, car, freedom, they don't need a man to go to a bar. For Brazilian women it's different, we need one. They like that, and they, the Brazilian women, like to be looked after by them. The women look at something and say, 'that's lovely,' and the men buy it for them. The men like this dependence and the women like the men's attitude" (Fortaleza, January 2002).

The ideas on Brazilian temperament are incorporated into the intense level of sensuality those interviewees consider marking their own styles of being women in a positive way. "We are hotter," says a girl considered the queen of the main nightclub in Praia de Iracema (Fortaleza, February 2002). In the words of a thirty-five-year-old middle-class psychologist and native of Ceará who, though unconnected to prostitution, dates foreigners: "I think it is the thing of being open . . . of being happier . . . I think that the climate influences this, if you look at the people who live in cold countries, they are more closed . . . They say that we are 'hotter' . . . My libido is very strong" (Fortaleza, January 2001).

Negotiations

The unequal positions occupied by foreigners and native women in the sex tourism of the middle class are expressed in terms in which gender and nationality become indivisible. This intertwining can also be read through the "color" connected to foreigners and natives: the relations established through color complete the translation procedures that result in the appreciation of the styles of masculinity attributed to certain nationalities and in the sexualization of the natives.

When I say that color, indivisibly linked to nationality, is connected to more highly valued masculinities, I refer to the invariable label of whiteness connected to those styles of manliness. In procedures in which temperament marks the body, which is appreciated through aesthetic criteria, the most valued distinctive traits of masculinity are always associated with a beauty that contrasts with the ugliness attributed to the locals — and, I think, of aesthetic criteria such as judgments of beauty and taste (Overing 1996) — as being indivisible from a process of education of the senses. In this process regional criteria are set in motion: expressing political location, the ugliness is not linked to all Brazilian men but to the natives of Ceará, particularly those of the same strata as the interviewed women, the men who would be their potential partners. In the words of those interviewed:

> The men here, the majority, are shorter, the head is like this, the shape of the head is rounder, they have paunches, are laid back.

> The (poor) men in Ceará are so ugly it hurts. Ugly, with large flat heads, they appear grey because the sun is so intense, their ignorance is great.

The aesthetization involving men "from the outside" does not obey fixed physical patterns with any precision. The beauty allocated to foreigners combines attributes embodied by young or not-so-young men, with or without hair. A barmaid describes her foreign boyfriend in the following terms: "He measures one meter eighty [centimeters}, he's very tall, or one meter ninety, about that. He is bald and is thirty-eight years old. He has blue eyes, the color of the sea. He is handsome, very caring" (Fortaleza, January 2001). This beauty, expressing criteria used in constructing hierarchies within masculinities, is associated with whiteness, which is expressed in phenotypical traits: the color of the skin, hair, eyes. But this idea of whiteness linked to Europeans and addressing localization involves aspects that go beyond phenotype.

In an analogous manner, reading the native femininities made by these foreigners is characterized by color. One color, morena, synthesizes the intertwining of the differentiations embodied in the local women. Yet if whiteness characterizes the positively evaluated styles of masculinity, being moreno/a, used in the sexualization process, racializes the natives in a way that renders them inferior.

When speaking of morenas, on many occasions foreigners use color in descriptive terms: they have a skin which is not white or black. In an attempt to describe this color, one of the Italians interviewed alluded with gestures to the shape of the mouth and the nose, evoking phenotypical traits of African origin. By describing the local morenas/caboclas in these terms, he translates as African traits aspects that, from the local point of view, are related to an idea of indigenous ancestry.[16]

The foreigners interviewed in Fortaleza also use color in categorical terms, that is, in terms that, more than describing, possess an autonomy in relation to corporeal signs since they are linked to a classification (Kofes 1976, 72, 97). In the vision of foreign visitors, including some Latin Americans, the morena color, which acquires the erotic connotations connected with the mulatta, is intimately linked to Brazil and is associated with the "better woman" and with being "hotter." In the words of an Argentinean looking for sex: "The 'morenitas' are hotter. They want to do it more often, they have another way of behaving in bed, they like other positions . . . Argentinean women don't look at it in this way" (Fortaleza, December 2001).

In these respects, beyond specific tonalities and phenotypical traits in a classification which crosses different social classes and sexualizes women whether or not they are connected to prostitution, the natives are considered morenas, embodying the high level of sensuality associated with this color. The ambivalences that shade the appreciation of this color maintain relationships with the procedures for aesthetization, which, associated with femininities, places the beauty associated with Brazilians in a relatively inferior position. The Italian interviewees, enchanted with the sensuality they attribute to the natives of Ceará, openly express the superiority of their female compatriots. A fifty-five-year-old tourist of this nationality explains to me: "Italian women are more beautiful, but not for me. I like them. It's they who don't like me. It's true" (Fortaleza, February 2001).

By synthesizing the values that permeate this world, the aesthetization mirrors the unequal relations present in it. The beauty associated with whiteness and intimately connected to localization characterizes the more valued styles of masculinity that are embodied in the most valued nationalities. By contrast, the aesthetization expresses the subordinate place attributed to the native women who stand for the authentic Brazilian female: the hot mulatta.

In this unequal milieu, the main instrument used by native women who form relationships with sex travelers to cross over class barriers and guarantee the success and permanence of their affairs is performing the racialized identity allocated to them by the foreigners. They fully incorporate those attributes. As a young waitress explained: "What is it that they like in me? My color. Always, all of those who know me always say, they really love my color, you know? Because I am morena, I have curly hair, and I am friendly, tender, I am very natural, from the earth, that's what they always say" (Fortaleza, January 2000).

Effacing local and regional identity attributes and embodying sex tourists' translation of Brazilian national traits, these girls open paths that destabilize linear criteria of inequality. Integrating the transmission of a romantic and sexual knowledge in their relationships with the foreigners, they also negotiate, on the basis of the sexualization of which they are the objects, their positioning in these relationships. They seek in these sexual/romantic liaisons the possibility of crossing local class and racial barriers. In fact, some do, mainly by migrating invited by sex tourists. By the time I finished this research, approximately half of my female interviewees had traveled abroad. Some spent a few months in a European country, either working in the sex industry or living as temporary brides with the men who invited them. Part of the latter group remained in Europe, marrying sex travelers, leaving the sex markets, and forming transnational families. They return to Fortaleza during the holidays, showing off their success, thus feeding the dreams of girls who enter the sex tourism circuits (Piscitelli 2006).

Conclusion

Although cultures can be seen as sites of travel for others (Clifford 1997), the context analyzed here presents the particularity of also constituting a gateway for local residents, opening ways for traveling abroad. It also shows another specific aspect. Neither the opposition between foreign and native nor scrutinizing the opposite flux of ideas is sufficient to explain how cultural translation works in this universe. The power that stems from differentiated localizations is intimately connected with the processes of effacing, enhancing, and rewriting gendered identities. But in this world localization entails a series of diverse entangled levels. Understanding how these residents negotiate themselves in external relationships in this transnational space requires taking into account how they negotiate their local, regional, and national identities.

Through the unequal relationships formed with foreigners, some of the girls who participate in middle-class sex tourism escape from other inequalities they consider much worse: those of their local social fate in an "inferior" state and region in Brazil. While the transcultural translations activated in this context partially allow them a certain enlargement of their space for agency, I do not assume that their crossover practices are necessary liberatory. Studies that analyze the effects of sex tourism highlight that in places where aspects linked to international tourism are relatively new forces, it is not always easy to discriminate between permanence and alterations in gender configurations. Some few cases that point to the enlargement of spheres of feminine influence or decision are not sufficient to state that there are changes in these configurations. It would be necessary to be able to trace patterns and recurrences (Brennan 2004).

The modality of sex encounters analyzed that takes place in Fortaleza is connected to the search for opportunities of local women and to strategies to promote those chances, including the challenge of local norms by means of multilayered practices of cultural translation. However, their individual getaways are far from interfering in local, collective gender configurations. Finally, their means of escape from inequalities in the local spheres do not release them from being affected by other inequalities in their new lives abroad, linked to the place acquired by that racialized tropical sexuality in so-called First World contexts, in southern European countries. But that is another study (Piscitelli 2006).

Notes

1. *Sex tourism* is today considered a problematic term, because it is recognized that it does not have the clear boundaries attributed to it a few decades ago. Studies have shown that it cannot be reduced to prostitution; it is not only men that travel in search of sex, women also do it; finally, sex travelers are not always from developed countries. However, the term has acquired an emic status, incorporated in governmental and nongovernmental debates and policies and also by native populations.

2. In 1991, the rate of self-classified black population stood at 2.95 percent, while Pernambuco stood at 3.3 percent and Salvador at 20.2 percent. It is important to highlight that according to the Census of the Instituto Brasileiro de Geografia Estatística (1991), the brown (*pardos*) population in the three states is represented in roughly equivalent numbers: Ceará numbered 67.4 percent, Pernambuco 63.4 percent, and Bahia 69 percent. But the category pardos, while alluding to mixed race, might be connected to populations of African, indigenous, or African/indigenous descent.

3. Significant research material was collected between 1999 and 2002. This information was supplemented by interviews with women who maintain love/sexual relationships with foreigners, with tourists in search of sex of various nationalities, with expatriates, and with native men who form relationships with foreign women. I also carried out interviews with various agents involved in international tourism and/or local prostitution and obtained secondary data, statistics, and case studies from government agencies, educational institutions and nongovernmental organizations. This text was written on the basis of the information given by seventy-five interviewees, including foreign women who form relationships with native men, whose views are not analyzed here.

4. The initial part of this study was followed by ethnographic research carried out in May and June 2004 in the north of Italy, focused on the trajectories of women who migrated from Fortaleza invited by sex tourists (Piscitelli 2006, 2013). This fieldwork involved interviews with eight key people from various nongovernmental organizations dedicated to working with prostitution and traffic and with agents from the Brazilian consulate in Milan. In-depth interviews with twelve Brazilian women between the ages of twenty-two and thirty-eight and with five Italian men, husbands of some of these women, were carried out in various neighborhoods of Milan and in several cities relatively close by: Abbiategrasso, Voghera, and Verona.

5. His reading of these traits distinguished him from negative ideas voiced by other social thinkers and medical doctors (Carrara 2004).

6. Freyre's optimistic reading is reinforced compared to the perception of other authors of the same period who also considered the sexual dimension a major reference in the constitution of a Brazilian national character. According to Rago (1998), Paulo Prado perceived this dimension as the origins of the instinctive traits and the sadness that mark Brazilianness as the roots of the impossibility of evolution toward a certain modernity.

7. A highly popular song is "Não existe pecado ao sul do Equador," by Chico Buarque and Ruy Guerra.

8. The most popular song is "Olê Mulher Rendeira," by Zé do Norte.

9. In the national context, since the first decades of the twentieth century, several of these notions were implemented to produce a conception of the northeast as Other with reference to the richer states of Brazil's south. Connected to the idea of a "Deep Brazil," these perceptions were fixed by the newspapers published in the South (Barbalho 2004).

10. In the second half of the 1990s, Fortaleza was considered to have the second largest concentration of poor people in the country, 40 percent, closely following Recife (Coriolano 1998).

11. According to the national census of 2000 (Instituto Brasileiro De Geografia Estatística 2000), while the illiteracy rate in the country has risen to little over 13 percent, in the northeast it currently stands at 26 percent. In the whole country, around 27 percent of the population subsists on less than two minimum wages per household, but in the northeast this figure rises to more than 47 percent. In terms of the female population, statistical indicators pointed to the fact that women formed the majority among those who have the lowest wages (Fundo de População das Nações Unidas/IPLANCE 1996).

12. This industry is considered to be responsible for 5.5 percent of the gross national product and 3.3 percent of jobs, but the government expects these figures to rise (EMBRATUR 2001).

13. In 2001, the city received more than 1,450,000 Brazilian tourists and only 172,000 foreign visitors (Governo do Estado do Ceará, Secretaria de Turismo 2002).

14. For a discussion of the immense diversity of relationships linked to sex tourism see Fernandez (1999) and Kempadoo (1999). For the blurred boundaries between prostitution and other forms of sexual encounters in the frame of sex tourism see Oppermann (1999) and Cohen (1982, 1986, 1993).

15. Analogous distinctions have been traced in other contexts of sex tourism in Brazil, see Silva and Blanchette (2005).

16. Unlike what appears to happen in other contexts of sex tourism in Brazil, in Salvador and in Recife, where foreign tourists look for black girls (Carpazoo 1994; Dias Filho 1998), in Fortaleza, the "black blacks" are rejected by foreigners of various nationalities who sometimes assume that they themselves are racists.

PART IV

MOVEMENTS/FEMINIST/SOCIAL/POLITICAL/POSTCOLONIAL

CHAPTER FIFTEEN/*TRANSLENGUAS*/MAPPING THE POSSIBILITIES AND CHALLENGES OF TRANSNATIONAL WOMEN'S ORGANIZING ACROSS GEOGRAPHIES OF DIFFERENCE

MAYLEI BLACKWELL

When people, capital, cultures, and technologies cross national borders with growing frequency, effective transnational social movements organize not only across political boundaries of nation-states but across internal social, cultural, and structural differences as well. Grounded in our collective project exploring the transnational feminist politics of translation, this chapter theorizes a practice of *translenguas* (trans–language/tongue) to identify the ways in which activists are translating, reworking, and contesting meaning in the transnational flow of discourses between social movement actors in three different cross-border formations.

Transnational organizing has provided a space to represent political interests of those who are marginalized within their own national contexts, and it has also been a space to construct those interests, identities, and discourses—all essential in building cross-border alliances and coalitions (Alvarez et al. 2003). By analyzing women's social movement discourses and transnational imaginaries, this chapter challenges the firmly rooted assumption that theories and discourses of liberation travel from the global North to the South. By charting the migrations of social movement discourses and the complex negotiations used to develop cross-border and translocal ways of speaking, this essay illustrates how questions of difference are (mis)translated across borders to forge political coalitions, invigorate social practices of liberation, and create new transnational communities and networks. These lessons about transnational organizing draw on oral histories and archival sources I have gathered since 1998 in my work on mapping uncharted genealogies of difference—the gendered racial formations, sexual identities, and uneven terrain of power negotiated within U.S. and Mexican women's movements. My fieldwork and participant observations at meetings, marches, and rallies include regional Latin American feminist *encuentros*, numerous sectors of the Mexican women's movement, intensive work among the indigenous women's movement, and interviews with various factions of the lesbian feminist movement in Mexico as well as recuperative history work with Chicana and U.S. women of color social movements.

My research explores how the flow and entrapment of capital, cultures, and peoples shape differently situated political actors, forming what I call unaligned geographies of difference (Blackwell 2000). Unaligned geographies of difference is the analytic *terrain* from which to understand the possibilities and challenges of transnational feminist political coalitions and social movements, how actors from different social and structural locations engage in collective political action and how they account for and negotiate power differentials. While earlier ideologies of feminism foregrounded sameness—perhaps epitomized in the slogan "Sisterhood Is Global"—this analytic lens continues a tradition of scholarship that challenged the idea of women's solidarity based on the imposition of sameness or the idea that oppression based on gender could be separated from other forms of geopolitical (colonial and imperial), economic, racial, gendered, or sexual oppressions (Lorde 1983; Moraga and Anzaldúa 1983 [1981]; Mohanty 1984; Grewal and Kaplan 1994b; Shohat 1997).

In our current context of neoliberal globalization, the rapid transnational mobility of capital and power not only makes imagined communities of resistance more urgent, it often makes them more difficult to form because these same processes exacerbate deep cleavages of inequality while obscuring power differentials through the illusion of inclusion in market multiculturalism.[1] Transnational solidarity or cross-border imagined communities are further complicated by the fact that the political construction and social meaning of differences surrounding racial formation, class stratification, and gender and sexual identities is highly differentiated in local contexts. Beyond being different in national contexts, making transnational shared understanding of oppressions difficult, these formations are often radically different within national contexts and across translocalities (Appadurai 1995, 1996). Hence, the kind of translocalism I am identifying here involves actors who, despite being multiply marginalized in their national contexts, create linkages with social actors across locales to build new affiliations, solidarities, and movements.

The challenge of such a proposition is illustrated by Teresa Carrillo's work on binational Mexican and Chicana workers whose efforts to create a binational coalition, despite shared language, culture, and economic conditions, were frustrated by the stark contrast in how power is organized differently in two national contexts that border each other (Carrillo 1998). In Mexico, women workers in the *maquilas* confront class and survival issues, whereas in the United States these same issues of poverty are refracted through race. These unaligned geographies of difference have formed partly because of the organization of global capital locally. Whereas corporate globalization is often accused of homogenizing culture (or producing a global monoculture), the ways global capital organizes itself through locally specific formations of power makes shared meanings across contexts, and often, the local translation of transnational strategies difficult.

Transnational social and political actors negotiate vectors of power organized around axes of gender, sexuality, race, indigeneity, class, citizenship, and geopolitics through a form of translation that involves representational struggles over meaning, identity, strategy, ideology, and power. These struggles form what I call a *translenguaje*, which can be defined as a committed practice of transnational translation and is a key step in cross-border coalition building. To be a *translengua* is (1) to incite new political projects by reworking meanings in local contexts (localization); (2) to translate ideas across international and transnational contexts (transnational appropriation and reworking); or (3) to transform identities and movement meanings across translocalities without erasing differences. The transformation of politics translocally is linked to how regimes and technologies of globalization and transnational movements are captured, (mis)translated, and deployed by social actors to redefine their own relational subjectivities, create new strategies by localizing transnationalized discourses, or build new bridges of cross-border organizing. The following three cases of women's transnational organizing illustrate translenguaje as a cultural and political practice of translation movement that engages identities, discourses, solidarities, and concepts over uneven relations of power.

Lost, Found, and Stuck in Translation: (Trans)Localizing Third World
Solidarity, Translating U.S. Women of Color

Although much of the literature on transnational feminism and transnational social movements has focused on global linkages outside of the geographic territories of the United States, I want to call attention to how transnational political processes have fundamentally shaped feminist identities and politics within the United States. Here I want to explore the transnational feminist politics of translation—the possibilities and perils of translenguaje—by examining two transnational flows of social movement discourse surrounding the category of "women of color." The first example shows how activists critically translated a transnational political imaginary created by decolonization movements in the Third World to create solidarity and build political and affective ties among racially marginalized communities in the 1970s in the United States. Their translenguaje formed the basis of what became women of color feminist theory and political subjectivities. Yet when this discourse is trafficked across borders, what is lost in translation is how women of color feminist theory is reduced to an identity category, rather than a political project. In this case, I illustrate how a social movement discourse traveled, was translated, and, in an attempt to travel again, got lost or stuck in translation.

I ground the discussion in the Third World Women's Alliance (TWWA) as a vital root in the genealogy of U.S. women of color political projects that built interconnections between American Indian communities and peoples of the Asian, African, and Latin American diasporas in the United States in the late 1960s and early 1970s. Third World solidarity was not only the ideology that underwrote people of color as an alternative racial formation in the United States; in the hands of the TWWA, it was the glue that built political communities and bound together the political category women of color. This alternative genealogy is vital given that the literature on transnational feminism has often erased women of color theories and politics or viewed them as suspect transnational subjects by characterizing women of color feminist theory as quintessentially "domestic" or some essentialist staging of identity politics (Soto 2003). Rather than viewing women of color as fixed political and social subjects, the example of the TWWA illustrates how women of color became a gendered racial formation in the post–World War II era that had not existed in any other time in U.S. history. Some scholars historicize the emergence of women of color feminism through a critique of sexism in various civil rights, national liberation, or black/red/yellow/brown power movements of the 1960s or 1970s. Others focus on an antiracist critique of the women's liberation movement and often locate the origins of women of color feminisms in the publication of This Bridge Called My Back: Writings by Radical Women of Color (Moraga and Anzaldúa 1983 [1981]). What these views fail to account for historically is how this subject formation emerged more than a decade earlier within coalitions created between movements, where the collaboration among U.S. Third World women facilitated new political identities, visions of liberation, and communities of resistance. Understanding this third thread of emergence recuperates U.S. Third World feminism, the emergence of gender justice within national liberation struggles, and the importance of Marxian critiques of U.S. imperialism in constructing this U.S.-specific racial and political formation on the ground (Lowe 1997).

A key turning point for Third World women (especially those in North America) was the women's gathering in Vancouver in 1971 where Third World women activists gathered to discuss the wars in Indochina and building a common agenda of Third World liberation and women's emancipation (Wu 2010). This vision built on the legacy of liberation movements that had built on the Asian–African Conference in Bandung in 1955, at which delegates from across the world met in Indonesia to discuss the end of colonial rule.[2] The TWWA not only invented a political subjectivity capable of crossing national borders, by linking their struggles to a growing Third World liberation movement, but also provided analytical tools and a notion of solidarity that crossed racial, class, and community lines within the United States (Elbaum 2002; Pulido 2006; Young 2006).

Emerging as an independent organization out of the Black Women's Liberation Committee within the Student Non-Violent Coordinating Committee, the Black Women's Alliance began to include a broader base of women and eventually formed a coalition with Puerto Rican women in New York, changing their name to TWWA to reflect their new political orientation (Anderson-Bricker 1999; Blackwell 2000; Springer 2005).[3] Edited by Frances Beal, their newspaper, Triple Jeopardy: Racism, Imperialism, Sexism, published from 1971 to 1976, covered topics including African and Indochinese movements for decolonization; women deputies to China's National People's Congress; the role of women in revolutionary struggles in Yemen, Cuba, Vietnam, Albania, Guinea-Bissau, Puerto Rico, and Latin America; and the Palestinian struggle against the Israeli occupation. Critically, they translated a Third World Marxist orientation to analyze how neocolonial and capitalist exploitation affected women in U.S. Third World communities. The scope of this analysis could be seen in every issue of Triple Jeopardy's coverage of abortion, maternity leave, unemployment, affirmative action, child care, and the practice of sterilization on Puerto Rican, American Indian, and black women. Articles recounted local rent strikes, union actions, boycotts and anticorporate campaigns, critiques of racism, sexual politics, and U.S. policy, as well as solidarity statements from the prison movement as illustrated by a four-part series featuring a "rap" with Angela Davis. Other reports ranged from "Changing a Fuse" to "Meatless Recipes" to an exposé on platform shoes called "The Platform Peril" to self-help guides on "Vaginal Ecology" and "Guerrilla Theater."

Importantly, because the TWWA had critical participation by Puerto Rican women and the newspaper served a large Latina activist community in New

York, many issues of the paper were bilingual. There were several special issues in Spanish and many articles focused on Latin American women's struggles, the Puerto Rican independence movement, and the Chilean and Cuban solidarity movements. Their practice of translenguaje was a translation of Third World solidarity with a Marxist lens, which helped the women involved see how their oppressions were interconnected through histories of imperialism and global capitalism. Their unique "translation" and remixing of the liberation traditions and anticolonial struggles provided the critical imaginary for the coalitions they built among antiracist struggles in the United States (Kelley 2003). This rich analysis of multiple systems of power became the foundation of early women of color feminism, which at its core theorized the idea of simultaneous, overlapping oppressions that were later referred to as "intersectionality" by academics and legal scholars (Crenshaw 1991; Blackwell 2000; Burnham 2001).

Claudia de Lima Costa takes up the (un)translatability of the category women of color when carried to other geographies of difference (see the second introduction to this volume). She states, "In doing so, the history of identity construction, which will vary geographically and culturally, needs to be highlighted in every process of translation. . . . Political labels such as 'women of color' are not always translatable in Latin America, especially in certain contexts (e.g., Brazil) and in relation to more 'fluid' markers of race and, precisely, 'color.'" Critically, it is often the very same contexts in which color is more fluid in its construction that racism, racial power, and privilege function precisely on the denial of the existence of a color line. Although the (un)translatability of the category "women of color" is linked to the complex ways the racialization of color and phenotype are contextual, the troubled notion of color has often been problematized by women of color activists themselves. Other critics have stated that the category "Third World women" flattens out internal diversity between historical racialized communities of women not unlike the way that pan-Asian and pan-Indian identities flatten national or tribal differences in the terms American Indian and Asian American. This collapsing of difference is especially a problem if one looks at U.S. Third World women as a biological or sociological category rather than a political and coalitional project, open to contestation and conflict, as has been theorized by Chandra Mohanty (1991a).[4]

Women of color feminist theories are often lost (or, perhaps more accurately, stuck) in translation because instead of seeing women of color as a political project or coalitional identity, it is most often (mis)translated as a biological category that does not easily travel or cross national borders. Traffic without translation is the literal application of one meaning system to another. For example, the conflation of a coalitional political project with a racialized biological category is what would occur if the concept black women or black feminism in the United Kingdom were imported without translation. The project of black British feminism encompasses women from the African, Indian, Pakistani, and Caribbean diasporas. These coalitional and identity categories are not easily used in transnational organizing unless the concerns and coalitions, which are embodied in this formation, can be successfully translated.[5]

Although the difficulty of this "travel" does not foreclose the possibility of shared theoretical and social movement experiences across borders, the challenge can be seen in the tepid response of Latin American feminists to the Spanish translation of *This Bridge, Esta Puente, Mi Espalda* (Moraga and Castillo 1988), which did not speak directly to the racial, class, and sexual formations of women across borders. This critical point is important for understanding how and why theories travel and who serves as travel agents and border guards to theories because these relationalities and attachments are imbricated with power. Categories and theories developed by marginalized peoples, just as those social movement actors themselves, often have to navigate unequal relations of power at home before traveling or crossing a border. Just as in other forms of international travel, to obtain a visa, women of color feminist theories would have to show they had capital (money in the bank) before being granted the authority to travel. While race should not be mistranslated as a biological category, the experience of racial/ethnic marginalization or being multiply marginalized because of class, sexual orientation, race/ethnicity/ culture, gender, and immigration status is an experience that does indeed translate in many contexts.

North by South: Translating the Practice of Indigenous Autonomy into Grassroots Sovereignty in Indian Country

Although there is a long tradition of women's participation in American Indian international and transnational organizing, violence and a lack of resources are among the numerous challenges organizers face. According to longtime indigenous rights activist and cofounder of the Indigenous Women's Network (IWN), Ingrid Washinawatok (Minominee),

> The Indigenous Women's Network was founded back in 1984 when a
> group of the women got together to talk about what was happening
> in the communities. What was happening in families. Attitudes about
> women from the men, lots of foreign ways that had developed over
> these last couple of decades. Rises in domestic violence, rises in abuses.
> In 1984, we knew there was sexual abuse going in the community, but

that's not a traditional aspect of our culture. Alcoholism had already been part of the community for a number of years. Drug abuse, with the new drugs coming in. While treaty rights are important, while hunting and fishing rights are important, if women who educate the children are trying to protect themselves from all the abuse that is going on, it's a crisis situation. . . . That's how the Network got started.

IWN members have been active in their communities and advocated on their behalf at international gatherings, which they reported on in their publication, *Indigenous Woman*.[6] For example, IWN published "Indigenous Women Address the World," their platform for the UN Fourth World Conference on Women in Beijing, where Winona LaDuke (Ojibwe), who has served in the leadership of IWN, spoke at the NGO Forum.[7]

With roots dating back to the 1923 petition of the Mohawk Nation to membership in the League of Nations, native nations have used the international sphere to lobby for their land and treaty rights and petition against land seizures when their sovereignty rights were denied domestically. The re-emergence of American Indian internationalism as a strategy is tied to the forms of state violence and blockages to justice that the American Indian movements found in advancing their claims to rights and sovereignty in the 1970s. Although indigenous movements had been growing in number and strength in the Americas, the density of cross-border contacts increased around the numerous events organized to protest the quincentenary celebration of Columbus's so-called discovery of the New World in 1992 (see Dunbar Ortiz 1984; Brysk 1994, 2000). The United Nations declared 1992 "The Year of Indigenous Peoples"; that same year, Rigoberta Menchú was awarded the Nobel Peace Prize.[8] Emerging from native protest against the North American Free Trade Agreement (NAFTA) and a shared critique of globalization in terms of environmental, economic, and cultural devastation, the outpouring of support and solidarity with the indigenous people of Mexico during the Ejército Zapatista para Liberación Nacional (EZLN) uprising was widespread throughout Indian country. Almost immediately, delegations gathered supplies and material aid and packed into vans and drove from reservations and urban Indian centers in the North directly to Chiapas. The International Indian Treaty Council, the National Congress of American Indians, the Indian Law Resource Center, the Assembly of First Nations (Canada), and the Women's Indigenous Network all sent delegations to the embattled area, some within days of the uprising. Over time organizations like First Nations North and South of Albuquerque, New Mexico, created "indigenous to indigenous" networks to support long-term projects of self-sustainability and provide material aid for continuing spiritual and cultural celebrations.

Tribal councils passed resolutions in solidarity with the indigenous peoples of Chiapas and together with native nongovernmental organizations lobbied their representatives and offered technical aid. Many tribal newspapers and native media organizations and radio stations actively disseminated information and updates about the uprising and continued to cover news from Chiapas on shows such as *Native American Calling*, a native public interest radio show that broadcasts to 37,000 people on sixty stations across the United States and Canada or KILI Radio (*kili* means "cool" or "awesome" in the Lakota language), which is the largest Indian-owned and Indian-operated public radio station in the United States and serves listeners in an area spanning over ten thousand miles on the Pine Ridge, Cheyenne River, and Rosebud Reservations, as well as Rapid City, South Dakota. Lori Pourier (Oglala/Mnicoujou Lakota), a former director of the IWN, reported that "people from Pine Ridge, so far from the South, consistently knew what was going on through either the tribal council meetings, the radio (KILI), or organizing going on there."[9] Although reservation newspapers a decade ago rarely covered outside events, much less international news, there was widespread coverage in U.S.-based native community newspapers, in particular *News from Indian Country* (Wisconsin), the *Yakama Nation Review* (Washington), and *Daybreak* (Barreiro 1994).

The indigenous struggle for rights in Mexico in the 1990s coincided with the consolidation of the neoliberal state project, especially after the implementation of NAFTA, which meant that indigenous rights were selectively coopted to fit within what Charles Hale calls the cultural logic of neoliberalism or neoliberal multiculturalism (Hale 2002). These state policies seemingly address movement demands without actually enacting meaningful legal and structural reforms to ensure those rights while establishing a discourse through which to regulate "good" and "bad" indigenous subjects. To illustrate, in 1992 the Mexican government amended article 4 of the constitution to recognize the pluricultural nature of Mexico in a largely symbolic gesture (Speed and Sierra 2005). At the same time, NAFTA was being negotiated and, to enter NAFTA, then-president Carlos Salinas de Gortari dismantled the *ejido* system, the collective land tenure system guaranteed by the Mexican revolution that was vital to the livelihood of many indigenous and peasant communities, opening the way to the privatization of land to individual title and corporate ownership (Hinley 1996). In 2001, the government passed the Indian Rights Bill, which failed to meet the most basic agreements of the San Andrés Accords, the agreement previously signed by the government and the EZLN. This new law was criticized by the National Commission for Human Rights and by the International Labor Organization for violating Convention 169, which recognizes indigenous peoples rights to their own customs, institutions, languages, and beliefs, which Mexico ironically ratified in 1992. These forms of state recalcitrance have led the indigenous rights movement in Mexico to continue to pursue forms of autonomy outside of the purview of the state. Women have been key actors in articulating a different practice of autonomy that does not rely solely on the state to grant them rights (Blackwell 2004, 2012; Speed 2006).

American Indian women activists in the United States have effectively localized their solidarity work with the people of Chiapas into their own organizations. Using translenguaje or translocal translation of Zapatismo and the vision of indigenous autonomy elaborated by the broader indigenous movement in Mexico, activists have reinvigorated their practices of grassroots sovereignty in Indian country. Building on international solidarity among native peoples, this process of translation acknowledges an indigenous identity that encompasses shared histories of colonization and aspirations toward indigenous rights, but what is translated in this case is not just the right to indigenous autonomy but the *practice* of autonomy. Indigenous women activists throughout Mexico have developed what I call a practice of autonomy, outside the purview of the state, that pushes beyond rights discourse to put indigenous autonomy into practices within daily life and communal social worlds (Blackwell 2004, 2009; Speed 2006).

Several key figures in IWN's early leadership led or traveled with delegations to Chiapas, including Winona LaDuke, Lori Pourier, Ingrid Washinawatok and Anne White Hat. Many women in the leadership of IWN were engaged in local community work, in addition to being on the forefront of international work at the United Nations or international solidarity work. Although moving in and between scales of power to struggle for sovereignty has been an effective strategy, it has also been costly (Blackwell 2006).[10] It takes tremendous resources, networks, and training, which native communities (who are among the poorest in the nation) can rarely afford. There is a delicate balance between international and local work, and many activists have stepped away from international work because it takes them away from their local community building and organizational commitments. For this reason, it is even more critical to translate transnational work locally.

Lori Pourier, executive director of the First Peoples Fund, an organization that offers capacity building to Native American artists, traveled to Chiapas, where her experiences reaffirmed the need to create programs to promote autonomy for native artists. According to Pourier, "Most tribes are caught up in a checkerboard of land base and federal development policies that make it so our land bases are not even ours. It [traveling to Chiapas] was a wake-up call for me . . . because it's really about economic survival at the most basic level."[11] She has translated Zapatista ideas of autonomy into her own vision of leadership development for native artists to receive training and acquire the tools necessary to become their own advocates in marketing their work while protecting their integrity and making a living from their art without the middleman.[12] This translocal translation of indigenous autonomy has helped a new generation of artists become autonomous and resist the long history of cultural, economic, and artistic exploitation that native artists have faced. Within the IWN, Pourier also created the Emerging Activist Leadership Program, which selected leaders for a multiyear program to teach them to apply the principles of autonomy and community-based know-how to a project each leader designed and implemented over the period of the grant. Participants included Crystal Echohawk (Pawnee), who worked as a special envoy to American Indian communities and the EZLN. After a solidarity trip to Chiapas, Echohawk joined the Commission for Democracy in Mexico, where she served as the national coordinator with a special focus on "building relationships between Indian Country and the Indigenous people of Chiapas and of Mexico."[13]

Another participant, Anne White Hat, a Lakota organizer, translated these principles into a project she is building with other community members on the Rosebud Reservation called the *Sicangu* Way of Life. White Hat traveled on two delegations to Chiapas; the first a Pastors for Peace delegation and the second a native delegation organized by Cecilia Rodriguez and Crystal Echohawk. Increasingly, indigenous women activists shared and translated their experiences to illustrate the link between colonial and state violence and other forms of domestic and intimate violence. While traveling to Chiapas, White Hat was moved by the "parallels to our own history. Like the massacre in Acteal . . . it sort of really hit home because we have had those experiences right here, you know, at Wounded Knee."[14] Traveling with veterans of the American Indian movement, native activists from the United States discussed the similarities of the paramilitary tactics used in Chiapas and their experiences with the Federal Bureau of Investigation, state violence, and the Counter Intelligence Program (COINTELPRO) in the 1970s. Furthermore, she was inspired by the concept of the practice of autonomy and how people with ever fewer resources, who live in a violent militarized zone, continue to revitalize indigenous traditions, knowledges, and community-based practices. She states:

> Now in the work we do at home, I see us as resource rich. I see the potential we have in our community that people don't realize or don't open their eyes to. Really seeing that we have a lot in our communities that we are not tapping into; resources that we have just forgotten. That is what

we are doing with herbal cooperative. It is a kind of community organizing work that involves connecting our people back with the land again. To be able to take care of ourselves instead of having to drive two and a half hours to Indian Health Services to wait three hours, just to be given Tylenol. Instead, we could go in our back yard and have that relationship again to the plant nation and take care of our families and ourselves.[15]

As a fellow in IWN's Leadership Program, White Hat developed the idea of Sicangu Way of Life by talking with women in her community who were frustrated with the lack of a quality health care system and saw the need to return to traditional medicine work with "the plant nation in order to reclaim the power we have to heal ourselves and keep our communities healthy with what is around us."[16] Sicangu Way of Life is a project "to reclaim the ways of life that have enabled us to survive since creation. Now is the time to reclaim this knowledge because we can't continue to be dependent." The other project the group is working on is their reproductive health initiative, with the idea of having a birthing center with Lakota midwifery. "Our ultimate goal is to be able to train Lakota midwives again. We are looking at rebuilding our nation from the first breath of life essentially and the ceremony that goes with pregnancy and childbirth. . . . We need to bring back this tradition and reclaim this knowledge. . . . We started with birth education classes because we have the highest rate of teen pregnancy in the United States, you know, back home on the reservation."[17]

Through this translocal translation of indigenous autonomy, participants in the Sicangu project started working with medicinal plants as a way to reclaim Lakota healing knowledge and also combat a form of colonialism that is manifest in the body. White Hat reflects, "Diabetes and other diseases like tuberculosis are not just diseases that came through to us, they are rooted in our loss. It takes generations to come back around and I see us coming back around. You know how they speak of seven generations? We are in that generation."[18] Furthermore, this translation of autonomy becomes its own local practice of autonomy (Forbis 2006). While the Sicangu project was established as an herbal cooperative and an economic development venture designed to promote community building and wellness through traditional plants and healing education, it also realigns Lakotas with their ancient philosophies and relationships. It helps participants assume their traditional relationship to the land as keepers of He Sapa, the Black Hills of South Dakota that are sacred to the Lakota, and share collective responsibility for the well-being of the land.

Lengua a Lengua: *Discursive Migration and the Politics of Translation in Cross-Border Lesbian Feminist Organizing*

Based on cautionary tales from travels with Mexicana and Chicana lesbian feminist organizers, the third and final case focuses on how different political cultures converge, translate, and conflict within a rich regional transnational history of lesbian feminist organizing in Latin America and the Caribbean. I focus specifically on transnational organizing across the U.S.–Mexico border to map the uneven ideological and social movement terrain that inflects relationships between cross-border actors and organizing. Human rights frameworks, identity narratives, and organizing logics travel and translate in different political contexts, and these discursive migrations serve as a site from which to examine how power and meaning are negotiated across social and cultural differences, power differentials, and national political arenas.

Studying the history of transnational networking among lesbian feminists has illustrated that often the most contested site of translation surrounds identity categories themselves. Lesbian feminist, queer, women of color, and LGBT serve as nodes of meaning through which struggles over power, self-definition, autonomy, imperialism, and solidarity converge and are negotiated. As such, they can help us understand the stakes in the transnational politics of political translation. Identities are compelling, contested, and often messy sites of affective politics. Transnational social movements frequently involve translating notions of identity that include struggles over meaning, regional identities, and local forms of autonomy that negotiate local and global discourses over uneven relations of power and geographies of difference. In 1986, several Latin American activists went to the Dutch-based International Lesbian Information System conference and decided to start their own Latin American network, "aimed at keeping everyone informed and distributing reports convening the violation of lesbian rights. The idea was to create an institution similar to the IGA, the International Gay Association (which later included Lesbians and became ILGA)" (Mogrovejo 2000). The difficulties of translating the logic of identity categories were felt at the highly anticipated first gathering of the lesbian feminist movement in Latin America in 1987. Organizers of the Encuentro Lésbico Feminista rejected how the funding for the meeting stipulated that everyone in attendance be a "lesbian," which excluded those who did not adopt this identity and many allies. This link between international funding and the imposition of identity categories was rejected by activists who called lesbian separatism a reactionary policy that would lead to the creation of a lesbianometer.[19]

The first Encuentro Lésbico Feminista in Taxco, Mexico, in 1987 was a key moment in the genealogy of Chicana and Mexicana lesbian transnational activism. Large contingents of Latina lesbians came from Los Angeles and a sizable contingent came from northern California's Bay Area. Several key Chicana lesbian scholars attended, including Yvonne Ybarro Bejarano, who wrote one of the only reports on the Encuentro in English, and Lydia Otero, who recalled that $9,000 was raised to send a contingent from Lesbianas Unidas, a Latina lesbian organization in Los Angeles (Yarbro-Bejarano 1989). Various political cultures converged and conflicted, and the different political contexts from which organizations emerged produced seemingly insurmountable differences. Some at the Encuentro condescendingly viewed the U.S. Latina organizations as merely social groups. Some U.S.-based activists viewed their Latin American counterparts as polarizing and exclusionary. Although political differences were debated vigorously, not much was productively resolved at this first regional meeting. One key debate was whether Latinas or the exiled Latin American community living in the United States and Europe should be included in the Latin American Encuentro or were they fundamentally First World? During the long debates on many of the big political questions, participants shared cultural productions, poetic performances, political manifestos, marched in the street together, fell in love, made new friendships, and engaged in other kinds of debates. Although the attempt to form a Latin American and Caribbean lesbian feminist network did not fully consolidate as anticipated, what did emerge was a social movement network dense with affective ties of love, friendship, erotic relations, and solidarities, if not a shared political platform.

While I've discussed how identities (rather than political projects) become (mis)translated, some transnational organizing efforts have been foiled by the ways in which even willing transnational partners conflict and (mis)translate political logics (Alvarez 2000). The National Latina/o Lesbian and Gay Organization (LLEGO), the first national U.S. Latina/o GLBTQ group, began to build bridges to Latin America and the Caribbean by holding several international meetings. Despite goodwill on the part of LLEGO and their partners in the Caribbean and Latin America, the first Encuentro in 1997, organized by Puerto Rican GLBT activists, many of whom were also *independistas*, or activists who support the independence of Puerto Rico, had a conflict/*choque* of transnational organizing logics. The hosts were insulted when LLEGO invited a White House representative to speak at the conference, which to the LLEGO leadership based in Washington, DC, was an important step in forging a U.S. Latino and Latin American GLBT alliance. Yet it magnified the convergence and disjuncture between an anti-imperialist political culture of the GLBT leaders from Puerto Rico and LLEGO's form of Washington policy advocacy (Quiroga 2000).

A rich site for understanding the complexity of translational processes of translation is the twenty-five-year history of networking among Chicana and Mexicana lesbian activists. For example, leaders of the Mexican lesbian movement visited the United States in the 1980s and tried to work with organizations like Lesbianas Unidas of Los Angeles. Luz Calvo, a member of Lesbianas Unidas, recalls a visit from leading Mexican lesbian feminist activist Yan Marie Castro, the founder of the famously named Seminario Marxista Leninista de Lesbianas Feministas (Marxist Leninist Seminar of Lesbian Feminists) that revealed the difficulties the movements had finding common ideological ground, even though they shared many of the same struggles.[20] The Mexican organizers did not understand why Chicanas and Latinas in the United States seemed preoccupied with race, because at that time, they linked their understanding of oppression to a Marxist-Leninist theory of social change. Chicana lesbians felt a need to vindicate their rights based on race, class, gendered, and sexual forms of oppression simultaneously based on their lived, material conditions and their multiple marginalizations from the radical social movements in which they had participated.

Other sites of incommensurability include encounters between the lesbian caucus of the National Association for Chicana and Chicano Studies (NACCS) and the Mexican lesbian feminist organization LesVoz. In 1998, NACCS descended on Mexico City. The lesbian caucus was organized by a founding generation in 1990 (Gonzalez 1998) and embraced a largely Latina lesbian separatist identity. Because the site committee was in Mexico City and most lesbian caucus members were in the United States, Mariana Pérez Ocaña and Juana Lisea of LesVoz were asked to be the lesbian caucus representatives to the Mexico City site committee. They had a difficult time participating due to the sexism and homophobia of the men on the committee. They resigned from the committee and proposed that the lesbian caucus of NACCS and LesVoz hold a separate event together.[21] LesVoz works from an autonomous lesbian feminist standpoint developed after a long history of lesbian activism in Mexico where lesbians have felt excluded from both the feminist and the gay and lesbian movements, despite their historic participation in both (Mogrovejo 2000).[22] While lesbian organizers have been leaders of many other social struggles such as labor organizing, many never found the space to vindicate their own rights or, from the point of view of Les Voz, to create their own lesbian feminist political culture.[23]

Because Chicana lesbians in NACCS had struggled for fifteen or twenty years to transform the organization from the inside, they were not willing to join their Mexican lesbian counterparts in completely' rejecting the organization and meeting separately despite the declared separatism of many of the founding generation. Because of their historic struggle to end homophobia within NACCS, members did not feel that holding a countermeeting to the one they had long struggled to be a part of was a viable political option. LesVoz, on the other hand, refused to work within what they saw as corrupt political or patriarchal spaces. In this instance, it was not just the identities or organizational logics that did not align, but how the geographies of difference inform the ways that power is articulated in different contexts. Although there was a commitment to working translengually, across differing languages, identities, logics, and discourses, and they shared the strategy of lesbian separatism, how each group defined what that meant tactically varied in each context. Creating a space for autonomy by forming a caucus within an organization was very different from forming an entirely separate organization, and yet both groups were harassed and widely criticized by their counterparts at the time of their formation. Despite their differences in political culture and ideology, the Lesbian Caucus participated in the conference and in several alternative events with LesVoz.

As for the Mexican counterparts, who formed one particular current of the autonomous lesbian movement in Mexico, there was a lot of political tension surrounding the organization. That same year, in 1998, they had formed Enlace Lésbico with many other groups who were challenging the sexism of mixed gay and lesbian groups as well as assuming an independent posture in relation to political parties. These local tensions were not always readably translated by Chicana lesbian activists who attended their first event during the *semana cultural* with LesVoz and were surprised to see LesVoz leave the stage they were presenting on in protest of Patria Jimenez, who had just been elected to the lower house of the Mexican congress on the PRD (Partido de la Revolución Democrática) ticket. LesVoz, along with members of Enlace Lésbico, had circulated a strong critique of the ways members of the LGBT community were being coopted by political parties without any kind of democratic deliberation with movements. They rejected the notion that the political elite could decide who represents the movement in the electoral arena or more broadly who legitimate LGBT representatives are. Informing this critique was a long history of corporatism that virtually guaranteed that if one leader appeared on a political ticket, the whole movement would vote with that party—the kind of hierarchy the Enlace Lésbico was challenging.

Sustained dialogue and communication continued between members of the Lesbian Caucus and LesVoz and many of the organizations in Enlace Lésbico (even long after that formation became much smaller due to in-fighting). One site through which dialogue, communication, and solidarity could continue to develop was the Lesbian March that Mexican lesbian activists organized. The Marcha Lésbica was among the first in Latin America and continues to be in the only country besides Brazil to have their own Lesbian March. Those organizations remaining in the Enlace Lésbico formed the Organizing Committee of the Lesbian March (Comite Organizador de Marcha Lésbica [COMAL]), asserted a separate lesbian presence and visibility to challenge the commercialization of gay pride, its collusion with a neoliberal agenda, as well as what they see as their erasure in LGBT formations. Although COMAL was widely criticized by other gay and lesbian organizations in Mexico City, other activists who joined explicitly challenged the discourse of pride and its relevance for the region as a reflection of U.S. imperialism and cultural hegemony in the definition and commercialization of gay, lesbian, and transgender life and the erasure of its indigenous and local roots. On March 21, 2003, the organizers of the first-ever Lesbian March, attended by 2,500 people, proclaimed that after twenty-five years of organizing, they needed "autonomous spaces that do not compromise our ethics in the construction of a society that is critical of heterosexism, neoliberalism and other fundamentalisms through the First Lesbian March of Mexico and Latin America." They continued, "We want as lesbians to have a public voice that is autonomous, heterogeneous, positive and free. The march will be an expression of our rebellious spirit as lesbians."[24] Although local movement dynamics in Mexico interact with global forces in ways that transform the local and the global, organizers refused the globalization of pride and enlisted an alternative grassroots globalism of lesbian feminists throughout Mexico, Central America, and Latinas living in diaspora in the United States and Mexico, who attended the march in good numbers.

Part of the developing translenguaje between U.S. Latina lesbians and Les-Voz was influenced by the fact that the Mexican counterparts called specifically for their own autonomous organizing spaces and benefited from having Chicana and Latina solidarity to help break their isolation from other sectors of the movement. Yet the (mis)translation of autonomous lesbian feminist identity often conflicted with the queer women of color stance that U.S. activists took and was one of the main topics of debate in a binational meeting organized by Mexican and Chicana activists the day before the Third Marcha Lésbica on March 25, 2006. With almost one hundred Chicana, Latina, and women of color activists present in Mexico City, this debate provided an illuminating window onto the practice of translenguaje and its successes and failures. One Chicana traveling with the U.S. contingent said she, a bisexual, did not feel included in the Lesbian March. This particular formation of lesbian feminist activists from Mexico firmly rejected the inclusion of transgendered women based on both their own negative experiences in Mexico as well as a view that "queer" discourse and transgender inclusion was an import of the North's queer agenda and ideology. Many organizers who came from a queer woman of color formation were challenged by their own commitment to transgender inclusion to drop or amend the "women" in women of color. Despite unaligned geographies of difference and differing histories of identity and struggle, they came to a collective stance to offer solidarity to the Mexican lesbian feminists and celebrate the power of their organizing.

This practice of translenguaje was developed among activists committed to carrying out their political projects through art, video or filmmaking, poetry, and performance. Indeed, a central strategy of translengua has been to bring art and culture to the center of the politics of liberation.[25] In another twist of translenguaje, these new forms of dialogue and translation brought about another kind of intersection. As many lesbians of color have always done, often serving as key organizers in immigrant, labor, antiwar, socialist, feminist, or Chicano movements, many present at the Third Lesbian March spoke of the mobilization of immigrants all over the United States that same day in protest of anti-immigrant legislation in Congress. Then spontaneously, but perhaps not surprisingly, given the kind of dense linkages mentioned, many like-minded individuals found each other on May 1, 2006, when 1 to 1.5 million people marched together for immigrant rights in Los Angeles. Marching with the leadership of the Garment Workers Center, who participated as part of the Multi-Ethnic Immigrant Worker's Organizing Network, activists brought translengua back to the streets of Los Angeles by changing the May 1 chants, "Quien no brinca es migra" (Those who are not jumping are *migra*), to the chants from the Marcha Lésbica, "Quien no brinca es buga" (Those who are not jumping are straight). The result was another kind of translenguaje or translating across social movement sectors. When activists began chanting "Bucha con Bucha, estamos en la lucha" (Butch with butch, we are in the struggle!), many organized immigrant workers joined in the chant.

To be a translengua entails cultivating a community practice of transnational feminist translation as a key step in coalition building. In this labor of coalition (see chapter 16 in this volume), it is essential to "know each other's histories," as Mohanty and Alexander (1996) suggest, but it is also necessary to understand how those histories and geopolitics shape our ability to speak to each other as situated actors. Although there may be deep ideological differences about strategy, political identity, and the boundaries of inclusion and exclusion, this case illustrates that a willingness does exist to translate and accept some level of difference and sometimes discomfort—to be translenguas. Indeed, many of the women involved with Tongues (a Los Angeles–based queer women of color organization) and other queer women of color activists organized Tongue to Tongue, a gathering that took place in September 2007 in response to the call by Mexican activists to hold the next Lesbian March in Los Angeles. While activists were inspired by the Mexico City Marcha Lésbica, this vision was difficult to translate locally because they were challenged by other Los Angeles activists who did not have that history of transnational connection. Although activists from Mexico City did attend, ultimately the event became a means of building local queer women and trans people of color political community and was highly successful and well attended. The Tongue to Tongue event became a critical dialogue among movement activists in Los Angeles to move beyond inclusion and visibility to build a broad framework of political work and dialogue based on economic justice, transgender inclusion, race and ethnic relations, health care, immigration, and the development of sustainable international solidarity.

Conclusions

Understanding transnational organizing through geographies of difference confirms the idea that the effect of globalization for women is almost always mediated by local relations of power. Marginalized (or subaltern) political actors have to navigate these local entrapments of power to reach the transnational level. While it is usually the way power is configured in the local arena that launches women's social movements to the transnational level of action, not enough attention is given to translocal configurations and negotiations of power—specifically race, gender, and sexual orientation. Categories like *women of color*, *LGBT*, or *queer* do not always translate well transnationally or across borders in expected ways, and they are often viewed as identity categories rather than political projects. Perhaps terms like *women of color*, *LGBT*, or *queer* would be more useful if divested from the desire to export a universal project and grounded in the political projects, communities of resistance, and visions for social change that are context-specific and historically situated. The incommensurability or impossibility of translation (faithless or otherwise) jettisons the "we are the world" tendency of many U.S. activists. We do not have to be each other (or labor under the fiction of sameness) to work together politically.

To be a translengua in transnational organizing is to recognize how power is structured in each context, and negotiates rather than glosses over power differences and requires a critical practice of translation of everyday political meanings, practices, and organizing logics. These forms of translengua include translation between scales of power as well as between contexts (Blackwell 2006). This can be seen in the ways native women activists translated the meaning of indigenous women's practice of autonomy locally into their sovereignty projects, creating a translocal indigenous dialogue. These strategies offer many U.S. social justice activists a model for conducting transnational solidarity work. For example, a critique of the dominance of U.S. activists at nongovernmental organization forums and the World Social Forum is that they dominate the space numerically, given the unequal access to travel resources, and also that many do not link their work back into grassroots action. Activists from the global South often critique U.S. activists in these settings by reminding us that if we just took care of our end locally by shifting U.S. economic and military policy, their work in the global South would be much easier.

By closely examining different kinds of transnational translations, this chapter has outlined the ways in which difference and internal movement diversity travel over uneven circuits of power in transnational organizing and how this form of political affiliation also creates new, not always equal, channels of symbolic power, access to resources, and status within movements locally. The way discourses migrate or are localized, reworked or contested over geographies of difference and transnational, national, and local scales of translation is highly charged. The way social movements align and frame themselves within these discursive formations can translate into new forms of solidarity, visibility, and resources both symbolic and material in the form of cultural capital.

Translenguaje requires deep learning and respect to build movements across geopolitical, national, identity, and ideological borders. Understanding the ways our allies are marginalized in their own contexts and how we are positioned ourselves helps us better situate and strategize new political projects that challenge neoliberal globalization. This continues Adrienne Rich's (1986 [1984]) notion of a politics of location that acknowledges how we are complexly situated among systems of power, especially geopolitical power, and how those locations affect our transnational solidarity and organizing efforts.[26] These emerging practices of translenguas are creating a new range of possibilities for transnational and translocal organizing and have created new languages, translation, interpretation, and analytical arts that help us see that another world is not only possible but that we, along with movements worldwide, are creating it together.

Notes

1. Others refer to this as neoliberal multiculturalism or corporate multiculturalism (Gordon and Newfield 1996; Hale 2002).

2. See Ella Shohat's important work on reclaiming this history through the nonaligned movement (Shohat 1997).

3. Frances Beal interview with author, September 21, 2002, Oakland, California (tape recording).

4. Feminist activists and theorists have been concerned with how theory travels over uneven terrains of power and meaning for some time. The Chicana feminist theorist Chela Sandoval discusses how the typologies of hegemonic feminism in the United States erased the flexible, tactical, and differential forms of oppositional consciousness formed by U.S. Third World women (Sandoval 1991). Sandoval's notion of U.S. Third World feminisms was based on a "new form of transnational alliance" and a solidarity across "the social movements of the 1960's and 1970's," bonding "activists of color in the Civil Rights, Anti-war, Black, Chicano, Asian, Native, Student, Encounter Group, Women's and Gay liberation movements" (Sandoval 1995).

5. For parallel interventions made by "black" women in Britain, see Amos and Parmar (1984) and Grewal et al. (1988). Social movement theorists call this process frame resonance, in the way issues are framed across contexts, but what I am arguing is the need for a translation of political subjectivities.

6. For more information on the American Indian women's movement see Women of All Red Nations (1980), Ohoyo Resource Center (1981), Green (1990), Jaimes and Halsey (1992), Jaimes-Guerrero (1997), and Ramirez (2007).

7. I thank Andrea Smith for sharing her files from the NGO Forum of the Fourth World Conference on Women with me.

8. Recognizing that a year was perhaps not long enough to address indigenous people's struggles for survival worldwide, in 1993 the United Nations announced that the Decade of Indigenous People would take place between 1995 and 2004. Two goals of the decade were to establish a permanent forum in the UN for indigenous peoples and pass a Draft Declaration on the Rights of Indigenous Peoples by the UN General Assembly. On September 13, 2007, the UN General Assembly adopted the UN Declaration on the Rights of Indigenous Peoples following more than twenty years of debate within the UN system and an enormous effort on the part of indigenous activists and their allies. See Escárcega (2010).

9. Interview with Lori Pourier conducted by the author, November 30, 2003.

10. Violence and even death has also been part of the cost of this international solidarity. For example, in 1999 Ingrid Washinawatok, a founding IWN member, was murdered along with Lahe'ena'e Gay and Terence Freitas, who accompanied her on a humanitarian mission in solidarity with the U'wa people of Colombia. Part of the American Indian Movement of the 1970s, Ingrid Washinawatok was one of a generation of activists who, after suffering state violence and murder in response to their efforts, turned to the United Nations on the advice of their elder's counsel. Washinawatok had been sent by the movement to Cuba to learn Spanish and had traveled extensively, meeting with native peoples in Latin America over decades. "Statement by the Indigenous Women's Network," March 8, 1999. Eventually the FARC claimed responsibility and issued a public apology.

11. Pourier interview.

12. In other instances, organizations of native and Chicana women have formed out of their solidarity work in Chiapas. This is the case with the organization Hermanas en la Lucha of Denver, Colorado (Sampaio 2004).

13. *Indigenous Woman* magazine, 1992.

14. Interview with Anne White Hat, conducted by the author, December 21, 2003.

15. White Hat interview.

16. White Hat interview. At the time of this interview, the *Sicangu* Way of Life project has incorporated in the state of South Dakota and was in the process of applying for nonprofit status.

17. White Hat interview.

18. White Hat interview.

19. It should be noted that this strategy is not static; in other times these same activists would use forms of exclusion or separatism in the name of autonomy.

20. Interview with Luz Calvo, conducted by the author, September 15, 1999. For a history of the Mexican lesbian movement, see Mogrovejo (2000).

21. Interview with Mariana Pérez Ocaña, conducted by the author, March 19, 1999.

22. Interview with Gloria Careaga Perez, conducted by the author, March 19, 1999, Mexico City.

23. Ocaña interview.

24. Organizing documents of COMAL and digital recording of the event, 2003.

25. As an actor in this history, I facilitated several meetings and an event between LesVoz organizers and Tongues, a queer women of color collective of cultural producers, in 2004 and 2005. In 2005 LesVoz had invited Chicana lesbian artist Alma Lopez to present as part of their semana cultural, and the Los Angeles–based Tongues began to collaborate with LesVoz through their binational meetings and the Lesbian March. In addition, continued relationship building from Chicana and Latina connections to LesVoz brought together a large delegation of the Mujeres de Costa Central that began in 1999 when Juana Lisea came to the University of California, Santa Cruz, for the summer institute for Social Change across Borders.

26. See Grewal and Kaplan (1994a) for a rich elaboration of Rich's concept of a politics of location.

CHAPTER SIXTEEN/QUEER/LESBIANA DIALOGUES AMONG FEMINIST MOVEMENTS IN THE AMÉRICAS

PASCHA BUENO-HANSEN

Upon my return to Lima, Peru, in 2006, I met up with a friend as she prepared for an LGBT (lesbian, gay, bisexual, and trans) fundraising event. As we sipped beer, arranged chairs, and chatted on the hot February evening, we talked about feminist constructions of sexuality. I asked her what she thought of the term queer in relation to the terms included in LGBT and shared with her the way we worked with queer to reinforce the inclusion of sexuality in the radical politics of women of color feminisms at the University of California, Santa Cruz (UCSC). She quickly dismissed it as another abstract concept that does not distinguish the specific political struggles of lesbianas. "Even with LGBT, note the L comes first to increase the visibility of lesbianas; gay men tend to dominate public political spaces. Besides the fact that queer doesn't do anything to gain public space for lesbianas, it is imposed from the North. Those kinds of power dynamics are why we need meetings like Diálogo Sur/Sur LGBT, which took place in Quito a few years ago," she said as she gestured to another friend's T-shirt that sported the insignia of that conference.[1]

From 2005 to the present, I have been part of ongoing conversations regarding the use of queer as related to women of color feminisms through my involvement with a collaborative writing group that grew out of the UCSC Research Cluster for the Study of Women of Color in Collaboration and Conflict (the WOC Research Cluster). Queer as an adjective asserts the central role of lesbians in the formation of women of color feminisms. Because issues of lesbianism are commonly erased from women of color feminisms on their reception in most heteronormative audiences, *queer* forces the issue of sexuality back into the discussion.[2] Using *queer* also asserts our contemporary sexual politics, which includes gender and sexual continuums. This assertion pushes against the possibility of reading "women," "lesbian," or "feminist" as essentialist identity categories based on the male/female binary.

What types of dialogues are necessary to build solidarity between feminist political projects that take up apparently contradictory uses of *lesbiana* and *queer*? This chapter explores one such possible dialogue between a *movimiento de lesbianas feministas* and a queer women of color feminist movement.

When taking the politics of location seriously, we find it useful to begin with the social positions of the members of each group. The lesbianas feministas in Peru described here participate in Lesbianas Independientes Feministas Socialistas (LIFS), which was formed during the first LGBT national gathering, or *encuentro*, in 2005. LIFS is composed of women of varied ages, from their late twenties to their early fifties. Though most of them live in Lima, they represent varied ethnic backgrounds and include women from the Amazon, the Andes, and the coast. LIFS members work as nongovernmental organization (NGO) staff, business administrators, and schoolteachers, among other occupations; a few are unemployed. When they invited me to join in early 2006, we jokingly inaugurated "LIFS international." We have varied political trajectories, including combinations of socialist, feminist, religious, popular theater, and LGBT organizing, which make for a rich diversity of approaches to lesbian political activism. All members take part in knowledge production and theory building in relation to a shared political project and the commitment to being "out"—*fuera del closet*.

I have yet to come across nonacademic spaces in the United States in which activists commit significant time to theoretical reflection on their political activism as they do in LIFS. The closest I have come to such an approach has been working within women of color feminist activist spaces linked to academia. I underscore the porous boundary between the intellectually engaged political practice of a group like LIFS, and a "politically engaged intellectual practice" found in some corners of academia (Fregoso 2006a, 431). Emphasizing the connection facilitates building alliances between similar political projects, albeit in different spaces of struggle. The members of the WOC Research Cluster see our work as inherently connected to struggles for social justice, and we are active in a wide spectrum of issues in addition to our interventions in academia.

The five of us in the writing collaborative began working together in January 2005. This collective effort started in a "Women of Color Feminisms" writing seminar directed by Angela Davis. After studying the collaborative writing and anthologizing practices of women of color feminists, we decided to give it a try.

At that time, we were all doctoral students in our mid-twenties to mid-thirties. We identified with and against the terms *queer, dyke, lesbian, feminist,* and *women of color* and were all active participants of the WOC Research Cluster. Like members of LIFS, we have diverse political formations and histories of organizing and activism that include women of color film festivals, women's rights, Latin American and Middle Eastern political solidarity, student organizing, LGBT/queer community organizing, Xicana *indígena* organizing, and all the combinations thereof.

Friendship is the basis of both groups' ongoing interchanges, activities, and collective theorizing. Luz del Alba Acevedo (2001), citing María C. Lugones and bell hooks, asserts that instead of sisterhood, we should consider friendship as a model for historically and politically contextualized feminist solidarity. Such an approach provides a way of negotiating heterogeneity by sharing stories and interpretations of lived experiences, thereby building trust. LIFS and the writing collaborative both dedicate long hours to getting to know each other, forging friendships across our different struggles, contexts, and perspectives. We cook meals, eat and drink together, share secrets, and work though tense moments when everyone feels like either running away or exploding.

Furthermore, the opening passage is based on a transnational friendship in that we are familiar with one another's contexts. My Peruvian friend lived in Santa Cruz for a few years, and we worked together at an NGO that provides services for women dealing with domestic violence or sexual assault. During this time we were active in women of color and Latina/Chicana political spaces, specifically around issues of violence against women. Moving in the other direction, I have traveled to Peru throughout my life to visit family and friends and more recently to do research.

Over the past eight years or so, LIFS and the writing collaborative are the spaces in which I have come to find myself as a queer Latina/lesbiana of Peruvian heritage in the United States and Peru. My identity construction in the interstitial spaces between these movement formations drives my interest in theorizing solidarity. LIFS and the writing collaborative do not have a formalized relationship, therefore this is a virtual dialogue, inspired by a desire to further connect the disparate contexts that make me whole. The question at hand—how to construct solidarity between differently situated feminist political projects—is a priority for activist intellectuals and intellectual activists globally (see chapters 15, 19, and 20 in this volume). LIFS and the writing collaborative work with identity categories as tools in a shared struggle to name themselves, achieve visibility, define a political project, and construct utopian futures. Both groups straddle the tension between using fixed identity categories and deconstructing these same categories. Therefore, this virtual dialogue demands an approach to feminist political solidarity that can contain conflict and contradiction, such as the friendship model.

The next section outlines the theoretical frame that holds the dynamism of multiple movement approaches to naming and visibility, in relation to their varied histories and contemporary contexts. To facilitate dialogue, throughout the chapter I pose key questions each group might ask the other. This exploration begins by looking at how each group names itself in a section titled "Self-Naming." To examine why each organization has the emphasis it does, the section titled "Learning Each Other's Histories" examines historical and contextual issues. Last, the section "Political Projects and Visibility Strategies," situates the use of *lesbiana* or *queer*, explaining what each group actually does, how they do it, and their spaces of intervention.

Theoretical Frame

Both feminist movements seek to claim their existence and create spaces from which to stand and speak, whether in academia, international forums, NGOs, or the streets. When the shared struggle for self-naming and visibility is brought into focus, the identity categories used to mobilize, whether lesbiana or queer, can be understood as discursive tools. Rather than points of irreconcilable division, understanding identity categories as tools in a struggle to disrupt mechanisms of erasure opens the possibility of solidarity across movements.

In differing ways, LIFS and the writing collaborative bridge the contradiction between using fixed identity categories such as lesbiana or woman of color and deconstructing these categories. As Peruvian/Mexican lesbiana feminista Norma Mogrovejo explains, while fixed identity categories run the risk of reifying oppressive social structures, these same categories can be powerful tools of resistance and unity (Mogrovejo 2001, 292). In their differing contexts, both movements' naming strategies wrestle with the "impasse between deconstructive cultural strategies and category-supportive political strategies" (Gamson 1995, 391). Meaningful dialogue can only occur in a space that can hold naming and visibility strategies that run the gamut between fixed and deconstructivist approaches to identity.

In this space of tension and negotiation, movements build "the network of relationships that will allow subjects to construct their identity" (Quiroga 2000, 17). José Quiroga's emphasis on a network of relationships draws attention to the inner workings of collectivity, taking the discussion out of the realm of intractable differences in terms. Reading Quiroga's focus on a network of relationships expansively, I understand it to hold space for multifaceted and dynamic identities and the varied political commitments of the social actors involved. Therefore, attending to a network of relationships includes the difficulties and asymmetries inherent to dialogue between groups.

A friendship model of feminist solidarity maintains a capacious frame for dialogue. Acevedo (2001) writes about her participation in the Feminist Latina Group: "What I experienced was a kind of friendship built through disagreements, critical discussions, and caring constructive arguments directed to enrich rather than diminish and discredit our personal lives and work. This experience led me to imagine an alternative framework to sisterhood as a model of feminist solidarity. Such a model has to be anchored in friendship and based on strength derived from women's different experiences, socioeconomic diversity, pluralistic political practices, and multicultural identities" (261–62). This alternative model of feminist solidarity does not presuppose getting along, unanimity or consensus. As Acevedo underscores, "dialogue is always a contested terrain for building feminist alliances" (2001, 262).

My location has led me to understand the importance of cultural translation as a means to facilitate dialogue between ostensibly incompatible political positions in differently situated locations. As Claudia de Lima Costa explains, "Many feminists, in trying to find productive ways of establishing dialogues across diverse and dispersed feminist communities in the articulation of transnational alliances, have resorted to the practice of translation as a privileged site for the negotiation of difference in a world of increasing cross-border movements and cross-cultural contacts" (see Introduction to Debates, this volume).

Cultural translation is critical for facilitating friendship-based feminist solidarity because it urges us to take time, step out of our own worlds for a moment, and get to know each other's struggles within context. Cultural translation is the dynamic and necessarily incomplete process of mediation across discursive, political, linguistic, and geographic borders and power asymmetries, which facilitates alliance building across movements (Carr 1994, 156). This virtual dialogue takes to heart the implications of cultural translation.

Accountable dialogue must displace dominant voices and social positions of privilege "through practices of translation that make visible the asymmetrical geometries of power along the local-regional-national-global nexus" (Introduction to Debates, this volume). Just as global sisterhood has been critiqued for subsuming the diversity of feminist struggles into a singular definition, queer can be equally problematic, as the LIFS member in the opening passage argues. Combining queer women of color feminisms and Latin American lesbian feminisms under a queer unifying umbrella buttresses historic and structural inequalities. Therefore, the virtual dialogue sets up an exchange of naming practices, histories, political projects, and visibility strategies. As Costa asserts, productive dialogue is a "daunting political and epistemological challenge" (Introduction to Debates, this volume). Attention to the dynamics of disequilibrium is critical for forging accountable conversations based on solidarity. The fundamental disagreement in the terms *lesbiana* and *queer* casts a shadow on the already formidable challenge of opening productive political exchanges.

Self-Naming

In the context of Peru, LIFS asserts that *queer* lacks a political project. Although it is fashionable among the academic crowd to talk about queer theory, it dilutes the struggle for basic rights. As gay feminist human rights activist Crissthian Manuel Olivera Fuentes (2006) writes, Peruvian culture suffers from sexism, heterosexism, and homo/lesbo/transphobia, erasing and marginalizing those who are different. As long as this is happening, it is important to account for discriminatory acts and name vulnerable groups so that their rights can be defended and exercised. Although names are used to oppress, names are also tools for the defense of rights. For example, at the Organization of American States Inter-American Commission for Human Rights public hearing titled "Sexual Orientation Discrimination in Peru," held in Washington in March 2006, a LIFS representative demanded recognition by the state. "Historically, marginalized peoples need to be named to remind society of their inclusion in the existing system of social protection. This claim is necessary because it goes to the heart of social change. If excluded subjects are not named, then their rights are left at the mercy of restrictive interpretations" (Estudio para la Defensa 2006).

LIFS's position reflects this sentiment with the further specification that the identity formation and political project associated with *lesbiana* is inseparable from *feminista*. LIFS, given its feminist emphasis, prioritizes the defense of and advocacy for women's rights alongside heterofeminists. This emphasis also calls for independence from male domination, which takes the concrete form of gays maintaining control over LGBT spaces. For example, in 2006, shortly after the exchange that opens this essay, a group of lesbianas broke away from the Movimiento Homosexual de Lima (MHOL), an institutionalized coalitional space for the LGBT community in Lima. For more than a decade, the lesbianas of MHOL ran weekly workshops, organized events, and provided counseling and advocacy. Yet their relations with the gay men and trans women became increasingly tense as they began to assert a feminist political agenda. In 2006, the lesbianas could no longer accept being spoken for, having their ideas stolen, and being relegated to a secondary position. After many heated discussions, the lesbianas left MHOL to name their autonomous existence as lesbianas feministas, breaking with the few lesbianas who decided to stay at MHOL. Shortly thereafter, the break-off group joined LIFS. In such a context, autonomous spaces are necessary to build individual and collective identity as well as articulate self-determined political projects. Lesbiana feminista might appear to be an essentialist identity formation, affirming a radical feminist agenda based on sex difference. But the political project in which it is embedded holds deconstructionist tendencies in that it is *una lucha por el contenido del termino*—a struggle for the meaning and significance of the term.[3]

LIFS might ask the writing collaborative how *queer* assists in defining a political agenda. The relevance of *queer* in women of color feminisms at UCSC reflects the political activism and intellectual production by key faculty and the graduate student WOC Research Cluster. The context is shaped by hardwon recognition of LGBT rights and an established LGBT presence in public political spaces on and off campus. I am in no way suggesting that UCSC is an LGBT utopia, much less for queer women of color feminists, only that some struggles have been won. Therefore, the generations coming up find ourselves/ themselves in a context in which we/they have access to "out" lesbian/queer women of color feminist mentors and can work with *queer* precisely because a minimum level of legitimacy has already been gained.

As mentioned, *queer* as an adjective does not erase the central role of lesbians in the formation of women of color feminisms, but is a vehicle for asserting it. Although *queer* does nothing to increase lesbian visibility in Peru, when brought together with women of color feminisms in the United States, the term functions to recenter questions of sexuality. In a simultaneous and somewhat contradictory way, *queer* also calls on the radical potential held within the rupture of fixed categories that form the basis of social hierarchies. This echoes queer women of color feminist contemporary cultural production, political organizing, and community building.

For this reason, the writing collaborative enacts a twofold strategy. By claiming queer women of color feminisms, the group rides the productive tension between fixed identity categories and the radical potential of queer politics through the deconstruction of identity categories. Women of color feminisms are historically grounded in an analysis of material oppression. *Queer* disables the normalizing regime of essentialist readings of women of color feminisms. Michael Warner writes, "The preference for 'queer' . . . rejects the minoritizing logic of toleration or simple political interest-representation in favor of a more thorough resistance to regimes of the normal" (1993, xxvi). Queer women of color feminisms resist "regimes of the normal," while retaining identity categories for self-naming as an integral part of political struggle.

To understand why lesbianas feministas and queer women of color feminists name themselves as they do, they must be situated within their historical contexts. The Peruvian lesbian feminist movement finds its roots within the Peruvian radical feminist agenda, emphasizing the problem of heteropatriarchy. Women of color feminisms grow out of the fissures between ethnic nationalist and feminist movements in the United States, underscoring multiple oppressions associated with race, gender, sexuality, and class. The writing collaborative might ask LIFS if they were concerned with the possible exclusions inherent in using *lesbiana*. Are only biological women included? What about trans women?

The second Latin American and Caribbean Feminist Encuentro, which took place in Lima in 1983, played a critical role in opening the national discussion on lesbianism in Peru. About 350 women attended the first workshop on lesbianism to take place at an Encuentro. According to Nancy Saporta Sternbach and coauthors, this workshop marked the beginning of a lesbian presence challenging homophobia and heterosexism within the movement (Sternbach et al. 1992, 220). Many women courageously came out in this public forum. However, the Encuentro's reception of lesbianism contrasted sharply with its reception of racism and national sociopolitical problems.

A series of incidents revealed the tensions. First, while the workshop on lesbianism was widely attended, two other workshops, on racism and the national sociopolitical situation of Peru, were forced to conduct their meetings in the corridors of the conference center because they were not afforded a space.[4] Second, during the days of the Encuentro at the Country Club del Bosque, Lima suffered a three-day power outage.[5] Because the Country Club del Bosque had its own generator, the Encuentro continued its schedule, impervious to the darkness blanketing the city. Finally, one of the main labor unions, the Confederación General de Trabajadores del Perú, had called a national strike and the wives of Andean miners had organized a march on Lima to voice labor demands. There was no organizational effort on the part of the Encuentro to collaborate with the union or the miners' wives gathered some kilometers away. This series of incidents speaks to the class and race differences that have historically stymied feminist efforts in Peru. Similarly, the newly emergent lesbianas feministas found themselves struggling with the social distances between lesbians of different class backgrounds.

In 1984, the burgeoning lesbiana feminista movement found national expression through Grupo de Autoconciencia Lésbico-Feminista (GALF). From its inception, GALF adopted feminism as the ideological and theoretical framework for its consciousness raising (Mogrovejo 2000, 307). GALF first publicly enunciated its presence in a feminist meeting, with a generally positive yet mixed response. The group's position was autonomous in relation to the feminist movement and MHOL, the mostly male group established in 1982. GALF aligned with the idea that *lesbianismo* is not only an erotic practice but also a political project that stands against heteropatriarchy. Mogrovejo explains: "The lesbian actively rejects [men] and chooses women, challenging the established political system that obligates relations between men and women to be based on domination, the gendered division of labor, the imposition of sex for serial reproduction" (Mogrovejo 2000, 48–49). GALF built its strength through various lesbian feminist spaces of expression and organizing: two cafés, La Otra Cara de la Luna and Aguas Vivas; a mimeographed bulletin, Al Margen; and cultural events (Mogrovejo 2000, 309).

The issue of class difference became a major challenge to GALF in its consciousness-raising work. Whereas the GALF members were mainly middle-class, the spaces they opened attracted working-class lesbians. The ensuing discussions revolving around survival defied their feminist consciousness-raising model and exposed its limitations in responding to issues such as lack of employment opportunities, health services, and safe housing. In the worst cases, these cross-class exchanges reinforced historic paternalist relations. Yet overall, the years during which these discussions took place were intensely productive in closing previously uncontested social distances.[6]

In 1986, the International Lesbian Information Service organized its eighth conference in Geneva, for the first time inviting women from Latin America, Africa, and Asia. The goal was to develop an international network for lesbian feminist communication and political strategizing. The conference participants also decided to organize the first Latin American and Caribbean Lesbian Feminist Encuentro to take place in Mexico in 1987 (Mogrovejo 2000, 241). The changing political climate in Peru made it impossible to sponsor the second Lesbian Feminist Encuentro in 1989 as planned. In 1987 the police raided a dance club frequented by lesbians, claiming that minors were present. Several lesbians were detained and the media spun negative publicity for a week by repeatedly showing the video of the women's faces coming out of the club during the prime news hour.[7] At the same time, due to the escalation of the internal armed conflict, President Alan García's administration declared a curfew and suspended constitutional rights.[8] These conditions caused a closure of public political space that stunted the growth of the LGBT movement.

In 1990, due to internal struggles and the difficulties related to working within the context of highly institutionalized feminist and homosexual movements, GALF stopped functioning as an autonomous collective (Mogrovejo

2000, 316).[9] One of the main difficulties was that MHOL's institutional capacity and access to resources attracted lesbians away from GALF, causing divisions.

For the lesbianas feministas in this story, the creation and establishment of LIFS in 2005 and 2006 forced a shift in the basis of coalitional work, heightening the recognition of their presence and political agenda within the larger LGBT community.[10] LIFS understands lesbians to be biological women; no trans women participate in LIFS. Although there are a few trans women that are activists with public profiles, generally trans women in Peru are not organized around feminist activism. Instead, they create survival communities of mutual care to address their social vulnerability. Due to lack of access to education and employment, many trans women depend on prostitution as a means of subsistence or start their own small businesses, commonly beauty salons. Therefore, the perspectives, struggles, and political agendas of lesbianas feministas and trans women do not have that much overlap from day to day. Furthermore, LIFS asserts that many trans women activists retain a masculinist attitude and do not share a feminist political vision. As LIFS member Esther Rodríguez asserts, "Right now we do not have enough in common that unites us as feministas." She also suggests that trans women need to strengthen their voices and develop their own agendas.[11]

The collaborative writing group might respond by arguing that queer, in its best light, makes an intergenerational connection with women who feel more identified with "lesbian" or "lesbian of color," thereby claiming histories, legacies, and genealogies under erasure. Queer women of color feminisms build on this history, yet with a contemporary twist because younger generations are more familiar with queer than lesbian and envision community more broadly to include trans and gender-fluid people.

Queer makes space for gender fluidity and nonconformity. As Juana María Rodríguez asserts, the term queer "creates an opportunity to call into question the systems of categorization that have served to define sexuality" (Rodríguez 2003, 24). Therefore, queer indicates a conceptual and analytical orientation toward sexuality, or the "formation of homosexualities" (Butler 1993, 229), denaturalizing heterosexuality yet leaving the question of actual sexual orientation slightly ambiguous.[12] Placing queer with women of color presses the bounds of "women" to include self-identified women and women who have transitioned to men. The construction is a work in progress with many raging debates.

Although it may seem that the writing collective takes an entirely deconstructivist approach, it never lets go of theorizing gender, race, sexuality, and class through collective reflection on and analysis of lived experiences. Cherríe Moraga and Gloria Anzaldúa (2002) write of "a theory in the flesh" as "one where the physical realities of our lives—our skin color, the land or concrete we grew up on, our sexual longings—all fuse to create a politics born out of necessity." Self-naming and sharing stories are central to bridging "the contradictions in our experience" (21). This collective and embodied theorizing practice links to a political agenda of social justice and creative expression, often making it poorly understood in academia.

In a reflection on the legacies of women of color feminisms, Angela Davis explains that it can be understood as both "a body of literature defining a field of inquiry" and "a community of scholars who identify with the field as a mode of solidarity" (2004, 4). As an object of study, women of color functions as a fixed identity category: as a method of study it is informed by critical reflection about subject positioning and structural inequalities. Yet much confusion has developed around the relationship between the field of inquiry and community of scholars (who identify as women of color feminists). The easy way out of the confusion is to conflate the two legacies: assume the texts and the material bodies are the same. This line of reasoning has been used to critique approaches such as "theory in the flesh," assuming that women of color feminists don't take seriously questions regarding "the constructed nature of experience, how the subjects are constituted as different in the first place, . . . and how one's vision is structured" (Scott 1992, 25). There is a much more nuanced negotiation at play in that women of color feminism can be associated with an identity category for political mobilizing and with a method of analysis. Those who identify with women of color feminists as a community of scholars commonly hold a militant commitment to social justice for oppressed peoples. As Moraga and Anzalúda write, "We are interested in pursuing a society that uses flesh and blood experiences to concretize a vision that can begin to heal our 'wounded knee'" (2002, 21). Simultaneously, those who use women of color feminist methods of study prioritize critical reflection about subject positioning and structural inequalities whether they identify as women of color feminists or not.

LIFS and the writing collaborative's theoretical elaboration of *queer* and *lesbiana* has everything to do with claiming an identity, defending one's rights, and collectively dreaming and theorizing emancipatory futures. These multiple processes are held in tension rather than conflated. The movement articulations discussed thus far navigate between knowledge production derived from lived experience, theories in the flesh, and the political stakes involved in naming and visibility. The two groups constantly explore the productive tension between fixing and unfixing identities. For LIFS *lesbiana* is a mobilizing term for political activism; at the same time LIFS is deeply invested in the struggle to shift the meaning of the term. As Evelyn Blackwood and Saskia E. Wieringa write, "the use of the term 'lesbian' is a political move to maintain visibility and independence as well as a refusal to limit the boundaries of the topic" (1997, 21). LIFS also employs deconstructive strategies to make interventions in systems of oppression, as the next section illustrates. Similarly, the writing collaborative claims a fixed political identity while pressing its limits.

Political Projects and Visibility Strategies

By getting to know each other's trajectories, the historical and contextual logics behind naming come to the fore. If a name enunciates a sociocultural and political presence, visibility strategies are how movements make that name known and intervene in the spaces that matter to them. Both groups straddle the tension between essentialist and deconstructionist naming practices and their political interventions further elucidate how they negotiate this tension. In pursuing a dialogue, the next question the groups might ask each other is, how are your politics expressed in your practices, and in what spaces do you engage? LIFS speaks out and claims public space through women's sports, demonstrations, marches, and regional encuentros. These actions work to challenge stereotypes about lesbianas and shift popular perception. The writing collaborative intervenes in academic spaces by participating in conferences, connecting with like-minded groups, and publishing "Building on 'the Edge of Each Other's Battles': A Feminist of Color Multi-dimensional Lens," in the Hypatia special issue "Interstices: Women of Color Feminist Philosophy" (Santa Cruz Feminist of Color Collaborative 2014). Both groups prioritize building networks of mutual support based on friendship and engage with manifesto writing as a method of disseminating their political projects, making themselves visible, and building political solidarity with other groups.

Within the Latin American lesbian feminist movement, according to the Mexican lesbiana feminista Claudia Hinojosa, visibility is a principal strategy for public education, which symbolically challenges the impunity associated with homophobia and heterosexism (2004, 16). In discussing issues of visibility in Latin America with regard to lesbianas, Quiroga writes, "The system created highly codified visibilities—once again as these related to men, although the fact that women were always already 'invisible' did not mean that they were 'outside' the taxonomical circuits" (Quiroga 2000, 13). Lesbianas feministas historically rebel against their status as always already invisible by naming themselves and inserting their political project into public discussions.

Testimony is a powerful strategy for visibility and political advocacy. At the UN conference on Human Rights in Vienna in 1993, the international press described the Tribunal on Violations of Women's Human Rights as one of the most notable events of the conference. Rebeca Sevilla, a founding member of

GALF, presented a testimony at the tribunal titled "Persecution, Impunity and the Hidden Life of Lesbians in Peru." Echoing the crisis of invisibility that Quiroga points out, she asserts, "While we are not given permission to exist, we are not noticed. While our rights are not recognized, while our control over our bodies and lives is denied, while our economic independence is kept out of reach, we are being denied our personhood" (Sevilla 2000, 188). Through the testimony, Sevilla claims an identity and makes her political struggle visible.

Besides grand international acts, literal play—sports—is another way of claiming public visibility. In the context of the generalized invisibility of lesbians in Lima, women's *fulbito* games are a key to building trust and opening public spaces. Fulbito is *futbol*—soccer—but on a smaller concrete playing field, with six on each team. Harnessing the national respect for futbol, women use play to bend the parameters of heteronormativity. According to Maria Lugones (1997), play is fundamental to developing a sense of collectivity and creating self-referential language and ways of being. Women's fulbito games open public spaces where girlfriends feel safe(r) to live their relationships and get to know one another. The lesbian feminist movement organizes women's fulbito tournaments, bringing together women from all sectors of Lima and thereby opening a playful and informal space across classes while increasing visibility and shifting meaning in the national symbolic realm.

LIFS is careful with its visibility strategies because widespread homophobia gives any self-representation effort the most negative connotation possible. When LIFS launched a campaign titled *Insurgencia Sexual* (Sexual Insurgency) members thought carefully about how to convey their political project. "We propose sexual insurgency as an idea and political action to confront the reality of our countries and the region. Our desire is to spark and arouse our hearts, to realign our bodies through insurgent action founded upon dialogue and debate."[13] During the initial discussions regarding the campaign, one LIFS member voiced concerns that this title may reify the negative visibility of lesbians as morally corrupt sexual deviants who suffer from nymphomania. Much time has also been spent discussing when and where it is appropriate to chant the group's signature call and response: "Insurgencia!" "Sexual!" It was decided not to spontaneously do the chant in public locales, as bold and transgressive as it may feel in the moment. The chant is part of a political project that necessitates a context to be understood, such as participation in the yearly Pride march or activities surrounding October 13, the day of Lesbian Rebellions (*Rebeldías Lésbicas*). Negative visibility is a huge liability that must be avoided at all costs. These concerns regarding visibility reflect a desire to strategically deconstruct negative stereotypes, replacing them with self-affirming definitions of *lesbiana*.

Visibility is a complicated matter, because meanings attached to names cannot be controlled, as Judith Butler explains. "As much as it is necessary to assert political demands through the recourse to identity categories, and to lay claim to the power to name oneself and determine the conditions under which that name is used, it is also impossible to sustain that kind of mastery over the trajectory of those categories within discourse. This is not an argument against using identity categories, but it is a reminder of the risk that attends every such use" (Butler 1993, 227–28). LIFS is well aware of the risk that Butler points out and strategizes its interventions in the most advantageous contexts in which it has the best chance of successfully challenging the content of the term *lesbiana* that serves to oppress.

The writing collaborative also is concerned with visibility, but in the context of academia. While striving to make histories and methods of analysis visible, the group broadens networks of collaboration and support. Claiming self-referential visibility stands against the workings of invisibility and hypervisibility. For example, the anthology *This Bridge Called My Back* (Moraga and Anazldúa 1983 [1981]) is generally accepted as the origin moment of women of color feminisms. The hypervisibility of *This Bridge Called My Back* in course syllabi, for example, erases the vast amount of collaboratively produced books, essays, articles, conferences, poetry, interviews, films, and other genres of expression that have both preceded and followed the edited volume. The second erasure due to the hypervisibility of *This Bridge Called My Back* is related to the heterosexism with which it is received. Agreeing with Anzaldúa, the writing collaborative asserts, "There has been a lack of attention paid to the centrality of queerness and lesbianism within the text. I argue for the importance of acknowledging that the theoretical formulations of 'theory in the flesh' within *Bridge* are undeniably linked to the experiences, activisms and political perspectives of radical lesbians of color."[14] Emphasizing the rich genealogy of women of color feminisms and the central contribution of lesbians counters both invisibility and hypervisibility.

At conferences and other public engagements, speaking with a collective voice and making comprehensible our collaborative method honors the legacy of women of color feminisms and provides a model for others to try it out. Because academia privileges single-authored texts, it is hard to find support for such a time- and energy-consuming endeavor that will not garner maximum points toward tenure. As the writing collaborative points out, "It takes work to be together in solidarity. We must listen to each other and not take for granted that because we both identify as 'women of color' we came to this identity in the same way or that we have the same experiences in the world."[15] Yet this practice is critical for our collective survival within academia because we carve a space in which we can feel whole and also challenge each other to stretch and grow in a way that integrates our personal, political, spiritual, and intellectual dimensions. All of these efforts insert us in larger networks of mutual support and survival that come to shift the contours of the acceptable within academia. We are part of retention networks for queer students of color, attract prospective students who are looking for such spaces, and influence the pedagogical, conceptual, and methodological approaches within the fields we inhabit.

One shared visibility strategy of LIFS and the writing collaborative is the production of manifestos. This textual expression is elaborated collectively through ongoing discussion and reflection. Both the writing collaborative and LIFS work on manifestos as points of departure for alliance-building dialogues. As Quiroga argues, in reference to manifestos, "they intervened in the economy of desire: the promise was more important than its fulfillment; wanting was more important than having; the project was more enticing than the realization of the project" (Quiroga 2000, 5). A manifesto is both the process and product of writing a shared vision based on claiming a collective identity and political project. Through ongoing discussions and reflections, networks of relationships are formed, identities are constructed and deconstructed, and alliances are built and dissolved.

The writing collaborative came together to produce a text reaffirming the relevance of women of color feminisms. "We are a dedicated group of radical women of color feminists who theorize through collaboration and honor the multiple women of color feminist legacies from which we grow and are inspired."[16] We initiated writing our text in manifesto form with the goal of intervening in academia by engaging in and fomenting knowledge production overtly derived from interpretations of lived experience. "We live and work in our contradictions, as individuals and as a collective, using our collaboration to acknowledge and keep in tension our different paths as women, feminists, activist-scholars, artists and radical women of color."[17] This style of knowledge production makes explicit its relationship to the social position of the knowledge producers and their political agendas.

Manifesto writing emerges from the deep desires voiced through intimate moments of speaking ourselves. The manifesto highlights the political project of women of color feminisms, alongside the method of analysis and identity category, embracing the tensions between them. We loosen the fixed identity category, reinvigorating it with dynamism by inserting *queer*. In this way, the political project reinvents meaning and content in response to the historical moment. The writing collaborative's internal opening, documented in the form of manifesto, reclaims movement and flux.

The manifesto is a founding practice for LGBT and left movements in Peru and Latin America in general. In 1982 Oscar Ugarteche wrote "Sobre los

Movimientos de Liberación Homosexual en América Latina," a manifesto that founded MHOL.[18] LIFS has circulated its own manifesto, titled "The Desire that Runs through Our Bodies and Latin America Is Possible!!!"[19] and holds meetings with other groups to discuss it. Polemical conversations have strengthened relationships with groups such as PachaAlterna, a radical student group in Lima. Furthermore, each discussion has informed revisions to the manifesto. At the VII Encuentro Lésbico-Feminista de Latinoamerica y el Caribe, in Santiago, Chile, in February 2007, LIFS prepared a bulletin including the manifesto-in-process and held a workshop to discuss it. The workshop opened a space for the give and take of ideas and sharing of information, political insights, and concerns at a regional level.

Given LIFS's emphasis on the identity category of lesbiana feminista, its manifesto is surprisingly deconstructivist in its politics. It militates against structural and cultural exploitation and dares to dream past the categories and barriers that limit emancipatory thought. "Because we live in a dictatorship of machismo, misogyny and lesbophobia, we have the legitimate right to defend ourselves and to be insurrectionary: going out into the streets and refusing to cook without any pay, raise children without social security, have sex without pleasure or get pregnant without choice."[20]

Although LIFS doesn't embrace the fluidity of sexual identities, it does engage in the deconstruction of society and the symbolic order that queer politics promotes. The last lines of the manifesto embody the desire to transgress. "We are committed to filling all public space with color, images, messages and love, to kiss with pride, to practice the sports that we want, just as we are committed to directing the State, the political parties and our lives. We create the conditions for women to determine their own identities and find their own well-being."[21]

LIFS's manifesto continues to shift to more fully express the desires and hopes of those engaged in it. As their manifestos illustrate, LIFS and the writing collaborative aim to radically transform society, which drives them to straddle essentialist and deconstructivist tendencies.

Conclusion

This virtual dialogue examines how two distinct groupings of feminist activists might negotiate the tension between essentialist and deconstructivist approaches to making identity claims, naming themselves, and struggling for visibility on their own terms. By using a friendship model for feminist solidarity attentive to the network of relationships through which people form their identities, this dialogic analysis attunes itself to the logics behind the words.

Following Quiroga's suggestion to "privilege the network of relationships that will allow subjects to construct their identity" (Quiroga 2000, 17) enables the sharing of histories and struggles. This exploration brings light to how each group negotiates the tension between tightening and loosening identity categories, how they strategize for visibility, and how they express desires and visions through manifestos.

This virtual dialogue visits the sticking points between queer/lesbiana feminist movements in the Américas. Although fundamental disagreements exist, when we can come to know each other in ways that are accountable to relations of power, we can respectfully challenge each other to shift and grow. Even when doing this, we fight, disagree, and sometimes break up. We continually construct our utopian futures in the present despite the difficulty of forging and sustaining such alliances.

Between the collaborative writing group in Santa Cruz and LIFS in Lima, I found a network of relationships that has allowed me to construct and sustain myself. Over the years, I have sought refuge in these spaces and offered strength when others find themselves struggling. Inspired by the beauty of participating in these seemingly disparate groups committed to survival and radical transformation, this chapter reflects my own "theoretical, political, personal, and intimate" crossings (see the first introduction in this volume). The issues raised by this virtual dialogue pertain to contemporary dialogues now occurring in more "material" forms among feminist movements in the Américas.

Although *queer* has not been taken up in Peru, there are other locations, such as Puerto Rico and the Dominican Republic, in which it has found resonance. As Jossianna Arroyo notes regarding Puerto Rico, "there are some activist groups that prefer to use 'queer' or 'raro (a)' as a political term, arguing for public-social spaces for alternative sexualities, bisexualities, or to contest the clear intervention of the state in the censorship of the lives of its citizens" (Arroyo, 2006, 11). Jaqueline Polanco (2006) explains that the Dominican LGBTIR (*lesbianas, gays, bisexuales, transexuales, transgéneros, intersexuales, raras/os*) movement, in which *queer* translates to *raras/os*, holds possibilities for new solidarities and alliances across sexualities. This example illustrates a carefully negotiated discursive travel that found echo in the Dominican Republic without necessarily imposing an agenda from the north. LIFS would surely question if the Puerto Rican and Dominican lesbianas feministas feel represented and included in the use of "queer." Such dialogues and debates animated the eighth Encuentro Lesbico-Feminista de Latinoamerica y el Caribe in Guatemala in 2010. Questions of who can attend fueled divisiveness. Only biological women? Trans women? Trans men? Gender-fluid people?

Although the friendship model of feminist solidarity does not presuppose getting along all the time, it does suggest that we pay closer attention to each other's struggles, listen to each other's concerns and demands, and respect differences that are not easily comprehended. This reflection is an invitation to partake in (or incitement to continue partaking in) such historicized and contextualized dialogues with the goal of solidarity within and between queer/ lesbiana feminist movements.

Notes

1. The Diálogo Sur-Sur LGBT is an international space for LGBT people from Asia, Africa, Latin America, and the Caribbean to develop analyses and proposals to counter the multiple forms of discrimination that affect them in the context of globalization (see León and Mtetwa 2003). All translations are the author's.

2. Questions of sexuality have always been central to women of color feminist work. The use of *queer* calls for a recognition of this submerged heritage. There is much more to say about this, but to get started see Cherríe Moraga and Gloria Anzaldúa's contribution to *This Bridge Called My Back*: "We are the colored in a white feminist movement. We are the feminists among the people of our culture. We are often the lesbians among the straight" (Moraga and Anzaldúa 2002, 21).

3. Personal communication with Esther Rodríguez, LIFS member in Lima, January 2010.

4. Lucrecia Bermúdez and Luciana Padilla interviews by author, San Francisco, August 8, 2007.

5. In 1980, a Maoist organization, the Peruvian Communist Party–Sendero Luminoso, instigated an internal armed conflict. One of their strategies was to cut off the capital by bombing electricity plants to cause power outages, among other tactics.

6. Padilla interview.

7. Bermúdez interview.

8. The parties involved in the internal armed conflict included the armed forces, the Peruvian Communist Party–Sendero Luminoso, and the Movimiento Revolucionario Tupac Amaru, which was founded in 1980 and lasted until the mid-1990s.

9. GALF was reestablished in Lima in the 1990s with a focus on cultural-artistic activities. In 2001, the organization launched the online magazine *Labia*. According to Luciana Padilla, GALF did not continue community outreach programming due to the initial difficulties in dealing with class differences experienced in the 1980s (Padilla interview).

10. In comparison, in the United States there are more coalitional spaces that allow room for organizations to express their own politics. With more groups and spaces, there is less of a need to battle it out in the kind of restricted and highly charged institutionalized coalitional space that MHOL became.

11. Personal communication with Esther Rodríguez in Lima, January 2010.

12. Although the term can be used to indicate same-sex orientation, trans, and bi, it is also used by straights to affiliate themselves with antihomophobic politics (Butler 1993, 230).

13. From LIFS Boletín *Insurgencia Sexual* 1, no. 1, enero 2007. "Proponemos la insurgencia sexual como idea y acción política para enfrentar la realidad actual en nuestras países y la

region. Nuestro deseo es encender nuestros corazones y sacudir nuestros cuerpos a través de un accionar insurgente que tiene como base el diálogo y el debate de las ideas."

14. Women of Color Collaborative Writing Group, "Radical Women of Color Feminisms: The Interconnectedness of Identity Formations, Political Projects and Methodologies," roundtable opening statement, Mujeres Activas en Letras y Cambio Social conference, August 2006, UCSC.

15. Women of Color Collaborative Writing Group, "Radical Women of Color Feminisms."

16. Women of Color Collaborative Writing Group, The Lens, unpublished manifesto, UCSC, March 2005.

17. Women of Color Collaborative Writing Group, The Lens.

18. Manifesto published in Conducta Impropia, boletín 6, Lima, mayo 1993.

19. "Manifesto Insurgencia Sexual: ¡¡¡El Deseo que Recorre Nuestros Cuerpos y América Latina, es Posible!!!"

20. From LIFS Boletin Insurgencia Sexual 1, no. 1, enero 2007. "Por vivir en la dictadura del machismo, la misoginia y la lesbofobia, tenemos derecho a la legítima defensa y la insurgencia: saliendo a las calles, renunciando a cocinar sin pago alguno, a criar sin seguro social, a tener sexo sin placer y a embarazarnos sin decidir."

21. From LIFS Boletin Insurgencia Sexual 1, no. 1, enero 2007. "Nos comprometemos a llenar todo espacio público de color, mensaje, imagen y amor, a besarnos con orgullo, a practicar los deportes que nos da la gana, así como, a dirigir el Estado, los partidos y nuestras vidas. Buscamos crear las condiciones para que las mujeres puedan determinar su identidad y conseguir su propio bienestar."

CHAPTER SEVENTEEN/LEARNING FROM LATINAS/TRANSLATING
OUR BODIES, OURSELVES AS TRANSNATIONAL FEMINIST TEXT

ESTER R. SHAPIRO

The tools and terms of translation, a field of growing interdisciplinary interest, have gained attention in health and public health. The U.S. National Institutes of Health used the concept of translation to create a new "roadmap" improving application of laboratory-based research findings in clinical and community settings, particularly in addressing health disparities. The World Health Organization and the U.S. Department of Health and Human Services proposed health equity agendas calling for cross-sector partnerships and mobilization to reduce barriers and improve access to social resources determining health outcomes (Health and Human Services 2011). Partnerships generating knowledge capable of inspiring social change require new approaches that go beyond traditional one-directional translation models emphasizing expert textual authority and demanding fidelity, addressing complexities of communication and power. Issues of gender, power, and equity are especially relevant when health knowledge crosses borders dividing disciplines, cultures, professional preparations, and community roles and goals. When translating texts with potential to inform and transform, inspiring active engagement and participation in critical spheres of personal, professional, and political life, it becomes crucial to understand connections between textual translation and processes motivating transformative individual and collective action. This chapter uses reflexive ethnography (Latina Feminist Group 2001b; Nagar 2002) with organizational and textual analyses based on Paulo Freire's critical pedagogy (2000) to analyze an experience of learning from personal, textual, and political translation in practice: my Cubana Americana border-crossing journey as coordinating editor of the Spanish-language cultural adaptation of *Our Bodies, Ourselves* (*OBOS*), the influential U.S. feminist health text.

OBOS, first published in 1969, is currently in its eighth English-language edition (2011). Women throughout the world heard *OBOS* as a clarion call heralding a revolution, the first offering women accessible health information while making connections to feminist social critique and movement mobilization. The book spoke to readers' personal struggles and strivings through the power of testimonials; feminist analysis; accessible health information on forbidden topics, including abortion, contraceptives, diverse sexualities, and natural childbirth; and examples of individuals and organizations working for change. Connecting millions of women to feminist movements, *OBOS* has been deeply influential for generations of feminists. Yet few scholars have critically assessed the history, evolving textual strategies, or connections to activist projects for "one of U.S. feminism's most famous (and favorite) projects" (Davis 2007, 5).

The Boston Women's Health Book Collective (BWHBC) has supported twenty international translation projects with technical assistance and seed funding, including two Spanish-language editions, *Nuestros Cuerpos, Nuestras Vidas* (*NCNV, Our Bodies, Our Lives*, 1973 and 2000). Publication of a Spanish-language translation in 1972 coincided with international women's health and rights meetings and was distributed to emerging feminist organizations throughout Latin America. Moldering yet still cherished copies of the 1973 edition hold places of honor at documentation centers and on feminists' bookshelves, just as *OBOS* copies from early editions were valued by its many U.S. and international readers as a radicalizing text. By 1985, *OBOS* editions became more encyclopedic in length, reflecting expansion and professionalization of the U.S. women's health movement (Norsigian et al. 1999; Wells 2010) and presenting challenges for international women's organizations translating the text for very different cultural and political contexts.

The second edition of *NCNV* (2000), initiated in 1990 as a new Latin American edition, was edited by a work group of Boston Latinas which I chaired, the only translation/adaptation project coordinated from Boston. Originally translated from English to Spanish with limited cultural adaptation, the project was transformed into a transnational "trialogue" through evolving, conflictual, negotiated collaboration between three perspectives, none of them uniform. First was the English version of *OBOS* and the U.S. feminist models and methods it embodied; second, work by an editorial team of U.S. Latinas working within BWHBC, assigned to create a text for Latin America and the Caribbean; and third, texts and materials from Latin American and Caribbean feminist organizations and activists, who provided feedback on chapters and information based on local and regional work. Our Boston-based Latina editorial committee predictably experienced conflicts over national, racial, educational, and organizational positions as they shaped our view of this trialogue. Yet we shared a vision of creating a transnational text that could speak to women of Latin American and Caribbean descent, wherever in the world we found ourselves. To do so, we had to intentionally identify areas of difference and resolve conflicts, translating text addressing women's personal health while conveying culturally and politically meaningful, inspiring messages about how the region's women were transforming their lives, communities, and societies.

Using feminist ecosystemic understandings of dynamic, intersectional processes linking individual, organizational, and social change (Shapiro 2005), I apply concepts from U.S. border crossing and Third World feminisms to articulate how including U.S. Latina perspectives helped re-vision the text's relationship to both local and transnational feminist movements, creating an empowering world-traveling text, "translocating" knowledge while identifying opportunities for transformative political action. NCNV was deliberately designed to be read, interpreted, and used differently as it traveled, engaging Spanish-speaking readers in multiple spaces and building empathy, recognition, and political connections across borders. Using methods from critical pedagogy and reflexive autoethnography, I identify critical moments in our evolving editorial trialogue, assessing textual differences and confronting translational conflicts around meanings and their political locations, resulting in a transformed text. I highlight hopes that we could preserve links between textual meanings and political mobilization and heartbreaks as we discovered unanticipated barriers in navigating the politics of feminist organizing and global publishing. Exploring organizational, political, and economic/global publishing dimensions of successes and failures helps illuminate relationships between activist communications, political methods, and movements, clarifying the possibilities and challenges of translating transnational feminist organizing while locating it within highly specific place-based "cultures of politics."

U.S. Latinas come from all over Latin America and the Caribbean, representing diverse nationalities, political and economic circumstances of migration, and generations. In addition, U.S. Latinas settle in different regions, encountering divergent receiving communities, in turn creating distinctive dynamics of language, race, culture, educational, and economic opportunity within ecologies of acculturation and potential transculturation. A powerful foundation of Chicana feminist writing theorizing border-crossing consciousness and action (Sandoval 2000b; Hurtado 1996) is increasingly being expanded by

Latinas from Puerto Rico, Cuba, Central America, and Latin America (Latina Feminist Group 2001b; Lugones 2003b). Puerto Rican feminists on the island and the U.S. mainland offer especially meaningful work bridging Latin American and Caribbean-based feminist activism and U.S. Latina perspectives (Warren 2003; Shapiro 2005). U.S. Latina immigrants working as academic/activists in gender justice can make distinctive contributions in translating feminist activisms across U.S. divides of race, ethnicity, class, and educational status, while remaining associated with global Third World feminisms through connections with their nation of origin. However, border-crossing learning requires processing our own "lived experience of transnationalism," emerging from specific encounters between personal histories, academic locations, and activist roles. We strive to learn from shifting relocations as academics whose work is considered too applied or interdisciplinary; as cultural outsiders in ethnocentric U.S. feminist organizations; as women in patriarchal Latino community-based organizations; as "Third World" women whose Caribbean Spanish is found primitive by European sensibilities; and as "Latina gringas" whose Spanglish marks us as undereducated in our nations of origin's language, culture, and politics.

As academics contributing to an understanding of feminist politics in translation, our personal and disciplinary locations also offer lenses clarifying some meanings and obscuring others. I first became interested in translation as a way of understanding my intergenerational migration history within a Cuban–Eastern European–Jewish American family. My extended clan of cousins launched gender-traditional families, branding my feminist aspirations as rebelliously disloyal. Seeking to understand reproduction and transformation of gender within families, I used clinical/developmental systems psychologies with feminist sociology and community health promotion to study the construction of gendered selves through culturally grounded intergenerational family life cycle transitions as lives collide with politics and history (Shapiro, 1994a, 1994b, 1996, 2001). I bring this deeply personal, theoretical, and methodological lens to evolving understandings of my lived experience of transnationalism in cocreating NCNV, as my life and work were transformed through confrontations with shifting feminist locations of language, culture, and politics. Text and embodied relationships, organizations, and feminist movements became new reflecting mirrors, offering new ways to consider lived experiences of cultural intersections, insights that helped formulate new questions in transforming the text. This process forced me to become newly acquainted with my internalized gringa feminist self, inspired by OBOS and other feminist sources, as an immigrant adolescent. I reconnected with my long-submerged eight-year-old self, enduringly afraid to confront my Spanish-language illiteracy and enduringly loyal to unacknowledged family rules forbidding political involvement. In my academic home as a clinical psychologist, apprenticeship with OBOS and NCNV transformed my work to focus on health promotion education as a catalyst linking personal wellness, gender justice, and broader social change.

Translations toward transnational collaborations take place at shifting, specific intersections of personal, relational, and collective experiences and material circumstances. To contribute from our perspectives as U.S. Latinas, our editorial team reflected on deeply personal, political, dynamic locations and how language reflecting ideas and values might shift for audiences crossing multiple regional borders. U.S. Latina and Latin American/Caribbean feminisms share approaches to grassroots organizing but have different "cultures of politics," linking individual women, activist organizations, and global movements for gender justice and social change (Alvarez 1998b). Interdisciplinary, comparative perspectives highlighting complexities of Latina experience in transnational settings help address intersections of gender, class, race, language, and ethnicity as sites of oppression and as powerful resources for resistance. Working in coalitions or partnerships, recognizing differences while sharing goals for gender equity, requires "strategic reflection" (Shapiro and Leigh 2005) capable of moving between intimate politics of personal experience and structural politics of social action as evoked by specific project goals and organizational contexts. Latin American, Caribbean, and U.S. women of color feminisms, systematically theorizing border-crossing consciousness and applying participatory methods within activist networks, were crucial to our learning from intersections of immigrant lives and activist texts, helping us construct a Latina working group linking personal and social change. These relationships, dialogues, and reflections on border-crossing political practices became embodied in a transformed text.

Our Bodies, Ourselves *across Cultures and Generations*

OBOS emerged from feminist consciousness-raising approaches to activism. A group of twelve young feminists met at a 1969 Boston workshop titled "Women and Their Bodies" and formed a mutual education group to prepare women's health materials they could share. Participants explored their own experiences, conducting research while critically examining sources, generating knowledge whose embodied intimacy, clarity, and feminist politics offered a compelling alternative to medicalized patriarchal discourse on women's health. OBOS offered multivocal personal testimonials, accessible information about women's health and reproduction, a powerful feminist critique of patriarchal health systems and political economics of health, and resource bibliographies with connections to feminist activists working to transform health and social contexts. Initially through feminist networks, and subsequently through commercial publication and distribution, the book became a friend and guide to millions of women who did not (yet) consider themselves feminists but wanted to understand themselves within profound social transformations. Because publication coincided with international meetings in women's health and rights, the book quickly circulated globally, first in English and later through translation/ cultural adaptation projects as women's organizations emerged to address gender inequality in specific local contexts. Among these was *Nuestros Cuerpos, Nuestras Vidas* (1973), a direct translation of the 1972 edition into Spanish distributed throughout the United States, Latin America, and the Caribbean, which in both the original English and the Spanish translation became highly influential in Latin American activism.

As U.S. feminisms achieved recognition and growing professionalization, scholars, policy makers, and activists began to specialize in their own spheres, and subsequent editions of *OBOS* reflected these changes. *OBOS* initially emerged from direct feminist action, but these links were later deemphasized as women entered health care and academia and *OBOS* became one book among others in the women's health marketplace it helped create (Wells 2010). Yet precisely this link between activism and knowledge captivated our attention as Latinas learning how Latin American and Caribbean feminist movements approached women's health and rights as vehicles for social change. The Latin American feminists we encountered moved easily between academia, activist organizations, health services, and government or public policy positions, their work informed by these overlapping roles. I began to see how feminist analysis and activism, influenced by assumptions from U.S. and European feminisms, privileged professional expertise and specialization in both academics and health care.

Recent studies of *OBOS* international editions (Davis 2007) and its influence on global feminist organizations (Thayer 2000) suggest that comparative analysis further clarifies *OBOS*'s embedded methodologies. Kathy Davis argues that *OBOS* traveled cross-culturally through women's organizations embedded in very different local realities, thus avoiding the trap of "feminism-as-cultural-imperialism." Davis locates *OBOS* in U.S. second-wave feminist discourse with its vision of universal sisterhood, celebration of individuality, and emphasis on consumer activism. However, she suggests that recognizing each woman as "the ultimate authority over her own bodily experiences" subverted the North American text's authority in speaking for all women everywhere. To Davis, the process by which *OBOS* was created informed by feminist epistemology, rather than the text alone, was the inspirational traveler: "The image of a group of (lay)women collectively sharing knowledge about their embodied experiences seems to be what fired the imagination of women in different parts of the world and served as an invitation to do the same" (2007, 240). Davis concludes with a "strange feeling I can only describe as hopefulness" about U.S. feminism in translation, arguing that the process of reading collectively while challenging society's gendered structures permitted OBOS to travel. Her analysis focuses on textual strategies of feminist epistemology and oppositional consciousness, rather than connections between texts and activist communities working for political change. Historically, connections between translation/adaptation projects and local feminist movements differed, as some were generated within mass-market publishing houses (i.e., European editions in the 1970s) whereas others emerged from feminist organizations using health education for social change (i.e., the South African edition, published postapartheid in 1996).

Furthermore, although OBOS successfully traveled to diverse cultural settings, knowledge gained from those travels has rarely made a return trip. Millie Thayer (2000) studied the feminist Brazilian group SOS Corpo as they encountered early editions of OBOS and perhaps the 1973 Spanish translation as well. She documented how SOS Corpo adapted OBOS methodologies of collective self-help and construction of feminist knowledge, shifting emphasis from "women and health" to "gender and citizenship." Thayer, who as an adolescent participated in BWHBC guerrilla theater on women's reproductive health, returned to Boston after completing her research. She was surprised to discover an organization unchanged by these exciting developments in Latin American and global feminism: the learning process was a one-way street. Because feminists culturally adapting OBOS must translate not only text but also women's inspirations and strategies for change in particular political and cultural contexts, international adaptation projects offer important lessons for understanding vital links between individual feminists, activist groups, and social change. Their translations can speak across cultures and generations while offering a critical lens for understanding OBOS as a product of U.S. politics and history on the return trip.

A conversation concerning cultural and political translation also took place within the collective, focused on needs of U.S. Latinas. Elizabeth McMahon Herrera, a Colombian immigrant and BWHBC founder, joined the organization in 1976 and created Amigas Latinas en Acción Pro-Salud (ALAS, Latina Friends in Health Advocacy) as a BWHBC-affiliated collective inspired by the 1973 NCNV. The group began work on a Spanish cultural adaptation for U.S. Latina immigrants. After completing a chapter on sexuality, they decided that reaching Latinas required accessible health education materials and outreach methods. Their work evolved to include conducting health promotion workshops using participatory arts, such as theater and film. ALAS critiques resulted in changes to OBOS editions, as the English text began to include more diverse women's voices, but without changing fundamental cultural and political assumptions. ALAS critiques were revisited during the NCNV translation process, as the Latina editorial group rediscovered the purpose and power of ALAS's participatory approach and made it central to reconceptualizing NCNV.

Nuestros Cuerpos, Nuestras Vidas *as an Evolving Translation Project*

The proposal for creating a new translation and culturally meaningful political adaptation of NCNV was initiated in 1990. Founding members of BWHBC conducted a workshop at the fifth Latin American and Caribbean Feminist Encuentro in San Bernardo, Argentina, seeking to identify an organization within the growing Latin American and Caribbean women's health movement to coordinate an OBOS translation/adaptation. However, no single group could undertake the project while sustaining its own work at a time of significant growth for the regional women's movement. Encuentro workshop participants proposed that BWHBC coordinate the translation/adaptation project from Boston, working with regional groups to adapt chapters in their area of activism. I first became involved in 1993, when Herrera asked me to review OBOS 1992 and suggest cultural adaptations for a Latin American edition. Considering the region's diversity, I proposed applying principles of Freire's participatory education (Freire 1994, 2000), inviting readers to complete the text by applying its tools to their own circumstances. Once the project began, I was asked to join NCNV's Editorial Committee and BWHBC's first diverse board of directors in their transition from founder-directed collective to nonprofit organization.

Beginning in September 1994, BWHBC assembled an editorial team of Boston Latinas to coordinate a cultural adaptation in collaboration with Latin American and Caribbean feminist and women's health organizations. Initially planned as a limited, two-year editorial process, NCNV took five years to complete. Furthermore, these were five tumultuous years in the BWHBC's struggles to evolve from homogeneous collective with a long, shared history of informal decision making to nonprofit organization with a racially and culturally diverse staff and board and formal structures (Main 1998; Wells 2010). NCNV became a case study for challenges of translation across not only languages but also differing personal, generational, national, and cultural visions of politics of women's lives and possibilities for social change.

Negotiating differences in political perspectives became entangled with organizational practices and power relationships that paralleled struggles for growth in other feminist organizations. The transition to a hierarchical, nonprofit organization required work plans, supervision, and accountability, as well as methods of sharing knowledge held by the highly experienced, close-knit founders with a diverse group including younger women as decision makers. This tumultuous workplace transition triggered power struggles over diversity and decision making (Main 1998), coinciding with financial crises due to diminishing royalties from book sales. The organization survived this critical transition by reaffirming the central role of OBOS and its international translation/adaptation projects in the group's identity and administration, diversifying sources of funding to include new grants and private donations, and working with a board of directors with management experience and a smaller staff.

These transitions presented significant challenges to the NCNV editorial process. However, many of the problems with the translation/adaptation project emerged from limited understanding of rigorous demands in producing high-quality translation requiring communication across distances. The work plan also required collaboration within the organization, especially documentation center librarians and staff working on international projects, yet no senior staff or any librarians read or spoke Spanish. By that time, the organization had limited funds for participation in international meetings. These were a primary focus of regional planning, especially Latin American/Caribbean participation in the 1995 UN Conference on Women in Beijing, central to training activists for regional feminist organizing (Alvarez 1998b; Petchesky 2003). Latina project directors, editors, and Latin American/Caribbean contributors working as part-time staff, volunteers, or consultants lacked necessary knowledge of how the organization's advocacy networks contributed to the considerable work of creating new OBOS editions and how those resources could support NCNV's adaptation. ALAS, experienced in translating and culturally adapting the text from its earlier history, was viewed as an outreach group whose community-based work with low-literacy Latinas was not relevant to textual adaptation. The single part-time ALAS staff member assigned to our initial NCNV Latina editorial group, along with the single Latina administrative assistant, were asked to participate without any shifts in their other responsibilities.

Organizational battles over resources and "ownership" of vision and direction affected relationships among Latinas with distinctive organizational roles, diverse nationalities, different social class and educational backgrounds, and different degrees of Spanish-language literacy. The first NCNV project director left abruptly after negotiating the initial translation. The second project director, a Puerto Rican public health activist well connected to social movements, inherited a poor translation, collaborators emphasizing medical rather than activist organizations, and a timeline that ignored major delays. The Latina editorial committee initially blamed the previous coordinator for these problems. Gradually we recognized a recurring pattern in which individual women lacking long-established knowledge and networks shared by experienced founders were hired to undertake ambitious projects with unrealistic timelines and limited funding but were expected to pour volunteer time into its completion. This strategy, problematic in volunteer activist organizations, was untenable for a nonprofit workplace striving for equity and accountability. When combined with efforts to diversify staff, these practices added a layer of unintentional, often implicit yet deeply affecting, interpersonal and institutional racism to the frustrating workplace experiences of staff members of color (Main 1998).

In this organizational context, the Latina working group experienced our own tensions concerning racial and national differences. The one part-time ALAS staff member, a community theater director and performer, resented demands made by the better-funded and -staffed NCNV project and insisted on editing only selected chapters. At first, the NCNV work group interpreted her refusal personally rather than politically and organizationally, as reflecting unacknowledged social class privilege and regional differences. Later, in a reconfigured Latina editorial group working closely with ALAS, we reinterpreted these conflicts as resulting from artificial splitting of ALAS and NCNV implicitly privileging text over outreach, high expectations relative to resources for both projects, limited organizational understanding of cultural and political dimensions in translation/adaptation, and lack of sovereignty for Latinas implementing project changes.

My dual role as member of NCNV's editorial team and its sole board member during key project and organizational transitions became a source of tremendous learning and significant tension. Latina staff and consultants on the editorial team did not have my privileged access to the organization's broader work or decision-making process, nor did they experience the same conflicts of interest resulting from my fiduciary responsibilities to the struggling organization as a whole. As our editorial group worked to address difficulties in editing a massive cultural adaptation of a complex international text, we became more aware of ways BWHBC, steeped in its shared history with OBOS, neither spoke our language nor understood our cultures of gendered lived experiences and social movement politics. As a newcomer, I lacked "insider" knowledge of informal networks and resources required in producing an OBOS edition. I constantly navigated different textual, organizational, and political cultures, moving between conversations, knowledge, and activism situated within Latin American and Caribbean feminisms, within U.S. Latina feminisms, and within English-speaking U.S. text, organizations, and feminist movements.

Only in retrospect could we see recurring patterns in which structural inequalities in distribution of material and information resources, within an organization whose values led members to deny that these inequalities existed, created double binds. Staff and founders with different locations in the organization's history and current structure contested the organization's "Good Story" (the preface title in pre-2005 editions). Some viewed it as enduringly egalitarian, others as experiencing understandable conflicts during a transition of authority, and still others as unjust and oppressive. Problems of different levels in experience, knowledge, and power were compounded by hiring women of color without consistently passing on knowledge or access to networks necessary for completing ambitious work plans. Founded as a labor of revolutionary love within the women's movement, BWHBC remained financially afloat only because founders continued to volunteer time or accept relatively modest salaries and no royalties. As BWHBC created new management structures, they discovered that competitive salaries were higher than those earned by staff/founders after decades of experience.

With the departure of two Latina project directors during the organization's crises, I became unexpectedly more involved with completing NCNV as a volunteer staff/board member and experienced my own problematic overinvestment within this role. Initially, I volunteered to work on overseeing the process and representing NCNV within BWHBC rather than editing chapters. As a U.S.-educated Cuban American, my limited Spanish literacy was inadequate to writing Latin American feminist and health texts. However, when BWHBC's financial and administrative crisis intensified my involvement in the final editorial phase, doing so forced me to face the painful sense of language loss and illiteracy in my native language, itself offering valuable insights toward a transformed text.

Creating a Transnational Trialogue in Women's Health Activism

True dialogue resulting in substantive collaboration is a gratifying, complex, potentially conflictual, and contentious process. Our trialogue between North American feminisms, U.S.-based Latina activism, and Latin American and Caribbean feminist movements required constant reflection on differences arising at multiple levels of meaning, planning, and practice. In addition to a flawed work design privileging the English-language version and its cultural assumptions, we experienced enormous barriers communicating with far-flung feminist groups politically engaged with civil wars, repressive dictatorships, and democratic transitions where gender activism played a crucial role. Some groups had only telephones, others had fax machines; a rare few had computers, but with incompatible systems and occasional lethal viruses. Latin American groups receiving poorly translated chapters and short turnaround times still succeeded in contributing substantive adaptations reflecting their extraordinary commitment to regional activism. Two Latin American groups representing different regions received each chapter, and our Boston Latina editorial group was charged with reviewing and integrating adaptations while making modest additions. We selected the brief mental health chapter adapted in Puerto Rico and Peru to evaluate our process, immediately confronting a major problem. Inviting Latin American groups to adapt translations of U.S. concepts already imposed these North American understandings, with groups reluctant to pose new questions framed by alternative perspectives. The OBOS mental health chapter was biased toward professionalized psychotherapy practice (Wells 2010), and the adaptations presented reflections on professional psychotherapy dominated by psychoanalysts in Peru and by U.S.-trained psychologists in Puerto Rico. Asked how they had chosen this relatively narrow focus, both groups responded that had we invited them to write about feminist mutual help or community activist practice, they would have written very different chapters. Without additional discussion, translated OBOS chapters imposed powerful frames within which adaptations necessarily privileged U.S. assumptions, not always explicit, favoring individualism and biomedicalization.

Perceiving critical differences in political perspectives as offering alternative pathways through the text, we changed the order of sections and chapters so that NCNV could better reflect Latin American experiences. Beginning with the 1985 edition through 2005, OBOS was organized into five sections with twenty-eight chapters, beginning with the section titled "Taking Care of Ourselves" and its first chapter, "Body Image." This section included chapters on nutrition and diet, movement and exercise, addictions, violence against women, psychotherapy, and environmental health. The next sections were "Relationships and Sexuality," "Sexual Health and Controlling Our Fertility," "Pregnancy and Childbirth," and a concluding section, "Knowledge Is Power," with chapters on health systems, organizing for change, and international feminist movements. We felt "Body Image" as an entry point lacked cultural and political congruence with Latin American experiences. We changed the order of sections so NCNV would begin with "Knowledge Is Power" and an adapted chapter on the Latin American and Caribbean feminist movements as part of global feminism.

The next major challenge for the NCNV project emerged as adaptations came in and editors alerted us to the poor quality of initial translations. Many projects underestimate the skill and time required to produce high-quality translations, especially problematic when addressing complex dynamics of gender, culture, and power. Inattention to translation quality reflected the project's marginalization when compared to OBOS's meticulous attention to accessible, inspiring language. We proposed expanding time and resources needed to in-corporate a high-quality rewrite into final editing, arguing that an accessible, inspiring voice conveying scientific information and feminist analysis was fun-damental to OBOS's methodology. With political and financial support from a newly diversified BWHBC board and executive director, we hired a gifted Puerto Rican health administrator and translator who shared our understanding of politics and translation methods to radically rewrite the text.

Bridging Latin American and U.S. Latina Audiences

From the beginning, our Latina editorial group was charged with reflecting Latin American feminist organizations and communities rather than our own border-crossing experiences. A Latin American and Caribbean edition itself presented great complexity, as each country in that region had its own rap-idly shifting political dynamics and material conditions within which women struggled for equality. However, shortly after we began our work, BWHBC was asked to create a Spanish edition for U.S. Latinas. The book *Like Water for Choc-olate* (by Laura Esquivel), thanks in part to a film by the same name (1992), had become a Spanish-language best-seller in the United States (Esquivel 1993), and publishers sought to capture that market. Enthusiastic about reaching U.S. Latinas but opposed to circulating two separate books in Spanish, we shifted to a transnational edition, using *OBOS*'s own textual strategy for addressing differences. *OBOS* speaks in the voice of a shifting editorial *we* that sometimes refers to all U.S. women, sometimes to a particular group's experience, clar-ifying the referenced *we* in specific contexts while using this rhetorical strat-egy to encourage active, critical reading of the text beyond a traditional frame (Wells 2010). We chose a similar textual strategy, with each *we* located within a specific narrative context, speaking to Latin American and Caribbean women wherever in the Americas we happened to reside, while asking readers to assess the relationship between text and their own settings. This editorial solution illustrates how a transnational approach included diasporic realities, requiring that an active reader visualize and connect to local particularities with the goal of recognizing differences and constructing deliberative forms of political sol-idarity. Once all collaborators agreed to work toward a transnational edition, we also felt freer to participate as Latinas in contributing to the text.

Proceeding with a re-visioned editorial process, we identified key organi-zations from different regions as consultants, using BWHBC's links as part of a worldwide feminist network of documentation centers. Partnering with regional centers as well as with the Latin American and Caribbean Women's Health Network, the Pan American Health Organization, and the Center for

Women's Information and Empowerment (Bolivia), which was in charge of the regional campaign for legalization of abortion, we incorporated regional materials while selecting key chapters for reorganization. We learned that Latin American and Caribbean documentation centers were frequently housed within organizations offering feminist health services using holistic, participatory methods. Often these organizations were also involved in regional activist campaigns, which leveraged UN agreements to promote women's empowerment and sovereignty in reproductive rights, often taking advantage of political transitions. Exposure to these cultures of politics and activist methods helped us revisit assumptions embedded in BWHBC's practice of positioning NCNV as more valued text, whereas ALAS was counterposed as less valued outreach.

When we began working as a Latina editorial committee, the organization saw ALAS as a participatory arts education group only relevant to low-literacy Latinas and completely independent from NCNV as a text. Once work on NCNV began, this implicit undervaluing of ALAS became more overt. NCNV was underfunded relative to the financial and social capital accrued through OBOS's thirty-year history and network of experienced contributors, but "better off" than ALAS, whose part-time staff positions were funded using modest grants from local foundations for targeted health education outreach. Just when financial and administrative crises resulted in resignation or voluntary layoffs of all Latinas on staff, BWHBC received grants for the ALAS project supporting collaboration, capacity building, and outreach to other Latina community-based organizations using a completed NCNV. The BWHBC board questioned whether any Latina project could have sufficient autonomy to ensure its integrity and doubted the organization's capacity to expand ALAS while completing NCNV at a time of crisis. I argued that by reconceptualizing ALAS and NCNV as parts of an integrated whole, we could hire a project director to design participatory education workshops while collaborating with community organizations to expand local activist networks. In this way, we could support both the text's completion and distribution.

Because NCNV was still being edited when we expanded ALAS staffing, the Latina outreach team became critical to the final editorial process. We were able to significantly revise key chapters based on feedback from community workshops, particularly the chapter on intimate relationships and sexuality, and rewrote textual transitions to highlight participatory methodologies. We re-visioned our new ALAS/NCNV work as connecting text to strategies characterizing Latin American and Caribbean women's health movements. We began to understand ALAS as introducing participatory education methods characteristic of Third World women's health movements, which lacked influence in BWHBC because of significant cultural differences in textual/political approaches. We shifted the discourse on participatory methods, giving them centrality and noting their consistency with OBOS's origins. We saw these methods as eroded through gradual, not always explicit or examined accommodation to consumerism, professionalization, and biomedicalization, as OBOS's content expanded and textual complexity increased without corresponding changes to explicitly locate the text within evolving political analysis and activist methods addressing these changes (Wells 2010). Emphasizing participatory methods helped counter U.S. publishing and media forces, which defined OBOS as just one more book among many in the crowded women's self-help marketplace, undermining its continuing revolutionary intent.

Conceptual and methodological reframing permitted us to use ALAS/NCNV outreach to incorporate work building local, national, and transnational connections between our Boston working group, an emerging U.S. movement in Latina reproductive health and rights, and growing Latin American/Caribbean feminist and women's health movements. We built a collaborative bridge between community-based participatory health education, feminist organizations working in research and policy roles, and networks connecting grassroots work with research and policy at national, regional, and international levels. The process helped us re-vision the text as embodying activist methods, images of mutually supportive relationships, and political pathways linking individual women to feminist groups and a feminist movement throughout the Americas.

Our work reconfiguring the adaptation process also drew increasingly on Latina and women of color feminist theorizing in the United States. A great deal of the literature on women's and feminists' transnational organizing emphasizes work centered in international settings rather than U.S. communities of color. However, a growing literature on Latino communities emphasizes the impact of border crossing and transnational migration experiences on U.S. Latinas (Velez-Ibanez and Sampaio 2002). Frameworks exploring transnational terrains from the standpoint of U.S. Third World communities argue for relational, process-oriented perspectives examining the historical unfolding of power relations as expressed in everyday life practices in local contexts (Naples and Desai 2002; Velez-Ibanez and Sampaio 2002). Engendering these perspectives through the study of everyday transnationalism, we could better map pathways by which women's everyday survival strategies offered opportunities for personal and collective empowerment (Shepard 2006). Transnational activism in women's health offered theory in practice supporting the articulation of linked processes of personal, organizational, and social change capable of creating "virtuous circles" expanding women's empowerment and reproductive and resource rights (Shapiro 2005).

Grounded in local partnerships, we helped create a local network, Latinas, Salud y Alternativas (Latinas, Health and Alternatives). We organized exploratory meetings in San Juan, Puerto Rico; in New York City; and at the Latin American and Caribbean Feminist Encuentro in the Dominican Republic, expanding transnational collaborations with activist organizations for book distribution while exchanging ideas with groups organizing within Latin American, Caribbean, and U.S. Latina feminist reproductive rights movements. Nurturing dialogues between community-based participatory health education and activism within grassroots organizations, on the one hand, and feminists working in national, regional, and transnational forums, on the other, helped support a social change strategy using global accords on gender equality as a source of leverage, while maintaining local connections (Alvarez et al. 2003; Petchesky 2003; Vargas 2003; Gonzalez 2010). Members of our work group visited Taller Salud in Puerto Rico and its documentation center during family trips to the island. Nirvana Gonzalez, founder and director of Taller Salud's documentation center and active in the regional movement since the first encuentros, became a crucial guide to important historical, conceptual, and methodological materials. Puerto Rico has a unique location as a U.S. territory with a status many regard as reflecting colonial power inequalities. Nonetheless, Puerto Rican feminists had independent ties to US, Caribbean and Latin American movements, uniquely positioning them to inform transcultural adaptation. Most Latinas on the editorial team were Puerto Rican– or Caribbean-born and -identified, and we began to examine regional tensions between more theoretically oriented Southern Cone feminist writings and works emphasizing participatory methods emerging from other regions and better addressing regional ethnic and racial diversities.

Finally, our Latina working group felt a deep respect and sense of responsibility to BWHBC, its founders, and OBOS history as transformative text. Our trialogue referenced 1992 and 1998 OBOS editions, while engaging founders who remained active in both the organization and in editorial updates to expand our understanding of their history and purpose. Individually and collectively, founders were unfailingly supportive of our work and generous in reflecting on emerging questions. As the group continued to struggle with its transition to a diverse, nonprofit organization, all of us had high hopes for NCNV as a vehicle for expanding the vision and inclusiveness of BWHBC's work. Yet supporting collaboration and equity in principle does not necessarily translate into reflection on organizational practices implicitly or inadvertently protecting a privileged status quo. Women of color usually entered as younger, less experienced staff, making it difficult for them to challenge organizational practices undermining their work. My own privileged position as an academic who earned my salary elsewhere and experienced support from diverse intellectual and activist networks outside the organization offered resources for critical reflection unavailable to other women of color.

Once NCNV neared completion, the power dynamics in an organization whose influence came from publishing a famous text began to change. Latinas were no longer represented by a relatively devalued, underfunded theater arts group for low-literacy women. We were now represented by and representing a text viewed as a major product of the BWHBC. As the organization continued to struggle to expand funding sources and staff diversity, NCNV as a Latina/ Latin American text was featured in proposals and publicity. Furthermore, because our editorial work had required systematic reflection on textual and political strategies embodied in the two texts, we were informed critics of the English-language edition. During the editorial phase, we conducted critiques in house in consultation with founders, feeling a responsibility to preserve fundamental OBOS principles in its trialogue with Latina and Latin American feminisms. As we completed the text and planned the next steps, we moved into more contentious areas of strategies for NCNV publicity, including explicit references to differences between NCNV and OBOS as texts.

Text as Culturally Embodied Relationships in Practice

The final phase of cultural adaptation built on these steps toward textual revisioning, in which the initial plan asking Latin American groups to respond to North American chapters was problematized, and the trialogue generating the book's voice, imagery, and politics shifted its center of gravity to privilege Latin American, Caribbean, and U.S. Latina perspectives. We made some key translation decisions emphasizing mutual help over individualism and professionalism, including translating self-help as ayuda mútua (mutual help) (because no one takes care of themselves by themselves) and self-esteem as amor propio (self-love). We also reframed the individualistic "You have the right to take care of yourself" with the more culturally congruent "You can't take care of others if you don't also take care of yourself."

Probably the most radical rewriting resulted from questioning the total absence of religion and spirituality in the English-language edition, resulting in two major changes in NCNV. First, we used the holistic health chapter to bridge sections on individual health and critiques of biomedicalization in health services, using imagery, poetics, and activist examples based on indigenous health and spirituality throughout the region. Second, we used work by Católicas por el Derecho a Decidir (Catholics for Free Choice) within the abortion chapter to locate reproductive choices as arduous ethical decisions made by so many of the world's women as they evaluated under what circumstances they could best care for the lives they were responsible for, present and future. Women in the region were willing to risk an illegal abortion and potential death or incarceration, rather than bring a child into the world when they could not take care of it. Invoking difficult reproductive choices made by poor women all over the world and rights not just to choose abortions but to receive society's support in bearing and raising healthy children and families offered an ethical framework more consistent with broader social justice movements and U.S. women of color reproductive justice movements (Silliman et al. 2004).

In the final editorial phase, we used participatory pedagogy principles to ensure that testimonials of lived experience, knowledge based on critical perspectives, and action based on personal reflection and solidarity were culturally meaningful and inspiring. We added poetry to key passages, drawing from rich traditions of regional women writers speaking eloquently of struggles and transcendence. We regarded book and section introductions as strategic thresholds, inviting readers into shared conversations. The text moved from women's testimonials to experientially grounded political analysis, offering inspiring visions of activists in practice. In a textual embodiment of NCNV's own "Border-Crossing Story," we reflected on our shared learning as a transformative journey toward wholeness with political, spiritual, and healing dimensions. NCNV also includes extensive resource bibliographies of publications and exemplary Latin American, Caribbean, and U.S. groups and programs. Finishing the book, our ALAS/NCNV understanding of its embodied methods moved us to reimagine our border-crossing text as nurturing relationships and supporting transnational movements for gender justice. We believed learning from the transnational work would inform the organization on our return trip.

Challenges to Transnational Collaboration

As we began publicity, we entered two more contentious and publicly visible arenas: the role of ALAS/NCNV participatory education and organizing methods within the larger organization's priorities and critiques of OBOS implicit in comparisons with NCNV, which appeared in publicity for the new book. Founders experienced in dealing with antifeminist media backlash worried that direct criticism of OBOS could be used to undermine both projects. I was concerned that limited critical engagement with diverse women's changing life circumstances distanced new generations and communities of women. Our ALAS/NCNV publicity proposals emphasized campus/community connections and outreach not just "for Latinas only." With NCNV's successful launching and commendations for the adaptation, I became increasingly invested (and overinvested) in NCNV's potential as a tool that might increase BWHBC's commitment to participatory methods and transnational collaborations.

Our ALAS/NCNV group envisioned the text as a tool for feminist movements organizing in Latin American, Caribbean, and U.S. Latina communities, whose vision it reflected. We hoped to build on the extraordinary media access OBOS enjoyed as a U.S. feminist icon, provoking curiosity in both U.S. and Latin American media about Latina/Latin American feminisms. We also hoped to leverage the impact of NCNV's publication to incorporate participatory methods into BWHBC's work for strategic planning. Unfortunately, we confronted more unyielding barriers in this phase. Our Latina work group couldn't persuade an organization highly experienced with English-language book publicity that Spanish-language readers required different publicity and outreach strategies. Furthermore, we lacked power to implement methods for publicity and distribution as part of systematic political organizing strategies. Finally, our lovingly crafted transnational edition collided with realities of Latin American and Caribbean book publishing and distribution, still dominated by publishing in Spain.

Differences in how we and BWHBC founders understood the political opportunities presented by a book tour were intensified by changes in economics and the politics of globalized publishing and media. This was compounded by gaps in coverage of Spanish-language readers by U.S. publishers and of Latin American and Caribbean readers by their European counterparts. These converging realities created significant barriers to implementing plans using NCNV as a means to support feminist organizations and movements. Part of OBOS's enormous power as an accessible feminist text emerged from endorsement by mainstream media, which brought it to women not otherwise reached by feminist organizations. Our ISIS International collaborators in Chile, whose center housed a feminist communications network, believed the timing was right for commercial publication. Emerging at a critical juncture in the region's changing political, economic, and gender landscapes, NCNV could offer feminist tools as women confronted contradictory demands for employment within changing economies and enduring sexism, paralleling U.S. women's dilemmas in the early 1970s to which OBOS so eloquently spoke. Regional feminist communications networks could use NCNV to insert reproductive health and rights into public conversations, expanding dialogues connecting private endorsement of reproductive choice with political campaigns for legalized abortion (Lamas 2002).

A commercial publishing contract opened access to mainstream media, but the economics and politics of global publishing created tremendous obstacles for U.S. sales and insurmountable barriers for Latin American distribution.

Simon and Schuster, profiting from millions in OBOS sales but fearing losses on their Spanish-language imprint, refused to publish NCNV unless OBOS royalties covered all costs. Random House, then involved in multiple mergers, contracted NCNV then canceled during production, further delaying publication. Seven Stories Press published NCNV to inaugurate their Spanish-language publications, hiring an experienced Latin American editor but lacking any other staff, from typesetters to publicists, who understood Spanish or appreciated the need for culturally tailored publicity. In the United States, NCNV received favorable national media and solid sales for U.S. Spanish-language publishing. Like OBOS, the Spanish text is available to clinics for substantial discounts, providing accessible distribution beyond individual book sales. BWHBC hoped Latinas would distribute the book through feminist networks, but neither bookstores nor feminist networks operate in the same way in reaching U.S. Spanish-language readers.

NCNV's Latin American distribution required a publisher with rights in Latin America, as U.S. publishers are heavily taxed and lack regional distribution. Unfortunately, Seven Stories Press sold the foreign rights to Debate, a Barcelona-based publisher owned by Plaza & Janes with no experience selling women's health or self-help books. In earlier drafts, I titled this chapter "'Your Spanish Is too Caribbean, Strange to the Sensibilities of Western Thought': A U.S. Latina Lens on Hope and Heartbreak in Translating *Our Bodies, Ourselves* as a Transnational Feminist Text." I quoted the Debate editor's memorandum listing changes to the NCNV Latin American edition for a Spanish audience, who they claimed would be mystified by references to primitive religions and offended by ungrammatical Spanish. We were dismayed to learn that due to international publishing laws compounded by Spanish publishing's enduring bias against colloquial language from former colonies, our meticulous trialogue could be arbitrarily judged by editors in Barcelona as not appropriate to a First World to First World dialogue between the U.S. English-language edition and readers in Spain. Plaza & Janes's editors peremptorily reedited the Latin American edition to reflect First World women's realities in Spain. Debate editors eliminated chapters on the Latin American feminist movement, feminist critiques of health care systems, and organizing for change. They reedited others, declaring the holistic health chapter "strange to the sensibilities of Western thought" because of its reference to indigenous women's sacred healing arts.

Advised that a long, costly legal battle would not guarantee victory, we decided that lack of accessible reproductive health information in the region and intact chapters on abortion legalization, domestic violence, and AIDS justified proceeding with publication. Sadly, the revised "First World" edition was neither well promoted nor widely distributed in Spain or Latin America. Legal limits on Latin American distribution of the U.S. edition remained a significant barrier to NCNV reaching its intended audience. Given changing global politics of gender inequality and economic marketplaces, our goal to position NCNV in the public eye as an inspiring reflection of regional feminisms and an accessible vehicle for personal empowerment and gender equality required thoughtful strategies. In both U.S. and Latin American settings, partnerships between college students, university professors, and community-based organizations suggest such possible strategies.

In the absence of feminist networks in the United States to build political capacity, a traditional book tour was not effective. However, campus visits organized by women's studies and women's health faculty activists suggested an alternative approach through which NCNV could become a catalyst to build networks, organizational capacity, and campus–community collaborations. On some campuses, like the University of Wisconsin, Madison, or San Diego State University, Latina students planned annual conferences connecting students, faculty, and staff with families and communities, offering opportunities for student leadership development and mentorship through empowering educational programs. At other locations, women's studies, women's health, and public health programs housed feminist faculty who brought NCNV to their campuses for academic presentations on NCNV's cultural adaptation, using the opportunity to connect with colleagues in other academic programs and community women's health providers and activists.

The Latin American and Caribbean Women's Health Network (RSMLAC), with its program Universidad Itinerante (Itinerant University), offers another model of educational outreach deliberately structured to raise consciousness and create strategic alliances between campus and community activists. RSMLAC is a regional coordinating network of organizations, networks, and individuals producing published materials and promoting activist campaigns in women's health and human rights, especially sexual and reproductive rights (Gonzalez 2010). Since 1998, RSMLAC has offered international courses on "Gender Perspectives in Health" as part of a regional Universidad Itinerante. This educational initiative pairs a local university's gender studies program with at least one local feminist organization to work with RSMLAC's regional experts in developing week-long intensive courses linking campus and community participants from different sectors in addressing areas of shared concern. The program strengthens the capacity of both organizations to develop women's leadership in policy and governance, while establishing stronger local connections to regional campaigns. The ways academic activists in the global South create value with far more limited resources became part of the inspirational message we sought to communicate across borders.

We began work with RSMLAC exploring ways to use Universidad Itinerante's model in building connections between universities and U.S. Latina organizations. This collaboration proved complex due to significant differences in "translating" feminist organizations across borders. National U.S. Latina feminist organizations working on reproductive rights have historically lacked support from white feminist organizations and Latino organizations reluctant to address abortion rights. Our NCNV U.S. launch in 2000 had been planned with the National Latina Institute for Reproductive Health, then based in Washington, and its Latina summit planned for September 2000, but the organization abruptly closed for lack of funds. The institute reorganized in New York, focused on developing local grassroots leadership supporting Latina reproductive rights. U.S. Latinas in politically influential positions rarely connect to local grassroots reproductive rights organizing. Many Latina leaders find that feminist organizations remain predominantly white, and male-dominated Latino organizations fear alienating religious constituencies. We remain hopeful that campus–community partnerships offer spaces for developing Latina leadership incorporating gender perspectives on "undivided rights."

Translocation Lessons Learned

Latina re-visionings and lessons described in this final section remain works in progress. Our Latina lens on transnational collaborative processes, emphasizing participatory methodologies, helped transform NCNV as text. However, we encountered many barriers in translating participatory methods systematically linking text to women of color movements organizing for reproductive justice. For BWHBC's 1999 strategic planning process, our NCNV working group organized a panel in which women of color shared strategies for participation in cross-racial community organizing. We suggested that OBOS could be updated with lessons learned from NCNV by shifting emphasis from text to participatory methodologies, systematic community outreach, and coalition building, using new opportunities afforded by new technologies. The South African Women's Health Project, whose visually beautiful and pedagogically accessible book based on OBOS provided an inspiring example of cultural adaptation, chose not to publish a second edition as an encyclopedic text, instead focusing on locally adaptable materials useful in politically empowering health promotion workshops. The 2005 edition of OBOS made significant changes toward a more accessible book, which were taken even further in the 2011 edition. For the first time, OBOS includes sidebars featuring the work of the global translation/adaptation projects, including NCNV's use of Catholics for Free Choice to frame an ethical stance on abortion. NCNV remains useful to U.S. Latina organizations, supported by an online public health curriculum for *promotoras* (health educators), and to Latin American and Caribbean organizations. As a bridge for transnational organizing, NCNV remains a thwarted promise and hopeful possibility.

In sum, this chapter recounts steps in the transcultural transformation of a U.S. activist text through remapped relationships linking women's lives, feminist organizations, and social movements across different cultures of politics. Our Latina work group's critical engagement with OBOS as historically and politically located, by sharing reflections with each other, with Latin American and Caribbean collaborators, and through texts and works representing their movements, helped clarify cultural misunderstandings while shifting power differentials. We identified commonalities while recognizing differences in NCNV's border-crossing story. Continuing work leveraging NCNV's potential usefulness toward transnational collaborations requires appreciating vulnerabilities and celebrating persistence among all partners in the trialogue. With a culturally transformed text as meeting point, NCNV's embodied methods can illuminate and inspire new coalitions building on opportunities for mutual learning and constructed solidarities. Appreciating the power of feminist organizations to multiply individual efforts, I participate in Latin American/ Caribbean feminist networks and in local and national Latina and multiracial reproductive rights networks, each offering a window onto the other. I have learned from productive conflicts between Haitian and Dominican women at the 1999 Dominican Republic Encuentro confronting issues of discrimination, language, and citizenship; from voices of new generations, diverse sexualities, and diaspora women at the 2003 Costa Rican Encuentro; and from indigenous women on preserving cultural traditions while promoting gender equity at the 2009 Mexican Encuentro. I share transnational lessons learned with diverse, predominantly immigrant students as a teacher in an urban public university, helping them appreciate how life experiences can connect to and inform movements for social change. Traveling with *Our Bodies, Ourselves* and *Nuestros Cuerpos, Nuestras Vidas,* I have learned new steps toward shared choreographies supporting change.

CHAPTER EIGHTEEN/WOMEN WITH GUNS/ TRANSLATING GENDER IN *I, RIGOBERTA MENCHÚ*

VICTORIA M. BAÑALES

In thinking about the topic of translation in relation to I, *Rigoberta Menchú: An Indian Woman in Guatemala* (Menchú and Burgos-Debray 1984), some of the associations that might immediately come to mind are Elizabeth Burgos-Debray's manipulations and reordering of the text, or Arturo Taracena's disclosures that he, along with several others, secretly partook in some of these textual reorderings.[1] Still, for some of us, David Stoll's (1999) polemic allegations that Menchú's testimony contains factual/textual discrepancies, and the multiple discussions enabled by this controversy, may also come to mind. Then, there is the question of language and culture: Menchú is a Maya Quiché woman who provides her testimony in Spanish to a Venezuelan anthropologist (Burgos-Debray) in France. The text has since been translated into multiple languages, including the English version referenced in this chapter. The fact that the text was originally an oral project that was later edited and transcribed by another (or others) also raises issues and questions about its multilayered translation and production process. These issues and more highlight the way in which this text, perhaps more so than others, has been heavily marked by a series of polemical and unresolved translation dilemmas.

However, I am not primarily interested in delving into these types of translation issues, many of which have already been extensively written about. Instead, I am more interested in a different type of translation issue, one that deals with I, *Rigoberta Menchú*'s rich gender representations, which, judging from the available critical literature, appear to have been lost in translation. A main concern of this chapter, then, revolves around a different type of translation or mistranslation issue: the alarming lack of gender analyses in relation to this book. For example, although hundreds of articles and dozens of important anthologies and books have been produced on *I, Rigoberta Menchú*, only a very small handful of scholars have drawn attention to the text's representations of gender (see, e.g., Marín 1991; Sternbach 1991; Bueno 2000; Matthews 2000). The more widely anthologized and influential critics, though not denying their exceptional and timely contributions, read *I, Rigoberta Menchú* as representative of a racial, ethnic, national, cultural, and/or class-based "collective" community at the expense of gender and sexuality.[2] More often than not, the tendency is to read and interpret the book's textual representations of Maya women's revolutionary efforts as emblematic of "collective" indigenous resistance struggles at large while ignoring the ways these women participate as explicitly gendered ethnic subjects.

Several important questions arise. Why are ethnicity, culture, class, and other categories of difference readily translatable and gender is not? What accounts for this imbalance? Is it that gender differences are not emphasized enough in *I, Rigoberta Menchú*? Or is it our own personal reluctance as critics to deal with gender in our scholarly renderings of this particular text? Does the text somehow impede a feminist, gender analysis? Is there something about Menchú's *testimonio* that makes gender untranslatable? Is it the text (or our readings and interpretations of it) that makes gender untranslatable, particularly when Menchú repeatedly echoes a "communal" and "collective" struggle? Are gender and "collective" indigenous struggles of resistance irreconcilable, making it impossible to link them? After all, one could argue, the text speaks for a collective community inclusive of "all poor Guatemalans" (Menchú and Burgos-Debray 1984, 1).

While not denying these important communal dimensions, this chapter demonstrates that gender and sexuality relations are deeply central to the text —from the military regime's sexualized forms of racial aggression against Maya peoples, to indigenous women's armed participation in the struggle for liberation and open defiance of the Ejército's violent enforcement of racialized gender codes. In an assessment that rethinks notions of collectivity and difference, I argue that Maya women participate in the revolution not simply as ethnic selves but as gendered ethnic subjects whose status as "women" in fact fuels their collective struggles of resistance. Furthermore, as indigenous women take up arms, guns acquire new gendered meanings and cultural significations that move beyond traditional representations of militaristic, phallic weapons of destruction. As I show, indigenous women's revolutionary struggles in *I, Rigoberta Menchú* openly defy and challenge dominant racialized gender and sexuality discourses that represent indigenous women as essentially passive, penetrable, and apolitical. When I refer to "women with guns" (or "men with guns," for that matter), I am referring not only to real, historical bodies and weapons but also their metaphorical significations, which include all forms of women's participation in the (traditionally male) realms of politics and war.[3] I contend that not engaging in an intersectional analysis inclusive of gender and sexuality occludes many important aspects of I, Rigoberta Menchú, leaving us with partial and single-sided — and to a certain extent misguided antiracist and paternalistic — understandings of this very important text.

What is it that makes the text's gender representations seemingly inaccessible or untranslatable? Why the shortage of gender analyses? Is it the testimony's "collective" emphasis that impedes the translation of gender? While not denying the larger, collective dimensions of testimonios — most testimonios do literally and figuratively claim to represent larger communities — this tendency of overemphasizing plurality or collectivity, as Eva Paulino Bueno (2000) adroitly observes, often effectively serves as a means of brushing gender questions aside. She writes, "The study of testimonies has become the construction of a form that, on the one hand, effaces the individuality and the gender of its authors and, on the other, promotes their identity exclusively as representatives of their communities" (2000, 119). Part of the problem no doubt stems from the false opposition set up between dominant notions of collectivity (as the forgoing of difference) and difference (as the forfeiting of collectivity). The importance of dispelling this false binary logic cannot be overstated. To treat the collective as if it is irreconcilable with gender differences is to ignore the gendered inflections that shape Menchú's collective account. As feminist critics remind us, sameness (community, collectivity) and difference (gender) are not mutually exclusive categories, and, as such, it is at once possible to read Menchú's testimonio as emblematic of a larger community that is also specific to Maya women's issues.[4] For instance, although I, Rigoberta Menchú presents us with a collective history of "all poor Guatemalans" (Menchú and Burgos-Debray 1984, 1), the text nonetheless makes sharp distinctions between the lives of indigenous men and women in the war-torn region of El Quiché. To cite a specific example, whereas Menchú's account shows the ways in which entire Maya communities (men and women) are heinously tortured and violated, the text is more than explicit in pointing to the ways rape primarily occurs along gendered lines, a context in which male ladino or ladinizado soldiers forcefully rape indigenous women, often impregnating and even murdering them. As Menchú explains, "when soldiers come to our area they usually catch girls and rape them — they don't care who they are or where they're from" (Menchú and Burgos-Debray 1984, 137).

Notwithstanding the centrality of these kinds of representations, gender remains a fleeting and untranslatable category in most renderings of the text. By not addressing gender or sexuality, such analyses ignore the ways gender and sexuality are always informed by and intersect with other categories of difference. As Lynda Marín writes, reading Latin American women's testimonial texts "requires us to see that gender . . . is a critical instrument in the rewriting of that history in which these testimonials are embedded" (1991, 58). Such a reading, she continues, entails negotiating and straddling (rather than polarizing) "this tension [between] Latin American women's testimony['s] . . . stated project—to speak in a unified way for a people in struggle—and its unstated project—to do so in a way that negotiates truthfully among the various positions of inequality that women occupy in their cultures—which pervades this writing and most curiously marks it" (Marín 1991, 55). Recognizing and naming this productive site of "tension"—as opposed to ignoring or inadequately dealing with it—permits us to move away from overarching critical analyses of I, Rigoberta Menchú that erase or neutralize gender difference. As Bueno states, "these women speak out not simply as political beings, but as female beings from a specific culture" (2000, 130). Bueno's ideas call for a situated knowledge approach, one in which we are invited to look more closely at Menchú's culture, history, positionality, location, and so on to avoid producing an overarching analysis that might unintentionally erase important differences. By the same token, Marín highlights the ways in which "Latin American women's testimonials bring back women's bodies, which have been, if it's possible, doubly disappeared, to the field of humanity. In the reading of these testimonials, it is the subjectivity of women, rooted as it is in women's bodies and women's experience that mediates what we hear, see, feel, know" (1991, 59). This is not to suggest a natural essence (biological or otherwise) to the lived experiences of women (or men). Indeed, as feminist critic Joan W. Scott (1992) reminds us, experience, too, is in and of itself always ideologically and discursively constructed. Nonetheless, testimonial subjects do encompass gendered subjectivities, and generally speaking, their identities, voices, experiences, viewpoints, and realities will be discursively, ideologically, and historically shaped by the particular genders in which they are socially and culturally located.

Although these feminist theoretical observations are useful in shedding some light on the "overwhelming disdain of gender" (Bueno 2000, 131) we encounter in scholarly analyses of I, Rigoberta Menchú, these discussions still do not adequately explain why, at times, even some feminist critics have resisted or shied away from performing a substantial gender analysis of the text. For example, renowned feminist scholars like Doris Sommer (1996), Mary Louise Pratt (1996, 2001), or Stacey Schlau (1996) have produced excellent and thought-provoking essays on Menchú's testimonio, touching on themes of language, discourse, community, power, and resistance, but their works nonetheless sidestep the issue of gender. By the same token, while Nicaraguan feminist writer Ileana Rodríguez (1996, 2001) critically analyzes representations of Salvadoran revolutionary women's gender transgressions in her readings of Claribel Alegría's *They Won't Take Me Alive* (Alegría and Flakoll 1987), she avoids performing the same kinds of gender readings in her analysis of *I, Rigoberta Menchú*. It is imperative to ask why the representations of gender differences in *They Won't Take Me Alive* become readily transparent and translatable while *I, Rigoberta Menchú*'s extensive attention to gender differences becomes lost in translation.

In assessing this critical inattention to gender, I choose to think of these omissions as political deliberations rather than gross oversights. For one, it can be argued that *I, Rigoberta Menchú* is a text that can be perceived as problematic for some feminist critics. Although the text's representations undeniably reflect an autochthonous, revolutionary feminist praxis, it can hardly be labeled "feminist" (at least not by Western, "First World," metropolitan standards), and Menchú herself is highly critical of Western forms of liberal feminism, even though, properly speaking, she does not specifically name them as such. Furthermore, although feminists may rejoice at the text's representations of revolutionary indigenous women—described as courageous, defiant, and brave, often even more so than their indigenous male counterparts—they may find themselves less enthused or deeply at odds with other textual moments in which gender relations are less favorably represented. For example, Menchú's descriptions of Maya gendered cultural roles and forms of male privilege within her community are, perhaps, representations with which scholars championing the text might prefer not to engage. By the same token, although machismo is critiqued in the text, it is at times done insufficiently, quite often explained as a nontroubling aspect within the community or a cultural, ancestral phenomenon that simply is.

To provide a textual example of this, in "Birth Ceremonies" (chapter 2), Menchú describes the ways an indigenous boy's birthing ceremony, unlike that of a girl, includes an extra day of rituals:

> When a male child is born, there are special celebrations, not because he's male but because of all the hard work and responsibility he'll have as a man. It's not that *machismo* doesn't exist among our people, but it doesn't present a problem for the community because it's so much part of our way of life. The male child is given an extra day alone with his mother. The usual custom is to celebrate a male child by killing a sheep

or some chickens. Boys are given more, they get more food because their work is harder and they have more responsibility. At the same time, he is head of the household, not in the bad sense of the word, but because he is responsible for so many things. This doesn't mean girls aren't valued. Their work is hard too and there are other things that are due to them as mothers. Girls are valued because they are part of the earth, which gives us maize, beans, plants and everything we live on. The earth is like a mother which multiplies life. So the child will multiply the life of our generation and of our ancestors whom we must respect. The girl and the boy are both integrated into the community in equally important ways, the two are inter-related and compatible. Nevertheless, the community is always happier when a male child is born and the men feel much prouder. (Menchú and Burgos-Debray 1984, 14)

Whereas male newborns in these birthing rituals are associated with respon-sibilities of hard work outside the home, females are associated with mother-hood and birthing. According to the rituals, men's labor is what marks men as different from women. As Menchú explains, it is not that men are valued (or, conversely, that women are devalued) for their gender per se but that men's lives to a certain extent will be hard(er); as such, the ceremony of boys requires an additional day of rituals and more food to compensate for the extra hardships that await men in life. Furthermore, these traditions, Menchú notes, are in ac-cordance with Maya Quiché customs, which must be respected. To this, she adds, machismo is not seen as a grave problem within the community "since we must take our customs into account" (The original Spanish version reads: "no es tanto que el machismo no exista, pero no es un elemento dificultoso en la comunidad ya que de hecho vamos a tomar en cuenta las costumbres"; Menchú and Burgos-Debray 1985 [1983], 35, translation mine). Elsewhere in the text Menchú likewise says: "In our culture we often treat the man as something different—the woman is valued too, of course—and if we do things we must do them well. First because they are our men, and second, because it's a way of encouraging them, in the same way our ancestors did for their men" (Menchú and Burgos-Debray 1984, 214). Although she is quick to note that women are also highly valued and esteemed, Menchú's commentary nonetheless points to an ancestral cultural norm in which men are attributed special status by virtue of being different. As she explains, "it is a special stimulus that our ances-tors also had towards men" ("En segundo lugar porque es un estímulo espe-cial que tenían también nuestros antepasados hacia el hombre"; Menchú and Burgos-Debray 1985 [1983], 239, translation mine). For some feminist critics, these types of commentaries will surely raise eyebrows. How do we translate and interpret this text which, on the one hand, represents indigenous women as heroic participants in the struggle, yet on the other hand seems to accept machismo and other forms of male privilege within the community?

It is important to note that Menchú's explanations as to why men are afforded special status in her community, particularly with regard to the birthing ceremonies, do not take into account the ways the implementation of a sexual division of labor—whereby indigenous men are relegated to the work sphere and indigenous women tend to the family—directly participates in a socially constructed gendering process that ascribes different roles and value systems to men and women. Furthermore, a close reading of I, *Rigoberta Menchú* suggests that indigenous women's lives are no less difficult than men's—in fact, at times, women are represented as having it much harder. For example, the text describes how indigenous women must not only attend to the family and home but also work alongside indigenous men in the *fincas*, often carrying small children on their backs and nursing in between work intervals. Even when pregnant, "women go on working just as hard in the fields" (Menchú and Burgos-Debray 1984, 10). Menchú further elucidates: "Women work and are exploited as well. Women work picking coffee and cotton, and on top of that, many women have taken up arms and even elderly women are fighting day and night" (Menchú and Burgos-Debray 1984, 221). In fact, at one point Menchú's heavy labor is such that she says, "I was like a boy, chopping wood with an axe, or with a machete" (Menchú and Burgos-Debray 1984, 43). In yet another section she says, "My work was almost the same as my father's" (Menchú and Burgos-Debray 1984, 194). Indeed, when we take women's labor (within and outside the home) into account, the separation between male versus female forms of labor and the different value systems ascribed to these in the birthing ceremonies become highly contradictory. Likewise, if we look at other aspects of indigenous women's lives as represented in the text—for instance, the high mortality rate of children, the deep suffering of mothers, rape and other forms of sexual violence against women by military men—notions of male versus female "hardship" prove highly problematic and deeply relative.

For First World metropolitan feminist readers, representations like these, in which gender contradictions are paramount, will no doubt occasion certain levels of discomfort, proving challenging or difficult for scholars who, on one hand, want to critique and draw attention to the patriarchal tendencies within these customs, yet, on the other hand, would like to do so in a way that respects Maya worldviews and cultural differences. Might it be easier to ignore these types of gender contradictions, allowing them to remain untranslatable? Furthermore, if we take into account how these indigenous practices, traditions, ceremonies, and rituals function as powerful resistance mechanisms against assimilation or forms of cultural genocide, engaging in a gender critique of these cultural practices proves doubly challenging and risky. Perhaps this is why Menchú sometimes chooses to deemphasize the gendered aspects of these rituals, focusing instead on their deep cultural significance and historical value for indigenous survival. As scholars in solidarity with the text, then, might it not be best or more politically correct or respectful to selectively and strategically distance ourselves from engaging in gender questions, concentrating instead on other important aspects of Menchú's testimonio—this, especially given the text's larger urgent political message and our desire to support and side with it wholeheartedly? Might it not be better to leave these troublesome representations of gender aside? After all, we might add, it is well known that revolutionary organizations often asked women participants to hold their gender-related questions for a later date for the sake of the more immediate, pressing social issues. Should we not also, then, hold our own gender-related questions—for the sake of the text, Menchú, leftist revolutionary cause, or Maya Quiché culture? Certainly, too, nobody wants to risk being accused of "paternalistic" ethnocentricities, a charge Menchú already ascribes to foreign, female outsiders who come into her community advocating forms of women's liberation and other ideas that simply do not apply to the indigenous context and contemporary urgent-historical moment (Menchú and Burgos-Debray 1984, 221). Avoiding the question of gender altogether is a simple and effective way to get around these delicate cultural, historical, and textual issues while at the same time staying out of harm's way. Perhaps this explains why many scholars, including feminist critics, tend to deemphasize the text's gender aspects, focusing instead on its "collective" and broader communal dimensions.

Regardless of whether intentional strategy is at play here, such silencing creates a new set of problems. For one thing, not dealing with the issue of gender by engaging in selective (and perhaps "safer") critical readings of the text is in and of itself a reverse form of paternalism. To cite feminist critic Rey Chow, it is a kind of academic "fascist" undertaking, a type of misguided antiracism by which we project our own desires, fears, and fantasies onto the text, whereby Menchú becomes an "idealized other" (Chow 1998b, 29). Along similar lines, Bueno discusses the problematic ways that critics in the North American academy exalt texts that (to them) represent the "'natural goodness' or 'nobility' of the Indian" (Bueno 2000, 119) while rejecting other (and, as a result, less renowned) testimonial texts—for instance, Brazilian Carolina Maria de Jesus's text *Child of the Dark* (1963)—that fail to conform to or resist scholars' desires for a particular and more acceptable testimonial subject model. *I, Rigoberta Menchú* might satiate scholars' longings for "the ideal witness," "a 'communal being' who cannot set herself apart in terms of her individuality, much less her gender" (Bueno 2000, 131), but such fulfillment of desires occurs only through a selective reading process in which particular aspects of the text are exalted and other (perhaps less favorable) parts are actively repressed.

Not to be taken as a position in support of Stoll (1999), I want to make clear that mine is a critical attempt at recuperating a feminist reading of *I, Rigoberta Menchú* by translating—rather than silencing or ignoring—the complex gender representations widely discussed and elaborated by Menchú in her testimonio.[5] Certainly if we read *I, Rigoberta Menchú* in all of its complexity, especially with regard to gender, it, too, like *Child of the Dark*, fails to conform to prescribed colonial paradigms and expectations. I say *colonial* because, as Bueno observes, echoing Gayatri Spivak, "even the most committed ethnographer or solidarity worker carries with her, embedded in the very core of her intellectual project, the traces of a colonial construction of the Other" (2000, 122–23). By silencing or disavowing certain parts of Menchú's testimonio, particularly those pertaining to gender that might prove too controversial or culturally sensitive, we fail to let Menchú speak on her own terms and instead authorize ourselves to decide when and where it is appropriate for her to speak. All good intentions aside—assuming that such a selective reading process is done with the best of all intentions (i.e., to "protect" or guard the text [or ourselves] from unnecessary, harmful criticism)—we thrust Menchú into a colonial "noble savage" position, not trusting that she can hold her own ground. By the same token, we altogether miss the ways in which, even when gender contradictions arise, the text itself actively responds to, resists, complicates, or counters these same contradictions via other representations.

For example, I have already talked about the ways representations of women in the text—as mothers, exploited workers, targets of sexual violence, and so forth—override and complicate these representations, although men are represented in Maya birthing ceremonies as facing deeper hardships in life. Furthermore, even though male sons are said to be valued and privileged in the community, especially by other (adult) men, Menchú repeatedly talks about the special bond she shares with her father. "I was my father's favourite," she tells (Menchú and Burgos-Debray 1984, 52). By the same token, although boys are afforded special outdoor privileges—girls, we are told, "don't play. . . . Girls have to learn to look after things in the home, they must learn all the little things their mothers do" (Menchú and Burgos-Debray 1984, 82)—it is Menchú, rather than her brothers, who travels with her father to the capital city at a relatively young age. Menchú also reveals how, although girls are not allowed to climb trees—"mothers think it's scandalous" (Menchú and Burgos-Debray 1984, 83)—girls defy these rules when parents aren't watching. In fact, she candidly adds, "I used to like climbing to the top of trees, but only when my mother wasn't looking" (Menchú and Burgos-Debray 1984, 83). A more poignant transgression of these gendered cultural norms is Menchú's choice not to marry or bear children.[6] This decision, as well as her longings and aspirations to learn Spanish, run deeply contrary to indigenous women's maternal cultural roles as represented in the birthing ceremonies as well as elsewhere in the text where indigenous values and traditions are discussed. As Menchú says, "Knowing that I had to multiply the seed of our ancestors and, at the same time, rejecting marriage . . . that was a crazy idea" (Menchú and Burgos-Debray 1984, 224; ellipsis in original). Elsewhere in the text she adds, "I've got more or less the same attitudes as [boys] have, getting mixed up in different things in just the same ways as my brothers" (Menchú and Burgos-Debray 1984, 194).

What these examples illustrate is how the everyday material lives of indigenous women as represented in the text do not always conform to or mirror Maya Quiché gendered cultural norms and expectations. The relationship between custom and lived practice is neither linear nor transparent but represented as an ongoing, complex negotiation process wherein cultural traditions and gender roles, while maintaining the signature of an ancestral past, continuously shift according to changing historical needs. Furthermore, as violent conditions increase in El Quiché, traditional gendered cultural roles as represented in the text become less demarcated, as both indigenous men and women equally engage in collective struggles of resistance. As Sommer (1996) adroitly highlights, "the trick [in our readings of the text] is not to identify the correct discourse . . . and to defend it with dogmatic heroism, but to combine, recombine, and continue to adjust the constellation of discourses in ways that will respond to a changeable reality" (153). To this she adds: "No one ideological code is assumed to be sufficient or ultimately defensible for . . . Rigoberta . . . instead, [she] inherit[s] a plurality of codes that intersect and produce a flexible and fissured political subject" (1996, 157). Although Sommer's comments here do not address the topic of gendered subjectivities, her keen observations are nonetheless useful in helping us translate and thus better understand the gender complexities that are represented in I, Rigoberta Menchú. Indeed, Menchú's resistance organizing actions, her collaborative work within the Peasant Unity Committee, her mother's community leadership role, the two younger sisters' guerrilla activity, as well as other examples of women's resistance efforts and armed struggles point to the ways in which indigenous female gender roles are never fixed or static but highly complex, myriad, and deeply transformative.

In fact, several of the text's most memorable and captivating moments revolve around the capture and disarmament of (ladinizado Indian) soldiers by indigenous women. For example, Menchú talks about a fourteen-year-old indigenous girl who uses her feminine beauty and sexual appeal as weapons with which to lure a solider into the community's captivity. Though there are multiple dangers involved in the girl's actions—as Menchú notes, "it was a miracle they didn't rape her" (Menchú and Burgos-Debray 1984, 137)—the plan proves to be successful. In fact, precisely because rape and other institutional forms of sexual violence against indigenous women are endemic to the Guatemalan army, the young girl's strategy of posing as sexual bait succeeds in luring and trapping the soldier. Once he is distracted and caught off guard, the soldier is held at fake gunpoint by the community and forced to relinquish his weapons. Although those participating in the scheme—four women, including Menchú, and one man—do not know how to use the confiscated arms, they successfully foil the captured soldier. As Menchú humorously recalls: "I thought it was really funny, it's something I'll never forget. . . . We took his rifle, his big rifle, and a pistol, and we didn't even know how to use the pistol. I remember that I took the soldier's pistol away and stood in front as if I knew how to use it but I didn't know anything" (Menchú and Burgos-Debray 1984, 137). Following his capture and disarmament, the soldier is tied up, blindfolded, and taken to an area where he is presented to the community at large. Indigenous women and men, we are told, reprimand and admonish the soldier for abandoning his indigenous ways, siding with the enemy, and especially raping and violating indigenous women. As Menchú describes, mothers and fathers "begged him to recount his experience when he got back to the army and to take on the role, as a soldier, of convincing the others not to be so evil, not to rape the women of our race's finest sons, the finest examples of our ancestors" (Menchú and Burgos-Debray 1984, 138). Although the community eventually sets the soldier free, ironically, we are told that he is later captured and killed by the army. As Menchú tells, "We didn't kill the soldier. The army itself took care of that. . . . They said the law says that a soldier who abandons his rifle must be shot. So they killed him" (Menchú and Burgos-Debray 1984, 139).

Similarly, the text details another incident in which a ninety-year-old indigenous woman's courageous actions lead to the capture of one soldier, killing another, and scaring off several others—despite the old woman's frail condition and the fact that, unlike the heavily armed soldiers, she is equipped with only an ax. Notwithstanding the woman's age, rape remains a constant threat. As Menchú points out, "those murderers were so criminal they didn't respect anyone's life, neither old people nor children. They like raping old people and children" (Menchú and Burgos-Debray 1984, 145). In a state of confusion and fear, however, the soldiers mistake the old woman for a guerrilla fighter, thus giving her the upper hand. As in the previous case, the captured soldier is admonished by the community, only this time young indigenous female survivors of rape join the choir of angry voices, giving testimony to their painful experiences, which they describe to the soldier as "monst[rous]" and "unbearable" (Menchú and Burgos-Debray 1984, 148). Like the former soldier, he is also set free, although, as Menchú notes, "perhaps [the army] killed him now" (Menchú and Burgos-Debray 1984, 149). As the soldier explains prior to his release, "If I lay down my arms, I'm the army's enemy" (Menchú and Burgos-Debray 1984, 148)—meaning that in the eyes of the military regime, he who abandons his weapon is a dead soldier.

Given the strict ideological links between the gun, masculinity, and power, it comes as little surprise that the soldiers' disarmament by enemy forces carries dire consequences. Taking guns is a symbolically castrating gesture, one that strips the soldiers of their military power and virile essence. As such, they become akin to masculine frauds or suspect males who must be exterminated by a Guatemalan army that has zero tolerance for weakened, disgraced soldiers. Moreover, the fact that the soldiers are captured and neutralized not by dangerously armed, male guerrilla forces but unarmed indigenous women represents an even more serious blow to their masculinity. The women's appropriation and usage of the soldiers' weapons subverts dominant patriarchal (and patriotic) national imaginings in that it destabilizes the discursive relationship between the gun and ladino masculine power, demonstrating the ways in which indigenous women, too, can extract (resistive) power from the phallic weapon. Furthermore, these gender transgressions illustrate the ways binary constructs between masculine and feminine, ladino and Indian, public and private, and active and passive are never as stable and rigid as they are made out to be in dominant discourses. Indeed, if a ninety-year-old indigenous woman—one who has no idea how to operate a gun—can successfully disarm and disempower a male soldier, then neither is the gun the sole or natural property of ladino/ladinizado military men nor is power masculine by essence or divine right. Ladino phallic power is denaturalized and demystified as "the fiction[s] of absolute power" (Scarry 1985, 27), and these fictions as represented in the text are securely grounded in racialized notions of sexual difference.

Whereas the soldiers are previously represented in the text as virile and all-powerful—this is especially made evident in the torturing and killing of Petrocinio as well as the raping to death of Menchú's mother—in a chiastic turn of events they are later depicted as disempowered, lacking, frightened, and impotent by virtue of having been disarmed by the pueblo. By contrast, indigenous community members, particularly women, are represented as brave, strong, courageous, and remarkably savvy. Indeed, in the capturing of the soldiers, it is indigenous peoples who now have the guns under their possession and control, and as such, they, rather than the soldiers, (momentarily) authorize and dictate power. It is important to stress, however, that the power of the gun here operates not as a way of enforcing violent social hierarchies (as in the case of the Guatemalan military regime) but as a means of resistance, self-defense, and cultural survival. As Menchú repeatedly states in her testimonio, engaging in acts of violence is not a choice but a necessity in a situation where peaceful political negotiations fail to become an option. Furthermore, the risks are paramount—that is, torture, rape, disappearance, and death. As such, violence is not a cause célèbre in the text and, in fact, is represented as a last resort in a situation where all other means of attaining social justice are futile. In fact, unlike her sisters, Menchú ultimately rejects the *via armada* and opts instead for a political path. Her leadership, organizing efforts, and voice become her main weapons.

Notwithstanding the dangers, indigenous women's revolutionary efforts are represented as highly integral to the struggle. In fact, as violent conditions dramatically escalate in El Quiché, Maya women's gendered cultural roles become increasingly politicized, inextricably linked to the revolution. For example, toward the end of the text Menchú describes meeting up with her father after undergoing a long separation by virtue of their extensive travels and political organizing efforts. She describes how Vicente Menchú, on seeing his daughter, proudly and playfully remarks to his comrades, "This badly brought up daughter has always been a good daughter" (Menchú and Burgos-Debray 1984, 183). Given the context of war and social struggle, to be a "bad" daughter is in essence to be a "good" daughter. Subverting gendered ancestral norms becomes a historical necessity in the face of the military regime's massive-scale violence and genocidal campaigns against indigenous peoples. As the Commission for Historical Clarification reports, over 83 percent of the estimated 200,000 lives that were massacred or disappeared during the armed conflict were Maya; of these losses, 93 percent have been attributed to the army (Commission for Historical Clarification 1999, 85–86). As such, to defy conventional gender roles by engaging in unruly and subversive indigenous political acts, although no doubt deeply threatening to a military state that relies on the policing of rigid gendered racial/ethnic boundaries, becomes, in the words of Vicente Menchú, a positive indigenous daughterly attribute. As Tace Hedrick writes, to be a "good" daughter is to engage in "bad" acts by "break[ing] the imposed silence of social and political forces both within and without her own community that mandate against the entrance of women into the public, political sphere" (1996, 231).

To cite another example wherein Menchú is expected and encouraged to take an active role within the revolutionary struggle, following the multiple tragic deaths of her family members at the hands of military soldiers, she describes feeling utterly devastated at the horror of it all to the point that she suffers a ruptured ulcer. She describes feeling hopeless, lacking the necessary health and motivation to return to her political organizing efforts: "I was in bed for fifteen days. I remember that that was when I got an ulcer. It was after my mother died. I was very ill. I wanted to go out after that, but I told myself that I just could not do it" (Menchú and Burgos-Debray 1984, 237). At this point Menchú has a powerful dream wherein her parents pay her a special visit, and her father conveys an important message to his daughter: "Then I dreamed about my mother and my father. My father said: 'What you are doing is not right, my child. You are a woman. That's enough of that!' And my father's words acted like a medicine and cured me straight away. So with my spirits raised, I left the house where I was staying" (Menchú and Burgos-Debray 1984, 237).

Menchú's health and political energies are reanimated by virtue of being reminded by her father that her politically inactivity "is not right" and that she is "a woman." According to the logic of Vicente's statement, it is precisely because she is a woman that she needs to overcome her inert physical condition and political lethargy. As such, her femaleness binds her to a political ethos; conversely, her political commitments make her a woman. In either case, being a woman, according to her father, presupposes a direct relationship to a political/public revolutionary role. Far from being oxymoronic or antithetical, women and politics are represented as coterminous and mutually dependent. No doubt, Vicente's representation of what it means to be a woman complicates traditional national gender norms wherein women are imagined as essentially apolitical and bound to the family or home. His words of strong admonition quickly restore her spirits, returning her to the political and public sphere, which, according to her father, is where she belongs.

Yet Menchú's revolutionary role is authorized by not just her father but also her mother. As she describes, her mother continuously reminds her that her duties as a woman are to serve the political needs of her community. At one point, for example, she tells her daughter that "women must join the struggle in their own way . . . any evolution, any change, in which women had not participated, would not be a change, and there would be no victory" (Menchú and Burgos-Debray 1984, 196). Elsewhere in the text, the mother tells her daughter: "I don't want to make you stop feeling a woman, but your participation in the struggle must be equal to that of your brothers. But, you mustn't join as just another number, you must carry out important tasks, analyse your position as a woman and demand your share" (Menchú and Burgos-Debray 1984, 219). Menchú's mother's words are important because they point to a strong affirmation of indigenous women's equal participation in the revolutionary struggle. Rather than ascribing to male standards of "sameness" (and the devaluing of difference that goes along with that), her mother emphasizes the equal participation of indigenous women as "women" (rather than as or like "men"). Thus, the goal is not to leave her gender behind and join a mass of genderless bodies but to aid her brothers in the collective struggle "as a woman."

By contrast, whereas indigenous women's political acts of gender insubordination are represented in the text as historical necessities that are integral to the struggle, these very same acts are depicted by the military regime as deeply threatening and punishable via violence. As more than evidenced in the gang rape and death of Menchú's mother, indigenous women meddling in politics are brutally punished for "stepping out of line." Even so, indigenous women as represented in *I, Rigoberta Menchú* demonstrate an indefatigable revolutionary commitment to the survival of indigenous cultural values, traditions, and ways of life. In fact, as Menchú's younger (twelve-year-old) guerrilla sister affirms, the military regime's counterrevolutionary efforts further animate (rather than thwart) indigenous women's participation in the movement. According to the sister, death is not a sign of defeat but one of revolutionary triumph and victory: "'What has happened is a sign of victory. It gives us reason for fighting. We must behave like revolutionary women.' 'A revolutionary isn't born out of something good,' said my sister, 'he [sic] is born out of wretchedness and bitterness. This just gives us one more reason. We have to fight without measuring our suffering, or what we experience, or thinking about the monstrous things we must bear in life.' And she made me renew my commitment completely and showed me how cowardly I'd been in not accepting all this. This encouraged me a great deal."[7]

Like the dream in which Vicente counsels his daughter and reanimates her political energies, here the younger sister's words allow Menchú to reflect positively on the situation while simultaneously calling attention to her "cowardly ways as a woman" ("Y, cabalmente, me hacía confirmar y me hacía ver mi cobardía como mujer de no aceptar muchas veces todo eso"; Menchú and Burgos-Debray 1985 [1983], 262, translation mine). To feel "cowardly" is to go against one's political duty as a woman, and such political duty, as articulated by the younger sister, is to be active in the struggle as a committed revolutionary. As the younger sister elsewhere poignantly puts it: "I can only honour my mother's banner by taking up arms. For me, there's no other choice" (Menchú and Burgos-Debray 1984, 244). Her words, which carry deep counternational sentiments, are a pledge not to the "banner" of the nation but to that of the violated and murdered indigenous mother. Her statement is a call to arms against the nation-state and also a symbolic resignification of the body of Guatemala as pueblo (as opposed to *Patria*)—and this pueblo is represented as violated, indigenous, and maternal. In the sister's words, only by taking to arms and engaging in political acts of gender insubordination can the indigenous mother's honor and pueblo's dignity be restored.

From representations of indigenous women's myriad, complex roles within their communities to textual dialogues that directly address and theorize gender relations, I, Rigoberta Menchú points to the deep relevance and centrality of indigenous women's participation as gendered ethnic subjects within organized collective struggles of resistance. As Menchú states, "it is unbelievable. Mothers with their children would be putting up barricades, and then placing 'propaganda bombs,' or carrying documents. Women have had a great history" (Menchú and Burgos-Debray 1984, 233). Yet far from being a celebratory account of women's participation in armed struggles, Menchú's testimonio highlights the real dangers that indigenous women face in openly challenging the military state. In a world where the very notion of indigenous "women with guns" denaturalizes the tautological links between politics, power, and ladino masculinity, racialized forms of sexual terror become the primary mechanism through which indigenous women suspected of subversion are brutally punished and subordinated. As mentioned before, violence is never celebrated in the text; in fact, violence is primarily represented as a means of self-defense and cultural survival. Menchú states: "We don't do [this] because we want power, but so that something will be left for human beings. And this gives us the courage to be steadfast in the struggle, in spite of the danger" (Menchú and Burgos-Debray 1984, 233).

Notwithstanding the multiple dangers and risks, one thing cannot be understated: indigenous women's emergence into the public and political (masculine) sphere of armed struggle, although not without violent consequences, destabilizes and reconfigures dominant Guatemalan racialized gender and sexuality discourses that represent indigenous women as essentially passive, inactive, silent, weak, penetrable, docile, apolitical, lacking, and so on. As Menchú's testimonio illustrates, women's participation in the struggle asserts subjective presence, political agency, survival, resistance, and deep cultural affirmation. The fact that indigenous women successfully organize, resist, and at times bear arms, disrupts the discursive, dominant, and all-too-familiar alignment between "men and guns" and, more important, brings to light the social construction (rather than essence) of gender and sexuality as represented in ladino patriarchal racist ideologies and institutions. Indigenous "women with guns" as a representational possibility in I, Rigoberta Menchú illuminates the ways power relations are never fixed and immutable but rather the historical, manmade (literally and figuratively) products of complex social institutions that can be ultimately challenged, resisted, and reconfigured.

To sidestep the issue of gender when critically reading and analyzing this text is to overlook some of I, Rigoberta Menchú's most compelling and important teachings regarding the rich, complex, and changing gendered ethnic subjectivities that are produced as a result of Guatemala's historical circumstances. While delving into a gender analysis might seem polemical or risky for some critics, an even greater risk, as I have explained, is to ignore or downplay the centrality and deep relevance of gender in I, Rigoberta Menchú. Although we may never successfully resolve all myriad language and cultural translation issues in this book, looking closely at and acknowledging (rather than repressing) the text's ample, complex, and richly detailed representations of gender can at least help unearth and recuperate some of its buried gender truth effects, which have remained, for one reason or another, deeply lost in translation.[8]

Notes

1. Although Burgos-Debray contends that she did not significantly alter Menchú's account, Stacey Schlau highlights how the prologue alone contains evidence of at least eight ways that Burgos-Debray changed it (Schlau 1996, 178). Moreover, although the Venezuelan anthropologist maintains that she was the sole compiler and editor of Me llamo Rigoberta Menchú, the Guatemalan historian and scholar Arturo Taracena reveals in an interview that he and several others also played an active role in producing the text. According to him, given Menchú's limited Spanish (at the time), the editorial process entailed "work[ing] on the grammatical coherence, everything having to do with syntax, gender, number, and tenses, which Rigoberta did not dominate very well then. . . . It was my task to eliminate all repetitions" (Taracena 2001, 85). In addition, scholars have much critiqued Burgos-Debray's prologue (appearing as the introduction in Ann Wright's English translation), which represents Menchú in infantilized ways that grossly replicate class and race stereotypes.

2. For example, although I, Rigoberta Menchú is a text to which important scholars like John Beverley and Marc Zimmerman devote considerable attention in various books, a substantial gender analysis is lacking in their writings. More often than not, attention revolves around issues of marginality pertaining to ethnicity, race, class, language, nation, or cultural politics, whereas gender is treated as irrelevant or secondary to these other categories. See, for instance, Beverley (1993), Zimmerman (1995). The edited compilation of essays by René Jara and Hernán Vidal (1986), Testimonio y Literatura—one of a handful of available and important books on the testimonio—also discusses testimonial literatures in gender-"neutral" ways. We encounter a similar problem in Allen Carey-Webb and Stephen Benz's (1996) anthology, Teaching and Testimony: Rigoberta Menchú and the North American Classroom, which fails to include essays that significantly treat the topic of gender. Although several of the contributors (Robin Jones, Catherine Ann Collins, and Patricia Varas) discuss using the text in women's studies or gender-related course units, their essays curiously sidestep issues of gender. Even Stacey Schlau's (1996) essay, "Passion and Politics: Teaching Rigoberta Menchú's Text as a Feminist," fails to adequately deal with gender. Although Tace Hedrick's (1996) "Rigoberta's Earrings: The Limits of Teaching Testimonio" engages in a substantial gender analysis, it does so only briefly (three pages). Likewise, the book The Rigoberta Menchú Controversy, edited by Arturo Arias (2001), hardly addresses gender issues, although the topic under consideration—a white male university

professor and anthropologist attacking the credibility of a Guatemalan indigenous woman's testimony—urgently merits such attention. Even Georg M. Gugelberger's (1996) edited volume, *The Real Thing: Testimonial Discourse and Latin America*, which contains some of the most cited and important essays on Menchú's *testimonio* (by Beverley, Zimmerman, Doris Sommer, George Yúdice), fails to critically take on the issue of gender.

3. "Women with guns" alludes to U.S. director John Sayles's (1997) film *Men with Guns.* The film is an adaptation of Guatemalan American Francisco Goldman's (1992) novel *The Long Night of the White Chickens.*

4. See, for example, Scott (1990) and MacKinnon (1987). Although these works primarily refer to (U.S.) legal debates on women's equality, I find their main theoretical concepts —gender difference versus equality/sameness—useful in thinking through and negotiating alternative ways in which to read Latin American women's *testimonios.*

5. Stoll argues that the wide championing of *I, Rigoberta Menchú* by the academic left has created a scenario wherein Menchú has become akin to a hagiographic untouchable, allowing for what he sees as a political distortion of the historical "facts." For more on the subject, see Arias (2001).

6. Menchú eventually married and became a mother.

7. In the original Spanish version, no (explicit) male pronouns are used: "'Un revolucionario no nace a causa de algo bueno,' decía mi hermanita. 'Nace a causa de algo malo, de algo doloroso'" (Menchú and Burgos-Debray 1985 [1983], 262).

8. The phrase "truth effects" is borrowed from Beverley's (1996) influential essay.

CHAPTER NINETEEN/TRANSLOCAL SPACE OF AFRO-LATINIDAD/ CRITICAL FEMINIST VISIONS FOR DIASPORIC BRIDGE-BUILDING

AGUSTÍN LAO-MONTES AND MIRANGELA BUGGS

That confrontation with heavyweight intolerance carried me through our
Civil Rights Revolution and into our resistance to the War Against Vietnam and
then into the realm of gender and sexual and sexuality politics. And those
strivings, in aggregate, carried me from Brooklyn to Mississippi, to South Africa
to Nicaragua, to Israel, to Palestine, to Lebanon and to Northern Ireland, and
every single one of those embattled baptisms clarified pivotal connections among
otherwise apparently disparate victories, or among apparently disparate events
of suffering, and loss.—June Jordan, *Some of Us Did Not Die*

The opportunity is one of understanding by translation a much larger act,
a much more faithful act, a more loving act, a more disruptive act, a more
deeply insurgent act than the finding of linguistic equivalences.
—Lydia Liu, *Translingual Practice*

"You wont find 'Olive' listed anywhere on the reading list," writes June Jordan
in her travel narrative "Report from the Bahamas" (2002, 216), referring to the
erasure from canons of U.S. black and women's studies of her Afro-Caribbean
maid at the "Sheraton British Colonial" hotel, where she was staying on vacation. Jordan's brief piece is charged with revealing examples of the travails
and contradictions of travel and translation across multiple borders and locations (national, ethnic-racial, class, gender, sexual, etc.). In a strikingly honest
self-reflexive narration of North/South class divides between "people of color"[1]
she writes, "We will jostle along with the other (white) visitors and join them
in the tee shirt shops or, laughing together, learn ruthless rules of negotiation
as we, Black Americans as well as white, argue down the price of handwoven
goods at the nearby straw market while the merchants, frequently toothless

Black women seated on the concrete in their only presentable dress, humble themselves to our careless game" (Jordan 2002, 212). This story challenges facile versions of solidarity among "blacks" and/or "women," and troubles univocal notions of sameness based on categorical concepts of gender, race, sexual, and class identities. At the same time, it reveals a search for common ground and complex unity, seeking to construct a global ethical-political project of liberation standing from recognition of real differences. Contrary to implicit assumptions of transparency and unmediated instant coalition building and community making on the basis of presumed common oppressions, the feminisms (which can be called Afro-diasporic, decolonial, women of color/Third World) championed by Jordan and Maria Lugones embody a translocal politics of travel and translation as key elements in a methodology for the production of radical political communities and critical political identities across borders. This involves communicative practices based on a politics of translation geared toward forming and negotiating meanings, critical knowledge, and a sort of political community seeking to forge reflexive solidarities.

The critical cosmopolitanism expressed in the opening quote by Jordan moved her to travel from the black liberation movement to gender and sexual politics, as well as from Brooklyn to South Africa, Nicaragua, Palestine, and Northern Ireland. This cross-border politics of translocation and translation, is what Lugones characterizes as "world traveling" and as a "deeply insurgent act" geared to build "complex unity" (Lugones 2003c). Coalition building across subject-positions and social spaces has been at the heart of the translocal and transcultural feminist epistemology and politics championed by intellectual activists such as Jordan and Lugones.

Thinkers-activists like Jordan and Lugones, along with others working within this vein, have proposed that what is needed for our millennium is a "politics of decolonization" (Alexander and Mohanty 1997) that analyzes and contests the "socioeconomic, ideological, cultural, and psychic hierarchies of rule . . . their interconnectedness, and their effects on the disenfranchised" (Alexander and Mohanty 1997, xxviii). This feminist radical politics of decolonization seeks to challenge the "hierarchies of rule" and the colonial legacies of race, gender, class, sexuality, and nation that constitute modern/colonial constellations of power. This decolonial project acknowledges the colonial origins and legacies of racism, sexism, capitalism, and heterosexism and poses a liberatory undoing of these intersecting modes of oppression.

Feminist decolonial politics are concerned with pervasive kinds of justice, addressing and combating intersecting spheres of injustice. Decolonial feminisms practice a politics of antiracism, anti-imperialism, and anticapitalism. These politics are prowoman, proqueer, and pro–LGBT liberation; they are antipatriarchal, antiheterosexist. These intersectional politics and commitments toward liberation are at the heart of translocal feminist discourses. Translocal feminist imaginaries are ideas, projects, and movements that travel across nations, borders, and identities. The notion of translocality combines multiple mediations of self, power, and culture that link local, regional, national, and global scenarios, configuring a more complex concept of location and perspective that we conceptualize as a decolonial politics of translocation.

In tune with this feminist political and epistemic project, this chapter connects the African diaspora in the Americas to decolonial feminist liberatory practices and imaginaries. Overlapping and intertwined Afro-diasporic communities, and their black consciousness and antiracist social movements, are primary examples of historical and potential articulations of decolonial politics. We are most interested in decolonial analyses of Afro-Latin@ diasporas as a translocal borderland and a bridging identification located in between and against hegemonic and androcentric narratives of blackness and Latinidad. This requires several analytical moves, and we begin by exploring the African diaspora as a potential site for insurgent political work and translocal organizing, highlighting the borderland/interstitial/nepantla space of Afro-Latin@s in constellations of identity, power, and positionality across contexts. Taking a feminist perspective, we "gender" the African diaspora and engage with women of color/black feminisms in alignment with coloniality of power/decolonial currents.[2] We aim to articulate a feminist Afro-diasporic politics that includes Afro-Latinidad. This move entails pluralizing geographies and historical agencies through the concepts of intertwined diasporas and the politics of decolonization and translocation and envisioning a translocality that is politically engaged with Afro-diasporic concerns as well as being rigorously feminist in its outlook and liberatory imagination.

Translocality, Feminisms, and the African Diaspora

Arguably, geohistorical transnational categories like the African diaspora and the black Atlantic are crucial for analyzing translocal networks that weave diverse histories of peoples of African descent within the modern/colonial capitalist world system. This implies a diasporic world historical framework as a schema for analyzing race, gender, class, sexuality, and nation across Afro-descendant communities in the Americas.

In an important article, Tiffany Patterson and Robin D. G. Kelley (2000) argue that diaspora is both a process and condition. They write: "As a process [diaspora] is constantly being remade through movement, migration, travel, and imagined through thought, cultural production, and political struggle.

Yet as condition, it is directly tied to the process by which it is being made and remade . . . the African diaspora exists within the context of global race and gender hierarchies" (Patterson and Kelley 2000, 20).

The analysis of the African diaspora as a *condition* linked to world historical processes of capitalist exploitation, Western/white domination (geopolitical and geocultural), and modern/colonial state-formation, and as a *process* constituted by the cultural practices, everyday resistances, social struggles, and political organization of "black people as . . . transnational/translocal subjects" (Patterson and Kelley 2000, 22) is analytically sound. We add a third dimension: the African diaspora as a political project of affinity and liberation founded on a translocal view of community making and a global decolonial politics of liberation.

There are distinct definitions and discourses of diaspora. For instance, we don't define the African diaspora simply as people of African descent located outside of the African continent but as a translocal space that we read as condition, process, and project. In particular, we understand the Afro-American[3] diaspora as a montage of local histories across nations and contexts interwoven with common conditions of racial, political-economic, and cultural oppression and by family resemblances grounded not only in commensurable historical experiences of racial subordination but also in cultural affinities and similar (often shared) repertoires of resistance, intellectual production, and political action.[4] Thus, the African diaspora as a multicentered historical field and as a complex and fluid geocultural formation and domain of identification, cultural production, and political organization is framed by world historical processes of domination, exploitation, resistance, and emancipation as well as by decolonial liberatory longings. If the African diaspora, as a condition of dispersal and a process of displacement, is founded on forms of racial violence and terror that are central to modernity, it also signifies a cosmopolitan project of articulating the diverse histories of Afro-descendant peoples. As such, it is a space for creation of translocal intellectual/cultural currents and political movements involving Afro-descendant activists and thinkers who interact and affect each other across nations.

This conceptualization of an African diaspora forms part of a decolonial project of liberation embedded in the cultural practices, intellectual currents, social movements, and political actions of Afro-diasporic, transnational, and translocal subjects across the Americas, not bounded by national narratives of belonging. The project of diaspora as a search for liberation and transnational community making is grounded in the conditions of subalternization of Afro-diasporic peoples and in their historical agency of resistance and self-affirmation.

Nonetheless, most accounts of the African diaspora tend to marginalize considerations of gender and sexuality and are often androcentric in imagining diasporic politics.[5] Invocations of diaspora from Afrocentric and black nationalist viewpoints tend to recycle pan-Africanist internationalist analyses and politics. In contrast, postnationalist analyses of the African diaspora criticize pan-Africanism for holding an essentialist view of African/Afro-diasporic cultures and a nationalist ideology which allegedly overlook differences (class, gender, sexual, ethnic).

The existence and influence of gendered and racialized hierarchies in diaspora discourses creates a terrain on which to theorize conditions and political projects that are relevant to feminist decolonial politics. Diaspora politics predictably cross borders, as the historical process of diaspora forges interconnectedness among black peoples across nations and is an important contextualization for theorizing translocal feminisms. Such border crossings require a politics of translation to facilitate communications, mediations, and negotiations.

Black feminist theory and politics, with their political epistemic attention to articulations/intersections of race with class, gender, and sexuality, provide important tools for the analysis and transformation of modern/colonial constellations of power and knowledge including the capitalist world economy, empires, nation-states, cultural logics, families, formations of intimacy, and the self.[6]

Black feminists have redefined the theory, history, and politics of the African diaspora.[7] Black cultural critics such as Carole Boyce Davies have greatly contributed to redefining the parameters of black literature by weaving together a global diasporic field of black women writers. Black feminist scholars like Michelle Stephens and Michelle Wright have performed feminist critiques of Afro-diasporic cultural, intellectual, and political traditions as not only led by male figures but also characterized by a masculine gaze and project. Their gendering of the African diaspora has redrawn the character and multidimensionality of diasporic consciousness.

Gendering the Afro-diasporic imaginary is necessary to draw a more complex and concrete picture of black humanity that not only includes women as agents and cocreators of Afro-diasporic life and thought but sees issues of gender and sexuality as constitutive of black identity, black life, and black liberation. Gendering the diaspora involves a feminist critique of the patriarchal forms, mediations, and practices that constitute both modern/colonial regimes of power and social relations in the diaspora itself. Gendering the diaspora involves analyses of the intersections of gender, race, and sexuality in the making and shaping of diasporic Black subjects, histories, and movements. It is necessary to have a diasporic feminist analysis to fully understand and map the histories of peoples of African descent in the modern world, "to make visible social lives which are often displaced, rendered ungeographic" (McKittrick 2006, x). Feminist perspectives of diaspora expose the limits of masculinist standpoints, which omit the centrality of gender and the realities of patriarchy and sexism in the creation of New World subjects in general and in Afro-descendant realities in particular. In its essence, feminist decolonial politics proposes a more comprehensive liberatory politics and articulates a more fully decolonial Afro-diasporic consciousness. Including women in conceptualizations of black personhood and analyzing gender as an organizing force in the formation of racialized identities central to Afro-descendant histories gives insight into contemporary diasporic realities and strivings toward liberation across the diaspora.

A commitment to "gendering" African diaspora discourses implies important epistemic breaks and political imperatives that challenge the masculinist voice and character of mainstream ideologies of global blackness, that center women's histories and feminist perspectives, and that recognize the significance of gender and sexual difference power within the multiple subjectivities that constitute Afro-diasporic selves.

The practices, ideas, and movements that we call Afro-feminism or black feminism have a long history. In the Anglophone world a key referent is Sojourner Truth's challenge to white feminists in the nineteenth-century first wave of feminism with her maxim "Ain't I a woman?" Similarly to Gayatri Spivak, we contend that deep subalternity and radical alterity are particularly located in the normalized untranslatability and unrepresentability of black women from the lower echelons of the social ladder, such as Olive, the maid in Jordan's travel story. Hence, recasting the voices and valorizing the historical agency of black women should be a primary task of subalternist historiography. There is a sea of hidden histories of black women. The habitual denial of their everyday lives, cultural creations, intellectual contributions, political participation, and leadership is a staple of pervasive racist cultures. A decolonial antidote is the rise of black women's history as a legitimate field of research in the United States. In Latin America it is now also emerging, as shown in publications like a recent Cuban anthology named *Afrocubanas* (Rubiera Castillo and Terry 2011), which traces Afro-Cuban feminism back to the nineteenth century. The histories of black women in Latin America are just beginning to be written, representing an imperative task for rethinking and rewriting the region and the diaspora. Another meaningful story is that of the early twentieth-century Afro–Puerto Rican anarcho-sindicalist feminist Luisa Capetillo, who struggled for a sort of libertarian socialism seeking women's liberation, the end of class exploitation, and free love.

Bringing to light and visibility the historical struggles, creations, and knowledges of black women and the longue durée of Afro-feminisms should be framed translocally, hence involving practices of translation. This political epistemic engagement entails deploying and developing traveling theories to articulate the myriad disparate yet intertwined histories and knowledges of women in/of Afro-American diasporas and beyond.

Diasporas and Borderlands: Women of Color, Third World, Black, Decolonial Feminisms

A U.S.-based political-intellectual movement with multiple currents named as "women of color," "Third World feminism," "black," "multicultural," or "transnational" feminisms emerged in the 1960s and 1970s. The movement served as a space to elaborate theoretical critiques and political opposition to global, national, and local modes of domination, revealing the workings of patriarchy through all social spaces and institutions (from the capitalist world economy and the modern nation-state to formations of intimacy) while recognizing the agency of racially oppressed women in historical struggles and social movements and in the forging of alternative worlds (see Moraga and Anzaldúa 1983 [1981]; Grewal and Kaplan 1994b; Mohanty and Alexander 1996; Mohanty, Russo, and Torres 1991). Many of these feminists have roots in and ties to various parts of the world, many having been involved in activism in the global South/Third World and in community-based work and university teaching in the United States among people of color and immigrant communities. Along with providing a powerful critique of hegemonic middle-class white feminism and its imperialist foundations and sensibilities, these feminisms have stressed the simultaneous importance of understanding the historical bases of present-day coloniality and global capitalism. They have also insisted on intersectional analyses as crucial to the project of theorizing and conceptualizing questions of race, gender, cultural identities, and the experience of diaspora.

To understand and fight the multiple oppressions forming a complex matrix of power has a longer history in the feminisms of the African diaspora. Another revealing example is Claudia Jones, who joined the U.S. Communist Party during the 1930s Depression to champion struggles against her triple oppression (class, gender, and race) as a black working-class woman who framed her politics as part of a more universal project of emancipation, as demonstrated in Carole Boyce Davies's (2008) book *Left of Karl Marx*. Her Caribbean ancestry and being based in such an Africana crossroads as Harlem speak of the diasporic character of her identity and politics. Jones was not an exceptional figure but was representative of the best of a political generation of black radical feminists as shown on Dayo Gore's (2011) *Radicalism at the Crossroads: African American Women Activists in the Cold War*.

Black feminisms and their critiques and politics are crucial for understanding the feminisms of the global majorities that W. E. B. Du Bois named as "the darker races of the world." For instance, Ella Shohat's *Talking Visions: Multicultural Feminism in a Transnational Age* argues for a feminist transnational and polycentric multiculturalism/interculturalism "[that] entails a profound re-conceptualization and restructuring of intercommunal relations within and beyond the nation state" (Shohat 1999, 2). This concept of "revolutionary intercommunalism" was coined by Black Panther Huey Newton in 1974. As an Israeli-born Sephardic Jew, Shohat engages in political practices of translation between Sephardim and American Black Panthers. In this vein, she views multicultural feminism as a standpoint that genders diaspora by looking beyond the nation. In the context of our translocation/translation to and with Afro-diasporic worlds, this raises new kinds of questions about Afro-descendants across the Americas as well as the polyvocal spaces of Afro-Latinidades. Her critical multiculturalism can relate to decolonial projects of interculturalism championed by movements of Afro-descendants and indigenous peoples in Latin America and specifically to the ways they articulate politics and projects of depatriarchalization and decoloniality to use languages of current communal feminisms of indigenous women in Bolivia. This should also entail politics and practices of translation.

Similarly, Gloria Anzaldúa's twentieth-century imagining of Chicana identities, "la conciencia de la mestiza" (1990), poses borderlands as a context of clashing histories and transnational encounters. This corresponds to Rose Brewer's assertion of the "polyvocality of multiple social locations" (1993, 13), and her emphasis on "diasporic connections" between women can also be extended to the potential for cross-border Afro-Latin@ connections, as can Chela Sandoval's "decolonizing movements for emancipation in global affinities and associations" (2000b, 45), and M. Jacqui Alexander and Chandra Mohanty's (1997) "politics of decolonization." Through the work of these women of color/transnational/multicultural feminists we can see a political praxis and analytical frame emerging that can evoke dialogues across and within diasporas. This succession of translations accounts for a dialogue between two key theoretical tropes (or concept-metaphors), namely, borderlands, associated with the translocal/transnational space of power, culture, and agency between Mexico and the United States, and diaspora, whose main referents usually are historical dispersions of African and Jewish peoples across the planet.

Instead of simply counterposing diasporas and borderlands, we suggest that they could be combined as tools of traveling theory. Playing this drum, we analyze the African diaspora as a black borderlands, as a geohistorical field with multiple borders and complex layers.[8] Similarly, Claudia Milian Arias's attempt to "reconceptualize two foundational models," namely, Anzaldúa's "borderlands" and Du Bois's "double consciousness," as a way to construct links between black studies and Latino studies based on a "relational theory of race" is another important move. Her proposal of "an open double consciousness" constitutes a useful extension of the analytical and political value of the concept insofar as it "allows the mixture of blackness to correspond with brown mestizaje, alongside the mixture of ideologies that shape these figurations via gender, class, and sexuality" (Milian 2006). Milian's comparison of Du Bois's double consciousness with Anzaldúa's alien consciousness could also be aligned with Sandoval's notion of "differential consciousness," recognizing that this latter notion supposes and implies an oppositional and transformative politics and praxis.[9] This border/diasporic decolonial imaginary has informed politically and intellectually fruitful coalitions between U.S. black and U.S. Latina feminists pursuing general goals of liberation and decolonization.

Women of color/transnational and multicultural feminisms recognize the realities of interlinked histories and advocate for the project of "forging alternative epistemologies and imaginative alliances" (Shohat 1999, 2). These feminist imaginaries advance a particular consciousness of cross-national and comparative gendered racial and cultural formation and the potential for cross-national alliance making, grounded on a powerful notion of feminist solidarity. These feminist theories and imaginaries stem from long-term intellectual and political coalitions between black, Latina, Asian, Middle Eastern, Pacific, and Native American women in the United States and transnationally. Again, this entails practices and politics of translation that ought to be analyzed, to understand how theories and politics travel in translocations of spaces and subject positions.

This strand of critique and politics is based on "an antiracist feminist framework, anchored in decolonization and committed to anticapitalist critique" (Lao-Montes 2007, 121). The links of antipatriarchal with antiracist struggles transit through different political perspectives ranging from institutional to radical forms of feminism. For instance, Afro-Latin American feminisms (especially Afro-Brazilian ones) were key in elevating the question of racism as a primary issue in transnational constellations of feminisms as demonstrated in the 1995 Beijing World Conference on Women. On a more radical note, the "unbounded promise of decolonization" (Mohanty 2003a, 1) entails combating all forms of oppression (class, race, gender, sexual, geopolitical, epistemic, governmental) in all social spheres and at all scales (local, national, global). Decolonizing economy, polity, knowledge, culture, and subjectivity, grounded on the kind of vision that the Chicana feminist scholar Emma Perez theorizes as a "decolonial imaginary" (Perez 1999) to change our lens and inform transformative praxis. This perspective and horizon informs a rising mode of feminist critique and politics denominated decolonial feminism.

Decolonial feminisms — as named and elaborated by theorists such as Ochy Curiel, Claudia de Lima Costa, Juliana Florez, Diana Gomez, Rita Laura Segato, and Mara Viveros (among others) — build from traditions of black/women of color/Third World women feminisms to develop a political epistemic perspective against the multiple regimes of domination (capitalism, imperialism, patriarchy, racism) that configure the complex matrix we call (following Quijano 2000) the coloniality of power. Arguably, a contribution of decolonial feminisms, which distinguishes it from analogous feminist formations such as postcolonial feminisms, is that its critical theories and radical politics are largely drawn from vernacular knowledges of indigenous and Afro-descendant subaltern communities. In other words, decolonial feminisms tend to engage in a strategy of double critique that using the critical imagination of the Afro-diasporic world could be described as, on one hand, exercising Caliban's reason, where you curse the master with his own tools/concepts (to paraphrase Audre Lorde), and, on the other hand, pursuing a Maroon (Cimarrona or Quilombola) epistemology where the categories and critical visions primarily come from subaltern counterpublics like indigenous communities in Bolivia and Guatemala and Afro-diasporic religious spaces with strong cosmologies such as Candomble in Brazil and Osha in Cuba. This counterpoint of Caliban with Cimarron rationalities corresponds to two political forms — the former to a politics of rights and extending the meaning of citizenship, and the latter to a subaltern counterpublic that tends to build alternate spaces of power autonomous from hegemonic institutions.

The critical theory and radical politics of decolonial feminisms converge in crucial ways with the analytics and decolonial project of intellectuals/activists who analyze and seek to transform capitalist modernity from the perspective of the coloniality of power at the same time that it critiques their relative blindness to the centrality of patriarchal power, gender, and sexuality. Decolonial feminisms analyze modernity from a world historical perspective and understand power as a complex matrix that integrates class exploitation and capital accumulation with ethnoracial, cultural-epistemic, and gender-sexual domination.

Decolonial feminisms (black, Third World, women of color) offer a complex understanding of history, culture, gender, and diaspora, along with a liberatory vision of translocal/transnational connections among differentially located women from the so-called darker races of the Earth. These kinds of feminist praxis and their conceptual groundings help us map the multilayered formation of gendered diasporic cultures and the interconnections between black communities across the Americas. These frameworks are useful for gendering African diaspora studies and addressing the African diaspora as translocal political and cultural spaces. In this way, feminisms could be translocal, diasporic, and decolonial.[10]

Afro-diasporic decolonial feminists from Latin America (represented by intellectuals like Ochy Curiel and Mara Viveros) engaged in practices of translation and recontextualization of black/women of color/Third World feminisms for the context of Latin America, working with concepts of diasporas as spaces of difference and places to build what Lugones calls "complex unity" or solidarity gained in the intersection of multiple chains of oppression and corresponding strategies of liberation. In these travels and translations of feminist theory and politics, the signifier *black* and *Afro-descendant* tends to translate better than *women of color* (which in many Latin American contexts could be a euphemism for not naming blackness) or *Third World*, which is a political identity that had more salience in the 1970s and 1980s. A remarkable achievement of translocal feminist politics of translation is how the concept of intersectionality, which was coined by black feminists in the United States (particularly Kimberlé Crenshaw and Patricia Hill Collins), is now widely used not only by black and indigenous women but by mainstream Latin American feminists. This has moved many, more in the North than in the South, to question whether the critical edge of the concept of intersectionality is beginning to get lost in translation.

Another key theoretical contribution of U.S. women of color feminism is the concept of "politics of location" (see Alarcón 1989; Frankenberg and Mani 1993; Grewal and Kaplan 1994b) that relates the "multiple mediations" (gender, class, race, sexuality, etc.) (Mani 2003) that constitute the self to diverse modes of domination (capitalism, patriarchy, racism, imperialism) and to distinct yet intertwined social struggles and movements. Building from this formulation, we propose the concept of politics of translocation to link geographies of power at various scales (local, regional, national, global) with the subject positions (gender/sexual, ethnoracial, class, etc.) that constitute the self.[11] Afro-American diasporic subjects are translocal; although Afro-descendant peoples are connected to nationality, they are also interconnected across nations, inscribed within larger geohistorical constellations (the Atlantic, the Americas, global blackness, the modern/colonial capitalist world system). At the same time, black identities are mediated by a myriad of differences (class, gender, sexuality, place, generation). Afro-diasporic subjects can simultaneously be national (Afro-Cuban), local (Louisiana), regional (Afro-Latin American), and global (cosmopolitan black intellectual/activist). In sum, the notion of African diaspora signifies an ocean of differences and a contested terrain inscribed by distinctive gendered ideologies, political agendas, and generational sensibilities, thus forming a truly translocal borderland.

Afro-Latinidades: Pluralizing African Diaspora Spaces

In mapping African diaspora spaces, we need to historicize them, specify their diversity and complexity while analyzing their linkages. Earl Lewis's concept of Afro-American communities as "overlapping diasporas" (1999) is useful in understanding diversity and articulation within the African diaspora. We coined the concept of intertwined diasporas to signify the plurality of histories and projects articulated within the African diaspora. We also emphasize the world historical entangledness of multiple genealogies of diasporic formation (African, South Asian, and East Asian diasporas composing a Caribbean diaspora space) and the transdiasporic character of world cities' populations (working classes and new immigrants as subaltern modernities). We also locate Afro-descendants—in particular Afro-Latin@s in Latin America, the Caribbean, and the United States—across the Americas as the focus of our imagining of translocal blackness.

We conceptualize Afro-Latinidades within world historical/decolonial perspectives that call attention to race, racialization, social power, and Afro-descendant histories and realities in Latin America. When elaborated as a category for decolonial critique and a critical political identity, Afro-Latin@ difference reveals and recognizes hidden histories and subalternized knowledges that unsettle and challenge dominant (essentialist, nationalist, imperial, patriarchal) notions of Africanity, Americanity, and Latinidad.[12] Such a lens allows us to conceptualize a black Atlantic and Afro-America where Afro-Latin@s have historically played important roles, while holding Latinidad generally as a trans-American/translocal diasporic category. Thus, Latin@/Americanism should be redefined and challenged to account for the histories of Afro-diasporic subjects, whereas African diaspora discourses should become more nuanced and pluralized in light of Afro-Latin@ histories. Afro-Latinidades are marginalized from hegemonic narratives of Africanity, blackness, Latinidad, and Hispanicity and therefore from the corresponding world regional (black Atlantic, Latin America, Afro-America, Afro-Caribbean) and national definitions of identity and community. For this reason, Afro-Latinidad as a subalternized diasporic form of difference should be transformed into a critical category that deconstructs and redefines all of the foregoing narratives of geography, memory, culture, and self.

In the Americas, processes of nationalization of memory, language, and identity are reflected in nationalist narratives in which white, male, Euro- and mestizo-American[13] elites are assumed to represent national and regional subjecthood, while subaltern racial others (blacks, *Indios*, Asian-descendants) are marginalized or virtually erased from national imaginaries.[14] In African diaspora studies that focus on the realities of black peoples in the United States, the Anglo Caribbean, and Europe, Afro-Latin@s tend to be invisibilized or marginalized from most mappings. At the same time, African diaspora perspectives need to play a more important role in Latin@ and Latin American studies, with a more strenuous acknowledgment of the presence and particularities of Afro-descendant communities in the region. In this work, we make Afro-Latinidades central to our envisioning of translocality, diaspora, and feminist liberatory thought.

In light of the patterns of marginalization and erasure discussed here, Afro-Latin@s are diasporic subjects who tend to transgress essentialist conceptions of self, memory, culture, and politics. The conventional identity categories such as "blacks" and "Latinos" overlook or undervalue the plurality and diasporicity of Afro-Latin@s. As such, Afro-Latinidades demonstrates the limits of categorical definitions of blackness and Latinidad at the same time that it expands the translocal possibilities of diaspora discourses.

Histories of exclusion and subalternization inform historical processes of community making, the constitution of black publics and expressive cultures, and the rise of black struggles for recognition, democracy, and social justice. Hence, there should be a redefinition of the concept of African American to signify a complex, diverse, and transnational diasporic identification that encompasses the histories, cultures, and identities of Afro-descendants across the Americas (see Hanchard 1997). In this register, *double consciousness* then refers to Afro-diasporic expressions of belonging and citizenship based on diverse Afro-American identifications with place and space within (Palenque de San Basilio in Colombia) and beyond the nation (Afro-Andean geographies). African Americans and Afro-America can be represented as creolized, polyphonic diasporic spaces, translocal crossroads, black borderlands.

In mapping the multiple genealogies of Afro-American communities we can account for their heterogeneity and multiple connections. For instance, Afro–North America is in fact a shifting historical formation, an ongoing process continuously redefined by the diverse cultural, political, and historical constellations of Afro-descendants from the United States, the Caribbean,

Latin America, Europe, and the African continent. In turn, along with a powerful Afro-descendant presence throughout the island, the eastern region of Cuba is largely of Haitian and West Indian descent, whereas Afro-descendant communities in Central America have roots in the Anglophone Caribbean and the Afro-indigenous Garifuna people the British expelled from Saint Vincent in 1789 after realizing their inability to colonize them. Various Latin American societies have involved (often underinvestigated and sometimes hidden) histories of enslavement—hence the presence of contemporary Afro-descendant communities—along with various migrations of black peoples from other parts of the Americas to the region. Also, world cities like New York and Paris have been for many years diasporic crossroads and Afro-diasporic borderlands where Afro-descendants from different places meet, develop ties, and reach out to other peoples and diasporas.

The fact of black presence across the Americas and the play of differences within the Afro-American diaspora calls for a politics of translation, not only in the narrow sense of linguistic translations but also in the broader sense of cultural and political translations to facilitate communication and organization, to create the conditions to construct the diaspora as a decolonial project across nations and borders. As we argued through this chapter, such a decolonial project of liberation necessarily means to critique and combat the workings of patriarchal power through the whole fabric of society from the forms of the self to state regimes, all the way to formations of empire and the capitalist structures of the world economy, as evident in the theoretical practices of decolonial feminisms.

Intertwined Diasporas in the "Belly of the Beast"

Afro-American subjects/peoples are intertwined diasporas in their history, ethnic composition, cultural expressions, and political projects. Perhaps the clearest example of the diasporicity and translocality of Afro-Latinidades are Afro-Latin@s residing in the United States, who are situated in between blacks and Latin@s in the U.S. national space at the same time that they link Afro–North Americans with Afro-descendants south of the Rio Grande (see Márquez 2000). However, short-sighted analytical and political perspectives that are held as common sense in both academy and public culture across the Americas keep feeding the tendency to divide black and Latin@s (and black and Latin@ studies) as sharply distinct and even opposing domains of identity, culture, and politics.

In analyzing black–Latin@ coalitions we should observe Afro-Latin@s' multiple identities and affiliations. An outstanding example from the 1960s is Denise Oliver's (a U.S. Afro-American) double membership in the Black Panthers and the Young Lords. In their platform, the Young Lords advocated an Afro-Indio identity. As an Afro–Puerto Rican and founder of the famed research center, Arthur Schomburg used the pen name Guarionex, who was a Taino warrior chief.[15] Afro–Puerto Rican writer Piri Thomas, in his classic Nuyorican novel *Down These Mean Streets* (1997 [1967]), articulates with clarity how sharp distinctions between blacks and Latinos produce disturbing dilemmas for mulatto subjects like him. Thomas narrates how after agonizing about whether he was "black" or "Puerto Rican" he realized that he was both, an Afro-Latino. He realized that his blackness and his *mulataje* were not in contradiction but constitutive of both his Puerto Rican and Afro-Latino identities. In this context the concept of mulatto does not mean a racial hybrid between black and white and/or a brown product of *mestizaje*, but is rather used to signify how resisting the invisibility of Afro-Latinidad, Afro-Latin@ difference could transgress and transcend ethnoracial binaries.[16]

If we view blacks and Latin@s as distinct groups, their relationship should be represented in its diversity and complexity. This means recognizing the "patterns of cooperation, conflict, and ambivalence" as put by political scientist Mark Sawyer (2010, 528). There is a growing scholarship on black and Latin@ relations that analyzes the actual and potential roles of Afro-Latin@s "bridging identities." This strand of research has taken important steps in identifying sources of conflict while analyzing bonds and potential forms of coalition building. Researchers have shown how similar histories and conditions of black and Latin@ subaltern sectors (and to some extent middle strata) account for shared sensibilities informing campaigns against racial discrimination (for affirmative action, mass incarceration of black and Latin@ youths), urban injustices (in housing, education, and health care), and economic inequality (living wage, union organizing).[17] This should not deny how different forms of racism (antiblack sentiments among Latin@s) and xenophobia (nativism of black and Latin@ U.S. citizens), and various political agendas and ideologies (ethnic-racial competition of black and Latin@ political classes), are sources of black–Latino conflict. Our task is to develop conceptualizations of identity and solidarity to apprehend the articulations of power and culture embedded in different definitions of blackness and Latinidad and distinct forms of black and Latin@ politics.

Liberal politics in the United States produce simplistic notions of justice, community, and coalition building. Often the basis of cultural and political affinity embraces a dehistoricized sense of ethnicity, the downplaying of class and gender differences, and the marginalization of labor and feminist organization. In this logic, political coalitions that are most often emphasized may be ethnic based yet operate in the mainstream electoral arena, whereas social movement organizations such as community–labor coalitions, broad-based alliances for racial justice, feminist of color alliances, black–Latin@ gay and lesbian networks, and the myriad institutions and informal networks that compose an emerging wave of collective action north and south of the Rio Grande are written out. The forms of power and difference (class, gender, race, ideology) that distinguish Latin@ identities and agendas are erased, hence producing a false sense of sameness and a superficial notion of Latin@ "community." This results in a minimal concept of democracy as formal representation and of justice as a share of the pie for the ethnic community. Concerns about the relation between democracy, difference, freedom, and justice that give substance to these ethical-political principles are absent. Fundamental differences among Latin@ political traditions, ideologies of power, and projects are also ignored.

Nicolas Vaca's critique of 1960s discourse on alliances between U.S. people of color and the connection between U.S. minority struggles and Third World liberation movements has implications for black–Latin@ studies and their racial, class, gender, and sexual politics (Vaca 2004). Vaca's liberal gaze ignores domination (imperialism, racism, patriarchy) and exploitation (neoliberal capitalism) at the global level and its connections with regimes of inequality (class, ethnoracial, gender, sexual) at national, regional, and local scales in the United States. In contrast, women of color/transnational/multicultural feminism anchors a politics of decolonization in a critical analysis of the articulations of capitalism, imperialism, racism, and patriarchy from the local to the global. Its coalitional politics of sisterhood promotes alliances among women of color as part of a broad-based movement for radical democracy and social justice. The feminisms embraced here critiqued and challenged the patriarchal character of the nationalist discourses of the 1960s at the same time they framed their analyses of domination in a world historical decolonial politics of liberation against interlocking systems of class, racial, and sexual oppression.

Third Wave of Feminisms and the Rise of Afro-Latina Women

The turn of the twenty-first century marked the rise of a third wave of feminism. We contend, against arguments that we live a "postfeminist" condition or simply an era of the mainstreaming of feminisms, that these are also times of "sidestreaming feminisms" to signify the global influence of feminist politics, epistemologies, and ethics across an array of social movements and spaces, as Sonia E. Alvarez explores in her introduction to this volume. This necessarily requires elaborating and enacting a politics of translation to communicate and negotiate between multiple subject positions embodied in subjects-agents, acting in a vast variety of social spaces that intersect at different scales. This is what we call a politics of translocation.

As we have argued in this chapter, black feminisms (or Afro-feminisms) have a long history of linking women's struggles against patriarchy with anti-imperialist, anticapitalist, and antiracist movements not only in local and national scenarios but within translocal (diasporic and global) frames. In the long tradition of Sojourner Truth, Julia Capetillo, and Ida B. Wells, in the 1980s and 1990s black women were the first to organize diasporic networks of Afro-descendants in Latin America and the Caribbean. In 1992, the Network of Afro-Latin American and Caribbean Women was organized in the Dominican Republic. The network is still active and provided some of the principal leaders of the now relatively robust web of black social movements and Afro-descendants working in nongovernmental organizations, states, and international institutions in the Americas. Now it is organized in the United States, and the name was changed to Network of Afro-Latin American, Caribbean, and Diaspora Women to signify border crossings and its translocal character.

Afro-feminisms are now integral to the political culture of the field of black politics in Latin America and the Caribbean. Black feminists are key leaders at all levels of organization, patriarchal practices are challenged from community spaces to high sites of government, and feminist discourses and political epistemic lenses are now appropriated and elaborated by a new generation of Afro-feminist activist-intellectuals such as Rossih Martinez and Aurora Vergara in Colombia, Rocio D. in Peru, and Esther Pineda in Venezuela. In this new wave of Afro-feminisms in Latin America, the practice of translation (literal, epistemic, political) of concepts, arguments, and texts from black and women of color feminisms in the United States is significant. Key concepts such as intersectionality (from black feminism) are increasingly part of the critical vocabulary and toolkit of the rising feminisms of Afro-descendant women in the region who grow together with an increasing level of organization and activism of black women throughout diasporic spaces in Nuestra Afroamerica.

We end by giving two brief examples from Colombia that show the rise of Afro-diasporic decolonial feminism among a new generation of black women. The first is a visit by Angela Davis in September 2010; she was invited by two black feminist professors, Mara Viveros and Ochy Curiel, to present at the master's in gender studies at the Universidad Nacional in Bogotá. This visit turned into a highly inspirational moment, especially for Afro-Colombian young women activists. We can still see on the Facebook profiles of many Afro-Colombian women the strong expressions of identification with Davis's critique of capitalism, racism, and patriarchy as paradigmatic of their own political sensibilities. The other example is the last Latin American Feminist Encounter, which happened in Bogotá in November 2011. Here, the language of decolonial feminism was used both in the official meeting at the Tequendama Hotel and the meeting of "autonomous feminists" that was held in parallel, partly in protest for having a feminist gathering in a hotel associated with the military. In this context, a group of Afro-Colombian feminists read a sort of manifesto that highlighted the idea that "you cannot be a feminist if you are racist" and carried a banner with that slogan that captured media attention.

In light of the emergence of black feminisms in the South and the ongoing translations from North to South, an important task is to promote travels and translations from South to North. It is imperative that the vernacular wisdoms and feminist political epistemic lens of Afro-Latin@ women travel and get valorized as equal partners from South to North, to pluralize and enrich feminist cultures, to foster decolonial projects of liberation, grounded on Afro-diasporic reciprocity and solidarity.[18]

Notes

1. The very category "people of color" is not easily translatable to political-cultural scenarios outside the United States, where it gained meaningful political and intellectual values as one of the critical political identities created in the wave of social movements of the 1960s and 1970s.

2. In short, gendering African diaspora discourses implies important epistemic breaks and political imperatives, including revisiting and challenging the masculinist character of mainstream ideologies of global blackness, centering women's histories, feminist perspectives, and critiques of androcentrism, recognizing the significance of gender and sexual difference among the multiple mediations of power and subjectivity that constitute Afro-diasporic selves. In exposing masculinist standpoints, the project of gendering the diaspora puts the fact of gender on the map, further politicizing the questions of knowledge production and inclusion and deepening the liberatory possibilities of Afro-diasporic politics. In other words, what is at stake in advancing a more fully decolonial Afro-diasporic consciousness is the feminist insistence on antipatriarchal and antiheterosexist politics as much as antiracism.

3. Our use of *American* here connotes the entirety of the Americas, not just the United States.

4. For the concept of family resemblances see Wittgenstein (1968).

5. James Clifford (1997) observes that gender is outstandingly absent from diaspora discourse in general. Patterson and Kelley (2000) discuss the importance of gendering analyses of the African diaspora. We are bracketing the question of sexuality in this article. However, this should not mean a denial of the centrality of mediations of sexuality in world historical constellations of power and hence in social movements, expressive cultures, and forms of subjectivity. The sheer absence (for the most part) outside of feminist

critique and queer theory of an analysis of the sexual logics and libidinal economies inscribed in diaspora discourses in general, and of Afro-diasporic trajectories in particular, implies an urgent need for an eroticization of critical theory and historical analysis.

6. See, among others, McClintock (1995), Mies (1998), and Stoler (2002).

7. See among others, Boyce Davies (1994), Hill Collins (2000), Gunning, Hunter, and Mitchell (2004), Nassy Brown (2005), and McKittrick (2006).

8. Clifford (1997) distinguishes "borderlands" and "diasporas" as two different spatial formations and as frameworks for identification and politics, at the same time that their meanings and dynamics intersect.

9. See Sandoval (2000b). Also see Allen's (2003) problematization of the Du Boisian concept of double consciousness.

10. Women of color and black feminists in the United States have highlighted the existence of a "Third World" in the "First World" based on an analysis of the structural, historical, and economic positioning of nonwhite communities in the discriminatory societies of the North. Thus, the fashioning of the idea of "U.S. Third World feminism" attempts translocal linkages among the realities of women of color across regions as a politics of solidarity and affinity of women in the global North/"First World" with women in the global South/"Third World."

11. Agustín Lao-Montes proposed a politics of translocation in the introduction to the coedited volume *Mambo Montage*. See Lao-Montes and Davila (2001).

12. In this formulation the concept of Afro-Latin@ difference, insofar as it designates subjects whose experience and knowledge are otherized and subalternized by hegemonic Occidentalist discourses, constitutes a form of "colonial difference" (Mignolo 2000). Hegemonic Occidentalist discourses of race in Latin America include a narrative of mestizaje, predicated on a norm of Hispanization and the denial and denigration of blackness and Africanness. Afro-Latin@ difference exists on the margins of hegemonic narratives about Latin@ identities as always mixed, nearly white, linked more to Spain than to Africa.

13. In Latin America, a hegemonic narrative of mestizaje/mixedness informs national and transnational narratives of belonging.

14. Clearly there are substantive differences, for instance, between racial regimes in the United States and Latin America, and in different national contexts of racial hegemony, which are complicated by local and regional particularities and historical changes over time. However, after recognizing significant differences and historical contingencies, we argue that the above-described dynamic of racial domination and representation characterize the overall pattern of racial formation in the Americas.

15. Taino is the name given to the people who inhabited Puerto Rico at the time of Christopher Columbus's arrival.

16. For two fairly promising elaborations of concepts of mulatto, mulataje see Arroyo (2003) and Buscaglia (2003). Also see Martínez-Echezábal (1990). The signifier mulatto, similarly to mestizo, is conventionally used to connote a false image of "racial democracy" in Latin America, in the Hispanic Caribbean, and among U.S. Latinos. However, analogous to the way Anzaldúa redefined the "new mestiza" to develop a theory and politics of identification stemming from the play of differences, the concept of mulatto can serve as a conceptual and political tool to challenge racial reasoning and to analyze "race" through its multiple mediations and myriad historical articulations.

17. See, among others, Jennings (1994), Betancur and Gills (2000), and Dzidzienyo and Oboler (2005).

18. An example of translations from South to North is an upcoming issue of the journal *Meridians* in which the editors (a collective from the project "Afro-Latin@ Diasporas: Black Cultures and Racial Politics in the Americas" from the University of Massachusetts, Amherst along with Kia Caldwell of the University of North Carolina, Chapel Hill) are translating texts from Afro-Latin American feminists, such as the Brazilian theorist Sueli Carneiro, into English.

CHAPTER TWENTY/TRANSLATIONS AND REFUSALS/
RESIGNIFYING MEANINGS AS FEMINIST POLITICAL PRACTICE

MILLIE THAYER

In the late 1970s, a group of young feminists, speculums in hand, gathered in each other's living rooms in the city of Recife, in northeast Brazil. Together they conducted gynecological self-exams, studied herbal remedies for common ailments, and talked about sexuality and relationships. In 1980, they founded an organization, SOS Corpo (SOS Body), and began to do outreach to women in the poor neighborhoods of the urban *periferia*, hoping to spread the gospel of bodily knowledge to those with little access to it.

These young women were part of a long history of feminist activism in Brazil, and in Latin America more broadly, stretching back to the mid-nineteenth century. Beginning in the 1970s, working-class women fought for day care and against the high cost of living, while their middle- and upper-class counterparts founded women's studies programs or fought male dominance in clandestine antidictatorial opposition parties. Over time, cross-class alliances were formed between the groups of activists. Although fraught with power, these liaisons nonetheless changed both sets of allies and contributed to impressive victories toward the end of the century for feminists in countries like Brazil (Hahner 1990; Miller 1991; Teles 1993).

Latin American feminist movements also reached across borders, establishing international relationships, first within the region and, in the early twentieth century, with movements in the global North.[1] The contours and timing of "waves" of feminist activity differed from one region to another, and the vagaries of history meant that the directionality of cross-border influences was not always predictable (Miller 1991). At certain historical moments and in particular situations, the innovations of Latin American feminists flowed North, helping shape the practices of movements there (Miller 1990). More often, however, global inequalities and political scenarios conspired to ensure that feminist discourses from Europe and the United States crossed borders more freely. The late 1960s, when dictatorship in Brazil still restricted and shaped activism, feminism in the North was experiencing a revival, and new forms of global capital were on the roam, was one of these latter times.

In 1969, the radical women's health movement had burst onto the scene in Boston, with the publication of *Our Bodies, Ourselves* (Boston Women's Health Collective 1971), a health manual that sought to empower women by providing accessible information about their bodies. In Europe, too, a self-help movement was urging women to take charge of their own health as a vehicle toward liberation. These strategies were linked with consciousness-raising, through which participants traced the connections between their intimate experiences of oppression and gendered structural inequalities.

The discourses around women's bodies and empowerment, and the practices linked to them, soon began to travel. By 1980, *Our Bodies, Ourselves* had been translated into eleven languages. By 2008, there were twenty-nine foreign-language editions, as well as innumerable unofficial translations and adaptations of the original.[2] Travelers from the global South encountered flourishing women's health movements in Europe and the United States and carried their inspiration home with them, where it took root among the local feminist activism already reemerging in Latin America and elsewhere. Among these visitors were young women from Recife. Some had headed North with a backpack to see the world; others had been exiled in Europe during the years of dictatorship in Brazil, until an amnesty law was passed in 1979. When the exiles and travelers returned home, they brought new ways of thinking about feminism, which were selectively appropriated—and transformed—by local Brazilian movements.

This chapter examines the kinds of translations produced by women's movements in northeast Brazil as they moved concepts across borders from one context to another. In some cases, these translations have crossed class lines, in others they have trespassed national boundaries; either way, the efforts to convey meaning—or reject it—have global implications. The process, as we shall see, has not always been without incident. Feminist movements have sometimes struggled over translations, and on occasion they have also refused dominant conceptions, "translating back" to more powerful interlocutors.

In what follows, I argue that translations—or refusals to translate—play a strategic role for social movements and represent a significant form of political agency, particularly in the context of cross-border relations. By resignifying

meanings, feminist and other movements construct alliances, defend themselves against discursive aggressors, and express their own visions. In the
hands of political actors, language is more than simply words, and translation
must take account of the social practices linked to discourse. I argue that for
feminist movements the most dangerous meanings abroad in the contemporary world are those linked to the market together with the practices that instantiate them. On the one hand, social movements struggle to interrupt these
destructive discourses; on the other, they deploy translation to facilitate collaboration with allies.

The chapter grows out of my own efforts to understand and translate transnational feminist relationships for an academic audience (Thayer 2010). It is
based on fifteen months of ethnographic research in Brazil between 1995 and
2005 with the two women's organizations described here. In addition, I conducted interviews with seventy-five activists and their allies, did research in
organizational archives, and attended international feminist conferences in
Brazil and Mexico. As a researcher from the global North, I, too, was entangled
in complex transnational power relations with my subjects, a fact that may have
made me particularly aware of the contingency of processes of translation.
Though I have endeavored to present what I "heard," my understandings were
as compromised by my location as were any of those I studied, and my account
must be read with that in mind.

Translation in the Feminist Counterpublic

With the resurgence of feminism in some parts of the world in the late 1960s,
feminists working in the United Nations and other international institutions
began pressing for greater attention to women's issues (Galey 1995; Antrobus
2004; Snyder 2006). In response, the United Nations declared the International
Women's Decade, kicked off by a conference in Mexico in 1975, which drew the
attention and energies of feminists from around the world. At this event, and at
subsequent UN conferences in succeeding decades, feminists lobbied official
delegations and held unofficial parallel gatherings. By the 1990s, these contacts had borne fruit in transnational campaigns and global networks around
every imaginable theme.

Partly through this process and partly through other, less institutionalized
connections, a political space was created that stretches across geographic and
social borders and includes a broad diversity of players, from academic theorists to working-class organizers, from professionalized urban activists to rural
peasant women, from representatives of national state entities to sympathetic
international development agency staff. Feminists at different locations within

this vast, heterogeneous "counterpublic" are linked not only to varying national political cultures and institutions but also to publics organized around other markers, such as race, class, and local region.[3] For this reason, movements speak distinctive "dialects" or sometimes even "languages." Constructions of issues and goals, choices of strategies and tactics vary to the point where communication, let alone discursive borrowing and alliance, seems daunting.

Yet these diverse women's movements increasingly contend with parallel or related sets of malevolent forces. Their encounters with the "scattered hegemonies" represented by states, development industries, global markets, and religious fundamentalisms create powerful (if only partially overlapping) interests and identities. In this context, the project of translation among them becomes both newly possible and all the more pressing (Grewal and Kaplan 1994b).

Social movements are constituted by their relations with interlocutors, those located within and those on the margins of or outside their counterpublics. In effect, movements are bundles of relationships, charged nodes in larger political arenas. The affiliations that generate collective identities embrace a spectrum ranging from overtly antagonistic to mutually supportive, with shades of ambiguity in between. SOS Corpo, for example, was a nexus of links between middle- and upper-class feminists, working-class women, the state, antidictatorial political parties, and the Catholic Church in Brazil and the international population establishment, development agencies, UN entities, women's health movements, and academic feminists in the global North. To this, we could add their multiple horizontal relations with women's movements in Asia, Africa, and elsewhere in Latin America, forged through international conferences and other forms of global activism, including the periodic Latin American and Caribbean feminist "Encontros." Conceptual translations, like the reinterpretations of feminist self-help discourse made by members of the Recife nongovernmental organization (NGO), facilitate or intentionally impede these relationships and frame the ways that movements confront foes or collaborate with their allies.

In the past two decades, scholars studying a wide variety of geopolitical contexts have focused attention on the relations among feminists, exploring the challenges of translations across class, race, ethnicity, and national borders. Some of these authors have followed the travels of academic feminist theories, seeking to understand their itineraries and reception in distinctive cultural and political circumstances (see John 1996; Costa 2000; Mani 2003). Others have analyzed the encounters of gender-based movements as they struggle for mutual understanding of potentially incompatible strategic agendas and conceptions of feminism (see Narayan 1997; Carrillo 1998; Shih 2005).

At the nexus of these two groups of theorists, Kathy Davis (2007) traces the multiple translations of *Our Bodies, Ourselves* as an iconic text, but one rooted in movement practices beyond the academy. Like her, I found feminists in Brazil grappling with novel ideas, which also had a material dimension, expressed through their activism.

The diversity among feminisms is often accompanied by profound disparities between movements in terms of their access to resources. Together, difference and inequality create obstacles to communication and the construction of coalitions and ensure that translations, even among allies, always involve negotiations across power relations. Economic inequalities underlie the dominant directionality of discursive flows from North to South (and, as some would say, from West to East), rather than in the reverse direction. The power of large publishing houses, well-funded academic venues, and more easily accessible grants all contribute to the primarily one-way travel of discourses. Constructions of the North as the locus of grand theorizing and the South as the site of its humble cases serve to legitimate this state of affairs.

But the picture is more complex than a simple story of North–South cultural diffusion. For one thing, as Claudia de Lima Costa points out, some kinds of theories are more privileged than others in these flows. She finds that Euro-American poststructuralist feminist theories, for example, arrived in Brazil much later and with greater difficulty than did their masculine counterparts (Costa 2000). For another, inequalities within both North and South create hierarchies of discursive flow internal to each region. Voices from more advantaged sites, such as universities, are more likely to reverberate around the world than are those from less advantaged locations in the same region, such as organizations of working-class women.

On occasion, texts and ideas do move from South to North. Social movement actors, as I will show, have sometimes managed to seize control of their own stories and political discourses, translating and pushing them across borders to be heard by more privileged audiences. But the reversal of flows does not in itself represent a challenge to discursive dominance by Europe and North America. The literature of translation studies has both reflected and critiqued the gendered marauding style of those from the North who pillage the cultural work of less powerful language groups, distorting it in the process of making it accessible to the speakers of English or other European languages.[4] It is an issue of not just which way the discursive current moves but what the political dispositions of the "translators" may be. Although certain Northern theories may arrive in places like Brazil by muscling their way into academic or social movement discourse with the support of powerful institutions, concepts and practices of politics may also be strategically appropriated and relocated by local political agents. In doing so, movements negotiate their differences and wage cultural struggles over the meaning of feminism (Davis 2007).

In the process of resignification, the inappropriate, the unwanted, and the untranslatable are left behind as new modes of enactment allow activists to construct fresh understandings. The outcome is discourses that are "partial and composite" in Mary John's (1996) words, made up of multiple elements picked up in their travels from one context to another. There are no "original" meanings to go back to, only a continuous process of translation (Tsing 1997).

Appropriating and Translating: "Women's Bodies"

In the early 1980s, the actions of feminists in sos Corpo appeared to replicate the small group consciousness-raising and individualized self-help practices of U.S. and European radical feminism. But it was an awkward fit for a movement in a newly democratizing polity and in a society with one of the most unequal distributions of wealth in the world. Members of the Recife NGO, like many feminists in Brazil, had been participants in left movements against the dicta-torship that ruled the country from 1964 to 1985, and their quest for feminist self-knowledge went hand in hand with commitments to social justice. Though the group continued to speak the language of women and the body, it didn't take long before their feminist practices diverged from those of the movements in the global North.

In effect, feminists in this corner of the global South engaged in a process of political translation, appropriating discourses from Boston and elsewhere and reworking them to fit their own circumstances. The process of resignifi-cation took place in the interstices between discourse and practice. Imported concepts came loosely linked to particular, Euro-American feminist practices. In Brazil, however, these couplings came undone and were reconfigured by activists as they engaged with a very different set of constituencies and institu-tions, which required new kinds of meanings.

The northeast was the poorest region of Brazil, and health conditions were dire for much of the population. Access to adequate health care and safe, reli-able contraception was limited; as a result, maternal mortality was high, steril-ization rampant, and diseases, such as cervical cancer, epidemic (Portella 1989; BEMFAM/DHS 1991; Ávila 1995). Responding to the desperate needs in the per-iferia, sos members' first move was to shift focus from discussions of sexual pleasure to activism around reproductive health, from producing sociodramas on "frigidity" to conducting research on sterilization and campaigns against cervical cancer.

sos's self-help practices found little echo in the working-class *bairros* around

Recife, and they were soon eclipsed by a second development: the group's growing engagement with a rapidly democratizing state. Feeling a sense of urgency about improving medical care for millions of poor women across the country, members seized an opportunity in the early 1980s to join the Ministry of Health in designing a new national women's health program and training medical personnel in gender-sensitive practices.

In the course of their practice, there was a third change: the transformation of the NGO's constituency. SOS, like its radical feminist counterparts in the global North, was initially an all-women's organization, in which the hiring of a male night watchman for the office occasioned heated controversy. Over time, SOS members increasingly found themselves working with mixed groups of men and women as they trained health professionals, worked with women's organizations linked to male-dominated unions and neighborhood associations, and encountered the familial networks in which their female constituents were embedded.

In a final shift, the emphasis on individual empowerment through consciousness-raising, dominant among many feminist movements in the North, gave way in Brazil to broader alliances with the women's, community, labor, and political organizations that had earlier opposed the authoritarian regime. In the 1980s, during the Ronald Reagan and Margaret Thatcher years, while feminists in the North watched their gains erode, Brazilian feminists and other social movements were participating in the process of creating a new, postdictatorship constitution. The document that was approved in 1988 reflected significant victories for women, though their implementation required ongoing mobilization and political pressure (UN Development Fund for Women 1998).

These shifts in feminist practices represented, in effect, political translations of concepts fashioned in other circumstances.[5] Brazilian feminists drew on Northern discourses of women and bodies that resonated to some degree with their experiences as young, middle- and upper-class urban women. But their own location in a context whose class configurations, culture, and political alignments differed starkly from those faced by European and American feminists called for distinctive tactics and ultimately new meanings. More obviously than in the case of most movements in the global North, feminism in Brazil did not have the luxury of being only about women, nor could challenges to gender subordination be undertaken entirely apart from the state. Threatened bodies demanded survival strategies as well as pleasures, and individual processes of change were, by necessity, linked to collective efforts for social transformation.

SOS members seized the language of radical feminism in the global North and resignified it for their own purposes through their practices. In time, however, the disjuncture between words and their forms of implementation grew too wide. Euro-American discourses of "women's bodies" and understandings of "empowerment" could no longer, by themselves, make sense of feminism in the Brazilian context, if they ever had. In 1990, the organization appropriated a new, more fitting discourse—that of "gender"—and once again began the process of translating meanings and linking them to new political practices.[6]

Constructing Rural–Urban Alliances

Translations are fundamental to political relationships across social divisions, as well as national boundaries, serving as a vehicle to convey the meanings that make these liaisons possible. Organizations like sos that are characterized by a denser set of relationships or that straddle class, regional, or national borders and have greater access to resources, play a particular role in the translation process. They frequently act as discursive brokers for other, less privileged or well-connected movements in the same geographic area. In this role, feminist brokers import "foreign" discourses and practices, resignifying and disseminating them to their network of allies, as sos did with "women's bodies." These organizations may also serve as interpreters of local working-class women's lives or ideas for global publics. Their translations often generate tensions around inequalities of discursive power, as well as new possibilities for conceiving feminist political action, as the following section shows.

Cross-Class Collaborations

The members of sos Corpo began their outreach in the marginal neighborhoods that encircled the well-to-do center of Recife, and their alliances soon expanded to include a grassroots organization of peasant smallholders and agricultural laborers, the Movement of Rural Women Workers (MMTR), in the semi-arid interior of northeast Brazil. The *sertão*, as this region is known, has an iconic place in the national imagination, representing the poor and ostensibly uncivilized past that modern, urban Brazil claims to have transcended (Albuquerque Júnior 2004). Its image rests as much on the patriarchal gender arrangements as on the feudal relations between rancher and peon, which are thought to define the region. There is certainly no disputing its poverty and marginality. Cyclical droughts, which can go on for years, threaten crops and animals, making agricultural subsistence daunting or impossible.

MMTR members, who live in clusters of homes scattered across the parched rural landscape, are largely invisible to development planners, politicians, and feminists beyond Brazil. When the movement was founded in 1980, rural women did not have rights to land, pensions, maternity benefits, drought relief, or membership in the agricultural unions that defended the interests of their class (Heredia 1979; Spindel 1987; Deere and Léon 2001). Even when they won some of those rights, it was years before they had access to the state identity cards that would allow them to register property, take out loans, receive pensions — to exist, that is, in the eyes of the state. In their private lives, rural women often faced restrictions on their freedom of movement, surveillance of their sexuality by male family members, and the endless and lonely burdens of child-rearing and arduous household tasks (Diniz, Mello e Souza, and Portella 1998).

In the mid-1980s, the MMTR made contact with SOS Corpo in Recife, several hundred kilometers away from its headquarters in the sertão. The rural organization's leaders had begun efforts to strengthen self-esteem among their constituency at the most intimate level — the body. Using slides borrowed from a local priest, they had shared knowledge about human anatomy with MMTR members and encountered eager curiosity in their audience. Feeling their own expertise on the subject to be limited, leaders asked SOS members to come out and hold a workshop that would help the women explore their relationships to their own bodies. They also cautioned the urban feminists to go slowly, fearing that they might intimidate MMTR members or impose alien worldviews. Heeding this advice, when SOS representatives came to the sertão, they transposed their radical feminist discourse into a different register, using the pedagogy of popular education. Rather than lecturing about the centrality of women's bodily experience, they took an inductive approach, asking MMTR members to create a visual timeline showing the most significant events in their lives. As the group reflected on this exercise, it became clear that many, if not most, of these events revolved around the body: adolescence and menstruation, loss of virginity, marriage, childbirth, infant deaths, and menopause.

Over the years, SOS Corpo members were invited to come out to the sertão many times to lead workshops on health, sexuality, and reproductive rights, and the two groups also collaborated on a variety of campaigns directed toward the state. SOS saw rural women as part of a broader working-class constituency with which they hoped to construct cross-class alliances in the fight to transform gender and other social relations. The MMTR saw SOS as an ally and source of feminist pedagogy and knowledge, in part gleaned from its transnational connections. At the same time, leaders insisted on the rights of rural women to define their own gender politics and took great care to articulate the urban feminist discourse with the class-based and religious ideologies of their constituency. It was a complex translation that both sides contributed to and that formed the basis of their alliance. Over time, the gaps between the two grew less formidable—SOS presentations and publications incorporated insights learned from the MMTR about rural gender and class relations, and the peasant farmers and agricultural laborers of the rural movement increasingly spoke directly about sexuality and rights to social citizenship. Despite their affinities, power relations persisted. The stark differences in access to resources between the two organizations made translations themselves an object of struggle.

Contending Translations: "Rural Women"

Over the space of a decade after its founding, SOS Corpo went through dramatic structural changes: by 1990, the small collective of women had metamorphosed into a professionalized NGO with a staff, an office, and a budget of several hundred thousand dollars. More and more, like other feminist organizations in Latin America, it engaged with the state and other national actors, participated in transnational networks, and depended on international sources of funding.[7] SOS leaders increasingly saw the NGO's role as a kind of feminist think tank whose findings could inform policy debates, rather than as a collective of popular educators who directed their efforts primarily toward working-class women.

In the early 1990s, SOS asked the MMTR to participate in a research project on gender and reproductive rights. The rural organization agreed, and SOS staff held focus groups and conducted interviews with MMTR members to elicit their experiences of sexuality and family relations, health and social reproduction, work and activism. The material was analyzed by Brazilian researchers and combined with similar data from participants in a domestic workers' organization in Rio de Janeiro and working-class housewife activists in São Paulo. Based on these data, they produced a chapter for a book that included contributions from seven countries around the world (Diniz, Mello e Souza, and Portella 1998). The project was coordinated by a feminist academic and an NGO consultant based in the United States.

In effect, through this project, the rural women were being asked to translate them*selves*, that is, the meanings they attached to their embodied lives, for a wider audience. In their translations, MMTR members did not convey a fixed "essence" of rural womanhood but shared their own constructions of gender relations in the sertão. Accepting the challenge not only strengthened their relationship with SOS Corpo, it was also linked to their struggles for visibility vis-à-vis more distant actors, such as the state and international development agencies, as well as other kinds of potential allies within and beyond Brazil.

Through their participation in writing the chapter, SOS Corpo staff then engaged in a second process of translation in which they linked the experiences of MMTR members to those of the domestic workers and urban housewives they had also studied. Though the essay made distinctions among and within the three marginalized constituencies of Brazilian women, the effect was to suggest parallel experiences, if not always identical ones. All of the groups, according to the chapter, faced the inaccessibility of information about sexuality and reproduction, significant health risks surrounding pregnancy and childbirth, resistance from men to sharing domestic tasks, and a lack of supportive social policies, among other difficult circumstances. The authors concluded that the Brazilian women they interviewed all sought to expand their space for decision making with respect to reproduction and sexuality, whether through activism in the public sphere, through the use of contraceptive methods (including sterilization), or through reinterpretations of religious scriptures to support their reproductive choices, including abortion. In making these claims, the authors constructed a constituency, illustrating the common interests of its members and verifying their potential as social change actors.

Through the retranslation of their self-representations, rural Brazilian women were made visible as political subjects and inserted into a transnational network of activism. Although their relationships beyond Brazil remained primarily virtual, the construction of rural women in the book, along with their participation in international women's conferences, constituted them as members of a larger feminist counterpublic, whose shared interests and struggles linked them to others around the world.

SOS's participation in the book project reinforced their leadership role at a national level and garnered international exposure, prestige, and connections. In recognition of the contributions of their rural research subjects, NGO staff returned to the sertão to present the results of the study in a workshop. It was yet another process of translation, in which an academic version of rural women's experiences was transposed back to a popular idiom, using visual representations as well as verbal ones. MMTR leaders expressed satisfaction with this exchange, apparently accepting the retranslations of their lives that had been made.

However, there was another chapter to the story. A few years later, at a 1998 regional MMTR meeting held during my fieldwork, members discovered that SOS was holding a seminar on rural women for NGO representatives from around the region, at a cost equivalent to $200 a head — a substantial sum for an impoverished region. The MMTR had neither been informed nor invited to participate. The reaction was furious: "How are they going to discuss rural issues if *we* are the ones who live that reality?" asked a member at a regional meeting. "We're going to *pay* to attend? *We're* the ones who taught them!" There was a palpable sense that something very intimate had been stolen from them—their local knowledge and understandings of their own lives. Once translated—and then retranslated by others—the meanings of their bodily experiences had slipped from their hands. "They appropriated all of our 'production'—the reality of the countryside," exclaimed an outraged MMTR member.[8]

A struggle ensued. The rural group fired off an angry letter, expressing in strong language their sense of betrayal at what they called "foul play"—the theft of their self-knowledge, seemingly for use by SOS for its own purposes, as well as other evidence of what they viewed as SOS's disrespect and self-interested behavior. The MMTR authors reminded SOS of their historically close relationship, demanded an apology, and insisted on a meeting to discuss the issues. The NGO's leaders responded swiftly and negotiations ensued. Although I was not party to the discussions, it was apparent that the antagonisms had been mitigated, and the two groups continued working together. In 2000 they embarked on a collaborative research project; this time MMTR members were trained as researchers and participated, along with SOS staff, in discussions of the theoretical framework and interpretations of results.

In a sense, the conflict I observed was a struggle for control over the women's translations of themselves. What had begun as an effort to claim visibility in the wider world, as well as strengthen ties with an urban ally, had created tensions over the ownership of meaning, inequality of access to resources, and relations of power. The struggle was intensified by the fact that the reciprocal translations between SOS and the MMTR took place in a larger context, in which market relations were increasingly threatening to restructure social movements and their alliances, as well as the lives of their members.

International Funding and the Extension of the Market

The potency of discourse lies not only in language but in its material expressions and effects. Intangible concepts or words are not the only things transferred between sites within the feminist counterpublic; so too is the concrete activity through which ideologies are materialized. As we have seen, discourses around gender or women's bodies spun off from Northern feminisms came attached to particular kinds of activist practices, such as consciousness-raising or gynecological self-help exams. Ideologies less compatible with feminist goals carry with them a more sinister set of enactments with which feminist translations must engage.

Over the past few decades, discourses that extol and amplify the power of the market have spread in tandem with flows of capital. They have fundamentally reshaped the political terrain for feminists, both North and South, exacerbating preexisting inequalities and promoting commodified relations of exchange among them. These discursive developments threaten to undermine longtime feminist alliances and weaken collaborative efforts for gender and social justice.

Messages from the Market

Latin American feminists have encountered market-based discourses and the practices that instantiate them in large part through their members' increasing links to the arena of development funding. Beginning in the 1970s, feminist development activists pressed Northern states, international development institutions, and private donor agencies to expand funding for women's and gender-related projects in Asia, Africa, and Latin America. Over time, gender-based funding won a place within many of these institutions, and staff members were hired to administer programs directed toward what were known as "Third World" women.

The dramatic expansion in the 1980s and 1990s of international development aid paralleled the reduction of state capacities as prescribed by the neoliberal New Policy Agenda. Funding flowed from bilateral, multilateral, and non-governmental sources in the global North to the newly minted "third sector" in Latin America, as well as other regions of the world.[9] By the late 1990s, SOS Corpo had become dependent on development funding from abroad and the MMTR was beginning to seek grants as a means to help amplify its voice. The funding served to expand their range of influence and made possible significant gains for women in the region. The MMTR had leveraged its small grants to win support for women's leadership at the national level of the rural workers' union confederation Confederação Nacional dos Trabalhadores na Agricultura (CONTAG) and had successfully pressed the state to recognize rural women as citizens by making identity cards accessible to them. SOS had made inroads into the regional and national health systems, training state health workers, and designing policy. Thanks to the persistent efforts of its staff, Recife was one of the first cities to allow abortion to be conducted in a public hospital, and the NGO's educational campaigns around AIDS and cervical cancer reached hundreds of thousands of women. Though clearly these campaigns involved much more than money, the support from donor agencies played an important role in making them possible.

Nevertheless, participation in aid circuits came at a price. As NGOs proliferated in Latin America, and as development aid to the region declined or shifted its targets, competition for funding among women's organizations intensified.[10] Feminist movements increasingly faced scrutiny from donors with their own agendas and requirements. The agencies' growing demands to demonstrate the utility and effects of grants created pressure on women's organizations to produce both visible outcomes and evidence of the "authenticity" of their knowledge and constituencies. With few state resources and little local philanthropy to provide alternative sources of income, feminists had scant room for maneuvering.

In this context, the knowledge of rural women's bodily experience became an exchangeable commodity, necessary for legitimating movements in the eyes of potential funding sources, as well as for constructing political alliances. Sonia Alvarez (1999) notes the tendency among Latin American feminist NGOs to develop a kind of "hybrid identity"—part professionalized institution, part politicized feminist organization. SOS was no exception, and both sides of its dual identity generated pressures to produce knowledge about working-class women that would be legible beyond the bairros and the sertão. On one hand, as an NGO without its own grassroots membership, SOS's legitimacy with development agencies in the global North rested on its ability to demonstrate its connections to working-class majorities. On the other hand, its aspirations to help build a movement for gender and social justice similarly required the production and dissemination of information about poor women's lives and struggles.

For their part, MMTR members may not have initially seen their life experiences as objects of exchange or as the grounds for potential connections beyond the sertão. However, their encounters with allies, such as SOS, and with international funding agencies led to a new appreciation of the value that their constructions of their lives might hold in a global marketplace of aid, as well as in feminist coalitions. In a sense, MMTR members were empowered at the very moment they saw power threatening to slip from their hands. As "rural women" entered the aid market and acquired the status of a valued commodity, control over their translation became an object of contention between the MMTR and its urban allies.

In the new global political economy, not only did the lives of women in northeast Brazil become objects of exchange, but more and more often their movements encountered dominant meanings that undermined their efforts, disparaged their abilities, or measured their success in terms alien to them as collective actors dedicated to transformative social change.

The following two anecdotes will illustrate how Brazilian feminists refused the unwanted—and perhaps unintended—meanings that came attached to international funding, and how they sought to translate back to their more powerful counterparts. The power of rural women to interpret their own realities became a weapon of sorts in a discursive conflict with potentially significant material consequences.

At a northeast regional meeting of the rural women's movement that I attended in 1998, it was apparent that money had become a pressing concern. Frustrations were rising over the lack of success of the organization's funding applications, as well as over unreasonable agency demands and timelines. More broadly, members were upset over the continual implication that rural women, if they were "seen" at all by agencies in the global North, were not "heard." Instead, they were viewed as backward, illiterate, and incapable of carrying out the projects they proposed.

Several years earlier, for example, MMTR representatives had sought funding to organize a meeting for rural women workers from all over Latin America and the Caribbean. A donor agency representative, previously quite supportive of their cause, responded by saying that she did not feel they were ready to take on such an ambitious event, involving some two hundred people from twenty countries. They called her to a meeting to express their fury at what they saw as paternalism and to defend their capacities and the political importance of the gathering. Her organization subsequently became one of the sponsors of the first Latin American and Caribbean Rural Women Workers' Encounter, held in Fortaleza in 1996.

At the 1998 meeting that I attended, the MMTR went beyond defensive maneuvers. The organization invited one of its allies in the funding world—a staff member of a German agency based in Brazil—to translate into plain language the history, procedures, and underlying interests of the development agencies. The goal was to educate members about the world of international funding and learn how to be more effective in their fundraising strategies.

The rural women present wanted to know who would be interested in their cause and how they could acquire funding—what did the agencies want to hear? Though the MMTR's organizational needs were palpable, members expressed skepticism about donor motives. "What are their objectives in helping me?" asked one woman, and another observed, "No one gives anything without receiving something in return." In her presentation, the speaker did her best to answer their questions, describing the different kinds of agencies, their priorities and criteria for funding, as well as the larger global political economy in which they were situated.

In the discussion afterward, the rural women shared their difficulties navigating agency expectations and communicating their message. When grants were written in their colloquial language without recourse to terms, such as *gender*, fashionable in the funding world, they were judged by donor agencies as lacking in sophistication. On the other hand, when staff wrote proposals using the discourse of the educated middle class, members were unable to understand or defend them in meetings with evaluators, and the authors were accused of manipulation. "We need," said one MMTR member, "to learn to speak the language of 'doctors.'"

Rather than abandoning their own language, MMTR members adopted a different strategy to make themselves heard. They decided to invite a group of donor agency representatives to the sertão to make the rural context more tangible to them. The plan was to show these visitors around, so they could see the problems of distance, transportation, and poverty the rural women faced. As hosts, MMTR members would have agency representatives ride in the backs of trucks over dusty, rutted roads; visit their blazing hot fields and humble homes; and share bowls of rice, beans, and *farofa* (manioc flour). The highlight of the visit was to be a performance of a sociodrama for their guests—an improvised negotiation session in which rural women would play the part of both applicants and funders. In the skit, they would reenact the arrogance and humiliations they had experienced in the course of seeking grant monies, so that agency representatives could see the relationship from the rural women's perspective. The goal of their plans was not just to refuse the demeaning discourses that so often circulated around rural women but to use their power to signify—to translate back. By making their own versions of life in the sertão visible and audible to their visitors from the global North, MMTR members would provide a context for understanding the challenges they faced in their struggles against the oppressions of gender and class.

TRANSLATING BACK: "ACCOUNTABILITY"

In its own way, SOS Corpo, the urban NGO, also refused unwanted meanings and sought to translate back to the international funding agencies on which it had come to depend. Ideologies that preached deference to the capitalist market were initially carried around the world by international institutions, such as the World Bank, the International Monetary Fund, and the bilateral aid programs of powerful nations, as well as by transnational corporations. The private nongovernmental agencies, which often received funding from these sources and in turn financed women's organizations in the global South, also played a part in disseminating the discourses of "efficiency," "results," and "accountability." These discourses were expressed in requirements and procedures that subtly reshaped—or sometimes overtly restructured—the practices of grantees around the world (Clark et al. 2006).

In the 1990s, SOS was experiencing growing pressure from its donors for what was referred to as "accountability." The term had a certain resonance with social movements in Brazil, given the victory over dictatorship in the mid-1980s and the country's new process of democratization. Demands for the accountability of the regime to its citizens had been part of the lexicon of the opposition and continued to be an object of struggle in the postdictatorial period. In the political sense, accountability signified transparency, democracy, and an end to corruption—values espoused by the larger left community of which women's organizations like SOS were a part. It referred to the accountability of ruling political institutions to their newly empowered constituents.

In this sense, the term had a pull that was hard to resist. But in the context of neoliberalism and in the hands of donor agencies, it acquired a different set of meanings. Though agencies sometimes pressed their grantees to demonstrate responsiveness to the communities they claimed to serve, they were above all concerned to guarantee that the organizations receiving funding were responsive to their own requirements as donors. The lines of accountability, in other words, more often ran upward (rather than downward) in terms of relations of power.

Then, too, in the hands of the agencies, the term took on meanings that were more closely linked to business than to politics. To be accountable was not to be democratic, but to demonstrate "results" of the investment made by the donors in one's work. Results, in turn, were understood to be quantifiable, to represent in countable units steps taken in a linear movement toward specified objectives. In this form, they would serve as ammunition for nongovernmental aid agencies under pressure to convince state officials, multilateral institutions, and corporate funders, as well as individual donors in the United States and Europe, that their money was being well spent. Some measureable outcomes—such as decreased rates of violence, poverty, and disease—were clearly desirable. However, the imposition of quantifiable criteria created growing pressures for social movement organizations to engage in often meaningless number-producing activities, rather than those aimed at less tangible but perhaps more enduring effects, such as the development of critical consciousness.

The emphasis on upward accountability to those who controlled the purse strings also sometimes led to instrumental relations among women's movement organizations. The tensions between SOS and the MMTR over the seminar on rural women may be a case in point. As NGOs sought to demonstrate their efficacy and efficiency to donors, there was less incentive or opportunity for time-consuming collaboration with grassroots movements that produced few immediately visible results. An NGO dependent on international funding might find it tempting—or necessary—to appropriate the knowledge of others for its own purposes, rather than engaging in the painstaking process of creating meanings together.

To resist the pressures toward unequal and commodified relationships, NGOs like SOS Corpo have found ways to both refuse and reinterpret the narrow concept of accountability and transform its practice. They have sought to change its content, shift its directionality, and unsettle the power relations surrounding its implementation. An initial moment of refusal occurred in the mid-1980s when SOS Corpo rejected a grant from a U.S. government–funded organization because of its political restrictions. In 1984, the Reagan administration had instituted the so-called global gag rule, conditioning all U.S. funding to private institutions overseas on a pledge not to promote abortion in any of their activities. SOS declined the much-needed funds, signaling its unwillingness to be accountable to a policy that undermined its responsibility to its own feminist mission.

A few years later, in 1988, SOS took another step toward constructing equitable relations with its donors, helping found an organization called the Network among Women (Red Entre Mujeres), which included program officers from NOVIB (a Dutch nongovernmental development agency) and its Latin American grantee organizations working on gender issues. The network aimed to democratize South–North relations around funding and sponsor critical discussions about the entanglements of gender and development aid. By 1994, there were eighty participating organizations in thirteen countries, along with NOVIB representatives and women from other Dutch organizations.

Through the network, grantees worked to strengthen South–South links, creating a "platform of counterparts" that could serve as a vehicle for dialogue with NOVIB and other donor agencies around the terms of their aid. They generated critiques of particular donor policies and insisted on their own identities as autonomous producers of knowledge, rather than needy victims dependent on Northern largesse. At the same time, Latin American organizations reversed the international relations of power to offer support to beleaguered feminists in European agencies with a questionable commitment to gender equity. At a meeting of NOVIB grantees in the Netherlands in the late 1980s, Latin American participants insisted that the agency could not pressure its so-called partners to incorporate gender in their projects without also addressing its own internal gender inequalities. Staff later credited that insistence for the Dutch agency's decision to institute a form of affirmative action in its personnel policies.[11] Finally, the Latin American organizations worked together with Dutch feminists to lobby European governments for more funding for women's and gender-based projects in the global South. They strategized and acted as allies in a common struggle, giving substantive meaning to the often empty phrase "international cooperation."

In these ways, SOS Corpo and other Network participants shifted the relations of power underpinning traditional foreign aid practices in a more horizontal direction. In so doing, they implicitly resignified the familiar discourses of "accountability" and "results." Accountability, in their translation, was not just a means of exacting compliance from the South with the criteria of the North. Instead, it required a mutual commitment to advancing the cause of gender and social justice. "Results" were not to be demanded only of the organizations in the South, but also of Northern governments and development agencies, who would be expected to demonstrate their own progress toward shared social goals.

The network itself dissolved in the late 1990s, but the South–North dialogue promoted by this experiment, as well as by other, less formal contacts between donors and grantees, bore fruit in new ways of thinking about evaluation practices and criteria among more progressive members of the donor community. In 2006 the Association for Women's Rights in Development, a feminist NGO based in Toronto and Mexico City, sponsored a conference titled "Where's the Money for Women's Rights?" to discuss issues raised by fundraising and North–South relations around development aid. In one plenary session, representatives of social change–oriented donor agencies—the Women's Fund Network, the Women's Environment and Development Organization, and Action Aid International—shared new models for evaluating the effectiveness of their own work as well as that of their grantees. These models reflected a view of change as a political (rather than a technical) process and sought to challenge relations of power, rather than simply providing charity for the less fortunate. Criteria for success included intangibles, such as "developing critical consciousness," "empowering women," and "reframing issues," as well as more easily measurable indicators and mechanisms for evaluation including peer and external reviews.

How these new systems are carried out in practice and whether they live up to their promises are empirical questions, subject to ongoing negotiation between grantees and donors. The point being made here is to signal the ways that the critiques by feminist grant recipients from Latin America and other regions have provoked rethinking among sympathetic European and U.S.–based donors. The new versions of "accountability" evident in these evaluation systems are a sign of the power of Southern feminist organizations to refuse prevailing meanings and counter them with alternative value systems.

Translation, or its refusal, is a strategic political act in the hands of social movements, whether it involves sharing knowledge to foster an alliance or interrupting a dominant discourse to defend autonomy. The stakes represented in these processes are high. The capacity to transpose discourses among allies is an urgent necessity in the context of contemporary global capitalism, aggressive states, and expansive fundamentalisms. As their enemies increasingly transcend borders, feminist movements must also find ways to make disparate and shifting realities at least partially understandable to one another as the basis for political engagement between them. Borrowings of discursive resources, struggles around strategies, and negotiations of shared agendas within a counterpublic are possible only insofar as movements are able to make sense of their distinctive "dialects."

The ability to refuse entry to dominant meanings that travel all too easily is also critical. Social movements face particular dangers in the newly unleashed discourses of the market. Embedded in management procedures, investment patterns, public policies, and international funding criteria, powerful ideologies shape lives and reproduce themselves in daily practices. The ability of global capitalism to restructure material life — to become flesh — has allowed its discourses to cut across differences and to aspire, as Anna Tsing (1997, 2005) would say, to universality. Though hegemonic status may yet be elusive, discourses based in competitive relations of exchange nonetheless threaten to restructure in their image, not only work and family, education, and leisure but social movement practices and alliances as well.

Contemporary feminist movements around the world have encountered neoliberal discourses in different forms. Many activists, like those described here, have worked to block the path of these discursive invaders, interrupting imposed translations and seeking to protect themselves from their toxic effects. At times, movements have gone further, building the strength to talk back by representing alternative meanings in their own languages and practices.

However, translating back is a tenuous strategy, which requires certain conditions to succeed. Grassroots organizations like the MMTR, for example, could only hope to be heard by those who already identified with their gender-based struggles and were receptive to the kinds of pressure they could exert. Their ability to convey their own meanings to donors was based partly on the fact that rural women and their more powerful counterparts in the funding world shared overlapping identities that located them in the same transnational counterpublic. On the other hand, NGOs like SOS Corpo, with a greater array of cultural and material forms of capital, were able to reach beyond feminist circles, but only by adopting practices and forms of communication that gave them entrée to the state, as well as to the international development industry. In institutionalizing its structure and professionalizing its feminist practices, the NGO came more and more to resemble the powerful interlocutors with which it sought to negotiate.

For each of these northeast Brazilian women's organizations, translating against the current meant forging relationships with more powerful allies both in Brazil and in the global North. In the process, each faced different kinds of dangers. By making themselves legible to donors, MMTR members gained material and political solidarity, but they also risked the kind of commodification that led them to conflicts with SOS Corpo. "Rural women" could become a confining as well as an empowering category, a means of exoticizing and dividing constituencies, thereby limiting their possibilities and subjecting them to the designs of others.

For NGOs like SOS Corpo, who sought to disseminate their feminist politics by engaging in the world of donors and the state, perhaps the danger lies in learning to speak the language of power all too well. There is always a risk of becoming so transparent to dominant forces that movements lose their relative autonomy and their capacities for critical vision. By entering the corridors of power, these feminist NGOs extend their reach and possibilities of impact but must also constantly struggle to sustain collaborative relations with and accountability to movements of working-class women.

There are perils facing feminist actors who seek to resist dominant discourses by translating back, but the dangers of remaining mute must also be considered. Development discourse, like that of human rights described by Rosalind Petchesky (2003), is a "discursive field of power relations," with which feminists have little choice but to engage in one way or another. If Brazilian women's movements do not translate themselves, providing their own constructions of the world as they see it, their lives and needs may be interpreted and manipulated by others, well intentioned or otherwise. In any case, maintaining control over their own meanings—insofar as this is possible—requires ongoing vigilance in the context of their transnational feminist alliances.

Beyond the blurred boundaries of the counterpublic, where feminist translations face even greater challenges, lie the institutions that generate discourses and practices of the capitalist market. Feminist movements in Latin America have long understood that their discursive struggles must also have a material dimension and they have fought for redistribution, as well as recognition (Fraser 1997). Beyond that, going on the offensive against gendered political and economic structures requires constructing links to other counterpublics—organized around class, race, ethnicity, sexuality, and other markers of identity—which also suffer their effects. The process of building transnational alliances against neoliberal markets and for gender and social justice will call for new kinds of strategic translations among movements.

Notes

A longer version of this chapter appeared in *Feminist Studies* 36(1) (Spring 2010): 200–230, reprinted here by permission.

1. Following the practice of activists in Latin America, I have chosen to use the language of "North" and "South" to denote the differences between early industrializing and late industrializing nations. In spite of their limitations, I find them useful in reminding us of the historical differences in development trajectories and global distributions of wealth.

2. For accounts of the processes involved in translating *Our Bodies, Ourselves*, see Davis (2007) and Shapiro (2005). See also Shapiro, chapter 17 in this volume.

3. I have borrowed and extended the conception of the counterpublic developed by both Felski (1989) and Fraser (1997).

4. For examples of both perspectives, see Venuti (2000).

5. Tsing (1997) uses this concept in the context of environmental movements.

6. For further discussion of this process, see Thayer (2000, 2010).

7. Alvarez (1999). Similar trends toward professionalization were seen in the United States, though for a somewhat different set of reasons. See Ferree and Martin (1995).

8. All translations are my own.

9. The number of nongovernmental European development agencies, an important source of funding for social movements in Latin America, grew from 1,600 in 1980 to 2,970 in 1993, and their spending rose from $2.8 billion to $5.7 billion in current dollars; Hulme and Edwards (1997, 4).

10. A study of women's organizations by Clark et al. (2006) found that agencies were shifting their funds to larger organizations and away from those with budgets under $100,000. In the same study, 74 percent of those from Latin America reported that their funding in 2005 had decreased relative to 2000, the highest percentage reporting a decline of any region of the world. Latin American survey respondents also reported greater conditionalities and a tendency for donors to channel larger proportions of their aid through states, resulting in less money being available to NGOs or social movements, a narrowing of the issues that would receive support to the least controversial, and more bureaucracy involved in applying for and receiving funding.

11. Papma and Sprenger (1994, 207).

Abreu, Capistrano de. 1975 [1899]. Sobre uma História do Ceará. In *Obras de Capistrano de Abreu: Caminhos Antigos e Povoamento do Brasil*. Rio de Janeiro: Civilização Brasileira / MEC.

Acevedo, Luz del Alba. 2001. Speaking among Friends: Whose Empowerment, Whose Resistance? In *Telling to Live: Latina Feminist Testimonios*, ed. Latina Feminist Group, 250–62. Durham: Duke University Press.

Acevedo, Marta. 1970. Women Fight for Their Liberation: Our Dream Is in a Steep Place. In *La Cultura en México*, supplement of *¡Siempre!*, no. 901 (September 30).

Aguasaco, Carlos. 2004. La Poesía Del Cuerpo y El Cuerpo de La Poesía: A Propósito de El Incansable Juego. *Hybrido* 6:56.

Ahluwalia, Pal. 2005. Out of Africa: Post-Structuralism's Colonial Roots. *Postcolonial Studies* 8(2): 137–54.

Aïnouz, Karim. 2006. *O Céu de Suely*. DVD.

Alarcón, Norma. 1989. Traddutora-Traditora: A Paradigmatic Figure of Chicana Feminism. *Cultural Critique* 13: 57–87.

———. 1990. La Literatura de la Chicana: Un Reto Sexual y Social del Proletariado. In *Mujer y Literatura Chicana: Culturas en Contacto*, ed. Aralia López Gonzalez, Amalia Malagamba, and Elena Urrutia, 207–12. Tijuana: El Colegio de Mexico y El Colegio de la Frontera.

Albuquerque Júnior, Durval Muniz de. 2004. Weaving Tradition: The Invention of the Brazilian Northeast. *Latin American Perspectives* 31(2): 42–61.

Alegría, Claribel, and D. J. Flakoll. 1987. *They Won't Take Me Alive: Salvadoran Women in Struggle for National Liberation*. Trans. Amanda Hopkinson. London: Women's Press.

Alencar, José de. 1876 [1865]. *Iracema*. Sao Paulo: Edicões Melhoramentos.

Alexander, Bryant Keith. 1999. Performing Culture in the Classroom: An Instructional (Auto)Ethnography. *Text and Performance Quarterly* 19(4): 307–31.

Alexander, M. Jacqui, and Chandra Talpade Mohanty. 1997. Introduction. In *Feminist Genealogies, Colonial Legacies, Democratic Futures*, ed. M. Jacqui Alexander and Chandra Talpade Mohanty, xiii–xlii. New York: Routledge.

Alfonso, Louise Prado. 2006. Embratur: Formadora de Imagens da Nação Brasileira. Master's thesis, Universidade Estadual de Campinas, Instituto de Filosofia e Ciências Humanas, São Paulo.

Allen, Ernest. 2003. DuBoisian Double Consciousness: The Unsustainable Argument. *Massachusetts Review* 43: 217–53.

Allende, Isabel. 1982. *La Casa de los Espíritus*. Barcelona: Plaza y Janés.

———. 1985. *The House of the Spirits*. Trans. Magda Bogin. New York: Knopf.

———. 1999. *Hija de la Fortuna*. New York: Harper Libros.

———. 1999. *Daughter of Fortune*. Trans. Margaret Sayers Peden. New York: HarperCollins.

———. 2000. *Retrato en Sepia*. Buenos Aires: Editorial Sudamericana.

———. 2001. *Portrait in Sepia*. Trans. Margaret Sayers Peden. New York: HarperCollins.

———. 2005. *El Zorro: Comienza la Leyenda*. Barcelona: Plaza y Janés Editores.

———. 2005. *Zorro*. Trans. Margaret Sayers Peden. New York: HarperCollins.

Almeida, Miguel Vale de. 2000. *Um Mar da Cor da Terra: Raça, Cultura e Política da Identidade*. Oeiras: Celta.

Alvarez, Sonia E. 1998a. Feminismos Latinoamericanos. *Revista Estudos Feministas* 6(2): 265–84.

———. 1998b. Latin American Feminisms "Go Global": Trends of the 1990's and Challenges for the New Millennium. In *Cultures of Politics / Politics of Culture: Re-Visioning Latin American Social Movements*, ed. Sonia E. Alvarez, Evalina E. Dagnino, and Arturo Escobar, 293–324. Boulder, CO: Westview.

———. 1998c. Los Feminismos Latinoamericanos se Globalizan en Los Noventa: Retos Para Un Nuevo Milenio. In *Género y Cultura en América Latina*, ed. María Luisa Tarrés, 89–136. Mexico City: El Colegio de Mexico.

———. 1999. Advocating Feminism: The Latin American Feminist NGO "Boom." *International Feminist Journal of Politics* 1(2): 181–209.

———. 2000. Translating the Global: Effects of Transnational Organizing on Local Feminist Discourses and Practices in Latin America. *Meridians: Feminism, Race, Transnationalism* 1(1): 29–67.

Alvarez, Sonia E., Elisabeth Friedman, Erica Beckman, Maylei Blackwell, Norma Chinchilla, Nathalie Lebon, Marysa Navarro, and Marcela Ríos Tobar. 2003. Encountering Latin American and Caribbean Feminisms. *Signs: Journal of Women in Culture and Society* 28(2): 537–79.

Amos, Valerie, and Pratibha Parmar. 1984. Challenging Imperial Feminism. *Feminist Review* 17: 3–20.

Anderson, Benedict. 1991. *Imagined Communities: Reflections on the Origin and Spread of Nationalism*. New York: Verso.

Anderson-Bricker, Kristin. 1999. Triple Jeopardy: Black Women and the Growth of Feminist Consciousness in SNCC, 1964–1970s. In *Still Lifting, Still Climbing: African American Women's Contemporary Activism*, ed. Kimberly Springer, 49–69. New York: New York University Press.

Antrobus, Peggy. 2004. *The Global Women's Movement: Origins, Issues and Strategies*. New York: Zed Books.

Anzaldúa, Gloria. 1987. *Borderlands / La Frontera. The New Mestiza*. San Francisco: Spinsters / Aunt Lute Books.

———. 1988. La Prieta. In *Esta Puente, Mi Espalda: Voces de Mujeres Tercermundistas en los*

Estados Unidos, ed. Cherrie Moraga and Ana Castillo, trans. Ana Castillo and Norma Alarcón. San Francisco: ISM Press.

———. 1990. La Conciencia de la Mestiza: Towards a New Consciousness. In *Making Face, Making Soul / Haciendo Caras: Creative and Critical Perspectives by Feminists of Color*, ed. Gloria Anzaldúa, 377–89. San Francisco: Aunt Lute Books.

———. 2000. *Interviews / Entrevistas*. Ed. Analouise Keating. London: Routledge.

———. 2002. Speaking in Tongues: A Letter to Third World Women Writers. In *This Bridge Called My Back: Writings by Radical Women of Color*, 3rd ed., ed. Cherríe Moraga and Gloria Anzaldúa. Berkeley, CA: Third Woman.

———. 2005. La Consciencia de La Mestiza / Rumo a Uma Nova Consciência. *Revista Estudos Feministas* 13(3): 704–19.

Anzaldúa, Gloria, and Analouise Keating, eds. 2002. *This Bridge We Call Home: Radical Visions for Transformations*. New York: Routledge.

Appadurai, Arjun. 1990. Disjuncture and Difference in Global Cultural Economy. *Public Culture* 2(2): 1–24.

———. 1995. The Production of Locality. In *Counterworks: Managing the Diversity of Knowledge*, ed. Richard Fardon, 204–25. New York: Routledge.

———. 1996. Sovereignty without Territoriality: Notes for Postnational Geography. In *The Geography of Identity*, ed. Patricia Yaeger, 40–58. Ann Arbor: University of Michigan Press.

Apter, Emily. 2001a. Crossover Texts / Creole Tongues: A Conversation with Maryse Condé. *Public Culture* 13(1): 89–96.

———. 2001b. On Translation in a Global Market. *Public Culture* 13(1): 1–12.

———. 2006. *The Translation Zone: A New Comparative Literature*. Princeton, NJ: Princeton University Press.

Ardito Vega, Wilfredo. 2001. Peruanos en Chile: Buscando una Nueva Oportunidad. *La Insignia* (April 23).

Arias, Arturo, ed. 2001. *The Rigoberta Menchú Controversy*. Minneapolis: University of Minnesota Press.

Arp, William, Marilyn K. Dantico, and Marjorie S. Zatz. 1990. The Immigration Reform and Control Act of 1986: Differential Impacts on Women? *Social Justice* 17(2): 23–39.

Arredondo, Gabriela, Aída Hurtado, Norma Klahn, Olga Nájera-Ramírez, and Patricia Zavella, eds. 2003. *Chicana Feminisms: A Critical Reader*. Durham: Duke University Press.

Arroyo, Jossianna. 2003. *Travestismos Culturales: Literatura y Etnografía en Cuba y Brasil*. Pittsburgh: Nuevo Siglo.

———. 2006. "To Queer or not to Queer": Coloniality, Feminism and New Research Agendas. *Latin American Studies Association Forum* 37(3): 10–12.

Asher, Kiran. 1997. "Working from the Head Out: Revalidating Ourselves as Women, Rescuing Our Black Identity": Ethnicity and Gender in the Pacific Lowlands. *Current World Leaders* 40(6): 106–27.

———. 2000. Mobilizing the Discourses of Sustainable Economic Development and Biodiversity Conservation in the Pacific Lowlands of Colombia. *Strategies: Journal of Theory, Culture and Politics* 13(1): 111–25.

———. 2007. Ser y Tener: Black Women's Activism, Development and Ethnicity in the Pacific Lowlands of Colombia. *Feminist Studies* 33(1): 11–37.

———. 2009. *Black and Green: Afro-Colombians, Development, and Nature in the Pacific Lowlands of Colombia*. Durham: Duke University Press.

———. 2012. The Footwork of Critique [Commentary on Joel Wainwright's interview with Kojin Karatani]. *Dialogues in Human Geography* 2(1): 53–59.

Ávila, Maria Betânia. 1995. *PAISM: Um Programa de Saúdepara o Bemestar de Gênero*. Recife: SOS Corpo.

Azeredo, Sandra. 1994. Teorizando sobre Género e Relações Raciais. *Revista Estudos Feministas* (Número Especial): 203–16.

Bacon, David. n.d. International Solidarity—Oaxacan Style: Cross-Border Organizing at the Grassroots. http://dbacon.igc.org/Mexico/23OaxacanSolidarity.htm.

Bakhtin, Mikhail. 1988. Formas de Tempo e de Cronotopo No Romance Ensaios de Poética Histórica. In *Questões de Literatura e de Estética; A Teoria do Romance*, 211–362. São Paulo: Hucitec.

Bandia, Paul. 1995. Is Ethnocentrism an Obstacle to Finding a Comprehensive Translation Theory? *Meta* 40(3): 488–96.

Banerji, Nirmala. 1981. Testimony of a Working Class Woman. *Economic and Political Weekly* 16(41): 1651–53.

Barbalho, Alexandre. 2004. Estado, Mídia e Identidade: Políticas de Cultura no Nordeste Contemporâneo. *Alceu* 4(8): 156–67.

Barbeitos, Arlindo. 1997. Une Perspective Angolaise sur le Lusotropicalisme. In *Lusotopie*, ed. Déjanirah Couto, Armelle Enders, and Leonard Yves, 309–26. Bordeaux: Institut d'Etudes Politiques.

Barber, David. 2001. Rumi Nation. *Parnassus: Poetry in Review* 25(1/2): 176.

Barreiro, José. 1994. Native Response to Chiapas. *Akwe: Kon Journal* 11(2): 78–80.

Bassnett, Susan. 2007. Culture and Translation. In *A Companion to Translation Studies*, ed. Piotr Kuhiwczak and Karin Littau, 13–23. Clevedon: Multilingual Matters.

Basu, Amrita. 2000. Globalization of the Local / Localization of the Global: Mapping Transnational Women's Movements. *Meridians* 1(1): 68–84.

Beck, Ulrich. 1992. *Risk Society: Towards a New Modernity*. London: Sage.

Bedregal, Ximena. 1995. Memoria y Utopía en el Movimiento Feminista: Un Diálogo con Mercedes Olivera. In *En Chiapas ¿y las Mujeres Qué?*, ed. Rosa Rojas, 185–89. Mexico: CICAM.

Behar, Ruth. 1993. *Translated Woman: Crossing the Border with Esperanza's Story*. Boston: Beacon.

Belausteguigoitia, Marisa, and Martha Leñero. 2006. *Fronteras y Cruces: Cartografía de Escenarios Culturales Latinoamericanos*. Mexico: PUEG/UNAM.

Belausteguigoitia Rius, Marisa, ed. 2009. *Güeras y Prietas: Género y Raza en la Construcción de Mundos Nuevos*. México: PUEG-UNAM.

Belausteguigoitia Rius, Marisa, and María del Socorro Gutiérrez Magallanes. 2013. Chicana/o and Latina/o Literary Studies in Mexico. In *The Routledge Companion to Latino/a Literature*, ed. Suzanne Bost and Frances R. Aparicio, 95–106. New York: Routledge.

Bell, Steven. 2003. The Development of Modern Health Promotion. In *The Social Significance of Health Promotion*, ed. Theodore MacDonald, 18–28. New York: Routledge.

BEMFAM/DHS. 1991. Pesquisa sobre Saúde Familiar no Nordeste. Brazil: BEMFAM/DHS.

Beneria, Lourdes, and Gita Sen. 1981. Accumulation, Reproduction and Women's Role in

Economic Development: Boserup Revisited. *Signs: Journal of Women in Culture and Society* 7(2): 279–98.

Benhabib, Seyla. 1995. Subjectivity, Historiography, and Politics: Reflections on the Feminism/Postmodernism Exchange. In *Feminist Contentions: A Philosophical Exchange*, ed. Seyla Benhabib, Judith Butler, Drucilla Cornell, and Nancy Fraser. New York: Routledge.

Benjamin, Walter. 1969. The Task of the Translator. In *Illuminations*. New York: Schocken Books.

Bernstein, Nina. 2005. Language Barrier Called Health Hazard in E.R. *New York Times*, April 21.

Betancur, John, and Dave Gills, eds. 2000. *The Collaborative City: Opportunities and Struggles for Blacks and Latinos in US Cities*. New York: Garland.

Beverley, John. 1993. *Against Literature*. Minneapolis: University of Minnesota Press.

———. 1996. The Margin at the Center: On Testimonio. In *The Real Thing: Testimonial Discourse and Latin America*, ed. Georg M. Gugelberger, 23–41. Durham: Duke University Press.

Bhabha, Homi K. 1988. The Commitment to Theory. *New Formation* 5: 5–23.

———. 1994. *The Location of Culture*. New York: Routledge.

Biron, Rebecca E. 1996. Feminist Periodicals and Political Crisis in Mexico: *Fem, Debate Feminista* and *La Correa Feminista* in the 1990s. *Feminist Studies* 22(1): 151–69.

Blackwell, Maylei. 2000. *Geographies of Difference: Mapping Multiple Feminist Insurgencies and Transnational Public Cultures in the Americas*. Ph.D. diss., University of California, Santa Cruz.

———. 2004. (Re)Ordenando el Discurso de la Nación: El Movimiento de Mujeres Indígenas en México y la Práctica de la Autonomía. In *Mujeres y Nacionalismo: De la Independencia a la Nación del Nuevo Milenio*, ed. Natividad Gutiérrez Chong, 193–234. Mexico City: UNAM.

———. 2006. Weaving in the Spaces: Transnational Indigenous Women's Organizing and the Politics of Scale. In *Dissident Women: Gender and Cultural Politics in Chiapas*, ed. R. Aída Hernández, Shannon Speed, and Lynn Stephen, 240–318. Austin: University of Texas Press.

———. 2009. Zones of Autonomy: Gendered Cultural Citizenship and Indigenous Women's Organizing in Mexico. In *Gendered Citizenships: Transnational Perspectives on Knowledge Production, Political Activism, and Culture*, ed. Kia Lilly Caldwell, Kathleen Coll, Tracy Fisher, Renya K. Ramirez, and Lok Siu, 39–54. New York: Palgrave Macmillan.

———. 2012. The Practice of Autonomy in the Age of Neoliberalism: Strategies from the Indigenous Women's Movement in Mexico. *Journal of Latin American Studies* 44(4): 703–32.

Blackwood, Evelyn, and Saskia E. Wieringa. 1997. Introduction. In *Female Desires: Same-Sex Relations and Transgender Practices across Cultures*, ed. Evelyn Blackwood and Saskia E. Wieringa, 1–38. New York: Columbia University Press.

Bloom, Harold, ed. 2002. *Isabel Allende. Modern Critical Views Series*. Philadephia: Chelsea House.

Bobo, Jacqueline. 1995. *Black Women as Cultural Readers. Film and Culture*. New York: Columbia University Press.

Boserup, Ester. 1970. *Women's Role in Economic Development*. New York: St. Martin's.

Boston Women's Health Book Collective. 1971. *Our Bodies, Our Selves*. Boston: New England Free Press.

———. 1998 [2005]. *Our Bodies, Ourselves*. New York: Simon and Schuster.

———. 2000. *Nuestros Cuerpos, Nuestras Vidas / Our Bodies, Our Lives*. New York: Seven Stories.

Boullosa, Carmen. 1991. *Son Vacas, Somos Puercos: Filibusteros del Mar Caribe*. México: Era.

———. 1997. *They're Cows, We're Pigs*. Trans. Leland H. Chambers. New York: Grove.

Bourdieu, Pierre, and Loïc Wacquant. 1999. On the Cunning of Imperialist Reason. *Theory, Culture, and Society* 16(1): 41–58.

Boyce Davies, Carole. 1994. *Black Women, Writing, and Identity: Migrations of the Subject*. New York: Routledge.

———. 2008. *Left of Karl Marx: The Political Life of Black Communist Claudia Jones*. Durham: Duke University Press.

Braidotti, Rosi. 1994. *Nomadic Subjects: Embodiment and Sexual Difference in Contemporary Feminist Theory*. New York: Columbia University Press.

———. 2000. The Way We Were: Some Post-Structuralist Memoirs. *Women's Studies International Forum* 23(6): 715–28.

Braidotti, Rosi, Ewa Charkiewicz, Sabine Häusler, and Saskia Wieringa, 1994. *Women, the Environment and Sustainable Development: Towards a Theoretical Synthesis*. London: Zed Books.

Braschi, Giannina. 1998. *Yo-Yo Boing!* Pittsburgh, PA: Latin American Literary Review.

Brennan, Denise. 2004. Women Work, Men Sponge, and Everyone Gossips: Macho Men and Stigmatized/ing Women in a Sex Tourist Town. *Anthropological Quarterly* 77(4): 705–33.

Brennan, Timothy. 2001. The Cuts of Language: East/West of North/South. *Public Culture* 13(1): 39–64.

Brewer, Rose M. 1993. Theorizing Race, Class, and Gender: The New Scholarship of Black Feminist Intellectuals and Black Women's Labor. In *Theorizing Black Feminisms: The Visionary Pragmatism of Black Women*, ed. Stanley Myrise James and Abena P. A. Busia, 13–30. London: Routledge.

Bruner, Edward. 1989. Of Cannibals, Tourists and Ethnographers. *Cultural Anthropology* 4(4): 438–45.

Brysk, Alison. 1994. Acting Globally: Indian Rights and International Politics in Latin America. In *Indigenous Peoples and Democracy in Latin America*, ed. Donna Lee Van Cott, 271. New York: St. Martin's.

———. 2000. *From Tribal Village to Global Village: Indian Rights and International Relations in Latin America*. Stanford: Stanford University Press.

Budge, David. 1998. Burden of Being a Mother's Tongue. *Times Educational Supplement* (September 11): 32.

Bueno, Eva Paulino. 2000. Race, Gender, and the Politics of Reception of Latin American Testimonios. In *Going Global: The Transnational Reception of Third World Women Writers*, ed. Amal Amireh and Lisa Suhair Majaj, 115–47. New York: Garland.

Bunster, Ximena. 1985. A Leader of Her People. *Womens's Review of Books* 3(1): 11–12.

Burnham, Linda. 2001. The Wellspring of Black Feminist Theory. Working Paper Series 1, Women of Color Resource Center, Oakland, CA.

Buscaglia, Jose. 2003. *Undoing Empire. Race and Nation in the Mulatto Caribbean*. Minneapolis: University of Minnesota Press.

Butler, Judith. 1993. *Bodies that Matter*. New York: Routledge.

Caldwell, Kia L. 2000. Fronteiras da Diferença: Raça e Mulher no Brasil. *Revista Estudos Feministas* 8(2): 91–108.

Camacho, Michael E. Madsen. 2001. *The Politics of Progress: Constructing Paradise in Huatulco, Oaxaca*. Irvine: University of California Press.

Canclini, Néstor García. 2001. *Consumers and Citizens: Globalization and Multicultural Conflicts*. Minneapolis: University of Minnesota Press.

Candelario, Ginetta. 2007. *Black behind the Ears: Dominican Racial Identity from Museums to Beauty Shops*. Durham: Duke University Press.

Cantú, Lionel. 1999. *Border Crossings: Mexican Men and the Sexuality of Migration*. Ph.D. diss., University of California, Irvine.

———. 2000. Entre Hombres / Between Men: Latino Masculinities and Homosexualities. In *Gay Masculinities*, ed. Peter Nardi, 224–46. Thousand Oaks, CA: Sage.

———. 2002. De Ambiente: Queer Tourism and the Shifting Boundaries of Mexican Male Sexualities. *GLQ: A Journal of Lesbian and Gay Studies* 8(1): 139–66.

Carey-Webb, Allen, and Stephen Benz, eds. 1996. *Teaching and Testimony: Rigoberta Menchú and the North American Classroom*. Albany: State University of New York Press.

Caro, Pamela, and Marco Kremerman. 2005. Chile, Menos Pobreza, Más Desigualdad. Santiago: CEDEM / Fundacón Terram.

Carpazoo, Ana Rosa Lehman. 1994. *Turismo e Identidade—Construção de Identidades Sociais no Contexto do Turismo Sexual entre Alemães e Brasileiras na Cidade do Recife*. Master's thesis, Universidade Federal de Pernambuco.

Carr, Robert. 1994. Crossing the First World / Third World Divides. In *Scattered Hegemonies*, ed. Inderpal Grewal and Caren Kaplan, 153–72. Minneapolis: University of Minnesota Press.

Carrara, Sergio. 2004. Estratégias Anticoloniais: Sífilis, Raça e Identidade Nacional no Brasil do entre-guerras. In *Cuidar, Controlar, Curar: Ensaios Históricos Sobre Saúde e Doença na América Latina e o Caribe*, ed. Gilberto Hochman and Diego Armus, 427–54. Rio de Janeiro: Editora Fiocruz.

Carrillo, Teresa. 1998. Cross-Border Talk: Transnational Perspectives on Labor, Race, and Sexuality. In *Talking Visions: Multicultural Feminism in a Transnational Age*, ed. Ella Habiba Shohat, 391–411. New York: New Museum of Contemporary Art / MIT Press.

———. 2004. Watching over Greater Mexico: Mexican Initiative on Migration. In *Alambrista and the US–Mexico Border*, ed. Nick J. Cull and David Carrasco Albuquerque, 103–23. New Mexico: University of New Mexico Press.

———. 2007. The Best of Care: Latinas as Transnational Mothers and Caregivers. In *Technofuturos: Critical Interventions in Latina/o Studies*, ed. Nancy Raquel Mirabal and Agustín Lao-Montes, 191–212. Lanham, MD: Lexington Books.

Casen 2003. Documento Mujer. Santiago, Septiembre 2004. http://www.mideplan.cl /admin/docdescargas/centrodoc/centrodoc_234.pdf.

Castañeda, Xochitl, and Patricia Zavella. 2003. Changing Constructions of Sexuality and Risk: Migrant Mexican Women Farmworkers in California. *Journal of Latin American Anthropology* 8(2): 126–50.

Castel, Robert. 1991. From Dangerousness to Risk. In *The Foucault Effect: Studies in Governmentality*, ed. Graham Burchell, Colin Gordon, and Peter Miller, 281–97. Chicago: University of Chicago Press.

Castellanos, Rosario. 1958. *Balún Canán*. Mexico: Fondo de Cultura Económica.

———. 1989. *The Nine Guardians*. Trans. Irene Nicholson. London: Faber and Faber.

Castro, Mary, and Leila Lavinas. 1992. Do Feminismo ao Gênero: A Construção de um Objeto. In *Uma Questão de Gênero*, ed. Albertina O. Costa and Cristina Bruschini, 216–51. São Paulo: Editora Rosa dos Tempos / Fundação Carlos Chagas.

Centro Cultural Indígena. 2002. Mujer Mapuche: Emigración y Discriminación. Working Paper Series 10, Centro Cultural Indígena, Area Femenina. http://www.mapuche.info /mapuint/conacinfo20700.pdf.

Cepeda, Wendy. 1987. Al iniciar la primavera: Seis mujeres poetas hurgan sus creaciones. *Listín Diario*, July 30.

Céspedes, Diogenes, and Silvio Torres-Saillant. 2000. Fiction Is the Poor Man's Cinema: An Interview with Junot Díaz. *Callaloo: A Journal of African-American and African Arts and Letters* 23(3): 892–907.

Céspedes, Karina Lissette. 2007. Talking across Latinidades: Disindentificatory Feminism in El Mundo Surdo. In *Technofuturos: Critical Interventions in Latina/o Studies*, ed. N. R. Mirabal and A. Lao-Montes. New York: Lexington Books.

Chambers, Iain. 2010. Theory, Thresholds and Beyond. *Postcolonial Studies* 13(3): 255–64.

Chaney, Elsa M. 1998. Ni "Muchacha" ni "Criada": Las Trabajadoras del Hogar y su Lucha por Organizarse. In *Género y Cultura en América Latina*, coord. María Luisa Tarrés, 263–81. Mexico: El Colegio de México.

Chaney, Elsa M., and Mary G. Castro. 1989. *Muchachas No More: Household Workers in Latin America and the Caribbean*. Philadelphia: Temple University Press.

Chávez-Silverman, Susana. 2004. *Killer Crónicas: Bi-Lingual Memories*. Madison: University of Wisconsin Press.

———. 2010. *Scenes from la Cuenca de Los Angeles and Otros Natural Disasters*. Madison: University of Wisconsin Press.

Chávez-Silverman, Susana, and Frances R. Aparicio. 1997. *Tropicalizations: Transcultural Representations of Latinidad*. Hanover: University Press of New England.

Children Valuable as Cultural Interpreters. 2004 (April 1). *USA Today* 132(2707): 10.

Choque, María Eugenia. 1998. Colonial Domination and the Subordination of the Indigenous Woman in Bolivia. *Modern Fiction Studies* 44(1): 10–23.

Chow, Rey. 1995. *Primitive Passions: Visuality, Sexuality, Ethnography, and Contemporary Chinese Cinema*. New York: Columbia University Press.

———.1998a. *Ethics after Idealism*. Bloomington: Indiana University Press.

———. 1998b. The Fascist Longings in Our Midst. In *Ethics after Idealism: Theory, Culture, Ethnicity, Reading*, ed. Rey Chow, 14–32. Bloomington: Indiana University Press.

Christian, Barbara. 1987. The Race for Theory. *Cultural Critique* 6: 51–63.

Chungara, Domitila, and Moema Viezzer. 1978. "Si me permiten hablar . . . " *Testimonio de*

Domitila, Una Mujer de Las Minas de Bolivia. Historia inmediata. Mexico: Siglo Veintiuno Editores.

Circulará Nuevo Libro de Yrene Santos. 2003. http://www2.todito.com/paginas/noticias /122294.html (accessed March 6, 2005).

CLADEM. 2004. Reporte Alternativo. http://www.cladem.org/espanol/regionales /monitoreo_convenios/DESCChile-nov2004.asp.

Clark, Cindy, Ellen Sprenger, and Lisa VeneKlasen, with Lydia Alpizar Durán and Joanna Kerr. 2006. *Where Is the Money for Women's Rights? Assessing Resources and the Role of Donors in the Promotion of Women's Rights and the Support of Women's Organizations.* Mexico: AWID / Just Associates.

Clark Hine, Darlene, and Jacqueline McLeod, eds. 1999. *Crossing Boundaries: Comparative History of Black People in Diaspora.* Bloomington: Indiana University Press.

Clifford, James. 1988. *The Predicament of Culture: Twentieth Century Ethnography, Literature, and Art.* Cambridge, MA: Harvard University Press.

———. 1997. *Routes: Travel and Translation in the Late Twentieth Century.* Cambridge, MA: Harvard University Press.

Cocco De Filippis, Daisy. 1988. *Sin Otro Profeta Que Su Canto: Antología de Poesía Escrita por Dominicanas.* Santo Domingo: Taller.

———. 2000. Yrene Santos. In *Para que no se olviden: The Lives of Women in Dominican History,* 152. New York: Ediciones Alcance.

Cocco De Filippis, Daisy, and Sonia Rivera Valdés, eds. 2000. Yrene Santos. In *Conversación entre Escritoras del Caribe Hispano,* 87–90, 153–56. New York: Centro de Estudios Puertorriqueños.

Cohen, Erik. 1982. Thai Girls and Farang Men: The Edge of Ambiguity. *Annals of Tourism Research* 9: 403–28.

———. 1986. Lovelorn Farangs: The Correspondence between Foreign Men and Thai Girls. *Anthropological Quarterly* 59(3): 115–27.

———. 1993. Open-Ended Prostitution as a Skilful Game of Luck. Opportunity, Risk and Security among Tourist-Oriented Prostitutes in a Bangkok Soi. In *Tourism in South-East Asia,* ed. Michael Hitchcock, Victor T. King, and Mike Parnwell, 155–78. New York: Routledge.

Cohen, Suzanne, Jo Moran-Ellis, and Chris Smaje. 1999. Children as Informal Interpreters in GP Consultations: Pragmatics and Ideology. *Sociology of Health and Illness* 21(2): 163.

Commission for Historical Clarification. 1999. *Guatemala: Memory of Silence.* Guatemala City: Litoprint.

Community Reading Series. 2002. http://www.joinercenter.umb.edu/Programs/Literary %20Programs/Community%20Reading%2020Series/Community%20Reading%20 Series.htm (accessed March 3, 2005)

Comunicación e Información de la Mujer. 2001. Este Mes se Celebrará el IV Encuentro de Escritoras del Caribe Hispano. April 4, 2001. http://www.cimac.org.mx/noticias /01abr/01040408.html.

Conde, Rosina. 1994. *Women on the Road.* San Diego: San Diego State University Press.

Constable, Nicole. 2006. Brides, Maids, and Prostitutes: Reflections of the Study of "Trafficked" Women. *Journal of Multidisciplinary Studies* 3(2): 1449–90.

Coriolano, Luzia Neide. 1998. *Do Local ao Global—O Turismo Litorâneo Cearense*. Campinas: Papirus.

Corrêa, Mariza. 1982. Repensando a Familia Patriarcal Brasileira (notas para o estudo das formas de organização familiar no Brasil). In *Colcha de Retalhos*, ed. Maria S. Kofes Almeida et al., 13–28. São Paulo: Brasiliense.

———. 1996. Sobre a Invencao da Mulata. *Cadernos Pagu* 6(7): 35–50.

Costa, Albertina de Oliveira. 1996. Women's Studies in Brazil, or the Tightrope-Walking Strategy. In *Brazilian Issues on Education, Gender, and Race*, ed. Elba Siqueira da Sa Barretto and Dagmar M. L. Zibas, 37–47. Sao Paulo: Fundação Carlos Chagas.

Costa, Albertina O., and Cristina Bruschini, eds. 1992. *Uma Questão de Gênero*. São Paulo: Editora Rosa dos Tempos/Fundação Carlos Chagas.

Costa, Ana Alice Alcántara, and Cecilia Sardenberg. 1994. Teoria e Praxis Feminista na Academia: Os Nucleos de Estudos Sobre a Mulher nas Universidades Brasileiras. *Revista Estudos Feministas* 2: 387–400.

Costa, Claudia de Lima. 1998a. O Tráfego do Gênero. *Cadernos Pagu* 11: 127–40.

———. 1998b. *Off-Center: On the Limits of Theory and Lived Experience*. Ph.D. diss., University of Illinois, Urbana.

———. 2000. Being Here and Writing There: Gender and Translation in a Brazilian Landscape. *Signs: Journal of Women in Culture and Society* 25(3): 728–59.

———. 2003. As Publicações Feministas e a Política Transnacional da Tradução: Reflexões do Campo. *Revista Estudos Feministas* 11(1): 254–64.

———. 2004. Feminismo, Tradução, Transnacionalismo. In *Poéticas e Políticas Feministas*, ed. Claudia de Lima Costa and Simone Pereira Schmidt, 187–96. Florianópolis: Mulheres.

———. 2006. Lost (and Found?) in Translation: Feminism in Hemispheric Dialogue. *Latino Studies* 4(1–2): 62–78.

———. 2009. A Urgência do Póscolonial e os Desafios dos Feminismos Latinoamericanos. *Terceira Margem* 13(22): 70–85.

Crenshaw, Kimberlé. 1991. Mapping the Margins: Intersectionality, Identity Politics, and Violence Against Women of Color. *Stanford Law Review* 43: 1241–99.

Cusicanqui, S. Rivera. 1991. *Pachakuti: Los Aymara de Bolivia Frente a Medio Milenio de Colonialismo Chukiyawu*. Lima: Taller de Historia Oral Andina.

Cusicanqui, Silvia Rivera, and Rossana Barragán, eds. 1997. *Debates Post Coloniales: Una Introducción a los Estudios de la Subalternidad*. La Paz: Editorial Historias.

Dankelman, Irene, and Joan Davidson. 1988. *Women and the Environment in the Third World: Alliance for the Future*. London: Earthscan.

David, Eduardo. 1998. *Gay Mexico: The Men of Mexico*. Oakland, CA: Floating Lotus.

Davis, Angela. 2004. Legacies of Women of Color Feminism. Paper presented at the Cultural Studies Colloquium, University of California, Santa Cruz, October 6.

Davis, Kathy. 2002. Feminist Body / Politics as World Traveller. *European Journal of Women's Studies* 9(3): 223–47.

———. 2007. *The Making of Our Bodies, Ourselves: How Feminism Travels across Borders*. Durham: Duke University Press.

Daykin, Norma, and Jennie Naidoo. 1995. Feminist Critiques of Health Promotion. In *The*

Sociology of Health Promotion, ed. Robin Bunton, Sarah Nettleton, and Roger Burrows, 57–68. New York: Routledge.

Deere, Carmen Diana, and Magdalena León. 2001. Empowering Women: Land and Property Rights in Latin America. Pittsburgh: University of Pittsburgh Press.

De Kooning, Anouk. 2005. Global Dreams: Space, Class, and Gender in Middle Class Cairo. Ph.D. diss., University of Amsterdam.

Dias Filho, Antonio Jonas. 1998. Fulôs, Ritas, Gabrielas, Gringólogas e Garotas de Programa: Falas, Práticas, Textos e Imagens em Torno de Negras e Mestiças, que Apontam para a Construção da Identidade Nacional, a partir da Sensualidade Atribuída à Mulher Brasileira. Master's thesis. Universidade Federal da Bahia, Salvador.

Díaz, Ximena. 2004. La Flexibilización de la Jornada Laboral. In El Trabajo se Transforma: Relaciones de Producción y Relaciones de Género, ed. Rosalba Todaro and Sonia Yáñez. Santiago: CEM.

Diniz, S. G., C. de Mello e Souza, and A. P. Portella. 1998. "Not Like Our Mothers": Reproductive Choice and the Emergence of Citizenship among Brazilian Rural Workers, Domestic Workers and Housewives. In Negotiating Reproductive Rights: Women's Perspectives across Countries and Cultures, ed. Rosalind P. Petchesky and Karen Judd. New York: IRRRAG / Zed Books.

Domínguez, Nora. 2000. Diálogos del Género o Como no Caerse del Mapa. Revista Estudos Feministas 8(2): 113–26.

Duany, Jorge. 2008. The Puerto Rican Diaspora: Transnational Circuits of Culture, Politics, and Economics. Presented at The Hospitable US: Transacting Hemispheric Agency, Human Rights and Border Epistemologies Workshop, University of Connecticut, Storrs.

Dunbar Ortiz, Roxanne. 1984. Indians of the Americas: Human Rights and Self-Determination. New York: Praeger.

Dzidzienyo, Anani, and Suzanne Oboler, eds. 2005. Neither Enemies nor Friends: Latinos, Blacks, Afro-Latinos. New York: Palgrave.

Ehrenreich, Barbara. 2002. Maid to Order. In Global Woman: Nannies, Maids, and Sex Workers in the New Economy, ed. Barbara Ehrenreich and Arlie Russell Hochschild, 85–103. New York: Metropolitan Books.

Ehrenreich, Barbara, and Arlie Russell Hochschild, eds. 2002. Global Woman: Nannies, Maids, and Sex Workers in the New Economy. New York: Metropolitan Books.

Elbaum, Max. 2002. What Legacy from the Radical Internationalism of 1968? Radical History Review 82 (Winter): 37–64.

Eltit, Diamela. 1983. Lumpérica. Santiago de Chile: Planeta / Biblioteca del Sur.

———. 1997. E. Luminata. Trans. Ronald Christ. Santa Fe, NM: Lumen.

El Hilero. 1998. Mujeres . . . Con Olor y Sabor a Chiyangua: Una Entrevista. Cali, Colombia.

Ellis, Kathryn. 2000. Welfare and Bodily Order: Theorizing Transitions in Corporeal Discourses. In Social Policy and the Body: Transitions in Corporeal Discourse, ed. Kathryn Ellis and Hartley Dean, 1–22. Basingstoke: Macmillan.

EMBRATUR, Departamento de Estudos e Pesquisas Mercadológicas, Instituto Brasileiro de Turismo. 2001. Estudo da Demanda Turística Internacional.

Escárcega, Sylvia. 2010. Authenticating Strategic Essentialisms: The Politics of Indigenousness at the United Nations. Cultural Dynamics 22(1): 3–28.

Escárcega, Sylvia, and Stefano Varese, eds. 2004. *La Ruta Mixteca: El Impacto Etnopolítico de la Migración Trasnacional en los Pueblos Indígenas de México*. Mexico City: UNAM.

Escobar, Arturo. 1995. *Encountering Development: The Making and Unmaking of the Third World*. Princeton, NJ: Princeton University Press.

———. 2008. *Territories of Difference: Place, Movement, Life, Redes*. Durham: Duke University Press.

Esquivel, Laura. 1989. *Como Agua para Chocolate: Novela de Entregas Mensuales con Recetas, Amores y Remedios*. México: Editorial Planeta.

———. 1992. *Like Water for Chocolate: A Novel in Monthly Installments with Recipes, Romances and Home Remedies*. Trans. Carol Christensen and Thomas Christensen. New York: Doubleday.

———. 1993. *Como Agua para Chocolate*. New York: Doubleday.

Esteva, Gustavo. 2002. Patriarcado y Sexismo. *Proceso* 1365 (December 29): 26–28.

———. 2003. Racismo y Sexismo: Dos Caras de La Ceguera Dominante. *Proceso* 1367 (January 12): 60–61.

Estrada, Andrea. 2010. Found in Translation: Susan Jill-Levine's Artistry. *UC Santa Barbara Today* (Spring): 6–7.

Estudio para la Defensa de los Derechos de la Mujer y el Movimiento Homosexual de Lima. 2006. *Documento Expuesto en la Audiencia Temática "Discriminación por Orientación Sexual en el Perú" ante la Comisión Interamericana de Derechos Humanos*. Washington, DC.

Evaristo, Conceição. 2003. *Ponciá Vicêncio*. Belo Horizonte: Mazza Edições.

EZLN. 1994. *Documentos y Comunicados*. Mexico: ERA.

———. 1995. *Documentos y Comunicados*, vol. 2. Mexico: ERA.

Fairbairns, Zoë. 1988. Wages for Housework. *New Internationalist*, no. 181 (March). http://www.newint.org/features/1988/03/05/wages/ (accessed March 19, 2012).

Falcon, Sylvanna. 2006. "National Security" and the Violation of Women: Militarized Border Rape at the US-Mexico Border. In *Color of Violence: The Incite! Anthology*, ed. Incite! Women of Color Against Violence, 119–29. Cambridge, MA: South End.

Fanon, Frantz. 1967. *Black Skin, White Masks*. New York: Grove.

Felinto, Marilene. 2004. *As Mulheres de Tijucopapo*. Rio de Janeiro: Record.

Felski, Rita. 1989. *Beyond Feminist Aesthetics: Feminist Literature and Social Change*. Cambridge, MA: Harvard University Press.

Fernandes, Leela. 2000. Nationalizing "The Global": Media Images, Cultural Politics and the Middle Class in India. *Media, Culture and Society* 22(5): 611–28.

Fernandez, Nadine. 1999. Back to the Future? Women, Race, and Tourism in Cuba. In *Sun, Sex, and Gold: Tourism and Sex Work in the Caribbean*, ed. Kamala Kempadoo, 81–89. Lanham, MD: Rowman and Littlefield.

Ferré, Rosario. 1976. *Papeles de Pandora*. México: Joaquín Mortiz.

———. 1991. *The Youngest Doll*. Lincoln: University of Nebraska Press.

Ferree, Myra Marx, and Patricia Yancey Martin, eds. 1995. *Feminist Organizations: Harvest of the New Women's Movement*. Philadelphia: Temple University Press.

Flores, Juan, ed. 1993. *Divided Borders: Essays on Puerto Rican Identity*. Houston, TX: Arte Público.

Flores, Juan, and George Yúdice. 1993. Living Borders / Buscando América: Languages of

Latino Self-Formation. In *Divided Borders: Essays on Puerto Rican Identity*, ed. Juan Flores, 199–252. Houston, TX: Arte Público.

Forbis, Melissa M. 2006. Autonomy and a Handful of Herbs: Contesting Gender and Ethnic Identities through Healing. In *Dissident Women: Gender and Cultural Politics in Chiapas*, ed. Aída Hernández Castillo and Lynn M. Stephen, 176–202. Austin: University of Texas Press.

Fosse, E. and Roeiseland, A. 1999. From Vision to Reality? The Ottawa-Charter in Norwegian Health Policy. *Internet Journal of Health Promotion* 1, http://www.rhpeo.net /ijhp-articles/1999/1/index.htm.

Foster, David William. 1994. On Translating Miguel Méndez. *Bilingual Review* 19(3): 83.

Foucault, Michel. 1990. *The History of Sexuality*, volume 1. Trans. Robert Hurley. New York: Random House.

———. 1997. On the Genealogy of Ethics: An Overview of Work in Progress. In *Ethics: Subjectivity and Truth*, ed. Paul Rabinow. New York: New Press.

Fox, Jonathan, and Gaspar Rivera-Salgado. 2004. Building Civil Society among Indigenous Migrants. In *Indigenous Mexican Migrants in the United States*, ed. Jonathan Fox and Gaspar Rivera-Salgado, 1–68. San Diego: Center for U.S.-Mexican Studies, UCSD.

Franco, Jean. 1994. A Touch of Evil: Jesusa Rodríguez's Subversive Church. In *Negotiating Performances: Gender, Sexuality, and the Theatricality in Latin America*, ed. Diana Taylor and Juan Villegas, 159–75. Durham: Duke University Press.

———. 1998. Defrocking the Vatican: Feminism's Secular Project. In *Cultures of Politics, Politics of Cultures: Re-visioning Latin American Social Movements*, ed. Sonia E. Alvarez, Evelina Dagnino, and Arturo Escobar. Boulder, CO: Westview.

Frankenberg, Ruth. 1997. Local Whiteness, Localizing Whiteness. In *Displacing Whiteness*, ed. Ruth Frankenberg. Durham: Duke University Press.

Frankenberg, Ruth, and Lata Mani. 1993. Crosscurrents, Crosstalk: "Race," Postcoloniality, and the Politics of Location. *Cultural Studies* 7(2): 292–310.

Fraser, Nancy. 1997. Rethinking the Public Sphere: A Contribution to the Critique of Actually Existing Democracy. In *Justice Interruptus: Critical Reflections on the "Post-Socialist" Condition*, 69–98. New York: Routledge.

Fregoso, Rosa Linda. 2006a. On the Road with Angela Davis. In *The Chicana/o Cultural Studies Reader*, ed. Angie Chambram-Dernersesian, 431–40. New York: Routledge.

———. 2006b. The Complexities of "Feminicide" on the Border. In *Color of Violence: The Incite! Anthology*, ed. Incite! Women of Color Against Violence, 130–34. Cambridge, MA: South End.

Freire, Paulo. 1994. *Pedagogy of Hope*. New York: Continuum.

———. 2000. *The Paulo Freire Reader*. Ed. Anna Maria Freire and Donaldo Macedo. New York: Continuum.

French, John D. 2003. Translation, Diasporic Dialogue, and the Errors of Pierre Bourdieu and Loïc Wacquant. *Nepantla: Views from the South* 4(2): 375–89.

Freyre, Gilberto. 1954 [1998]. *Casa Grande e Senzala: Formação da Família Brasileira sob o Regime de Economia Patriarcal*. Rio de Janeiro: Livraria José Olympio Editora.

Friedman, Susan. 1998. *Mappings: Feminism and the Cultural Geographies of Encounter*. Princeton, NJ: Princeton University Press.

Fry, Peter. 1995–96. O Que a Cinderela Negra Tem a Dizer Sobre a Política Racial no Brasil. *Revista USP* (28): 122–36.

Fuertes, Denisse. 1987. Al Iniciar la Primavera: Recital poético. *Nuevo Diario* (April).

Fundo de População das Nações Unidas / IPLANCE. 1996. Ceará Mulher 1, 1, Fortaleza.

Galey, Margaret E. 1995. Women Find a Place. In *Women, Politics, and the United Nations*, ed. Anne Winslow, 11–27. Westport, CT: Greenwood.

Galindo, María. 2006. Evo Morales y la Descolonización Fálica del Estado Boliviano. *Ephemera* 6(3): 323–34.

Galindo, María, and Rosario Adrián. 2005. *Mujeres Creando*. London: Republicart / Goldsmiths University of London.

Gálvez, Thelma, and Rosalba Todaro. 1989. Housework for Pay in Chile: Not Just Another Job. In *Muchachas No More: Household Workers in Latin America and the Caribbean*, ed. Elsa M. Chaney, Mary Garcia Castro, and Margo L. Smith, 307–22. Philadelphia: Temple University Press.

Galvin, Rose. 2002. Disturbing Notions of Chronic Illness and Individual Responsibility: Towards a Genealogy of Morals. *Health: An Interdisciplinary Journal for the Social Study of Health, Illness and Medicine* 6(2): 107–37.

Gamson, Joshua. 1995. Must Identity Movements Self-Destruct? A Queer Dilemma. *Social Problems* 42(3): 390–407.

Gaspar de Alba, Alicia. 2005. *Desert Blood: The Juárez Murders*. Houston: Arte Público.

Gates, Henry Louis. 1989. *The Signifying Monkey: A Theory of African-American Literary Criticism*. New York: Oxford University Press.

Gentzler, Edwin. 2001. *Contemporary Translation Theories*. Clevedon: Multilingual Matters.

———. 2003. Interdisciplinary Connections (Translation, Theory). *Perspectives—Studies in Translatology* 11(1): 11–24.

Giacomini, Sônia. 2006. Mulatas Profissionais: Raça, Gênero, e Ocupação. *Revista de Estudos Feministas* 14(1): 85–101.

Giddens, Anthony. 1991. *Modernity and Self-Identity. Self and Society in the Late Modern Age*. Cambridge: Polity.

Gilroy, Paul. 1993. *The Black Atlantic: Double Consciousness and Modernity*. Cambridge, MA: Harvard University Press.

———. 2001. *O Atlântico Negro: Modernidade e Dupla Consciência*. São Paulo: Editora 34; Rio de Janeiro: Universidade Cândido Mendes, Centro de Estudos Afro-Asiáticos.

Glantz, Margo. 1981. *Las Genealogías*. México: Martín Casillas.

———. 1991. *The Family Tree*. Trans. Susan Bassnett. London: The Serpent's Tail.

Goldman, Francisco. 1992. *The Long Night of the White Chickens*. New York: Atlantic Monthly Press.

Goldstein, Donna M. 2003. *Laughter Out of Place: Race, Class, Violence, and Sexuality in a Rio Shantytown*. Berkeley: University of California Press.

Gómez-Barris, Macarena. 2009. *Where Memory Dwells: Culture and State Violence in Chile*. Berkeley: University of California Press.

Gonzalez, Deena. 1998. Speaking Secrets: Living Chicana Theory. In *Living Chicana Theory*, ed. Carla Trujillo, 46–77. Berkeley: Third Woman.

Gonzalez, Nirvana Rosa. 2010. Reviewing Our History, Charting New Roads. *Women's Health Journal* 3: 22–29.

González-Gimbernart, Esther. 1996. Coreografía de la Imagen. *Letras Femeninas* 22(1–2): 155–56.

Goodman, Emily Jane. 2010. Landmark State Law Protecting Domestic Workers Takes Effect. *Gotham Gazette*, November 29, 2010. http://www.gothamgazette.com/article /law/20101129/13/3420 (accessed November 11, 2011).

Gordon, Avery, and Christopher Newfield, eds. 1996. *Mapping Multiculturalism*. Minneapolis: University of Minnesota Press.

Gore, Dayo. 2011. *Radicalism at the Crossroads: African American Women Activists in the Cold War.* New York: New York University Press.

Governo do Estado do Ceará, Secretaria de Turismo. 2002. *Ceará, Terra da Luz: Indicadores Turísticos 1995/2001*. Fortaleza.

———. 2010. Conjuntura do Turismo no Ceará: Janeiro a Dezembro de 2009, Balanço do Turismo. http://www.setur.ce.gov.br/categoria1/copy4_of_estudos-e-pesquisas /document_view (accessed June 3, 2010).

Gray, Herman. 2005. *Cultural Moves: African Americans and the Politics of Representation.* Berkeley: University of California Press.

Gray, Herman, and Macarena Gómez-Barris, eds. Forthcoming. *Nation and Difference*. Minneapolis: University of Minnesota Press.

Green, Rayna. 1990. American Indian Women: Diverse Leadership for Social Change. In *Bridges of Power: Women's Multicultural Alliances*, ed. Lisa Albrecht and Rose Brewer, 61–73. Philadelphia: New Society Publishers.

Grewal, Inderpal, and Caren Kaplan. 1994a. Introduction: Transnational Feminist Practices and Questions of Postmodernity. In *Scattered Hegemonies: Postmodernity and Transnational Feminist Practices*, ed. Inderpal Grewal and Caren Kaplan. Minneapolis: University of Minnesota Press.

———, eds. 1994b. *Scattered Hegemonies: Postmodernity and Transnational Feminist Practices.* Minneapolis: University of Minnesota Press.

Grewal, Shabnam, Jackie Kay, Liliane Landor, Gail Lewis, and Pratibha Parmar, eds. 1988. *Charting the Journey: Writings by Black and Third World Women*. London: Sheba Feminist Publishers.

Grosz, Elizabeth. 1994. *Volatile Bodies: Toward a Corporeal Feminism*. Sydney: Allen and Unwin.

Grueso, Libia, Carlos Rosero, and Arturo Escobar. 1998. The Process of Black Community Organizing in the Southern Pacific Coast Region of Colombia. In *Cultures of Politics / Politics of Cultures: Re-Visioning Latin American Social Movements*, ed. Sonia Alvarez, Evelina Dagnino, and Arturo Escobar, 196–219. Boulder, CO: Westview.

Guano, Emanuela. 2002. Spectacles of Modernity: Transnational Imagination and Local Hegemonies in Neoliberal Buenos Aires. *Cultural Anthropology* 17(2): 181–209.

Gugelberger, Georg M., ed. 1996. *The Real Thing: Testimonial Discourse and Latin America.* Durham: Duke University Press.

Guimarães, Antônio Sérgio Alfredo. 1999. *Racismo e Anti-Racismo no Brasil*. São Paulo: Editora 34.

———. 2002. *Classes, Raças e Democracia*. São Paulo: Editora 34.

Gunew, Sneja. 2002. Feminist Cultural Literacy: Translating Differences, Cannibal Options. In *Women's Studies on Its Own*, ed. Robyn Wiegman, 47–65. Durham: Duke University Press.

Gunning, Sandra, Tera W. Hunter, and Michele Mitchell, eds. 2004. *Dialogues of Dispersal: Gender, Sexuality, and African Diasporas*. Oxford: Blackwell.

Gupta, Akhil, and James Ferguson. 1992. Beyond "Culture": Space, Identity, and the Politics of Difference. *Cultural Anthropology* 7(1): 6–23.

Hahner, June Edith. 1990. *Emancipating the Female Sex: The Struggle for Women's Rights in Brazil, 1850–1940*. Durham: Duke University Press.

Hale, Charles, R. 2002. Does Multiculturalism Menace? Governance, Cultural Rights and the Politics of Identity in Guatemala. *Journal of Latin American Studies* 34(3): 485–524.

Hall, Nigel. 2004. The Child in the Middle: Agency and Diplomacy in Language Brokering Events. In *Claims, Changes, and Challenges in Translation Studies*, ed. Gyde Hansen, Kirsten Malmkjær, and Daniel Gile, vol. 1, 285–96. Amsterdam: J. Benjamins.

Hall, Stuart. 1996. When Was "The Post-Colonial"? Thinking at the Limit. In *The Post-Colonial Question: Common Skies, Divided Horizons*, ed. Iain Chambers and Lidia Curti, 242–60. New York: Routledge.

———. 2003. Pensando a Diáspora: Reflexões Sobre a Terra no Exterior. In *Da Diáspora: Identidades e Mediações Culturais*, ed. Liv Sovik, 25–50. Belo Horizonte: Editora UFMG.

Hanchard, Michael. 1997. Identity, Meaning, and the African-American. In *Dangerous Liaisons: Gender, Nation, and Postcolonial Perspectives*, ed. Anne McClintock, Aamir Mufti, and Ella Shohat, 230–39. Minneapolis: University of Minnesota Press.

———, ed. 1999. *Racial Politics in Contemporary Brazil: Comparisons with the U.S. Case*. Durham: Duke University Press.

Haraway, Donna. 1991. A Cyborg Manifesto: Science, Technology, and Socialist-Feminism in the Late Twentieth Century. In *Simians, Cyborgs and Women: The Reinvention of Nature*, 149–81. New York: Routledge.

———. 1994. Um Manifesto Para os Cyborgs: Ciência, Tecnologia e Feminismo Socialista na Década de 80. In *Tendências e Impasses: O Feminismo Como Crítica da Cultura*, ed. Heloísa Buarque de Hollanda, 243–88. Rio de Janeiro: Rocco.

———. 1997. Race: Universal Donors in a Vampire Culture: It's All in the Family. Biological Kinship Categories in the Twentieth-Century United States. In *Modest_Witness@ Second_Millenium. FemaleMan@_Meets_Oncomouse: Feminism and Technoscience*, 213–65. New York: Routledge.

Harcourt, Wendy, and Arturo Escobar, eds. 2005. *Women and the Politics of Place*. Bloomfield, CT: Kumarian.

Health and Human Services. 2011. *Action Plan to Reduce Racial and Ethnic Health Disparities: A Nation Free of Disparities in Health and Health Care*. Washington, DC: Office of Minority Health. http://minorityhealth.hhs.gov/npa/files/Plans/HHS/HHS_Plan_complete.pdf (accessed July 22, 2013).

Hedrick, Tace. 1996. Rigoberta's Earrings: The Limits of Teaching Testimonio. In *Teaching and Testimony: Rigoberta Menchú and the North American Classroom*, ed. Allen Carey-Webb and Stephen Benz, 223–35. Albany: State University of New York Press.

Heilborn, Maria Luisa, and Regina Barbosa. 2003. Sexuality Research Training in Brazil. In *Handbook of Sexuality Research Training Initiatives*, ed. Diane Mauro, Gilbert Herdt and Richard Parker, chapter 9. New York: Social Science Research Council.

Heilborn, Maria Luisa, and Bila Sorj. 1999. Estudos de Género no Brasil. In *O Que Ler na Ciência Social Brasileira*. São Paulo: Anpocs.

Hemmings, Clare. 2005. Telling Feminist Stories. *Feminist Theory* 6(2): 115–39.

———. 2011. *Why Stories Matter: The Political Grammar of Feminist Theory*. Durham: Duke University Press.

Heredia, Beatriz Maria Alasia de. 1979. *A Morada da Vida: Trabalho Familiar de Pequenos Produtores do Nordeste do Brasil*. Rio de Janeiro: Paz e Terra.

Hernández, Tanya K. 2003. "Too Black to Be Latino/a": Blackness and Blacks as Foreigners in Latino Studies. *Latino Studies* 1 (March): 152–59.

Hernández Castillo, Rosalva Aída. 2001. Entre el Etnocentrismo Feminista y el Esencialismo Etnico. Las Mujeres Indígenas y sus Demandas de Género. *Debate Feminista* 24 (October): 206–29.

———. 2006. Zapatismo and the Emergence of Indigenous Feminism. In *Dispatches from Latin America: On the Frontlines against Neoliberalism*, ed. Teo Ballvé and Vijay Prashad, 229–42. Cambridge, MA: South End.

Hicks, Diana, and Jonathan Potter. 1991. Sociology of Scientific Knowledge: A Reflexive Citation Analysis; or, Science Disciplines and Disciplining Sciences. *Social Studies of Science* 21(3): 459–501.

Hill Collins, Patricia. 2000. *Black Feminist Thought*. New York: Routledge.

Hinley, Jane. 1996. Towards a Pluricultural Nation: The Limits of Indigenismo and Article 4. In *Dismantling the Mexican State*, ed. Robe Aitken, Nikki Craske, Gareth Jones, and David E. Stansfield, 225–43. New York: St. Martin's.

Hinojosa, Claudia. 2004. Gritos y Susurros: Una Historia sobre la Presencia Pública de las Feministas Lesbianas. *Cotidiano Mujer* 39 1/2 (February). http://www.cotidianomujer .org.uy/2004/39ycairo3.htm.

Hirsch, Marianne. 1994. Pictures of a Displaced Girlhood. In *Displacements: Cultural Identities in Question*, ed. Angelika Bammer, 71–89. Bloomington: Indiana University Press.

———. 2001. Surviving Images: Holocaust Photographs and the Work of Postmemory. *Yale Journal of Criticism* 14(1): 5–37.

Holanda, Sérgio Buarque de. 1959. *Visão do Paraíso: Os Motivos Edênicos no Descobrimento e Colonização do Brasil*. São Paulo: Companhia Editora Nacional Editora da Universidade de São Paulo.

Hollanda, Heloísa Buarque de. 1992. Os Estudos Sobre a Mulher e Literatura no Brasil: Uma Primeira Avaliação. In *Uma Questão de Gênero*, ed. Albertina de Oliveira Costa and Cristina Bruschini, 54–92. Rio de Janeiro: Editora Rosa dos Tempos / Fundação Carlos Chagas.

———. 1998. The Law of the Cannibal or How to Deal with the Idea of "Difference" in Brazil. Paper given at a conference at New York University, April 20, New York City.

Hondagneu-Sotelo, Pierrette. 2002. Families on the Frontier: From Braceros in the Fields to Braceras in the Home. In *Latinos Remaking America*, ed. Marcelo M. Suárez-Orozco and Mariela M. Páez, 259–73. Berkeley: University of California Press.

———. 2007. *Religion and Social Justice for Immigrants*. New Brunswick, NJ: Rutgers University Press.

Horowitz, Daniel. 1998. *Betty Friedan and the Making of the Feminist Mystique: The American Left, the Cold War and Modern Feminism*. Amherst: University of Massachusetts Press.

Hull, Gloria T., Patricia Bell-Scott, and Barbara Smith, eds. 1982. *All the Women Are White,*

All the Blacks Are Men, but Some of Us Are Brave; Home Girls: A Black Feminist Anthology. Old Westbury, NY: Feminist Press.

Hulme, David, and Michael Edwards. 1997. NGOs, States and Donors: An Overview and Key Issues. In NGOs, States and Donors: Too Close for Comfort?, ed. David Hulme and Michael Edwards, 3–22. New York: St. Martin's.

Human Rights Watch. 2011. ILO: New Landmark Treaty to Protect Domestic Workers. Press release, June 16. http://www.hrw.org/news/2011/06/16/ilo-new-landmark-treaty -protect-domestic-workers (accessed on November 20, 2011).

Hurtado, Aida. 1996. The Color of Privilege: Three Blasphemies on Race and Feminism. Ann Arbor: University of Michigan Press.

Ibarra, María de la Luz. 2007. Mexican Immigrant Women and the New Domestic Labor. In Women and Migration in the U.S.-Mexico Borderlands, ed. Denise A. Segura and Patricia Zavella, 286–306. Durham: Duke University Press.

Iglesias, Norma. 1985. La Flor Más Bella de la Maquiladora. Mexico: SEP.

———. 1997. Beautiful Flowers of the Maquiladoras: Life Histories of Women Workers in Tijuana, trans. Michael Stone and Gabrielle Winkler. Austin: University of Texas Press.

Illo, Jeanne Frances. 2005. "Politics" and Academic Feminist Theorising: Reflections on Women's Studies in Asia. Australian Feminist Studies 20(47): 195–205.

Inda, Jonathan Xavier. 2006. Targeting Immigrants: Government, Technology, and Ethics. New York: Blackwell.

Instituto Brasileiro De Geografia Estatística. 1991. Censo Demográfico 1991.

———. 2000. Censo Demográfico 2000.

———. 2001. Pesquisa Nacional de Amostra por Domicílio.

Instituto Nacional de Salud Pública. 2008. Encuesta de Salud y Derechos de las Mujeres Indíge-nas. Cuernavaca, Mexico.

Jaimes, M. Annette, and Theresa Halsey. 1992. American Indian Women: At the Center of Indigenous Resistance in North America. In The State of Native America: Genocide, Colonization and Resistance, ed. M. Annette Jaimes, 311–44. Cambridge, MA: South End.

Jaimes-Guerrero, M. Annette. 1997. Civil Rights versus Sovereignty: Native American Women in Life and Land Struggles. In Feminist Genealogies: Colonial Legacies and Demo-cratic Futures, ed. M. Jacqui Alexander and Chandra Talpade Mohanty, 101–21. New York: Routledge.

Jacobs, Barbara. 1987. Las Hojas Muertas. Mexico City: Era.

———. 1993. The Dead Leaves. Trans. David Unger. Willimantic, CT: Curbston.

Jara, René, and Hernán Vidal. 1986. Testimonio y Literatura. Minneapolis: Institute for the Study of Ideologies and Literature.

Jardine, Alice. 1988. Gynesis: Configurations of Woman and Modernity. Ithaca, NY: Cornell University Press.

Jennings, James, ed. 1994. Blacks, Latinos, and Asians in Urban America: Status and Prospects for Politics and Activism. Westport, CT: Praeger.

Jesus, Carolina Maria de. 1963. Child of the Dark: The Diary of Carolina Maria de Jesus. Trans. David St. Clair. London: Penguin Books.

John, Mary E. 1996. Discrepant Dislocations: Feminism, Theory, and Postcolonial Histories. Berkeley: University of California Press.

Johnston, Paul. 2004. The Blossoming of Transnational Citizenship: A California Town Defends Indigenous Migrants. In *Indigenous Mexican Migrants in the United States*, ed. Jonathan Fox and Gaspar Rivera-Salgado. San Diego: Center for U.S.-Mexican Studies, UCSD.

Jordan, June. 2002. *Some of Us Did Not Die*. New York: Basic Books.

Kabeer, Naila. 1994. *Reversed Realities: Gender Hierarchies in Development Thought*. London: Verso.

Kaiser, Susana. 2005. *Postmemories of Terror: A New Generation Copes with the Legacy of the "Dirty War."* New York: Palgrave Macmillan.

Kandiyoti, Deniz. 1998. Gender, Power and Contestation: "Rethinking Bargaining with Patriarchy." In *Feminist Visions of Development*, ed. Cecile Jackson and Ruth Pearson, 135–51. London: Routledge.

Kaplan, Caren. 1994. The Politics of Location as Transnational Feminist Critical Practice. In *Scattered Hegemonies: Postmodernity and Transnational Feminist Practices*, ed. Iderpal Grewal and Caren Kaplan. Minneapolis: University of Minnesota Press.

———. 1996. *Questions of Travel: Postmodern Discourses of Displacement*. Durham: Duke University Press.

Kelley, Robin D. G. 2003. *Freedom Dreams: The Black Radical Imagination*. Boston: Beacon.

Kempadoo, Kamala. 1998. Migrations and Tourism: Introduction. In *Global Sex Workers: Rights, Resistance, and Redefinition*, ed. Kamala Kempadoo and Jo Doezema, 99–103. New York: Routledge.

———. 1999. Continuities and Change: Five Centuries of Prostitution in the Caribbean. In *Sun, Sex and Gold: Tourism and Sex Work in the Caribbean*, ed. Kamala Kempadoo. Lanham, MD: Rowman and Littlefield.

———. 2004. *Sexing the Caribbean. Gender, Race and Sexual Labour*. New York: Routledge.

King, Katie. 2001. Productive Agencies of Feminist Theories: The Work It Does. *Feminist Theory* 2(1): 94–98.

Kinzer, Stephen. 2003. America Yawns at Foreign Fiction. *New York Times*, July 26.

Kirkwood, Julieta. 1986. *Ser Política en Chile: Las Feministas y los Partidos*. Santiago: FLACSO.

Knapp, Gudrun-Axeli. 2005. Race, Class, Gender: Reclaiming Baggage in Fast Travelling Theories. *European Journal of Women's Studies* 12(3): 249–65.

Kofes, Suely. 1976. *Entre Nós, os Pobres; Eles, os Negros*. Master's thesis, Unicamp.

Kresge, Lisa. 2007. *Indigenous Oaxacan Communities in California: An Overview*. California Institute for Rural Studies, November. http://www. cirsinc. org/Documents/Pub 1107.

Kuhiwczak, Piotr, and Karin Littau. 2007. Introduction. In *A Companion to Translation Studies*, ed. Piotr Kuhiwczak and Karin Littau, 1–12. Clevedon: Multilingual Matters.

Kuznesof, Elizabeth. 1989. A History of Domestic Service in Spanish America, 1492–1980. In *Muchachas No More: Household Workers in Latin America and the Caribbean*, ed. Elsa M. Chaney, Mary Garcia Castro, and Margo L. Smith, 17–36. Philadelphia: Temple University Press.

Lacan, Jacques. 1985. El Estadio del Espejo Como Formador de la Función del Yo [Je] Tal Como Se Nos Presenta en la Experiencia Psicoanalítica. In *Escritos II*. Mexico: Siglo Veintiuno.

La Fountain-Stokes, Lawrence. 2008. Trans/Bolero/Drag/Migration: Music, Cultural Translation, and Diasporic Puerto Rican Theatricalities. *WSQ: Women's Studies Quarterly* 36(3–4): 190–209.

———. 2011. Translocas: Migration, Homosexuality, and Transvestism in Recent Puerto Rican Performance. *e-misférica* 8 (1). http://hemisphericinstitute.org/hemi/en/e -misferica-81/lafountain.

La Jornada. 2006. Mujeres de AL Exigen más Espacios Políticos. . . . *La Jornada*, March 9. http://www.jornada.unam.mx/2006/03/09/054n1soc.php.

La Segunda. 2006. *Dónde Viven los Nuevos Ministros: Por sus Barrios los Conoceréis*. April 12. http://www.lasegunda.com.

Laldyada. 2005. Naked Song. In *Other Women's Voices—Translations of Women's Writing Before 1700*. http://home.infionline.net.

Lamas, Marta. 1986a. La Antropología Feminista y la Categoría de "Género." *Nueva Antropología. Estudios Sobre la Mujer: Problemas Teóricos* 30.

———. 1986b. El Movimiento de las Costureras. *Fem*, no. 45 (April–May).

———. 1994. El EZLN, El Vaticano: El Aborto y el Estado Mexicano. *La Jornada* 29 (April). Rpt. in *Chiapas ¿Y las mujeres qué?*, ed. Rosa Rojas, 1:139–42. Mexico: CICAM.

———. 2002. Mujeres en Debate. *Proceso* 1364 (December 22): 33–34.

———. 2003. Género: ¡Bienvenido un Debate tan Necesario! *Proceso* 1366 (January 5): 58–59.

———. 2006. Betty Friedan. *Proceso* 1528 (February 12): 73.

Lao-Montes, Agustín. 2007. Afro-Latinidades: Bridging Blackness and Latinidad. In *Technofuturos: Critical Interventions in Latina/o Studies*, ed. N. R. Mirabal and A. Laó-Montes. New York: Lexington Books.

Lao-Montes, Agustín, and Arlene Davila, eds. 2001. *Mambo Montage: The Latinization of New York*. New York: Columbia University Press.

Larkosh, Christopher. 2002. Translating Woman: Victoria Ocampo and the Empires of Foreign Fascination. In *Translation and Power*, ed. Maria Tymoczko and Edwin Gentzler, 80–98. Amherst: University of Massachusetts Press.

Larson, Linda. 1994. A Culture Fights for Survival. *English Journal* 83(8): 105–6.

Latina Feminist Group. 2001a. Introduction. Papelitos Guardados: Theorizing Latinidades through Testimonio. In *Telling to Live*, ed. The Latina Feminist Group. Durham: Duke University Press.

———. 2001b. *Telling to Live: Latina Feminist Testimonios*. Durham: Duke University Press.

Lau Jaiven, Ana. 1987. *La Nueva Ola del Feminismo en México*. Mexico: Planeta.

Lauretis, Teresa de. 1994. A Tecnologia do Gênero. In *Tendências e Impasses: O Feminismo Como Crítica da Cultura*, ed. Heloísa Buarque de Hollanda, 206–42. Rio de Janeiro: Rocco.

Lefevere, André. 1992. *Translation, Rewriting, and the Manipulation of Literary Fame*. New York: Routledge.

Lemaire, Ria. 2000. Metaforizar: Des-metaforizar, Re-metaforizar—Qual é a Verdade que (não) se quer Revelar? O Caso de Casa-Grande e Senzala. *Rivista di Studi Portoghesi e Brasiliani (Roma)* 2: 125–39.

León, Irene, and Phumi Mtetwa, eds. 2003. *Globalization: Alternativas GLBT. Dialogo Sur/Sur GLBT*. Quito, Ecuador: Enero.

Lewis, Earl. 1999. To Turn as on a Pivot: Writing African Americans into a History of Overlapping Diasporas. In *Crossing Boundaries: Comparative History of Black People in*

Diaspora, ed. Darlene Clark Hine and Jacqueline McLeod, 3–32. Bloomington: Indiana University Press.

Lillis, Theresa, Ann Hewings, Dimitra Vladimirou, and Mary Jane Cury. 2010. The Geolinguistics of English as an Academic Lingua Franca: Citation Practices across English-Medium National and English-Medium International Journals. *International Journal of Applied Linguistics* 20(1): 110–35.

Lipsitz, George. 1993. *The Possessive Investment in Whiteness: How White People Profit from Identity Politics*. Philadelphia: Temple University Press.

Liu, Lydia H. 1995. *Translingual Practice: Literature, National Culture, and Translated Modernity: China 1900–1937*. Palo Alto, CA: Stanford University Press.

Logan, Kathleen. 1997. Personal Testimony: Latin American Women Telling Their Lives. *LARR* 32(1): 199–211.

Lorde, Audre. 1983. *Sister Outsider: Essays and Speeches*. Freedom, CA: Crossing.

Los más leidos. 2002. Revista [A]HORA (1,279) (November 4). http://www.ahora.com.do /Edicion1279/SECCIONES/libros.html (accessed June 19, 2007).

Lovera, Sara, and Nellys Paloma, eds. 1997 [1999]. *Las Alzadas*. Mexico: Centro de Información de la Mujer A.C. y Convergencia Socialista.

Lowe, Elizabeth, and Earl E. Fitz. 2007. *Translation and the Rise of Inter-American Literature*. Gainesville: University Press of Florida.

Lowe, Lisa. 1997. Angela Davis: Reflections on Race, Class and Gender in the USA. In *The Politics of Culture in the Shadow of Capital*, ed. Lisa Lowe and David Lloyd, 303–23. Durham: Duke University Press.

Ludec, Nathalie. 1999. México: Mujeres Hacia la Emancipación y la Afirmación. In *Mujer, Creación y Problemas de Identidad en América Latina*, ed. Roland Forgues. Mérida, Venezuela: Universidad de los Andes.

Lugones, Maria. 1990. Playfulness, "World" Traveling, and Loving Perception. In *Making Face, Making Soul / Haciendo Caras: Creative and Critical Perspectives by Women of Color*, ed. Gloria Anzaldúa. San Francisco: Aunt Lute.

———. 1997. Playfulness, "World"-Traveling, and Loving Perception. In *Feminist Social Thought: A Reader*, ed. Diana T. Meyers, 148–59. New York: Routledge.

———. 2003a. Introduction. In *Pilgrimages/Peregrinajes: Theorizing Coalition against Multiple Oppressions*, 1–39. Lanham, MD: Rowman and Littlefied.

———. 2003b. *Pilgrimages/Peregrinajes: Theorizing Coalition against Multiple Opressions*. Lanham, MD: Rowan and Littlefield.

———. 2003c. Playfulness, "World"-Traveling, and Loving Perception. In *Pilgrimages/ Peregrinajes: Theorizing Coalition against Multiple Oppressions*, 77–102. Lanham, MD: Rowman and Littlefied.

———. 2007. Heterosexualism and the Colonial/Modern Gender System. *Hypatia* 22(1): 186–209.

Lutz, Catherine. 1995. The Gender of Theory. In *Women Writing Culture*, ed. Ruth Behar and Deborah Gordon, 249–66. Berkeley: University of California Press.

MacDonald, Theodore Harney. 1998. *Rethinking Health Promotion: A Global Approach*. New York: Routledge.

Machado, Lia Zanotta. 1997. Estudos de Gênero: Para Além do Jogo entre Intelectuais e

Feministas. In *Gênero Sem Fronteiras*, ed. Mônica Raisa Schpun, 93–140. Florianópolis: Editora Mulheres.

MacKinnon, Catherine. 1987. Difference and Dominance: On Sex Discrimination. In *Feminism Unmodified: Discourses on Life and Law*, 32–45. Cambridge, MA: Harvard University Press.

Mahmood, Saba. 2005. *The Politics of Piety: The Islamic Revival and the Feminist Subject.* Princeton, NJ: Princeton University Press.

Maia, Suzana. 2009. Intersections of the Transnational: Brazilian Dancers in New York City's Gentlemen's Bars. *Vibrant* 6(1): 37–64.

———. 2010. Brazilian Women Crossing Borders. In *Gendering Border Studies*, ed. Jane Aaron, Henrice Altink, and Chris Weedon, 1:63–82. Cardiff: University of Wales Press.

———. 2012a. Identificando a Branquidade Inominada: Corpo, Raça e Nação nas Representações sobre Gisele Bündchen na Mídia Transnacional. *Cadernos Pagu* (UNICAMP) 38:309–41.

———. 2012b. *Transnational Desires: Brazilian Erotic Dancers in New York.* Nashville: Vanderbilt University Press.

Main, Shelly. 1998. Our Feminist Institutions, Ourselves. *Sojourner* 23: 10–14.

Mainardi, Pat. 1970. The Politics of Housework. In *Sisterhood Is Powerful*, ed. Robin Morgan, 447–54. New York: Vintage Books.

Mani, Lata. 2003. Multiple Mediations: Feminist Scholarship in the Age of Multinational Reception. In *Feminist Theory Reader: Local and Global Perspectives*, ed. Carole R. McCann and Kim Seung-Kyung, 364–77. New York: Routledge.

Marcos (Subcomandante). 1994. Letter to Marta Lamas. *La Jornada*, May 11. In *Chiapas, ¿Y las Mujeres Qué?*, vol. 1, ed. Rosa Rojas. México: CICAM.

———. 2009. Siete Vientos en los Calendarios y Geografías de Abajo. http://enlacezapatista .ezln.org.mx/2009/01/04/tercer-viento-un-digno-y-rabioso-color-de-la-tierra-tercer -mesa-del-3-de-enero/.

Marcos (Subcomandante) and Julia Pachecho. 2004. *Relatos del Viejo Antonio.* Ediciones Desde Abajo.

Marcos, Sylvia. 2002. Carta a Proceso. *Proceso* 1365 (December 29).

Marín, Lynda. 1991. Speaking Out Together: Testimonials of Latin American Women. *Latin American Perspectives* 18(3): 51–68.

Márquez, Francisca. 2002. Innovación Institucional en la Formación Laboral con Perspectiva de Género: El Programa de Habilitación Laboral para Mujeres de Escasos Recursos—CHILE. In *Diálogo Social, Formación Profesional e Institucionalidad*, ed. Anne Caroline Posthuma. Montevideo: Cinterfor.

Márquez, Roberto. 2000. Raza, Racismo, e Historia: Are All of My Bones from There? *Latino Research Review*, no. 4: 8–22.

Martínez-Echezábal, Lourdes. 1990. *Para una Semiotica de la Mulatez.* Madrid: Ediciones Jose Porrua Turanzas.

Martínez-Márquez, Alberto. n.d. *Cuatro Poetas Mujeres Actuales de la República Dominicana.* http://www.geocities.com/poeta_invitado/poetas_dominicanas.html (accessed June 16, 2007).

Martínez Pizarro, Jorge. 2003. *El Mapa Migratorio de América Latina y el Caribe, las Mujeres y el Género.* New York: United Nations Publications.

———. 2003. *El Encanto de los Datos: Sociodemografía de la Inmigración en Chile según el Censo de 2002.* Serie Población y Desarrollo N° 49, Diciembre. Santiago: Cepal.

Marx, Anthony W. 1998. *Making Race and Nation: A Comparison of South Africa, the United States, and Brazil.* Cambridge: Cambridge University Press.

Masiello, Francine. 2000. Conhecimento Suplementar: Queering o Eixo Norte/Sul. *Revista Estudos Feministas* 8(2): 49–62.

Matthews, Irene. 2000. Translating/Transgressing/Torture. . . . In *Frontline Feminisms: Women, War, and Resistance,* ed. Marguerite R. Waller and Jennifer Rycenga, 85–112. New York: Garland.

McCallum, Cecilia. 2005. Racialized Bodies, Naturalized Classes: Moving through the City of Salvador da Bahia. *American Ethnologist* 32(1): 100–117.

McClintock, Anne. 1995. *Imperial Leather: Race, Gender and Sexuality in the Colonial Contest.* New York: Routledge.

McElhinny, Bonnie. 2003. Theorizing Gender in Sociolinguistics and Linguistic Anthropology. In *The Language and Gender Handbook,* ed. Janet Homes and Miriam Meyerhoff, 21–42. Oxford: Basil Blackwell.

McGregor, Sue. 2001. Neoliberalism and Health Care. *International Journal of Consumer Studies* 25(2): 82–89.

McKittrick, Katherine. 2006. *Demonic Grounds: Black Women and the Cartographies of Struggle.* Minneapolis: University of Minnesota Press.

Melo, Hildete Pereira de. 1989. Feminists and Domestic Workers in Rio De Janeiro. In *Muchachas No More: Household Workers in Latin America and the Caribbean,* ed. Elsa Chaney and Mary Garcia Castro, 245–70. Philadelphia: Temple University Press.

Memmi, Albert. 1977. *Retrato do Colonizado Precedido Pelo Retrato do Colonizador.* Rio de Janeiro: Paz e Terra.

Menchú, Rigoberta, and Elizabeth Burgos-Debray. 1985 [1983]. *Me Llamo Rigoberta Menchú y así me Nació la Conciencia.* Mexico: Siglo Veintiuno Editores; Havana: Casa de las Americas.

———. 1984. *I, Rigoberta Menchú: An Indian Woman in Guatemala.* Trans. Ann Wright. London: Verso.

Meredith, Paul. 1998. Hybridity in the Third Space: Rethinking Bi-cultural Politics in Aotearoa / New Zealand. Paper presented at the Te Oru Rangahau Maori Research and Development Conference, July 7–9, Massey University. http://lianz.waikato.ac.nz /PAPERS/paul/hybridity.pdf.

Mies, Maria. 1982. *The Lace Makers of Narsapur: Indian Housewives Produce for the World Market.* London: Zed Books.

———. 1998. *Patriarchy and Accumulation on a World Scale: Women in the International Divison of Labor.* London: Zed Books.

Mignolo, Walter. 2000. *Local Histories / Global Designs: Coloniality, Subaltern Knowledges, and Border Thinking.* Princeton, NJ: Princeton University Press.

———. 2006. *The Idea of Latin America.* Cambridge: Blackwell.

Milian Arias, Claudia. 2006. Playing with the Dark: Africana and Latino Literary Imaginations. In *The Blackwell Companion to African-American Studies*, ed. Lewis R. Gordon and Jane Anna Gordon, 554–67. Cambridge: Blackwell.

Miller, Francesca. 1990. Latin American Feminism and the Transnational Arena. In *Women, Culture, and Politics in Latin America*, ed. Emilie Bergmann, Janet Greenberg, Gwen Kirkpatrick, Francine Masiello, Francesca Miller, Marta Morello-Frosch, Kathleen Newman, and Mary Louise Pratt, 10–26. Berkeley: University of California Press.

———. 1991. *Latin American Women and the Search for Social Justice*. Hanover: University Press of New England.

Miller, J. Hillis. 1996. Border Crossings, Translating Theory: Ruth. In *The Translatability of Cultures: Figurations of the Space Between*, ed. Sanford Burdick and Wolfgang Iser, 207–23. Palo Alto, CA: Stanford University Press.

Minkler, Meredith. 2000. Personal Responsibility for Health: Contexts and Controversies. In *Promoting Healthy Behavior: How Much Freedom? Whose Responsibility?*, ed. Daniel Callahan, 1–22. Washington: Georgetown University Press.

Modleski, Tania. 1991. *Feminism without Women: Culture and Criticism in a "Postfeminist" Age*. New York: Routledge.

Mogrovejo, Norma. 2000. *Un Amor Que Se Atrevió a Decir su Nombre*. Mexico City: Plaza y Valdés.

———. 2001. El Movimiento Lésbico Latinoamericano: 25 Años de Herstoria. In *De Amores y Luchas: Diversidad Sexual, Derechos Humanos y Ciudadanía*, ed. Jorge Bracamonte Allaín, 283–97. Lima: Universidad Nacional Mayor de San Marcos, Centro de la Mujer Peruana Flora Tristán.

Mohanty, Chandra Talpade. 1984. "Under Western Eyes: Feminist Scholarship and Colonial Discourses." *boundary 2*(3): 333–58.

———. 1987. Feminist Encounters: Locating the Politics of Experience. *Copyright* 1: 30–44.

———. 1991a. Introduction: Cartographies of Struggle: Third World Women and the Politics of Feminism. In *Third World Women and the Politics of Feminism*, ed. Chandra Talpade Mohanty, Ann Russo, and Lourdes Torres, 1–47. Bloomington: Indiana University Press.

———. 1991b. Under Western Eyes: Feminist Scholarship and Colonial Discourse. In *Third World Women and the Politics of Feminism*, ed. Chandra Talpade Mohanty, Ann Russo, and Lourdes Torres, 51–80. Bloomington: Indiana University Press.

———. 1997. Women Workers and Capitalist Scripts: Ideologies of Domination, Common Interests and the Politics of Solidarity. In *Feminist Genealogies, Colonial Legacies, Democratic Futures*, ed. M. Jacqui Alexander, 3–29. New York: Routledge.

———. 2003a. *Feminism without Borders: Decolonizing Theory, Practicing Solidarity*. Durham: Duke University Press.

———. 2003b. Under Western Eyes: Feminist Scholarship and Colonial Discourses. In *Feminist Postcolonial Theory*, ed. Reina Lewis and Sara Mills, 49–74. Edinburgh: Edinburgh University Press.

Mohanty, Chandra Talpade, and M. Jacqui Alexander, eds. 1996. *Feminist Genealogies, Colonial Legacies, Democratic Futures*. New York: Routledge.

Mohanty, Chandra Talpade, Anna Russo, and Lourdes Torres, eds. 1991. *Third World Women and the Politics of Feminism*. Bloomington: Indiana University Press.

Molina, Sintia E. 1998. Duality and Displacement in the Dominican Literature in the United States. *Latino Studies Journal* 9(3): 65–85.

Molloy, Silvia. 2005. Postcolonial Latin America and the Magic Realist Imperative: A Report to the Academy. In *Nation, Language and the Ethics of Translation*, ed. Sandra Bermann and Michael Wood, 370–79. Princeton, NJ: Princeton University Press.

Monasterios, Elizabeth P. 2006. *No Pudieron con Nosotras: El Desafío de Feminismo Autónomo de Mujeres Creando*. Pittsburgh / La Paz: University of Pittsburgh / Plural.

Monasterios, Karin. 2007. Condiciones de Posibilidad del Feminismo en Contextos de Colonialismo Interno y de Lucha por la Decolonización. In *Reinventando la Nación en Bolivia: Movimientos Sociales, Estado y Poscolonialidad*, ed. Karin Monasterios, Pablo Stefanoni, Hervé Do Alto. Plural Editores.

Monsiváis, Carlos. 2002a. Del "Rescate del Género" y el Género del Rescate. *Proceso* 1363 (December 15): 58–59.

———. 2002b. De Obispos y Geología Social. *Proceso* 1362 (December 8): 68–70.

Montecino, Sonia. 1993. *Madres y Huachos: Alegorías del Mestizaje Chileno*. Santiago: Editorial Cuarto Propio-CEDEM.

Moraga, Cherríe. 2002. La Güera. In *This Bridge Called My Back: Writings by Radical Women of Color*, 3rd ed., ed. Cherríe Moraga and Gloria Anzaldúa. Berkeley, CA: Third Woman.

Moraga, Cherríe, and Gloria Anzaldúa, eds. 1983 [1981]. *This Bridge Called My Back: Writings by Radical Women of Color*. New York: Kitchen Table.

———. 2002. Entering the Lives of Others: Theory in the Flesh. In *This Bridge Called My Back: Writings by Radical Women of Color*, 3rd ed., ed. Cherríe Moraga and Gloria Anzaldúa. Berkeley, CA: Third Woman.

Moraga, Cherríe, and Ana Castillo. 1988. *Esta Puente, Mi Espalda: Voces de Mujeres Tercermundistas en los Estados Unidos*. San Francisco: ISM Press.

Moraña, Mabel, Enrique Dussel, and Carlos A. Jáuregui, eds. 2008. *Coloniality at Large: Latin America and the Postcolonial Debate*. Durham: Duke University Press.

Morawska, Ewa. 2003. Disciplinary Agendas and Analytic Strategies of Research on Immigrant Transnationalism: Challenges of Interdisciplinary Knowledge. *International Migration Review* 37(3): 611–40.

Moya, Paula M. L. 2002. *Learning from Experience: Minority Identities, Multicultural Struggles*. Berkeley: University of California Press.

Moya, Paula M. L., and Michael R. Hames-García, eds. 2000. *Realist Theory and the Predicament of Postmodernism*. Berkeley: University of California Press.

Nadasen, Premilla, and Tiffany Williams. 2010. *Valuing Domestic Work*. New Feminist Solutions Series, vol. 5. New York: Barnard Center for Research on Women, Barnard College. http://bcrw.barnard.edu/publication-sections/nfs (accessed November 11, 2011).

Nagar, Richa. 2002. Footlose Researchers, "Traveling" Theories, and the Politics of Transnational Feminist Praxis. *Gender, Place and Culture* 9(2): 179–86.

Naples, Nancy, and Manisha Desai. 2002. *Women's Activism and Globalization: Linking Local Struggles and Transnational Politics*. New York: Routledge.

Narayan, Uma. 1997. *Dislocating Cultures: Identities, Traditions, and Third World Feminism*. New York: Routledge.

Nassy Brown, Jacqueline. 2005. *Dropping Anchor, Setting Sail: Geographies of Race in Black Liverpool*. Princeton, NJ: Princeton University Press.

Nettleton, Sarah, and Robin Bunton. 1995. Sociological Critiques of Health Promotion. In *The Sociology of Health Promotion*, ed. Robin Bunton, Sarah Nettleton, and Roger Burrows, 39–56. New York: Routledge.

Niranjana, Tejaswini. 1992. *Siting Translation: History, Post-Structuralism, and the Colonial Context.* Cambridge, MA: Harvard University Press.

Norsigian, Judy, Vilunya Diskin, Paula Doress-Worters, Jane Pincus, Wendy Sanford, and N. Swenson. 1999. The Boston Women's Health Book Collective and *Our Bodies, Ourselves*: A Brief History and Reflection. *Journal of the American Medical Women's Association* 54(1): 35–40.

Norvell, John A. 2001. A Brancura Desconfortável das Camadas Médias Brasileiras. In *Raça como Retórica: A Construção da Diferença*, ed. Maggie Yvonne and C. B. Rezende, 245–68. Rio de Janeiro: Civilização Brasileira.

Nzomo, Maria. 1995. Women and Democratization Struggles in Africa: What Relevance to Postmodernist Discourse? In *Feminism/Postmodernism/Development*, ed. Marianne H. Marchand and Jane L. Parpart, 131–41. London: Routledge.

O'Dougherty, Maureen. 2002. *Consumption Intensified: The Politics of Middle-Class Life in Brazil.* Durham: Duke University Press.

Ohoyo Resource Center. 1981. *Words of Today's American Indian Women (Ohoyo Makachi).* Washington: U.S. Department of Education.

Olivera Bustamante, Mercedes. 1995. Práctica Feminista en el Movimiento Zapatista de Liberación Nacional. In *Chiapas ¿y las mujeres qué?*, ed. Rosa Rojas, 168–84. Mexico: CICAM.

Olivera Fuentes, Crissthian Manuel. 2006. Reflexionando sobre el Queer. http://www.demus.org.pe/Menus/Articulos/queer.htm.

Olsen, Tillie. 1979. *Silences.* New York: Delacorte / Seymour Lawrence.

Ong, Aihwa. 1988. Colonialism and Modernity: Feminist Re-Presentations of Women in Non-Western Societies. *Inscriptions* 3–4(2): 79–93.

———. 1996. Cultural Citizenship as Subject-Making: Immigrant Negotiate Racial and Cultural Boundaries in the United States. *Current Anthropologist* 37(5): 737–62.

Oppermann, Martin. 1999. Sex Tourism. *Annals of Tourism Research* 26(2): 251–66.

Orellana, Marjorie Faulstich, Lisa Dorner, and Lucila Pulido. 2003. Accessing Assets: Immigrant Youth's Work as Family Translators or "Para-phrasers." *Social Problems* 50(4): 505.

Ottawa Charter for Health Promotion. 1986. Ottawa: World Health Organization. http://www.who.int/healthpromotion/conferences/previous/ottawa/en/.

Overing, Joana. 1996. Against the Motion I. In *Key Debates in Anthropology*, ed. Tim Ingold, 261–71. London: Routledge.

Pabst, Georgia. 2004. Heartbreaking Translation: Boy's Winning Essay on Being Bilingual Tells of Sharing Sad News with His Mother. *Milwaukee Journal Sentinel*, December 16.

Papma, Adrie, and Ellen Sprenger. 1994. NOVIB and Gender: State of Affairs and Current Issues. In *Engendering Development*, ed. Maruja Barrig and Andy Wehkamp, 201–20. The Hague: NOVIB.

Paredes, Julieta. 2005a. Pronunciamiento de la Asamblea Feminista de Bolivia. http://www.rebelion.org/noticia.php?id=16401 (accessed May 14, 2006).

———. 2005b. Entrevista con una Feminista Boliviana, Mujeres Creando-Asamblea Feminista. http://www.anarkismo.net/newswire.php?story_id=734 (accessed June 18, 2006).

Paris Pombo, María Dolores. 2006a. *La Historia de Marta: Vida de Una Mujer Indígena por los Largos Caminos de la Mixteca a California*. Mexico City: Universidad Autónoma Metropolitana.

———. 2006b. Transiciones de Género y Etnicidad: Las Mujeres Triqui en el Valle de Salinas. In *Un Continente en Movimiento: Migraciones en América Latina*, ed. Ingrid Wehr, 131–42. Madrid: IberoAmericano.

Parker, Richard Guy. 1991. *Bodies, Pleasures, and Passions: Sexual Culture in Contemporary Brazil*. Boston: Beacon.

Parpart, Jane L., and Marianne H. Marchand. 1995. Exploding the Canon: An Introduction/Conclusion. In *Feminism/Postmodernism/Development*, ed. Marianne H. Marchand and Jane L. Parpart, 1–25. London: Routledge.

Parreñas, Rhacel Salazar. 2001. *Servants of Globalization: Women, Migration, and Domestic Work*. Palo Alto, CA: Stanford University Press.

———. 2005. *Children of Global Migration: Transnational Families and Gendered Woes*. Palo Alto, CA: Stanford University Press.

———. 2008. *The Force of Domesticity: Filipina Migrants and Globalization*. New York: New York University Press.

Passel, Jeffrey, and D'Vera Cohn. 2011. *Unauthorized Immigrant Population: National and State Trends, 2010*. Washington, DC: Pew Hispanic Center.

Patterson, Tiffany Ruby, and Robin D. G. Kelley. 2000. Unfinished Migrations: Reflections on the African Diaspora and the Making of the Modern World. *African Studies Review* 43(1): 11–46.

Paz, Octavio. 1985. *The Labyrinth of Solitude, and Other Writings*. Trans. Lysander Kemp. New York: Grove.

———. 1994 [1983]. *El Laberinto de la Soledad*. Mexico: FCE.

Peden, Margaret Sayers. 1987. Translating the Boom: The Apple Theory of Translation. *Latin American Literary Review* 15(29): 159–72.

Perez, Emma. 1999. *The Decolonial Imaginary: Writing Chicanas into History*. Bloomington: Indiana University Press.

Peri-Rossi, Cristina. 1984. *La Nave de los Locos*. Barcelona: Seix Barral.

———. 1989. *Ship of Fools*. Trans. Psiche Hughes. Columbia, LA: Readers International.

Petchesky, Rosalind P. 2003. *Global Prescriptions: Gendering Health and Human Rights*. New York: Zed Books / UNRISD.

Petersen, Alan R. 1996. Risk and the Regulated Self: The Discourse of Health Promotion as Politics of Uncertainty. *Journal of Sociology* 32(1): 44–57.

Piglia, Ricardo. 2005. *El Ultimo Lector*. Barcelona: Anagrama.

Pinho, Osmundo de Araújo. 2004. O Efeito do Sexo: Políticas de Raça, Gênero e Miscigenação. *Cadernos Pagu* 23: 89–121.

Pinho, Patricia de Santana. 2009. White but Not Quite: Tones and Overtones of Whiteness in Brazil. *Small Axe* 13(2): 39–56.

Pinto, Alberto Oliveira. 2007. O Colonialismo e a "Coisificação" da Mulher no Cancioneiro de Luanda, na Tradição Oral Angolana e na Literatura Colonial Portuguesa. In *A Mulher em África: Vozes de Uma Margem Sempre Presente*, ed. Inocência Mata and Laura Cavalcante Padilha, 35–49. Lisboa: Colibri.

Piscitelli, Adriana. 1996. "Sexo Tropical"; Comentários sobre Gênero e "Raça" em Alguns Textos da Mídia Brasileira. *Cadernos Pagu* 6–7: 9–34.

———. 1998. Gênero em Perspectiva. *Cadernos Pagu* 11: 127–40.

———. 2005. Viagens e Sexo On-line: A Internet na Geografia do Turismo Sexual Internacional. *Cadernos Pagu* 25:281–327.

———. 2006. Intérêt et Sentiment: Migration de Brésiliennes en Italie dans le Contexte du Tourisme Sexuel International. *Migrations Société; Le Grand Tournant: De l'Emigration à l'Immigration* (Colloque de Cerisy) 17(102): 105–25.

———. 2007. Shifting Boundaries: Sex and Money in the Northeast of Brazil. *Sexualities* 10(4): 489–500.

———. 2008. Looking for New Worlds: Brazilian Women as International Migrants. *Signs: Journal of Women in Culture and Society* 33(4): 784–93.

———. 2013. *Trânsitos: Brasileiras nos Mercados Transnacionais do Sexo*. Rio de Janeiro: EDUERJ/CLAM.

Pla Benito, Juan Luis. 1990. Silencio y Entrega en la Poesía de Yrene Santos. *Pliego De Murmurios* 9(104): 36.

Polanco, Jaqueline Jiménez. 2006. "Pájaras y maricones" "llegó la hora": Un Relato de Mi Experiencia en el Movimiento LGBTIR Dominicano. *Latin American Studies Association (LASA)* Forum 37(3): 15–18.

Pondrán a Circular Nuevo Libro de Poeta Dominicana Yrene Santos. 2003. LIBRUSA: Agencia Internacional de Notiças Literarias. http://www.librusa.com/noticias_200305 .htm.

Poniatowska, Elena. 1971. *Noche de Tlatelolco: Los Testimonios de Historia Oral*. México: Era.

———. 1975. *Massacre in Mexico*. Trans. Helen Lane. New York: Viking.

———. 1988. *Nada/Nadie: Las Voces del Temblor*. Mexico: Era.

———. 1995. *Nothing, Nobody: The Voices of the Mexico City Earthquake*. Trans. Aurora Camacho de Schmidt and Arthur Schmidt. Philadelphia: Temple University Press.

Pordeus, Ismael de Andrade, Jr. 2006. Cearensidade. http://enecom.oktiva.net/sispub /anexo/1071.

Portella, Ana Paula, ed. 1989. *Os Direitos Reprodutivos e a Condição Feminina*. Recife: SOS Corpo / Liber Gráfica e Editora Ltda.

Prada, Ana Rebeca. 2002. *Viaje y Narración: Las Novelas de Jesús Urzagasti*. La Paz: Sierpe/IEB.

———. 2005. The Collective of "Mujeres Creando" and Feminist Anarchism: Is Anzaldúa Translatable in Bolivia? Paper presented at the Spring Colloquim of the Chicano/Latino Research Center, April 1, University of California, Santa Cruz.

———. 2006. Nuestros Sueños son tus Pesadillas: La Marca de Mujeres Creando en la Piel de la Urbe Paceña. In *No Pudieron con Nosotras: El Desafío de Feminismo Autónomo de Mujeres Creando*, ed. E. Monasterios. La Paz / Pittsburgh: Plural Editores / University of Pittsburgh.

Pratt, Mary Louise. 1992. *Imperial Eyes: Travel Writing and Transculturation*. New York: Routledge.

———. 1996. Me llamo Rigoberta Menchú: Autoethnography and the Recoding of Citizenship. In *Teaching and Testimony: Rigoberta Menchú and the North American Classroom*, ed. Allen Carey-Webb and Stephen Benz, 57–72. Albany: State University of New York Press.

———. 1999. A Crítica na Zona de Contato: Nação e Comunidade Fora de Foco. *Travessia: Revista de Literatura* 38: 7–30.

———. 2001. I, Rigoberta Menchú and the "Culture Wars." In *The Rigoberta Menchú Controversy*, ed. Arturo Arias, 29–48. Minneapolis: University of Minnesota Press.

Price, Janet, and Margaret Shildrick. 1999. *Feminist Theory and the Body: A Reader*. New York: Routledge.

Proyecto Rios Vivos. 2000. *Proyecto Rios Vivos: Informe del Proyecto Final*. Cali, Colombia: Convenio Ecofondo, Fundación HablaScribe, Red Matamba y Guasá.

Pulido, Laura. 2006. *Black, Brown, Yellow and Left: Radical Activism In Los Angeles*. Berkeley: University of California Press.

Quijano, Anibal. 1997. Colonialidad del Poder, Cultura y Conocimiento en América Latina. *Anuario Mariateguiano* 9: 113–21.

———. 2000. Coloniality of Power, Eurocentrism, and Latin America. *Nepantla* 1(3): 139–55.

Quiroga, José. 2000. *Tropics of Desire: Interventions from Queer Latino America*. New York: New York University Press.

Rabassa, Gregory. 1991. Words Cannot Express . . . The Translation of Culture. In *Translating Latin America: Culture as Text*, ed. William Luis and Julio Rodríguez-Luis, 35–44. Binghamton: SUNY Binghamton Center for Research for Translation.

Radway, Janice A. 1984. *Reading the Romance: Women, Patriarchy, and Popular Literature*. Chapel Hill: University of North Carolina Press.

———. 1997. *A Feeling for Books: The Book-of-the-Month Club, Literary Taste, and Middle-Class Desire*. Chapel Hill: University of North Carolina Press.

Rago, Margareth. 1998. Sexualidade e Identidade na Historiografia Brasileira. In *A Sexualidade nas Ciências Humanas*, ed. Maria Andréa Loyola. Rio de Janeiro: UERJ.

———. 2001. Sexualidade e Identidade na Historiografia Brasileira dos Anos Vinte e Trinta. *Estudios Interdisciplinarios de América Latina y el Caribe* 12(1). http://www.tau .ac.il/eial/XII_1/rago.html.

Ramirez, Renya. 2007. Race, Tribal Nation, and Gender: A Native Feminist Approach to Belonging. *Meridians: Feminism, Race, Transnationalism* 7(2): 22–40.

Ramon, Maria Dolors Garcia, Kirsten Simonsen, and Dina Vaiou. 2006. Guest Editorial: Does Anglophone Hegemony Permeate Gender, Place and Culture? *Gender, Place and Culture* 13(1): 1–5.

Red Matamba y Guasá. 1997. Segundo Encuentro- Taller Sub-Regional de Organizaciones de Mujeres del Pacífico Caucano "Matamba y Guasá": Fuerza y Convocatoria de la Mujer del Pacífico Caucano. Timbiqui y Guapi, Cauca: Fundación Chiyangua de Guapi, Grupo de Promoción de Santa Rosa de Saija, Asociación Apoyo a la Mujer de Timbiqui, Asociación Manos Negras de Guapi.

———. 1997–98. Visión y Perspectiva Política y Organizativa de la Red De Organizaciones de Mujeres de Cauca: La Red Es Una Familia Numerosa. *Boletin Anual de Matamba y Guasá*, 13–17.

Renta, Priscila. 2007. Salsa Dance Performance: Latina/o History in Motion. In *Techno-futuros: Critical Interventions in Latina/o Studies*, ed. N. R. Mirabal and A. Lao-Montes. New York: Lexington Books.

Ribeiro, Margarida Calafate. 2004. *Uma História de Regressos; Império, Guerra Colonial e Pós-Colonialismo*. Porto: Afrontamento.

Rich, Adrienne. 1986 [1984]. Notes towards a Politics of Location. In *Blood, Bread and Poetry: Selected Prose, 1979–1985*, 210–32. New York: Norton.

———. 2002. Notas Para uma Política da Localização. In *Gênero, Desejo e Identidade*, ed. Ana Gabriela Macedo, 15–35. Lisboa: Cotovia.

Richard, Nelly. 1993. *Masculino/Femenino: Practicas de la Diferencia y Cultura Democrática*. Santiago: Francisco Zegers Editor.

———. 1998. *Residuos y Metaforas: Ensayos de Critica Cultural Sobre el Chile de la Transición*. Santiago: LOM Ediciones.

———. 2001. Globalización/Traducción/Diseminación. Paper presented at the seminar Intellectual Agendas and the Localities of Knowledge, October 2–5, Mexico City.

———. 2002. Experiência e Representação: O Feminino, O Latino-Americano. In *Intervenções Críticas: Arte, Cultura, Gênero e Política*, ed. Nelly Richard, 142–55. Belo Horizonte: Editora UFMG.

Ríos, Marcela, Lorena Godoy, and Elizabeth Guerrero. 2004. *¿Un Nuevo Silencio Feminista? La Transformación de un Movimiento Social en el Chile Postdictadura*. Santiago: CEM.

Rivera Cusicanqui, Silvia. 1991. *Bircholas: Trabajo de Mujeres: Explotación Capitalista y Opresión Colonial entre las Migrantes Aymaras de La Paz y El Alto*. La Paz: Editorial Mama Huaco.

———, ed. 1996. *Ser Mujer Indígena, Chola o Birlocha en la Bolivia Postcolonial de los Años 90*. La Paz: Subsecretaría de Asuntos de Género / Ministerios de Desarrollo Humano.

Rivera Cusicanqui, Silvia, and Rossana Barragán, eds. 1997. *Debates Postcoloniales: Una Introducción a los Estudios de la Subalternidad*. Trans. Alison Spedding, Raquel Gutiérrez, Silvia Rivera, and Ana Rebeca Prada. La Paz: Historias, SEPHIS, Aruwiyiri.

Rivera Garza, Cristina. 1999. *Nadie Me Verá Llorar*. México: Tusquets.

———. 2003. *No One Will See Me Cry*. Trans. Andrew Hurley. Willimantic, CT: Curbstone.

Rodríguez, Dora Elia. 1998. Las Cartas No Mienten I. In *En Las Fronteras del Cuento: Jóvenes Narradores del Norte de Tamaulipas*, ed. Orlando Ortiz. Mexico: Fondo Editorial Tierra Adentro.

Rodríguez, Ileana. 1996. Case B: Of Testimonial and Diaries: Narratives of Success and Failure. In *Women, Guerrillas, and Love: Understanding War in Central America*, trans. Ileana Rodríguez with Robert Carr, 157–67. Minneapolis: University of Minnesota Press.

———. 2001. Between Silence and Lies: Rigoberta Va. In *The Rigoberta Menchú Controversy*, ed. Arturo Arias, 332–50. Minneapolis: University of Minnesota Press.

Rodríguez, Juana María. 2003. *Queer Latinidad: Identity Practices, Discursive Spaces*. New York: New York University Press.

Rodriguez, Lilia. 1994. Barrio Women: Between the Urban and the Feminist Movement. *Latin American Perspectives* 21(3): 32–48.

Rojas, Jeannette Silva. 1996. Las Mujeres En Moviemiento: Cronica De Otras Miradas. In *Pacífico ¿Desarrollo O Diversidad?: Estado, Capital y Movimientos Sociales en el Pacífico Colombiano*, ed. Arturo Escobar and Alvaro Pedrosa, 205–18. Bogotá: CEREC y ECOFONDO.

Rojas, Rosa, ed. 1994. *Chiapas, ¿Y las Mujeres Qué?*, vol. 1. Mexico: CICAM.

———, ed. 1995. *Chiapas, ¿Y las Mujeres Qué?*, vol. 2. Mexico: CICAM.

Román, Miriam Jiménez, and Juan Flores, eds. 2010. *The Afro-Latin@ Reader: History and Culture in the United States*. Durham: Duke University Press.

Rosario Candelier, Bruno. 1988. Prólogo. In *Desnudez del Silencio*, ed. Yrene Santos, 5–6. Santo Domingo: Editora Búho.

Rose, Nikolas. 1996. Governing "Advanced" Liberal Democracies. In *Foucault and Political Reason: Liberalism, Neo-Liberalism, and Rationalities of Government*, ed. Andrew Barry, Thomas Osborne, and Nikolas Rose. Chicago: University of Chicago Press.

———. 1999. *Governing the Soul: The Shaping of the Private Self*. London: Free Associations Books.

Rovira, Guiomar. 1997. *Mujeres de maíz*. Mexico: Era.

Rubiera Castillo, Daisy, and Inés María Martiatu Terry, eds. 2011. *Afrocubanas: Historia, Pensamiento y Prácticas Culturales*. Havana: Ciencias Sociales.

Rubin, Gayle. 1978. The Traffic in Women: Notes on the "Political Economy" of Sex. In *Toward an Anthropology of Women*, ed. Rayna Reiter. New York: Monthly Review Press.

Ruiz, Albor. 1997. Where Words and Latin Culture Grow into Art. *Daily News* (New York), May 27.

Sahlins, Marshall. 1976. *Culture and Practical Reason*. Chicago: University of Chicago Press.

Said, Edward W. 1983. *The World, the Text and the Critic*. Cambridge, MA: Harvard University Press.

———. 2001. Representing the Colonized: Anthropology's Interlocutors. In *Reflections on Exile and Other Essays*, 293–316. Cambridge, MA: Harvard University Press.

———. 2003. Reflexões Sobre o Exílio. In *Reflexões Sobre o Exílio e Outros Ensaios*, ed. Edward Said, 46–60. São Paulo: Companhia das Letras.

Salazar, Gabriel, and Julio Pinto. 2002. *Historia Contemporánea de Chile IV: Hombría y Feminidad (Construcción Cultural de Actores Emergentes)*. Santiago: Editorial LOM.

Salisbury, María Cecilia. 1993. An Interview with Edith Grossman. *Translation Review* 11: 11–15.

Sampaio, Anna. 2004. Theorizing Women of Color in a New Global Matrix. *International Feminist Journal of Politics* 6(2): 181–206.

Sanchez-Crispin, Alvaro, and Alvaro Lopez-Lopez. 1997. Gay Male Places of Mexico City. In *Queers in Space: Communities, Public Places, Sites of Resistance*, ed. Gordon Brent Ingram, Anne-Marie Bouthillette, and Yolanda Retter, 197–212. Seattle: Bay Press.

Sanders, Jim. 2003. Kids as Translators? Language Barrier Creates Health Challenge. *Sacramento Bee*, April 13.

Sandoval, Chela. 1991. U.S. Third World Feminism: The Theory and Method of Oppositional Consciousness in the Postmodern World. *Genders* 12(10): 1–23.

———. 1995. U.S. Third World Feminism. In *Oxford Companion to Women's Writing in the United States*, ed. Cathy Davidson and Linda Wagner-Martin, 880–82. New York: Oxford University Press.

———. 2000a. Love as a Hermeneutics of Social Change, a Decolonizing *Movida*. In *Methodology of the Oppressed*, 139–58. Minneapolis: University of Minnesota Press.

———. 2000b. *Methodology of the Oppressed*. Minneapolis: University of Minnesota Press.

Sanjinés, Javier. 1991. From Domitila to "los relocalizados": An Essay on Marginality in Bolivia. In *Translating Latin America: Culture as Text*, ed. William Luis and Julio

Rodríguez-Luis, 185–96. Binghamton: SUNY Binghamton Center for Research for Translation.

Santa Cruz Feminist of Color Collaborative. 2014. Building on "the Edge of Each Other's Battles." *Interstices: Women of Color Feminist Philosophy*, special issue of *Hypatia: A Journal of Feminist Philosophy* 29:1.

Santiago, Esmeralda. 1994. *When I Was Puerto Rican*. New York: Vintage Books.

Santos, Boaventura de Sousa. 2002. Entre Próspero e Caliban: Colonialismo, Pós-Colonialismo e Inter-Identidade. In *Entre Ser e Estar: Raízes, Percursos e Discursos da Identidade*, ed. Maria Irene Ramalho and António Sousa Ribeiro, 23–85. Porto: Afrontamento.

———. 2004a. Do Pós-Moderno ao Pós-Colonial. E Para Além de Um e Outro. Paper presented at Conferência de Abertura do VIII Congresso Luso-Afro-Brasileiro de Ciências Sociais, Realizado em Coimbra, September 16–18, Disponível.

———. 2004b. El Foro Social Mundial: Hacia Una Globalizacíon Contra-Hegemónica. In *El Foro Social Mundial: Desafiando Imperios*, ed. J. Sen, A. Anand, A. Escobar, and P. Waterman, 330–43. Málaga: El Viejo Topo.

Santos, Yrene. 1988. *Desnudez del Silencio*. Santo Domingo: Editora Búho.

———. 1998. *Reencuentro*. New York: La Candelaria.

———. 2002. *El Incansable Juego*. Santo Domingo: Editorial Letra Gráfica.

———. 2013. *The Untiring Game*. Trans. Isabel Espinal. The Selected Works of Isabel R Espinal. http://works.bepress.com/isabel_espinal/4.

Saucedo, Renee. 2006. INS Raids and How Immigrant Women Are Fighting Back. In *Color of Violence: The Incite! Anthology*, ed. Incite! Women of Color Against Violence, 135–37. Cambridge, MA: South End.

Saunders, Kriemild. 2002. Introduction: Towards a Deconstructive Post-Development Criticism. In *Feminist Post-Development Thought: Rethinking Modernity, Post-Colonialism and Representation*, ed. Kriemild Saunders, 1–38. London: Zed Books.

Sawyer, Mark. 2010. Racial Politics in Multiethnic America: Black and Latin@ Identities and Coalitions. In *The Afro-Latin@ Reader: History and Culture in the United States*, ed. Miriam Jiménez Román and Juan Flores, 527–39. Durham: Duke University Press.

Sayles, John, dir. 1997. *Men with Guns*. Culver City: Columbia TriStar Home Video.

Scarry, Elaine. 1985. *The Body in Pain: The Making and Unmaking of the World*. New York: Oxford University Press.

Schlau, Stacey. 1996. Passion and Politics: Teaching Rigoberta Menchú's Text as a Feminist. In *Teaching and Testimony: Rigoberta Menchú and the North American Classroom*, ed. Allen Carey-Webb and Stephen Benz, 175–82. Albany: State University of New York Press.

Schutte, Ofelia. 2000. Cultural Alterity: Cross-Cultural Communication and Feminist Theory in North-South Contexts. In *De-Centering the Center: Philosophy for a Multicultural, Postcolonial, and Feminist World*, ed. Uma Narayam and Sandra Harding, 47–66. Bloomington: Indiana University Press.

Schwarz, Roberto. 2000. *Ao Vencedor as Batatas: Forma Literária e Processo Social Nos Inícios do Romance Brasileiro*. São Paulo: Duas Cidades / Editora 34: 9–31.

Scott, Joan W. 1988. *Gender and the Politics of History*. New York: Columbia University Press.

———. 1990. Deconstructing Equality-versus-Difference: Or, the Uses of Post-

Structuralist Theory for Feminism. In *Conflicts in Feminism*, ed. Marianne Hirsch and Evelyn Fox Keller, 134–48. New York: Routledge.

———. 1992. Experience. In *Feminists Theorize the Political*, ed. Judith Butler and Joan Scott, 22–40. New York: Routledge.

———. 2002. Feminist Reverberations. *Differences: A Journal of Feminist Cultural Studies* 13(3): 1–23.

Seminar on Feminism and Culture in Latin America. 1990. *Women, Culture and Politics in Latin America*. Berkeley: University of California Press.

Sen, Gita, and Caren Grown. 1987. *Development, Crises, and Alternative Visions: Third World Women's Perspectives*. New York: Monthly Review Press.

SERNAM. 2002. Habla la Gente: Situación de las Mujeres en el Mundo Laboral. Documento de Trabajo no. 77, October. Santiago.

Serrano, Margarita. 2005. Entrevista a Michelle Bachelet. *Diario el Mercurio*, July 24. Santiago. http://salvador-allende.cl/Michelle/archives.php?id=A2005071

Sevilla, Rebeca. 2000. La Persecución, la Impunidad y la Vida Clandestina de las Mujeres Lesbianas en Perú. In *Los Derechos de las Mujeres son Derechos Humanos: Crónica de una Movilización Mundial*, ed. Charlotte Bunch, Claudia Hinojosa, and Niamh Reilly, 186–88. Mexico: EDAMEX/Bridge.

Shapiro, Ester. 1994a. Finding What Had Been Lost in Plain View. *Michigan Quarterly Review* 33: 579–89.

———. 1994b. *Grief as a Family Process: A Developmental Approach to Clinical Practice*. New York: Guilford Press.

———. 1996. Exile and Professional Identity: On Going Back to Cuba. *Cultural Diversity and Mental Health* 2(1): 21–33.

———. 2001. Santeria as a Healing Practice: My Cuban Jewish Journey with Oshun. In *Healing Cultures: Practices in the Caribbean*, ed. Margarite Fernandez-Olmos and Lisbeth Paravisine-Gebert, 69–88. New York: Palgrave.

———. 2005. Because Words Are Not Enough: Latina Revisionings of Transnational Collaborations Using Health Promotion for Gender Justice and Social Change. *NWSA Journal* 17(1): 141–72.

Shapiro, Ester, and Jennifer Leigh. 2005. Toward Culturally Competent, Gender-Equitable Leadership: Assessing Outcomes of Women's Leadership in Diverse Contexts. In *Women and Leadership: Transforming Visions and Diverse Voices*, ed. Jean Lau Chin, Bernice Lott, Joy K. Rice, and Janis Sanchez-Hucles, 88–105. New York: Blackwell.

Shepard, Bonnie. 2006. *Running the Obstacle Course to Sexual and Reproductive Health: Lessons from Latin America*. Westport, CT: Praeger.

Sheriff, Robin E. 2001. *Dreaming Equality: Color, Race, and Racism in Urban Brazil*. New Brunswick, NJ: Rutgers University Press.

Shih, Shu-Mei. 2002. Towards an Ethics of Transnational Encounter, or "When" Does a "Chinese" Woman Become a "Feminist"? *differences* 13(2): 90–126.

———. 2005. Towards an Ethics of Transnational Encounters, or 'When' Does a Chinese' Woman Become a 'Feminist?'. In *Dialogue and Difference: Feminisms Challenge Globalization*, eds., Marguerite Waller and Sylvia Marcos, 3–28. New York: Palgrave Macmillan.

Shohat, Ella. 1997. Post-Third-Worldist Culture: Gender, Nation, and the Cinema. In

Feminist Genealogies, Colonial Legacies, Democratic Futures, ed. Jacqui Alexander and Chandra Talpade Mohanty, 183–213. New York: Routledge.

———. 1999. Introduction. In Talking Visions: Multicultural Feminism in a Transnational Age, ed. Ella Shohat, 1–64. Cambridge, MA: MIT Press.

———. 2001. Feminismo Fora do Centro. Revista Estudos Feministas 9(1): 147–63.

———. 2002. Area Studies, Gender Studies, and the Cartographies of Knowledge. Social Text 72(20.3): 67–78.

Shumaher, Shuma. 2003. Primeira Onda Feminista. http://www.mulher500.org.br/artigos _detalhe.asp?cod=9, 3/9/2003.

Sicilia, Javier. 2002a. Buscando una Bisagra. Proceso 1364: 30–32.

———. 2002b. La Opresión y la Máscara de la Libertad. Proceso 1363: 56–57.

———. 2003. La Miseria de los Derechos Reproductivos. Proceso 1367: 58–59.

Silliman, Jael, Marlene Fried, Loretta Ross, and Elena Gutierrez. 2004. Undivided Rights: Women of Color Organizing for Reproductive Justice. Cambridge, MA: South End.

Silva, Ana Paula, and Thaddeus Gregory Blanchette. 2005. Prostituição e Namoros Internacionais em Copacabana. Anales del I Congreso Latinoamericano de Antropología, Universidad Nacional de Rosario, Argentina.

Silva, Tony Simões da. 2002. Raced Encounters, Sexed Transactions: "Lusotropicalism" and the Portuguese Colonial Empire. Pretexts: Literary and Cultural Studies 11(1): 24–39.

Simon, Sherry. 1996. Gender in Translation: Cultural Identity and the Politics of Transmission. London: Routledge.

Snyder, Margaret. 2006. Unlikely Godmother: The UN and the Global Women's Movement. In Global Feminism: Transnational Women's Activism, Organizing, and Human Rights, ed. Myra Marx Ferree and Aili Mari Tripp, 24–50. New York: New York University Press.

Sommer, Doris. 1996. No Secrets. In The Real Thing: Testimonial Discourse and Latin America, ed., Georg M. Gugelberger, 130–57. Durham: Duke University Press.

———. 1999. Proceed with Caution, When Engaged by Minority Writing in the Americas. Cambridge, MA: Harvard University Press.

———. 2004. Bilingual Aesthetics: A New Sentimental Education. Durham: Duke University Press.

Sosa, José Rafael. 1988. Yrene y su Desnudez. Bicho (May): 3.

Soto, Sandra. 2003. Where in the World Are U.S. Women of Color. In Women's Studies for the Future, ed. Elizabeth Kennedy, 111–24. Durham: Duke University Press.

Sparr, Pamela, ed. 1994. Mortgaging Women's Lives: Feminist Critiques of Structural Adjustment. Atlantic Highlands, NJ: Zed Press.

Speed, Shannon. 2006. Rights at the Intersection: Gender and Ethnicity in Neoliberal Mexico. In Dissident Women: Gender and Cultural Politics in Chiapas, ed. Shannon Speed, R. Aída Hernández Castillo, and Lynn M. Stephen, 203–21. Austin: University of Texas.

Speed, Shannon, and María Teresa Sierra. 2005. Critical Perspectives on Human Rights and Multiculticulturalism in Neoliberal Latin America. PoLAR: Political and Legal Anthropology Review 28(1): 1–9.

Spindel, Cheywa R. 1987. The Social Invisibility of Women's Work in Brazilian Agriculture. In Rural Women and State Policy: Feminist Perspectives on Latin American Agricultural Development, ed. Carmen Diana Deere and Magdalena León, 51–66. Boulder, CO: Westview.

Spivak, Gayatri. 1988. Can the Subaltern Speak? In Marxism and the Interpretation of Culture, ed. Cary Nelson and Lawrence Crossberg, 271–313. Urbana: University of Illinois Press.

———. 1989. The Political Economy of Women as Seen by a Literary Critic. In *Coming to Terms: Feminism, Theory, Politics*, ed. Elizabeth Weed, 218–29. New York: Routledge.

———. 1990. *The Post-Colonial Critic: Interviews, Strategies and Dialogues*, ed. Sarah Harasym. New York: Routledge.

———. 1992. The Politics of Translation. In *Destabilizing Theory: Contemporary Feminist Debates*, ed. Michèle Barrett and Anne Phillips, 177–200. Cambridge: Polity.

———. 1993. The Politics of Translation. In *Outside in the Teaching Machine*, 179–200. New York: Routledge.

———. 1999. *A Critique of Postcolonial Reason: Toward a History of the Vanishing Present*. Cambridge, MA: Harvard University Press.

———. 2012. *An Aesthetic Education in the Era of Globalization*. Cambridge, MA: Harvard University Press.

Springer, Kimberly. 2005. *Living for the Revolution: Black Feminist Organizations, 1968–1980*. Durham: Duke University Press.

Stacey, Judith. 1988. Can There Be a Feminist Ethnography? *Women's Studies International Forum* 11(1): 21–27.

Stam, Robert. 2001. Cultural Studies and Race. In *A Companion to Cultural Studies*, ed. Toby Miller, 471–89. Oxford: Blackwell.

Stefoni, Carolina. 2003. *Inmigración Peruana en Chile. Una Oportunidad a la Integración.* Santiago: Flacso / Editorial Universitaria.

———. 2004. Inmigración y Ciudadanía: La Formación de Comunidades Peruanas en Santiago y la Emergencia de Nuevos Ciudadanos. *Política* 43: 319–36.

Stephen, Lynn. 2007. *Transborder Lives: Indigenous Oaxacans in Mexico, California and Oregon.* Durham: Duke University Press.

Stephenson, Marcia. 2003. Inscribing Gynetics in the Bolivian Andes. In *Chicana Feminisms: A Critical Reader*, ed. Gabriela F. Arredondo, Aida Hurtado, Norma Klahn, Olga Nájera-Fernández, and Patricia Zavella. Durham: Duke University Press.

Sternbach, Nancy Saporta. 1991. Re-membering the Dead: Latin American Women's "Testimonial" Discourse. *Latin American Perspectives* 18(3): 91–102.

Sternbach, Nancy Saporta, Marysa Navarro-Aranguren, Patricia Chuchryk, and Sonia E. Alvarez. 1992. Feminisms in Latin America: From Bogotá to San Bernardo. In *The Making of Social Movements in Latin America: Identity, Strategy and Democracy*, ed. Arturo Escobar and Sonia E. Alvarez. Boulder, CO: Westview.

Stevens, Cristina, ed. 2010. *Mulher e Literatura — 25 Anos: Raízes e Rumos*. Florianópolis: Editora Mulheres.

Stoler, Ann Laura. 1995. *Race and the Education of Desire: Foucault's History of Sexuality and the Colonial Order of Things*. Durham: Duke University Press.

———. 2002. *Carnal Knowledge and Imperial Power: Race and the Intimate in Colonial Rule.* Berkeley: University of California Press.

———. 2006. *Haunted by Empire: Geographies of Intimacy in North American History*. Durham: Duke University Press.

Stoll, David. 1999. *Rigoberta Menchú and the Story of All Poor Guatemalans*. Boulder, CO: Westview.

Stone-Mediatore, Shari. 2000. Chandra Mohanty and the Revaluing of "Experience." In

Decentering the Center: Philosophy for a Multicultural, Postcolonial, and Feminist World, ed. Uma Narayan and Sandra Harding, 110–27. Bloomington: Indiana University Press.

Suárez-Boulangger, Carlos. 1998. Latino Experience Focus of Writing Workshop. *Gatson Institute Report* (Fall): 6–8.

Subercaseaux, Elizabeth. 2000. *La Rebellion de Las Nanas*. Santiago: Grijalbo.

Tapia, Luis. 2011. *El Estado de Derecho como Tiranía*. La Paz: CIDES-UMSA.

Taracena, Arturo. 2001. Interview with Luis Aceituno: Arturo Taracena Breaks His Silence. In *Rigoberta Menchú Controversy*, ed. Arturo Arias, 82–94. Minneapolis: University of Minnesota Press.

Tarrés, María Luisa, ed. 1998. *Género y Cultura en América Latina*. México: El Colegio de México.

Taussig, Michael T. 1999. *Defacement: Public Secrecy and the Labor of the Negative*. Stanford: Stanford University Press.

Taveras Hernández, Juan. 1987. La Mujer es la Depositaria de la Vida. *El Nacional de Ahora*, April 6.

Teles, Maria Amélia de Almeida. 1993. *Breve História do Feminismo no Brasil*. São Paulo: Brasiliense.

Terry, Jennifer, and Jacqueline Urla, eds. 1995. *Deviant Bodies*. Bloomington: Indiana University Press.

Thayer, Millie. 2000. Traveling Feminisms: From Embodied Women to Gendered Citizenship. In *Global Ethnography: Forces, Connections, and Imaginations in a Postmodern World*, ed. Michael Burawoy, Joseph A. Blum, Sheba George, Zsuzsa Gille, Teresa Gowan, Lynne Haney, Maren Klawiter, Steven H. Lopez, Seán Obriain, and Millie Thayer, 203–33. Berkeley: University of California Press.

———. 2001. Transnational Feminism: Reading Joan Scott in the Brazilian Sertão. *Ethnography* 2(2): 243–71.

———. 2004a. *Negotiating the Global: Northeast Brazilian Women's Movements and the Transnational Feminist Public*. Ph.D. diss., University of California, Berkeley.

———. 2004b. Transnational Feminism as Field: Power, Solidarity and the Researcher. In *Negotiating the Global: Northeast Brazilian Women's Movements and the Transnational Feminist Public*, 228–40. Ph.D. diss., University of California, Berkeley.

———. 2010. *Making Transnational Feminism: Rural Women, NGO Activists and Northern Donors in Brazil*. New York: Routledge.

Thomas, Caroline, and Martin Weber. 2004. The Politics of Global Governance: Whatever Happened to "Health for All by the Year 2000"? *Global Governance* 10(2): 187–206.

Thomas, Piri. 1997 [1967]. *Down These Mean Streets*. New York: Vintage.

Thomaz, Omar Ribeiro. 2002. Tigres de Papel: Gilberto Freyre, Portugal e os Países Africanos de Língua Oficial Portuguesa. In *Trânsitos Coloniais: Diálogos Críticos Luso-Brasileiros*, ed. Cristiana Bastos, Miguel Vale de Almeida, and Bela Feldman-Bianco. Lisboa: Imprensa de Ciências Sociais.

Tinker, Irene, ed. 1990. *Persistent Inequalities: Women and World Development*. Oxford: Oxford University Press.

Tobar, Marcela Ríos, Lorena Gody, and Elizabeth Guerrero. 2003. *¿Un Nuevo Silencio Feminista? La Transformación de un Movimiento Social en el Chile Posdictadura*. Santiago: CEM y Editorial Cuarto Propio.

Todaro, Rosalba, and Sonia Yañez, eds. 2004. *El Trabajo se Transforma: Relaciones de Producción y Relaciones de Género.* Santiago: CEM.

Torres-Saillant, Silvio. 1998. Visions of Dominicanness in the United States. In *Borderless Borders: U.S. Latinos, Latin Americans, and the Paradox of Interdependence,* ed. Frank Bonilla, 139–52. Philadelphia: Temple University Press.

Traba, Marta. 1981. *Conversación al Sur.* México: Siglo Veintiuno Editores.

———. 1986. *Mothers and Shadows.* Trans. Jo Labanyi. London: Readers International.

Tricot, Tito. 2006. Democracia Formal y Derechos Indígenas. *Periódico Azkintuwe,* March 15. http://argentina.indymedia.org/news/2006/03/380780.php?theme=1.

Tsing, Anna Lowenhaupt. 1997. Transitions as Translations. In *Transitions, Environments, Translations: Feminisms in International Politics,* ed. Joan Scott, Cora Kaplan, and Debra Keates, 253–72. New York: Routledge.

———. 2005. *Friction: An Ethnography of Global Connection.* Princeton, NJ: Princeton University Press.

Twine, France Winddance. 1998. *Racism in a Racial Democracy: The Maintenance of White Supremacy in Brazil.* New Brunswick, NJ: Rutgers University Press.

Udayagiri, Mridula. 1995. Challenging Modernization: Gender and Development, Postmodern Feminism and Activism. In *Feminism/Postmodernism/Development,* ed. Marianne H. Marchand and Jane L. Parpart, 159–77. London: Routledge.

UN Development Fund for Women. 1998. *Bringing Equality Home: Implementing the Convention of the Elimination of All Forms of Discrimination against Women.* New York: UNIFEM.

Vaca, Nicolas C. 2004. *The Presumed Alliance. The Unspoken Conflict between Latinos and Blacks and What It Means for America.* New York: HarperCollins.

Vale de Almeida, Miguel. 1995. *Senhores de Si: Uma Interpretação Antropológica da Masculinidade.* Lisbon: Fim de Século.

Valentine, Vikki. 2005. Health for the Masses: China's "Barefoot Doctors." National Public Radio, November 4. http://www.npr.org/templates/story/story.php?storyId=4990242 (accessed February 23, 2011).

Valenzuela, Luisa. 1982. *Cambio de Armas.* Hanover, NH: Ediciones del Norte.

———. 1983. *Cola de Lagartija.* Buenos Aires: Bruguera.

———. 1985. *Other Weapons.* Trans. Deborah Bonner. Hanover, NH: Ediciones del Norte.

———. 1999. *The Lizard's Tail.* Trans. Gregory Rabassa. New York: Farrar, Straus and Giroux.

Vargas, Virginia. 2003. Feminism, Globalization, and the Global Justice Solidarity Movement. *Cultural Studies* 17(6): 195–205.

———. 2006. Las Nuevas Dinámicas Feministas en el Nuevo Milenio. *LASA Forum* 37(1): 34–36.

Velasco Ortiz, Laura. 2004. Organizational Experiences and Female Participation among Indigenous Oaxaqueños in Baja California. In *Indigenous Mexican Migrants in the United States,* ed. Jonathan Fox and Gaspar Rivera-Salgado, 101–21. San Diego: Center for U.S.-Mexican Studies, UCSD.

———. 2005. *Mixtec Transnational Identity.* Tucson: University of Arizona Press.

———. 2007. Women, Migration, and Household Survival Strategies: Mixtec Women in Tijuana. In *Women and Migration in the U.S.-Mexico Borderlands: A Reader*, ed. Denise Segura and Pat Zavella, 341–59. Durham: Duke University Press.

Velez-Ibanez, Carlos, and Anna Sampaio. 2002. *Transnational Latina/o Communities: Politics, Processes and Cultures.* Lanham, MD: Rowman and Littlefield.

Venuti, Lawrence. 1998. *The Scandals of Translation: Towards an Ethics of Difference.* New York: Routledge.

———. 2000. Translation, Community, Utopia. In *The Translation Studies Reader*, ed. Lawrence Venuti, 468–88. New York: Routledge.

Vianna, Hermano. 1999. *The Mystery of Samba: Popular Music and National Identity in Brazil.* Trans. John Charles Chasteen. Chapel Hill: University of North Carolina Press.

Wade, Peter. 1995. The Cultural Politics of Blackness in Colombia. *American Ethnologist* 22(2): 341–57.

Wainwright, Joel. 2008. *Decolonizing Development: Colonial Power and the Maya.* London: Blackwell.

Warner, Michael. 1993. *Fear of a Queer Planet: Queer Politics and Social Theory.* Minneapolis: University of Minnesota Press.

Warren, Alice E. Colon. 2003. Puerto Rico: Feminism and Feminist Studies. *Gender and Society* 17(5): 664–90.

Weber, Samuel. 2005. A Touch of Translation: On Walter Benjamin's "Task of the Translator." In *Nation, Language, and the Ethics of Translation*, ed. Susan Bermann, 65–78. Princeton, NJ: Princeton University Press.

Wells, Susan. 2010. *Our Bodies, Ourselves and the Work of Writing.* Palo Alto, CA: Stanford University Press.

Williams, Patrick, and Laura Chrisman, eds. 1994. *Colonial Discourse and Postcolonial Theory.* New York: Columbia University Press.

Winant, Howard. 1999. Comparing Contemporary Racial Politics in the U.S. and Brazil. In *Racial Politics in Contemporary Brazil*, ed. Michael Hanchard. Durham: Duke University Press.

Wittgenstein, Ludwig. 1968. *Philosophical Investigations.* Oxford: Blackwell.

Women of All Red Nations. 1980. *W.A.R.N. Report II.* Sioux Falls, South Dakota.

Writers Workshop Model: Hispanic Writers in the Schools. 2005. University of Massachusetts, Boston, March 3. http://dl.umb.edu/latino/workshop.html.

Wu, Judy Txu-Chun. 2010. Rethinking Global Sisterhood: Peace Activists and Women's Orientalism. In *No Permanent Waves: Recasting Histories of US Feminism*, ed. Nancy Hewitt, 193–220. New Brunswick, NJ: Rutgers University Press.

Xavier, Elódia. 2007. *Que Corpo é Esse? O Corpo no Imaginário Feminino.* Florianópolis: Mulheres.

Yarbro-Bejarano, Yvonne. 1989. Primer Encuentro de Lesbianas Feministas Latinoamericanas y Caribeñas. In *Third Woman: The Sexuality of Latinas*, ed. Norma Alarcón, Ana Castillo, and Cherríe Moraga, 143–46. Berkeley: Third Woman.

Young, Cynthia. 2006. *Soul Power: Culture, Radicalism, and the Making of a U.S. Third World Left.* Durham: Duke University Press.

Zavala San Martín, Ximena, and Claudia Rojas Venegas. 2005. Globalización, Procesos Migratorios y Estado en Chile. In *Migraciones, Globalización y Género en Argentina y Chile*, 150–91. Buenos Aires: Centro de Encuentros Cultura y Mujer (CECYM), Argentina; Cotidiano Mujer, Uruguay; Fundación Instituto de la Mujer, Chile; Movimiento Pro

Emancipación de la Mujer (MEMCH); Red de Educación Popular entre Mujeres (REPEM), Uruguay.

Zavalia, Juliana de. 2000. The Impact of Spanish-American Literature in Translation on U.S. Latino Literature. In *Changing the Terms: Translating in the Postcolonial Era*, ed. Sherry Simon and Paul St-Pierre, 187–206. Ottawa: University of Ottawa Press.

Zavella, Patricia. 2011. *I'm Neither Here nor There: Mexicans' Quotidian Struggles with Migration and Poverty*. Durham: Duke University Press.

Zimmerman, Marc. 1995. *Literature and Resistance in Guatemala: Textual Modes and Cultural Politics from El Señor Presidente to Rigoberta Menchú*, vol. 2. Athens: Center for International Studies.

Zlotnik, Hania. 2003. *The Global Dimensions of Female Migration*. *Migration Information Source*. Washington: Migration Policy Institute. http://www.migrationinformation.org.

SONIA E. ALVAREZ is Leonard J. Horowitz Professor of Latin American Politics and Studies and director of the Center for Latin American, Caribbean, and Latino Studies at the University of Massachusetts, Amherst. She has written extensively on social movements, feminisms, nongovernmental organizations, transnational activism, and democratization. Her current research centers on the articulation of race and antiracist politics among feminist movements in Brazil and on the "sidestreaming" of feminist discourses and practices into parallel social movements throughout the Latin American region. Alvarez has participated in Latina/women of color feminist, social justice, international solidarity, and antiracist activism since the 1980s and has maintained manifold connections with Brazilian, Latin American, and global feminist movements while theorizing with/about them.

KIRAN ASHER is associate professor of international development and social change at Clark University, Massachusetts. Her diverse research interests, grounded in two decades of field-based research in Latin America and South Asia, focus on the gendered and raced dimensions of social and environmental change in the global South. Her publications include a monograph, *Black and Green: Afro-Colombians, Development, and Nature in the Pacific Lowlands* (Duke University Press, 2009). She is currently working on a theoretical and political critique of the development theories and postdevelopment proposals by drawing on political-economic and feminist approaches in a postcolonial frame.

VICTORIA (VICKY) M. BAÑALES received her Ph.D. from the University of California, Santa Cruz, in literature with a parenthetical notation in feminist studies. Her dissertation is titled "Twentieth-Century Latin American and U.S. Latina Women's Literature and the Paradox of Dictatorship and Democracy." She is tenured English faculty at Cabrillo College, which is located along the coast of Santa Cruz in California, and lives with her husband, son, and three cats in Watsonville.

MARISA BELAUSTEGUIGOITIA RIUS is chair of the Gender Studies Program of the National Autonomous University of Mexico (UNAM). She earned her Ph.D. in ethnic studies, with emphasis on gender, race and sexuality, at the University of California, Berkeley. She is professor at the School of Humanities in the areas of Latin American studies, Latino and gender studies, and pedagogy at UNAM. She has written numerous articles on the topics of gender, race, sexuality, and border pedagogy analyzing processes of resistance of women in prison and indigenous women inside the EZLN and their fight for territory and voice. Since 2009 she has coordinated a project inside women's jails focused on justice, art, and pedagogy through the painting of murals. She has written six books: *Pedagogías en espiral* with Rían Lozano, *Güeras y prietas: Género y raza en la construcción de mundos nuevos*, *Enseñanzas desbordadas*, *Fronteras y cruces: Cartografía de escenarios culturales Latinoamericanos* with Martha Leñero, *Fronteras, violencia y justicia: Nuevos discursos* with Lucía Melgar, and *En la punta de la lengua*.

MAYLEI BLACKWELL is the author of *Chicana Power! Contested Histories of Feminism in the Chicano Movement*, which was a finalist for the Berkshire Conference of Women Historians Book Prize and also received honorable mention as one of the best books on Western women and gender history by the Western Historical Association. Her research has accompanied indigenous women's organizers in Mexico, feminist movements and sexual rights activists throughout Latin America, and more recently, farmworker women's organizing and indigenous migrant activism in the United States. She is associate professor in Chicana and Chicano studies and gender studies at the University of California, Los Angeles.

CRUZ CARIDAD BUENO is a Ph.D. candidate in the Economics Department at the University of Massachusetts, Amherst. Her dissertation, "A Knife Hidden in Roses: Development and Gender Violence in the Dominican Republic," explores the economic, political, and social variables associated with gender violence within the context of gender equity and the development paradigm. Her research is grounded in fieldwork she conducted as a participant-observer with women workers in the export processing zones and domestic workers in the Dominican Republic with funding from the Inter American Foundation's Grassroots Development Dissertation Fellowship. Cruz's research interests center primarily on the political economy of race, class, and gender. She loves to travel and run half-marathons.

PASCHA BUENO-HANSEN is assistant professor in women and gender studies at the University of Delaware. She received her Ph.D from the University of California, Santa Cruz, in politics, Latin American and Latino studies, and feminist studies. Bueno-Hansen is working on a book titled "Decolonizing Transitional Justice: A Feminist Analysis of Human Rights and Internal Armed Conflict in Peru." She has published articles in the *International Feminist Journal of Politics* and the *Journal of Peacebuilding and Development*. She is an affiliated faculty member of the Master's in Community Psychology program at the Pontifícia Universidad Católica de Peru.

MIRANGELA BUGGS is a doctoral candidate in Social Justice Education at the University of Massachusetts, Amherst, whose work is crafted in the intersections of women of color feminist thought, Afro-diaspora studies, education for critical consciousness, and the politics of decolonization. Her time as a student in Central America in the late 1980s and early '90s and her subsequent journey earning a master's degree in gender studies and feminist theory from the New School for Social Research began her process of transcribing/translating multiple realities pertaining to the United States and Latin America.

TERESA CARRILLO chairs the Latina/Latino Studies Department in the College of Ethnic Studies at San Francisco State University. Her teaching and research focuses on Latino politics with an emphasis on immigration and citizenship, reflecting her fascination with Latinos as political actors in a constant interaction with local, national, and transnational political forces. Carrillo comes from a large family from Tucson, Arizona, and earned a Ph.D. in political science from Stanford University. She is presently working on a book manuscript titled "Watching over Greater Mexico: Transnational Citizenship and Governance of Mexicans Abroad."

CLAUDIA DE LIMA COSTA teaches literary theory, feminist theories, and cultural studies at the Federal University of Santa Catarina, Florianópolis, Brazil, and is one of the coeditors of *Revista Estudos Feministas*, Brazil's premier feminist studies journal. She was a visiting professor at the University of California, Santa Cruz, and at the University of Massachusetts, Amherst, where she taught courses on feminist theories. She has published articles on the travels and translations of feminist theories and is presently doing research on the feminist decolonial turn in Latin America.

ISABEL ESPINAL has been translating between Spanish and English since she was five years old. She was born and grew up in Brooklyn, New York, attended the Massachusetts Institute of Technology, and eventually graduated from Princeton. She earned a master's of library and information science from the University of California, Berkeley, and has been a librarian since 1991. In 1993, a year after giving birth to the first of three children, she began writing, publishing, and translating poetry. In 2005, she obtained a master's degree in American studies from the University of Massachusetts, Amherst, and is currently in the last stages of a Ph.D. there. At UMass she is also the librarian for Afro-American studies and Native American Indian studies. She serves as vice president/president elect 2012–14 of REFORMA: The National Association to Promote Library and Information Services to Latinos and the Spanish Speaking and also as co-chair of the Green Party Latino Caucus for 2012–13.

VERÓNICA FELIU is a full-time Spanish instructor at City College of San Francisco. She has conducted research on Chilean feminisms with a focus on performance and identity politics.

MACARENA GÓMEZ-BARRIS is associate professor of American studies and ethnicity and sociology at the University of Southern California. She is author of *Where Memory Dwells: Culture and State Violence in Chile* (2009), and coeditor (with Herman Gray) of *Toward a Sociology of the Trace* (2010). She has published in journals including *Sociological Perspectives*, *Culture and Religion*, *Television and New Media*, and *Transmodernity*. She is coeditor with Licia Fiol-Matta of a special issue of *American Quarterly* on Las Américas (2014).

REBECCA J. HESTER received her doctorate in politics from the University of California, Santa Cruz. A strong advocate of social justice, Hester's interdisciplinary scholarship draws from the social sciences and the humanities to focus on questions of culture in medicine, the political economy of the body, health inequities, and biological citizenship. She is currently assistant professor of social medicine in the Institute for the Medical Humanities at the University of Texas Medical Branch.

NORMA KLAHN is professor of literature at the University of California, Santa Cruz. She received her Ph.D. from the State University of New York, Stony Brook, and taught at

Columbia University (1978–89). Her research focuses on Mexico and Latin America and cross-border Chicana/Latino expressions. Her work has appeared in *Revista Iberoamericana*, *Nuevo Texto Crítico, Debate Feminista, Studies in 20th Century Literature, Revista de la UNAM, MLN, Journal of Latin American Cultural Studies*, and *Tulsa Studies in Women's Literature*. She is coeditor of *Lugar de Encuentro: Ensayos críticos sobre Poesía Mexicana* (1987); *Los novelistas como críticos* (1992); *Las nuevas fronteras del siglo XXI* (2000); and *Chicana Feminisms* (2003). She has contributed chapters in *El arte de la ironía* (2007) with Carlos Monsiváis; *Independencia, revolución y revelaciones* (2010) with Agustín Yáñez; and *México: Migraciones culturales-topográfías transatlánticas* (2012) with Margo Glantz and Barbara Jacobs.

AGUSTÍN LAO-MONTES is associate professor of sociology at the University of Massachusetts, Amherst, where he is also affiliated with the Center for Latin American, Caribbean, and Latino Studies as well as with the departments of Afro-American studies and gender, sexuality, and women studies. He has published widely in the fields of African diaspora studies, decolonial critique, historical sociology, and political sociology. He is an intellectual-activist who participates in a variety of social movements and is especially active in networks of black movements across the Americas.

SUZANA MAIA is professor of anthropology at the Universidade Federal do Recôncavo da Bahia, Brazil. She has done various research projects on the theme of gender and globalization and is currently working with women leaders in the quilombola movement in Brazil, focusing on the relationship between universities and social movements.

MÁRGARA MILLÁN is a sociologist and has a Ph.D. in social anthropology from the UNAM (National Autonomous University of Mexico). She is full-time professor in the Faculty of Social and Political Sciences, UNAM, and member of the Center of Latin American Studies of the same faculty. She coordinated the research program Alternative Modernities and New Common Sense: Prefigurations of a Non-Capitalist Modernity, 2011–13. She has published on gender cultural politics of the zapatista movement, feminist critique, and cinema and gender cultural representations.

ADRIANA PISCITELLI is a feminist social anthropologist, professor at the University of Campinas (Brazil), Brazil National Science Research Council researcher, and senior researcher of the Unicamp's Centre for Gender Studies. Over the past twelve years she has been engaged in studies focusing on the transnational sex and marriage markets and carried out research on human trafficking. She is author of articles in *Brazilian Virtual Anthropology, Revista Etnográfica, Signs: Journal of Women in Culture and Society, Estudos Feministas*, and *Sexualities*. She also wrote "Between Trafficking Discourses and Sexual Agency: Brazilian Female Sex Workers in Spain" (in Tiantian Zheng, ed., *Sex Trafficking, Human Rights, and Social Justice*, 2008).

ANA REBECA PRADA teaches comparative literature and research methodology and is head of the Graduate Program in the Literature Department at Universidad Mayor de San Andrés (La Paz, Bolivia). She has recently published two essay collections: *Salto de eje* (2011), which has to do with her longtime work on women and writing; and *Escritos críticos* (2012), which deals with contemporary Bolivian narrative. After teaching gothic, crime, and science fiction narrative for several years, she is now turning to *modernismo*, having finished a group project on the Bolivian writer Alberto de Villegas and beginning another collective effort on the very well-known Bolivian *modernista* Ricardo Jaimes Freyre.

SIMONE PEREIRA SCHMIDT teaches literary theory and postcolonial feminist studies at the Federal University of Santa Catarina, Florianópolis, Brazil, where she also co-coordinates the research group on postcolonial studies and Afro-Latin-America. She was a visiting scholar at the New University of Lisbon (Portugal) and the Fluminense Federal University (Brazil). As a collaborator of the research group Africa, Brazil, Portugal: Literary Dialogues, she is presently working on the project titled "Memory Maps: Bodies and Territories in the Writings of Female Authors in the Portuguese Speaking Africa." She has published extensively on issues of gender and race in literary texts.

ESTER R. SHAPIRO is associate professor of psychology at the University of Massachusetts, Boston, and research associate at the Gaston Institute for Latino Research/Public Policy. Her scholarship and practice apply cultural/ecosystemic approaches mobilizing resources facilitating health and growth by linking individual, family, and social/community change. She was coordinating editor of *Nuestros Cuerpos, Nuestras Vidas* (2000), a Spanish-language transnational adaptation of an activist women's health text. She wrote *Grief as a Family Process* (1994) and is completing *Culture, Grief and Family Resilience*. A Cuban Jewish Eastern European immigrant, she writes on immigration impacts in her own family and is working on a memoir with recipes.

MILLIE THAYER is associate professor of sociology at the University of Massachusetts, Amherst, where she is affiliated with the Center for Latin American, Caribbean and Latino Studies and Women, Gender, Sexuality Studies. Her recent book, *Making Transnational Feminism: Rural Women, NGO Activists, and Northern Donors in Brazil* (2010), is an ethnography of cross-border feminist relationships and negotiations of difference and inequality. She is a coeditor of *Global Ethnography: Forces, Connections, and Imaginations in a Postmodern World* (2000) and *Beyond Civil Society: Social Movements, Civic Participation and Democratic Contestation* (forthcoming). Her two current projects—researching the mutual influences between feminism and other social movements in Nicaragua, and studying the challenges of economic and political sustainability for feminist movements in Brazil—extend her interest in activist translations.

Confederación General de Trabajadores del Perú, 328

contact zones, 22, 24, 89, 90, 119–20, 147n2

Convention Concerning Decent Work for Domestic Workers, 237

Convention 169, 307–8

Coordinadora Nacional del Movimiento Urbano Popular, 229

Correa Feminista, La (journal), 149, 157–58, 159, 161

Counter Intelligence Program (COINTEL-PRO), 309

"Crossing Borders" (Anzaldúa), 58, 61

Cueca Sola, La (film), 215

cultural citizenship, 271

cultural formation, 1, 17, 22, 384, 389

cultural translation, 6–7, 19, 56, 184; commodity culture and, 22; in performance, 210, 215; resignification and, 86; in sex tourism, 277, 279, 294–95; textual revisioning in, 356–57; transnational feminism and, 24, 88, 145, 210, 325; traveling theory and, 20, 190; world culture and, 135, 145–46

Curiel, Ochy, 390, 397

D., Rocio, 397

Davies, Carole Boyce, 385, 387–88

Davis, Angela, 303, 322, 331, 397–98

Davis, Kathy, 23, 345–46, 405

Daybreak (newspaper), 307

Daykin, Norma, 171

Dead Leaves, The (Jacobs), 51

Debate (publisher), 359

Debate Feminista (journal), 45, 53, 149, 156–57, 159, 162

Declaration on Primary Health Care, 170

deconstruction: in bilingualism, 133; birth of, 136; center-periphery discourse, 54; difference and, 26, 327; global feminism and, 23; in naming practices, 332; queer politics and, 336

Department of Health and Human Services (U.S.), 340

Department of Labor (U.S.), 230–31

Derrida, Jacques, 135–36, 145

Desert Blood (Gaspar de Alba), 48

"Desire that Runs through Our Bodies and Latin America Is Possible!!!, The" (LIFS), 336

Desnudez del silencio (Santos), 97

Diálogo Sur/Sur LGBT, 321

diasporas, 7, 242–43; African, 383–87; Afro-Latina, 242–43, 383, 387–94; intertwined, 15, 87, 302, 305, 315, 392, 394–96

Díaz, Junot, 102–3

Díaz, Ruth, 246, 248

Díaz, Ximena, 247

DIVERSA, 155

Doble Jornada, La (newspaper), 158

domestic service: citizenship and, 237–38; feminists on, 235–36; politicization of, 230–34; racism toward women of color, 255; silence around, 242; translations in, 225–28; undocumented labor in, 226; workers' rights movement, 226–28

Domestic Workers United, 231–32, 236

Domínguez, Nora, 22

Domínguez Santos, Rufino, 177

double, pedagogy of, 112–14, 120, 122–25, 389, 393

Down These Mean Streets (Thomas), 395

Du Bois, W. E. B., 4, 388, 389

Dussel, Enrique, 65

Echohawk, Crystal, 309

economic liberalization policies, 192

Ehrenreich, Barbara, 236, 247, 250–51

Ejército Zapatista de Liberación Nacional (EZLN), 158–59, 163, 306, 307

ejido system, 307

Ellis, Kathryn, 172

Eltit, Diamela, 51–52, 53, 61

E. Luminata (Eltit), 53

EMBRATUR. *See* Empresa Brasileira de Turismo

Emerging Activist Leadership Program, 309

Primer Congreso de Trabajadores de Casa Particular, 253

Proceso (journal), 164–65

PRODEMU. *See* Foundation for Women's Promotion and Development

Programa Nacional de Solidaridad (PRONASOL), 155

Promoción de la Mujer, 200

promotora model, 174, 176, 178–85

PRONASOL. *See* Programa Nacional de Solidaridad

prostitution: exotic dancers and, 270, 273; immigration laws and, 239n9; sex tourism and, 86, 280, 285, 287, 289, 290; transgender women and, 330

Proyecto de Salud Indígena, 174, 178

publishing, global, 358–59

queer(ness): self-naming, 326–27; theory, 57, 64, 143, 315–17, 326; use of term, 321–24, 325–26, 330, 337

Questão de Gênero, Uma (Costa/Bruschini), 144

Quiché, Maya, 368

Quijano, Anibal, 43

Quintrala, La, 215

Quiroga, Jose, 324–25, 332–33, 335, 337

Rabassa, Gregory, 41, 51

race, mixed, 87–88, 254, 259–61, 262, 283–84, 285–86

racism: in Brazil, 10, 88, 262, 267–68; in Chile, 248, 254; decolonial feminism on, 382–83, 389–90; difference and, 214, 218; discourse against, 63, 74, 98–99; domestic service and, 236, 255; in health promotion, 187n15; in immigration policies, 229; as imperialism, 25; internalized, 3, 242; in Mexico, 163; patriarchal, 3, 378, 389; postcolonial theory on, 143; in testimonios, 44; transportation of text and, 25; untranslatability in, 304; U.S. model of, 21–22; in women's organizations, 349

Radical Crossroads (Gore), 388

Radway, Janice, 103

Rago, Margareth, 280–81

Random House, 55, 359

rape, 154, 365, 373

reading: learning and, 189–90; as replicating, 114; transnational, 112–14, 115

Reagan, Ronald, 407

Red de Organizaciones Femeninas del Pacífico Caucano Matamba y Guasá. *See* Matamba y Guasá

Reina Sofía Museum, 67

relationality, 89

Report from the Bahamas (Jordan), 381

reproductive rights, 164–65, 361

Research Cluster for the Study of Women of Color Research in Collaboration and Conflict, 321

resistance, indigenous, 364–65, 374–77

Retrato en sepia (Allende), 50

Revel, Judith, 65

Revista Estudos Feministas (journal), 134, 138–44; citation practices, 141–44; editorials, 139–40; gender studies canon, 140–41

Revuelta, La (newspaper), 151, 152

Rich, Adrienne, 92, 318

Richard, Nelly, 45–46, 58, 61, 134–35, 137, 144, 150

Rivera Cusicanqui, Silvia, 58, 59, 62, 74, 244

Rivera Garza, Cristina, 52–53

Rivera-Salgado, Gaspar, 175

Rodriguez, Cecilia, 309

Rodríguez, Dora Elia, 47–48

Rodríguez, Esther, 330

Rodríguez, Ileana, 367

Rodríguez, Jesusa, 53, 157

Rodríguez, Juana María, 330

Rojas, Rosa, 157, 158, 159

Rovira, Guiomar, 48

RSMLAC. *See* Latin American and Caribbean Women's Health Network

Rubin, Gayle, 156

Ruiz, Samuel, 162–63

Ruskin, Donna Kaye, 5–6